# TUDOR COSTUME AND FASHION

by

## HERBERT NORRIS

With a New Introduction by
**RICHARD MARTIN**
Curator, the Costume Institute
Metropolitan Museum of Art

## DOVER PUBLICATIONS, INC.
Mineola, New York

*Bibliographical Note*

This Dover edition, first published in 1997, is an unabridged, corrected
republication in one volume of the work originally published in two
volumes by J. M. Dent & Sons Ltd., London, in 1938 under the title
*Costume and Fashion, Volume Three: The Tudors, Books 1 and 2.*

*Library of Congress Cataloging-in-Publication Data*

Norris, Herbert.
    Tudor costume and fashion / Herbert Norris.
        p.    cm.
    Reprint. Originally published: London : Dent, 1938. 2 v.
    Includes bibliographical references and indexes.
    ISBN 0-486-29845-0 (pbk.)
    1. Costume—Great Britain—History—Medieval, 500–1500.
2. Costume—Great Britain—History—16th century.  I. Title.
GT734.N67   1997
391'.00942—dc21                          97–19413
                                              CIP

Manufactured in the United States of America
Dover Publications, Inc., 31 East 2nd Street, Mineola, N.Y. 11501

# INTRODUCTION TO THE DOVER EDITION

HERBERT NORRIS was a scholar in the generation of twentieth-century universalists enamored of history as a pageant. His rich, visually expressive volume, *Tudor Costume and Fashion,* takes its title from his predilection for the extravagant panorama associated with costume and the special circumstances and evolution that connote fashion. Few historians have skillfully and subtly combined the two sensibilities with Norris's commanding sense of history. Norris looks at history not only as a series of tableaux enlivened by accounts of prominent men and women, but also as a vivid sartorial revelation of the class realities of an epoch.

Ironically, Norris employs consistent black-and-white image-making for most of his figures. These are precise, systematic renderings of the details of painting and documents that allow us to focus on specific aspects of coiffure, collar, or clothing construction. Norris's black-and-white portrait renderings are enriched by his articulate descriptions of color along with the techniques employed. Both iconic and didactic, these images show how an extrapolated likeness or salient feature can evoke an entire social fabric. Costume designers for theater and film will find in Norris's scrupulous images a reliable guide to period dress.

Norris's ambition was grand. His epic of history includes the inventories of great properties and accounts of the courts of church and state, but his descriptions also include the low-life rascal and vernacular witness. The delight that Norris shows in parsing the details of state robes and court dress is equally evident when he examines the everyday dress of the common man and woman; the details of regular seaman's trousers and clay pipe are as striking as the pattern pieces of religious garb or the detailed analysis of an escutcheon of royalty. Cognizant that the history of fashion is not solely a story of women (though he pays them ample attention), Norris chronicles the cogent elements of class, race, and gender in a comprehensive vision unrestricted by the blinkers of political correctness.

Norris's book is at once grand historical narrative and acute cultural analysis. He gives us the pattern pieces, silhouettes, descriptions of materials, and details that allow lace, cutwork, and embroidery to tell their own precise, evocative stories. Contemporary texts and descriptions are mingled with Norris's own analytical knowledge of the fashions.

More than half a century after Norris wrote this work, we know little more about fashion history than he did, perhaps even less. In the 1920s and 1930s, with conflicting ideologies struggling for world power, the fashion historian and bibliographer Hilaire Hiler wrote, in his monumental *Bibliography of Costume* (1939), that "the study of costume is quite without limits. . . . " Norris, too, saw the potential of costume history, viewing it as a kind of cultural grammar that yields insights into the urgent forces of history. Norris, who formulated his great work in the years between the world wars, believed that costume and fashions together would yield a coherent, cohesive picture of humanity. But in the 1920s and 1930s some were already using appearance and apparel to widen divisions of race, class, and gender; the ensuing war and holocaust dashed the visionary hopes of a whole generation of scholars.

One might wonder why the scale of effort represented in this volume is so rare today. Have we lost faith in the parade of history? Theory so clogs the arteries of vital history that some ignore the possibility that Clio may be inherently colorful and vivacious. Norris's exuberant, concrete approach can serve as a useful corrective to the elaborate cant that too often passes for historical writing these days.

In fact, Norris's work on Tudor history, stretching from the last years of the fifteenth century to the first years of the seventeenth, evinces the author's commanding sense of an evolving history, giving us noble surcoats, folkwains for transit, beguins as kerchiefs of a prefeminist religious order and of middle-class women. As always with Norris, we see such vivid personalities as Eleanor of Austria, Sir Thomas More, Henry VIII, Elizabeth I, Catherine de Medici, and common sailors, court jesters, and peasant women. These opulent, colorful years of history have never had a greater pageant master or a more precise limner than Norris.

Norris immerses the reader in an epic of visual history. There is a visionary splendor to Norris's enterprise that is absent from today's arid scholarly landscape. One celebrates this work in the wish that we might all strive toward a comparable exuberance, inclusiveness, and grandness of vision.

Curator, the Costume Institute                    RICHARD MARTIN
Metropolitan Museum of Art

'All manners of attire came first into the city and country from the court, which, being once received by the common people, and by very stage-players themselves, the courtiers justly cast off, and take new fashions (though somewhat too curiously); and whosoever wears the old, men look upon him as a picture in arras hangings. For it is proverbially said, that we may eat according to our own appetite, but in our apparel must follow the fashion of the multitude, with whom we live. But in the meantime it is no reproach to any, who of old did wear those garments, when they were in fashion. In like sort, many dances and measures are used in Court, but when they come to be vulgar and to be used upon very stages, courtiers and gentlemen think them uncomely to be used, yet is it no reproach to any man who formerly had skill therein.'

FYNES MORYSON: *Itinerary*, 1617.

'Immaculate costuming gives that confidence
which religion is powerless to bestow.'

Fig. 1. Penmynnydd, Anglesey, the Cradle of the Tudors

# FOREWORD

A DELAY of eleven years between the appearance of two consecutive volumes of a work of this magnitude—for Volume II was published so long ago as 1927—is much to be regretted, and indeed calls for some apology. The abundance of the material, which has necessitated a double volume, and the labour of producing over a thousand illustrations, will account for much of this delay: but the chief reason has been the intrusion of other work in connection with stage and screen. In carrying Volume III to completion I have been much heartened by the encouragement of that scholarly Tudor historian, the late Mr. Ernest Law, who was kind enough to write to me shortly before his death, 'No one is so well fitted for this undertaking as yourself.'

During the Tudor Period, continental fashions continued to influence those of the English nobility to an increasing extent; and for this reason brief introductory surveys of costume worn in France, Italy, Spain, and Germany have been given. In this volume, too, quotations from authorities have been printed in the same size type as the rest of the book; this may not be the conventional method, but I hoped that it will be appreciated by readers.

In reply to some criticisms and in anticipation of others, it may be said in the first place that even so large a number of illustrations does not allow space for many actual photographs of original sources. Moreover, a very extensive experience and many years of experiments with models have enabled me to show in diagrams the construction of various garments and articles of headgear. Again, to some readers the biographical details and descriptions of appearance and mannerisms, although the result of much painstaking research, have appeared irrelevant; and, indeed, I am informed that many actors purposely refrain from studying such matters because either

vii

author or producers (or perhaps both) hold views altogether at variance with the facts. Such details have been inserted, however, with due regard to their sartorial significance, quite apart from any historical interest.

It is again my pleasant task to thank my former helpers, Major and Mrs. D. S. Paterson; as also my publishers, Messrs. J. M. Dent & Sons Ltd., for their continued helpfulness and patience in considering my every request; to Macmillan & Co. for permission to quote the long extract from Major Martin A. S. Hume's *Philip II of Spain*; and Ernest Benn Ltd., for the extracts from the same author's *The Year after the Armada*.

For valuable work in translation from the original sources I am indebted to Marc Caulier, M. B. Elliott, Alice Maud Norris, Anthony Thorne, Mary Lowndes, Patrick Treble, James Wardrop, and Althea M. H. Westland.

Other kind friends have helped the production in various ways. Too numerous for individual mention here are the authors from whose works references have been taken, the owners of private collections of portraits, and the directors of Art Galleries, Museums, and Libraries at home and abroad; to all of these I wish to express my gratitude for their extensive and generous assistance.

I particularly wish to record my special thanks to J. Howard Brown for his valuable assistance in editing my manuscript.

HERBERT NORRIS.

Thame, Oxon.
*October* 1938.

# CONTENTS

## Book I

# CONTENTS

x

## Book II

# ILLUSTRATIONS

## IN COLOUR AND HALF-TONE

Note: For this edition, color plates, marked by an asterisk, appear between pages **170** and **171**.

## Book I

## Book II

# ILLUSTRATIONS

# IN BLACK AND WHITE

## Book I

# ILLUSTRATIONS

## Book II

# AUTHORITIES QUOTED

C. K. ADAMS
JAMES PETTIT ANDREWS, F.S.A.
KATHERINE ANTHONY
*Antiquarian Repertory*
*Archaeologia*
EDWARD ARMSTRONG, M.A.
WILLIAM A. BAILLIE-GROHMAN
*Bannatyne Club*
DR. CHARLES R. BEARD
*Biographies*
*Dictionary of National Biography*
MICHAUD's *Biographie Universelle*
W. J. BISHOP
PIERRE DE BOURDEILLE
BRANTÔME
MARY CROOM BROWN
J. HOWARD BROWN, B.Sc.
MURIEL ST. CLARE BYRNE, M.A.
*Calendars of State Papers*
ALBERT F. CALVERT, F.C.S., F.R.G.S.
*Camden Society*
FREDERICK CHAMBERLIN, LL.B., F.S.A., F.R.Hist.S.
G. E. CHAMBERS, F.S.A.
BARBARA McCLENAGHAN
SIR W. LAIRD CLOWES
CHARLES HENRY COOPER
F. H. CRIPPS-DAY
SIR LIONEL HENRY CUST, K.C.V.O.
THOMAS DELONEY
EDWARD DILLON
F. M. O'DONOGHUE, F.S.A.
HERBERT DRUITT
CAMILLE ENLART
JOAN EVANS, F.S.A., D.Litt., F.R.Hist.S.
CHARLES ffOULKES, C.B., O.B.E., Hon. D.Litt. (Oxon), F.S.A.
PATRICK FRASER-TYTLER
CANON FRANCIS W. GALPIN, M.A., F.L.S.
ARTHUR GARDNER
HEREFORD B. GEORGE
SEBASTIAN GIUSTINIAN
MRS. EVERETT GREEN
GEORG GRONAU
HENRY M. HAKE, C.B.E., F.S.A.
HALL's *Chronicles*
CHRISTOPHER HARE
HARRINGTON's *Nugae Antiquae*
G. B. HARRISON, M.A., Ph.D.
WILLIAM HARRISON
HELEN W. HENDERSON
WILLIAM HERBERT
A. J. HIPKINS, F.S.A.
CHRISTOPHER HOLFORD
MARTIN A. S. HUME, F.R.Hist.S.
GEORGE LELAND HUNTER
*Inventories*
A. JAQUET
MARGARET JOURDAIN
FRANCIS M. KELLY
VICTOR VON KLARWILL
ERNEST LAW, F.S.A.
ROBERT LESLIE

LOSELEY MSS.
DAVID LOTH
J. SEYMOUR LUCAS, R.A.
HENRY MACHYN's *Diary*
SIR FREDERICK MADDEN, F.S.A.
DE MAISSE's *Journal*
J. G. MANN, M.A., B.Litt., F.S.A.
*Manuscripts*
G. E. MAINWARING
JEAN H. MARIEJOB
SIR CLEMENTS ROBERT MARKHAM, K.C.B., F.R.S., D.Sc.
FRANCIS AND HUGH MARSHALL
JULIAN MARSHALL
DR. ERIC G. MILLAR
JOSEPH RAMÓN MÉLIDA
ANDRES MUÑOZ
NAUNTON's *Fragmenta Regalia*
PROFESSOR J. E. NEALE, M.A.
SIR NICHOLAS HARRIS NICOLAS, C.B., G.C.M.G.
C. C. OMAN
JEHANNE D'ORLIAC
*Oxford Dictionary*
MRS. BURY PALLISER
SAMUEL PEGGE
J. R. PLANCHÉ, Somerset Herald
A. F. POLLARD, M.A., Hon. Litt.D., F.B.A.
SIR WALTER SHERBURNE PRIDEAUX
FRANÇOIS RABELAIS
ANGELO S. RAPPOPORT, Ph.D., B.ès.L.
ARY RENAN
E. M. G. ROUTH
G. B. ARCHIBALD RUSSELL, Lancaster Herald
L. F. SALZMAN, M.A., F.S.A.
SIR GEORGE SCHARF
PHILIP W. SERGEANT, B.A.
GEORGE SLOCOMBE
G. F. HERBERT SMITH, M.A., D.Sc., F.R.A.S.
H. CLIFFORD SMITH, M.A., F.S.A.
*State Papers*
SIR WILLIAM STIRLING-MAXWELL, Bart.
J. M. STONE
STOW's *Chronicles* and *Annales*
RALPH STRAUS, B.A.
EDWIN W. STREETER
PHILIP STUBBES
LAWRENCE E. TANNER, F.S.A., M.V.O., B.A., M.A., F.R.Hist.S.
*Testamenta Vetusta*
C. J. S. THOMPSON, M.B.E., Ph.D.
G. A. THRUPP
ELEANOR E. TREMAYNE
GEORGE UNWIN
AYLMER VALLANCE
EUGÈNE EMMANUEL VIOLLET-LE-DUC
*Walpole Society*
*Wardrobe Accounts*
JOHN DOVER WILSON, C.H., M.A., Litt.D., F.B.A.
VIOLET A. WILSON
BRIG.-GEN. G. F. YOUNG, C.B.

# CHAPTER I

## THE REIGN OF KING HENRY VII
### 1485—1509

## CONTEMPORARY SOVEREIGNS

| | ENGLAND | SCOTLAND | FRANCE | GERMANY | SPAIN | SWEDEN | | DENMARK |
|---|---|---|---|---|---|---|---|---|
| | Henry VII | James III | Charles VIII | Frederick III | Ferdinand II | John II | = | John I |
| | | 1460–88 | 1483–98 | 1440–93 | 1474–1516 | 1483–1502 | | 1481–1513 |
| | | Margaret of Denmark | Anne of Brittany | Eleanor of Portugal | 1. Isabella of Castile | Christina of Saxony | | |
| | | | | | 2. Germaine de Foix | | | |
| 1485 | | | | | | | | |
| 1488 | | →James IV | | | | | | |
| | | 1488–1513 | | | | | | |
| | | Margaret Tudor | | | | | | |
| 1493 | | | | →Maximilian I | | | | |
| | | | | 1493–1519 | | | | |
| | | | | 1. Marie of Burgundy | | | | |
| | | | | 2. Bianca Sforza | | | | |
| 1498 | | | →Louis XII | | | | | |
| | | | 1498–1515 | | | | | |
| | | | 1. Jeanne of France | | | | | |
| | | | 2. Anne of Brittany | | | | | |
| | | | 3. Mary Tudor | | | | | |
| 1502 | | | | | | →Interregnum | | |
| 1503 | | | | | | →Swante Sture | | |
| | | | | | | Protector, 1503 | | |
| 1509 | Henry VIII | | | | | | | |

3

1485. Accession of Henry VII, 22nd August.
*Fulgens and Lucres* by Henry Medwall. The earliest English printed play, published 1485-90.

1486. Bartolommeo Diaz, Portuguese navigator, led an expedition fitted out by Joam II to the Cape of Good Hope.

1487. Rebellion of Lambert Simnel (son of an organ maker at Oxford). Crushed at Stoke, 15th June.

1490. Thomas Cromwell born, son of a blacksmith at Putney: destroyer of the famous shrines throughout the country. Executed 1540.

John Cabot arrives in England and settles at Bristol. Born during the first half of the fifteenth century at Genoa, he went to Venice in 1461. In 1496 he was granted by Henry VII 'the right to seek islands and countries,' and with his three sons sailed from Bristol in May 1497, reaching the American mainland the 24th June following. Date of death unknown.

Sebastian Cabot, born probably at Venice in 1474, was the second son of John. Accompanied his father in 1496, and eventually they discovered Newfoundland, Labrador, and Cape Florida; was later employed by Henry VIII until 1512. He then entered the service of Spain (with the exception of two years' banishment in Africa 1532) until 1547. Returning to England in that year, he was nominated first Governor of the Merchant Adventurers 1553, and died in London in the last quarter of 1557. His pension was paid in September of that year, but not in December. His portrait may be seen in the Bristol Art Gallery; another, by Lorenzo Lotto, belongs to the Earl of Harewood.

1492. Christopher Columbus discovered America, 12th October. Born about 1436 at Genoa (?), son of a woolcomber. Died at Valladolid, 1506.

Perkin Warbeck's Rebellion, 1492-9.

1494. War between France and Italy, until 1496.

1495. François Rabelais born at Chinon. A mendicant friar, author, and one of the most scholarly men of his age. Qualified as a physician. Died 1553.

1497. Cornishmen's Revolt.

1498. Desiderius Erasmus came to England. Born 1466 at Rotterdam. Secretary to the Bishop of Cambrai 1491. Bachelor of Divinity, Cambridge, 1505. Died at Basle 1536.

Vasco da Gama reached India by sea route round the Cape of Good Hope. Born about 1469 at Sines, Portugal. Died at Cochin 1524.

1498 (about). Edward Hall born, citizen of London, lawyer. Died 1547. His *Chronicle* extended from 1399 to 1547.

1499. Edward, Earl of Warwick (nephew of Richard III), the last Prince of the House of York, beheaded 24th November. Born in 1474/5 he was the only son of George, Duke of Clarence, and Isabel, daughter and coheir of Richard, Earl of Warwick and Salisbury.

1503. War between France and Spain. In this campaign the Chevalier Bayard (1476-1524) performed prodigies of valour.

Abuse of Privileges of the Church by ecclesiastics leads to the Pope allowing investigations to be made into various monasteries—the prelude to the political Reformation.

1504. John Colet became Doctor of Divinity. Born about 1467, son of a City knight. Dean of St. Paul's 1505. Founder of St. Paul's School 1510. Died 1519.

1505. Polydore Vergil, an Italian, commissioned by Henry VII to write a history of England. Born about 1470 at Urbino. Returned to Italy 1550. Died 1555.

Martin Luther entered an Augustinian monastery. Born 1483 at Eisleben, son of a miner. Excommunicated 1520. Translated the Bible 1522. Married a nun 1525. Died at Eisleben 1546.

1506. John Leland, the first English antiquary, born in London. He was at St. Paul's School and Christ's College, Cambridge. Appointed King's Antiquary 1533, and made his antiquarian tour 1534 to 1543. Rector of Haseley, Oxon, 1542. Died 1552. Author of *Itinerary* and *Collectanea*.

Nicholas Udall born. Wrote the first true English comedy, *Ralph Roister Doister*, 1553-4. Head master of Eton 1534. Head master of Westminster 1554. Died 1556.

1508. The League of Cambrai: France, Spain, and the emperor unite with many Italian powers against Venice.

Ferdinand Alvarez de Toledo, Duke of Alba or Alva, born. Present at the Battle of Pavia 1525. Sent to subdue the Netherlands 1567; recalled after six years. Called upon to suppress Portugal 1581. Died 1582.

1509. John Calvin, the Protestant Reformer, born at Noyon. Died 1564.

Death of Henry VII, and accession of Henry VIII.

# THE ARTS, 1485-1509

## Sculpture—Monumental Effigies (*continued from vol. ii, p. 354*)

Sculptured monumental effigies continue to afford valuable sources of information on costume throughout the period covered by volume iii.

As previously, the Gothic style prevailed: the figures were recumbent, i.e. lying on their *backs*, with their hands clasped; the heads of knights rested upon their helmets, while ladies had embroidered cushions to support them. At the feet were animals, usually from their heraldic achievements. Cushions were also used under the heads of civilians.

Weepers appear on many monuments at this time, and were in use sparingly almost to the end of the sixteenth century.

Men of rank were nearly always shown wearing full armour, sometimes with their mantles of office over it. Effigies of women are the most useful, because they are usually wearing their best dresses. What is so helpful about effigies is, that one can walk round them and examine details at close quarters.

(*Continued on p.* 145)

## Memorial Brasses (*continued from vol. ii, p. 354*)

Memorial brasses in England have been grouped broadly, by the eminent historian, Herbert Haines, into three main periods. The first covers the earliest examples, and finishes at the end of the fourteenth century; the second closes with the death of Henry VII; and the third surveys the sixteenth and seventeenth centuries.

The first period, and the major part of the second, have been dealt with briefly in volume ii of this work.

More brasses were laid down towards the end of the fifteenth century than during the periods previously described. They were used by all classes of the community, and great numbers commemorative of civilians are still in existence.

The artistic deterioration of memorial brasses continued. Over-abundance of shading and too much detail were introduced, which spoilt the composition; and conventionality of treatment became more noticeable. The metal used was thinner than before, and the engraving necessarily shallower.

To effigies of man and wife were frequently added groups of their children —the sons under the figure of their father, and the daughters under that of their mother. About the same time, figures of the deceased in the attitude of prayer were substituted for the older recumbent effigies.

5

The method of showing women with their heads in profile, or three-quarter, in order to display the headdress to better advantage, was still continued.

Lettering of the inscriptions was somewhat crowded: the older use of the Norman-French language and Lombardic capitals was superseded by Latin (and occasionally English), with Gothic letters.

The second period of the classification of brasses ends in 1509.

(Continued on p. 145)

### TAPESTRY (*continued from vol. ii, p. 356*)

Tapestries of the period comprised in this volume are divided into two classes:

Gothic, fifteenth century to 1515.
Renaissance, 1515 to 1615.

Tapestry characteristic of the period 1485–1509 is known as late Gothic, and was for the most part woven in French Flanders. After the fall of Arras in 1477 tapissers from that town settled in Bruges, Brussels, and Tournai. The following are some of these master-craftsmen: Stephen of Brumberghe, who worked thirty years on 'The Acts of the Apostles'; John Roubronck, Perquid d'Ervine, Peter van Oppenom, and John van der Brugghe. The men who were responsible for these masterpieces were artists as well as master-weavers, collaborating with the designer, and at their discretion altering the detail of a cartoon, choosing the colouring, and even introducing new figures into the composition, if, in their judgment, they considered the cartoon unsuitable for translating into tapestry.

In workmanship, colour, and design, tapestries of this period are second only in excellence to the earlier Gothic tapestries executed before 1480. Those made in Brussels during the period dealt with in this chapter, interwoven with gold and silver, are considered by some equal in beauty to those of an earlier date.

The costumes and accessories depicted in late Gothic tapestries are of the greatest value for study, particularly as the artist-cartoonist at this time designed his own figures, whether biblical, classical, historical, or 'up to date,' wearing fashionable contemporary dress.

The 'sets' are too numerous to mention here, but 'The Story of David' in the Musée Cluny contains ten panels rich with gold. They afford excellent material for the study of costume, etc., of this period, especially in some panels which depict Court scenes.

The 'Salvation Series' of tapestries consists of many sets, of which some were called 'The Story of the Seven Deadly Sins.' One set of the latter woven at Brussels about 1500 was purchased in 1521 by Cardinal Wolsey, to hang in the Legates' Chamber of his palace at Hampton Court, where some of them still remain. Reproductions of this set of tapestries are excellent illustrations of the dressing of morality characters during the last ten years of the fifteenth century.

'The Trojan War' series is an interesting set to be seen at Zamora Cathedral in Spain, of which there are several replicas by the same makers in public and private collections.

The tapestry in St Mary's Hall, Coventry, is said to depict Henry VI and Margaret of Anjou, but it is obviously dated about the year 1490 (see vol. ii, p. 355, and Figs. 6, 7, 69, and 145 of this volume).

Mention is made in vol. ii, p. 355, footnote, of the wonderful tapestries now at the Musée Historique Lorraine at Nancy, and described by Viollet-le-Duc as having been taken as loot by the Swiss from the camp equipment of Charles le Téméraire after the Battle of Granson in 1476. The authorities of the Musée have been kind enough to furnish minute details of the tapestries in their possession, from which it is certain that they were wrongly ascribed by Viollet-le-Duc. They were, in fact, not in existence at the time of Charles le Téméraire's death. The series represents 'The Condemnation of Banquet and Supper,' and was woven at Tournai in 1510. It is particularly useful for the study of costume, etc.

The tapestries actually taken by the Swiss in 1476 are now preserved in the Berne Museum. They are of the kind known as 'Gothic Verdure Armorial.' In such tapestries the whole surface is covered with flowering plants growing, as it were, in grass. Armorial bearings and initials are frequently set in the midst of this verdure, but they are useless to the student of costume.

The most wonderful collection of Flemish or late Gothic tapestries in existence belonged to ex-King Alphonso XIII of Spain. They are most interesting and informative for the study of costume and other details.

A fine set of four panels was made in the Netherlands for Philippe le Beau and his wife, Joanna, the sister of Henry VIII's first queen. The subject is 'The Story of the Holy Virgin,' and the set was designed, it is said, by Jan van Eyck. They are woven in silk, wool, gold, and silver, with the figures garbed in contemporary fashions. They adorned the private apartments in the Castle of Tordesillas on the Douro occupied by the unfortunate mad Queen Joanna [1] during her detention of forty-seven years. On this account, perhaps, they were affectionately cherished by her descendants.

Tapestries depicting the hunt were much in favour during the period under discussion, and examples can be found in many collections. The 'Chasse au Faucon' set in the Musée Cluny shows wonderful costumes of the time of Charles VIII.

Some subjects are working men and others peasants. A useful set showing the former, woven in the last decade of the fifteenth century, is to be found in the Musée des Arts Décoratifs, Paris.

(*Continued on p.* 145)

[1] See p. 63.

### ILLUMINATED MANUSCRIPTS

As stated on p. 356, vol. ii, the best illuminated manuscripts of this later period were produced in Flanders, where the art reached its highest point of excellence at the end of the fifteenth century and during the early years of the sixteenth. These were greatly prized by collectors of the period.

The figures are well proportioned, their clothes well defined, and the draperies arranged in very beautiful folds, though perhaps a little formal. Furniture and all kinds of useful everyday objects executed with neat draughtsmanship are to be found in the folios of these valuable works of art. Landscapes and architecture are treated in a very delightful manner, and full justice is done to atmosphere in depicting really lovely scenery. These pictures with their borders occupy, as a rule, a full page.

Borders consisted of a rather wide monochrome band decorated with naturalistic flowers—single blossoms of roses (see Fig. 54), carnations, cornflowers, pansies, daisies, etc. Often short sprays of these flowers were painted with their shadows to give the effect of their being laid on the background.

Fruit, especially the strawberry, was frequently introduced, and it was quite usual for insects of all kinds to be dotted about amongst the flowers and fruit.

The work of the French manuscript artists approached in excellence the finished style of the Flemish, in fact they were very close rivals; and their work shows strong affinities with Flemish art. Illuminated manuscripts produced in south-east France display Italian influences in the technique.

Long after the introduction of painting, Illum. MSS. continued to be produced in France, but very few Illum. MSS. were done in England at this period; most of those that were made here were the work of resident Flemish artists who had been invited over by those interested in their art.

(Continued on p. 148)

### PORTRAITS AND PAINTERS (continued from vol. ii, p. 356)

A very useful supplement to other authorities on costume is the study of portrait painting, an art which made considerable strides during the fifteenth century, and, towards the end of it, had attained a notable distinction.

Full-length portraiture was not attempted by the artists in this country, the head and shoulders only being depicted. Portraits were usually painted in oil upon wood, oak panels often being used, sometimes with semicircular tops (Fig. 2). Backgrounds were in gold, or a pattern was painted to represent a rich brocade. In front of the figure a parapet was often shown, covered with tapestry or brocade, on which the hands rested (see Fig. 226).

Since the time of Henry III no English sovereign took so much interest in art, or was so generously its patron, as Henry VII. His privy purse expenses abound with items relating to payments to artists: 'Thomas Paynter for paynting,' and 'Maynard the King's Payntour,' are two among the names recorded.

There is some doubt as to the existence of any creative school of English portrait painters at this period; but there is sufficient evidence that a few English painters, other than those already mentioned as being remunerated by Henry VII, were at work, many as copyists from Flemish original works. The portraits at Windsor of the kings from Henry V to Henry VII (*see* vol. ii, p. 356), and those of many other personages in various collections, were probably painted by Flemish artists. By command of Henry VII many copies of the portraits in the royal collection were probably made by English artists, chiefly for display at the Palaces of Westminster, Greenwich, and Sheen. They are now scattered throughout the land; some are still in the possession of private persons, and a number of them now belong to the Society of Antiquaries. These portraits are most valuable for the details of head attire, and especially of jewellery. The limited portions of the costumes they depict are those fashionable in western Europe during the reign of Henry VII.

Fig. 2. The Emperor Ferdinand I

Before the dawn of the sixteenth century, when HANS MEMLINC (1430–94) was at his prime, and JEROME BOSCH (1460–1516) was about to make his name, no Flemish artists of any repute considered it worth their while to give up their connections on the Continent and seek their fortunes in England. It has been suggested that JENIN GOSSART DE MAUBEUGE (1470–1534), better known as JAN VAN MABUSE, made short visits to this country to execute commissions before the year 1503, and some portraits of the reign of Henry VII are attributed to this artist.

The family of HOORENBAULT, established at Ghent from 1414 until 1544, were responsible for many portraits of continental notabilities, and, most likely, of some of their English contemporaries.

JEHAN BOURDICHON (1478–1516) was an artist of the Franco-Flemish school and became Court painter to Charles VIII and Anne of Brittany about 1495. He was also *valet de chambre* to the King.

Another artist of the same school, JEHAN PERRÉAL, known as JEHAN DE PARIS, was born at Lyons, where he painted as early as 1483. In 1497 he was appointed Court painter to Charles VIII and toured Germany and Italy, painting portraits of many distinguished people. He entered the service of the Archduchess Marguerite of Austria in 1504. In 1507 he painted several members of the French Court, under Louis XII, to whom he had been appointed Court painter.

BERNHARD STRIGEL, born 1460–1, was a prominent artist of the German school who painted portraits of the Emperor Maximilian, Mary of Burgundy, the Emperor Charles V in his youth, etc. He died in 1528.

Another artist of the German school, LUCAS CRANACH (or KRANACH), was born at Kronach in 1472. He was court painter to the Elector of Saxony, Frederick III, the Wise, from 1504 onwards. His portraits are very useful for the study of costume of the Maximilian epoch.

Chief, of course, of this school is ALBRECHT DÜRER, born at Nuremberg in 1471, son of a Hungarian goldsmith.

ANDREA SOLARI, born about 1460, was a Lombard-Milanese painter. He went to Flanders after 1509, but spent the latter part of his life in Italy, probably at Milan. His work is distinguished by the subtle modelling of the heads and its delicate execution. He died about 1515.

One of the greatest artists of all time was RAPHAEL SANZIO. He was born at Urbino on 28th March 1483, the son of Giovanni Sanzio or de Santi, an eminent artist of the Umbrian School. Entering the atelier of Pietro Perugino at Perugia in 1494, he remained there till 1503. His works, pictures, frescoes, designs for tapestries, etc., are notable for their grandeur of conception and calm realism of the loftiest ideal achieved by perfect harmony of grouping, colouring, and drapery. Raphael died on 6th April 1520.

Other artists of the Italian school are too numerous and well known to be included in these sections.

(Continued on p. 149)

# SECTION I: 1485–1509

## INTRODUCTION

The victory of Bosworth Field, 22nd August 1485, placed Henry Tudor, Earl of Richmond, on the throne as Henry VII.

This accession of the House of Tudor marks in English history the division between the Middle Ages and the Age of New Learning and New Faith, known as the RENAISSANCE.

It may be well to recapitulate briefly the sequence of events which brought about this new access of culture in England (*see* vol. ii, p. 467).

In 1453 the Turks captured Constantinople, which had been the home of Greek art and scholarship for a thousand years. Many of its treasures were dispersed—through ignorance as much as cupidity—countless examples of inestimable value were destroyed and the rest scattered far and wide. This completed the destruction and dissipation of art treasures begun by the first Fall in 1204.

The Turks were not left alone to garner the spoils. Such a rich harvest attracted a swarm of seekers, whose wealth or power gave them a chance of acquiring some of the loot. The process continued over many years. With a lively sense of intrinsic value as well as artistic merit, the de' Medici grasped the opportunity to acquire vast quantities of treasure, including a wealth of Illum. MSS., destined to have an incalculable influence on western culture. Successive popes did the same, sending agents to search for and purchase the scattered proceeds of the sack.

This gave a great impetus to the new cultural movement in Italy, which had begun much earlier to rival Byzantium as a centre of learning; indeed, the Renaissance period in Italy may be said to start with Petrarch (1304–74), and to reach its zenith during the pontificate of Leo X (Giovanni de' Medici, 1513–21).

The Renaissance influence in France was the outcome of the Italian wars, waged by Charles VIII, Louis XII, and Francis I.

Although these wars involved a tremendous waste of life and energy, their indirect benefits were of the highest value. In Italy the French had greatly widened their knowledge of the masterpieces of the arts and literature, mainly the literature of ancient Greece and Rome; this new appreciation emphasized the Italian influence on French thought and outlook which had been at work for the past century. It also wrought a marked effect upon French culture, and, largely through that nation, transformed the whole intellectual outlook of northern and western Europe. To this period the French gave the name of 'Renaissance' (new birth, regeneration). In the early years of the Tudor period, the Renaissance movement found its way to England through the enthusiasm of a few learned men; notably Bishop Fox, Confessor to the Lady Margaret Beaufort, Countess of Richmond. It was usually spoken of as the New Learning.

## ROYALTY AND NOBILITY—MEN: 1485–1509

### KING HENRY VII

Henry VII was born at Pembroke Castle on 26th July 1455.[1] In appearance his face was pale and long with small pretensions to good looks, but his features were regular, his eyes 'grey shining and quick,' and his hair 'yellow, like burnished gold.' In middle age it was dark brown. According to the

fashion of the time he was always clean-shaven, showing a red wart upon his right cheek. Of middle height, his figure was slight and well proportioned.

As a young man Henry Tudor was of a romantic and poetic disposition, much interested in Celtic lore and the genealogy of his own family; in fact, an antiquary of no mean order. Having spent many of his early years either in exile or as a prisoner, he developed much seriousness of mind. During the first part of his reign he was decidedly popular, and his pleasant expression and ready smile won all hearts.

'After the Death of the Ufurper [Richard III] and the Rout of his Army at Bosworth-field, Henry Earl of Richmond being, by his victorious Army,

Fig. 3. Badge of Henry VII

proclaim'd King, on the Twenty-fecond Day of Auguft, he foon after fat out for London, where, on the Way, he was met at Hornfey-Park [now Highgate] by the Lord Mayor and Aldermen, in their Scarlet Robes, accompanied by a great Number of Citizens on Horfeback, in Violet-colour'd Gowns, whence they conducted him to Shoreditch, where he was receiv'd by the feveral Corporations of the City in their Formalities, and thence by them conducted to St. Paul's Church, where, after having offer'd his Three Standards, he took up his Refidence in the Epifcopal Palace.'[2]

The three standards referred to were the Red Cross of St. George upon white silk: the fiery Red Dragon of the Tudors on parti-per-pale white and green

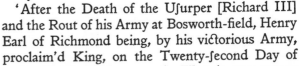

---

[1] This king's ancestry is given in vol. ii, p. 376 with footnote.
[2] William Maitland's *History of London*.

sarsenet, Fig. 4, and the Dun Cow of the Warwicks [1] on yellow tiretaine (Fig. 5). Henry VII was crowned 30th October 1485 at Westminster Abbey by Cardinal Bourchier, Archbishop of Canterbury. He was referred

Fig. 4. The Dragon Standard

to by his contemporaries as 'The King our Sovereigne Lord' and 'The Kings Highnes.'

His marriage took place at Westminster, 10th January 1486, and was celebrated 'with all religious and glorious magnificence' by Cardinal Bourchier. His bride was the Princess Elysabeth Plantagenet, eldest daughter of King Edward IV and Elizabeth Wydeville, and heiress of the Royal House of Plantagenet. This marriage led to the union of the Red Rose badge of the House of Lancaster and the Yorkist White Rose, resulting in what was called the Union or Tudor Rose, represented in blazon as 'a rose quarterly gules and argent barbed vert and seeded or' (see Fig. 53), but more commonly shown as a white rose charged upon a red one, barbed green and seeded gold (Fig. 316). Sometimes the Rose of Lancaster is blazoned gold.

The following is a description of Henry VII, written in 1598, by Edward Hall in his *Chronicle*:

Fig. 5. The Black Bull of the Nevilles

'He was a man of body but leane and spare, albeit mighty and strong therewith, of personage and stature, somewhat higher than the mean sort of men be, of a wonderful beauty and fair complexion, of countenance merry

[1] This 'dun cow' probably originated in a skeleton of an aurochs which was exhibited at Warwick Castle during the Middle Ages as the monster slain by Guy of Warwick. Point was given to the legend by the use of the Neville crest (a black bull's head) by the Earls of Warwick as a badge: this may have occurred either when Richard Neville married (1449) Anne de Beauchamp (1427–90), Countess of Warwick in her own right, or through Edward Plantagenet (born 1474/5, captive in the Tower, 1485–99, when he was beheaded) in right of his mother, the Lady Isabel Neville.

and smiling, especially in his communications, his eyes grey, his teeth single, and hair thin, of wit in all things quick and prompt, of a princly stomacke and haute courage.'

From another source, dated 1498, we learn that 'his Crown is, nevertheless, undisputed, and his government is strong in all respects. He is disliked, but the Queen beloved, because she is powerless. They love the Prince [Arthur] as much as themselves, because he is the grandchild of his grandfather [Edward IV]. Those who know him love him also for his own virtues. The King looks old for his years, but young for the sorrowful life he has led. One of the reasons why he leads a good life is that he has been brought up abroad. . . . Although he professes many virtues, his love of money is too great.'

In his youth, and at the time he ascended the throne, Henry VII must have dressed well, and in the manner expected of so important a man; but after the death of the Queen in 1503, he ceased to trouble overmuch about his own wardrobe, but was nevertheless jealous of his subjects if they made a better show of raiment than himself. It was about this time that Henry became silent, suspicious, and reserved, characteristics which were, no doubt, symptomatic of the avarice and parsimony of his remaining years. On the other hand, a contemporary writes: 'Though frugal to excess in his own person, he does not change any of the ancient usages of England at his Court, keeping a sumptuous table,' 600 to 700 persons sitting down to dinner, which cost the royal household £14,000 sterling annually. In earlier days his own personal expenses with that of his family amounted to £20,000.

In the year 1504, he started a campaign against the extravagant dress of his nobles and their retainers; and Edward Hall, within a few years of this event, states in his *Chronicle*: 'He sought out the penal laws, and put them into execution, and they that were found offenders, were easily at the beginning fined and scourged. After that he appointed two masters and surveyors of his forfaytes, ye one Sir Richard Empson [an infamous Minister and Master Court-Leech] and the other Edmund Dudley, both learned in the Laws of the realm. And these two persons contended, which of them by most bringing in might most please and satisfy his master's desire and appetite. Wherefore in the beginning, they armed with a company of accusers [commonly called promotors] which brought to them the names of the offenders, esteemed and regarded so much the gain of money, that they clearly forgot and banished out of their remembrance their duty present, the peril that might ensue, and the thank and goodwill that they might have obtained, and yet they had warning of great and sage persons to close their hands from such uncharit-able doings and cruel extremities, according to the Adage, the extremity of injustice, is extreme injury.'

John de Vere, Earl of Oxford, was one of these unfortunate offenders. He had entertained Henry VII most lavishly at Castle Hedingham, and with more ostentation in ceremonial, hospitality, and dress than his sovereign thought fit. The day after the termination of the King's visit the Royal attorney called upon the Earl and fined him 15,000 marks, equal to £10,000.

To offset these suggestions of craft and stinginess it is cheering to find items in the King's privy purse expenses enumerating rewards paid to various people on a liberal scale: 'My Lorde of Northumblande pleyers,' 1492; 'Three pleyers of Wycombe' and 'Frenshe pleyers,' 1494; and in 1495, 'Jakes Haute for disguysing.' It is probable that this versatile individual was a dabbler in what is now known as stage production, for not only is his name found 'Jakes Haute for the Tenes playe,' but 'Jacques Haulte [obviously the same man] for producing a disguysing' at Christmas 1498.

In 1502 there are entries: 'pleyers of St Albones,' and the following year, 'pleyers of Essex.' All these 'pleyers' were probably touring companies of actors.

The game of 'Tenyse' also interested Henry Tudor. He paid one shilling to Hugh Denes in 1494 for balls at the 'Paume play,' and two years later gave £4 'to the new pleyer of Tenes' (see p. 43).

An excellent comparison, made by the well-known biographer, Martin Hume, is here quoted: 'Ferdinand of Aragon [1] and Henry Tudor were well matched. Both were clever, unscrupulous and greedy; each knew that the other would cheat him if he could, and tried to get the better of every deal, utterly regardless, not only of truth and honesty, but of common decency. But, though Ferdinand usually beat Henry at his shuffling game, fate finally beat Ferdinand, and a powerful modern England is the clearly traceable consequence.'

Various portraits of Henry VII are to be found in Illum. MSS. and some contemporary paintings. One is at Windsor Castle. The head and shoulders portrait by Michiel Sithium in the National Portrait Gallery, London, No. 416, is pronounced by authorities to be an excellent likeness. In it the King wears an underrobe of black velvet and an overrobe of gold brocade and ermine, obviously a costume such as is seen in Fig. 11. His bonet is of blocked felt (see Fig. 111) and the collar of the Toison d'Or lies upon his shoulders. A red rose is held in the right hand. The recently discovered terra-cotta bust,[2] illustrated in *Old Furniture*, vol. v, p. 187, and the bronze effigy on his tomb in Westminster Abbey, are the last portraits of Henry VII. The King died 21st April 1509.

An Illum. MS. dated 1496 shows Henry VII in state dress at the age of forty-one, and Plate I is a drawing made from one of the miniatures which it contains. The King is wearing a robe, cut on similar lines to that shown in Fig. 561, vol. ii, but without the padding on the shoulders and the slit in the sleeves; it is long enough to trail upon the ground. This robe is of cloth of gold lined with miniver, which shows in the turned-back portions of the front and at the edges of the sleeves. It is girded at the waist by a jewelled belt; and a hooded cape surmounted by a jewelled collar covers the shoulders. Hardly any part of the purple underrobe is visible, except just below the

---

[1] Ferdinand is often referred to as 'Ferdinand II of Aragon,' 'Ferdinand V of Spain,' and 'Ferdinand the Catholic.'

[2] Now in the Victoria and Albert Museum, No. A 49–1935.

knee where the robe falls slightly apart. The crown is a band of moderate depth, jewelled, supporting four crosses patée alternating with four fleurs-de-lys, surmounted by two arches (the crown above shows four), with a ball, and a cross above their intersections. The King carries a sceptre with a fleur-de-lys above a double cross. The background is composed of the livery colours, white (silver) and green, of the House of Tudor, with the arms, supporters, and crown superimposed. King Henry was elected a

Figs. 6–7. Henry VII (*from the Coventry Tapestry*)

Knight of the Order of the Golden Fleece in 1491. He received the insignia from the Emperor Maximilian and was the first of the few English kings honoured by the grant of this famous Order. For details of the Order of the Golden Fleece see vol. ii, p. 402.

The Palace of Whitehall contained a famous and magnificent fresco, said to have been Holbein's finest work, painted in 1537. It portrayed Henry VII, Elysabeth of York, Henry VIII, and Jane Seymour.

This fresco was destroyed when the Palace of Whitehall was burnt in 1698. It is fortunate that Charles II had the foresight to commission a small copy of this fresco executed from the original by Remigius van Leemput in 1667, and now to be seen in Wolsey's Room at Hampton Court Palace. In this fresco Henry VII is dressed almost exactly like the nobleman shown in Fig. 8

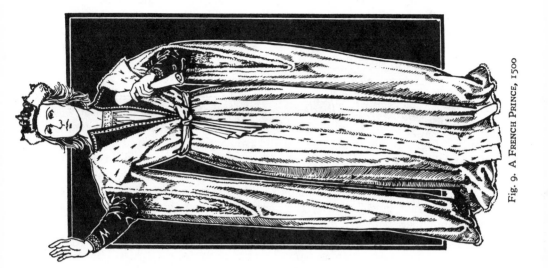

Fig. 9. A French Prince, 1500

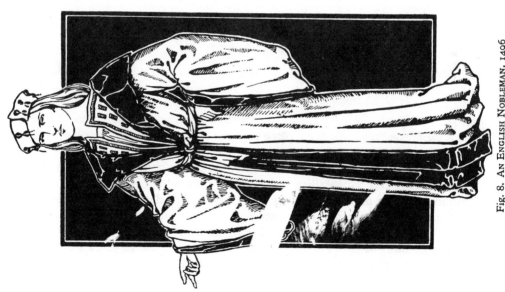

Fig. 8. An English Nobleman, 1496

except that his sleeves are slit vertically at elbow level.    The robe is of cloth of gold lined with ermine, the underrobe being of crimson velvet.    Above this costume is a long black silk scarf passed round the neck and hanging down the front on both sides.    The King wears the French bonet of black velvet, with a jewelled brooch and pendant pearl fixed on the right side.

Several portraits of Henry VII show him wearing a scarf, and in some cases, where a jewelled collar is worn, the scarf passes over this.    A portrait, No. 572–1882, in the Victoria and Albert Museum shows this King wearing a scarf of black velvet lined with brown fur.

Henry VII and his Queen were admitted to the Trinity Guild at Coventry in the year 1490, and there is no doubt that the figures in the tapestry (see vol. ii. p. 355) in St Mary's Hall there represent the King, his Queen, and Court.    Fig. 7 is a drawing constructed from this tapestry, and shows Henry VII kneeling at a prie-dieu covered with a piece of blue damask (see Fig. 198) on which is placed a missal and the Royal crown.    The King wears an ample gown with sleeves similar in shape to those seen in Fig. 8, and made of a large patterned gold brocade, the design of which is shown in Fig. 199, faced and lined with ermine—the only difference being that the revers are 'stepped' back.    On the chest is seen the upper part of the pourpoint, and a massive gold chain is wound twice round the neck.    The French bonet of black velvet is turned up with an embattled brim of ermine—a mode borrowed from Germany.

Another version of this gown shows some of the fullness front and back pleated or gathered into the shoulder seam (see Fig. 233).

## NOBILITY: MEN

After the Wars of the Roses, and as a natural consequence, the ranks of the old nobility were greatly diminished and their power gradually declined. Like all the Tudors, Henry VII disregarded the advantages and traditions of noble birth, and one of his great ambitions was the extermination of the medieval aristocracy.    In their place he sought to elevate unknown persons, not only men of wealth, such as the upper rural class and non-noble free landowners—the country gentlemen—but versatile, competent individuals, many of great ability.

'They all from time immemorial wear very fine clothes, and are extremely polite in their language. . . . In addition to their civil speeches, they have the incredible courtesy of remaining with their heads uncovered, with an admirable grace, whilst they talk to each other.'    This comes from an Italian —and Italians were renowned for good manners.

An English nobleman is represented in Fig. 8, which is taken from an Illum. MS. written and illustrated at Sheen, Surrey, in 1496.    It shows the Italian and Flemish influences.    This nobleman is wearing a robe like that described under Plate I, but without the fur cape.    Such robes are referred to by the name of 'SIMAR' in wardrobe accounts and other writings of this time.    It

is derived from 'chimer' or CHIMERE, which
was an ecclesiastical garment very like it in
shape. The robe shown in Fig. 8 is of plain
cloth of gold lined and turned back with black
velvet. The neck part is shaped as shown in
diagram, Fig. 10, somewhat on double-breasted
lines; the corner A is turned back wide on the
shoulders, forming revers. The back of the
neck is left quite plain, and it is important
to note that at this date no square collar is
attached to it, as in the later mode (*see*
p. 237). The robe is confined at the waist by
a narrow silk scarf, knotted with one loop and
two ends. The underdress is of crimson velvet, the front of the body part or pourpoint
is cut in the same manner as the black velvet

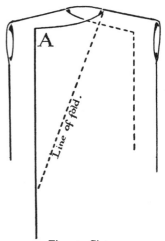

Fig. 10. Simar

revers, but these are not turned back. The pourpoint has a band of gold
passement at the edges, and is decorated with a series of gold billets (*see*
Fig. 428 (6), vol. ii). Frequently the edges of the pourpoint were caught

Fig. 11

Fig. 12

together by a silk lace and aiglettes. The French bonet is of crimson
velvet, the upturned brim being tied to the crown by black laces with
gold points.

Figs. 11 and 12 show the manner in which these long robes were draped when worn open up the front and without a girdle.

The drawing of the gentleman in attendance on Henry VII (*see* Fig. 6) shows a typical costume worn in England at this period by elderly men of rank.   His robe of rich brocade is waisted, and the skirt part, cut slightly on the circle, is gathered or pleated to the body part, the whole robe opening up the front.   Its low neck reveals the shirt beneath.   The robe is short, reaching below the calf.   The moderately close under-sleeves are treated in the newest fashion, derived from Germany, and decorated with a series of CUTTES through which the sleeves of the shirt puff.   The large pouch is slung on the right side by a cord passing through a ring.   Over this robe is an ample gown, cut on the semi-circular plan, the same length as the robe. It has a garded collar, which is unusual, and the sleeves are tubular as of old. The brim of the bonet is embattled in the same fashion as the king's, and curious shoes, without backs, are worn (*see* Fig. 174).   Attention is called to this early use of the word 'cuttes,' French 'crevés,' which then made their appearance in the decoration of fashionable garments.   This new mode originated from the sensation caused by the exploits of the warlike Swiss at this time (*see* p. 172).   Fig. 198 gives a design of the period such as was used in wearing damasks and brocades.   Fig. 201 is a design for embroidery in gold upon silk, satin, or velvet.

### Flemish, English, and French Fashions

The robe of the nobleman in Fig. 13, taken from a Flemish tapestry of this time, is somewhat similar to the others already shown, but worn loose and ungirded.   It is made of a spotted brocade lined with plain silk.   The fronts, as usual, are cut to form revers, but being of soft material drape into folds.

The sleeves are cut tubular as before, but the treatment of the top part is new.   They are secured to the garment at the back of the shoulders only, the unattached portion falling back and forming another pair of revers (the point of the left revers is marked A).   This nobleman has his right arm enveloped in the long sleeve, but the left emerges from the armhole and slit, the sleeve itself falling behind.   The robe, being open, exposes a garment often referred to—the paltock, now more generally called the pourpoint. This is fully described under Fig. 20.   The hair is worn long and locks are seen upon the forehead.   A new fashion is to cover the top of the head with a skull cap of jewelled network, over which various shaped hats are worn.   This one is a broad-brimmed beaver having a basin-shaped crown. It is worn very much tilted, to right or left, the brim being turned up at one side and down at the other, exposing a portion of the skull cap (*see* Headgear, Fig. 120).   The shoes are extremely broad in the toe—a reaction from the long pointed toe of Edward IV's time.   The natural shape, reaching midway between these two extremes, remained in fashion for only a brief time.

The nobleman, Fig. 14, is dressed like the preceding one with slight modifications. The drawing is made from the mural painting in the Lady Chapel at Winchester Cathedral and dates 1489. His costume proves how very closely the English aristocracy followed the fashions in vogue on the Continent. The robe is not so long as in Fig. 13, and the turned-back revers are of moderate proportions. The sleeves also are simpler, and have no lateral slit at elbow level, although such slits were frequently worn in England; neither are they extravagantly long, reaching only to the wrists.

Fig. 13. An Italian Noble        Fig. 14. An English Noble

The pourpoint of brocade is not open up the front, and reaches a little below the waist-line, the belt which carries the pouch passing over it. The neck opening is cut circular.

The beaver hat is the same as that just described, but no skull cap is seen.

In the drawing, Fig. 20, taken from a Flemish Illum. MS., is seen a gentleman of fashion who has discarded his long robe (similar to those described in the preceding pages). His costume consists of the following garments. First, the shirt, made of fine cambric, lawn, or silk, gathered into a band forming a square neck opening. Some shirts have the gathers at the neckband fixed in pleats or tucks [1] for about four inches in depth. This band was usually embroidered with a delicate design in fine black silk stitching, and the opening in front tied with a fine black or white lace. The full sleeves are also gathered or pleated on the shoulders into the neckband, and seamed

---

[1] Sometimes referred to as 'pynched.'

on the slant to the body of the shirt as shown by the dotted line in the diagram, Fig. 15. The sleeves, usually embroidered like the neckband, taper to the wrist, and are gathered into the wristband. Sometimes there was a narrow embroidered frill at the edge of the wristband. The fine black silk

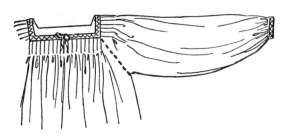

Fig. 15. Shirt

Fig. 16. Paltock

stitching frequently seen as a decoration to neck and wristbands of shirts shown in portraits, particularly those of Italian origin, is the 'Spanish work' described on p. 47. Great patience and skill were expended in the making of these shirts, and it was not beneath the dignity of great ladies of this period to make and decorate such garments for their menfolk. We know that Isabella the Catholic made and embroidered her husband's shirts, and

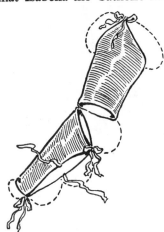

Fig. 17. Italian Sleeve

the first Governess of the Netherlands, Marguerite of Austria, sent to her father, the Emperor Maximilian, some which were received with great pleasure, and acknowledged in a letter from which the following is an extract: 'I have received by this bearer some beautiful shirts and HUVES [1] which you have helped to make with your own hand, with which I am delighted. . . . Our skin will be comforted with meeting the fineness and softness of such beautiful linen, such as the angels in Paradise use for their clothing.'

Returning to the description of Fig. 20, the next garment is the paltock or pourpoint. This little jacket could be cut all in one piece, with seams under the arms as in diagram, Fig. 16.

It finished at the waist-line, the two front edges being laced across over the shirt, but it was generally laced over a false piece called a stomacher, PLACARD, or 'placcate' made of some contrasting colour or material, or of brocade as in Fig. 13. There were many ways of treating the front of the pourpoint as shown in several of these drawings. Some opened out square in front, thus forming revers when turned back (see Fig. 8).

[1] 'Huves' and 'Hemets' are German expressions of the period for shirts. Charles V, referring to Edward VI, remarked that 'his hemet was never so nigh his skin as the King's Majesty's father was.'

The sleeves are made in two parts—an Italian fashion (Fig. 17). The upper part, seamed to form a cylinder, is secured sometimes by buttons, but more frequently tied by laces and aiglettes to the shoulder of the

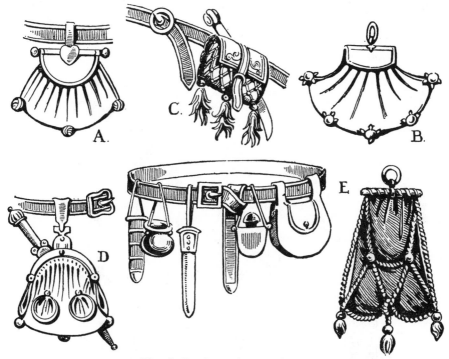

Fig. 18. Pouches and accessories

pourpoint. The lower part is also buttoned or tied to the upper, often left unseamed at the back, and sometimes tied round the arm. Between the open parts of these sleeves the full sleeves of the shirt are allowed to puff.

The hosen were drawn on and tied to the pourpoint as shown in the drawing, and described fully in vol. ii, p. 222. Between pourpoint and hosen the shirt is allowed to puff. Covering the division of the hosen up the front is the cod-piece, buttoned or tied at the top.

Pedules were not always worn over the hosen, but shoes or boots (see Footgear) of various shapes and colours, usually black, were indispensable.

Pouches of an elaborate nature (see Fig. 18) slung on waist or hip-belts were worn when required.

Fig. 19

On the head is the fashionable cap (see Fig. 119), made of material or of jewelled network (see Fig. 120), and usually tilted on one side. Such caps were worn on most occasions both indoors and out.

For the origin of the aiglet, aiguilette, or aiglette see vol. ii, pp. 222 and

365, the name being given to the metal tag or point at the end of a lace or cord.

Aiglettes and lacet, or lacets, are now coming into much more general use as means of fastening garments, and by degrees aiglettes became very rich and ornate. These lacets are best described as braid, woven in silk or cotton, and half an inch wide. Cords were also used, and they are seen in portraits

Fig. 20. Fig. 21. Fig. 22.

Fashionable Attire, 1485–1510

sometimes plaited in two or three colours: a gold or silver band clipped the end which frayed out below and appeared like a tassel (*see* Fig. 19).

The method of fastening the various garments mentioned in this book, when not definitely described, is usually obvious to the intellectual in any given case.

Simultaneously with the long robes just described a short surcote was worn. This was simply the long robe cut off at hip level, converting it into a short full coat.

Fig. 22 shows this garment worn by a fashionable young man of the upper classes. The drawing is made from one of the miniatures in the celebrated Flemish Illum. MS. 'The Romance of the Rose,' dated 1490. In the original illumination this surcote is pale grey, lined and turned back with pale rose colour. The long hanging tubular sleeves are bordered at the bottom with the same pale rose. The pourpoint, of old rose velvet, is fastened at the side, leaving the front plain. This descends a little below the waist-line, and is worn over a white shirt. Its sleeves are similar to those described under

Fig. 23. Diagram of Surcoat                    Fig. 24

Fig. 20. The hat is of rose-coloured beaver, worn over an emerald green cap, and is surmounted by a panache of rose, white, and black ostrich feathers. Hosen are in a lighter shade of rose colour, with buff pedules turned down to show their yellow ochre lining, and the shoes are black.

Fig. 21 shows the back view of one of these short surcotes. It is cut on the semicircular principle (*see* diagram, Fig. 23), which makes it set smoothly on the neck and shoulders, whence it hangs in radiating folds to the bottom edge.

Fig. 24 gives another version of the same surcote. This drawing is taken from a French Illum. MS. dated 1500, and in the original the pourpoint, 'cutte' diagonally on the chest, is of black velvet; the sleeves are of the same velvet and cut in one piece; they are open down the back showing the full sleeve of the shirt. The surcote is of gold brocade lined with shot blue and mauve silk. The hosen are a pinkish heliotrope; pedules ochre and shoes black. The bonet held in the hand is of vermilion velvet decorated with gold laces and aiglettes, and a gold brooch or ouche. This young man is in the act of respectfully 'valing his bonet,' that is, he politely raises his hat.

Fig. 25. This drawing of a young noble shows the short surcote with tubular sleeves [1] similar to that in Fig. 22. It is here lined with a brocade, and is turned back as usual to form revers. The very full, wide sleeves are pleated on the shoulders, open at elbow level, and made smaller at the wrists. The arm is enveloped in the right sleeve, the hand coming out at the bottom and well *pushed up* on to the upper arm ; the left one comes out of the opening at elbow level. The pourpoint is of a large-

Fig. 25

patterned brocade, cut square at the neck, belted at the waist, and descending to the hips. Close-fitting sleeves of the style shown in Fig. 17 but of different material are attached to it. The long hosen are partially covered by long boots of soft leather lined with some rich fabric, and turned down at the top. The square toes should be noticed. The bonet is fastened over the right eye by a rich jewel from which hangs a peardrop pearl.

[1] This figure, 25, should be compared with Fig. 568 in vol. ii, p. 413; they are very much alike, so that either the short coat was in fashion at an earlier date, or the portrait of Richard III was painted while the style of Fig. 25 was popular. If the latter theory is correct, the portraits of the other fifteenth-century kings, mentioned on p. 356 of vol. ii, must have been painted (possibly by his order) in the reign of Henry VII and in the fashion of his time.

Fig. 26

Figs. 27–28.
A SEIGNEUR AND HIS LADY (*from a Flemish Tapestry*)

The woodcut, Fig. 26, showing a young gentleman ready to 'go a-maying,' comes from a French calendar for the year 1497. His shortened surcote, belted at the waist, has revers of fur on the front and sleeves. The hat, worn over a cap like the one shown in Fig. 119, has a large crown of cloth or felt; the brim is turned up with fur and the hat decorated with a long plume. The hosen appear to be all in one with the foot part.

Fig. 29. Fulgens

The craft of the woodcut and metalcut artists is a valuable study. Woodcuts should be examined carefully by students of costume as, in addition to their other interesting features, they give clear definition of all details. They are chiefly the work of French, German, and Italian craftsmen who, during the first half of the sixteenth century, produced them in great numbers. Those by English artists are rare.

The seigneur, Fig. 28, walking with his lady is taken, by kind permission of Sir William Burrell, Bart., from a panel of Flemish tapestry dating about 1490. The whole costume is characteristic of the mode followed by the aristocracy in western Europe at the end of the fifteenth century. The short coat is similar to that described under Fig. 22, and is worn over the same kind of underdress. The sleeves are of the same cut, though shorter, but fixed to the armhole in the manner shown in diagram, Fig. 23. The drawing shows again the fashionable trick of carrying one sleeve on the arm, while allowing the other arm to emerge from the side slit. This practice is first referred to in vol. ii, p. 408. The hat is of the fashionable type, but the shoes show a difference mentioned under Footgear, p. 114.

The drawing, Fig. 29, is an interesting one. It is reproduced from a woodcut of the earliest known English costume design, made for a play *Fulgens and Lucres* by Henry Medwall, and published 1485–90. It was designed for an actor of the time in the character of the Emperor of Rome! The 'period' of the costume is conspicuous by its absence—it is simply modern —the dress of a fashionable young man of the reign of Henry VII, combining Flemish influences. The design thus betrays a lack of concern for historic accuracy strangely peculiar to some theatrical ventures. In the same tradition are the productions of the eighteenth and some of those of the nineteenth and twentieth centuries. One can be charitable and assume that their perpetrators knew no better. Even in these days of research and lending libraries, do we not find equal divergence from fact?

Returning to the illustration, Fig. 29, the robe, very similar to those already described, and worn widely open in front, 'was in effect a goune cut in the middle.' Often one of the lower corners was caught up and draped from the waist-belt, revealing the decorative hose beneath. This mode of wearing the 'shemew' or simar was adopted by persons of rank—the garment

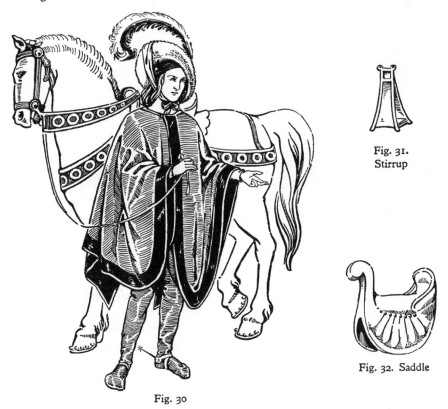

Fig. 30

Fig. 31.
Stirrup

Fig. 32. Saddle

was frequently very richly embroidered, or, as in the present example, made of a large-patterned Renaissance brocade, lined and faced with fur. It is worn over a tunic, decorated with cross-bars, and descends to just above the knees. The usual headgear, 'Massy Chain,' hosen, and footgear are worn.

The noble young horseman in Fig. 30 is Flemish in style, but since the Illum. MS. from which this drawing is taken was executed at Sheen, Surrey, it may be safely said to depict an English fashion. Diagram, Fig. 33, gives the shape of the cloak. This young man wears his cloak fastened round the neck in the usual way, with the side portions D and E draped over the arms. The opening G hangs down the middle of the back, conveniently for riding. These cloaks were made of fine cloth—this one is red, and is bordered *inside* and out with black cloth or velvet edged with gold: and if required for smart

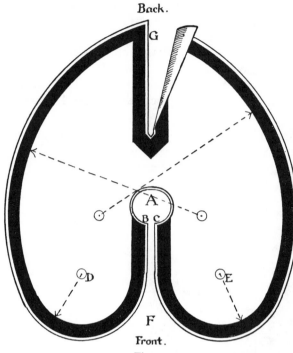

Fig. 33

occasions they would be lined with silk. Cloaks for wet weather would be made of felt; and despite their curious shape they were very useful for riding as the sides D and E covered the thighs. This attractive get-up comprises also a chic white beaver hat, turned up at one side and tied with a pink scarf over a blue cap, plumed with a long ostrich feather, half white half black. The boots are soft buff leather, and long-necked spurs are worn. The horse furniture is of coloured leather ornamented with gold, and the saddle, Fig. 32, is an elaborate piece of leatherwork in colour and gold.

Fig. 33 shows the cut of the cloak worn by Fig. 30 and Fig. 34 with the centres of the front curves marked at D and E. A is the neck opening, and BC the points that fasten at the neck. F is the front and G the back with slit. The border with gold edging encircles the cloak inside and out except at the neck opening which is edged only with gold.

Fig. 34 shows the same shaped cloak worn in a different manner. The right-hand portion, D, is thrown over the left shoulder with the circular neck part drawn tight under the right arm and over the left shoulder. The left corner of the neck opening, C, is drawn over the left shoulder and tucked in behind the first throw of the cloak.

To gain proficiency in the Art of

Fig. 34

the Manage, or training in horsemanship, young gentlemen were sent to Italy where, at the academies of Naples and Ferrara, they were *initiated in the exigences of the* haute école.

With the dawn of the sixteenth century a new sleeve appears. It was, in fact, a revival of one worn during the latter part of the fourteenth century (*see* vol. ii, Fig. 353, p. 250). This sleeve, Fig. 35, had what may be called a 'faked puff,' really consisting of an extra full sleeve above the foundation. The sleeve itself, only the lower part of which is visible, was cut in one piece, with a seam running the whole length of the front, and another seam at the back *from elbow to wrist only*. The upper part was covered by a piece of the same material, wider, and long enough to form a puff when gathered or pleated

Fig. 35

into the armhole and again just below elbow level. This is plainly seen in the diagram, Fig. 35, and in Plate III A and Fig. 274.

The young man—a gentleman or gentleman-at-arms—Fig. 36, shows an eccentric style which was in vogue among English, French, and Flemish coxcombs during the first years of the sixteenth century. It was much influenced by foreign modes. The pourpoint or jacquette with a narrow basque is much decorated, and is open up the front to display the stomacher. Being cut very open at the shoulders, it had to be secured across the chest by a strap, tied with one loop and two ends. The wide sleeves have the same decorative pattern as the jacquette and reveal close undersleeves. The waist-belt, with sword, belt, pouch, and dagger, help the line of the elegant figure. The hat is on the same lines as the bonet in use at this time, the brim being cut in battlements in the German fashion, and a feather coquettishly droops over the left ear. The hosen are parti-coloured and striped, and the usual square-toed high boots are worn.

Fig. 36. A Gentleman-at-Arms

The reader will have recognized in this figure the familiar knave on playing cards, whose conventional garb is based upon those worn by the coxcombs of the time, while those of the kings and queens on playing cards are similarly adapted from the regal costume. One has only to refer to Fig. 148 and Plate V to understand whence the queens derive their headdresses.

The sinfulness of apparel is a favourite topic rubbed in by moral fanatics of all periods. Here is an excerpt from *Narrenschiff* or *The Grete Shyppe of Fooles of the Worlde* by Sebastian Brant, first printed in Basle, 1494:

'Ample bonets, with low necks . . . great hats that is set all upon one side, gowns long, full of pleats, and the sleeves as large as a sack. Cloaks bended with divers colours. The gowns have double re-braced collars.' This 'is the guise of the infidels, of the Turks and Saracens vile and abominable.'

These indignant comments might have been written to describe many of the costumes referred to in this chapter.


## FRENCH FASHIONS

### CHARLES VIII

#### King of France, 1469–98

Charles VIII, l'Affable, King of France, 1483–98. Born in 1469, the son of Louis XI and Charlotte of Savoy, 'he was the most affable and sweetest natured prince in the world.' In 1489 he married Anne, heiress of Duke François II of Brittany, and 'thus Bretagne came under the French power, to the unspeakable grief of all its subjects.' A very beautiful portrait of Charles VIII by Andrea Solari is in the Louvre, from which Fig. 114 is made.

In a French Illum. MS. dating about 1490 there is a portrait of this king at about the age of twenty-one, and therefore almost contemporary with the Illum. MS. mentioned in the description of Plate I. In this he wears a robe similar to that in Plate I, made of gold brocade lined and turned back with sable. The sleeves are a trifle wider, and no cape or hood of fur is worn with it; but the robe is turned back at the neck forming right-angled revers, and a heavy gold chain with pendant is spread widely over the shoulders. The little that is seen of the underdress is of crimson velvet; and the fashionable black velvet bonet, with circular jewelled brooch and peardrop pearl, is worn.

This type of dress was universal throughout western Europe, and its vogue amongst the nobility lasted from about 1480 to 1510. It was definitely of Italian origin which dictated the fashions of the civilized world at this time. Examples of this type of costume are frequently seen in paintings by Italian artists, notably those of Vittore Carpaccio (c. 1455–c. 1522).

For a description of the people and life at the Court of Guidobaldo, Duke of Urbino, reference should be made to the *Boke of the Courtier* by Count Baldassare Castiglione (born 1478, died 1529), who spent the years 1504 to 1508 in the entourage of the Italian duke.

Charles VIII—that genial monarch and man of taste—died in 1498 at the early age of twenty-nine.

In Fig. 9 is seen a 'Prince of France' taken from an Illum. MS. dating about 1500. The robe with long tubular sleeves is of blue cloth of gold, lined and turned back with ermine. The arrangement of the revers is the same as described under Fig. 9 and diagram, Fig. 10. This robe is confined around the waist, either by a silk scarf or by a jewelled belt. The underdress, which has been already described (*see* Fig. 20), is of black velvet with a narrow band of gold passement, open to show the shirt with the embroidered neckband. The headgear is the French bonet of blue velvet, turned up with sable, having a coronet set inside it—a fashion first noted under King Henry VI (*see* Fig. 534, vol. ii).

## ITALIAN INFLUENCES

### BASES

A distinct type of garment made its appearance in western Europe during the reign of Henry VII.

Its earliest form was not unlike the tunic shown in Fig. 532, vol. ii, and mentioned on p. 388 of the same volume, except that it was sleeveless. The important item which developed later into a distinctive separate garment was the skirt—sometimes descending as far as the knees—and referred to as the BASE or BASES. It originated in Italy, where it continued to be worn during the remainder of the fifteenth century. It is represented in paintings by Benozzo Gozzoli (1469), Andrea Mantegna (1474), etc., and later by Raphael (1512) (*see* Fig. 218).

The wars conducted in Italy by Charles VIII and Louis XII during the latter part of the fifteenth and the beginning of the sixteenth century introduced this fashion into France. It became the vogue in western Europe, especially in Germany, during the reign of the Emperor Maximilian; and with variations remained in fashion in England long after Henry VIII ascended the throne.

The name 'Bases' was given to the skirt part of the garment which was often detached from the upper part and worn separately, being buckled or tied round the waist. Bases were semicircular skirts worn with both civil and military dress, often over complete suits of armour (*see* Fig. 38). They are sometimes referred to in modern writings as 'military skirts.' Frequently they are represented in this manner in Illum. MSS., statuary, etc., dating from the late fifteenth to the early sixteenth century: their use was general in Germany, and Albrecht Dürer has left many examples in his drawings. It was usual for the bases—the complete skirts—to be composed of a series of corrugations (*see* Fig. 39), the stiffly lined material being attached at intervals to braids underneath, the braids running at right angles to the corrugations (*see* Fig. 40). Another method was to use padding between the material and the lining, sewn down in vertical lines radiating from the waist to the hem.

The surface of the bases, usually composed of very rich brocade, was sometimes of a single colour. Other examples show wide stripes of two colours, and materials forming alternating corrugations (*see* Figs. 38, 218, Plate VI, and 219), thickly padded and sewn down on a thick foundation, or held by heavy braids as previously described. In some cases horizontal bands of different colours or materials crossed the pleats. When worn for riding bases were open up the front, and they were always open down the back. Sometimes the back portions overlapped. The armour of the time was modelled on the lines of bases or military skirts; this part was then called 'jamboys.'

In the picture gallery at Windsor Castle there is an altar-piece of the Anglo-Flemish school dating about 1508. In it Henry VII and his family are shown in company with St. George, who wears bases in red and white stripes over armour. Numerous illustrations of the Emperor Maximilian show that he wore a military skirt of some very rich large-patterned brocade over his armour, or jamboys. Such an illustration is provided by one of the woodcuts in Dürer's 'Triumphal Arch,' which shows the Emperor receiving from his wife, Marie, the armorial bearings of Burgundy (*see* Fig. 42).

## Louis XII

### *King of France, 1462–1515*

Louis XII, le Père du Peuple (*see* Figs. 38 and 113), one of the few entirely estimable kings of France (1498–1515), was born 1462, the son of the Duc d'Orléans and great-grandson of Charles V, King of France. He married first Jeanne (born 1462), daughter of Louis XI, whom he divorced. He married secondly, in 1498, Anne of Brittany, widow of Charles VIII, and thirdly in 1515, Mary, daughter of Henry VII of England.

On ascending the throne of France, Louis XII assumed the titles of King of Jerusalem, King of the Two Sicilies, and Duke of Milan, the last two involving him in the Italian wars. A religious, sweet-natured man, fond of learning, he possessed an economical spirit rather exceptional among crowned

Fig. 37.
Badge of Louis XII

Fig. 38. KING LOUIS XII OF FRANCE, 1498
After Jean Bourdichon

heads. 'I prefer to hear my courtiers laugh at my parsimony than see my people mourn at my extravagance' was his answer to a courtier who suggested that his economical habits savoured of niggardliness. Always good-natured, Louis forsook for the gratification of his young bride of sixteen years the humdrum habits of his later life, and at the age of fifty-two indulged in all kinds of excesses. 'He used to dine at eight in the morn, but to please his fair young wife, he put off his dinner until twelve. And instead of going

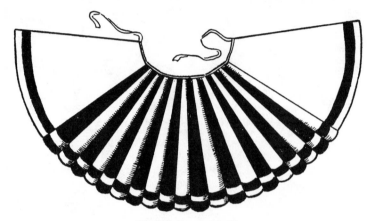

Fig. 39. Bases, outside

to bed at six, he was now tempted sometimes to sit up till midnight.' Louis XII died in 1515 after three months of connubial bliss.

There is in existence a portrait group which includes Louis XII, representing him kneeling and surrounded by various saints. It dates about 1498. The king wears a fully developed version of the bases or military skirt, and this is probably one of the earliest extant examples of its climax. Fig. 38 is a drawing made from this portrait. It shows the bases, made of brocade, fixed in corrugations and edged with two bands, the upper one ornamented with 'cuttes.' It has a body part decorated with cross-bar embroidery, and thickly padded. The wide sleeves of an under-tunic, probably of leather, show on the upper arms which are encased in rerebrace, coude, or elbow cops and vambrace; the legs are covered by cuisses, genouillères or knee cops, jambs, and solerets. The background of Fig. 38 is taken from an Illum. MS. in the Bibliothèque Nationale, Paris, depicting this king in a similar attitude and costume. It is composed of strips of silk about fifteen inches wide, of two alternating colours, sewn or (as shown in some examples) tied together. A twelve-inch letter L, crowned, is worked in gold at equal intervals in lines across the fabric, alternate lines shifting to half spaces. This type of wall hanging, or dorsal, was much in use during the fifteenth century, and large sums were spent upon them. Thus, in 1499, even the parsimonious Henry VII paid no less than £522 10s. to Antony Corsse 'for a clothe of an estate conteyning 47½ yerds. £11 the yerd.'

Very few actual specimens of bases are still in existence. One, in the Metropolitan Museum, New York, is of brocade, having a large pattern of blue on a ground of gold. It is not open up the front but laps over behind, being fastened round the waist by straps. Fig. 39 shows the outside view of a military skirt or bases laid out flat. It is more than a semicircle, the pleats or corrugations radiating from the waist. It measures twenty-one inches from the waist to hem and four yards round at the lower edge. The

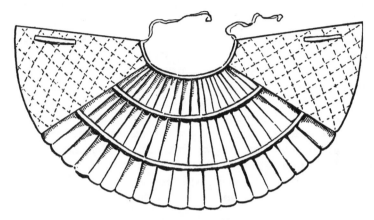

Fig. 40. Bases, inside

waist measures twenty-three inches. In this example the back parts are without pleats. Fig. 40 is the inside view of the same garment. Twenty pleats or corrugations occupy the front part, each pleat kept in place internally by two bands of heavy braid. The back parts, right and left, are quilted behind the pleats. The lining throughout is of heavy linen, and the whole garment is padded with flax more than half an inch in thickness.

## THE EMPEROR MAXIMILIAN, 1459–1519

The Emperor Maximilian, son of the Emperor Frederick III and Eleanor of Portugal,[1] was born 22nd May 1459. He married Marie of Burgundy (*see* vol. ii, p. 402) 19th August 1477, and was crowned at Aachen, 9th April 1486, with the Diadem of Charlemagne as 'King of the Romans.' His second wife (1494) was Bianca Maria (born 1473, died 1512), daughter of Galeazzo Maria Sforza, Duke of Milan, and Bona of Savoy. Elected Emperor in 1493, he was proclaimed Holy Roman Emperor in the Cathedral of Trent by consent of Pope Julius II, 1508.

The Emperor Maximilian is one of the most charming personalities in the catalogue of European monarchs. Considered the handsomest man of his time, he is described as of a noble countenance. He had bright, honest,

[1] See p. 202. This empress must not be confused with her great-granddaughter, Eleanor of Portugal, Queen of Francis I.

animated brown eyes, and an aquiline nose, but his clean-shaven jaw protruded and the lower lip was thick and long, a widely known characteristic feature of the Hapsburg family.[1]  His complexion was pale, his hair fair, inclined to auburn, worn falling on his shoulders in the fashionable style.  His figure was well proportioned and moderately tall.

During the greater part of his life he was full of energy; a fearless and unrivalled hunter, he sought relief from strenuous affairs of state in the joys of the chase.  A writer on divers subjects, a patron of art—a personal friend of Albrecht Dürer—he was also a proficient blacksmith, a great lover of animals, and a skilled veterinary surgeon.  Renowned as a gallant warrior and organizer of the Landsknechten, he was a most courteous knight, and genial and generous to all, both great and small, who came under his notice.  He was equally beloved by his army and subjects, who affectionately named him 'Kaiser Max.'  Maximilian had his weaknesses: he was extravagant and vainglorious, with an inordinate pride of family, while an exaggerated self-confidence led him to evolve marvellous schemes which he could never carry out.  Throughout his reign he was handicapped by inadequate financial resources; but despite manifold disappointments he retained great tenacity of purpose, excellent spirits, and good temper.  A model husband, father, and grandfather.  In the autumn of his life this great man showed a strong dislike of innovations, whether military, political, or social.  He died 12th January 1519.

Fleuranges, referring to Maximilian in his memoirs, says: 'His death was a great pity, as he was a good prince, and kept all Christendom awake; for when he could not accomplish anything himself, he showed the way to other people.'

An interesting portrait of Maximilian at about the age of sixteen is to be found in the Harleian MS. 6199, British Museum.  It shows him wearing the crimson velvet robes of the Toison d'Or (see vol. ii, p. 403).  His long yellow hair is surmounted by a flat cap having three upright quills attached to a jewel in front.

The following is a contemporary description of the young Archduke at the age of eighteen (1477), as he made his triumphal entry into Ghent to claim his bride: 'Gallantly riding a mighty chestnut horse, clad in silver armour [2]

---

[1] In connection with this commonly accepted family trait, it is of interest to compare the popular tradition with the following extract from a record by Brantôme. 'I have heard,' he says, 'a lady of the Court of those times relate as follows: "Once when Queen Eleanor, passing through Dijon, went to make her devotions at the Chartreux monastery of that town, she visited the venerable sepulchres of her ancestors, the Ducs de Bourgogne, and was curious enough to have them opened, as many of our kings have done with theirs.  She found them so well preserved that she recognized some by various signs, among others by their mouths; on which she suddenly cried out: 'Ha! I thought we got our mouths from Austria, but I see we get them from Marie de Bourgogne, and the Ducs de Bourgogne our ancestors.  If I see my brother the Emperor again, I shall tell him so, or else I shall send him word.'"' Queen Eleanor was the granddaughter of the Emperor Maximilian and of his wife, Marie of Burgundy.  The brother she mentions was the Emperor Charles V.  If she was right, how was it that the Emperor Maximilian—who was *not* of the House of Burgundy—possessed this characteristic projecting jaw?

[2] For a reproduction of the original drawing of this armour see *The Connoisseur*, vol. xliv, p. 15. At Hampton Court Palace there is a picture by Hans Burgkmair, which shows Maximilian, at a later date, wearing full armour and mounted upon an armoured charger.  It illustrates perfectly the description given above.

with uncovered head, his bright flowing locks bound with a diadem of pearls and precious stones, Maximilian appeared so glorious in his young majesty, so strong in his manliness, that I knew not which to admire most, the beauty of his youth, the brave show of his manhood, or the rich promise for the future. He was a joy to behold, that splendid man!'

There is a drawing of the young Archduke in the museum at Nuremberg. It dates 1477 and is reproduced in Fig. 41. The gown has close-fitting sleeves, open at the elbows, with a turned back cuff at the wrists. The waist-belt, through which a dagger is stuck, is spirally bound with a narrow band of silk like a crest wreath which ties with a loop and two ends in front. It is somewhat surprising to find at this early date the ends of the silk cut in two points like modern ribbon. The collar of gold chain is wound twice round the neck on the left shoulder *underneath* the gown and over the right outside it. The hat has a crown in the Italian style (*see* Fig. 125), turned up with ermine. It is worn over a small cap like those shown in Figs. 117 and 119 with one corner sticking up over the right eye. The shoes have rather wide toes and low backs with the instep cutte in three rows. Gloves are carried.

Fig. 41. The Archduke Maximilian, 1477 (*from a drawing at Nuremberg*)

Maximilian's marriage ceremony is depicted in one of the bas-reliefs on his tomb at Innsbruck. In it the bridegroom is wearing a doublet with bases, and an overrobe of brocade like that in Fig. 9 in shape. The assembled nobles wear costumes of a period much later than the date of the marriage, and the details, therefore, should be studied with this fact in mind. The explanation is that nearly all the reliefs were executed by Alexander Colin of Malines, and not completed until March 1566.

Fig. 42 is a reproduction of a panel from Albrecht Dürer's design for a triumphal arch, dated 1515. In it is seen Marie of Burgundy presenting to Maximilian the shield of arms of her inheritance—the Dukedom of Burgundy. The Emperor is crowned and in military equipment. Over this he wears bases composed of two wide horizontal bands of gold brocade and two of velvet, finished with a narrow band of brocade at the hem. The imperial crown, as worn by Maximilian, surmounts his armorial bearings in the left-hand corner.

Numerous engravings and drawings illustrate a variety of works on Maximilian's life. He is usually represented wearing a robe similar to those shown

Fig. 42. THE EMPEROR MAXIMILIAN, and Fig. 43. MARIE OF BURGUNDY

From Dürer's engraving for a Triumphal Arch, dated 1519

*By courtesy of the British Museum*

in Figs. 9, 11, and 12, made of gold brocade, plain velvet or silk, furred with ermine or sable: on his yellow hair there may be a velvet bonet or a coronet.

In later life, as Dürer shows him, the Emperor Maximilian was more soberly clad, chiefly in black velvet and sable, and usually wearing a typical German hat such as that seen in Fig. 368.

It was occasionally remarked that this famous potentate was somewhat shabby in his dress, but 'with an indescribable carriage of dignity withal.'

Fig. 44. The Emperor Maximilian in hunting kit (c. 1510)

The wardrobe of a keen sportsman like Maximilian was not complete without a hunting outfit. In 1496 we have a record of a meet at the Benedictine Abbey of Mals, at which he was present attended by fifty nobles in gorgeous hunting apparel, with falcons on their wrists, and escorted by a hundred Landsknechten with their characteristic long spears (see Fig. 224). The Emperor himself, always a dignified personality, was attired simply in his usual hunting costume of plain grey cloth, the collar of the Toison d'Or which he nearly always wore, a lion skin draped across his back and thigh, and a purple velvet bonet (see Fig. 110). In his *Hunting Book*, written and illustrated in 1499, we find Maximilian wearing a tunic of grey cloth, with bases, and with sleeves large at the shoulders and getting smaller towards the wrists where they turn back to form cuffs. The hat is of felt, with a low crown and upturned brim coming to a point in front. The black boots come well up the thigh and are square-toed.

Fig. 44 is made from the various figures in Bernard van Orley's cartoons (see p. 147) representing the Emperor about 1510. In all the figures his dress consists of a tunic with bases of grey cloth, having large puffs on the shoulders slashed with black, and a hood surmounted by a purple velvet bonet—his usual winter hunting dress.

Discrimination should be exercised in studying the costumes and armour indicated in the twenty-eight life-size bronze figures representing members of the Hapsburg Dynasty, which stand as a bodyguard around the sarcophagus of the Emperor Maximilian in the Hofkirche at Innsbruck; many of them are purely fantastic. Those which are reliable from the point of view of authentic detail are the following: Philippe le Beau; Kunigund, daughter of Frederick III; Eleanor of Portugal and Marie of Burgundy (these four are the work of Gilg Sesselschreiber of Munich, 1502–18); Bianca Maria Sforza; Marguerite of Austria; Philippe le Bon; Charles le Téméraire; Ferdinand of Aragon, and the Emperor Frederick III, all six of which were finished by Stefan Godl between 1518 and 1534. The effigy of the Emperor himself, the work of Louis de Duca, an Italian, from a model by Master Colin, was not placed in position until 1584.

### THE ARCHDUKE PHILIPPE LE BEAU, 1478–1506

The only son of the Emperor Maximilian and Marie Duchess of Burgundy, Philippe le Beau was born in 1478, and besides being King of Spain was Sovereign of the Netherlands in his mother's right. He married Joanna of Castile (*see* p. 62) in 1496. They spent much time in Flanders, and their court, modelled on that of Duke Philippe le Bon, was very elaborate and splendid.

The Archduke was handsome, well built, of a joyous character and pre-disposed to pleasure. A keen sportsman and fine horseman, good-natured, liberal, and amiable, quick-witted and religious, he hated court etiquette. Over-indulgent in sport, cold water killed him.

The portrait of Philippe le Beau, mentioned on p. 63, shows him in full armour of the period, with a pointed helmet surrounded by a jewelled crown. His surcote is blazoned with the armorial bearings of Austria, Burgundy, and Spain. A long mantle of brocade, lined with ermine, is worn over it, and surmounted by an ermine cape with the Collar and Pendant of the Golden Fleece above it.

During his visit to England, Philippe received from Henry VII the insignia of the Garter; and returned the compliment by creating Henry, Prince of Wales, a Knight of the Golden Fleece. He died 1506.

### FERDINAND V OF ARAGON, 1452–1516

Ferdinand, son of Juan II of Navarre and Aragon, was born 1452, married Isabella of Castile in 1469, and succeeded as Ferdinand V in 1479.

In January 1492 (the year in which America was discovered), the Moors were defeated at Granada and driven from Spain. Those that became Christians, known as 'Moriscos,' were allowed to remain. Expulsion of the Jews followed at once, much to the detriment of Spanish commerce. Ferdinand married secondly, in 1505, Germaine de Foix, aged twenty-one, the spoiled and petted niece of Louis XII of France. He died in 1516. His

PLATE II A. ISABELLA, QUEEN OF CASTILE     PLATE II B. FERDINAND V, KING OF ARAGON
Portraits by unknown artists.    Windsor Castle.    *By gracious permission of H.M. the King*

dress in the portrait, Plate II B, of red and gold brocade, is made on the same lines as the robes shown in this chapter. He wears a black velvet bonet, and his hair is very dark brown, almost black.

## 'TENYSE'

The game of 'tenyse' had been an exercise indulged in by gentlemen for some time previously. The poet Gower first mentions 'tennes' in a ballade dating about 1400. It was derived from the 'jeu de paume,' the French game of fives, and was originally played with the gloved hand, the palm of the glove being padded for striking the ball.

Tennis was also known in France, for it was while playing tennis in 1484 that the Duc d'Orléans was made acquainted with the fact that a plot was being hatched against him. Magnificent entertainments were given at the Castle of Blois by Louis XII in honour of the visit of the Archduke of Austria, Philippe le Beau, and his wife Joanna, which occurred in December 1501. On this occasion it is recorded that the French king played the 'jeu de paume' with the young Archduke, who was an enthusiast for this pastime. It is probable that he was responsible for the introduction of the 'racquet' into England; for we have it on contemporary authority that in 1506 Philippe, while paying an enforced visit to England (driven ashore at Weymouth, while on his way from Flanders to Spain), played a match in the 'tenes court' at Windsor, with a racquet. His opponent was the Marquess of Dorset (nephew of Elizabeth Wydeville and first cousin to the Queen) who used the older fashion of a gloved hand, receiving a handicap of fifteen. Philippe's devotion to this exercise appears to have been the cause of his death, for his last illness was brought about by drinking too much cold water when over-heated by the game, 25th September 1506. At this period the game was played with hard balls on a covered court.

(*Continued on p.* 194)

## PERFUMES AND POMANDERS

Perfumes and sweet-smelling ointments were little known in England until the fifteenth century. Even then only the wealthiest ladies and gentlemen used them as great luxuries. There are, however, a few scattered references to perfumes in the fourteenth century.

Fragrant gums, known as 'spices,' found their way occasionally into England at a somewhat earlier date, being imported chiefly from Arabia and the Orient.  Merchants who dealt in these scarce commodities were called 'spicers'; and from them the monopoly eventually passed to the apothecaries.

Italy was the centre of the manufacture of perfumes, produced mainly by the monks, who appear to have been very skilled in their distillation.  Venice was the chief place of export.

The chief ingredients employed were ambergris, musk, and civet.  Ambergris is a solid fatty substance, speckled grey in colour, ejected by whales, and found floating on the sea or on the coasts of India and China.  It is very

Fig. 45. Pomander

costly, and its price in the Middle Ages was never less than twenty shillings per ounce.

Ambergris was mixed with other scents, thereby increasing their fragrance.  Musk and civet are both obtained from animals.

The perfume concocted from these scents was called 'pomandre,' pome-ambre, an apple of ambergris, because the perfume was made up into little balls: the word 'pome' was applied to any spherical object such as an apple or ball, while 'ambre' was a name given to perfume in general.  These small balls were kept under perforated lids in small boxes called 'cassolettes' or 'printainers,' made of choice woods, ivory, or gold, often set with jewels.

In the fourteenth century the name 'pomandre' was first applied, not as previously to the perfume itself, but to the ornamental container—the POMANDER.

Some inventories of the fourteenth and fifteenth centuries mention them: Charles V of France had twelve; and Henry IV and Henry V of England each had pomanders.  Fifteenth-century pomanders were ball-shaped, generally of filigree goldsmith's work composed of two semi-spheres hinged together; each section had a perforated hinged lid, so that two kinds of scent could be kept in each pomander. Surmounting the clasp was an ornament securing a small chain which terminated in a ring (Fig. 45). This type of pomander was hung from a gentleman's waistbelt, or was sometimes carried in the hand with one finger slipped through the ring. About the middle of the fifteenth century mention is made of 'a pomander for use as a pendant to a lady's girdle.'

Henry VII spent various sums upon perfume and pomanders as his privy purse expenses testify. For example, in 1492 'a box of pomand 10s.,' and in 1498 for 'Muske and Awmber £17 5s.' During the first years of the sixteenth century pomanders were more frequently used, as they were found convenient to place to the nostrils in the event of unpleasant vapours being encountered. They also acted as a disinfectant.

(*Continued on p.* 271)

Fig. 46. XVth Century

## EMBROIDERY

*Introduction.* It is felt that some knowledge of the crafts of embroidery and lace, and also the characteristic designs used at different periods, will be helpful to those interested in the study of costume.

Certain types of embroidery or needlework are generally assumed to have originated at the periods best known for their production; but, in many cases, investigation has disclosed examples much earlier in date than that fixed by the popular belief. Stump work, associated mainly with the seventeenth century, is a case in point, its earliest appearance in England being found in the fifteenth century.

Early embroidery and garments decorated with needlework have been dealt with in vols. i and ii of this work.[1]

From the sixth century, monks and nuns in England were noted for their proficiency in designing and working embroideries. Many private individuals of the upper classes also excelled in the broderer's art, ladies of the aristocracy frequently being sent to convents to study the craft and to acquire skill with the needle.

[1] *See* Indexes, vol. i, p. 289, and vol. ii, p. 472.

Numberless references to embroidery are to be found in early writings, and many names of professional broderers engaged in royal and noble households occur in wardrobe accounts and privy purse expenses. These persons were chiefly employed in embroidering ecclesiastical vestments and furnishings, although they did some personal and domestic work for lay employers.

In the fourteenth century the craft of weaving brocaded and other patterned materials had reached a high standard; this fact is responsible, in a measure, for the decline in the art of the needle during this and the fifteenth century.

In spite of many vicissitudes, professional broderers were formed into a company in 1430, and with them were amalgamated the more ancient Company of Tapissers. Notwithstanding this stimulus, however, the unsettled state of the country, resulting from the Wars of the Roses (1453–85), still prevented any further developments in style and technique being achieved: in fact, the broderer's art remained practically at a standstill during the fourteenth and fifteenth centuries. All extant specimens of needlework dating between 1485 and 1500 display the technique common to these centuries.

Latin names for various types of needlework were in use during its best periods throughout Europe, and the following list may be of interest:

*Opus Anglicanum*, the name given to the early type of English needlework, which was the best of its kind from Anglo-Saxon times until the end of the thirteenth century. This was executed in chain stitch and a fine split stitch, which gave the effect of slight modelling, and a certain richness to the figures and subjects portrayed (*see* vol. ii, p. 64).

*Opus Consutum*. Sections of needlework stitched together, *appliqué* or cut-out work. Figures and motifs were shaped out of silk, satin, velvet, or linen, and sewn to a ground. The faces and limbs of figures were worked in thin lines of brown silk, or they were sometimes painted. The draperies were shaded with stitching and outlined, the edges being finished with silk stitching, gold thread, or cord. Practised in England during the fourteenth century—a hundred years before the birth of Botticelli, who is said to have invented the process!

*Opus Filatorium*. Thread embroidery on network—darned work.

*Opus Pectineum*. Woven or comb work, in imitation of embroidery; woven with the aid of a comb-like instrument.

*Opus Phrygium*. Passing, or gold work—hence 'passement.' Flat gold or gold outline embroidery was known long before the Christian era; the women of Phrygia excelled in the art, and this type of needlework is named after them. In post-Christian centuries thick raised gold thread was used, in imitation of goldsmith's work and carvings. Narrow thin strips of the gold metal were whipped around threads of silk or twine. This work is sometimes referred to as *Aurifrisium*.

*Opus Plumarium*. Feather stitch. Long stitches close together, laid on lengthwise, and overlapping one another like the plumage of a bird.

*Opus Pulvinarium*. Cross or canvas stitch, covering squares counted by threads of the basic fabric. French: *point comptée*. Much used in oriental embroidery. Being of a coarse strong stitching it was chiefly used to embroider cushion covers, foot carpets, etc. Sometimes called 'cushion work.'

*English Work.* The name given to the later variety of *Opus Anglicanum.* It was embroidery of laid stitches in gold thread, and usually formed a background for figures and motifs worked in silk. The faces and limbs of figures were worked in split stitch with fine black outlines, the draperies in thickly laid stitches of shaded colour; or they were sometimes worked in 'basket' or cross-bar stitch.

*Nuns' Work.* Needlework resembling modern needle point. So called since the fourteenth century.

'Pricking clouts' is a fifteenth- and sixteenth-century expression for embroidering.  (*Continued on p.* 224)

## SPANISH WORK

About the year 1490 a type of needlework, originating in Spain, had reached France and Flanders. Embroidery in black silk as a decoration for garments was known in England before the end of the fifteenth century, therefore the theory that it was introduced by Katherine of Aragon should be regarded as another unsubstantiated legend. But it was popularized in England when Katherine came as the bride of Arthur, Prince of Wales, in 1501.

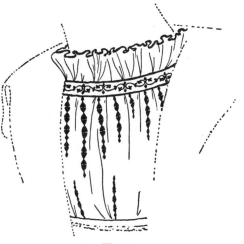

Fig. 47

It was known as 'Spanish stitch,' 'Spanish work,' or 'Black work,' its characteristic being black silk embroidery on linen or fine 'Holland cloth,' and was at first worked in 'line,' 'stroke stitch' or 'double running.' [1]

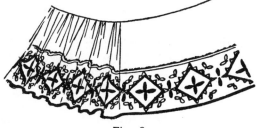

Fig. 48

Some examples found in portraits of the late fifteenth or early sixteenth century show an edging, less than a sixteenth of an inch wide, of black silk, in overcast or buttonhole stitch, used for overcasting the edge of the lawn frill.

Fig. 47 illustrates a design, executed in 'coral' stitch, used on the neck-band of a shirt. The pendant motif, of solid work or 'satin stitch,'

[1] Sometimes referred to in modern times as 'Holbein stitch.'

is repeated in varying lengths at about two-inch intervals on the shirt, and amongst the gathers or folds.

Fig. 48 gives another example of Spanish work, double-running stitch, used as a decorative edging to the frill of a shirt cuff.

Fig. 49 gives yet another design of the same date, also in coral stitch, used for a similar purpose. The small detached leaves are probably knot stitch.

(*Continued on p.* 225)

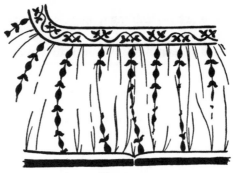

Fig. 49

## CUTWORK

During the Middle Ages monks and nuns monopolized, among other crafts, the art of working with the needle intricate patterns on fine lawn, linen, or network, chiefly for the decoration of church vestments. This style of embroidery was known as 'cutwork.' It was exceptional for private individuals to wear it, until it came into universal use during the first part of the sixteenth century, not only for the decoration of church vestments, but for Court and civil costumes.

Cutwork was embroidered in various ways, in buttonhole stitch, whipped stitch, drawn thread, or darned work.

Threads of linen fabric were drawn and *cut* out to form vacant spaces, the remaining threads being overcast with buttonhole stitch and fashioned with the needle into various geometrical forms.

Another method was to wind threads round a small frame, interlacing them so as to form a network; and for more elaborate designs threads were crossed and recrossed diagonally through the network. Beneath this was set a piece of linen, and with the needle the network was sewn to it, by edging round those parts of the pattern that were to remain opaque. When this was completed the superfluous linen was *cut* away. Later, this was called 'point coupé.'

In yet another way patterns were *cut* out in linen, applied to net, and their edges overcast.

Patterns were also darned on net; but as this type required no cutting it comes under the head of *Opus Filatorium.*

Italy, always at that time in advance of other nations in matters of art, had known cutwork for some time previously, and used it during the second half of the fifteenth century for personal adornment.

What is no doubt the earliest representation of cutwork in England, worn by an Englishwoman, is to be seen in the portrait (Plate XII) of the Princess

Fig. 50

Mary Tudor at the National Gallery. It is a very fine embroidery in white silk or thread on white lawn; the edge is composed of little dots—picot—and the design is scrollwork. This cutwork is sewn just inside the square neck opening.

Fig. 50 shows this cutwork embroidered on fine lawn. It is probably of Italian workmanship.

Another person of importance who used cutwork was Cardinal Wolsey, whose rochets were decorated with cutwork at the neck, on the shoulders, the edge of the sleeves, and at the bottom hem.

It is more than likely that this cutwork was also Italian in origin.

Fig. 51 shows a design of cutwork in use at this time, and is taken from a portrait of John Fisher, Bishop of Rochester and Saint (born 1459, bishop 1504, executed 1535), whose rochet is trimmed with it. The pattern is of linen, buttonholed on to a foundation of network threads, interlaced in

Fig. 51

squares and diagonally. The illustration (Fig. 51) shows one section as it was worked on a frame; and many of these, of the same design, were joined together to form a long strip, garded at both edges by two rows of linen joined together with cross-stitching.

In wardrobe accounts of the first half of the century the term 'laced linen' is sometimes encountered. This reference applies to cutwork decoration, not to lace.

Cutwork is the origin of lace (see p. 230).

### THE ORIGIN OF STUMPWORK

A rich and effective type of embroidery was used for the decoration of church vestments, especially for the orphreys and borders of copes, etc. Figures of saints, armorial bearings, and other subjects were first drawn out

on linen, which was then tightly stretched upon small frames.   Certain parts
of these figures were designed to be in relief, and, for this purpose, padding
of cotton, wool, or hair was laid on, and the whole figure then embroidered in
silks on the same principle as described under *Opus Consutum*.   When complete the figure was cut out, backed by paper to prevent the linen foundation
from fraying, and then mounted upon some rich material—silk, velvet, or
cloth of gold—the edges being oversewn with silk thread or gold cord.   This
style was the origin of the stumpwork associated mainly with the seventeenth
century.

For centuries it had been the custom for persons of the upper classes to
present to the church the rich apparel which they had worn on some auspicious
occasion, for conversion into vestments and altar coverings.

(*Embroidery continued on p.* 224)

### THE YEOMEN OF THE GUARD

It is commonly supposed that the costume worn to-day by the Yeomen of
the Guard is the same as that in use when the corps was first formed.[1]

The history of their costume which follows, showing its variations from
reign to reign, will prove this idea to be a misconception, and at the same time
may be entertaining to many of those interested in the corps.

There are two theories with regard to the origin of the name 'Beef-Eater'
or 'Beefeater.'   The first suggests that the word is a corruption of the
French 'buffetier,' an officer who attended the buffet (sideboard) or 'dressoir'
(*see* vol. ii, p. xii), whereon were displayed the gold and silver vessels and the
special viands and wines used at state banquets.   From early times officers of
the guard were stationed by these buffets, and, since Tudor times, this privilege has belonged to the Yeomen of the Guard, hence the term 'buffetier'—
beefeater—was vulgarly applied to them.

The second, less credible, story concerns a scurvy trick said to have been
played on the Abbot of Reading by Henry VIII.

Having disguised his portly person in the character and habit of a Yeoman
of the Guard, the King was invited to dine with the abbot.   The burly 'yeoman,' his lusty appetite increased by the ardour of the chase, ate voraciously
from a large joint of roast beef, much to the chagrin of the fastidious abbot,
who cried: 'I would give an hundred pounds on the condition I could feed so

[1] When the author first saw the opera *The Yeoman of the Guard* he was quite certain that the
liveries of the guard were wrong, and set about proving that this was so.   The brief history given
above is the result.

heartily on beef as you do. Alas! my weak and squeamish stomach will hardly digest the leg of a small rabbit or the wing of a chicken!'

A few weeks later the abbot was committed a close prisoner to the Tower, and for a short time fed on bread and water. At length roast beef was set before him, and the abbot acquitted himself with a valour accentuated by his fast. To his alarm and discomfiture the King unexpectedly entered the apartment, claiming the £100 which the abbot had so lightly promised for the restoration of his appetite for roast beef.

The remedy was severe, and the physician's fee high; but the money had to be paid before the abbot was released. Never afterwards could he see or think of a Yeoman of the Guard without associating him with a beef-eater.

Such a prank naturally amused the Court, and, indeed, percolated quickly to the gossips of the town. It is interesting to reflect that the nickname of this honourable corps may perpetuate a practical joke played long ago, by the bluff and merry King Hal!

In the first year of his reign (1485) Henry VII, issued a decree as follows:

'Wherefore, for the safeguard and preservation of his own body, he constituted and ordained a certain number as well of good archers as of diverse others persons being hardy, strong and of agility to geve [give] daily attendance on his person, whom he named "Yeomen of his Garde," which president men thought that he learned of the French King when he was in France.'

A description of the dress of the Yeomen of the Guard is found in a notice of the marriage of Arthur, Prince of Wales, in 1501. They wore sleeveless tunics of green and white damask—the Tudor livery colours—stripes 'goodly embroidered both on their breasts before and also on their backs behind, with round garlands of vine branches beset before richly with spangles of silver and gilt, and in the middle the Red Rose [1] beaten with goldsmith's work; the which were of the chosen persons of the whole country; proved archers; strong, valiant, and bold men; with bright hawberts in their hands; to the number of three hundred; evermore standing by the ways and passages upon a row in both the sides where the King's Highness should from chamber to chamber, or from one place to another, at his goodly pleasure be removed' (*see* Plate III A).

The earliest authentic representation of a Yeoman of the Guard is given in a document dated 1527, which shows a yeoman in the characteristic dress of an earlier date than the document, in point of fact that of the reign of Henry VII. In details the livery is the same as that just described, namely: a tunic, with a skirt or 'base' of damask, striped with the Tudor livery colours of white and green. An important detail is that the stripes shift or are counterchanged at the waist-line—a method frequently encountered. On the breast and back of this livery, as first worn, was embroidered a red rose surrounded by a vine branch or wreath in gold. A detail drawing of this is shown in Fig. 52. Under this tunic the pourpoint, with sleeves shaped as

---

[1] The Red Rose of the House of Lancaster.

described under Fig. 35 was worn, its colour in the original document being a mauvish pink: the bonet is of the same colour, the rose vermilion, and the sword belt, scabbard, and shoes black.    There was no particular rule as to the colour of these undergarments, which might vary in different members of the detachment, but the tunic or livery jacket was 'uniform' for all.

Fig. 52

The arms carried were 'bright hawberts' of gilt, bows and arrows, and also a sword suspended from a belt attached to the waist-belt.

It is recorded that each man had three changes of livery: one for state occasions, one for ordinary use, and one for watching. The state livery is shown in Plate III A. The ordinary livery consisted of the same shaped tunic or jacket, in green and white stripes, but made of cloth.    The third or 'watching' livery is invariably described as 'russet' (see vol. ii, p. 65, and vol. iii, p. 371), but its shape is unknown; in all probability it was the everyday dress of ordinary working people.    When they 'made watch' nightly, they were 'girt with their swords, or with other weapons ready, and harness about them.'

The corps was divided into two sections, Halberdiers and Archers.    On certain occasions the former were mounted, and sometimes, though rarely, the Archers also.

In number the smallest complement of the corps was two hundred, of whom one hundred were mounted.    Both detachments were frequently employed on active service.

(Continued on p. 289)

Fig. 53. Tudor Rose Quarterly

## ROYALTY AND NOBILITY—WOMEN: 1485–1509

### ELYSABETH OF YORK

#### Queen of Henry VII, 1466–1503

Elysabeth Plantagenet, born 1466, was the eldest of the six daughters of King Edward IV and Elizabeth Wydeville.    Her sisters were:

Mary, born 1467, died 1482.
Cicely married John Viscount Welles and d.s.p.

Anne married Thomas Howard II, Duke of Norfolk, K.G., in 1495, and died in 1511 leaving no surviving issue. Her effigy is in Framlingham Church.

Bridget became a nun at Dartford, Kent, and died in 1517.

Katherine, born at Eltham Palace in 1479, and married Sir William Courtenay, K.B., and died 1527. Their only son, Henry, Earl of Devonshire and Marquess of Exeter (1498–1539), had an only son, Edward Courtenay, Earl of Devonshire, born 1526, d.s.p. 1556.

This queen usually signed her name 'Elysabeth.' She was of fair complexion with hair of pale gold like her mother, Elizabeth Wydeville. Of a complacent and charitable disposition, she was beloved of her people and had the good sense to leave government and politics alone. It must not be forgotten, however, that Elysabeth was in justice a Queen Regnant, being the lawful heiress to the crown (*see* vol. ii, p. 414), her husband, Henry VII, having won it by the sword.

As a little girl the Princess Elysabeth Plantagenet of York would have been dressed as shown in the drawing of the Princess Margaret of Clarence (vol. ii, Fig. 571) who was three years younger

Fig. 54. Late Fifteenth-century Rose

than Elysabeth. Close-fitting sleeves, in place of the long hanging ones, could be worn with this garment. As a young woman she wore a fashionable costume as shown in Fig. 576 or 577 (vol. ii).

The Princess's marriage took place in 1486 and her coronation in the following year.

The children of Henry VII and Elysabeth were:

Arthur, Prince of Wales, born 1486. Married in 1501 Katherine, daughter of Ferdinand V, King of Spain, but d.s.p. 1502.

Henry, Prince of Wales, afterwards King Henry VIII.

Margaret, born 1489, married first in 1503 James IV, King of Scotland, and was the mother of James V, and grandmother of Mary Queen of Scots.

She married secondly in 1514 Archibald Douglas, Earl of Angus, whose only daughter, Margaret, married Matthew Stuart, 4th Earl of Lennox, Regent of Scotland, and became the mother of Henry Stuart, Lord Darnley (born 1545), and Charles Stuart, 5th Earl of Lennox, the father of Arabella Stuart.

The Queen-Dowager married thirdly in 1526 Henry Stuart, Lord Methven. She died in 1539.

Mary was born in 1498 and married first in 1514 Louis XII of France; secondly in 1515 Charles Brandon, Duke of Suffolk.

Their only daughter, Frances, married Henry Grey, Marquess of Dorset, afterwards Duke of Suffolk (beheaded 23rd February 1554), and had three daughters:

> Jane, born 1537, who married in 1553 Lord Guyldeford Dudley (beheaded 12th February 1554).

> Katherine married first Henry Lord Herbert, and secondly Edward Seymour, Earl of Hertford, and left issue.

> Mary married in 1553 Martin Keys, groom-porter to Queen Elizabeth. She died in 1578 and their younger daughter, Eleanor, married Henry Clifford, Earl of Cumberland, and left issue.

Queen Elysabeth died on her birthday 1503.

As the spouse of a husband notorious for his niggardliness, Elysabeth

Plantagenet faced her difficulties in the spirit of a good wife, and practised shrewd economy regardless of her position as Queen of England! She was, alas, frequently in arrears with the payment of her bills, both domestic and personal, and one often finds in household accounts of this time items such as this: 1497: 'Delivered to the Quenes grace for to pay hir detts, which is to be repayed £2,000.' An entry perhaps explained by the fact that the Queen often had to find money for the maintenance of her sisters.

With her own wardrobe she was ever thrifty. Her gowns were often mended and re-shorn (see vol. ii, p. 188), or 'raised'—that is, had a new nap set upon the material. Frequently the fabric was turned and re-made or freshly trimmed, newly hemmed and beaten out at the bottom.

Fig. 55. Lute    New bodies were even added to old gowns.

To-day, when dressmakers select their professional names with such finicking fantastic taste, it is refreshing to learn that a Queen of England's 'Yeoman of the Queen's Stuff' (for that was what the dressmaker was called) possessed the commonplace name of Maistre John Belly.

Elysabeth's frugality in personal adornment was in striking contrast to her liberal expenditure in the encouragement of music. Her taste in that art is well known, and it was inherited by her son and two daughters, Margaret, Queen of Scotland, and Mary, Queen of France. Largely through her interest and

Fig. 56. Dulcimer

influence music now became increasingly an accomplishment and pastime of the aristocracy. From earlier times the lute (Fig. 55) and harp were in general use, but at this period the ancestor of the modern piano appeared.

It was called the 'claregalls' or 'clarichord,' and was itself an improvement on the older 'dulcimer' (Fig. 56).

The dulcimer was similar to the earlier 'psaltery' (Fig. 57). Both were boxes in which the strings were of gut or wire. The psaltery was played by plucking its strings with the fingers: whereas the strings of the dulcimer were struck by small hammers. The 'clarichord,' so spelt in the Leckingfield *Proverbs*, is first mentioned in 1404. The earlier instrument was rectangular in shape with nine keys and six strings all of the same length.

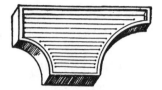

Fig. 57. Psaltery

Later on separate bridges were introduced to shorten the higher pitched strings, and the box was reduced in shape accordingly (Figs. 58 and 59). Even the parsimonious Henry contributed with moderate generosity to the

art of the musician. He paid William Newark £1 for composing a song in 1492, and in 1502 13s. 4d. to William Cornish, junior, of the King's Chapel, for the setting of a Christmas carol. In addition to music, the relaxations of society at this period included the recitation of prose and verse; also witnessing the performances of players, and listening to the 'disour,' a teller of stories. A 'disar' was an actor or clown, hence any fool was so called. 'Dizard' is a variant of the same name. 'A Dizzard or common vice and jester counter-fetting the gestures of any man, and moving his body at him list.'

Fig. 58. Clavichord

Dancing and the morris dance were much indulged in; and a primitive kind of masque called a 'disgysing,' in which 'Ladyes and gentilmen dressed up and performed interludes,' was engaging the interest of the courtiers and the upper classes.

The frolics of the jester (*see* Fig. 335 taken from an Illum. MS. of this time) diverted the court or family circle.

Queen Elysabeth's jester bore the common name of 'Patch' (*see* p. 300); his salary was 6s. 8d. Thomas Blakall was 'the Kinges foule,' who received the same sum. Prince Henry's jester was called 'Goose.'

Fig. 59. Clavichord

The Lord or 'Abbot of Mysrewle' to the royal household was named Ringeley, and on several occasions he received a gift of £5.

For quieter moods there were the games of chess and cards. 'Primero' [1]

---

[1] For the manner of playing the game, *see* Nares's *Glossary*, where it is fully described. A picture painted in the late sixteenth century, belonging to the Earl of Derby, shows four gentlemen playing this game.

and 'Imperial' were those most frequently played. In 1502 it cost 'the Quenes grace upon the Feast of S. Stephen for hure disporte at Cardes this Christmas, c/-.'

'Tabuls' (the old name for backgammon) and dice were also popular. 'The Quenes grace' was put to some expense on many occasions by playing these games, which were permitted as pastimes for the Royal children, who also played cards for high stakes, even on 'Sondays.' On one occasion, Prince Henry, aged nine, lost as much as £3 6s. 8d.

Palaces in Tudor times were divided into two parts or 'sides': the king residing on his side accompanied by his suite, and the queen on hers with her ladies. The king and queen only dined together at state banquets, or on some formal occasion, and then at separate tables, as this was more convenient when being served by the important officials of the household. At other times they dined separately in their own suites of rooms. The aristocracy sat down to dinner at 11 a.m., and often spent two or three hours over the meal. Games and pastimes usually took place after the most important meal of the day—supper, served at six o'clock. The more frivolous society folk gave what were called 'voides,' equivalent to the cocktail parties of to-day. Ipocras in golden cups and comfits on golden platters were handed round to the assembled company.

Fig. 60. Chair of Estate (*from painted glass*)

A French maxim recommends 'To rise at five and dine at nine, to sup at five and sleep at nine, is the way to live to ninety and nine,' but it is doubtful if it was followed by the aristocracy.

The middle classes took their chief meal at midday, and their evening repast at seven or eight o'clock. As for the lower orders, they fed when they could and when they had anything in the larder.

In Queen Elizabeth's reign the hours for meals remained much the same.

A contemporary description of Elysabeth's coronation robes is given as follows: The queen was 'royally apparelled, in a kyrtle of white cloth of gold of damask, and a mantle of the same suit, furred with ermine, fastened before her breast with a great lace [cord], curiously wrought of gold and silk, and rich knobs of gold at the end, tasselled; her fair yellow hair hanging down plain behind her back, with a *calle of pipes* over it, and wearing on her head a circle of gold richly garnished with precious stones.' The word 'kyrtle' was used in a twofold sense, sometimes for a jacket or bodice only, and sometimes for the petticote. A full kyrtle was always a jacket and petticote. A half kyrtle was either one or the other (*see* vol. ii, p. 358). The shape of the dress is described under Regal Costume (vol. ii, chap. vi). The headdress was simply the caul (*see* Fig. 130); the network made of gold thread (*see* vol. ii, p. 463). On top of this was worn a gold crown; in all probability *not* the crown of a queen consort but a crown regnant as shown in Plate I.

This figure is taken from the portrait of Queen Elysabeth in the altar-painting at Windsor. It is said to have been painted about 1508, five years after the death of Elysabeth; and in it she is represented in the regal robes she wore during the last ten years of the fifteenth century. Her gown is of blue velvet, having

Fig. 61. Border, 1487

down the front bands of ermine reaching below the waist, in a manner similar to that worn in Fig. 605, vol. ii, but clasped with rubies and diamonds. The sleeves are close-fitting, with turned-up pointed cuffs of ermine.

The mantle is crimson velvet, lined with ermine, and is fastened across the shoulders by gold cords and tassels.

The crown is worn above the gable headdress, and from a jewelled lace, wound twice round the neck, is suspended a beautiful gold and jewelled cross.

The Coventry Tapestry shows Queen Elysabeth in 1490 wearing a gown fashioned exactly like that shown in Fig. 66. It is made of a large-patterned gold brocade, bordered with ermine, the wide sleeves being lined with the same. Her elaborate headdress is shown in detail in Fig. 146.

## The Lady Margaret Beaufort

### Countess of Richmond, died 1509

The Grande Dame of this time, described by her confessor, Bishop Fisher, as 'a Scholar and a Saint' was Margaret, Countess of Richmond, the daughter and heiress of John Beaufort, 3rd Earl and 1st Duke of Somerset, and great-granddaughter of John of Gaunt, Duke of Lancaster.

The Lady Margaret Beaufort married, first, Edmund Tudor, Earl of Richmond, and was the mother of King Henry VII. At the earl's death, in 1456, she married Sir Henry Stafford; and Thomas, 2nd Lord Stanley and 1st Earl of Derby, became her third husband.

During her married life her taste in dress was simple, and in the fashions of the second half of the fifteenth century. There is a portrait extant [1] which shows her wearing a gown of dull red velvet, having the square neck-line bordered with gold and jewels; her headdress is similar to that worn by Elysabeth of York (Plate IV)—a fact which dates the portrait about 1500.

---

[1] This belonged to the late Gibson Cullum, Esq. *See* Tudor Exhibition Catalogue, 1890.

It is on record that the countess had some rich costumes, of velvet and cloth of gold, to be worn at court on special occasions.

The portrait in the National Portrait Gallery, London, painted about 1485, represents her as a widow, though without conventional widow's dress. Her gown is of dull red velvet and grey fur: she wears a *black* barbe (the sole indication of widowhood) under a white frontlet of embroidery, and a hood-piece of gold damask.

Becoming a widow for the third time in 1504, she took the vow of celibacy at Bishop Fisher's hands. In portraits at St John's College, and Christ's College, Cambridge, she is seen wearing widow's weeds complete, which indubitably she had earned (*see* Fig. 149). This lady was the foundress of both these colleges. She played a prominent part in setting her son upon the English throne, and was also the authoress of a useful document on cere-monial.

Margaret died 29th June 1509, and is buried in Westminster Abbey, where a beautiful bronze effigy perpetuates her memory. 'At her death she had thirty kings and queens allied to her within the fourth degree either of blood or affinity.' (From Bishop Fisher's funeral sermon.) 'Since her death she has been allied in her posterity to thirty more.' (Thomas Baker.)

### Nobility: Women

#### *English, Flemish, and French*

The type of dress worn by noble ladies of the first part of this reign is shown in Plate IV, and closely resembles that worn by the lady in Fig. 576, vol. ii, the only difference being in the body part and neck opening. In some cases the gown was made all in one; but the latest mode was to have BODICE [1] and skirt separated at the waist-line, which was masked by a narrow scarf of contrasting colour, tied in front with one loop and two ends. The 'pair of bodies' were fairly tight-fitting, and finished off square at the neck with a band of embroidery and sometimes fur, showing at the shoulders a part of the underdress. Inside this was seen the fine lawn tucker, gathered into an embroidered neck-band, or drawn in close by a silken cord. A band of

---

[1] The name 'bodice' (*see* vol. ii, Fig. 550 and p. 399) is used in this volume at this early date as a more understandable alternative for 'corset,' although the former word did not come into use until late in the sixteenth century. The latter was often applied to the bodice in contemporary writings, but it is thought advisable to restrict the use of this name to 'stays.' Bodice, the outer garment; corset and stays, the tight-fitting body support worn underneath.

passement set with jewels frequently followed the outline of the neck and sometimes descended down the front of the dress. The close-fitting sleeves were finished off at the wrists with cuffs of fur or velvet. Skirts were cut

Figs. 62, 63, 64. Noble Ladies, c. 1495

as shown in diagram, Fig. 546, vol. ii, and decorated at the bottom edge with deep borders of fur or velvet.

The drawing, Plate IV, represents Queen Elysabeth in a gown of plunket celestyne (sky-blue) velvet furred with ermine and banded with gold set with rubies. For full state a rich mantle was worn over this type of dress; and it was the custom for the mantles of royal and noble ladies to display their armorial bearings (see Plate V). In Plate IV the queen is wearing the new kind of headdress or hood which is associated entirely with the reign of Henry VII. For a full description of it, see under Figs. 151 and 152. The union Badge of the red rose of Lancaster and the white rose of York is surmounted by the crown imperial (see p. 117), and beneath the rose is the Badge of the Beaufort family — the portcullis — adopted by the Tudors.

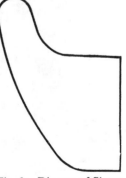

Fig. 65. Diagram of Sleeve

Later in the reign, and before 1496, the fashion for wearing a wide full sleeve, rather square in shape, was revived. It was introduced from the Continent, where it reappeared at a somewhat earlier date, especially in

France and Flanders. It is worn by the three ladies (Figs. 62, 63, 64, and shown in diagram, Fig. 65). In some cases this square sleeve was cut with a close-fitting armhole, as in Figs. 62 and 63, and in others it is rather bulky round the upper arm (Fig. 64). In all cases the edges were turned back showing the lining of fur or different-coloured material.

Another mode was to have the body part of the gown without sleeves, worn over another body of a contrasting colour with sleeves of the shape just described. The neck openings were of different kinds. Fig. 63 shows a style which is sometimes met with in the earlier part of the fifteenth century, and is similar to Fig. 605, vol. ii. The waist is girdled in the manner there shown with a handsome belt and massive clasps. In the original Illum. MS., from which this drawing is taken, the gown is of red velvet.

Fig. 64 shows the back of another contemporary dress. Its back is open down to the waist, the edges being laced across an undergarment. The front view of this is shown in Fig. 142 where

Fig. 67.
Diagram of Sleeve

Fig. 66. French

Fig. 68. Flemish

it is laced widely across the breast and down to the waist-line. Attention is called to these two drawings, Fig. 64 and Fig. 142, which explain the origin of the term 'a pair of Bodies.' It will be observed that the body garment is in two distinct parts, laced together both back and front. The lady wears a gown with the body part cut all in one with the skirt. Some of the fullness is caught with an ornament at the back of the waist, whence the chief lines of drapery radiate.

Skirts were cut on the semicircular plan, and, as previously, were frequently raised and held in the hand, or draped over or under the arm.

When skirts were of less ample dimensions it was the mode to attach the hem at the centre of the back to a button at the back of the waist. With this method it was necessary to have the lining, thus shown to advantage, of rich material, often fur. Similarly, a larger portion of the underdress was displayed and this in consequence was composed of beautiful material or brocade (see Fig. 62).

For the headdresses of these ladies see p. 99.

The lady in Fig. 66 is taken from a French Illum. MS. of the last years of the fifteenth century. The simplicity of this costume, and the beautiful lines of the drapery carried out in a rich shade of rose-coloured velvet, in contrast to the black velvet headdress, are very striking, and are typical of a well-dressed noble lady of this time. This figure introduces a new fashion, a revival of one of the mid-fifteenth century, in which the sleeves finish in a point instead of a square, and taper from the armhole to the lowest point of

Fig. 69. English

the opening as shown in diagram, Fig. 67. The open part was usually turned back to show the lining of a contrasting colour or material, frequently fur. This is shown to advantage in Fig. 68. This lady's gown has the neck opening cut somewhat high, but open a little way in front, turned back to form small revers, and fastened on the chest by a jewelled ornament. A heavy gold chain surrounds the neck. The waist is confined by a sash-girdle, and the trailing skirt, without a border, is held up in the left hand, showing the underdress. The headdress is dealt with on p. 102.

The lady walking with the seigneur (Fig. 27) is dressed in the same style, but the divided top of the body is not turned back in revers. Her gown is of some rich large-patterned brocade, but she wears a different kind of headdress.

The general style of costume worn by the noble ladies attending Elysabeth of York, as depicted in the Coventry Tapestry, is shown in Fig. 69. They all wear gowns, modelled on the lines of those shown in previous drawings, but one has long and rather wide hanging sleeves, with a longitudinal slit at elbow level through which the arm passes. The close-fitting under-sleeve, decorated with bands of gold and 'cuttes,' is of the German fashion; and the large hanging cuffs to the sleeves of the white cambric camise are rather exceptional, although a few of these tapestried ladies wear them.

The headdress is interesting, as it is probably the earliest (1490) representation of the 'gable headdress,' of which a full description is given under Fig. 145.

The costume in which that important young lady, Marie of Burgundy, is represented in the woodcut shown in Fig. 43 may be that which she actually wore, but is more likely to be in the fashion of the time of Dürer's woodcut.


## SPANISH STYLES

### Isabella of Castile, 1451–1504

Isabella, daughter of Juan II of Castile and Leon, was born 1451. Married Ferdinand of Aragon in 1469, and succeeded her half-brother Enrique IV as Queen in her own right, 1474. This marriage brought about the Union of Spain.

The introduction of the Inquisition (1476–80) shows her to be neither scrupulous nor tender-hearted, though inspired by high aims. Very dignified, devout, and a Great Lady, she made Spain one of the greatest powers in Europe. After a reign of thirty years she died in 1504.

Her dress of red and gold brocade in the portrait (Plate II A) appears to be of the same make as shown in Fig. 66, and the painting suggests that the headdress is arranged very much like that in Fig. 248. Her hair is brown. This portrait with that of her husband hangs in the Holbein Room at Windsor Castle. They are mentioned in the Royal collection of Henry VIII, and it is pleasant to think that the Princess Katherine may have brought the portraits of her parents with her into England.


### Joanna

### Queen of Castile, 1479–1555

The lives of these two daughters of Ferdinand V, King of Aragon, and Isabella, Queen of Castile—Joanna, born at Toledo, 6th November 1479, and Katherine of Aragon—very were sad ones. Joanna was morbidly affected by her mother's religious zeal, and there is little doubt that she was mentally unbalanced in early life. After the death of her mother in 1504, her father Ferdinand exaggerated her condition, in order to make it the pretext for nominating himself regent on her behalf at the time she succeeded her mother as Queen of Castile. Ferdinand's appointment was contested by Joanna's husband, but she was indifferent and allowed her father to reign. The loss of her husband, Philippe le Beau, in 1506, at the age of twenty-eight, sent

Joanna into the depths of despair, from which she never recovered, her affliction developing later into acute anti-religious insanity. She is frequently —rather unkindly—referred to as 'Joanna the Mad' or 'Jeanne la Folle.' The Castle of Tordesillas, on the banks of the Douro, was the residence of Queen Joanna for the greater part of her widowhood, and here she died in 1555.

Fig. 70

The triptych in the Musée Royal, Brussels, painted by Jacques van Laethem, furnishes the details of the costume illustrated in Plate V. In the two side panels are very fine portraits of Philippe le Beau and his wife Joanna, both wearing full state dress.

Fig. 71

Philippe's costume is described on p. 42, and Plate V is adapted from the portrait of the Queen. She wears a gown of rich brocade of the type much used in the fifteenth century; the background of gold woven with a pattern in gold outlined with red silk. The gown fits the figure, and has wide sleeves lined with red velvet and shaped as shown in the diagram, Fig. 67. It descends into a full skirt with train brought round and held in the left

Madame Eleanor aged iiii yeres.

Fig. 72

Duke Charles aged ii yeres and a half.

Fig. 73

(After Mabuse, Imperial Museum, Vienna)

hand. The plastron of miniver is edged at the neck and down the front with a band of jewels set in gold mounts (see Fig. 70). The purple and gold sidepieces under the neck opening belong to the underdress, and the pattern of the embroidery is given in Fig. 71. The state mantle, lined with miniver, displays the quarterings of the Hapsburg and Spanish armorial bearings. Some of them are visible. Sicily is seen on the right shoulder with the Lion of Leon underneath, and at the bottom a part of Ancient Burgundy above the Lion of Brabant. On her left shoulder is seen Austria above Ancient Burgundy repeated, and beneath the golden castle of Castile. An explanation of the hairdressing is given under Fig. 141, the headdress, Fig. 159, and the coronet, Fig. 181.

The children of Philippe le Beau and Joanna were:

Eleanor, the eldest (*see* p. 204). Fig. 72.

Charles (*see* p. 180). Fig. 73.

Isabel, born 1501, married in 1515 Christian II of Denmark. They were the parents of the celebrated Duchess of Milan. Queen Isabel died in 1526.

Ferdinand, born 1503 (*see* Fig. 2), married in 1521 Anne of Hungary (*see* Fig. 393). Emperor (*see* Fig. 2).

Marie, born 1505, married in 1521 Louis II, King of Hungary, and died 1564.

Catalina, born 1507, married Joam III of Portugal.

## KATHERINE OF ARAGON

### *Princess of Wales, 1485 until 1509*

JOANNA'S younger sister, Katherine of Aragon, was born 15th December 1485. On 14th November 1501 she married Arthur, Prince of Wales, and was left a young widow in April 1502. Katherine was no beauty, although in her youth she had some pretensions to good looks, and at the time of her first marriage, when aged sixteen, a certain grace of girlhood. Her complexion was light and her features rather hard and statuesque. She had black eyes and ruddy fair hair, which are not uncommon among Castilians. A head and shoulders portrait of Katherine, a lovely painting by Michiel Sithium, at the time of her marriage is in the Kunsthistorisches Museum, Vienna, and is reproduced in Plate X. It shows this young princess in Anglo-Franco-Flemish dress, wearing the early type of French hood as represented in Fig. 162. The halo was painted in at a later date. The black velvet body is shaped like that seen in Fig. 66, and the lawn tucker is drawn square round the neck and edged with black silk stitchery.

Even in Tudor times the most important feature of a society wedding was the clothes worn by the contracting parties and guests—and in those days public interest centred in masculine attire, as well as in feminine adornments. The marriage of Arthur, Prince of Wales, and the Princess Katherine was no exception. This sartorial 'event' took place '14 Nov. 1501, Sunday and the day of S. Erkenwald, and all London was agog to see the show.' An eyewitness of the princess's entry into London apologetically enumerates the wonders of the occasion: 'The costly apparel, both of goldsmith's work and embroidery, the rich jewels, the massy chains, the stirring horses, the beautiful bards,[1] and the glittering trappers,[1] both with bells and spangles of gold. I pretermit also the rich apparel of the princess, *the strange fashion of the Spanish nation*, the beauty of the English ladies, the goodly demeanour of the young damosels, the amorous countenance of the lusty batchelors. I pass over the fine engrained [coloured, dyed] clothes, the costly furs of the citizens, standing upon scaffolds, railed from Gracechurch St to Paul's. What should I speak of the *odoriferous* [2] scarlets, and fine velvets and pleasant furs, and rich chains which the Mayor of London with the Senate, sitting on horseback at the Little Conduit in Chepe, ware upon their bodies and about their necks. I will not molest you with rehearsing the rich arras, the costly tapestry, the fine cloths of silver and of gold, which did hang in every street where she passed.'

Of the bridal garments another writer of the time interestingly relates:

'The garments of the Lord Prince and Princess both were of white satin; but (for the strange dyversity of raiment of the country of Spain to be discryvyn) she were that time and day of her marriage upon her head a coif of white silk with a border of gold, pearl, and precious stones being of an inch and a half in breadth,[3] the which covered the great part of her visage, and also a large quantity of her body toward her waist and middle; her gown very large both the sleeves and also the body, with many pleats, much like unto men's clothing. And after the same form the remen'nt of the Ladies of Spain were arrayed; and beneath their waists certain round hoops, bearing out their gowns from their bodies, after their country's manner.'

This was also the first appearance in this country of the famous FAR-THINGALE. A description of it is given under Noble Ladies, *temp.* Henry VIII, p. 199.

Another gossip tells us that the Princess Katherine made her entry into London riding on a mule and that she wore 'a litill hatte fashounyd like a cardinall's hatte with a lase of gold at this hatt to stay hit.' This was a shiny-black circular Andalusian hat, with a wide brim and a low crown, such as may be seen in Spain to-day. The gold cord or lace, tied under the chin, secured it to the head, and the hat was worn over a red coif embroidered with gold 'covering the ears in the Venetian fashion.'

To Katherine of Aragon is due the introduction of Spanish interests into England, so that from this point sections on Spanish styles will be inserted.

In Spain, costume in general underwent many vicissitudes owing to the

---

[1] See vol. ii, p. 341.     [2] Garments were frequently perfumed.
[3] For a similar headdress see Fig. 130.

long-standing, though somewhat ineffective, custom of the sovereign, chiefly at the instigation of the Cortes, issuing 'pragmatics,' or sumptuary laws. The Cortes were the two chambers of legislative assembly of Spain, the most important being the Cortes of Castile, which included the representatives of eighteen cities. For two and a half centuries past there had been continual conflict between the Cortes and the people, who tenaciously ignored their decrees.

As soon as Ferdinand and Isabella had firmly established their joint sovereignty over united Spain, a pragmatic of 1495 decreed against the wearing of extravagant apparel, and especially the use of gold and silver woven into materials and into embroideries.

The Christianized population of southern Spain, the Moriscos, were extremely proficient in weaving gold and silver and in embroidery, particularly the latter. Their gold and silver embroideries on velvet were in great demand for Church vestments and Royal trappings, and the semi-oriental fabrics of Andalusia were much sought after by all Europe. Gold was plentiful, as it was finding its way into the country from the newly discovered Indies, and the ingenious and industrious weavers and broderers provided the world with textiles of exceptional splendour to their own very great advantage. A pragmatic issued in 1498 very seriously crippled this flourishing industry. It is true that the weaving of gold brocade had been stopped by the previous decree, and supplies were now imported from abroad. To replace this fabric all sorts of strange devices and novelties were introduced in the manufacture of silks.

The silkworm had been reared in Spain for many centuries (*see* vol. i, pp. 213 and 218), and silk weaving was of a very high standard, and the finest in Europe; yet a pragmatic was issued in 1499 stringently forbidding the manufacture, sale, and use of silk except for linings. This staggering blow was tempered to prevent total ruin by a decree that no raw silk from abroad was to be introduced into Spain, and only Spanish-reared silk could be used. This again was somewhat relaxed to the extent of allowing silk to be *worn*. But this was not the weavers' contention. They did not want to wear the silk themselves, so much as to make it for other people to wear; consequently their industry languished and never entirely recovered.

### The Lady Margaret Tudor

*Queen Consort of James IV of Scotland, 1489 until 1509*

There have been many distinguished Margarets in our English royal families. They include the following:

1. Margaret, daughter of Edward the Exile, son of Edmund Ironside, King of England and last of the Saxon princes in succession to the throne. She was heiress of her brother Edgar the Atheling, and married in 1070 Malcolm Ceanmor, King of Scotland. Canonized as St. Margaret.

2. Margaret, elder daughter of Henry III, married Alexander III of Scotland.

3. Margaret, daughter of Edward I, married John, Duke of Brabant.

4. Margaret, daughter of Edward III, married John Hastings, Earl of Pembroke.

5. Margaret, daughter of Richard, Duke of York.   Duchess of Burgundy.

6. Margaret, daughter of George, Duke of Clarence.   Countess of Salisbury.

7. Margaret, daughter of Henry VII.   Queen of Scotland.

8. Margaret, daughter of James I.   Died young.

9. Margaret, daughter of the Duke of Connaught.   Late Crown Princess of Sweden.

10. Margaret, daughter of King George VI.

The first of them to fall within the scope of this present volume is Margaret Tudor, elder daughter of Henry VII.

It is perhaps unfair to describe her as an extravagantly dressy woman; but undoubtedly she was no niggard, either in clothes or husbands. She was a woman of decided personality and charm, and it so happens that some illuminating details of her expenditure on dress are still extant. Her marriage portion was £10,000, and £1,000 was allowed her per annum for personal expenses.

Some extracts from wardrobe accounts of this Princess dated 1499 are as follows:

'Nine yards of green velvet, edged with purple tinsel, for a gown, and as much buckram as will line the same.

'A kirtle of tawny damask lined with black, and linen cloth behoveful thereto.

'A kirtle of black satin, lined with black and linen sufficient for the same: with as much black velvet as will edge both the said kirtles.

'Two pairs of hosen, knit.

'Two ells of riband silk for girdles.

'One ounce of lacing ribands for the gown and kirtles aforesaid.

'Seven ells of linen cloth for SMOCKS.

'One gown of crimson velvet, edged with fur.   £13 15s. 6d.'

Wardrobe indentures name amongst other items for Princess Margaret's use, a bed of green velvet with curtains of crimson and green. Her horse litter, also used as a Bed of State, was of cloth of gold with silk and gold fringe, embroidered with the Royal Arms of England, and covered with blue velvet. Her litter-men wore green and black liveries; those of her footmen were of green cloth of gold and white.

In the Bibliothèque at Arras there is a small drawing of the Princess Margaret, together with one of her future husbands, King James IV, showing her wearing the same kind of gable-headdress and gown as worn by her mother in Plate IV.

When Margaret Tudor journeyed to the north to marry James IV in 1503, she was met by a brave array of the Scottish nobility, and we are told that 'the Scottes that day, I assure you were not behind, but far above the English, both in apparel and rich jewels and massy chains . . . and many ladies having their habilments partly set with goldsmith's work, garnished with pearl and precious stones with their gallant and well-trapped horses, which was comely to see.'

The King laid himself out to play the gallant and well-dressed bridegroom, for he 'ordered expressly from France, costly robes, doublets, jackets of cloth of gold, embroidered satin and purple velvet richly furred,' and he met his bride, 'arrayed in a jacket of crimson velvet bordered with cloth of gold, his lure behind his back, his beard something long.'

Fig. 74. A Lure

A lure was a falconer's decoy. When the hawk had failed to take his quarry, the lure was cast into the air by the long cord to entice the bird back to his master's gloved fist. Fig. 74 shows a lure made of a braided pad to which the wings of a bird are attached. At the end of the cord is a bell.

The Princess Margaret made her state entry into Edinburgh wearing a gown of cloth of gold, shaped like that shown in Fig. 66; and her marriage to King James took place at Holyrood, 8th August 1503. On this occasion the bride was gowned in white damask flowered with gold; and the bridegroom's costume was fashioned of the same material.[1] Fortunately, the bill for both wedding garments is extant. Here it is:

| | £ | s. | d. |
|---|---|---|---|
| Item for one steik [piece] of white damask flowered with gold, containing 33 ells 1 quarter, which was one gown to the King and another to the Queen, and part remained thereof, for each ell, £4 15s. 8d. | 157 | 18 | 9 |
| Item for buckram to the King's gown | | 3 | 0 |
| Item for 4 ells taffety to line the said gown, each ell 14s. 8d. | 9 | 16 | 0 |

[1] During the latter part of the fifteenth century, and the first part of the sixteenth, it was the fashion, when kings and queens appeared together in public, that their garments should always be made of the same material.

|  | £ | s. | d. |
|---|---|---|---|
| Item for 2 ounces silk to be cords to the said gown    .    . |  | 7 | 0 |
| Item for 7 ells taffety to line the queen's gown of white damask, each ell 13s. 8d.    .    .    .    .    .    .    .    . | 5 | 7 | 0 |
| Item for lining cloth to the sleeves of the same, and to the body from the waist up    .    .    .    .    .    .    .    . |  |  | 16 |
| Item for 1 ell Scots black to take up the plaits of the same    . |  | 2 | 0 |
| Item for 3 ells crimson velvet to the said gown to border it, each ell £4 12s. 8d.    .    .    .    .    .    .    . | 13 | 10 | 0 |
| Item to two men that sewed the same gown    .    .    . |  | 8 | 0 |
| *Treasurer's Account*, 20th July 1503. | 187 | 13 | 1 |

Another description records that Margaret was robed in a dress of white damask, lined and bordered with crimson velvet, the material for which was the same as that of her husband's costume; and was presented to her by him. 'Her long fair hair floated loosely over her shoulders: upon her head she wore a rich netted tissue veil which hung down to her feet, and over it a golden crown studded with pearls and other gems, also a gift of the King.' The remodelling of this crown for Margaret's use cost the Royal Exchequer the sum of £90.

In early times a queen-consort did not sit by the side of the king upon the dais of the throne. In the later medieval period the custom arose of the queen sitting on a stool, at first by the side of the dais and later upon it, though she sometimes stood. James IV of Scotland was the first to change this, and to create a precedent by ordering a chair similar to his own for Queen Margaret.

(*Continued on p.* 199)

## MARGUERITE, ARCHDUCHESS OF AUSTRIA

### *Duchess of Savoy, 1480–1530*

Another Grande Dame of Europe at this time was Marguerite, only daughter of the Emperor Maximilian and Marie of Burgundy (*see* vol. ii, p. 402). This Archduchess of Austria was born at Brussels, 10th January 1480. At the age of two years she was betrothed to the Dauphin Charles, and forthwith sent to France and placed under the guardianship of the Lady Anne de Beaujeu, the daughter of Louis XI, at Amboise. There she received much kindness and an excellent education, and it is interesting to note that one of the companions of her early childhood was Louise of Savoy (*see* chap. ii, pp. 215 and 218).

Repudiated by the French as their future queen, Marguerite was sent back to Flanders in 1493, where she lived at Namur until 1497. In this year her father arranged a diplomatic marriage for her with Don Juan, heir to the

Spanish throne. The wedding took place at Burgos with due ceremony and magnificence, but in less than a year she was left a widow. For two years of her widowhood the Archduchess remained in Spain, but returned in 1500 to the Court of her brother Philippe le Beau. It was impossible that so charming a woman should remain long a widow! The next year she wedded Philibert II le Beau, Duke of Savoy, who was not only a very handsome man but a brilliant soldier. Fate, so often unkind to royal ladies, did not spare misfortune to Marguerite. In 1504 the Duke died from a chill caused by overheating during the chase. As a memorial, his wife erected the beautiful church at Brou near the town of Bourg-en-Bresse, Burgundy, for the glorification of which she employed the most famous architects and sculptors that Europe could produce. In 1507 the Archduchess Marguerite was created Governor or Regent of the Netherlands, and from this time forth she devoted herself to the regency and the interests of her father and orphan nephews and nieces. Her rule was one of the happiest and most prosperous periods in the history of Flanders.

Fig. 75. Marguerite, Archduchess of Austria, aged 14: 1494 (*after Peter van Coninxloo*)

During the greater part of her life the Archduchess Marguerite was an indefatigable correspondent, the letters she wrote to her father being quite famous. These were a great solace to the Emperor Maximilian as she communicated much valuable advice to him on many subjects, exercising extreme tact and displaying great intelligence in any matter to which she gave her attention. In fact, it is said she possessed 'political insight far more true and clear-sighted than her father.'

The Archduchess Marguerite of Austria, Duchess of Savoy, died 1530 and was buried at Brou.

In the Imperial Museum, Vienna, is a portrait head of the Archduchess at the age of fourteen. Fig. 75 is a drawing of it. Fig. 388 represents her in middle age wearing a headdress favoured by her in later life. The type of dress worn with it, for ordinary occasions, is shown in Fig. 349. The robe she wears in her effigy at Brou is of brocade with wide-open sleeves, and in the stained-glass window she is shown wearing over this robe a mantle displaying the armorial bearings of Austria impaling Savoy. Her headdress is a network caul surmounted by an archduchess's coronet. The inventory of her furniture, plate, tapestries, pictures, etc., in French, is of great interest.

## Anne, Duchess of Brittany

### *Queen-Consort of Charles VIII and of Louis XII of France, 1476–1515*

ANNE, twice Queen-Consort of France, daughter of François II, Duke of Brittany and heiress of her father, was born 1476, and married first in 1491 Charles VIII; secondly in 1498 Louis XII, immediately following his divorce from his first wife Jeanne, daughter of Louis XI.

Anne of Brittany was a great rival of Louise of Savoy (mother of the heir presumptive to the Crown of France); she was ostentatious, and in order to enhance her exalted position formed a great court of ladies. 'Her suite was very large of Ladies and young girls. She had them taught and brought up wisely; and all, taking pattern by her, made themselves wise and virtuous.' [1] Queen Anne discouraged the attendance of these ladies at public festivities, and only suffered them to appear upon occasions of ceremony. Anne of Brittany also organized a personal bodyguard, 'and so formed a second band of a hundred gentlemen,—for hitherto there was only one; and the greater part of the said new guard were Bretons, who never failed, when she left her room to go to Mass or to promenade, to await her on that little terrace at Blois, still called the Bretons' Perch.' [2]

This illustrious lady was plain of feature, shrewd, and clever in her own way, but somewhat narrow-minded and bourgeoise in her tastes. One of her legs was shorter than the other: this originated the vogue among the court ladies and women of fashion for walking with a limp.[3]

To the same Queen was due the introduction of the fashion of wearing black clothes for mourning: all earlier queens of France having worn white as evidence of bereavement.

It is entertainingly recorded that Anne 'was so affected at the death of her first husband, Charles VIII, that she put on black instead of the usual Royal weeds which were white; and yet she married speedily a second mate.' Also 'that her second husband paid the same compliment of black mourning for her decease, and like her sought another spouse as soon as decency would permit.'

Anne of Brittany died 21st January 1515 and was buried 12th February in the Church of St. Denis, where a beautiful tomb was erected, surmounted by kneeling effigies of Louis XII and herself.

[1] Brantôme.                                        [2] Ibid.
[3] A vogue repeated in modern times; see vol. vi, pp. 164–5.

### UNDERCLOTHES

Ladies' underclothes deserve some attention.

They were not numerous, consisting first of an undermost garment, which was a direct descendant of the Roman camisia and Norman camise. This was the equivalent of the men's shert, and was known by the original Anglo-Saxon name of 'smock,' though sometimes referred to as the SHIFT. The garment, made of silk, linen, or cotton, was white, and reached from neck to ankle. It was usually gathered at the neck, and had fairly wide sleeves gathered at the wrist where they were often decorated with stitchery or cut-work. No reference to garments intended to cover the lower limbs of the female sex at this period has been found.

A petticote, frequently referred to as the kyrtle (*see* vol. ii, p. 429) was worn over the smock. Climatic considerations governed the number of petticotes worn, and the material of which they were made. The uppermost petticote was made of some rich fabric, since it was invariably exposed to view when the dress was raised.

Fig. 76. Border

# SECTION II: 1485–1509

## MIDDLE AND LOWER CLASSES

### INTRODUCTION

The great changes which took place among the various grades of society constituting the middle classes were not complete until the early years of the sixteenth century.

Since the Wars of the Roses the professional and commercial classes had gradually risen into prominence, and, by the time Henry VII ascended the throne, were becoming an important factor in the development of the country. It has been said that the monarchy was based on individualism, which superseded the old ecclesiastical system, and on commerce, which replaced feudalism.

The professional class became more conspicuous than hitherto by reason of the assistance they rendered their sovereign in the legal and other methods of despoiling wealthier subjects. Their efforts increased his exchequer so handsomely that it was unnecessary for the King to apply to Parliament for money.

The merchant class (*see* vol. ii, p. 462) was a growing influence; and Henry VII, like his successors, desired to increase the new commercial spirit: he therefore gave his encouragement to trade, realizing that the growth of commerce provided a useful counterbalance to the power of the old nobility. The assistance given by the King to the merchants of Bristol and other ports in their attempts to make discoveries in the New World, greatly stimulated trade and shipping; and as a natural consequence the prosperity of the middle classes increased in a marked degree. This access of wealth is commented upon by an Italian who visited England during the reign of Henry VII. Remarking that London had no buildings in the Italian style, but of timber or brick like the French, he added that the Londoners lived comfortably. The city abounded with every article of luxury, as well as with the necessaries of life, but the most remarkable thing that struck him was the wonderful quantity of wrought silver, not only in private houses but in the shops. In one single street, named the Strand, leading to St. Paul's, there were fifty-two goldsmiths' shops full of rich silver vessels—salt-cellars, drinking cups, basins to hold water for the hands, 'for they eat off that fine tin, which is little inferior to silver'—pewter. 'There is no small innkeeper, however poor and humble he may be, who does not serve his table with silver dishes and drinking cups. . . . No one, who has not in his house silver plate to the amount of at least £100 sterling, is considered by the English to be a person of any consequence.'

The lower classes were also affected by these changes, but to their detriment at this time, chiefly on account of the great increase in the wool trade. Already country gentlemen had realized the advantages of enclosing much of their land for sheep farming, instead of cultivating crops.   Much of the land which had been used formerly by the peasants for growing their own vegetables and grain, was enclosed by hedges for use as sheep-runs and pasture, and ploughland, common land, and waste land shared the same fate.

This change in the established order caused intense poverty, discontent,

Fig. 77. A Physician          Fig. 78. Doctor of Medicine

and unemployment, and created serious conflict between the upper and lower middle classes.

These conditions imposed considerable strain upon the Justices of the Peace—landed country gentlemen—appointed to administer the law in country districts.   Their difficulties were increased by the flotsam and jetsam of disbanded armies, of vagabonds, cut-throats, and thieves, and even bands of robbers, who overran the woods, which then spread over large tracts of country, and infested the highways.

### PROFESSIONAL

The study of academic robes is too wide a subject for inclusion in this book; nevertheless some brief references to them may be useful.   In vol. ii a sergeant-at-law of the fourteenth century is given in Fig. 371.   The costume remained more or less the same as the usual official dress during the fifteenth century. During this period judges wore the same shaped garments, but in scarlet, and occasionally purple, according to their rank: budge was the fur used for lining and edging the garments. A small black silk scarf tied round the waist now appears.

A physician of the fourteenth century is illustrated in Fig. 369 of the same volume. In the fifteenth century the ordinary everyday dress of a physician consisted of a long black gown, ungirded, having loose sleeves edged with

Fig. 79. Robert Fairfax, Doctor
of Music

Fig. 80. A Notary

white fur, a hooded cape lined with fur, and a high, black, felt, brimless, basin-shaped cap.

Fig. 77, taken from a late fifteenth-century Illum. MS., shows a physician wearing a long black gown, without fur, and a black cap. A hooded cape, unlined or lined with fur, would be worn when not attending to the business of the sick room. The academic robes of a Doctor of Medicine varied like those of all others. The full academic robes of a Doctor of Medicine, Oxford, late fifteenth century, are shown in Fig. 78. Over the ordinary black gown is worn a short cloak of red. Often the cloak was seamed up a short distance from the hem leaving an opening for the hands to pass through, and over it a red scarf or tippet. A green hood was the distinguishing colour of the faculty of medicine during the reign of Henry VII. This is thrown back on to the shoulders, and on the head is a close-fitting felt skull-cap or pileus of black, with a point on the crown.

A Doctor of Divinity usually wore as full academic robes a girded cassock, fur cape, sometimes called a tippet, and a pileus, with or without a point on top.

A Doctor of Canon Law wore a cassock, fur cape, and pileus.

For a Doctor of Civil Law, see Fig. 323.

Fig. 79 is based on a sketch made in 1643 of the brass in St. Albans Abbey to the memory of Robert Fairfax (born 1470, died 1529), an eminent musician and composer. The brass has long since disappeared and only the indent in the Presbytery now remains. Fairfax was organist to the abbey during the last years of the fifteenth century, and the organ he used, given by

Fig. 81. A Squire        Fig. 82. A Gentleman

Abbot John de Wheathampstede in 1438, was considered the finest in England. He held the office of chanter in 1502, took his degree of Doctor of Music at Cambridge in 1504, Oxford in 1511, and was Gentleman of the King's Chapel in 1509. The gown he wears is simple, made of dark silk or cloth in the fashion of the late fifteenth century (refer to Fig. 560, vol. ii, and Fig. 8, vol. iii) and faced with fur. For another Doctor of Music, see p. 156.

The Notary (Fig. 80) (William Long by name, a brass to whose memory is in St. Mary's Tower, Ipswich) wears a plain gown with wide sleeves edged with a roll of fur; a similar roll surrounds the neck opening. A penner and inkhorn exactly like those in use a hundred and fifty years earlier (see vol. ii, Fig. 370) are slung through his waistbelt. He carries his circular fur hat over his left shoulder by its drapery or liripipe, in the approved fifteenth-century manner.

### GENTRY

Fig. 81 is a drawing of the squire from Guyot Marchant's *Death Dance*, published in Paris, 1485. He wears a patterned tunic reaching to the thighs, showing the gathered shirt on the breast crossed by bands of the same braid which surrounds the open front. The sleeves are of different material, open up the back seam to reveal the shirt sleeve, and fastened on to the tunic. The

Fig. 83. A Gay Young Gentleman

Fig. 84. A Gentleman

sleeveless surcote has already been described under the Nobility, but this one is of simpler make, and descends just below knee level. The cap of felt has a shaped crown, the brim being only two-thirds round the head at the back, and from it springs a modest plume. His hosen are of cloth. The shoes are similar to the one shown in Fig. 171 but decorated.

A smart young gentleman is shown in Fig. 82, but his style is a little out of date. His blue tunic is of the shape worn during the reign of Henry VI. He is, however, the hero of that wonderful Illum. MS. *Roman de la Rose*, dated 1490. At the edge of the tunic is a heavy blue silk fringe, and gold chains hang about his neck. Gold bells shaped like shells (*see* inset), a revival of an earlier gewgaw, are hung by chains from the waistbelt. The cap, of rose colour to match his hosen, is decorated with long fringe in gold and rose colour. (Sometimes a tassel was attached to the top of the crown. *See*

Headgear, p. 97.) His black shoes, very pointed in the toe, are in the fashion of Edward IV's reign.

The young gentleman shown in Fig. 83 is described in the calendar (*see* p. 28), whence he is taken, as 'full blooded with the nature of the air—moist and hot; he is goodly, luxurious, amiable, a child of nature, joyful, singing, laughing, and gracious. Of the nature of the monkey, that is to say, when he has drunk too much, is the more joyous with the ladies, and naturally loves clothes of bright colour such as scarlet, violet, and fine colours.' He is

Fig. 85. A Country Gentleman          Fig. 86. A Merchant

therefore garbed in a fashionable gown, as worn by the Nobility, in some bright colour. The sleeves are fairly close-fitting and turn back at the wrists to form cuffs. A large rough beaver hat is worn at a rakish angle, over a small cap of the same shape as that shown in Fig. 119. He carries a falcon on his gloved wrist.

A coloured illustration of a young gentleman clad like the last is to be found in Provost Thackeray's *Missal* (1480–90) in the Library of King's College, Cambridge. He is represented in Fig. 84. His costume is very gorgeous, and consists of a tunic with detached sleeves of black velvet. His hosen are vermilion, and he wears high boots of ochre-coloured leather. The surcote is of cloth of gold, lined and turned back with brilliant blue silk. It has narrow sleeves turned back with blue at the wrists, but they are worn off the arms and hang behind from the shoulders. The angular hat of black fur is decorated with a heron's plume fixed at the side by a jewelled cross, and is worn over a vermilion cap like Fig. 119.

Fig. 85 is a country gentleman, or he might be the owner or freeholder of a small farm but does not rank as a gentleman. He wears a belted tunic reaching to just above the knee, hosen, and footgear similar to those worn in Fig. 28. Over these garments he wears during the winter months a long gown with loose sleeves composed of substantial cloth. Above this is worn an old-fashioned hood, and on top a basin-shaped felt hat with an upstanding brim.

Fig. 87. A Quoystrele

Fig. 88. A Crinkler

## MERCHANTS

Andrew Jones, a cider merchant, is shown on an incised slab, dated 1497, in the crypt of Hereford Cathedral (Fig. 86). He wears the usual merchant's cloth gown with wide sleeves and circular roll collar (compare with Fig. 582, vol. ii). His leather pouch is worth noticing; the inset shows a similar one taken from a brass of the same date.

## LOWER CLASSES

The unpleasant-looking man (Fig. 87) of doubtful social standing, probably what was known as a 'Quoystrele' or base fellow, comes from a missal dating between 1480 and 1490. His jacket is blue, with scarlet collar and cuffs bound with brown leather. Close-fitting green drawers are worn, the red hosen being laced with red to the waistbelt underneath. The felt hat and the leather shoes are black.

The man in Fig. 88 is of the swashbuckler type, a 'crinkler'; that is, a trickster or 'a bravo, a swashbuckler, one that for mony and good cheere will follow any man to defend him and fight for him, but if any danger come, he runs away the first and leaves him in the lurch.' 'A roister, cutter, swaggerer, one that's ever vaunting of his own valour.' He is distinctly well dressed. There is an attempt at display—the fashionable 'placard,' his under-sleeves 'cutte' at the wrists, and a skull-cap worn under a black felt hat.

Fig. 89. A Messenger                    Fig. 90. A Workman

Fig. 89 is a messenger about to deliver a letter, and in the act of respect-fully removing his hat. He is taken from a woodcut of the period which shows very clearly the cloak with hood, tunic, girdle, pouch, knife, gartered hosen, and boots, the method of folding a letter, which resembles a modern envelope, and the seal. Letters were carried in a pouch or bag known as a 'male' (French: *malle*).

A working man of this period is seen in Fig. 90. The cut of his tunic, buttoned up the front, is clearly defined. The hat, worn over a skull-cap as shown in Fig. 93, is of rough felt or straw, and has a cord round it through which a wooden spoon is thrust. This was the usual way of disposing of his table implement. On his legs he wears cloth hosen, to which are added cloth gaiters bound under the knee and round the ankle. His shoes are thick and clumsy. The pouch fastened round the waist is an interesting and useful article, which was originally produced by tying a square piece of cloth, corner-wise, round the waist (*see* Fig. 91). This one is more carefully made. The material is pleated on the left side to form a substantial belt, and the top edge, which forms the flap, is indented. This is tied to the bottom part of the pouch, and from it hang three cords passing through wooden balls. This man carries a hoe in his right hand and a plumb line in his left.

Fig. 91 is a countryman, a villager, or 'goeman,' who is wearing over his

Fig. 91. A Goeman       Fig. 92. A Peasant

shirt a cloth tunic with fairly wide sleeves, and over that a sleeveless leather jacket. His felt hat is of an old-fashioned shape and he wears coarse cloth hosen and leathern shoes. His pouch is simply a folded piece of cloth tied round his waist by the twisted pointed ends, a primitive version of that just described.

The peasant (Fig. 92) enjoying a pull from his bottle is taken from the same missal as Fig. 84. Over his shirt he wears a leathern jacket bound at the edges and buttoning up the front. The round black fur cap is in the style of the fourteenth century (*see* vol. ii, Figs. 317, 391, and 583). His thighs are bare; red hosen, turned down below the knees, and black leather shoes are worn. A steel sharpener for the scythe is slung from the cord at his waist.

The gaffer carrying his ducks and hens to market (Fig. 93) was perhaps a man of some importance.   If he owned the small piece of land he cultivated he was known as a 'yeoman,' but if he only rented it he was but a small 'farmer.'   He is dressed much like the other figures shown.   His cap and boots should be noticed, and particularly the basket of ducks strapped to his back, as also the key of the henhouse hanging below.

The reaper (Fig. 94) is not so undressed as the peasant, although he must

Fig. 93. Peasant

Fig. 94. A Farm Hand

feel the heat of the day, because he has covered his head with a cloth sur-mounted by a wide-brimmed sun-hat of straw.   In other respects his costume is similar to Fig. 90.


## MIDDLE-CLASS WOMEN

### GENTRY

Simplicity and line are two of the chief points which constitute beauty, and this gentlewoman of 1490 (Fig. 95) justifies this statement.   The sleeve-less gown, with a one-and-a-half-inch border of black velvet round the square neck and a narrower one round the armhole, is worn over a different-coloured under-robe, with full sleeves.   The black velvet hood is shaped like that shown in Fig. 155, but the right side is draped over the top, and a V of black descends the forehead.   An elaborate headdress-pin is her only ornament. The table and silver ewer are contemporary.

The gentlewoman (Fig. 96) represents Alice Tame, taken from the brass, 1500, in Fairford Church to the memory of her husband, John Tame, Esq., Merchant of London. He is represented wearing a complete suit of armour, and is immortalized by the church which he began to rebuild (it was finished by his son, Sir Edmund Tame), and by its beautiful stained-glass windows. It is said that John Tame captured the Flemish ship which was carrying them as a present to the Pope, and erected them at Fairford, where they have been preserved practically intact ever since and are famous throughout the world.

Fig. 95. A Gentlewoman, 1490

Mistress Alice wears a kirtle (*see* vol. ii, p. 97) of the best Flemish cloth, cut all in one. It fits well around the bust and waist, the folds of the semicircular skirt radiating from about hip level. The close-fitting sleeves have pointed cuffs of fur; the wide neck opening rises to a point, and is outlined with a band of colour or embroidery showing an undergarment. The leathern girdle ornamented with metal is worn loose, with one end passing through a buckle and the long end hanging almost to the feet. Such belts had been fashionable in the days of Richard III (*see* Fig. 576, vol. ii). Her headdress consists of a hemispherical cap in some bright colour, and to its edge is attached a gable-pointed band of black velvet with a line of gold passement. A second and wider piece, a segment of a circle, of black velvet hangs at the back.

Fig. 96. Mistress Tame, 1500

The Church of St Mary, Thame, is rich in

brasses of the fifteenth and sixteenth centuries. One is shown in Fig. 97 to the memory of Alice, second wife of Geoffrey Dormer, who died in 1502: the

brass is of this date, though the lady lived until 1513. Of county family, she is dressed in the prevailing fashion adopted by gentlefolk in the reign of Henry VII. Fig. 98 is an interpretation of the said brass, which may be of considerable assistance to the student in visualizing the human form from the conventional figure in the brass. Mistress Alice's gown is fashioned on the same lines as shown in Figs. 96 and 99, but the neck is cut square and filled in with a kerchief, and the skirt hangs in heavy folds to the ground — a proof that the gown is made of substantial cloth. The gable head-dress is formed on the same

Fig. 97.      Fig. 98.
Marjorie Dormer, 1502

principle as that described under Fig. 155, and the girdle is similar to that shown in Fig. 96, only more elaborate.

### MERCHANTS' WIVES

Mistress Jones (Fig. 99), wife of the cider merchant of Hereford (Fig. 86), wears a cloth gown or kirtle similar to that shown in Fig. 96. The neck and wrists are finished with dark fur, probably marten ; and a kerchief of fine linen or lawn is folded inside the neck opening. The girdle is an important feature; it is made of leather in its natural colour, black, or perhaps red, and having a row of ornamental metal bosses. At the ends are five-petalled roses linked to a quatrefoil, from which is hung, by a long loop of silk, an ornament of metal-work. Another girdle of different design is shown

Fig. 99. Mistress Jones, 1497

in Fig. 100. The headdress is decidedly old-fashioned, dating back to the first half of the fifteenth century (*see* vol. ii, Figs. 600 and 615), and the veil is laid over the top.

## LOWER CLASSES

Fig. 101 is a country girl: although she comes from a Flemish tapestry, her dress is typical of that worn by English women. Her whole-piece gown is simple, and fits the figure fairly well, being laced up the front. A girdle or belt could be worn, but in this drawing the waist is encircled by a pouch ingeniously contrived from a square of material folded cornerwise as described

Fig. 100. Girdle     Fig. 101. Country Girl     Fig. 102. Country Woman

under Fig. 91. The sleeves are cut straight without any shaping, and, when necessary, the ends can be rolled back up the arm. The hood is one that was much used by this class during the latter half of the fifteenth century. Her shoes are of leather or felt.

The country woman (Fig. 102) is dressed in much the same manner, but her overdress is shorter and shows an under-petticote. It laces up the front of the body and has a small turned-down collar to the smock. Her headdress of white linen is shaped as shown in Fig. 618, vol. ii, and she has twisted the tubular part around her head.

The country woman (Fig. 103) arguing with the old gammer has adopted the practical and very usual method of buttoning on long sleeves over those of her smock, now that she has finished her work.   The body part with short sleeves fits loosely, and is turned up round the waist.   This and the separate skirt are of a coarse brown material, braided with black at the neck, on the sleeves, and at the hem.   A white apron is tied round the waist under the body part.   The extra sleeves are grey, and have a coloured border at the top and wrists.   The headdress is a piece of linen tied round the head.

Fig. 103.            Fig. 104.                              Fig. 105. A Beggar
          An Altercation

Fig. 104 wears a body and skirt cut all in one and of a dark colour.   The manner of tucking up the skirt was general among this class.   The linen headrail is all in one piece, and tied up to form a cap and wimple.

For a more elaborate arrangement of a linen headrail see Fig. 166.

Fig. 105 represents a beggar-woman between the years 1480 and 1560. She has clothed her person in any material available; patched, threadbare, and ragged, as the result of years of wear and tear.   For warmth she has procured a piece of deerskin which she has laced about her as a body-covering. Pieces of skin clothe her feet and legs, and she carries an extra wrap over her shoulder.   In her hat, rescued from some rubbish heap, she fastens her spoon, and suspended from her waist is an old girdle to which is attached her cooking utensil or dish.   This, the usual stock-in-trade of the medieval and Elizabethan beggar, and known as a 'clap-dish' or 'clack-dish,' has a lid hinged to the bowl, and would often be used as a clapper to attract attention, and to solicit alms from passers-by. It is referred to in literature of the time; and the following are two excerpts. Lucio in *Measure for Measure*, III. ii, says: 'Who? not the duke? Yes, your beggar of fifty; and his use was to put a ducat in her clack-dish.' Jane Shore in *Sonnets* by Thomas Deloney (1593) states that 'I beg'd my bread with clacke and dish.' It is also the origin of the old saying: 'A woman's tongue is like a beggar's clap-dish.'

Fig. 106. Embroidered Border

# SECTION III: 1485–1509

## HAIRDRESSING: MEN

The style of hairdressing as worn by the men of fashion during the reign of Henry VII had its origin at the Court of Burgundy as has been already noted on p. 433, vol. ii (Fig. 108 shows this style). All the hair is brushed to radiate from the crown of the head: it forms a fringe on the forehead and flows in locks well on to the shoulders behind. Fig. 109 shows similar hairdressing, but the fringe lies straight and flat on the forehead.

Fig. 107              Fig. 108

Very often the back hair was arranged in a smooth mass which lay upon the shoulders as shown in Fig. 110. It was parted in the middle, and either flowed curtain-like over the temples or formed a fringe on the forehead.

Fig. 115 gives a back view of the head of a fashionable young man. The hair is dressed smoothly on the head; but below, starting level with the nape of the neck, it is arranged in ringlets. In front the hair was parted in the middle.

Fig. 9, taken from a French Illum. MS. dating about 1500, shows a much simpler style of hairdressing. The hair is straight and brushed out to set away from the head. Another simple style, worn by less fashionable men, is shown in Fig. 107. It was that generally adopted throughout the fifteenth century and described under Fig. 607 B in vol. ii. Fig. 117 shows moderately short wavy hair.

Henry VII dressed his hair in the modified fashionable style, as shown by his portraits (Fig. 111). The hair was parted in the middle, and fell to the shoulders in waves, either naturally or by artifice.

In a portrait of the Emperor Maximilian (Fig. 110), painted when he was aged about forty, by Bernhard Strigel, his hair is worn long, falling round the head and over the forehead in a stiff mass as though it were a wig. Towards the end of his days the emperor was painted by Dürer, and in this portrait he is wearing hair in the ordinary fashion. Fig. 368 is a drawing made from it.

*Beards.* Among the aristocracy and fashionable men, except for some old gentlemen (*see* Fig. 85), beards on the upper lip and chin were the exception according to portraits and illustrations of this time. They were, however, more

Fig. 109

general on the Continent, but not so much so in France. Some portraits of Flemish and Italian noblemen show beards in the ordinary close-cut style (*see* Fig. 122). This also applies to many German notabilities.

## MIDDLE AND LOWER CLASSES

The professional class does not appear to have adopted the ultra-fashionable style of hairdressing. The different members are usually shown wearing their hair arranged more or less like that shown in Fig. 107, and they were nearly always clean-shaven. The well-dressed young gentlemen, of course, followed the dictates of fashion as shown in Figs. 108 and 109. (*See also* Figs. 81, 82, 83, and 84.)

Men of the lower orders are often shown in Illum. MSS. wearing their hair about four inches in length, wavy and bushy, or straight and lank, or even curly, as they thought fit. Figs. 87, 88, and 90 are good examples of characters whose hairdressing is not fashionable, but in the traditional style. It must be remembered that at no time during the sixteenth century did the lower classes have their hair cut close to the head.

There was no particular style of hairdressing worn by the peasants, as may be seen on referring to the different figures illustrating their section; such men wore beards or not, as it pleased them, and the styles in which their beards were trimmed varied indefinitely.

FIG. 110

FIG. 111

FIG. 112

FIG. 113

Fig. 110. THE EMPEROR MAXIMILIAN.   After B. Strigel
Fig. 111. KING HENRY VII     Fig. 112. THE FRENCH BONET
Fig. 113. KING LOUIS XII.   After Jehan Perréal
*By gracious permission of H.M. the King*

## HEADGEAR

### The French Bonet

The French bonet was fashionable during the reign of Henry VII. It was constructed as described in vol. ii, p. 436. The vertical edges of the brim sometimes overlapped, as in Fig. 8: but it was more usual for a portion of the turned-up brim to be cut away, leaving a space of from two to three inches, the separated portions being caught together by a lace either fastened behind the brim and tied as in Fig. 116, or passing through them and tied as in

Fig. 114. Charles VIII of France (*after Andrea Solari*)

Fig. 112. Figs. 233 and 118 give other examples of the method of fixing the brim in an upward position. The opening could be worn at the side (generally left) of the head; and sometimes the brim continued in one piece all round, without an ornament (*see* Figs. 12 and 110), or with a medallion as in Figs. 11 and 114.

When the brim was void for a space it was sometimes attached to the crown by a series of laces, each tied in a loop with two ends finishing with aiglettes; perhaps a medallion would be added, as in Fig. 24. The prince shown in Fig. 9 wears a bonet having the brim turned up with ermine, with a coronet set inside, after the manner described under Fig. 534, vol. ii. Another variation of the brim, whether made of fur or velvet, was to embattle the edge in the German fashion, as shown in Figs. 6 and 7.

Bonets were usually made of black velvet, but various colours were

sometimes used. In contemporary descriptions of ceremonies and processions one often finds it stated that the courtiers had velvet bonets of
different colours. Figs. 8, 24, 116, 118 and Plate VI are examples.

The decoration of the bonet, apart from laces, consisted usually of a
medallion or brooch, in goldsmith's work, often supplemented with enamel
or jewels—or both. This was fixed
to the brim, nearly always over the left
eye or on one side of the open brim.
A favourite subject for the decoration
of brooches or ouches was the figure of
a popular saint, in embossed gold or
enamels. The portrait of Charles
VIII (Fig. 114) shows one such ouche,
fixed to the left side of his French
bonet, the all-round brim slightly
turned down over part of it.

Fig. 115

A portrait of Louis XII (Fig. 113)
shows a medallion in gold, engraved
with the figure of a saint, and fixed
to the side of the crown-part in the
space left visible between the ends of
the open brim, the band of black velvet
which connects the edges passing *over*
the medallion. The curious cuts at
the temples should be noticed.

Fig. 118—from an Illum. MS. dated
1500—gives a smart bonet of crimson
velvet. The brim, back, front, and
left side are laced to the crown by a
band of gold, passed twice round and
tied on the right.

The back view of a bonet is shown
in Fig. 115. In the original illustration
it is scarlet, and the gold cord which
attaches one upstanding brim to the other is itself fixed to a gold button at the
back of the left-side brim, to ensure the correct angle. The tall plumes are
blue, having gold ornaments set part of the way up the quills, and are fixed to
the same button which holds the cord. The coquettish angle of the cap and
plumes was much affected by smart young men throughout western Europe
at the end of the fifteenth century.

A portrait [1] by Bernhard Strigel, dated 1507 and representing a nobleman
of the court of the Emperor Maximilian, shows him wearing a black velvet
bonet, its upturned brim being decorated with gold buttons, and with gold
cords laced through and through the brim. The visible portions of the

[1] Sold in 1925 for £15,000.

FIG. 116

FIG. 117

FIG. 118

FIG. 119

Figs. 116–19. FASHIONABLE HAIRDRESSING AND HEADGEAR

cord are threaded with at least nine jewelled finger-rings—a form of ornamentation suggesting a more mundane spirit than that of this gentleman's contemporaries who displayed figures of saints.

Towards the end of the fifteenth century a new type of hat made its appearance. Whether of Flemish or Italian origin is uncertain, but it was the height of fashion in both countries and was also worn in France and England. This hat had a basin-shaped crown, and a wide brim which was always worn turned up in one place, either at the side or in front. The Flemish nobles in Figs. 13, 21, 22, and 28, and the English nobles in Figs. 14, 29, 30, and 34, wear this hat in various ways. It was always worn over a cap (see Fig. 119) in a plain

Fig. 120.          Fig. 121.          Fig. 122.
Italian Coifs

bright colour, or over a skull-cap or coif (see Fig. 120) of gold network, often set with jewels (see Fig. 13).

In Fig. 30 the large beaver hat and cap are secured by a scarf of silk tied over both. In Fig. 21 the scarf passes over the crown of the hat and through holes at the sides. This drawing shows that the wide brim was sometimes slit at right angles.

Cords, after the style of those attached to the Greek petasos (see vol. i, p. 50), were used when the hat was pushed back off the head on to the shoulders. When decorated with feathers, like Fig. 21 or Fig. 22, it had a curious effect of a bird's wings or tail projecting from the wearer's back—considered very chic by the well-dressed man.

These large hats were made principally of blocked beaver in various colours —white, fawn, black, pink were the favourite tones. Often a long ostrich plume, as shown in Figs. 21, 30, and 34, or a quill (see Figs. 26 and 29), was stuck up inside the brim. Sometimes a panache of any number of exceedingly long ostrich plumes, in many different colours, stood up high above the crown as in Figs. 22 and 28.

Ostrich feathers were unknown in western Europe until the fourteenth century, when the first mention of them is made in literature. They appear as an heraldic charge in the time of Edward III. During the reign of Henry V, ostrich feathers and other plumes were more extensively used in hats and also for the adornment of helmets. They were very expensive in the fifteenth century, and were not generally used in profusion until the period dealt with in this chapter.

Fig. 120 shows one type of coif worn under these large hats. It is composed of gold network set at the intersections with jewels *and worn very much on one side.* An Italian coif (Fig. 122) has the gold frame-work radiating from a centre motif. It is taken from a portrait by Paolo Morando Cavazzola (1489–1522). Fig. 121, taken from a portrait dating 1523 by Lorenzo Lotto (1480–1556), is a later development of the Italian coif which is much more like a turban. It is composed of dark coloured silk or velvet, embroidered with gold with a circular motif in front. It may be presumed that these coifs

Fig. 123

or skull caps composed of network, silk, velvet, or cloth, *and their tilt*, were introduced into Italy from Germany at a much earlier date—possibly by a member of the princely family of Hohenstaufen of Waiblingen. This latter name was Italianized into 'Ghibellines.'

A cap something like the French bonet was also in use, made of felt, cloth, or velvet in various colours, blocked or shaped with the crown and brim all

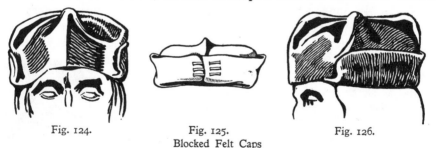

Fig. 124.     Fig. 125.     Fig. 126.
Blocked Felt Caps

in one. Sometimes the brim was slit in one place, sometimes in two. Fig. 119 shows a cap of bright scarlet having one slit. A similar one with a point on the top is shown in Fig. 117, but in this case the front brim is narrower than the back which slightly turns up. In the original illustration, dated 1490, this cap is 'sanguine-in-grain'—petunia. Another variety is shown in Fig. 20. Some of these caps are shown in drawings in this chapter, worn under other headgear. The back view (Fig. 123) is an example. A round black beaver hat is perched at an angle on the left side, a golden-yellow feather rises from

inside the rolled brim and droops down the back on the right.    Underneath
the beaver is a cap of crimson velvet, shaped like that shown in Fig. 119.
The jewelled brooch on the side of the beaver fastens the two together.    The
date of the original illustration is 1500.

A close-fitting skull-cap of felt, known at this time as 'pileus,' was worn

with academic robes chiefly by Doctors of
Divinity and Medicine.    One is seen in
Fig. 78.    'Makers of these caps were called
Birretarii, that is commonly called capper,
hurrer, or knitters of caps.'

There was another kind of blocked felt
cap much worn by sober-minded men: of
Italian origin, it is shown in Fig. 125.    It
had the upstanding brim divided at the sides
and laced together.    The crown was moderately close - fitting to the head and rose to
a point in the centre.    An English example
of a simple blocked cap of black felt worn
by a student is shown in Fig. 127.    The
diagram, Fig. 128, shows its shape with the
brim turned down.    When it was turned up
the corners were buttoned together.    Fig. 111
is from a bust of Henry VII, and shows a
cap of a similar kind, but with a ridge front
and back instead of a point in the centre.    The
brim is turned up at the back only, and lined
with fur.

Fig. 127. A Student

The cap seen on the effigy of Henry VII (on his tomb in Westminster Abbey
designed by Pietro Torrigiano of Florence) is more elaborate (see Fig. 124);
it rises in ridges front, back, and sides: the brim is at the back only, where it
is turned up or down (see Fig. 126).

A different kind of hat is shown in Fig. 82.    It has
a high bag-shaped crown of pleated or gathered material,
finished with a tassel at the top and having an upstanding brim (see also Fig. 129).    Sometimes fringe took
the place of the tassel, and hung over the crown.    Caps
of knitted wool were in use among the middle classes, and
these were close-fitting or skull-caps; some were on the
lines of the French bonet and others bag-shape.

Fig. 128

With few exceptions there was nothing exceptional in the headgear of the
professional and middle classes, excluding certain cases which are mentioned
in the description of their dress.    This also applies to the lower classes.
On referring to the various figures it will be found that most of their headgear has already been shown and described, and that there was nothing new.
Details of some will be found in vol. ii, Chaps. IV and VI.

Headgear plays an important part in etiquette of the period, most of which was borrowed from the Court of Burgundy.

When two gentlemen met, the *inferior* raises his hat with his left hand and kneels on one knee, his right hand clasping the other's right hand. Another form of greeting between two gentlemen was for the inferior to hold his hat in his left hand, to take both hands of the superior and then touch elbows with elbows, the forearms pressing against each other; and finally kiss.

A method of welcoming is illustrated in an Illum. MS., wherein a gentleman in civil dress hastens out of his castle gate, hat in left hand, and *grasps* the right hand of an approaching knight in armour, also bareheaded, with

Fig. 129

great eagerness. Although the hat was removed when greetings were exchanged, it was often retained in the house. Calendars for January frequently show a man sitting at home by the fire with his hat on.

## HEADDRESSES

Ladies' headdresses of the Tudor period are very varied in character and design. They are complicated in construction, and not easy to copy with accuracy. To provide a reliable basis for convincing reproductions, the explanations and diagrams which follow are given, as the result of much research and experiment.

It will be seen that the drawings are lettered throughout in a uniform manner according to the following formula:

| | | |
|---|---|---|
| A . . . | The cap or coif |
| B . . . | The band |
| BB . . | The curtain |
| C . . . | The semicircular hood |
| D . . . | A small head-veil |
| E . . . | The rigid front of the gable, referred to at this time as a 'frontlet' |
| F . . . | The pad on the forehead |
| G . . . | The lappets of the cap A or their substitute |

| | | | |
|---|---|---|---|
| H . | . | . | An extra band |
| I J K | . | . | Points of the gable |
| L M | . | . | First slits |
| N O | . | . | Portions between slits |
| P Q | . | . | Second slits |
| R S | . | . | Embroidered band |
| T . | . | . | Diamond back-piece |

The various headdresses of the early part of this reign demonstrate the interesting transition from the *Hennin,* shown in Fig. 619, vol. ii, to the Tudor, shown in Fig. 380 of this volume.

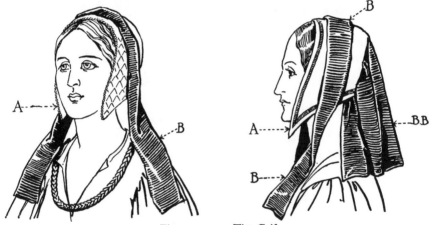

Figs. 130, 131. The Coif

Examine Fig. 130. First of all there is the foundation—a coif, which has descended from its ancestor, the steeple cap in vol. ii, Fig. 619 (1), through

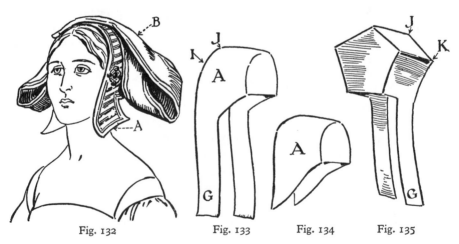

Fig. 132      Fig. 133      Fig. 134      Fig. 135

the stages of exaggeration shown in Fig. 619 (2), (3), and (4); thence by way
of its truncated cone form, Fig. 619 (5), and receding into the flowerpot-
shaped cap in Fig. 619 (6). The reduction of this last cap into the shape
shown in Figs. 68, 130, and 131 of this volume took place about the time
of Henry VII's accession; and this form, with some later additions, was
in vogue during the whole of his reign and, with further additions, that of
his successor.

Fig. 130 represents one version of the fashionable headdress. The close-
fitting cap or coif, A, was of some rich material, generally cross-barred with
gold and jewels, and often embroidered. This jewelled coif can also claim kinship with the network caps worn in Italy at this period, which will be familiar
to students through the portrait of Beatrice d'Este, Fig. 140. Princess

Fig. 136                                    Fig. 137

Katherine of Aragon wore a coif of this kind. In the year 1514 she is
described as wearing 'on her head a cap of cloth of gold, covering the ears
in the Venetian fashion.'

Its ordinary shape, as worn by English, French, and Flemish ladies, is
shown in Fig. 134. Pearls or drop ornaments were frequently used to
decorate the edge framing the face, and sometimes the entire edge. Over
this coif was placed a band, B, of double material, about forty inches long by
four or five inches wide, often of black velvet, and sometimes richly embroidered. This band was pinned to the coif in places, the ends hanging
down over the shoulders.

Refer back to Fig. 68, where one side of the band has been folded up and
fixed coquettishly to the top of the coif. The lady in Fig. 62 has turned up
the right end of the black velvet band—this arrangement suggests a gable
and probably gave the idea for the design of later headdresses.

Fig. 131 shows another example of this headdress. In this the coif, A, is
of some plain material, edged with passement, and it should be noticed that
the points are more acute. The band, B, is worn as before described; but
to the seam of the back section of the coif is fixed a small semicircular piece

or curtain, BB, of black velvet or embroidered material, draping the back of the headdress and falling in regular vertical folds well on to the shoulders. Sometimes this part, BB, was a semicircular piece placed on the head *under*

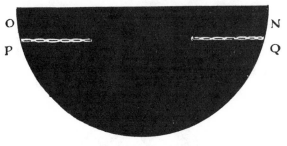

The Semicircular Hood of Black Velvet C.

O            N

P            Q

Fig. 138.

the coif, in which case the back section of the coif remained visible, the drapery or curtain falling from under it.

Another version of Fig. 130 is shown in Fig. 132. Here the coif, A, is made of material arranged in tucks at right angles to the edge, and overlaid with a narrow band of material or passement. In place of the sharp points in Fig. 131, this coif shows the beginning of the lappets shown at a later stage in Fig. 133. Notice that the coif is fixed to the hair by a jewelled ornament. The band, B, in Fig. 132[1] is made of stiffened lawn or cambric, about sixty inches long and from five to six inches wide. A favourite method of arranging it was to fasten the ends back again on top of the coif.

The chic headdress shown in Fig. 136 is either evolved from the hood, seen in diagram, Fig. 138, folded and draped over the head; or it is the band, B, worn on top of a close-fitting cap or coif (unseen in both cases) as in Fig. 130.

Fig. 137 is definitely the same type of headdress with the band B draped over a coif. No hair is seen, but a V loop of black velvet lies on the forehead. A similar arrangement of the band is worn by the lady in Fig. 62. Both these headdresses are taken from an Illum. MS. dating 1490.

Fig. 139 proves that some bright young things in Tudor society considered it very piquant to wear a man's French bonet. This headdress is taken from

Fig. 139

the same Illum. MS. as the lady representing 'England.' Over a close-fitting coif of purple silk, cross-barred with gold cord and edged with passement, is perched a bonet of scarlet silk edged with gold, having the brim slit in one place over the left eye.

[1] Headdresses of very similar design may be seen to-day worn by French peasants.

The Princess Mary I also affected a rakish tilt with hats. When riding a white palfrey to meet the Dauphin, in a dress of crimson cloth of gold, she wore 'a shaggy hat of crimson silk cocked over her left eye.' The expression 'shaggy' refers to a method of weaving silk with loops which, being cut, resemble fur. The Musée des Arts Decoratifs, Paris, has a portrait of her wearing a square cap of black velvet at a very much more exaggerated angle—completely covering her right ear.

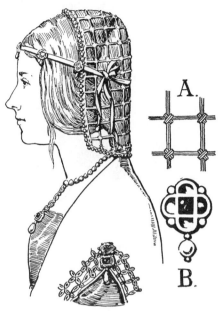

Fig. 140. Beatrice d' Este
(*after Leonardo da Vinci*)

The well-known portrait (Fig. 140) of Beatrice d' Este by Leonardo da Vinci (1452 – 1519), affords a fine example of the Italian coif which formed the basis of many kinds of headdress. The network is composed of two strands of gold cords bound together at the intersections by the same (*see at* A); all round the edge is a row of pearls. The gold band which binds the coif to the head has ornaments (*see at* B) spaced along it, in the form of a quatrefoil in gold with a pearl set in each angle: a large drop pearl is suspended from each quatrefoil, and a pearl is fixed to each end of the band.

## HAIRDRESSING

The style of hairdressing shown in Fig. 141 is that worn by Joanna of Castile (Plate V). The hair is quite smooth, probably oiled or pomatumed, and parted in the centre from forehead to nape; the side portions are brought round the neck *under* the ears and taken up the side of the cheeks on to the top of the head. Here it is fixed in a small pad of hair.

This was more or less the method of dressing the hair during this period and the first half of the sixteenth century. It formed a firm foundation on which to secure the various headdresses worn.

When the hair is seen on the forehead it is parted in the middle and waved over the temples. With many of the headdresses described the back hair is entirely concealed by the coif or curtain; but sometimes it is left flowing, and is visible below it.

An exceptionally attractive style of Italian hairdressing is shown in Fig. 142. It is taken from the *Horae* dating about 1490, and once owned by Isabella of

Aragon, daughter of Alphonso II, King of Naples. The hair is parted in the centre, the back part divided into two tresses which are bound with narrow silk. After the head has been covered with a net of gold cord and

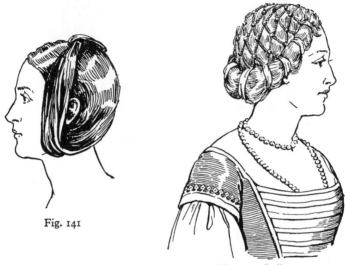

Fig. 141

Fig. 142. Italian

pearls, the two tresses are crossed at the nape, brought round the side of the head and the ends tucked in above the forehead.

(*Continued on p.* 108)

## HEADDRESSES, *continued*

The headdress seen in Fig. 63 is of Flemish origin, and consists of two hemispherical gold cauls, worn over the ears and enclosing the hair, surmounted by a cap of gold having an upstanding brim (*see* Fig. 143). A small twist of hair brought down V-shape on the forehead takes the place of the usual waved hair, and is a revival of a previous fashion, referred to on p. 445, vol. ii.

This headdress could be worn with a band, B, as shown in Fig. 63, or with the velvet hood, C (Fig. 144), turned back off the face revealing a portion of the gold caul on either side. This hood was semicircular and consisted of a piece of black velvet (*see* diagram, Fig. 138). It measured about fifty inches by twenty-five inches, and was lined with coloured or white silk.

At the same time, the hood alone was much in fashion as a headdress. It is shown in Fig. 148, and is cut like Fig. 138, but with slits at the dotted lines P and Q. The portions O and N usually hung in front of the shoulders. This same headdress or hood is seen worn by the ladies in Figs. 27, 64, and 66. In this last figure it is worn over a gold network coif or cap. The front edges were often decorated with pearls, gold balls, or peardrop pearls. Various caps, as well as network coifs, could be worn under this hood if desired.

FIG. 143

FIG. 144

FIG. 145

FIG. 146

Figs. 143, 144, 145. FASHIONABLE HEADDRESSES
Fig. 146. QUEEN ELYSABETH.   From the Coventry Tapestry

Over the hood queens and noble ladies wore their coronets, set at a backward angle on the head, *behind* the turned-back lining, as shown in Fig. 148. This headdress is the original of that seen on queens in playing-cards (*see also* Plate V).

Fig. 147                    Fig. 148

Fig. 149.  Margaret, Countess of Richmond

## THE GABLE HEADDRESS

*Also known as the Pedimental, Pyramidal, Kennel, or Diamond-shaped Headdress*

The evolution of the various headdresses just described into the characteristic Tudor 'gable' is an absorbing but complicated study.

The first stage showing a definite gable character is seen in Fig. 150. It is the semicircular hood, C, differently arranged from Fig. 148. The straight edge of the semicircle has had added to it a decorated band, RS, of cloth of gold or black velvet edged with a passement, and a further pair of slits, L and M, partly separated this from the hood. The material between I and K (*see* diagram, Fig. 153, as well as Fig. 150) is made rigid, and in the form of a gable, with a ridge at J. The coif, A (see other drawings), is certainly worn

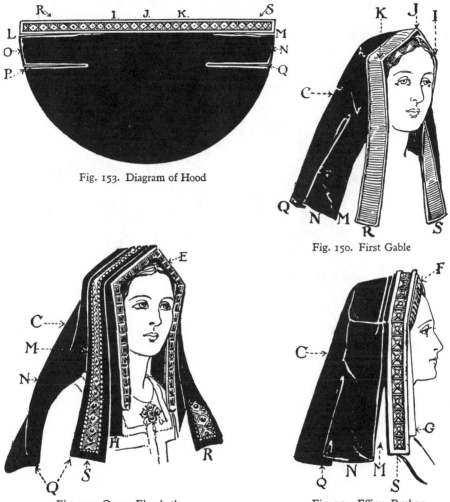

Fig. 153. Diagram of Hood

Fig. 150. First Gable

Fig. 151. Queen Elysabeth

Fig. 152. Effigy, Ruabon

as a foundation for the hood although unseen, and the hair of this lady is waved on the temples and done in a coil on the nape of the neck—sometimes it might be allowed to flow down the back.

In an Illum. MS. dated 1500 another arrangement of this black velvet semicircular hood is shown (Fig. 147). The front part is slightly stiffened and creased into a fold which comes on the forehead, and is there fixed with a pin to the white head-veil, D, or folded linen coif.

The apparently elaborate headdress (Fig. 156) is composed of a front part edged with gold ornaments; but, in place of the semicircular hood, a rectangular piece of double black velvet hangs from the back of the gable.    This is slit for a certain distance up the centre and normally hangs down, but this lady has turned up both sections on to the top of the headdress: the divided portions overlap slightly, and their bottom edges come well on to the forehead.    Under this is worn a dark cap, straight-edged with right-angle corners, extending below the level of the chin, and under this again is a close-fitting

Fig. 154                Fig. 155                Fig. 156

white coif as a foundation for the whole structure.    A similar headdress is shown in Fig. 241.

The lady in Fig. 155 is wearing the cap, A, slightly gabled, and over it an arrangement of the hood, C, which suggests a bag-cap with a curtain falling from it down the back.    The front is turned back to show the lining, and fixed to the cap by a jewelled brooch.    The monument to the Dawtry family in Petworth Church, from which this headdress is taken, dates 1527.    It is to the memory of an elderly woman who has retained the fashion of her youth —a habit with many old ladies of the country gentry class from time immemorial—which accounts for this late fifteenth-century headdress being worn at so late a date.

The three-quarter back view of a similar headdress is shown in Fig. 154. This is simply the semicircular black velvet hood, illustrated in diagram, Fig. 138, with a string inserted and drawn up sufficiently to form a covering for the cranium.    This was a method of achieving the bag-cap (Fig. 155);

and also suggested the placing of caps of other shapes at the back of the hood (*see* Fig. 96).

In Fig. 149 the headdress of a widow is seen, worn by Margaret Beaufort, Countess of Richmond, and mother of King Henry VII. It consists of the barbe (*see* vol. ii, p. 191), a distinctive item of widow's weeds, over which is worn a veil or headcloth, D, which would be fixed by pins to the barbe. On the back of the head is placed the black velvet hood, C, lined with black silk, and over all the band, B, of horizontally pleated linen embroidered with black silk and surrounded by a plain linen border. The hood takes the place of the black veil shown in vol. ii, Fig. 571, and the band has been added as a concession to the modern mode.

The headdress of the lady (Fig. 69) in attendance on Queen Elysabeth in the Coventry Tapestry is shown enlarged in Fig. 145. On her head she has placed, first, a small white coif, A; to this is fixed a second coif, also white, tucked, and bordered with gold. It is made *rigid* by the insertion of wire or parchment at the edge, bent gablewise to give the point at the top, the bend on either side of the temples, and the sloping line on to the cheeks. On top of this again is a third coif, worn far back on the head, and made of orange velvet bordered with wider gold. To the back of this is fixed a semicircular drapery—the curtain, BB—of crimson velvet striped with gold.

Although the headdress shown in Fig. 146 is similar in some details to the last (i.e. the coif and the back drapery), it does not suggest the gable, but has more the character of the headdresses shown in Figs. 130 and 131. It is worn by Queen Elysabeth in the Coventry Tapestry, and consists of two coifs, one on top of the other. The first is orange, outlined with narrow gold, and has large pear-shaped pearls hanging all round its edge; the second coif is of crimson velvet, with a wider gold edging. The semicircular back drapery, or curtain, BB, is of deep blue velvet, bordered with crimson and gold; narrow gold bands are set diagonally, alternating with rows of pear-shaped pearls. The crown (*see* Jewellery) takes the form of a frontal coronet.

In Fig. 151, taken from portraits of Queen Elysabeth, the headdress is now definitely of the gable type. In addition to the cap-like coif, A, used as a foundation, a stiffened cap (Fig. 135), shaped to the outline of the box-like or dog-kennel structure, was worn as a basis for the headdress. To its front edge, surrounding the face, is fixed a narrow edge-on band of gold, E, the FRONTLET, set with rectangular rubies placed close together. Behind this, and fixed to the cap, is a covering of black velvet, marked H. On top of this is worn the semicircular hood, C, as described under Fig. 150, with an elaborately decorated band, RS, placed on the straight edge of the hood—a decorative addition to the plain lappets seen in Fig. 148. This band, RS, is partly separated from the hood by slits, L and M, as shown in the diagram, Fig. 153.

The edge-on band of gold, E, surrounding the face is referred to in wardrobe accounts of the time as the 'frontlet.' 'Frontletts of golde for the Quene iiijd,' is an item in the privy purse expenses of Elysabeth of York.

In every representation of the gable headdress the band of gold embroidery,

RS, always falls in front of the shoulders, with the remaining part of the hood falling behind.

In Fig. 152 the only visible parts of the cap which replaces A (*see* Fig. 135) are the lappets, G.    On this box-like cap is fixed the semicircular hood of black velvet, C (*see* diagram, Fig. 138).    Its band, S, of gold embroidery or passement, often set with jewels, is about two and a half inches wide.    The additional slits, L and M, parallel to P and Q, and about six or eight inches away, give a double-fold effect at N.

The gable headdress was nearly always made of black velvet; but there are instances of some being made in crimson velvet.

Queens and noble ladies wore their crowns or coronets on top of this headdress, encircling the apex of the gable, as shown in Plate II and Fig. 315.

(*Continued on p. 323*)

## HAIRDRESSING

The hair in all these figures is waved on the temples, and in some cases allowed to flow on to the shoulders and show below the hood.   Fig. 152 shows the newest treatment, which became fashionable shortly after the dawn of the sixteenth century.   The hair is concealed by a piece of striped silk, F; this has been folded to a width of about two inches or three inches, slightly padded, and bound round the head, brought up the sides of the head above the ears, over the temples, and crossed in the centre of the forehead.   This pad fills the cavity between the forehead and the angles of the gable—it is seen to better advantage in Figs. 379 and 380.   The side hair, encased in silk, was also used to form these pads.   An alternative was to bring forward coils of hair, bind these spirally with bands of silk not more than half an inch wide, and cross them on the forehead to form a filling between the gable and the head.

Fig. 157. Stained Glass, King's College, Cambridge

(*Continued on p. 449*)

## FLEMISH HEADDRESSES

Quite distinct from the gable headdress, but contemporary with it, is a Flemish headdress much in fashion and shown in Fig. 157. Most of the representations of this headdress in England and France are to be found in paintings and tapestries by Flemish artists; but English and French ladies adopted it on occasion. The first item is a coif of stiffened white linen, shaped like Fig. 133. The nipped fold on the forehead, and the manner in which the ends turn up, are very characteristic. Over this is placed the familiar cap, A, edged with pearls. The third item is a melon-shaped cap, the shape of which can be seen in many of Dürer's drawings. It has a stiff foundation, and is covered with tucked folds of gold tissue in alternating diagonal directions, widely banded at right angles to the face with gold set with rubies and pearls. A number of varieties of this type of headdress were in fashion at this time.

Fig. 158. After Bernardino dei Conti

## SPANISH-ITALIAN HEADDRESSES

Fig. 159. Joanna of Castile

A profile head-and-shoulders portrait of a Spanish (or Italian) lady, by Bernardino dei Conti (1450–1525), reproduced in Fig. 158, shows a method of wearing the veil in Spain at this time. This figure shows a side view of the headdress worn by Isabella of Spain (Plate II A, see also Fig. 248). The dark hair is parted in the centre, and descends smoothly, though with a slight wave, well on to the cheeks. A white gauze veil, with a beautiful embroidered border and bound by a fillet of jet, passes over the back of the head: it is tied low in the nape by a black lace which is brought round to the front of the bodice. The remainder of the hair forms an encased pigtail down the back. The dress is of black velvet, made with sleeves shaped close at the shoulders and wrists and wide at elbows. The sleeves are tied to the bodice, which is moderately short-waisted, by black velvet laces. The skirt is full with a slight train. The whole of the upper part of the dress is decorated with rows of fancy network, finished with tassels in gold, blue, and silver.

Fig. 159 gives the headdress of Joanna of Castile, Plate V, on a larger scale. The hair is arranged as described under Fig. 141, and on top is placed a coif similar to that shown in Fig. 130, of red velvet or silk edged with a gold trimming of the design of Fig. 160. Above this is placed the black velvet hood, having a band of passement or embroidery in gold at the edge (*see* Fig. 161). Where the hood is turned back on top of the head this band of passement is still in evidence, and the hood lining of red and gold tissue is brought forward to rest on the coif. The coronet is set well back on the hood, as in Fig. 148, *behind* the band of passement.

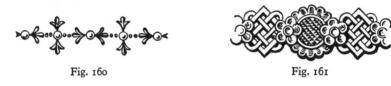

Fig. 160                    Fig. 161

### FRENCH HEADDRESSES

A form of headdress originating in France late in the fifteenth century developed into what came to be known in England as the FRENCH HOOD.

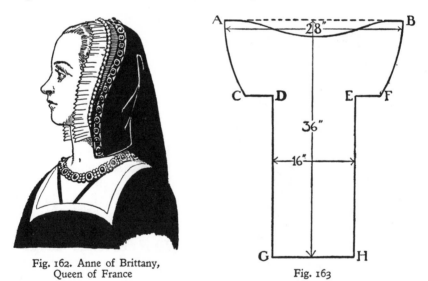

Fig. 162. Anne of Brittany,
Queen of France

Fig. 163

Its evolution at first sight appears somewhat involved, but the drawings, diagrams, and descriptions given hereafter will demonstrate that it followed a logical sequence of development.

One of the ancestors of the French hood is shown in Figs. 144 and 148, and a similar hood worn by Queen Joanna of Castile is seen in the drawing, Fig. 159, and Plate V. Yet another (Fig. 72), dated 1502, shows the top turned back, revealing the lining and resting on a cap of pleated gold gauze.

A later version of this early type, displaying the more characteristic features of the French hood, is shown in Fig. 162. This is taken from the portrait miniature of Anne of Brittany in a book presented to her and dates 1507. The back part is a development of the semicircular hood, shown in Figs. 148 and 138, and is now shaped like diagram, Fig. 163. It is made of black velvet and lined throughout with white or coloured silk. The front edge, AB, is slightly concave, and along it is set a band of jewels in gold mounts (Fig. 162). The edges marked CDG and FEH are seamed together, forming a tube which hangs down the back. This hood is placed on the head over a close-fitting cap edged with pearls, of which a small portion only is seen. Under this again, and resting on the hair, is a goffering of double gold gauze. In a medallion of Queen Anne of Brittany, struck at Lyons in 1499, she wears a crown set rather far back on this kind of headdress.

(*Continued on p.* 336)

### FLEMISH: THE BÉGUIN

Before proceeding further with the development of the French hood, another type of headdress must be considered. This is an essentially Flemish

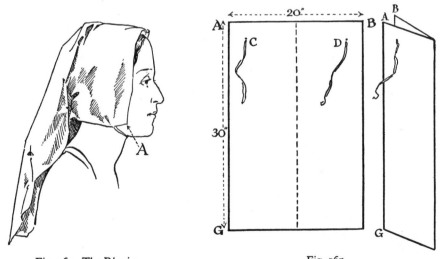

Fig. 164. The Béguin                    Fig. 165

headdress called a BÉGUIN, and is one of the several sources from which the French hood was derived.

Its origin is interesting. The Béguines were a religious order of women, founded, it is said, by Lambert le Bègue (the Stammerer), a priest who gave his name to the society he founded at Liège in 1173. The Order spread and became important in the thirteenth century, when organizations were established in several cities in Germany, Flanders, and France. Members of this Order wore a small white coif like that mentioned on p. 176, vol. ii, and henceforth the name béguin was given to this type of coif. At a later date a veil folded round the head was added, and to this also the same name was applied.

The collection of houses in which the religious women lived was called a 'Béguinage'; one of them still exists at Bruges, but in recent times the Order has dwindled to very small proportions.

The béguin was a very simple headdress—a rectangular piece of linen, lawn, or cambric; in fact, a headkerchief or couvrechef. It was much worn also by women of the laity in Flanders, and is often found in paintings by Flemish artists of the fifteenth and sixteenth centuries. The measurements of the rectangle varied, and there were many different ways of arranging it.

Fig. 166

Fig. 164 shows the simplest method, as worn by a Flemish woman of the middle and lower classes; diagram, Fig. 165, gives the details. The rectangle of linen, about twenty inches, AB, by twenty-five or thirty inches, AG, is doubled lengthways as shown by the dotted line, and the crease pressed. Tapes or fine cords are attached to positions (external when the béguin is folded) about three inches from the corners A and B as shown at C and D.

The béguin is then opened out; one end is placed on the head, with the crease downward, forming a slight dip on the forehead; and its long edges, at points about eight or nine inches from the extremities A and B, are pinned together at the nape, E to F.

The tapes, now inside the hood, are tied together under the chin, and the corners of the headdress flare slightly from the cheeks.

(Continued on p. 327)

A variety of headdresses worn by the lower classes is to be found in the drawings of them in their respective sections.

The young woman (Fig. 166) has ingeniously contrived to imitate the fashionable line in her head attire of white linen by pinching the edge into a point on the forehead like a gable headdress. It is worn over a wimple.

Simpler methods of arranging the headrail are shown in Figs. 103 and 104.

## FOOTGEAR, 1485–1509

The Cordwainers are one of the oldest guilds, but details of their earliest operations are unknown owing to the loss of all their records in the Great Fire of London, 1666.

The name is derived from the town of Cordova in Spain, whence the best leather, made of goat's skin and called 'cordwain,' was imported into England. Spanish leather had always been regarded as superior to any other, owing to the fact that the Moors of Spain were expert in dressing leather of a soft and durable nature either by tanning or tawing.

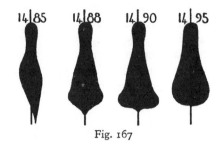

Fig. 167

The Cordwainers' Company included the curriers, girdlers, leathersellers, pouchmakers and pursers, tanners and shoewrights. The articles of leatherwork made by the latter were: ankle-leathers, boiling vessels, bottles, bridle thongs, flasks, halters, leather hosen, leather neck-pieces, pouches, trappings, wallets, and 'schon,' 'shoon,' or 'shon.'

A shoemaker was sometimes referred to in early times as a 'chaucer.'

St. Crispin is the patron saint of shoemakers.

The livery colours of the company were black and red. The date when they were adopted is not known, but it was probably in the fourteenth century.

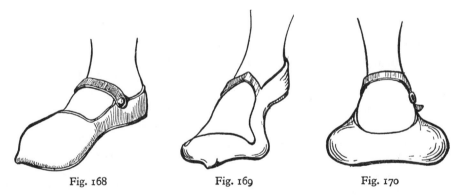

Fig. 168          Fig. 169          Fig. 170

The shape of the foot-part or sole of boots and shoes worn at the time of Henry VII's accession is shown in the sole plan, Fig. 167 (date 1485). Fig. 630, vol. ii, shows the type of shoe, and Fig. 636 the boot, then worn.

About 1488 the sides of the toe-part of boots and shoes began to bulge, but the point was still in evidence. About 1490 the sides increased in bulk, and it was in the early nineties that the point disappeared altogether, leaving the front of the shoe straight and wide and curving round to the sides of the foot.

Fig. 168 shows a shoe of the first years of Henry VII's reign. It is similar to Fig. 631, vol. ii, except that the back is a trifle lower, and the sides of the toes are more bulged. Fig. 169 is a shoe later in style, in use after 1490: it is considerably broader in the toe and cut very much lower at the back, sides, and over the instep. The shoe shown in Fig. 170, which dates about 1495, is very wide at the toe and round at the side. The point at the toe has now vanished. All these three shoes (Figs. 168, 169, and 170) have straps across the instep or ankle, fastened either with a buckle or button. 'Single soled with latyn buckles' is an item from a contemporary inventory. Latten was a metal very like brass. 'Double soled shoys' is another item frequently found.

In Fig. 20 the shoe is cut across the instep, the top part forming a wide band which is laced. This kind of shoe is to be seen in the tapestry, 'The Seven Deadly Sins,' at Hampton Court. Fig. 28 has ankle shoes fastened by a strap across a vertical slit on the instep.

Several shoes of this period have been unearthed lately from the city ditch in the precincts of the City of London: they are nearly all made of black

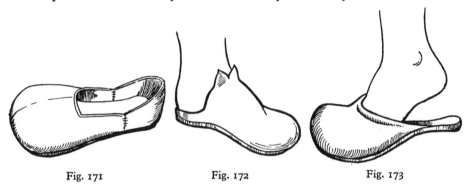

Fig. 171                    Fig. 172                    Fig. 173

leather: but whether their blackness is due to age or not is uncertain. In most contemporary illustrations of the commonalty, shoes are shown black. Fig. 171 is a drawing of one, the sole measuring eight and a half inches long and three inches at its widest part. The upper is nine inches long and the back of the heel two and a half inches high. This shoe has no fastening, but some have straps which buckle or button round the ankle. This is obviously a woman's shoe, such as was worn by women of all classes, from the queen to the spouse of the country gentleman. No decoration is evident. The material of these shoes was velvet, cloth, or leather, usually black but sometimes in colour. Long and trailing skirts hid the shoe to a great extent.

The queen's cordener was a certain Maister Rutte—a suitable name for a man of this craft in days when roads were quagmires and footpaths exceptional.

The heel covering in smart footwear became so narrow that the heel itself was left almost bare. Fig. 172 shows one of these shoes, worn by the Flemish gentleman (Fig. 22), and dates about 1495.

Shoes without any heel covering were in general use among the upper and lower classes about 1500. When the foot was bent the heel of the foot rose above the sole of the shoe, making a clatter as the wearer walked. The toe of this shoe (Fig. 173) is even more rounded than that of the last one.

Fig. 174 is a similar shoe, but the toe part follows the natural shape of the foot. It is made of cloth or velvet and ornamented with two bands of passement. Fig. 6 is wearing shoes of this kind.

It should be noticed that the young gentleman (Fig. 82) is wearing old-fashioned long-toed shoes, such as were in vogue during the reign of Edward IV! The notary (Fig. 80) and the cider merchant (Fig. 86) are also shod a little out of date; but these two persons do not aim at being in the fashion.

The shoes worn by the notary are shown in Fig. 175.

A more natural shaped shoe than Fig. 173 is shown in Fig. 176. It has a very thick sole which takes the line of the foot, and has a black leather upper. This kind of shoe or clog was often worn by middle-class people, and frequently by peasants.

The shoes of the two peasants (Figs. 91, 92) are medieval in type.

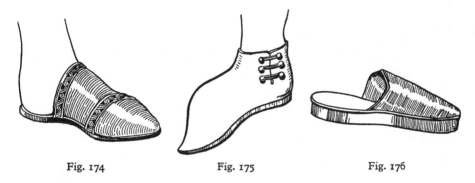

Fig. 174          Fig. 175          Fig. 176

Those worn by Fig. 87 are uncommon, being cut high at the back and buckled and strapped across an open instep.

Strong boots are worn under loose hosen by working men as shown in Figs. 90 and 94.

Coverings which became fashionable after originating as definitely practical protection to the hosen can be described as 'leg wear.' [1]

They were designed for use when walking in rough weather and muddy streets, or to slip on for riding as an alternative to long heavy boots, as is first seen in Fig. 22. They are the descendants of the peduals worn by the early Franks (*see* vol. i, p. 191), and resemble modern stockings. They were made of various materials, chiefly linen, and usually turned down at the top below the knee. The gentlemen (Figs. 24 and 28) are wearing them over their hosen. Various kinds of shoes were worn with them. Fig. 85 shows the same kind of leg coverings, made of thick material, probably felt or soft leather, combined with heavy soles transforming them into a kind of top-boot.

In Illum. MSS. of this period one sometimes finds illustrations of men and women with a shoe cast from one foot. These show how the foot-part of the hosen was finished, viz. the toe and heel uncovered, the hosen continuing

[1] Refer to boot-hose, page 457.

under the arch of the foot. As seen in Fig. 177 these primitive hosen are knitted and perhaps the knitter found it difficult to shape the toe and heel. In some instances the toes only were uncovered as shown in Fig. 178.

There was no great variety in the style of long boots worn during the reign of Henry VII. It will be observed, on referring to Figs. 9, 30, 34, and 36, that they are all very much alike.

Fig. 179 comes from an Illum. MS. dated 1490, and is characteristic of those generally worn at this time. Various kinds of leather were used in their making, some thick, giving a solid appearance to the boot, others of soft leather which produced folds around the leg, as seen in Fig. 179. They all had rounded toes, and most of them were turned down at the top; nearly all reached some distance above the knee. A few examples are to be found where the top of the boot is not turned down: in these instances the back was slit from the top to just above the top of the calf, as shown in Fig. 21.

Fig. 179

An item in a wardrobe account runs: 'Botews above the knee of tawny Spaynyssh leder' (botews being the name often given to long boots).

A pair of boots belonging to a man of no importance, taken from an Illum. MS. dating 1489 in the Winchester Chapter Library, is shown in Fig. 180. They are of brown leather reaching to the calf, and flexible enough to flop round the lower part of the leg.

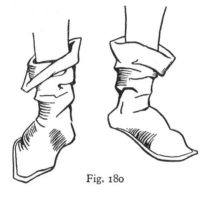

Fig. 180

## JEWELLERY, 1485–1509

This section should be read as a continuation of the corresponding jewellery section in vol. ii, Chap. VI, p. 453. The type of jewellery fashionable during the entire period altered but little: the style was determined mainly by the work of Flemish-Burgundian artists, as Italian influence had as yet scarcely shown itself in the art of the English goldsmiths. Goldsmiths were artists in metalwork, making vessels and ornaments for the church and private individuals. Gems and precious stones were cut, polished, and engraved by lapidaries, and the work of setting them and creating personal ornaments (often under the direction of an artist such as Holbein) was done by those goldsmiths who were jewellers. Goldsmiths were also bankers.

The Goldsmiths' Company is an ancient one, and was in existence in the reign of Henry II, 1180. It was incorporated by charter by Edward III in 1327, and confirmed by Richard II in 1394. Henry VII, by Inspeximus of his twentieth year, confirmed all the preceding charters. St. Dunstan was their patron saint. The date of the original grant of the shield of arms is unknown, the grant having been long since lost, and the date unrecorded at the College of Arms.

The armorial bearings (see Fig. 910) are: Quarterly, gules and azure, in the first and fourth a leopard's head or; in the second and third, a covered cup, and in chief two round buckles, the tongues fessewise, points to dexter, all of the third.

The livery colours in 1474 were violet and scarlet. In 1495 there is an entry in the company's records that the colours for that year were blue and crimson. Under Henry VIII (1512) the Goldsmiths' livery was a gown of violet with a hood particoloured violet and scarlet.

### CROWNS

A crown having arches, though not necessarily that of an emperor, was usually alluded to at this time as an imperial crown. The crown 'Imperiall,' as used by Henry VII, is shown in Plates I and IV surmounting the Royal coat of arms of the Tudors, which are supported by the Lion of England and the Dragon of Wales. It is made from a drawing dated 1500. The circlet is set with rubies and emeralds, and bears four crosses patée and as many fleurs-de-lys: four crocketed arches carry the ball and cross.

The crowns worn by the King and Queen in the same plate have only two arches. Other drawings of the crown of Henry VII are shown in Figs. 3 and 7, and in Plate IV.

Up to the end of the fifteenth century there had been no definite distinction between the crowns of the reigning houses of Europe, and Fig. 38 shows one of the first to attain a style of its own. It is the crown of France,

and in the illustration surmounts the helmet of Louis XII.   There are eight
fleurs-de-lys above the circlet, and a larger one rising from an arch (*see also*
Plate XXXVI).   A coronet of a Spanish Infanta is seen in Fig. 159.   It
should be noticed that it is placed far back on the head behind the turn-back
of the hood, the approved universal manner.   In the original painting, the

coronet is much confused with the trees
in the background; therefore Fig. 181 is
given showing a portion of it with the
detail on a larger scale.   The circlet of gold
is edged with a cord-like design, and on
it are lozenge-shaped jewels in gold mounts
with pearls at the angles: these alternate
with groups of seven pearls.   Above the
circlet rise leaf-like motifs, each set with
a central ruby and three pearls in the members: between the motifs a single large
pearl is raised.

Fig. 181. Portion of Coronet

An English version, but not placed so
far back, is worn by Elysabeth of York
(Fig. 146); here the circlet takes the form of a wide horseshoe beneath nine
fleurs-de-lys, each pair separated by a group of three pearls.

The Infanta Joanna lived part of her life in Flanders, and imbibed Flemish
influences.   The Coventry Tapestry, from which Fig. 146 is taken, is of
Flemish make, which probably accounts for the two crowns appearing somewhat similar.

### COLLARS

Collars of heavy rectangular, circular, or oval ornaments of goldsmith's
work, often set with jewels, were in great favour with royalty and the nobility
when in full or even semi-dress.   Fig. 182 is a part detail of a collar taken
from a portrait of Henry VII.   It is composed of a series of roses en soleil.

Fig. 182.                                    Fig. 183.

Sections of Collars

The three petals of the rose shown black are of green enamel in the original,
the two lower ones of white.   Alternate roses have these colours reversed.
Superimposed on the rose are the rays of the sun in gold, and in the centre is
a ruby in a gold claw setting.   The roses are linked by triple loops of gold
cord with fringed ends, each loop enclosing a pearl.   Another collar worn by

Henry VII is shown in Fig. 183. The seven-petalled rose is of gold and red enamel, with an emerald set in the centre. Two of the gold loops enclose round pearls, and the third a pear-shaped one.

In a portrait at Windsor Castle, Arthur, Prince of Wales, wears a collar (Fig. 184) in simpler design, of alternate red and white double roses linked by triple loops enclosing pearls, with two petals of red enamel in the angles. The centre rose only has three peardrop pearls.

A collar is mentioned in the inventory of the Prince of Wales, 1504, which describes 'a rose of rubies, set in a rose white and green with iij fayre perles, yeven by my Lord Chaumbrelayn poisaunt di oz.' In the same inventory there is a description of another collar belonging to this Prince, as follows : 'A collar of garters of gold, con't XXII garters and XXII laces, w't a George on horseback, poisaunt [weighing] togeders XXX oz di quart.' Also 'a collor of golde w't rede roses and white enamel w't pauncies [violas] w't wyres of pynnes.' That ladies

Fig. 184. Section of Collar

of the Royal family sometimes wore these collars of roses and knots is evidenced by the portrait of Queen Elysabeth of York at Hatfield House.

Nicholas, Lord Vaux, who received knighthood from Henry VII after the Battle of Stoke, was present at the marriage of the Prince of Wales in 1501; and on this occasion, Stow informs us, 'he wore a gown of purple velvet adorned with pieces of gold so thick and massy, that besides the silk and furs it was valued at a thousand pounds, as also a collar of SS, weighing eight hundred pounds in nobles.' In his will, proved 1523, he left his three daughters £1 each.

## NECK CHAINS

Edward Hall frequently refers in his *Chronicle* to 'massy chains' worn by the nobility and wealthy people. These chains, although rich, were not so elaborate as the collars, and were definitely composed of links, rectangular, circular, or oval in shape. Sometimes, however, the design varied, and consisted of spiral sections and linked motifs of goldsmith's work set with jewels.

These rich chains were bestowed by the sovereign and nobles upon their adherents and dependants as marks of favour, the extent of which was indicated by the weight of the chain. As much as £1,400 was the estimated value of a chain worn by Sir Thomas Brandon, Henry VII's Master of the Horse.

£600 was considered quite a reasonable sum to pay for a really good chain. The length of these distinctive ornaments was considerable, which, of course, added to the expense and weight. They were often wound round the neck and shoulders two or three times, and a mode of wearing them 'prisoner fashion' or transverse, that is over one shoulder and under the opposite arm, was quite usual (*see* Fig. 29). These 'massy chains' descended as heirlooms in families and are generally described with much detail in wills: Lord Mountjoy, 1485, left 'to Rowland, my son, a chain of gold with a lion of gold, set with diamonds.'

Gentlemen wearing rich chains are seen in Figs. 7 and 28.

Jewelled collars, when worn by ladies, were referred to as carcanets, and examples are seen in Figs. 69, 145, and 147. Chains were used also (*see* Figs. 68, 75, 130, and 143). Sometimes ladies wore both carcanet and chain, as shown in Figs. 69 and 145.

JEWELS

Fig. 185 is a jewel, four inches in length, worn by Henry VII on the placard of his dress in one of his portraits. The larger stones are rubies, and the smaller emeralds and sapphires, with small pearls intermixed and the whole set in gold. It is a good example of the term 'jewel,' which was very popular at this time and is found in many inventories. An interesting one is

Fig. 185. A 'Jewel'

mentioned as belonging to Henry VII, and called 'La Fleur de luce.' It was in the form of a fleur-de-lys pendant of gold set with many gems, 'wherein was a piece of wood of the True Cross' and weighed twenty-one and a half ounces. This substantial jewel, originally in the possession of the House of Hapsburg, was pawned by Philippe le Beau to Henry VII for fifty thousand crowns.

The astute Henry may have admired beautiful jewellery, for he acquired much and paid large sums for jewels; but knowing his money-making propensities one is inclined to think that he accumulated a rich store chiefly for its money value. In his privy purse expenses we find an entry: 'Jan. 15. 1492. Delivered by the Kinges commandement for diverse juels pledges oute of London for the household, £350.'

Then in May of the same year: 'Delivered by the Kinges commandement for diverse peces of cloth of gold, and for certain and many precyouse stones and riche perlis bought of Lombardes for the garnyshing of Salades, Shapues, and helemytez, agenst the King's noble voyage £3,800.' These items have nothing to do with edibles, but were for the purpose of enhancing his Royal pomp upon a trip abroad. This treasure might also be turned into hard cash if occasion required. In March 1501 an item is entered: 'Delivered and payd by the Kinges commandement for diverse and many juells brought oute of Fraunce agenst the marage of my Lorde Prince [Arthur] £14,000.'

The collection of magnificent jewels possessed by the House of Burgundy, some of which are mentioned on p. 459, vol. ii, was dispersed after the Battle of Granson in 1475 (*see* p. 171). Amongst these looted jewels was the ceremonial hat worn by Charles le Téméraire, reproduced in Fig. F, Plate XVIII, by reason of the multitude of jewels with which it was smothered. An account of it, written in German by Jacob Fugger (1459–1525), was translated into Latin; and now done into English is as follows:

'Moreover the said Charles, Duke of Burgundy, lost in the Battle of Granson . . . a hat no less elegant than magnificent, of which an exact account is hereunder.

'The hat was made of cloth of gold, and formed like the Italian hats nowadays; that is to say, that not only had it a brim or round margin moderately large for keeping off the sun, but also a similar round and raised crown. At the top of this ducal hat in the centre there was superimposed a long and pointed balas ruby inserted in a setting. Moreover, the whole hat was adorned round about with very precious pearls. In place of the hat-band above the brim was a golden garland in which sapphires and rubies of equal size were alternately inserted, and were parted from one another by three great oriental pearls to which were added pearls, two by two, set in the spiked extremities of the garland, above and below. In the front part of the hat was a very well wrought sheath of gold, adorned with diamonds, pearls and rubies, in which were inserted two feathers, one of which was red and the

Fig. 186. Rose Pendant

other white, and both of them shone with pearls and gold most magnificently as befitted the ducal dignity.

'Although therefore what we have already related as an eyewitness concerning the shape and adornment of this ducal hat, which may justly be compared with a ducal crown, be true, yet so that our heirs may be able in some way to see with their own eyes with what great riches Charles, Duke of Burgundy, was endowed, for that reason and for their own pleasure we will insert here a picture [Fig. F, plate XVIII] of the whole of this crested hat. For we have caused that hat to be dismantled, and the gems, having been thence removed and reset in various jewels and rings, we have sold together with the two feathers belonging to it, to the most Serene Prince Maximilian I, King of the Romans (1498), for [many] thousand florins; and for this reason also these jewels for the greater part have returned into the possession of the House of Burgundy.'

Among other jewels lost at Granson was a most precious heart-shaped ruby in a gold setting resembling a rose (Fig. 186). This was worn by Charles le Téméraire as a pendant, and was doubtless disposed of to one of the Fugger clients.

## ENSEIGNES, BROOCHES

Enseignes of gold and jewels for the bonet kept for a time the religious subjects inherited from the pilgrim's badge, and were often decorated with

Fig. 187. Enseigne

the figures of saints in gold. The Virgin and Child, St. John the Baptist, St. George, and St. Christopher were prime favourites. One is worn in the cap of Fig. 7, and another in Fig. 28. In Fig. 116 an enseigne of gold and enamel is set with a ruby and four pearls; Figs. 113 and 114 are examples of the style in which saints are enclosed in a decorated border. The one shown in Fig. 187 has an engraved border, with the figure of St. Catherine in gold and silver upon a background of enamel, diaper pattern above and plain below. Rings for sewing it on to the bonet are seen at the edge.

It was the mode to just break the line of the circle, perhaps by turning the brim down slightly over its edge as seen in Fig. 114. The band of the bonet passes right over the centre of the enseigne shown in Fig. 126.

## ENAMELS

Enamel as a decoration to jewellery had been used in earlier times, and towards the end of the fifteenth century flat surfaces—'en taille'—for backgrounds covered with translucent enamel were extensively introduced.

At the same time enamel on high relief, such as figures, flowers, scrolls, began to be more generally used by the goldsmiths of Italy, Germany, and France. Painted enamel originated with the Limoges artists in the fifteenth century, and was much in vogue.

Enamels were made in three styles: cloisonné (see vol. i, p. 206); Limoges (vol. ii, p. 62); and champ-levé, in which spaces in the metal were dug out and filled with enamel-paste which was permanently fixed by fusion. The metals used for the foundations were bronze and copper. After the fourteenth century this style was not very general.

The method of engraving gold and silver with incisions filled in with black alloy and burnished, a process known as niello, reached a very high standard in the fifteenth century, and many small pieces of jewellery were embellished in this manner. The goldsmiths of northern Italy were the most proficient in this craft, although the art of engraving was first practised in Germany.

Some artists of Italy who painted beautiful pictures were also masters of other artistic crafts, such as jewellery and designs for jewellery. Francesco Raibolini, known as Francia (1450–1517), was one of the most versatile. He painted on walls and glass, cut dies for coins, engraved niello, and as a goldsmith produced some exquisite masterpieces.

## Pendants

Pendants were very often made of two plates joined so as to leave a space for a relic between them; 'magical' pendants were formed in like manner and set with 'proofs' of natural or unnatural substances and of the unicorn's horn, which was really that of the narwhal, supposed to possess the power of detecting poison.

The front plate of such pendants was usually richly ornamented; and an elaborate one, or more likely a *reliquary*, is shown in Fig. 188. It is worn by Anne of Brittany in her portrait at the Louvre and dates 1500. It measures quite four inches in length, and has an enamelled background on which are set six jewels in irregular claw mounts between groups of small pearls. In the centre is the figure of St. John the Baptist, with what looks like a basket of eggs (or are they locusts?) on his lap. A nimbus of gold surrounds his head, and also the golden lamb on the top right of the pendant. An edifice of gold is on the opposite side.

Fig. 188. Pendant

The reliquary was most popular in Spain, and one of lozenge shape worn by Isabella the Catholic (Plate II) is reproduced in Fig. 189. Of gold, it has four rubies with a diamond in the centre, and four pearls at the edges, and is hung from a chain of woven links.

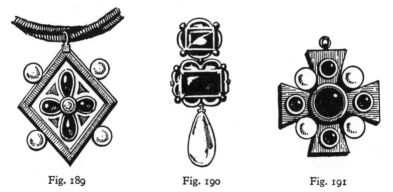

Fig. 189          Fig. 190          Fig. 191

The pendant or reliquary of Joanna of Castile (Fig. 159 and Plate V) has a heavy gold mount set with an oval ruby, and measures about three inches in length.

Fig. 190 shows the ornament or pendant on the shoulder of Beatrice d' Este

(Fig. 140) and is drawn on a larger scale; it is in two sections, each containing a jewel in gold mounts, from which a large peardrop pearl is suspended.

*Crosses*, usually hung round the neck, were much worn during the period 1460–1527. Behind the central jewel was a cavity in which a small relic might be kept. Fig. 191 is one such cross, made from a portrait of Ferdinand of Aragon. It is of gold, with five rubies and four pearls, and hangs from a red lace.

Queen Elysabeth (Plate I) has a Latin cross of gold set with rubies. Crosses and crucifixes, besides being worn round the neck, were frequently attached

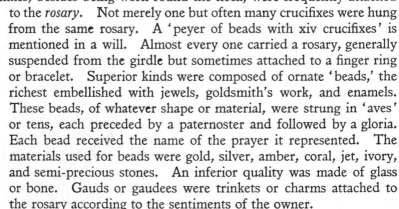

to the *rosary*. Not merely one but often many crucifixes were hung from the same rosary. A 'peyer of beads with xiv crucifixes' is mentioned in a will. Almost every one carried a rosary, generally suspended from the girdle but sometimes attached to a finger ring or bracelet. Superior kinds were composed of ornate 'beads,' the richest embellished with jewels, goldsmith's work, and enamels. These beads, of whatever shape or material, were strung in 'aves' or tens, each preceded by a paternoster and followed by a gloria. Each bead received the name of the prayer it represented. The materials used for beads were gold, silver, amber, coral, jet, ivory, and semi-precious stones. An inferior quality was made of glass or bone. Gauds or gaudees were trinkets or charms attached to

Fig. 192    the rosary according to the sentiments of the owner.

*Ornamental pins* were used by ladies to fix the black velvet hood on one side of the head. Usually the pin had a jewel or ornament hanging from it by a ring or small chain. One is shown in Fig. 192, which has a bevelled square of gold, with a ruby in a claw-setting and four pearls on the edges. A pear-shaped pearl hangs from it.

Other ornamental pins on headdresses are seen in Figs. 63, 64, 95, and 144.

### BRACELETS

Bracelets are ornaments which demand the bare skin as a foundation; and as sleeves during the Middle Ages, and also in Tudor times, covered the wrists few bracelets were worn. However, inventories and wills occasionally mention them, and an illustration of one may be seen in Plate XII.

A plain ring on the wrist, though unseen, was worn for the convenience of carrying the rosary.

The same applies to *earrings*, as most headdresses of this period almost covered the ears. On the Continent, bracelets and earrings were more generally worn, owing to the different style of sleeve and headdress. At a later date—1514—we find the Princess Mary I (Plate XII) and Eleanor of Austria (Plate XI) wearing earrings, but it must be borne in mind that both these ladies are wearing Spanish dress. Later still, the drawings of Catherine de' Medici (Figs. 525 and 543) show a peardrop pearl hanging from under her French hood, but that is exceptional.

As yet the *girdle* was worn entirely for utility—the belt, and as such its only decorations, if they can be so called, were the buckle and mordant.

From time to time during the whole course of the Middle Ages extra adornments in the form of metal plates were added, but girdles decorated in this manner do not come under the heading of jewellery.

Royalty and nobility of the same period did use jewels, often to a great extent, for the decoration of their belts, as mentioned under some of the

Fig. 193. Arms of the Girdlers' Company

figures in vol. ii. Girdle- and belt-makers formed an important fraternity, and as far back as 1449 were incorporated. They had armorial bearings granted to them by Henry VI, 1454 (Fig. 193), namely: Per fesse azure and or, a pale counterchanged: three gridirons of the last, the handles in chief. Crest, on a wreath, a demi-man proper, representing their patron St. Laurence (with Glory round his head or, issuing out of clouds of the first), vested azure, girt round the body with a girdle of the second, holding in his dexter hand a gridiron of the last, and in the sinister a book argent. Motto: Give thanks to God.

The original colours of the livery, it is said, were blue and gold, the same as Aaron's girdle.

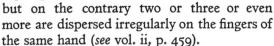

RINGS

How many rings should be worn on the fingers of one hand? That depends upon the wearer: according to portraits a single ring is often met with,

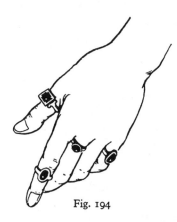

but on the contrary two or three or even more are dispersed irregularly on the fingers of the same hand (*see* vol. ii, p. 459).

Fig. 194 shows four rings, on the thumb and on the first, second, and fourth fingers: that on the forefinger is placed on the middle joint— quite a usual position on any finger. Wedding rings were seldom plain; they were generally worn on the third finger of the right hand during the Middle Ages. They were often engraved with a pattern, motto, or affectionate inscription; and, as proved by portraits of married women, not always worn.

Fig. 194

Fig. 195 shows an ecclesiastical ring of the late fifteenth century set with a sapphire. The shank is octagonal: the edges are bevelled and engraved. The jewel would be either square or round, the claws branching out to hold it.

A similar ring, dating about 1500, is shown in Fig. 196. This is in the

Fig. 195

Fig. 196

possession of the Right Reverend Bishop of Pella, and has a rectangular amethyst in a claw setting. The circle is engraved with the Five Mysteries. Only one other like it is known to the Victoria and Albert Museum authorities.

## GUILDS AND TRADE (*continued from vol. ii, p. 464*)

Trade with foreign countries was now in a much more flourishing condition than before, owing to the effects of the 'Great Treaty' of 1496 (*see* vol. ii, p. 462), and commerce with other countries than Flanders increased considerably. Venice had been, and still was, the chief emporium from which products of South Europe and the rich stores of India and China were shipped to this country.

Henry VII and Henry VIII both gave great encouragement to English trade, and during their reigns English ships, independently of other nations' merchant fleets, entered the Mediterranean. They brought back wonderful silken fabrics and new luxuries of every kind unheard of before.

Trade with the Baltic provinces was still very jealously guarded by the German merchants, who had their English headquarters at the 'Styleyard which is East of Dounegate,' or 'Dowgate in Thames Street.' There, Germans of the Hanseatic League or Hansa, which rose to its highest power in the fifteenth century, had certain privileges, and in consequence were very much disliked by the English merchants. The discovery of the New World (1492), and the opening of the Cape route to the Indies (1498), were destined to give an immense impetus to the shipping and commerce of western Europe, and governments were very willing to assist trade by granting charters to trading companies. Thus a charter of 1501 (following an earlier one of 1407, which gave the right of choosing their own governor) enabled the Merchant Adventurers to manage their own trade and to punish those who broke their rules.

As previously the best gowns or liveries of the city companies were of raye cloth, that is, striped or particoloured in the colours of their fraternity. Stow in his *Survey* tells how 'the liverymen of the city of London, and probably the burghers of other cities in England also, exclusive of the livery and badges belonging to their own companies, frequently complimented the Mayor by appearing in his: such of them as chose to do so gave at least 20s. in a purse, with the name of the donor marked upon it, and the wardens delivered it to the Mayor by the 1st of December; for which every man had sent to him Four yards of broadcloth rowed, or striped athwart, with a different colour, to make him a gown; and these were called rey-gowns, which were then the livery of my Lord Mayor, and also the Sheriffs, but each differing from the others in colours.'

The original shape of the gown as shown in Fig. 221, vol. ii, had undergone a slight change, and the livery gowns of Henry VII's time were almost the same in shape as shown in Fig. 561, vol. ii. The kind of fur used on them depended upon the means of the wearer. At this period the hood, particoloured in the colours of the company, was not worn but carried over the shoulder, the liripipe hanging in front on the left side, and the headgear—the French bonet, then in vogue—was worn in place of the hood.

### Weaving and Materials

Towards the latter part of the fifteenth century the weaving industry, which hitherto had been principally carried on in the towns, spread to the villages owing to the desire of the clothworkers to escape from the stringent rule of the Town Guilds. For centuries the various craftsmen had worked entirely on their own in their own homes. Up to the time when machinery was introduced, spinning and weaving was practised in the home, and re-garded not only as a part-liveli-hood, but as a relaxation from ordinary everyday work. This is why looms were set up in the living-rooms of cottages which were on the street. Many Acts of Parlia-ment had been passed from time to time for the prevention of fraud in the making of cloth and other materials. One, in 1483, con-demned 'various fraudulent and tricking methods of making wool-len cloths' and decreed that 'Ten-ters shall not be kept within doors, but alone in open places,' so that all might keep an eye on them lest

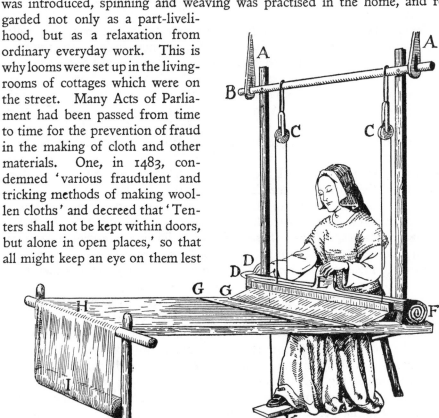

Fig. 197. A Fifteenth-century Loom

they stretch the cloth too much. For the same reason it was the rule that looms should stand in shops and rooms adjoining the thoroughfare in sight of every one, so that false working could easily be detected.

A medieval loom, in use at this time with a woman working at it, is shown in Fig. 197; it would be set up in her 'parlour' or living-room. This loom was easily erected, as can be seen in the drawing, the only part more or less permanently in position being the two loops, AA, hung from a beam. These support the cross-bar, B, to which the main part of the loom is attached: legs are fixed to the end of the frame only. The warp running lengthwise is wound on a roller, I, over a pole, H, and partly over and partly under the two rods, GG. The yarn is then carried through the healds, DD, which make the shed and allow the shuttle, thrown by the right hand in the drawing, to be sent flying through the shuttle-race. By means of the upright, E, the two sections of the warp, attached to the rods slung from the two pulleys, CC, are raised and depressed with each throw (from right to left—and left to right) of the shuttle. K is one of the pedals which raises and pulls down the healds, DD; and the woven cloth is wound round the roller, F.

In winter-time the spinster would sit by the fire and spin. In warmer weather she would plant herself by the cottage door and 'spin a yarn' to every gossip who gave her the opportunity. Women were not considered eligible for marriage till they had spun a regular set of bed furniture, and until their wedding day were called spinsters. A woman spinning is shown in Fig. 353.

## LIST OF MATERIALS

*Andly*, from aande, meaning broad. A kind of broadcloth.

*Barde, bayette*, harsh flannel.

*Blanket*, a soft and loosely woven woollen material, used as clothing by peasants. Made at Bristol and Witney.

*Bordat*, cloth used for covering furniture.

*Broadcloth*, mentioned in vol. ii, p. 123, but this refers to cloth of a certain width. Also applied to cloth of a close weave manufactured by John Winchecombe. A length measured 24 yards, and in breadth 'eight quarters between the lists.'

*Buckram*, a superior material used for wearing apparel. There was also an inferior quality used chiefly for lining garments.

*Buffins*, a coarse material like serge used for gowns of middle-class women.

*Burat*, a kind of ratine or twilled wool.

*Bureau*, a coarse woollen cloth in various colours.

*Canon's cloth*, coarse cloth like serge used for monastic habits.

*Cloth of gold* and *of silver*, see under *Gold*.

*Damask*, a material wholly of silk woven with a pattern, and made in Italy, chiefly at Genoa. It was supplied in great quantities to the whole of Europe at a high price, about eight shillings per yard.

*Duffel*, a stout milled flannel, with a blanket or napped surface woven extra wide and in all colours. Made at Witney and in western Europe.

'*Engrain*' or '*ingrain*.' Graine is the dye of cochineal, so that to dye with cochineal means to dye in fast colours, i.e. dye 'in grain.' Applied chiefly to scarlet, crimson, and purple.

*Foynys, foins*, the fur of the polecat.

*Gold, cloth of*, also *cloth of silver*. This very rich material continued to be much used by royalty and the nobility. It was woven with a warp of pure gold threads and a weft of silk, sometimes the warp and weft both being of gold, very similar to baudekyns. For the origin of this see vol. ii, p. 123, under 'Imperial,' and p. 147.

Another kind known as *'crimson* (or any other colour) *cloth of gold'* was woven with a coloured silk, and had the appearance of a colour-and-gold shot. These golden fabrics were chiefly imported from Venice through Lombard middlemen. 'Diverse peces of cloth of gold . . . bought of Lombards' occurs in Henry VII's privy purse expenses.

*Half-cloths* usually measured twelve yards long and were not to exceed sixteen yards, and 'eight quarters' wide.

*Holland cloth,* a superior kind of fine linen first made in Holland; also linen, although woven elsewhere, sent to that country to be bleached.

*Lukes,* a kind of velvet.

*Lynx* fur. The European kind was usually a dark grey, tinted with tawny orange; and variegated with dark spots and patches. The lynx of Asia and Africa was of a yellowish grey colour, and this fur was highly valued.

*Monk's cloth.* See *Canon's cloth.*

*Paper.* The first paper in Europe was made by the Moors in Spain in the eleventh century. A paper mill was established in Italy in 1297; and the earliest mention of paper being made in England occurs in a work printed by Caxton about 1490, where an allusion is made to John Tate, a papermaker. Two entries in Henry VII's household book, 1498–9, show that this King encouraged John Tate in the working of his paper mill at Stevenage, Herts. In 1503 three quires of paper cost sixpence.

*Passement.* See vol. ii, p. 463.

*Raye cloth,* the name of a cloth dyed in stripes in use since the twelfth century (*see* vol. ii, pp. 124, 188). In one or two documents of the late fifteenth century it is definitely stated that raye cloth was 'not coloured,' and the supposition is that the name was sometimes applied to an undyed cloth.

*Riban, ryben, reben*=ribbon.

*Silk,* see *The History of Silk,* vol. ii, Chap. V, p. 210.

*Silver, cloth of.* See under *Gold, cloth of.*

*Spangles,* first mentioned in the reign of Henry VII and often referred to as 'musers.' Small discs of burnished metal, usually flat.

*Stamine,* a worsted cloth of coarse make, manufactured in Norfolk and used for garments, also for wall-hangings.

*Straits,* a term relating to *narrow* width cloths, measuring twelve yards long and one yard wide.

*Tartan,* first mentioned in an inventory, 1474. A material of which the warp and woof are of different colours or stripes, introduced into Scotland (it is said) by Margaret of Denmark, Queen of James III.

*Tinsel, tinsen, tilsent,* a textile of gold or silver not so brilliant or substantial as cloth of gold, and used for trimming dresses. Black tinsel satin was a satin interwoven with fine strands of copper gilt. It was also made in colours.

*Tissue*, a particularly rich material in gold or silver, of thinner substance than cloth of gold.

*Tukes*, a kind of buckram.

*Velvet* was much used by royalty and the wealthy upper classes during the reign of Henry VII (*see* vol. ii, p. 463). Velvets in two piles, in which the pattern was raised above the ground, were known as 'pile on pile.'

*Vesses*, *weysses*, a cheap kind of worsted, made chiefly in Suffolk.

## PATTERNS

The pine motif dominated patterns in use during the fifteenth century, and this is well represented in Fig. 571, vol. ii, and also in Fig. 198. In both, the pine is enclosed in ogival lines which form another characteristic feature of fifteenth-century patterns. In Fig. 199 the pine begins to assume the character of the pomegranate, a distinctive motif in velvets and silks imported from Venice which makes its appearance after the middle of the century. Henry VII is wearing a gold brocade of this actual design in Fig. 7; variations of it were much used in weaving rich golden fabrics. Often the pattern was outlined in red silk, and the gown worn by Joanna of Castile (Plate IV) is of this type.

A more fully developed pomegranate pattern combined with the pine is shown in Fig. 200.

A fifteenth-century design for gold embroidery, or a silk woven with gold thread, is given in Fig. 201.

Another pattern of this period, given in Fig. 202, is a typical example of a velvet or silken material. The design is inspired by the blossom of the oleander, an Oriental plant cultivated in southern Europe but not introduced into England until a much later date (1596). It will be noticed that the design has something in common with the medieval five-petalled rose, but the leaf of the oleander is

Fig. 198. Pine Pattern

ignored, and the base of each motif is more or less fanciful.   The boldness of this
pattern is enhanced by being woven in a rich coloured velvet on a gold ground

Fig. 199.

Fig. 200.

Pine and Pomegranate Patterns

Fig. 201. Woven Design in Gold

Fig. 202. Oleander Motif

or on a silk of contrasting shade—another masterpiece of the Venetian craftsmen.
In Fig. 200 is given an Italian brocade of the second half of the fifteenth

century, embodying the pine and the pomegranate fruit, blossom, buds, and leaves.   Three colours at least, and perhaps four, are used in gold, velvet, and silk.

The oblique line of design is first seen in Fig. 573, vol. ii, in which the oleander is the chief feature; Fig. 203 is a later development of it.   This line of design when seen in a large piece of material leans towards the left, and now has a flower or leaf springing from it and crossing the main oblique branch.

Fig. 203. Oblique line of Design

## COLOURS

Some names of colours used during the Middle Ages are given in vol. ii, p. 124.   Many of these are found in writings of the early Tudor period.

'Isabella colour,' a shade of colour resembling flax-seed, seems to have originated during this reign.   The following information is due to the kindness of the Baron de Belabre:

'According to Spanish tradition, Queen Isabella of Castile, when besieged by the Moors in one of her strongholds, decided that something should be done to sustain the sagging courage of the garrison.   She must have had a sense of humour, for she made the curious vow (*Honi soit*, etc.) not to change her shift before the city was released.

'Alas, it was nine months later that the Queen and her ladies-in-waiting who had made the same vow were able to put on clean underlinen. The soiled garments were then solemnly hung in a chapel of the Holy Virgin as *ex voto* offerings, just as old regimental flags are hung in churches here. They had acquired through long use a certain tint which, when the romantic episode got known, became the vogue in Europe, and, of course, the brave Queen's name was given to this uncommon colour.'

(*Continued on p. 367*)

Fig. 204

## VEHICLES

(French, *véhicule*.    Latin, *vehiculum* from *vehere*, to carry)

As several references are made to litters and carriages, it is thought expedient to add brief descriptions of some of these.

### INTRODUCTION

Road-making was introduced by the Romans when they annexed Britain to their empire, but during the centuries after the evacuation these Roman-made roads were not kept in repair. Consequently, during the Anglo-Saxon and Norman periods, and in the Middle Ages, they were most unsuitable for wheeled vehicles, and journeys were made chiefly on horseback. Merchandise and personal luggage were usually transported on the backs of horses and mules. These animals walked in single file along narrow bridle paths, tracks, and rough country, with bales or panniers strapped across their backs. When wealthy people travelled, wagons with huge wheels were used to carry all necessities—clothes, furniture, plate, books, provisions, etc. A great number of retainers, henchmen, servitors, and artisans making a small army, accompanied the noble. All these had to be catered for, and, unless they put up for the night at the castle of some nobleman, they were accommodated in a monastery. On the other hand, pavilions for the more important personages might be erected at any stage *en route*. It was the duty of 'harbegiers,' who were sent on in advance to get everything in readiness for the travellers; or to arrange hospitality in other people's houses. This was known as 'harbegage.' The rest had to sleep where they could in barns or stables, under hedges or straw stacks, or even in the open.

## The Litter

In the twelfth century the litter came into use, and this mode of travelling became general amongst the upper classes, both in England and on the Continent. The majority of these litters held one person, and were reserved for ladies and invalids.

By travelling in this vehicle the occupier could make a journey along ill-kept roads, muddy tracks, and mountain passes with a certain amount of comfort. This accounts for the popularity of the litter from this date until the early sixteenth century, when its use was retained for ceremonial occasions with preference even over the wheeled carriage. One learns from contemporary writings that Royal and noble ladies travelled on horseback, but

Fig. 205. A Litter, Fifteenth Century

when approaching a town they dismounted and made their state entry in a horse litter. As the name implies, the litter was a bed formed like an oblong box, long enough to lie down in, and carried between two poles by men or horses. Rising from the main body of the litter were uprights carrying a semicircular roof composed of half-hoops and horizontal rods or pommels finished at the ends with circular plates, often highly ornamented. This erection was known as a 'bail.' The same kind of structure was also used to cover a bier or effigy, and an interesting example is to be seen covering the effigy of the Earl of Warwick on his altar tomb in St. Mary's, Warwick. It was then called a 'hearse.' The same name was given to a pedestal frame to hold candles.

The bail was usually covered with matting or some rich material; curtains, or blinds which rolled up and down, hung at the sides.

Fig. 205 shows a Royal litter of the reign of Edward IV. It is a reasonably good representative of litters in general during the fifteenth century. In the original miniature from which this drawing is made the entire frame is of wood overlaid with gold. The rods with circular ends forming the bail support the covering of cloth of gold, which descends to the panelled sides. One side is turned up over the top and shows the rose-coloured silk lining. The lady has risen from her reclining position, and is sitting on a stool.

The harness of the white horses is rose colour edged and embroidered with gold, and the saddles are black. A wide belt passes over these having a loop at the ends through which the poles or shafts pass, thereby supporting the whole weight of the litter. Rings are fixed to the shafts, and leather straps fasten them to the collar and saddle to prevent any backward or forward movement of the shafts. The rest of the harness is purely decorative. A driver sits the front horse, and sometimes a servant or small page was seated on the back one.[1]

In the account of expenses for the marriage of Pedro I, the Cruel, King of Castile, 1350, we find the entry of all materials that made up the litter of his bride, Blanche de Bourbon.

The covering of the bail consisted of five layers of material—first cloth of gold outside, and under it vermilion linen; next, waxed or oiled cloth to make it waterproof, and under that canvas finishing with vermilion écarlaté inside. Other items were: Three ounces of silk to embellish the windows; tassels, leather curtains and cords to the latter. Seven pieces of striped silk to form perpendicular bands over the outside of the covering, double stitched and ornamented with studs. A covering for the whole litter to keep it clean when not in use, made of some special material called 'Marbré de Saint-Odmer.' There was given 140 livres to a certain Robert de Troies for the shafts for this litter; for painting; for the embellished studs and other things which belong to it; for the pommels, rings, and pegs to enclose the litter; for all decorated leather; for the harness of two horses, including saddles, collars, and *avallouères*—breechings, the harness to be made of vermilion Cordova leather, decorated with gilded studs, and the saddle-bows to be painted front and back with the armorial bearings of the owner. The carpet covering was the personal property of the Queen. Two pieces of deep vermilion velvet, two large pieces of green sendal, a quarter and half of cloth of gold, and a half-ell of ultramarine camacas were all required for the upholdering, cushions, etc.

A noble personage who, though wounded in the tournament, attended the festivities in connection with the wedding of Charles le Téméraire and Margaret of York in 1467, appeared in 'a litter richly covered with crimson cloth of gold. The pommels were of silver with his armorial bearings enamelled on the ends, and all the wood-work was richly painted with devices. The litter was carried by two very beautiful and fiery black horses lavishly caparisoned in blue velvet with great studs of silver. The pages who rode these horses were clad in blue velvet heavily embroidered with gold, bonets of the same, and buff buskins without spurs; each carried a whip. Inside, the noble reclined on large cushions of rich crimson velvet placed upon a Turkey carpet; he was dressed in a long robe of tawny velvet, furred with

[1] The origin of the custom once seen of liveried servants holding on to the back of family coaches.

ermine, and wore his hood thrown back off his head.   The robe was open
up the sides, and the sleeves split in front, showing that he was clad in full
armour underneath.   A black velvet bonet completed the ensemble.   The
litter was escorted by four big handsome knights on foot, dressed in heuks,
with flowing sleeves of blue velvet, and each had a large baton or wand in
his hand.'

## THE CARRIAGE

### Chariot, chariette, charet, char

It was in the thirteenth century that the wheeled carriage was introduced
into Italy, and later France, either from Flanders or Hungary, both countries
being the pioneers of carriage building in the Middle Ages.   It is possible
that one of the earliest illustrations of a medieval French carriage, of which
Fig. 206 is a drawing, is in an Illum. MS. dating the middle of the thirteenth
century, in the Bibliothèque Nationale, Paris.   In construction it is a large
litter, borne on four wheels of equal diameter and covered with a bail consisting of seven semicircular pieces of wood joined by five transverse rods
or pommels.   The end side-panels are covered with heraldic devices below
and fleurs-de-lys above.   The front and back could be open or closed.   Over
the middle part is fixed on either side a blind or curtain which can be rolled
up.   The occupants sit on a seat extending the length of the carriage, and
could view the scenery from whichever side was more interesting.   This
carriage has no springs, the axle trees being fixed to the frame set rigid without any turning pivot.   How they managed to get round corners is a mystery,
unless the occupants disembarked and the footmen, who usually walked at
the sides, hauled the carriage round.

Like the litter these carriages had some pretensions to comfort, the interior
being furnished with soft cushions like a luxurious couch.   Should the
journey extend for a couple of days or more, it was possible, if necessary, for
the travellers to go to bed.

This vehicle is drawn by two horses tandemwise.   The shaft horse is harnessed with a wide collar from which straps are attached to the shafts and with
straps fixed under the saddle; both horses have narrow breast bands, breechings, and bridles, but no reins are shown.   The leading horse is attached by
rope traces to the shafts by means of a loop and peg.   A driver sits the shaft
horse, and carries a whip of moderate length.

Probably the first carriage to be used in England is to be seen in Fig. 207,
from the Louterell Psalter, which dates the early years of the fourteenth century.   It may have been imported from Flanders, and is similar in shape to
those used in France (Fig. 206) and Italy.   It is covered with a bail and open
at both ends.   Apertures in the rich covering were closed by curtains hanging
outside: in the drawing these curtains are raised and draped up over the top.

Fig. 206. Folkwain, Thirteenth Century

Fig. 207. Whirlicote, Fourteenth Century

Sometimes curtains were rolled up by cords or straps, particularly if they were made of leather.

The five horizontal rods or pommels are ornamented at the ends by grotesque heads such as one sees on carved stone corbels, and the bail cloth of incarnadine is embroidered with an elaborate scroll design. The panels of the sides have cusped motifs, and golden eagles displayed occupy the centres of the panels. At each end two fabulous creatures flank the sides. Underneath is fixed an ironbound cash-box or jewel-case, and rings are attached to the framework for fastening on packages or securing hounds. Five horses tandem-wise draw this cumbersome vehicle, driven by a groom on the shaft-horse carrying an excessively long whip: another driver rides the fourth horse, and the leader is riderless. The first four horses are harnessed by ropes with loops at the ends caught together by pegs. These ropes are fixed to an iron band on the wide collar, and a rectangular embroidered pad covers the shoulders of each horse. Other attendants walked at the sides.

These carriages were called 'whirlicotes,' derived from *whirling* or moving swiftly, and *cot* or house. Also 'folkwains,' when the travelling carriage contained several people.

We have a description of a French Royal chariot, covered inside and out with sky-blue velvet powdered with golden fleurs-de-lys. Beatrix, wife of Charles of Anjou, rode in this when they entered Naples in 1267.

The Lady Eleanor, Edward III's sister, paid John le Charer £1,000 for one in 1330. The first English queen to use a 'charet' was Isabella, wife of Richard II, for it is recorded that Roger Rouland received a Royal commission in 1397 to supply this lady with one which cost £400. In 1486 Elysabeth of York rode with the Countess of Richmond in a charet covered with cloth of gold, and drawn by six horses caparisoned in the same rich material. In a Flemish Illum. MS. is a miniature of a carriage and pair, dating 1500, and Fig. 208 is made from it. There is very little difference between this and the carriage shown in Fig. 207, which proves that the main principles of construction were not altered during the intervening period. The box-like body is panelled at the sides, and mounted on smaller wheels in front and larger ones behind. It is coloured brown decorated with gold. The bail and the two sets of pommels are of metal, and the covering or awning is of incarnadine silk embroidered and bordered with gold; the part which closed the opening or window is turned up over the top, showing that the covering is lined throughout with deep blue silk. No turning pivot is in evidence, and to the central shaft is now fixed a splinter-bar carrying two swingle-trees to which the traces are attached. These latter, of black leather, are fixed to the wooden collar mounted on a circular black leather pad. Black leather straps are looped round the horses' necks and hooked to the end of the shaft. The driver is seated upon a crimson cushion fixed to a pad and girth, to which the avallouère binding the horses' tails is also attached. One of the most interesting details is the early use of rectangular blinkers. These are arranged on the bridle in two different ways, and are of black and gold checks within a narrow border. The near horse is brown, the other white.

It was in 1474 that the Emperor Frederick III entered Frankfort in a covered carriage hung on leather straps to posts fore and aft and fixed to the axle-trees —a great improvement in comfort.

(*Continued on p. 374*)

Fig. 208. A Carriage and Pair, 1500

# CHAPTER II

## THE REIGN OF KING HENRY VIII
### 1509—1547

## CONTEMPORARY SOVEREIGNS

| | ENGLAND | SCOTLAND | FRANCE | GERMANY | SPAIN | SWEDEN | DENMARK |
|---|---|---|---|---|---|---|---|
| **1509** | Henry VIII | James IV | Louis XII | Maximilian I | Ferdinand II<br>King of All Spain, 1512 | | John I |
| **1512** | | | | | | →Sten Sture<br>Protector, 1512 | |
| **1513** | | →James V<br>1513–42<br>1. Magdalene of France<br>2. Mary of Guise | | | | | →Christian II<br>1513–23<br>Separated from Sweden<br>Dethroned, 1523<br>Isabel of Austria |
| **1515** | | | →Francis I<br>1515–57<br>1. Claude of France<br>2. Eleanor of Austria | | | | |
| **1519** | | | | →Charles V<br>1519–55<br>Isabella of Portugal = | Charles I<br>1519–56 | | |
| **1520** | | | | | | →Christian II<br>Deposed, 1520 | |
| **1523** | | | | | | →Gustavus Vasa<br>1523–60<br>1. Catherine of Sachsen-Larenberg<br>2. Margaret Ericson<br>3. Catherine Stenbock | Frederick I<br>1523–34<br>1. Anne of Brandenberg<br>2. Sophia of Pomerania |
| **1534** | | | | | | | →Christian III<br>1534–59<br>Dorothy of Larenberg |
| **1542** | | →Mary Stewart<br>1542–67 | | | | | |
| **1547** | Edward VI | | | | | | |

1509. Accession of Henry VIII.

1511. Alliance of England, Spain, the Empire, Venice, the Swiss, and the Pope against France—the 'Holy League.'

1513. Battle of Flodden Field; death of James IV, and with him perished the flower of the Scottish nobility.

1514. Peace with France and Scotland.

1515. Invasion of Italy by the French, and defeat of the Armies of the Emperor, Ferdinand of Spain and the Pope at the Battle of Marignano, 13th September.

Thomas Wolsey made Cardinal and Chancellor, born about 1471 at Ipswich. Rector of Torrington 1510; Canon of Windsor 1511; Prebendary of York 1512; Bishop of Lincoln and Archbishop of York 1514. Fall 1529. Died 1530.

1516. Robert Fabyan's *Chronicle* printed. Born second half of fifteenth century. Sheriff of London 1493. He 'made Fabian's Chronicle, a painful labour, to the honour of the City, and the whole realm.' Died 1513.

1520. The Field of the Cloth of Gold. Meeting between Henry VIII and Francis I.

1521. Henry VIII granted the title of Defender of the Faith by Pope Leo X for writing a book against Luther and Protestant doctrines.

The Conquest of Mexico by Hernando Cortes.

Renewed hostilities between Francis I and Charles V, lasting until 1529. 'Le chevalier sans peur et sans reproche' (Pierre du Terrail, Seigneur de Bayard) slain while crossing the river Sesia.

1525. Battle of Pavia between the armies of the Emperor and Francis I; the latter was captured and suffered a year's confinement in Madrid.

John Stow born in London. A tailor who devoted himself to the 'delectable study of antiquities.' Wandered over England collecting documents dispersed at the Dissolution for *Annales*, 1580. *Survey of London*, 1598. Died 1605; effigy at St Andrew Undershaft.

1529. The Conquest of Peru undertaken by Francisco Pizarro.

Charles V finally elected to the Imperial throne.

The French driven out of Italy: the Peace of Cambrai, 'La Paix des Dames,' settled by Louisa of Savoy (mother of Francis I) and Marguerite of Austria (Charles V's aunt).

1529–36. The Reformation Parliament.

1532. Alliance between Henry VIII and Francis I.

1534. The Act of Supremacy, by which the King of England became 'the only Supreme Head on earth of the Church of England.'

William Harrison born in London. Educated at St Paul's and Westminster Schools, at Cambridge 1551 and at Christ Church, Oxford, taking his B.A. in 1556. B.A. and Vicar of Radwinter, Essex, 1558. M.A. 1560 and Canon of Windsor. A topographer and chronologer. Wrote *Description of England* for the first edition of Holinshed's *Chronicles* 1578. Died 1593.

1535. Execution of Bishop Fisher and Sir Thomas More.

1536. Milan seized by the Emperor Charles V: Francis I declares war on him.

Suppression of the smaller monasteries begins.

Pilgrimage of Grace, headed by Aske and other gentlemen of the north. They took as their badge the five wounds of our Lord and demanded the dismissal of Cromwell, reunion with Rome, redress to the Church, and the total reversal of the Royal policy.

1537–40. Suppression of the greater monasteries.

1539. The Great Bible issued through the efforts of Archbishop Cranmer, and ordered to be set up in churches.

The Six Articles Statute.

Thomas Cawarden made Master of the Revels to Henry VIII. At the Dissolution he was granted Kenilworth. He kept all his theatrical props stored at the Monastery of Blackfriars. Stage-managed the pageantry in connection with Queen Elizabeth's coronation. Died 1559.

1540. L'Étoile, Pierre de, born in Paris. Grand audiencier de la Chancellerie. Author of *Journal de Henri III*, 1589, and *Journal de Henri IV*. Died 1611 and buried in the Church of Saint-André-des-Arcs.

1542. Portuguese trading ships first visit Japan; St Francis Xavier introduces Christianity in 1549.

1543. Henry VIII and Charles V conclude an alliance against France.

War with France and Scotland, until 1546.

1547. Death of Henry VIII and accession of Edward VI.

# THE ARTS, 1509-47

## SCULPTURE: MONUMENTAL EFFIGIES (*continued from p. 5*)

ALTHOUGH the Italian style was spreading over western Europe, monumental effigies in England still retained their Gothic characteristics. Figures continue to lie upon their backs upon tomb chests; but, as far as workmanship is concerned, some of the monuments erected during this reign are not up to the previous standard.

(*Continued on p.* 385)

## MEMORIAL BRASSES (*continued from p. 5*)

The third period of brasses commences with the accession of Henry VIII. Technique continued to show progressive deterioration during the whole of this reign: with few exceptions workmanship was coarser and weaker, and the practice of shading was still carried to excess.

Kneeling figures became more common.

(*Continued on p.* 385)

## TAPESTRY (*continued from p. 6*)

As a general rule it is impossible to give the exact date of the commencement of any period in art or costume; but, in the history of tapestry, it is fortunate that we have an outstanding landmark. The year 1515 marks the beginning of the definite style called 'Renaissance tapestry.' In this year Raphael was commissioned by Pope Leo X to design cartoons for the series of tapestries representing 'The Acts of the Apostles,' and within a short time the order was given to the Flemish tapissers at Brussels to start work.

Not being familiar with the technique of tapestry production, Raphael in his designs ignored the conventional methods of the tapestry weavers, which from their point of view were unsuitable for translation into fabric. His cartoons were so carefully drawn, every line defined, and every shade of colour minutely expressed, that nothing was left to the ingenuity and skill of the Flemish master-weaver. He had but to copy the cartoon to the smallest detail, and the artistic freedom he had enjoyed in earlier days was denied to him. It will be easily understood that the introduction of this new method into the art of the tapisser resulted before long in the artist-weaver declining into a mere master-craftsman.

The deterioration of tapestry-weaving in later times is attributable jointly to this cause and to the dearth of designers of Raphael's calibre.

Incidentally it is of interest to mention here that these cartoons [1] by Raphael for 'The Acts of the Apostles' were lost for a time. They reappeared about 1652, and, on the advice of Rubens, seven of them were purchased by Charles I. They are now deposited in the Victoria and Albert Museum.

A series of tapestries (not the originals) was woven from these cartoons, and came into the possession of Henry VIII. They decorated the walls of Windsor or Greenwich, where they remained until the effects of Charles I were sold by the Commonwealth. They are now in Spain.

An interesting set, entitled 'The Battle of Pavia,' was woven in the Netherlands, from cartoons by Bernard van Orley, and presented to the Emperor Charles V in 1531. They commemorate the battle fought in 1525, in which the French were routed and Francis I taken prisoner. These tapestries, as well as the small cartoons, are in the Louvre.

A very successful tapestry manufacturer in the first half of the sixteenth century was William van Pannemaker of Brussels, who was much patronized by the Emperor Charles V and the continental nobility.

In Henry VIII's reign, the Royal inventories mention much tapestry displayed in the various palaces of the King. At Greenwich alone there were seven sets of 'Hangynges of Arras' consisting of from six to twelve panels each. Three sets depicted Biblical subjects, and the others represented 'The Story of Youth,' 'The Seven Ages,' a hunting and hawking set, and 'Nine pieces of hangings of Verdoure of Sundry Sortes.'

Other references to tapestries and wall hangings will be found on p. 183.

Cardinal Wolsey spent vast sums of money on tapestries, and, in the inventory of his 'Rich Household Stuff,' mention is made of at least one hundred sets. On Wolsey's downfall all his tapestries and other household effects were confiscated to the King, and these helped considerably to swell the list set forth in the inventory of the Royal household stuff made at his death in 1547.

It is important to remember that the figures depicted in Renaissance tapestries are clothed in 'modern' dress when the subject is a contemporary one, but when the subject is ancient history (a very popular one) the figures are garbed in what the sixteenth-century artists imagined to be correct Roman or Greek styles. Even contemporary personages were sometimes represented in 'Roman' dress, although nearly always in conjunction with the coiffure which they personally affected.

This forms an important departure from previous practice. Unlike the artists of the Late Gothic period and their predecessors, these sixteenth-century craftsmen had at their disposal, for the first time, a certain amount of more or less authentic information derived from the revival of classic learning which was spreading over Europe during the early years of the Renais-

---

[1] Richard Duppa, writing from Rome about 1813, reports that the whole of the Raphael cartoons could be bought for 1,250 thalers.

sance Period—itself to a large extent the result of the indiscriminate scattering of art treasures and records which followed the Fall of Constantinople in 1453. The effects of this movement began to appear in England during the reign of Henry VIII.

## Hunting Tapestries

The ever-popular hunting tapestries are well represented during this period, notably in the set of twelve panels known as 'Les Belles Chasses de l'Empereur Maximilien,' designed by Bernard van Orley immediately after the Emperor's death in 1519. These cartoons are now in the Louvre. Van Orley was very careful that the details in these cartoons should be correct, although his animals are not too lifelike, and he is incorrect in some of his technical details. The opposite is the case with the Emperor and his retinue, whose costume dates before the year 1519, as we learn that both his daughter, the Archduchess Marguerite, and his granddaughter, Queen Marie of Hungary, were very particular that they should be correct, and themselves supplied the necessary information. It was not until the year 1528, or 1530, that the tapestries were completed. They were the property of the Emperor Charles V until they were captured by the French under the Duc de Guise at the fall of Metz in 1552. They are now in the Louvre where they are, or were, exhibited under the erroneous title of 'Les Belles Chasses de Guise.'

## Armorial Tapestry

Another kind of tapestry, as much in use during the sixteenth as in the fifteenth century, is the 'armorial' style already described in vol. ii, pp. 346 and 356.

Such hangings were usually composed of pieces of rich material—silk, satin, cloth, or even velvet—sometimes of one colour; and others consisted of widths of two different colours sewn together, embroidered with devices, badges, and coats of arms. The backgrounds of Fig. 38 and Plate IX are good examples.

## French Tapestry

Gilles and Jean Gobelin, the founders of a firm of tapestry weavers destined to be famous at a later date, lived in Paris during the reign of Francis I. For some generations members of this family were expert dyers; later they developed into rug, carpet, and tapestry manufacturers, and after a time their [1] tapestry reached quite a high standard.

---

[1] About 1664 the concern was purchased by Louis XIV, who converted it into a Royal factory in which some of the choicest examples of tapestry work were made.

### German and Swiss Tapestries

German and Swiss tapestries form a class of their own dating from the fourth decade of the sixteenth century. They are not in any respect imitations of the Franco-Flemish styles, but a definitely national product developed in Germany.

A Flemish tapisser, Seeger Bombeck, emigrated from Brussels to Saxony about this time and established himself there in business. He appears to have gone alone and there is no doubt he found it necessary to initiate Teutonic craftsmen into his art, for the results of his efforts are rather crude in treatment, and are obviously not the product of highly skilled weavers. All kinds of illustrations were copied as subjects, for lack of artists able to produce original designs.

These early German tapestries were usually small, being about one yard wide and three yards or more long. The best collections of German-made tapestries are to be found in Berlin, Nuremberg, and Basle.

(Continued on p. 385)

### ILLUMINATED MANUSCRIPTS (continued from p. 8)

Although the work of the manuscript illuminators continued to maintain its excellence for some years after the opening of the sixteenth century, one finds many Illum. MSS. obviously executed by second-rate artists. Invariably the drawing is faulty, and the figures are dwarfed; but this may be the method employed by the artist to show the importance of the person represented by the size of his figure. The Parliament Roll, referred to on p. 158, is a case in point: the minor personages in the procession are on a smaller scale than the peers spiritual and temporal. However, it is not the technique of these illuminators that should be the primary interest of students of costume; they should regard the figures rather as fashion plates of the period in which they were executed, and as such they are invaluable.

After the Reformation a great number of manuscripts, plain as well as illuminated, were destroyed as 'superstitious books,' thus depriving us of an incalculable number of first-hand authorities.

Miniatures, associated up to this time with Illum. MSS., began to appear in official documents as decorations of the initial letters, and frequently the subject was the reigning sovereign in regal robes. Fig. 292 is based on such initial miniatures.

(Continued on p. 475)

Portraits and Painters (*continued from p.* 10)

## Temp. Henry VIII

By the time Henry VIII ascended the throne a definite school of English artists had been established in England who preserved some of the traditions of medieval painting. The 'inferiority complex' was known among artists even in those days, for they ever welcomed the assistance and counsel of more accomplished painters from the Continent! Nevertheless, no English artist of any repute appeared until later in the century. Portraits of any note at this time are all by foreign artists, chiefly of the Flemish and Franco-Flemish schools, the more important of whom are enumerated below:

Jehan Perréal, a portrait painter of distinction, was sent to England in 1514 by Louis XII to design and supervise the trousseau of the Princess Mary. Her portrait, said to have been painted by Jean Perréal at this time, now hangs in the National Gallery, London (*see* Plate XII). It is also possible that this artist painted some of the early portraits and miniatures of Henry VIII.

Michiel Sithium or Zittoz, born in Flanders about 1455, was Court painter to Isabella the Catholic, Queen of Castile. He retained this office until the Queen's death in 1504, after which he was in the service of Marguerite, Archduchess of Austria, until the year 1516. Some of his portraits, including one of Isabella, are at Windsor.

Jean Clouet, born at Brussels in 1475, was the son of Jean Clouet, born 1431, who was Court painter to the Duke of Burgundy. His name first appears in 1516, and he became the chief painter at the Court of Francis I. His portraits belong to the period 1516–25. He died in 1541 and was succeeded in his office by his son François,[1] sometimes known as Janet, who was born at Tours between 1515 and 1520, and died about 1572.

Gerard Hoorenbault, born in Ghent about 1480. From 1516 to 1521 he was in the service of the Archduchess Marguerite. In the latter year he came to England and was appointed painter to Henry VIII. He married Margaret Saunders of Fulham; a brass to her memory is in the parish church there, and is dated 1529.[2] Gerard died in 1540. His son Lucas (died 1544) and his daughter Suzanna (born 1503, died 1545) were both distinguished painters.

Johannes Corvus or Jan Raf or Rave, admitted to the Guild of Painters at Bruges in 1512, came to England between 1510 and 1520 to execute various commissions. He returned to England in 1544 and was established at the Court.

Bernard van Orley, born in 1485, painted the youthful Charles V in 1515. He was Court painter to the Archduchess Marguerite, Regent of the Netherlands, a protégé of Raphael and a friend of Dürer. He died in 1542.

[1] Paul Jamot, of the Louvre, says his activity began about 1530!
[2] A head, in widow's weeds, on a lozenge-shaped plate, fixed to the east wall of the nave.

JOOST VAN CLEVE, born in 1490, painted Henry VIII and other distinguished Englishmen. His portraits can be identified by a deliberate foreshortening of the hands—a peculiarity of this artist.

HANS HOLBEIN the YOUNGER was born at Augsburg in 1495, son of Hans Holbein, also an artist and a pupil of Lucas Hoorenbault.

He came to England in 1526, but returned to Basle in 1529. He was back in England in 1531, and in 1536 received his first Royal commission for the portrait of Jane Seymour, now at Vienna. His first portrait of Henry VIII was painted when the King was forty-five; a fact much at variance with the popular belief that many of the earlier portraits of Henry VIII are attributable to this artist—in actual fact, all portraits previous to this date (1536) are certainly by others. The portraits of Henry VIII which are indisputably by Hans Holbein the Younger are: that in the possession of Earl Spencer at Althorp; a chalk drawing at Chatsworth; the Barber-Surgeons' (unfinished); the fresco at Whitehall (now destroyed), and the portrait in the National Gallery at Rome.

As Court painter, Holbein never lacked commissions to the day of his death, and few men or women of any social importance escaped his brush or crayon. His draughtsmanship was perfect, and his style, technique, and composition formed the models for the work of succeeding portrait painters. Full-length portraits and heads and shoulders, whether in oils, chalk, or crayon, miniatures, etchings, and wood-engravings, besides designs for jewellery and books, all manifested his genius. He was the greatest exponent of miniature painting of his time. The details of dress, which he delineated with minute and careful precision, are extremely valuable in the study of costume of this period. He died of the plague in 1543, and is buried in the Church of St. Catherine Cree.

After the death of Hans Holbein the Younger, many foreign artists came to England, including the following:

HANS EWORTH, EWOTTES, EWOUTSZ or HAUNCE EWOOTH, born at Antwerp, arrived in this country in 1543, and later completed some portraits which Holbein had left unfinished.

GERLACH FLICKE or FLICCIUS, known by his portrait in the National Portrait Gallery, London, of Archbishop Cranmer, 1546, was one of the four painters belonging to the school of Holbein.

CORNEILLE DE LYON, a Dutchman, settled at Lyons before 1536. He painted many small portraits on clear green, and sometimes blue or brown backgrounds, and may have been in England between 1541 and 1547. He died in 1574.

'Yet had the King in wages for limning divers others.'

PIETER BRUEGEL, a Fleming, was born in 1525. His pictures are valuable authorities for the costume of the Flemish, middle, and lower orders. He died in 1569.

Of the German school of portrait painters BERNHARD STRIGEL (died 1528) was still working; he and LUCAS CRANACH were two of the most prominent artists. The latter painted Charles V at various times from 1509 onwards. He was Court painter to the House of Saxony during the reigns of John (1525), John Frederick the Magnanimous (1532), and Maurice (1548–53). He died at Weimar in 1553. His son LUCAS, also a painter, was born in 1516 and died at Wittenberg in 1586.

Another important artist of this school was ALBRECHT DÜRER, employed during the years 1507–16 by the Emperor Maximilian, whose reign he has immortalized in drawings, paintings, and engravings. He died in 1528, and is buried in the churchyard of St. John, Nuremberg.

TITIAN, TIZIANO VECELLIO, the greatest painter of the Venetian school, was born at Pieve di Cadore, about eighty-six miles from Venice, in 1477 or 1480. Information with regard to his life previous to his thirtieth year is very meagre, but it is known that as a young man he worked in the studio of Giovanni Bellini. He became famous in the second decade of the sixteenth century, and after his first meeting with Charles V in 1530 he worked almost entirely for the Emperor and other members of the House of Hapsburg. His relations with Philip II began in 1548 and lasted until his death from old age on 27th August 1576.

GIOVANNI BATTISTA MORONI was born at Bondo, Bergamo, about 1525. His portraits of men are valuable for the study of costume. He died in 1578.

ALESSANDRO BONVINCIO MORETTO, born at Brescia about 1498, died in 1554.

An inventory of all portraits belonging to Henry VIII is extant. It gives very minute descriptions of each picture, many (if not all) of which are still in the Royal collections.

That extensive patron of art, Marguerite, Archduchess of Austria, possessed many paintings by famous artists, past and present, including Bernard van Orley; Hans Memlinc; Michel van Coxcyen (1499–1592); Jan van Eyck (1385–1441); Jan Cornelisz Vermeyen (1500–59); Roger van der Weyden (1400–64); Jan van Mabuse; Dieric Bouts (1400–75); Jacopo da Barbarj (1450–1516); Jerome Bosch (1460–1516); and Gerard Hoorenbault. These names are taken from the Archduchess's inventory made at the time of her death. The paintings are now dispersed all over Europe.

Canvas was used by Venetian artists throughout the sixteenth century, but in western Europe the use of canvas except for small pictures was rare. It was more extensively employed very late in the sixteenth century, and its use became general during the first decade of the seventeenth century. There are a few exceptions, of course. The portrait of Charles IX by Clouet (Janet) in the Kunsthistorisches Museum, Vienna, is one. It is painted on canvas and measures 7 ft. 3½ in. by 3 ft. 9⅜ in.

Holbein painted on oak panels even when the portrait was full-length; for example, that of the Duchess of Milan in the National Gallery, London.

The full-length portrait of Henry VIII by Hans Eworth at Trinity College, Cambridge, although measuring about 8 ft. by 4 ft. is painted on three oak boards three-quarters of an inch thick.

Artists of the sixteenth century do not seem to have discovered a satisfactory manner of representing diamonds, and so always painted them black.

Miniature[1] portraits came into fashion in England, amongst Royalty and the Nobility, during the early part of Henry VIII's reign.    They are usually referred to, in records of the time, as 'limnings.'

Early in the sixteenth century the only miniature portraits were those to be found interspersed amongst Illum. MSS. mostly executed during the two preceding centuries.    About this time someone conceived the idea of cutting out such a small portrait of an interesting personality and preserving it as a decorative feature in a frame.    The example was followed by others, and many of these old miniatures were inserted in plain or jewelled frames, ivory cases, or picture boxes.

The immediate result is an amusing instance of supply following demand, for very soon this new interest in an 'antique' mode brought the inevitable flood of 'modern examples,' and artists such as those enumerated below began to paint miniature portraits of notabilities of their own time.    Those which have come down to the present day are the work of such men as HANS HOLBEIN, GUILLAUME GEOFFROY, SIMON BINNINC, of Bruges, and his daughter, LEVINA TEERLINCK, GERARD and LUCAS HOORENBAULT, and the latter's sister, SUZANNA.    It is thought that these artists based their miniatures upon the life-size drawings executed by JEHAN PERRÉAL and JEAN CLOUET.

During the Middle Ages it was the custom to paint the walls of large and small chambers with subjects from scripture and history (see vol. ii, p. 134). These pictures were arranged in rows, one above the other, each one some two or three feet in height.

About the fifteenth century the subjects were divided by narrow wooden styles or battens; and a little later styles were added top and bottom.    About the same time painted portraits were often inserted into the panels of wainscoting.

The mural type of wall decoration went out of fashion early in the sixteenth century, but the use of pictures surrounded by styles was retained, thus originating the 'picture frame.'    Picture frames in fashion during the first part of Henry VIII's reign were painted black and relieved with gold lines, but they soon became more elaborate.    A 'frame of black Ibonye garnished with silver,' and a 'frame of wood wallnutte coloure,' are items mentioned in an inventory of Henry VIII.    Curtains of silk or sarsenet (frequently yellow) were hung in front of pictures, obviously to prevent them from fading.

[1] For the origin of this name see vol. ii, p. 12.

In the 'large faire wainscotted parlour' of Jack Winchecombe hung fifteen pictures covered with curtains of green silk fringed with gold.

A painting on a wooden board or panel was called a 'table,' and a painting on canvas is referred to as 'a steyned clothe.'

In the study of pictures relating to this period it is surprising to find many portraits of the same persons scattered through numerous picture galleries, museums, and private collections all over the country—all more or less similar in treatment, and obviously variants of the same originals, though differing in size. The explanation of this interesting fact is that, when portrait painting became fashionable, it was the custom for the subject of a portrait to have reproductions made, not necessarily identical, to present to his special friends. Henry VIII frequently bestowed a copy of his portrait, often painted on a small-sized table, upon some friend whom he wished to favour.

Painting of another type—decoration—had been practised for some time before the accession of Henry VIII. This King founded the Paynter-Stayners' Company, and instituted the office of Serjeant-Paynter to the King.

Paynter-Stayners' Hall was founded, in Little Trinity Lane, by JOHN BROWNE, who was the first to hold this office, 1511. He painted flags, banners, surcotes, horse-trappings, etc., and other adornments connected with the Royal household. He died in 1532 and was succeeded by Andrew Wright (died 1543). The third to hold office as Serjeant-Paynter to the king was an Italian named ANTONY TOTO, whose chief work was the decoration of Nonsuch Palace. Another Italian, VICTOR VOLPE, is mentioned as being at work in the year 1514. He assisted John Browne and was kept busy painting the 'ornaments' used at the Field of the Cloth of Gold. It is supposed that he was the artist who painted the two well-known pictures, one celebrating that event, and the other depicting the 'Embarkation of Henry VIII at Dover.' His name last appears in the household accounts in 1532, and he is known to have been an assistant to Antony Toto. NICHOLAS LYZARD was another Serjeant-Paynter who worked under Antony Toto.

(*Continued on p.* 387)

# SECTION I: 1509-30

### INTRODUCTION

After the rather dull time experienced during the latter years of the preceding reign, the accession to the throne of a handsome and jovial young Prince was acclaimed throughout the land with great rejoicings. England of Henry VIII's time is often referred to as 'Merrie England.'

Alas! it was not so merry for some. The burnings of the Reformation; the destruction of the monasteries, with the consequent forfeiture of many comforts previously enjoyed through their ministrations by the middle, lower, and destitute classes, to say nothing of the numerous heads rolling from the block, were poor aids to merriment.

## ROYALTY AND NOBILITY—MEN: 1509-30

### KING HENRY VIII, 1491 *until* 1530

It is much to be deplored that in any modern presentation in painting and on stage or screen Henry VIII is always shown as a corpulent elderly man, no matter at what period of his life the action is supposed to take place. Such lack of intelligent vision is amazing amongst people so cultured as ourselves.

Fig. 209. A Badge of King Henry VIII

The following quotation from *The Private Character of Henry the Eighth* (1932) by the most eminent authority on the period, Frederick Chamberlin, makes an admirable prologue to the biography of this King. It sums up in an excellent manner the mentality of the man-in-the-street of to-day concerning the facts of history.

'It is this *handicap* of more than ordinary sexual dangers, the six wives, and the cry of Bluebeard that have made Henry's name a byword in every country in the world. Dickens spoke of him as a "spot of blood and grease" upon the pages of England's history. The quip will never die—and it is all that the immortal writer *had* to say of the monarch—and one seldom hears more. The sneers and the ribald tale are all that have struck the public imagination. . . . Only the

154

six wives and their beheading—for such is the usual tale—are fastened in the mind.

'Not a word can the ordinary man tell of Henry's ability, his ceaseless industry, his tremendous personality, his driving power, his faithfulness to his task as ruler, his pride in his position, his determination that other rulers should acknowledge it, his great prowess as an athlete right up to the age of forty-four, his gigantic physique, his founding of the British Navy, his exceptional love for, and skill in, music, his high regard for scholars, his appreciation of painting and literature, his wide education, linguistic ability, and high standing as a statesman—not *one* of these things will the ordinary Englishman of to-day know—not one of them has he ever been taught.'

Henry was born at Greenwich Palace, 28th June 1491. He married Katherine of Aragon, the widow of his brother Arthur, Prince of Wales, 3rd June 1509. The King and Queen were crowned at Westminster by William Warham the 24th of the same month. It is said that all the orders for the coronation and for the late King's funeral were given by Queen Katherine. Henry VIII is the first English monarch who bore the title of 'majesty' following the example of the Emperor Charles V. He was addressed or referred to as 'His Most Gracious Majesty,' or 'The King's Most Excellent Majesty.'

The new King was eighteen years of age when he ascended the throne. He was in every way the child of the New Age, and his reign inaugurates the era of modern history. His appearance at this period was that of a healthy-looking, chubby-faced English boy, of a very fair complexion. His hair was gold tinged with red and his eyes blue.

A terra-cotta bust of Henry, obviously executed just before the death of Henry VII, was discovered a few years ago. An illustration of it can be seen in *Old Furniture*, vol. v, p. 196. Although the face appears to be that of an older man, it agrees with the description given by contemporary writers of about this date. The features are good, but the face is inclined to puffiness. No hair is seen on the forehead, but around the neck it is cut level with the mouth, slightly waved, and the ends rolled.

The cap is of the characteristic shape worn during Henry VII's reign, and the robe is of red, sleeveless, the fullness back and fronts gathered into the shoulder seams. It is lined ('turfed') and turned back with ermine, and worn over a gown with full sleeves of gold brocade.

As a youth, Erasmus tells us, 'he was a prodigy of precocious scholarship. Though his learning was superficial and carefully made the most of, he was, in effect, an apt and diligent student.' As he grew to manhood his amazing personal vanity led him to delight in sumptuous raiment, as will be found in the pages of this book. Henry spent on his wardrobe 16,000 ducats yearly. This is equal to about £8,000 in English money of that day; but if we consider relative value of money then and now, his expenditure on dress is equivalent to something like £120,000 in present-day currency. He is described as 'the best-dressed sovereign in the world: his robes are the richest and most superb that can be imagined: and he puts on new clothes every Holyday.' Henry VIII could afford it.  His crafty and politic father, old Henry, had initiated him into his own financial doctrine: that the command of ready money, gained no matter how, meant power.  Young Henry, though of a different nature from his father, made good use of his lesson; and why shouldn't he?  Old Henry left him 'ten millions of ready money in gold.'

Henry VIII was a patron of Letters and the Arts.  'Hans Holbyn,' 'Luke Hornebaund,' and others are mentioned in his privy purse expenses as having received payments for work done.  'Paynter-Stayners,' who were decorative artists, sometimes portrait painters, and often glorified house decorators, are frequently found in the list of the King's benefactions.  Nor were musicians forgotten.  The King himself was a musician of no mean order, besides being a composer of merit.  The anthem reputed to have been set to music by him, *O Lord, the Maker of all thyng*, is considered good enough to be used even to-day.[1]  A Venetian, Dionysius Memo, previously organist of St Mark's, Venice, was the Court organist to Henry VIII, and entertained the King and his friends for hours at a time.

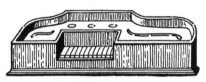

Fig. 210. Clavichord

Dr Tye should be mentioned here as an interesting musician and composer of church music of this time. Christopher Tye was born about 1497 and became fifth choir boy at King's College, Cambridge, in 1511.  He took his degree as Bachelor of Music in 1536 and became Master of the Choir at Ely Cathedral in 1541.  In 1545 he was made a Doctor of Music, but as there were no distinctive robes for musical graduates at this time he was permitted to wear the robes of a Doctor of Medicine (*see* p. 293).  In Queen Elizabeth's reign he was 'Gentleman of the Chapel Royal.'  Dr Tye restored church music after it had been almost ruined by the dissolution of the abbeys.  Thomas Tallis, born about 1510, was another eminent musician, composer of church music, and organist of Waltham Abbey.

From the inventory of Marguerite, Archduchess of Austria, we learn the names of some foreign musicians composing music at this time, to whom the Archduchess extended her patronage.  They are: Alexander, Antoine Brumel, Josquin des Prés, Compère, Henry Isaac, and Pierre de la Rue.

Henry VIII had his own orchestra or 'consort' as it was called.  It comprised a harp, dulcimer, trumpet, pipe, and tabor.  The musical instruments owned by him, according to an inventory dated 1547, were numerous and varied.

At this time the clavichord was constructed in a rather more elaborate shape (Fig. 210).  The strings were struck by pins attached to the ends of the keys, and damped by pieces of cloth, so as to produce a very soft sound.

---

[1] Musical authorities to-day ascribe the setting of this anthem to William Mundy (died 1591?). The words are from Henry VIII's Primer, 1545.

The virginal, in use at this time, may derive its name from the fact that it was a favourite instrument among the ladies, while the lute (Fig. 55) was preferred by the men.    The former was similar to the clavichord, but the action of the notes was different.    These had 'jacks' made of quills, whalebone, or leather, which hit the strings and rebounded.

Such seemly entertainments of high-class music were not always appreciated by the younger generation, who by organizing their own less highbrow amusements demoralized the taste of the court.    For instance, about 1519 certain young English gentlemen, having spent some time at the court of Francis I, where on several occasions they 'disguised themselves and with the king behaved in a foolish manner,' returned to England.    So completely had their heads been turned by their sojourn abroad that they were 'all French in eating, drinking, and apparel, yea, in French vices and bragges, so that all the estates of England were by them laughed at, the ladies and gentlemen were dispraised, so that nothyng by them was praised, but it were after the French turne.'    This behaviour, it is gratifying to learn, so upset every one at Henry VIII's not particularly squeamish Court, that the King agreed to dismiss these foolish and ill-behaved young men, and decided to reform the Court!

King Henry possessed his own interlude players: and it is interesting to remember that he was the first English king to give amateur theatricals, an example followed later by the English aristocracy and by many Courts of Europe.    He was passionately fond of gorgeous ceremonies, 'dysguisings' and pageants.    In 1513 the first masquerade ever seen in England was presented at Greenwich Palace before the King and his Court.    Besides composing music, Henry wrote verses to go with it; notably *Pastime with Good Company*. He played tennis, was an excellent archer, jouster, and horseman.

Amongst his other virtues Henry VIII can be reckoned as one of our sporting monarchs; for he kept horses or 'gueldings that did run' as well as 'Phillippes boyes' or 'riding boyes that ride the running horses,' otherwise jockeys.    They were dressed in doublets of green Bruges satin—a cheap variety—and white fustian; riding caps of black velvet with gold buttons, and 'parti-hosen.'    All these items for clothing the 'boys that ryde the kinges gueldings' were paid out of his own personal expenses.    For 'Phillippes boyes' see Fig. 333.

'Boyes of the Stabull' is another expression which often occurs.    They attended to the horses at the Royal stables at Holborn, until these were burnt down in 1534.    'All the king's horses and all the king's men' were then removed to temporary quarters at Charing Cross, in a building where the Royal falcons were kept to *mew* and moult, and called 'The Falcons' Mews' on that account.    These temporary stables eventually became permanent, but still retained the name of 'mews.'

Horse races were part of the entertainments given at the coronation of the Emperor Charles V, at Bologna, in 1530.    They were organized in the Italian fashion and run in the principal street.

In the library of Trinity College, Cambridge,[1] is a roll 10¾ inches wide by 24 feet long depicting Henry VIII going to Parliament in the year 1512. The drawings are rather crude; but they present a wealth of detail concerning costume and the order of precedence, as well as other interesting details, of great value to producers responsible for any spectacle of the period, which aims at accuracy rather than imaginative slapdashery.

The procession to 'Parleament holden at Westm̃ the iiijth day of February the thirde yere of oure Soueraigne Lorde Kyng Henry the viijth' consists of Church Dignitaries, the Regalia, the Sovereign, and finally the Peers in their several degrees in order of creation.'

First come the twenty-three 'mitered abbots' led by 'the Abbot off Tewkysbery' (Henry Beoly 1509), the last being the Abbot of Westminster (John Islip 1500–32). Next come the bishops, ranging from the Bishop of Bangor (Sir Thomas Skerryngton) to the nineteenth, the Bishop of London (Richard Fitzjames).[2] On either side of the bishops walk seven heralds in their various armorial tabards worn over long gowns of pinkish colour.

The Archbishop of Canterbury (William Warham, 1504–32), preceded by his chaplain and crossbearer, comes next escorted on either side by a mace-bearer and followed by an acolyte. The State Regalia are headed by the Garter King of Arms, wearing his tabard with the Royal arms, carrying a scroll in his right hand and bonet in his left.

Immediately following comes the Royal mace on the right flanked by the Bearer of the Sword of State.

Edward Stafford, third Duke of Buckingham (born 1478, beheaded 1521), in peer's robes follows, carrying the Cap of Maintenence.

The King (see Fig. 211) walks next under a canopy carried on golden poles by four acolytes. The canopy consists of small blue and gold squares with the Tudor rose in the centre, and bordered with fringe chequée in the Tudor colours of white and green. A duke carries the train of the King's long mantle, and is followed by two other dukes (see Fig. 212, but having the ducal gards upon their hoods).

Thomas Grey, Marquess of Dorset and Baron Ferrers of Groby (grandson of Elizabeth Wydeville) is the sole representative of his rank. Seven earls follow, headed by Henry Algernon Percy, Earl of Northumberland, and last Henry Stafford, Earl of Wiltshire.

The Lord Prior of St. John of Jerusalem, 1502–27 (Sir Thomas Docwra), is followed by twenty-one barons, starting with Henry, Lord Clifford, and ending with Baron Conyers.

From this illustration it would seem that Henry's personal appearance had not altered materially since 1508, the date of the last description. He wears a long robe with wide sleeves made of deep rose velvet, and lined and bordered

[1] There are two or three copies extant. One is in the British Museum and one in the Ashmolean, Oxford.

[2] Student at Oxford 1459; Fellow of Merton 1465. Translated from See of Chichester to London 1506. Died 1522.

with ermine (Fig. 211).   He has a hood and cape of the same, but, as these
were put on before the mantle, very little of them is seen except on the neck
and chest; the hood is turned back over the mantle in the usual manner.
The mantle of blue velvet is very long, lined and bordered with ermine.
Around the King's neck is a massive gold and jewelled collar.   Although a
sceptre is carried, the crown which might be expected to accompany it is
awaiting the King at the House of Peers, and Henry wears the usual black
velvet bonet with a jewel.   His black shoes have the fashionable round toes.

Fig. 212. A Duke or Earl

Fig. 211 (left).
King Henry VIII, 1510

This costume conforms to the type of regal dress worn by English kings during
many centuries, before and after Henry's time; but, as always, some detail,
cap, collar, shoe, or other item, marks the period of each individual king.

Fig. 213 is one of the twenty-three mitred abbots in a long black gown or
cassock with moderately wide sleeves edged with brown fur and girded at
the waist.   The mantle and hood are of a grey-purple, the latter very open
at the neck and falling well over the shoulders, the head part hanging for some
distance down the back.   A black blocked felt cap is worn, and the round-
toed shoes are those so much in vogue.   One of the nineteen bishops is shown
in Fig. 214.   They all wear convocation robes consisting of a white under-
gown girded by a black belt with gold buckle and chape.   The semicircular
mantle is of scarlet, surmounted by a white fur hood lined with scarlet
descending to the elbows, the head part being smaller and the cap a little
wider than those worn by the abbots.   Black shoes with round toes are worn.

Fig. 212 from the same source shows one of the earls in his Robes of Estate. For an earlier example of a peer refer to Fig. 519, vol. ii. In this the gards are placed on the right shoulder of the mantle. In Fig. 212 they have been transferred to the cape part of the hood which is worn *over* the mantle. The

Fig. 214. A Bishop

Fig. 213 (*left*).
A Mitred Abbot

surcote is worn under this as previously. The chaperon in Fig. 519, vol. ii, has been discarded for the biretta-shaped bonet.

All the ecclesiastics and the peers have their heads covered, but the officials are bareheaded.

The Venetian Ambassador in 1515 gives the following description of Henry arrayed in the robes of the Most Noble Order of the Garter:

'We entered a room where His Majesty was leaning against a chair,[1] which was covered with cloth of gold brocade, with a cushion of the same material, and a large gilt sword, under a canopy [2] of cloth of gold, with a raised pile.

[1] Refer to drawing of chair, Fig. 215.          [2] For canopy, see Fig. 292.

His Majesty was dressed as a Knight of the Garter, of which order he is the superior, and wore a very costly doublet, over which was a mantle of violet-coloured [1] velvet, with an extremely long train, lined with white satin; on his head was a richly jewelled cap of crimson velvet, of immense value, and round his neck he wore a collar, studded with many precious stones, of which I never saw the like.'

Another description by this Ambassador, given later in the same year, tells us that 'he wore a cap of crimson velvet, in the *French fashion*, and the brim was looped up all round with lacets and gold enamelled aiglettes. His doublet was in the *Swiss fashion*, striped alternately with white and crimson satin, and his hose scarlet, and all *slashed* from the knee upwards. Very close round his neck he had a gold collar, from which there hung a rough-cut diamond, the size of the largest walnut I ever saw, and to this was suspended a most beautiful and very large round pearl. His mantle was of purple velvet lined with white satin, the sleeves open with a train verily more than four Venetian yards in length. This mantle was girt in front like a gown,[2] with a thick gold cord, from which there hung large glands [3] entirely of gold, like those suspended from a cardinal's hat; over this mantle was a very handsome gold collar, with a pendant St. George entirely of diamonds.[4] On his left shoulder was the garter, which is a cincture buckled circular-wise, and bearing in its centre a cross gules on a field argent, and on his right shoulder was a hood, with a border [5] entirely of crimson velvet. Beneath the mantle he had a pouch of cloth of gold, which covered a dagger; and his fingers were one mass of jewelled rings.'

The 'cap of crimson velvet' was, in fact, in the Milanese fashion, which had already found its way into France. It was like that shown in Fig. 219, though feathers are not mentioned, or like Fig. 360.

The doublet 'in Swiss fashion' will be understood by referring to Plate VII A and Plate IX, and to the descriptions under each figure. Some writers of the time did not discriminate between Swiss and German—either term being applied to the same fashion. Henry's hosen were slashed in the manner shown in Plates III B and VII A.

Already in 1510 Henry VIII had made certain alterations and additions to the Insignia of the Order of the Garter (*see* vol. ii, pp. 241 and 242).

In the 'xix yere Henry VIII' Francis I was created a Knight of the Garter, and Henry made a Knight of the Order of St. Michael. 'The mantle of the latter Order,' says Edward Hall, 'was of cloth of silver embroidered with French knots and kocleshelles and the collar was the same deuise having hanging before the breast the image of St. Michael (*see* vol. ii, Fig. 565).

---

[1] This proves that Queen Elizabeth was not the first to change the colour from sky-blue to purple. See vol. ii, p. 241. Purple velvet cost at this time 41s. 8d. per yard.

[2] This statement is slightly misleading. The mantle was caught across the breast in the usual manner. See Fig. 338, vol. ii.

[3] 'Glands' refer to the spherical or barrel-like ornaments through which the cord passes.

[4] Probably inherited from his father, who only paid £18 in 1501 'for a George of Dyamonds' and again in 1503: 'To Master Shaa for a George of diaments, £4 4s.'

[5] 'Border' here refers to the liripipe worn border-fashion across the front.

Referring to Henry at the age of twenty-four, the Venetian Ambassador says: 'His Majesty is the handsomest potentate I ever set eyes on; above the usual height, with an extremely *fine calf* to his leg, his complexion very fair and bright, with auburn hair combed straight and short, in the French fashion, and a round face so very beautiful that it would become a pretty woman, his throat being rather long and thick.'

Again, writing in 1519, the same partial critic says: 'His Majesty is twenty-nine years old and extremely handsome: Nature could not have done more for him; he is much handsomer than any other sovereign in Christendom; a great deal handsomer than the King of France; very fair, his whole frame admirably proportioned.   On hearing that Francis I wore a beard he allowed his to grow, and, as it is reddish, he has now got a beard which looks like gold.'

An interesting record of Henry's tonsorial vagaries will be found on p. 311.

*Furniture* is not included in the scheme of this book, but it is realized that some excerpts describing various pieces will prove not only interesting but also useful, especially to those who may have a superficial knowledge of the furniture used during this period.   These further details may help them to visualize the surroundings in which the Tudors lived.

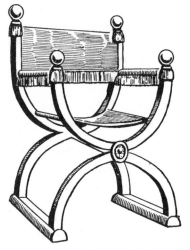

Fig. 215. A Typical Chair

Furniture in general use among the best people can be classified into three sections:

1. Furniture to put things on, such as tables and dressoirs (*see* vol. ii, p. 371).

2. Furniture to put things in, as armouries or cupboards, chests or coffers.

3. Furniture to sit or lie down on, such as benches, stools, chairs for important people, and beds.

All these pieces were strongly built, mostly in oak, and the work of the carpenter.

Mention of a chair in the Ambassador's description of Henry VIII raises the question of the appearance of these chairs, and incidentally of the rooms occupied by His Majesty.

Two illustrations in Henry's Psalter (Royal MS. 2 A xvi) depict rooms occupied by the King: one is decorated in the highly ornate Renaissance style, the walls, columns, arches, and floor being in different coloured marbles: another shows a typical Italian interior of coloured marble columns, pilasters, and arches, black walls, and floors of coloured tiles.   But his private apartment is much more likely to have been a timber-and-plaster-, or stone-walled, room with an oak-beamed ceiling, perhaps painted in reds, blues, or greens, and oaken floors; the walls hung with priceless pieces of tapestry.   The chair occupied by the King in one of these illustrations is shaped like Fig. 215 and covered with blue velvet. Upon the seat of such chairs, which were usually of canvas covered with material, was placed a cushion with two cords and tassels at each corner to tie round the frame to keep it in place. Chairs like this were covered with velvet in rich colours: vermilion, crimson, green, blue, or black. One is mentioned in an inventory as being covered with cloth of gold brocade: this refers to the frame-work, which was often entirely covered, seat, cushions, and footstool.

In 1543 the Princess Mary II sent a New Year's gift to her father of a chair, presumably of the shape shown in Fig. 215. The cost of covering it was £3 16s. 8d., and the embroidery came to £18.

These beautifully shaped chairs when used by very important people stood upon a dais or 'haut-pas,' and were placed in front of a dorsal (see vol. ii, p. 346 and Fig. 571) with canopy or 'sparver' of cloth of gold or brocade with armorial bearings embroidered thereon (see Fig. 60).

The ancestry of this type of chair dates back to the fourteenth century. One of this date is kept in York Minster, and a drawing of one is shown in Fig. 354, vol. ii. The height of the back varied and was sometimes higher than the occupant's head (see Fig. 571, vol. ii). Frequently they were made wide in the seat, especially during the Tudor and Elizabethan periods, and this type can be seen in Plates XXXIX and XLIII.

Fig. 216. An Italian Table

The contents of the King's privy chamber at Greenwich Palace are officially enumerated as follows in an inventory of the Royal household goods:

'A breakfast table of walnut tree: a round table covered with black velvet: a square table: a cupboard of wainscot: three *joined* [1] forms with three stools: a table and a pair of tressels: a Steele glass [a mirror of polished steel]: one pair of regals [a small organ with two manuals] with a case: one pair of tables [a backgammon board] of bone and wood in a case of leather: a pair of gridirons, a fire shovel, and a fire fork.'

Gridiron, gredel, andiron, was a horizontal bar, one of a pair, sustained on short feet, with an upright pillar, placed on either side of the hearth for supporting logs—a firedog. A richly carved oak mantelpiece surrounded the opening of the fireplace. There is no doubt that oriental rugs were placed in front of important pieces of furniture and about the floor in convenient positions.

Stools were much more used than chairs in all the palaces and great houses, where only privileged persons were entitled to occupy chairs. At Court functions no one but the King occupied a chair, stools being reserved for the ladies of the court. Stools were chiefly of oak, referred to as 'wainscot'

[1] See p. 619.

because they were made of oak boards of small scantling imported from the Continent and known as *wagenschot*—hence *wainscot*. Boards of smaller size were called 'clapboards.' The stools were rectangular in shape, and often of the X pattern (*see* Fig. 351); in a few instances cushions were tied on to the top.

Supplementing the above items of furniture at Greenwich were: 'A clocke: a painted table [a picture]: a standing glasse of steele: a branche of flowers wrought upon wyre: three combe cases of bone, furnished: four littel coffers for jewels: a chair of *joined* worke.'

### SOME OFFICERS OF A ROYAL HOUSEHOLD

The *Lord Great Chamberlain* controlled the household of the King, and with *Garter King of Arms* was responsible for the arrangements of all State ceremonies and Court functions. A *Vice-Chamberlain* relieved him of some of his duties, or even took his place when necessary.

The titles of the other Great Officers of the Household sufficiently explain their duties: these are the *Earl Marshal*, the *Lord Steward*, the *Private Secretary* and the *Keeper of the Privy Purse*, and the *Master of the Horse*.

Fig. 217. Ewer and Basin

*Esquires in Ordinary of the King's Body* had very responsible duties to perform. Usually they were knights, and each of them was entitled to two esquires and a page in attendance. They were near the King's person both day and night, and there were always two in immediate attendance 'to array and unarray him, watch day and night, and to dress him in his cloaths: and they be retainers to the Lord Chamberlain if anything lack for his [the King's] person or pleasaunce. Their business is in many secrets, some sitting in the King's Chamber, some in the Hall with persons of like service, which is called Knight's service.'

At the King's rising six esquires were in waiting as well as a page and a barber. His Majesty was 'but loosely dressed by these in his bedchamber, and proceeding into the privy chamber where the more finished and ornamental part of his costume was put on by the Gentlemen of the Privy Chamber.'

Two Esquires of the Body sat at the King's feet at meal times, in front of the table and sometimes underneath it;[1] at least two served the dishes, and another, receiving it from the Chief Butler, presented the cup. The basin

---

[1] See the duties of the two countesses at Anne Boleyn's coronation banquet, p. 266.

and ewer were handed by two others (Fig. 217). Indoors and out one esquire was always in readiness to carry the King's cloak, or render him any similar service. At night the Esquire of the Body held in his own person the combined powers of the Gentlemen Ushers, the Vice-Chamberlain, and the Lord Great Chamberlain, having the absolute command of the house above and below stairs. No business could be done, nor dispatches brought to the King, except through this officer.

*Esquires Extraordinary of the King's Body* were called in to assist on special occasions when required.

*Gentlemen of the Privy Chamber* were above the Esquires of the Body in social position, but had fewer duties to perform about the King's person. They were actually courtiers. It was one of their privileges to finish the robing of the King when he emerged from his bedchamber in the morning, and they formed his entourage on unimportant occasions as well as at state ceremonies. These gentlemen had their own personal attendants, and it seems that their number was not limited. They included esquires and pages.

*Gentlemen Ushers* had charge of the entrance to the various chambers of a palace or great house; they conducted into the Presence people who came on important business, and checked others. They had various other duties to perform.

A *Gentleman of the Bedchamber* had his bed in the same room as the King, and in the anteroom between the privy chamber and the bedchamber slept the *Groom of the Bedchamber*.

In the privy chamber slept two of the six Gentlemen of the Privy Chamber in waiting, and in the presence chamber the Esquire of the Body accompanied by two pages. All the temporary beds were put up and taken down under the supervision of the *Groom of the Wardrobe of the Beds*. Beyond, in the guard-room, was the watch, consisting of a certain number of the *Yeomen of the Guard*.

The *Yeomen of the Wardrobe* had the keeping of the King's clothes, and each morning brought those required to the door of the privy chamber and handed them over to one of the *grooms* or pages, who in turn delivered them to one of the six Gentlemen of the Privy Chamber 'to be ministered to the King's person as shall stand with his pleasure.' The gentleman who adjusted the mantle or other important outer garment was called the *Groom of the Stole*: it was a special honour to desire 'the person of the greatest estate' present to render this service.

A *Corps of the Yeoman of the Guard* was in general attendance at the palace, and two stood near certain of the officers of the household. A full company, together with the gentlemen pensioners, formed the King's escort at state functions, indoors and out.

The *Household of the Queen-Consort* consisted of *Maids of Honour* as organized by Anne of Brittany (*see* p. 71), *Ladies-in-Waiting*, *Gentlewomen of the Bedchamber*, and *Tirewomen*. The Queen had also her own *Lord Chamberlain*, *Steward*, *Secretary*, and *Keeper of the Privy Purse*.

The nobility formed their households upon the same principles.

The British Museum contains a document [1] full of enlightenment on the subject of clothes, etc., in use during the first years of Henry VIII's reign, and entitled:

'The Booke of Delyueraunce and Discharge of the Kings Standynge Warderobe of his Robes within the Towre of Londone. . . . James Worsley yoman of our said souveraigne lordes Robes & Keper of his said warderobe sithen the xxth day of december the viijth yere of our said souverane lordes most noble Reigne'—1517.   All the garments are specified under the following names with descriptions of materials used:

Mantelles; gownes and clothe of golde and velwete; coots and jaquetts and dobletts; GLAUDKYNS; placards, bases, trappers, and bards; gyrdells, or belts; copes and vestments of diuerse makings; hangyngs and chemberyngs; furres and sables and of powder'd ermyns; clothes of golde of dyuerse collours; tylsenttes of dyuerse collours; baudekyns; velvets; sattens, damasks, sarcenetts, dyaper, and lynnene clothes.

Below are descriptions of one item from each of the above:

'delyuered by the Kinges commandement to Nicolas Carewe a mantell of purpulle Tilsent furred with blacke bugie' [bogie; i.e. black lamb].

'They delyuered by the Kinges commandement to Sʳ william Sandes Knight a Gowne of grene velwete lyned with grene satten with xvj buttons of gold with a Jaquet of grene tylsent, doblet, & hose to the same.'

'Jaquet a crimosyn clothe of gold with slyves furred with bugie.'

'. . . to Sir Edward guylford a Riding cote of crimosyn cloth of golde of tissewe lined with white cloth of silver damaske silver and welted with the same.'

'ffirst delyuered by the Kinges commandment and my Lorde Cardynalles to Robert Amadas goldsmyth for the Kinges use—ccccxlviii ozs iij qrt of fine golde and Dccclj perles moche of a sorte that was taken of from the Kinges Cote thoone syde of purpulle velwete pyrled and thoder syde of white cloth of silver tyssewe.'

'xxi yds 1 qrt of white cloth of silver, cut and poynted upon cloth of golde with a border of the same richly embroidered for a Glaudkyn with wide slyves for the Kinges grace, and the same quantity of yellow cloth of golde upon satten for the lyning of the same Glaudkyn.'

[The word 'glaudkyn' is peculiar to wardrobe accounts and inventories of this period.   From the above description it would appear probable that the surcote is intended.]

'Item a swerde Gyrdell of lether set with Roses portcules studds buckell and pendaunte of golde.'   'Item a sworde Gyrdell of lether with aches & Eys with bokell pendaunt and studdes of golde.'

<hr />

[1] Harleian MS. 2284.

'Sent unto ye French King in January ao xijo { Item a Doblet of Russet cloth of gold
Item a Doblet of crimosyn satten
Item a Doblet of dammaske syluer } The placardes & fore-slyves of every of them richely embrauderd with dammaske gold.'

'Item delyuered by the Kinges commandment to the sergeaunt skynner iij quartes and ij slyves of a ffurre of sabullus spent for the furring of a nyght gowne for the Kinges grace.'

During the first half of this reign the ornate fashions of France influenced the costume of the English nobility to a very considerable extent. On the other hand, France itself was under the sway of other foreign fashions. These will be dealt with in the order in which they appeared.

Italian Influences, 1490–1520 (*continued from p. 33*).

Swiss or German styles, 1476–1547.

French Fashions, 1500–30.

## ITALIAN INFLUENCES

### BASES

Fig. 218 is a drawing founded on the paintings by Raphael. It shows the costume of an Italian nobleman dating between 1510 and 1520. He wears a striped padded tunic, with bases slit up the front and back: these are first mentioned under Fig. 38. The tunic is of two colours; and the manner in which the borders at the neck and hem are treated by counterchanging or shifting the two coloured stripes should be noticed. This treatment, alluded to under Plate III A, also takes place at the waist-line, where it was usually covered with a belt. The full sleeves of the pourpoint are of a different material, but nothing of this undergarment is seen at the low neck of the tunic. A shirt, gathered into a narrow neckband headed by a small frill, fills in the neck opening. The headgear is composed of a cap of network in gold and jewels, surmounted by a broad-brimmed hat of beaver or velvet with the edge cut out in battlements. The arrangement of the dagger, pouch, and sword is characteristic of the time, but the shoes follow the natural form of the foot.

Fig. 219 shows another costume derived from the same source. Sleeves were frequently largely puffed and well padded; in this instance they are divided quarterly in two colours, two materials, or both. This variety of arrangement also applied to the bases. Similarly the body part and neckband are per pale counterchanged. The headgear is described under Fig. 360.

In Plate VI is given the costume of a fashionable young English courtier, who was present among many others at the famous tournament held at

Fig. 218. Italian, 1510–20             Fig. 219. Italian, 1510–20

Westminster in February 1510 in honour of the birth of Prince Henry, who died seven weeks later. The 'Tournament Roll,' which illustrates this magnificent entertainment, is in the possession of the College of Arms, and Plate VI is adapted from one of the figures. There are many other beautiful costumes shown and the MS. abounds in details of every kind. The inspiration for the design of this costume is decidedly Italian, and proves that at this date Italian styles were generally adopted in England, as also in France. A description of this costume is as follows: The body part is blue cross-barred with gold, the neck and sleeve borders being of gold lozenges upon a green or blue ground. The bases are striped, plain green alternating with red and gold brocade. On alternate pleats the two separated bands at the hem are blue and gold counterchanged. The wide sleeves, attached to the body part or perhaps belonging to an underjacket, are of red and gold brocade of the same pattern used in the bases, and are lined with green, over moderately close-fitting under-sleeves of crimson velvet visible at wrists and elbows in the drawing.    Bonets shown in this tournament roll are of various colours—blue, green, red, as well as the more usual black velvet. The one shown in Plate VI is of blue velvet with the brim cut in two places; and the plume is per pale green and white. High boots of soft yellow leather are worn. The whole effect of this costume is decidedly gorgeous, not to say bizarre, and recalls the style of the kings and knaves on court cards, as referred to in the previous chapter (*see* p. 31).

Another representation of bases is to be seen in a figure of St. George by Lucas Cranach, about 1516, painted on a shutter of a triptych in the collection of H.M. the King at Buckingham Palace.    The saint is equipped in a full suit of German plate armour.    Tied round his waist is a military skirt composed of alternate horizontal bands of brocade and dark-coloured velvet. The skirt descends below the knees and is widely open up the front.    This painting is exceptionally helpful to students, as it demonstrates more clearly than any other evidence known to the author that military skirts were some-times worn over cuisse, knee-cops, and tassets (*see* Fig. 512). St. George wears one of the fashionable close-fitting caps of material covered with network (*see* Fig. 120), and a massy chain is wound twice round the neck.

In connection with bases an interesting story is told.    As High Constable of England and Ewer-bearer to the King, the Duke of Buckingham on one occasion was holding the basin for Henry to wash his hands before dinner, when, without ceremony or privilege, the upstart Wolsey dipped his hand in at the same time.    The basin tilted either by accident or as a reproof for the impertinence, and some water fell into the Cardinal's shoe, whereupon His Eminence in his irritation swore that 'he would sit on Buckingham's skirts,' otherwise the fashionable bases.    Next day the Duke appeared at court in a doublet without bases, giving as explanation for ignoring the mode, 'that he was resolved to disappoint the malice of Wolsey.'    This incident took place after 1515.    The execution of the Duke, as a consequence of charges brought against him by the spitefulness of the Cardinal, took place in 1521.

It is possible that Buckingham's example caused bases to go out of fashion shortly after this date.    However, the following entry occurs in a Royal ward-robe account for 1517: 'Item—to Sʳ Henry Guylford Knight to be kept for the Kinges use a Base with a placard of white cloth of gold of tissewe to were upon harness with a rich trapper of the same lyned with grene satene fringed with white silk and gold and lace of silke and gold.'

Another Italian fashion which influenced western costume was that of 'CUT HOSEN.' Figs. 220, 221, 222, and 223 give some examples. The first three are taken from a group in the picture 'The Trial of Moses,' painted by Giorgio Barbarelli, called Giorgione (1477–1510). Fig. 220 has the thigh part decorated with perpendicular cuttes with rosette designs embroidered at their extremi-ties.    Garters are tied below the knee.    Fig. 221 wears hosen cutte round the ɪower part of the thigh, with black laces over the cuttes forming two loops at the top and two loops and two aiglette ends at the bottom points.   The jackets or pourpoints of both these figures resemble those described in Chapter I. The man in Fig. 221 wears his shirt projecting between his pourpoint and the hosen.   The sleeves of these pourpoints are shaped as shown in Fig. 35.   Fig. 220 has the top part cutte vertically (*see also* Plate VII A).   The hosen worn by the man in Fig. 222 are even more fantastic.   The vertical cuttes are of various lengths decorated here and there with small loops, a row of loops finishing off their lower points.   The pourpoint worn by this

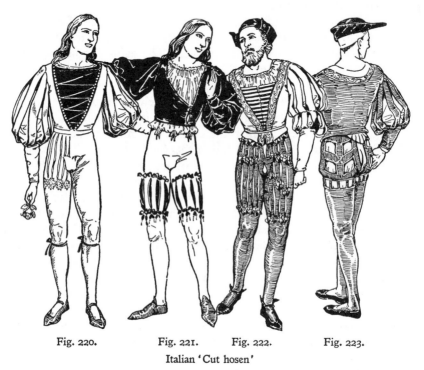

Fig. 220.          Fig. 221.     Fig. 222.          Fig. 223.

Italian 'Cut hosen'

figure comes from another source.   It has a horizontally striped placard and gold embroidery down the fronts and round the neck.   The sleeves are cutte in the same manner as Fig. 220, but the straps are caught in at elbow level.

Fig. 223 is taken from a figure in the painting representing Æneas Sylvius Piccolomini receiving the title of 'Poeta,' by Bernardino Benedetto, otherwise 'Il Pintoricchio' who was born at Perugia about 1454 and died 1513.   The top part of the hosen consists of sloppes divided down the middle, back, and front, and cutte to form bars, the upper part of the hosen being attached to them.   The pourpoint is the same shape as that worn by the preceding figure. Notice the end of the short shirt protruding below the waist-line.

It must be borne in mind that these styles were fashionable in Italy twenty years or so earlier than the period under discussion.

# COLOUR ILLUSTRATIONS

PLATE I.    KING HENRY VII AND QUEEN ELYSABETH (*see* p.15)

YEOMEN OF THE GUARD

PLATE III A.    1501–30 (*see* p.51)    PLATE III B.    1530–50 (*see* p.290)

PLATE IV.    QUEEN ELYSABETH OF YORK (*see* p.59)

Plate V.   JOANNA, QUEEN OF CASTILE (*see* p.63)

PLATE VI.    AN ENGLISH NOBLEMAN, 1510 (*see* p.168)

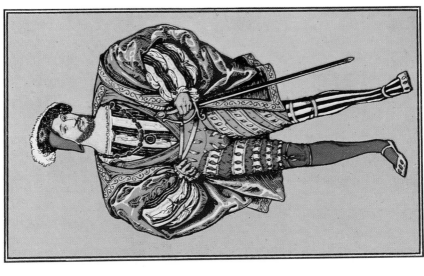

PLATE VII B.    FRANCIS I, KING OF FRANCE (*see* p.193)

PLATE VII A.    A LANDSKNECHT (*see* p.172)

PLATE IX.    KING HENRY VIII AT THE FIELD OF THE CLOTH OF GOLD, 1520 (*see* p.184)

HN.

PLATE XI.    ELEANOR OF AUSTRIA, QUEEN OF PORTUGAL, c.1518 (*see* p.204)

PLATE XIII. KING HENRY VIII, 1542 (*see* p.236)
After a portrait by Hans Eworth. Original at Trinity College, Cambridge.
By kind permission of the Master and Fellows.

PLATE XVI.   A NOBLE LADY OF THE COURT OF HENRY VIII, 1530–40 (*see* p.269)

PLATE XVII.    A NOBLE LADY, 1540–50 (*see* p.283)

PLATE XIX.    KING EDWARD VI, 1548 (*see* p.392)

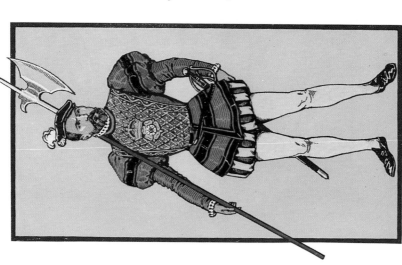

YEOMEN OF THE GUARD

PLATE XXIII A.    1550–75 (see p.422)    PLATE XXIII B.    1575–95 (see p.422)

PLATE **XXIV**.   THE LADY JANE GREY, 1553 (*see* p.426)
Watercolour by the author. By kind permission of Madame Tussauds, Ltd.

PLATE XXVI.    QUEEN MARY, 1554 (*see* p.441)
After a portrait by Hans Eworth. Original at the Society of Antiquaries.
By kind permission of the Committee.

PLATE XXVII.    QUEEN ELIZABETH IN CORONATION ROBES, 1559 (*see* p.485)
Portrait by Gwillim Stretes. Warwick Castle.
By kind permission of the Earl of Warwick.

PLATE **XXIX**.    QUEEN ELIZABETH, 1560–70 (*see* p.489)
Portrait by an unknown artist. Private collection.

PLATE **XXX**.    QUEEN ELIZABETH, 1570 (*see* p.492)
After a portrait attributed to Federigo Zuccaro. Original at Hampden House.
By kind permission of the Earl of Buckinghamshire.

PLATE **XXXIV**.    MARY STUART, QUEEN OF SCOTLAND, 1562 (*see* p.516)

PLATE XXXVI.　CHARLES IX, KING OF FRANCE, 1561 (*see* p.556)

PLATE XL.    QUEEN ELIZABETH, 1589 (*see* p.606)
Portrait by an unknown artist. Private collection.

PLATE XLVI.     PHILIP II, KING OF SPAIN, c.1580 (*see* p.673)

## LANDSKNECHTEN

### The Victory of Slashes and Puffs

The word means in German a lance or land knight and one of a chosen body of German soldiers.

'Lansquenets' were mercenary soldiers, who served on foot and were of great repute during the early years of the sixteenth century. The word 'lanzknecht' was also used for a German pikeman, billman, or halberdier.

During the Middle Ages the 'Confederate Germans called Swiss'[1] were sorely oppressed by the various continental powers, especially the Empire. Perhaps their greatest enemy was Charles le Téméraire, Duke of Burgundy. When he invaded Switzerland in 1475–6 he was utterly routed at Granson after fierce fighting by the Swiss; his army was destroyed, and his camp, abounding with untold riches, entirely sacked. Frantic destruction followed; and the Swiss, reduced by their poverty and hardships to rags and tatters, seized a wealth of treasure such as they had never before imagined. They demolished the wonderful pavilions in which the magnificent Duke and his equally magnificent entourage had been housed, and here follow the narrator's own words:

'All his [Charles le Téméraire's] tents were of silk, of several colours, which, the battle being ended, being all torn to pieces by the Swiss soldiers, of a part of one colour they made them doublets, of the rest of the colours breeches,[2] hose and caps, returning home in that habit; so ever in remembrance of that famous victory by them achieved, and their liberty recovered, even to this day they go still in their particolours' which 'consist of doublets and breeches, drawn out with huge puffs of taffatee or linen, and their hose party coloured of red and yellow, and other colours.'

At Nancy Charles le Téméraire[3] received his death-blow on Twelfth Eve, 1477, and the Swiss recovered their liberty. It was proved on this memorable occasion that men on foot lightly armed were more than a match for knights in full armour.

The Swiss had made their reputation for bravery, and from this time they became much in demand as mercenaries, being engaged by various War-Lords of different nationalities. In 1487, at the recommendation, curiously enough, of their former invader's widow, Margaret of York, Duchess of Burgundy, they joined the forces of John de la Pole, Earl of Lincoln, under the captaincy of Martin Schwartz, in the Lambert Simnel rebellion, where, however, these mercenaries were annihilated at the Battle of Stoke by Henry VII's archers. The Swiss carried 'hand fire machines' of the latest type but the old-fashioned bow and arrow prevailed. A nasty knock for firearms!

[1] In the sixteenth century they were frequently referred to as 'Switzers.'
[2] 'Breeches' are mentioned here before their time.
[3] For further details respecting Charles le Téméraire, see vol. ii, pp. 355, 357; Burgundy, pp. 400, 453, 459.

The Swiss victory over fifteen thousand Austrians at Dornach in 1499 finally won their independence: and in the same year, at the Peace of Basle, the Emperor Maximilian tacitly acknowledged that the Confederation, although nominally subject to the Empire, was practically independent.

Maximilian had a very great regard for these brave and lusty mountaineers, although they had fought continuously against his ancestors, and the father of his wife, Marie of Burgundy; and as early as 1482 he had set his heart on training and organizing them into a company of foot-soldiers, which ultimately became the envy and terror of Europe, and the finest fighters in the world. By the year 1511 Swiss mercenaries were entirely associated with Germany, and the name 'Landsknechten' was applied to them. They were sworn to the most severe discipline, but were allowed to retain their own costume, characterized by excessive slashings, puffings, particolour, and other eccentricities.

The fame of the Swiss armed forces, the Landsknechten, spread all over Europe, and much interest was taken in their extraordinary apparel. Originating as their costume did from dire necessity and patched together as best could be contrived from all manner of odd pieces, it revealed involuntarily many a peep of equally disreputable undergarments; but the fame of their military achievements fired the imagination of the courts of Europe, and fashionable Society imitated deliberately what had been a makeshift, making 'cuttes' and 'slashes' important additions to the tailor's vocabulary.

Plate VII A represents a typical Landsknecht in characteristic complicated costume of the early sixteenth century, by which time the Company was thoroughly organized. The white, but often dirty yellow, shirt is full and gathered into an upstanding neckband. The sleeves of the shirt are also full, and either these or the coloured linings of the outer sleeves are 'pulled through'[1] the straps of the sleeves and are visible. The scarlet jacket of the overdress is shaped to bulge round the figure: it is decorated with three different kinds of cuttes. The top cuttes of the jacket continue round the shoulder of the right sleeve. This sleeve is composed of narrow straps, all of them sufficiently long to bulge just above the elbow, part of the way down the forearm, and again at the wrist, where they are fixed to a narrow band. The left sleeve of purple, lined with orange, starts at the shoulder seam with a moderate-sized puff, followed by a smaller one, both with cuttes: next comes a large puff of straps, then two small ones with cuttes, almost elbow level: a large puff of straps comes almost to the wrist, where the sleeve finishes with two small puffs with cuttes. The clothing of the hips is divided per pale by a codpiece. The right of green is cut longitudinally and fits close. At hip-bone level is a strong piped heading; two puffs of straps finish above the knee with a small puff with cuttes; below the knee a puff of straps; and on the lower part of the leg a plain blue hose. On the left leg from the waist to above the knee is a covering composed of spiral bands in blue, ornamented along its entire length with cuttes showing yellow underneath, the hose striped scarlet and

---

[1] This expression was in use at this time. See Edward VI's *Journal*.

Fig. 224. LANDSKNECHTEN

white pushing up the lowest puff. A tied garter of purple is worn on the left leg only.

The head is covered with a close-fitting blue cap of cloth edged with loops, and decorated with five cuttes radiating from the centre (*see* Fig. 373). On this is placed, very much on the left side of the head, a hat of fawn felt with a normal basin-shaped crown, having a very wide brim cut at regular distances all round, each portion being turned back and fastened to the base of the crown so as to form stiff loops. (A similar hat is shown in Fig. 371.) Round the brim, at all angles, are placed ostrich plumes which vary in number, colour, and length. A cord, or cords, were often attached to the brim and hung in front so that the hat could be pushed off the head and lie on the back.

It was the general rule with this kind of costume to have the different parts in varying colours. Each section of straps would be loosely lined with a contrasting colour so that the lining could be pulled through the spaces between the straps.

The colours used were reds, blues, purples, greens, yellows, white, black, and buff, in all their variety of shades, but usually of the most glaring tones.

A battalion of these picturesque

Fig. 225. King James IV of Scotland.
From the Arras drawing
(*By kind permission of Emery Walker Ltd.*)

fellows arrayed in their gaudy clothes glowing beneath a forest of tremendously long lances of ash, often painted red, must have been an impressive sight. Fig. 224 shows two lines of them: those in the first row carry halberds, those in the second long lances. During a campaign in 1504, the Emperor Maximilian and his son entered Cologne in triumph, attended by Landsknechten in their multi-coloured costumes and carrying their red lances across their shoulders.

In 1505 a section of these Swiss mercenaries was engaged by Pope Julius II, who thus founded the Papal Swiss Guard.

## JAMES IV

### *King of Scotland, 1473–1513*

Amongst the brothers-in-law of Henry VIII, first mention must be made of James IV of Scotland, who was born in 1473, and succeeded to the throne in 1488. The drawing from which Fig. 225 is taken dates about the time of his marriage with the Princess Margaret, 1503 (*see* p. 68). There is in it sufficient evidence that he is dressed in the same style as that worn by the nobles of Henry VII's reign. There was a contemporary portrait of King James at Whitehall. Fig. 226 is a drawing made from a copy of it. It was painted some time after his marriage, and in it he wears fashionable English attire. He carries a falcon on his left wrist, and clasps a falconer's embroidered leather pouch in his right hand. (For a lure, *see* Fig. 74.) The underdress is of cloth of gold open to show the shirt with an embroidered neckband. The long outer robe is crimson silk, embroidered with a curious shell-like design in gold arranged diaper-wise. It is

Fig. 226. King James IV of Scotland
(*By kind permission of Captain Archibald Stirling*)

faced with black silk and turned back to show the lining of lynx fur. One detail worthy of notice is the manner in which the ends of the wide sleeves are treated. A wide band of black silk edged with lynx is tied with black laces across the wrists. The bonet of black velvet, with the brim tied on the right side, has a medallion or enseigne of gold fixed in front. The bonet is worn at a jaunty angle, over hair which falls well on to the shoulders.

It is said that James always wore an iron belt outside his doublet as a penance, as he never forgave himself for responsibility for his father's death.

James IV was slain at Flodden Field, 1513, and was buried at Richmond, Surrey.

For the biography of another brother-in-law, Louis XII of France, the first husband of the Princess Mary, see Chapter I, p. 34. His portrait is given in Figs. 38 and 113.

### CHARLES BRANDON

*Duke of Suffolk, 1484–1545*

The third brother-in-law, Charles Brandon, born 1484, was son and heir of Sir William Brandon, Henry VII's standard bearer at Bosworth, who was on that account singled out by Richard III and killed by him in personal encounter. This family is said to have been located at Brandon in Suffolk, whence they took their name, and where they carried on the business of woolstaplers (*see* verse below).

In 1509 Charles Brandon became Esquire of the Body to Henry VIII, and henceforth a personal friend and boon companion of the King, whom he much resembled. This tall, valiant, handsome young man was much involved in matrimonial alliances—he married four times. First, Margaret, daughter of the Marquess of Montagu, whom he divorced. Secondly, Anne, daughter of Sir Anthony Browne, Kt. This lady died before her spouse was created a Knight of the Garter in 1513, and Duke of Suffolk, 1st February 1514. He was sent in this latter year on a mission to Marguerite, Governess of the Netherlands, who expressed her opinion of Suffolk in a letter to the English Envoy, in these words: 'Knowynge . . . the vertwe & grace of his person, the wyche me semyde that I have not aproche yt.'

The Duke was present at the Princess Mary's marriage to Louis XII in 1514; and shortly after the King's death himself secretly wedded her in Paris as his third wife. This union inspired the following lines, referring to his origin:

> 'Cloth of Gold do not thou dispys
> Though thou be mached with Cloth of fries
> Cloth of friez be not thou to bould
> Though thou be mached with Cloth of Gold.'

Henry affected displeasure at this clandestine marriage; but Francis I looked favourably upon it: a fact which considerably modified Henry's wrath, as he regarded the French King's approval as likely to make the match more acceptable to the old English nobility, who regarded Suffolk as an upstart. Henry's irritation was perhaps even more effectively allayed by a conciliatory gift from Suffolk, who presented to him the plate and jewels which formed Mary's jointure as Queen-Dowager of France, together with a bond for £24,000.

Suffolk was present at the Field of the Cloth of Gold: he entertained King Henry and the Emperor Charles V at his residence in Southwark in 1522, and accompanied Henry to France in 1532. The Duke again became a widower in June 1533, and in the following September married his fourth wife, Katherine, daughter of Lord Willoughby d'Eresby.

The Duke of Suffolk died at Guildford in 1545, and was buried at Windsor at the King's charge. He left two sons, Henry (born 1537, died 1551) who succeeded as the second duke, and Charles (born 1539, died 1551).

In the portrait mentioned on p. 212 the Duke is shown dressed in the fashion of the later period described under Fig. 280, with the Collar of the Garter over his shoulders. The fashion depicted convinces the author that this portrait must have been painted at least fifteen years after the time of Suffolk's third marriage, although the date 1515 is assigned to the portrait by a very eminent authority.

Fig. 358 is a drawing made from a recently discovered head-and-shoulders portrait by Holbein of the Duke at the age of about fifty-six.

The remaining brothers-in-law are mentioned on pp. 53 and 54.

## THOMAS WOLSEY

### Cardinal and Archbishop, 1471–1530

Although, with few exceptions, ecclesiastical vestments do not come within the scope of this book, this chapter would be incomplete without some reference to the robes worn by that outstanding personality — Thomas Wolsey. He was born at Ipswich in 1471, the son of a wealthy grazier and wool merchant, whom his enemy, the poet and satirist, John Skelton (born 1460, died 1529), denounced as a butcher. Graduating at Magdalen College, Oxford, he later found favour with Henry VII, and in 1510 became associated with Henry VIII. From this moment his rise was speedy. A Prebendary of York in 1512, Archbishop of York, 1514; Cardinal and Lord Chancellor in 1515; and Papal Legate in 1518. He lost the favour of his Royal master in 1529.

Fig. 227 shows the Cardinal in full robes. Over his ordinary day clothes he wore a CASSOCK buttoned to the feet, with a very lengthy train and close-fitting sleeves reaching well on to the hands. This, like other items of the costume, was of cardinal-red silk.

Fig. 227. Cardinal Wolsey

Over it was placed the ROCHET of fine white lawn edged with cutwork,[1] with long sleeves full enough to ruck over those of the cassock. The sleeve

---

[1] Deep lace was exceptionally rare at this time. See Lace, Chapter II.

of the latter was turned back over the rochet sleeve, and looked like a cuff. The ecclesiastical chimere was a sleeveless tabard-shaped garment of red reaching just below the knee. The hood, with a deep full cape buttoned all the way down the front, came last, and over it the jewelled cross was worn.

The BIRETTA or pillion was of scarlet silk and of the orthodox sixteenth-century shape (*see* Headgear, p. 321).

The gloves were white kid, the cuff ending in two long points and buttons.

George Cavendish (born 1500, died 1561) (?) entered Cardinal Wolsey's service about 1526. In the biography of his master, finished in 1557, he records that Wolsey went to Westminster Hall apparelled as follows: 'His upper vesture was all of scarlet, or else of fine crimson taffata, or crimson satin ingrained, his pillion [biretta] scarlet, with a black velvet tippet [scarf] of sables about his neck, holding in his hand an orange, the meat or substance thereof being taken out and filled again with a part of spunge, with vineger and other confections against pestilent airs, the which he most commonly held to his nose, when he came to the presses, or when he was pestered with many suitors: and before him was born the Broad Seal of England, and the Cardinal's Hat, by some Lord, or some Gentleman of Worship right solemnly.'

It was also Wolsey's custom to carry a cane or rod. He would strike out with it or gnaw it when irritated. Skelton alludes to the Cardinal's habit in the following lines:

'In Chamber of Stars,
All matters there he mars;
Clapping his rod on the board,
No man dare speak a word;
For he hath all the saying
Without any renaying.
He rolleth in his Records;
He sayeth, How say ye, my lords?
Is not my reason good?
Some say, Yes, and some
Sit still as they were dumb.'

The Bishop of Palencia, who was in the entourage of the Emperor Charles V when he visited England in June 1522, well summed up the Cardinal when he said to the Venetian Ambassador: 'Really that fellow is a wonderful man; he chooses to interfere in everything, and to do all himself; one must act according to his fashion.'

It should be remembered that at the time when Wolsey became Lord Chancellor, Henry VIII was a man of twenty-four; and during the whole course of their friendship the King was a young man of fine figure and appearance. Plate IX is a good representation of him at this period. The fact has been obscured in the popular imagination by the vagaries of sundry playwrights and artists, whose inaccuracies, starting in the early nineteenth-century age of romanticism, have become traditional—so that every one is familiar to-day with representations of Henry and Wolsey together, both middle-aged and corpulent, whereas in truth Henry was the younger by twenty years.

On his exaltation in 1515 the pomp and magnificence which surrounded this Archbishop exceeded that of all his predecessors, even Thomas à Becket. His cardinal's hat [1] was borne by a nobleman and placed only on the high altar. His banquets were the last word in sumptuous feasting; he would seek out, regardless of the abnormal expense, such dishes and choice wines as the King had a particular liking for, whenever he was honoured with a Royal visit. The number of his household is given at five hundred, which was later increased to eight hundred persons, amongst whom were 'one Earl,[2] nine Barons, Knights, Gentlemen, and inferior Officers, about one thousand.' The gentlemen, it is noted, 'were clothed in livery coats of crimson velvet of the best, and chains of gold about their necks; and his yeomen and all his mean Officers were clad in fine scarlet, garded with black velvet, one hand breadth.' Other yeomen of the different departments, such as 'Yeomen of the Wardrobe,' wore 'orange-tawny coats and the Cardinals Hat with T. and C. for Thomas Cardinal embroidered upon them, as well upon his own servants coats, as all the rest of the Gentlemen,' including his bodyguard selected from the tallest men in the realm. Even the master-cook went about daily in velvet or satin with a gold chain.

When the Cardinal travelled he was accompanied by a huge cavalcade of sumpter horses (baggage horses), footcloth horses (riding horses), baggage mules, and wagons.

He 'expended vast sums on books, pictures, statues, and vestments, besides the great cost of the buildings,' such as Hampton Court, Christ Church College, and Cathedral, Oxford.

Much could be said of the worldly belongings of this ostentatious churchman. His tapestries are mentioned in the section dealing with that subject (see p. 146). Numerous inventories of his 'household stuff' are extant, but the following excerpt from Cavendish must suffice. 'Then my lord called his Officers before him [1529], and took account of all things they had in their charge, and in his gallery were set divers tables, upon which were laid divers and great store of rich stuffs, as whole pieces of silk of all colours, velvets, satins, musks, taffaties, grogarams, scarlets, and divers rich commodities. Also there were a thousand pieces of fine Hollands, and the hangings of the gallery with Cloth of Gold, and Cloth of Silver, and rich Cloth of Bodkin [3] of divers colours, which were hanged in expectation of the King's coming. Also of one side of the gallery were hanged the rich suits of Copes [4] of his own providing, which were made for colleges at Oxford and Ipswich, they were the richest that ever I saw in all my life; then had he two chambers adjoining to the gallery, the one most commonly called the Guilt Chamber,

---

[1] For origin, see vol. i, p. 50.    [2] Thomas Stanley (1485–1521), second Earl of Derby.
[3] Baudekyn.  See vol. i, p. 215.    [4] Forty-four in number, profusely loaded with jewels.

the other the Council Chamber, wherein were set two broad and long tables whereupon was set such abundance of plate of all sorts, as was almost incredible to be believed, a great part being all of clean gold, and upon every table and cupboard where the plate was set were books importing every kind of plate, and every piece with the contents and the weight thereof.'

When the dishonoured Cardinal took leave of his household, in 1529, he appeared 'in a rochet upon a violet gown like a bishop,' attended by his chaplains.

In the beginning of Lent, 1530, Cardinal Wolsey 'removed his lodging into the Charterhouse at Richmond, where he lay in a lodging that Dr Collet made for himself . . . and there they gave unto him shirts of hair, to wear next his body, which he wore divers times after.'

'He kept his solemn Feast of Easter at Peterborough, and upon Palm-Sunday he bare his palm, and went in Procession with the Monks, and upon Thursday he made his Maundy, having 59 poor people whose feet he washed and kissed; and after he had dried them, he gave every one of them twelve-pence, and three ells of good canvas to make them shirts, and each of them a pair of new shoes and a cask of red-herring.'

Overtaken with dysentery while at the Abbey of Leicester, Cardinal Wolsey died there in November 1530.

## The Emperor Charles V

### 1500 *until* 1530

The most powerful emperor since Charlemagne, and the most sincere of the trio of monarchs who shared public attention in Europe at this time, was Charles of Austria. Born at Ghent, 24th February 1500, he was the son of Philippe le Beau and Joanna of Castile, and heir to the German possessions of the House of Hapsburg, the territories of the House of Burgundy, and the Kingdom of consolidated Spain, Lord of all Italy, Sovereign of the New World —truly an imposing list! It is the more appropriate that he should be the first monarch to assume the title of 'majesty,' which was reserved for him at the Treaty of Cambrai in 1529. To this was added the prefix 'imperial.' Other monarchs of Europe followed the Emperor's example, preceding the title with distinguishing qualifications.

His appearance as a child may be seen in Fig. 73. In youth and as Comte de Flandres he is shown in Fig. 369. Of fair complexion, he had brown eyes and hair verging on auburn, and a nose slightly rounded on the bridge. A prominent jaw and a protruding lower lip were very noticeable.

Plate VIII A shows his appearance a year or two later, perhaps about fifteen or sixteen. The portrait is by Bernhard Strigel, and is now in the Borghese Galley, Rome. On the death of his maternal grandfather, Ferdinand of Aragon, he was proclaimed King of Spain at Brussels, January 1516, the rights of his mother having been set aside. On the 18th June 1519 he

PLATE VIII A. CHARLES, COMTE DE FLANDRES,
1506: Portrait by an unknown artist. Borghese Gallery,
Rome. *Photo by Mansell*

PLATE VIII B. CHARLES V, KING OF THE ROMANS,
1526: Portrait by an unknown artist
Private collection

was elected at Frankfort to the imperial throne. In 1520 he paid a visit to Henry VIII, and on 24th May landed at Dover 'under the Cloth of his Estate of the Black Egle all splaied on rich cloth of gold. In his retinue with him, were many noble menne, and many faire Ladies of his bloud as princes and princesses, and one Ladie as chief to be noted, was the princes Auinion [1] with many other nobles which landed with hym in high and sumptuous maner and great riches in their apparell.' He was met there by Henry VIII and all the Court and they spent Pentecost together at Canterbury.

Charles V had another interview with Henry VIII at Gravelines, 10th July 1520.

At Aachen on 23rd October 1520 Charles was crowned with the Iron Crown of Lombardy, as King of the Romans and Germany. In 1521 he found himself so much occupied in Spain that he relinquished to his brother Ferdinand his interest in the Austrian Hapsburg territories which they had inherited jointly; and thus the House of Austria was divided into two separate branches —the Spanish under Charles and the German under Ferdinand.

On a second visit to England in 1522, the Emperor was created a Knight of the Garter and wore the full robes of the Order, at Mass and in procession, at Windsor on 4th June.

A portrait of Charles in the year of his marriage (1526) is reproduced in Plate VIII B. The ceremony took place in March at Seville, his bride being Isabella, daughter of 'His Most Faithful Majesty' Emmanuel II, King of Portugal. The poor lady, Empress of half the world, was overwhelmed by her exalted position, and led as retired a life as the numerous Court functions which necessitated her presence made possible. Their children were:

Philip,[2] afterwards Philip II (see p. 404).

Maria, born 1528, married in 1548 Maximilian II and had seven children; died 1603.

Joanna or Juana, born 1535, married Joam III of Portugal. She is often styled Princess of the Brazils, and was left a widow in 1557, being nominated Regent of Spain by Philip II. In 1559 the Princess resigned, and retired to Abrojo, where she died in 1578.

The Emperor had a natural daughter, Margaret, born 1522, who married first Alessandro de' Medici, and secondly Ottavio Farnese, Duke of Parma. Their son, Alessandro (1545–92), married Maria of Portugal. Margaret died 1586. The Emperor also had a natural son, the celebrated Don Juan,[3] born 1547 and d.s.p. 1578.

[1] A misprint for 'Aragon.' This lady was 'Queen Germaine de Foix, the French woman, relict of the late King Ferdinand the Catholic, now married [in 1519] to the Marquis of Brandenburg.'
In the year following the death of her second husband in 1525, she married the Duke of Calabria. 'When Germaine de Foix arrived in England she may perhaps have been fat, lame, and ugly, as asserted by Sanuto and Castiglione; but on a variety of accounts she was one of the most remarkable of royal and state personages of the period.'
[2] It was to celebrate the birth of Philip that Charles killed a bull in the public square at Valladolid in the Spanish fashion, and thereby went far to overcome his unpopularity with his Spanish subjects.
[3] Perhaps more familiar as Don *John* of Austria.

Many descriptions of the clothes worn by Charles V are given in contemporary records. These prove that as a young man he was apparelled very gorgeously, and with great taste. His clothes were made on fashionable lines, but his headgear was in the Flemish style (*see* Headgear, p. 317). His Spanish subjects were somewhat unreasonable in their severe criticism of his so-called lavishness, and blamed him for introducing into Spain the elaborate extravagance of his grandfather's Burgundian court. Still, it must be borne in mind that Charles was a young man, and his exalted position demanded and excused magnificent display.

Full-length portraits of Charles V in early life are few, but there are many showing the head and shoulders, among them one by Mabuse (Budapest), another by Bernhard Strigel (Rome) (Plate VIII A), and a terra-cotta bust with a movable hat (Fig. 369) in the Gruuthuse at Bruges. In the Musée du Cinquantenaire, Brussels, is a panel of tapestry showing two figures of young Charles in full regalia. In the same panel there are also figures of his aunt Marguerite, his brother Ferdinand, and his three sisters.

(*Continued on p. 247*)

Some of the costumes worn during the visit of Charles V to Henry VIII in May 1520 are briefly described in the Venetian calendar. As they should prove of much interest to the student a translated summary is given.

*The Emperor* on the first day wore a simar or long robe (like Fig. 8 or 9), 'the right half of cloth of silver and on the left half of alternate stripes of gold and silver, lined with costly sables.'

On Whit Monday, 28th May, 'he wore a doublet, half of silver brocade, and half of alternate stripes of gold and silver, over which he had a simar of gold brocade lined with sables.'

*King Henry* was equally magnificent. 'The simar of the King of England was entirely of cloth of gold, lined with very beautiful lynx's fur, and round his neck he wore a very valuable jewelled collar. Both their majesties wore cloth caps with a brim [the French bonet] and two very superb jewelled ornaments.'

On another occasion he 'wore a doublet, one half of cloth of gold, the other half of grey velvet, girt with a jewelled belt; the doublet was slashed across in about six compartments, and joined by a quantity of buttons, all of which were balas rubies, sapphires, diamonds, and other sorts of jewels, and round his neck he had a jewelled collar, said to be worth more than 10,000 ducats. His cap or bonet of black velvet was edged and covered with white feathers.'

*The Prince of Orange*, a youth about eighteen years of age, was in the Emperor's entourage. 'His entire costume was of cloth of silver, striped longitudinally with cloth of gold, and so wide were the sleeves of his doublet, which were lined with cloth of gold, that they almost touched the ground; and his hose and doublet were joined in jacket fashion with three plaits [laces], his shirt being of red murrey sarsnet, which contrasted admirably with his white arms.'

At the second meeting between Charles and Henry at Gravelines, 9th July 1520, the Emperor wore a doublet of gold brocade chequered with silver brocade; and the King of England had a simar with a *galeto* wellnigh in the Spanish fashion. There is some doubt as to the meaning of the old Italian word *galeto*. It was most likely a cap of fur, false hair, or beaver.

'On Saturday, the 14th July, the Emperor at length departed, accompanied by the King of England and the Royal retinue. Both the Sovereigns wore doublets; the Emperor's was of silver and gold tissue in triangles; the King of England wore cloth of gold. They rode dapple-grey horses, both with very smart housings of cloth of silver, with knots.'

The dresses of the ladies are detailed on p. 213.

The 4th day of June 1520 is important in the history of costume, since it marked the opening of a period famous for its lavishly magnificent modes. The parade of fashion known as

## The Field of the Cloth of Gold

was the rendezvous of two Kings, 'His Most Excellent Majesty,' Henry VIII of England, and 'His Most Christian and Catholic Majesty,' Francis I of France, to each of whom beautiful and sumptuous attire in all its details was of paramount importance. Henry crossed over to France in his mighty galleon, the *Henri Grâce à Dieu*, with a retinue of 4,300 of England's nobility and lesser gentlemen, and 1,600 horses.

Queen Katherine was accompanied by the great ladies of her Court with their attendants to the number of 1,200.

In his *Chronicle* for 'xij yere' Edward Hall gives an account of this event.

The two Kings had agreed to meet on barren ground, so for this reason the plain between Ardres and Guines was selected, and converted into a twenty days' wonder. Temporary palaces were erected which to the wonderment of all beholders appeared as substantial as any stone-built castle. Henry had all his gigantic buildings constructed in England, shipped over piecemeal, and re-erected in France. They mimicked the architecture of the time, and suggested one side of an Oxford or Cambridge College quad. Interiors were decorated and furnished in a lavish manner. Edward Hall's graphic description of this galaxy of wealth and ingenuity is worth repeating. 'The walls of these temporary palaces,' he says, were 'inbowed [chambered, hung] and batoned [stretched on batons] with riche clothes of silk knitte, and fret with cuttes and braides and sundry newe castes, that the same clothes of silk shewed like bullions of fine burned gold, and the roses in lossenges. Rich and marueilous clothes of Arras wrought of golde and silk, compassed of many auncient stories. In euery chamber in place conuenient were clothes of estate, greate and large of clothe of golde, of Tissue, and rich embroidery, with Chaiers couered with like clothe, with pomelles of fine gold: and great cushyns of rich woorke of the Turkey making.' Tents and pavilions were hung, inside and out, with cloth of gold, cloth of silver, tapestries sent from England and Hallings of rich embroideries.

The establishment of the French King resembled a fabric fortress, having large and lofty pavilions surrounded by walls of canvas and towers of tents that suggested turreted ramparts. The banqueting hall in the centre, fifty yards square, was covered with cloth of gold and hung inside with blue velvet, embroidered with fleurs-de-lys in Cyprus gold, and supported by ropes of gold. Just as a banquet was about to commence, a sudden gale of wind wrenched away the tent pegs, broke the golden ropes, and overthrew the whole structure. Undismayed, the hosts postponed the banquet to the morrow, and re-erected the pavilion. Hall eulogizes in most enthusiastic terms the clothes worn by his own countrymen:

'He were much wise that could haue tolde or shewed of the riches of apparell that was amongest the Lordes and Gentlemenne of England, Cloth of Gold, Clothe of silver, Veluettes, Tinsins, Sattins embroudered, and Crymosyn sattens. The marueilous threasor of golde that was worne in Chaynes and Bauderickes, so great, so weightie, some so manifolde, some in colers of S, that the Golde was innumerable to my demyng to bee summed. Gentlemen, Squires, Knights, and every honest Officer of the Kyng was richly apparelled, and had chaynes of golde. Surely emong the Englishemenne lacked no riches, nor beautifull apparell or array.'

'The Kyng of Englande shewed hymself somedele forwarde in beautie and personage the moste goodliest Prince that euer reigned ouer the Realme of Englande; his grace was apparelled in a garment of clothe of siluer, of Damaske, ribbed with Clothe of Golde, so thicke as might bee, the garment was large, and plited verie thicke, and *canteled* of verie good *intaile*, of suche shape and makying, that it was marueilous to beholde.'

Plate IX is reconstructed from a bas-relief at the Hôtel de Bourgtheroulde, and represents Henry VIII as he appeared at the Field of the Cloth of Gold. This work was executed very shortly after 1520, and the costumes worn by the figures therein are of the period 1515–25. It is therefore more reliable as a guide than the celebrated picture recording the same subject and attributed to Vincent Volpe, now at Hampton Court, which was not painted until eighteen or twenty years after the event, when fashions had altered. This picture is, however, fairly correct as regards the lay-out, buildings, and temporary structures.

The 'garment' is the tunic with bases, 'canteled' or made with alternate stripes or 'plites' of damask (patterned cloth of silver in a design such as is shown in Figs. 198 and 199) and plain gold, each 'plite' padded 'so thicke as might bee' (as described under Fig. 38) and bordered at the bottom with a wide embroidered band, counterchanged, i.e. gold on the damask stripe and silver on the gold.   The upper part is striped in the same manner, and has a wide collar of miniver or ermine.   The large sleeves of the tunic are also counterchanged, one being of gold lined with silver and the other of silver damask lined with gold.   The rope-like girdle is of gold with a jewelled clasp, and the sword hangs from it on the left side.   The undergarment or doublet is of rose velvet, 'of verie good intaile,' i.e. *cut into* or slashed in the German or Swiss manner.   The bonet of black velvet, and the boots of yellow leather, also have cuttes.   A jewelled collar surrounds the neck and a BAUDERICKE of pearls, emeralds, rubies, and diamonds is worn, prisoner-fashion.   The whole costume is profusely bedecked with these jewels.   Henry of England was mounted on a Spanish charger on some occasions and, on others, on 'a courser of Naples barded.'   'The Courser which his grace roade on, was trapped in a marueilous vesture of newe deuised fashion, the Trapper was of fine golde in Bullion, curiously wrought, pounced, and sette with anticke [antique] woorke of Romayne Figures.'   The Master of the Horse, Sir Henry Guyldeford, led 'the Kynges spare horse, the which horse was trapped in a Mantellet front and backe piece, all of fine gold in Scifers, of deuice with Tasselles on Cordelles pendaunt, the Sadell was of the same sute and woorke, so was the hedde stall and raynes.'

The trapper of the king's mount was of pure gold 'pounced and sette,' i.e. embossed with figures of ancient Roman gods and warriors—with a mixture of Greek detail.   The 'mantellet' of the spare horse, covering chest and haunches, was decorated with hanging straps ending in tassels, alternating with cords and tassels; the complete suit being composed of Cyprus gold.

Francis I (Fig. 228), taken from the same bas-relief as Plate IX, made an equally imposing figure, according to Hall, who goes on to say: 'I then well perceiued the habliment royall of the French kyng, his garment was a chemew [chimer] of clothe of silver, culpond [cutte] with clothe of golde, of damask cantell wise, and garded on the bordours with the Burgon bendes, and over that a cloke of broched satten with gold of purple coloure, wrapped about his body trauerse, beded from the shulder to the waste, fastened in the lope of the first fold: This said Cloke was richly set with pearls and precious stones: This Frenche Kyng had on his hed a koyfe of damask gold set with diamonds and his Courser [a Spanish Genet] that he rode on was covered with a trapper of Tissue, broudered with deuise, cut in fashion mantell wise, the skirts were embowed and fret and frised woorke and knit with cordelles, and buttons Tasseled of Turkey making.   Raines and hedstall, answeryng of like woorke.'   These details are reproduced in Fig. 228, which is made from the Bourgtheroulde bas-reliefs.   The outline of this costume was not unlike that shown in Plate IX, except that Francis wore a cloak, the CHAMARRE similar to that shown in Fig. 283.   The tunic was of cloth of silver, cutte and embossed with a raised pattern in gold.   The bases were of vertical stripes of gold and silver damask, garded and bordered with embroidery in coloured silks. The chamarre of brocaded satin, bordered with pearls and jewels, was lined with purple and gold shot silk. This being caught at the waist by a button and loop gave the effect of being 'wrapped about his body trauverse' wise. The coif of damask gold set with diamonds was worn

Fig. 228. Francis I at the Field of the Cloth of Gold

under a hat. The hat of coloured velvet shown in Fig. 228, but omitted in Hall's description, was, in shape, like that worn by Henry VIII (Fig. 370). Two ostrich plumes were added to it. Hall gives detail of the coif, but this is absent in the bas-relief, otherwise the correspondence is complete on almost every point.

The horse trapper, made like a mantle, was of blue and gold tissue, the 'skirts' embroidered with fleurs-de-lys in trellis work, with a border edged with cords and buttons and tassels of 'turkey making' at the points. The stirrups took the form of leather slippers suspended from the stirrup leathers.

Although many formalities and conferences and much talk were the order of the day, no real benefits were derived from this meeting by either country. It cost an immense amount of money; and it is reassuring to be told that 'good feeling endured among all' from the highest to the lowest. 'The Kyng of England gaue to the Frenche Kyng a collor of Iewels of precious stones called Balastes [Balays, see vol. ii, p. 454], the Sanker [a pendant] furnished with great Diamantes and Perles. The Frenche Kyng gave to the Kyng of England a Bracelet of precious stones, rich Iewels and fayre.'

The grand tournaments or 'triumphs' which took place on various days were open to all comers. No small amount of dissatisfaction was felt because 'from the Court of the Emperor, nor of the Lady Marguerite's Court, nor of Flaūders, Babāt nor Burgoyn came neuer a persone to answere to the chalenge: By that it seemed that there was small loue between the Emperor and the Frenche Kyng.'

'Duryng this Triumph so much people of Picardie and west Flaūders drew to Guysnes to see yᵉ Kyng of England and his honor, to whō vitailes of the Court were in plentie, the conduicte of the gate ranne wine alwaies, there were vacaboundes, plowmen, laborers, and of the bragery, wagoners and beggers that for drunkennes lay in routes and heapes, so great resort thither came, that both knightes and ladies that wer come to see the noblenes, were faine to lye in haye and strawe, and helde theim thereof highly pleased.'

The two Kings, after many affectionate embraces, parted on the 24th June, and the next day Henry and his Court were at Calais. Thence he went to Gravelines in Flanders to meet the Emperor and his aunt Marguerite. 'When the French Kyng and his lordes had knowlege of yᵉ meeting of the Emperor and the Kyng of Englād in the Towne of Grauelynge they were therewith greatly greued.'

So ended 'the last and most gorgeous display of the departing spirit of Chivalry.'

The Venetian calendar gives numerous references to the costumes worn at the Field of the Cloth of Gold, and translations of some of them are set out below.

### King Henry VIII

5th June 1520. 'The king wore a simar of silver brocade, joined with silver cords, from the extremities of which hung beautiful pendent jewels, and round his neck he wore a jewelled collar of great price.' This garment was constructed in a similar manner to the skirt shown in Fig. 252. Later on the same day 'the King of England wore a very handsome and costly doublet of cloth of silver, with a waist girdle and TRAVERSA from the shoulder to the girdle, both of cloth of gold and studded with very beautiful jewels, and a black velvet bonet with jewels and black feathers.' On 7th June, Henry 'wore cloth of very rich silver 'soprarizo,' and a bonet of black velvet with black feathers. He wore a jewelled collar in lieu of a chain, of great value, and a jewelled belt besides, no less costly.'

The 'traversa' or baudericke was a band, usually of jewels worn from one shoulder, across the breast and under the opposite arm: it sometimes returned to the shoulder across the back (*see* Plate IX).

'Soprarizo' or 'soprariccio' was cloth of tissue: also applied to the richest velvet with a pile upon pile.

Later, when riding a bay courser, Henry 'wore a garment of brocade ribbed with crimson satin, and a hat ornamented with black feathers. He is a very handsome king, both in face and figure, and has a red beard.'

On the following day 'the king rode a light bay courser, and was dressed in a very beautiful doublet of cloth of silver, with a hood of cloth of gold at the back of his head, on which he wore a cap of black velvet, with a black feather which encircled the brim of the cap' or bonet—'bereta.'

*8th June.* 'The King wore a garment of ribbed cloth of silver, a cap of black velvet and black feathers, the Collar of the Garter, and a massive gold girdle. He rode a bay Neapolitan courser, on whose trappings and headpiece were a number of bells nearly the size of an egg, and which from their sound were of gold' (*see* Fig. 229).

Fig. 229.
Golden Bell

*12th June.* 'He wore a garment of cloth of gold, and in the belt [1] across the breast was a treasure of jewels, principally rubies and diamonds. The corrugations of his doublet and bases were loaded with precious stones. Round his neck was hung a large carbuncle, and in his bonet blazed a ruby.' This costume was obviously like that shown in Plate IX.

*18th June.* 'The King of England was dressed on the right side entirely in stiff brocade, on the left in russet velvet; and he had a St. George on horseback, with the dragon under his feet and the maiden in front of him; the velvet was diapered with red hearts transfixed with darts, and hands in the act of launching arrows all embroidered in gold.'

A description of the costumes worn by the guards attending both Henry and Francis is also given. 'On the [left-hand] side of the King [Henry] was his guard, 500 in number, dressed' as described on p. 290. 'They headed a squadron of 4,000 footmen.'

### King Francis I

*5th June.* 'The king wore a cap of black velvet with feathers of the same tone, and some large jewels in it very well set, estimated at 2,000 ducats. His doublet was embroidered with gold knots, the shirt protruding from the slashes, and the aiglettes being most beautiful jewels. His neck was bare. Over the doublet was a cloak or chamarre of cloth of gold embroidered, with a small cape or deep collar of the same. He wore white boots.' A description well illustrated in Fig. 228.

*6th June.* 'Next came the most Christian King, on a courser whose trapper

---

[1] The 'traversa.'

was completely covered with gold. He wore a doublet of stiff brocade, with a simar of black brocade all covered with precious stones.'

*7th June.* 'King Francis rode a very beautiful bay horse, caparisoned with embroidery and pearls. He himself wore a doublet of very costly cloth of gold and a cloak of the same material; his jerkin embroidered and slashed was of great value. On his breast he wore sundry rich and beautiful jewels, and likewise on his cap, which was of black velvet.'

On 10th June when entering Ardres, he wore 'a doublet of cloth of gold and silver tissue, and a very superb collar of precious stones. He rode a bay charger, given him by King Henry the day before.'

At a banquet on the same day Francis 'was dressed in royal cloth of silver all slashed, the slashes being joined with silver bosses, and instead of buttons his apparel was covered with the most beautiful pearls ever seen.'

*20th June.* 'The King of France was dressed in cloth of silver, embroidered all over in silver with clouds, shaded with murrey silk, edged with a label bearing the words "Tanquam nubes igne crepans" ["Like a cloud crackling with fire."] His plumes were white with purple tufts.'

On the 21st 'King Francis had his surcote of brocatel striped and garded with black velvet, and on the border were small squares, embroidered in silver shaded with black silk, each square being inscribed with a Latin letter joined to the next by a small

Fig. 230. The French King's Guard, 1520

silvet lacet, a very elegant design; and the letters together formed the word "Reciproce"' ['Turn back'].

On Sunday, the 24th, 'King Francis wore a garment of murrey brocatel, with a hood and hat in the German fashion, with yellow and murrey feathers.'

For descriptions of the ladies' costumes, see p. 214.

Of King Francis's guard it is stated: 'Then came the 100 Switzers of the Guard, in satin doublets of the King's colours, and hose to match, the plumes in their bonets being of the same hues—black, tawny, and white.' Fig. 230 is taken from the bas-relief mentioned on p. 184, and shows one of these French guards. The costume is, of course, founded on that originated by the Landsknechten, only not so fantastic.

A recently discovered portrait of universal interest showing Henry VIII at about the age of thirty is reproduced in Plate X B.   It was painted by Lucas Cornelisz (1493–1552), a Dutchman, who came to England at this time (1521). For further details, see Fig. 370.

Six years later we have a drawing of Henry VIII in an Illum. MS. showing him in state dress, Fig. 231.   This consists of a close-sleeved tunic with skirt of incarnate velvet with a border of gold embroidery.   It is cut very low on the chest showing a placard of cloth of gold; above it the shirt is seen.   The

Fig. 231. King Henry VIII, 1527          Fig. 232. English Nobleman, 1520–30

overrobe or surcote is also of cloth of gold lined and turned back with leopard. The Royal crown is set inside the brim of the French bonet, and a gold and jewelled chain passes twice round the neck; the sceptre is carried.   The legs are clothed in white hosen; the white square-toed shoes, straps, cuttes, and all, are edged with narrow black silk braid.

It is recorded that on the festival of St. Thomas of Canterbury, 29th December 1528, Henry appeared 'dressed in a doublet of cloth of gold with a raised pile and having at his side a dagger, on which he kept his hand the whole time.   He wore a surcote of gold brocade, lined with very beautiful lynx's skins: which apparel, combined with an excellently formed head and a very well-proportioned body of tall stature, gave him an air of Royal Majesty.'

The English noble of the decade 1520–30 (Fig. 232) apologizes for being out of his chronological sequence. He should follow Figs. 233 and 234; but being English his place is after his King whose costume has just been described. Both of them come from the same Illum. MS. dating 1527. The noble's tunic is not so close-fitting, nor is the skirt quite so supple as is shown in the earlier style of Fig. 234; the skirt has more the character of bases. Cuttes decorate the chest of the tunic, revealing the white shirt gathered into a narrow embroidered neckband, headed by a small frill. The close-fitting sleeves are of dark velvet.

The surcote of silk, with turned-back collar, in shape like that in Fig. 234, reaches to the knees. The sleeves introduce a new mode of German origin. They are very full, pleated into the armhole and into a band on the forearm (unseen), and are caught close round the upper arm, thus dividing the sleeve into two puffs. Each puff is cutte laterally, showing the lining.

The bonet has an all-round brim ornamented only by a medallion. A dagger with tassel is suspended from the narrow waistbelt, and both hosen and round-toed shoes are black.

## FRENCH FASHIONS

A French nobleman of the Court of Louis XII during the first years of the sixteenth century is seen in Fig. 233. He is wearing a tunic with bases which are not so stiff as heretofore, nor are they treated in corrugated stripes of different colours in the characteristic German and Italian manner. The tunic is made of gold brocade. The neck opening is cut square, revealing the shirt, and is edged with narrow fancy braid which also continues in a slanting line from the centre front to the left side of the waist, where the garment fastens. Two horizontal bands of the same braid decorate the bases, and a single band comes down the front. The left side of the bases is a flap-piece which fastens in the centre, the waistbelt covering the join. The sleeves are somewhat large, but narrow as they reach the wrist, showing the small fold of the shirt sleeve. A pouch with tassels is looped to the waistbelt.

The surcote, or overrobe, is of velvet without any ornamentation. It is not cut on the true semicircular plan; the side seams are slightly on the slope, and the fullness on the shoulders is gathered into a very narrow neckband and into part of the shoulder seam. A similar gathering of the surcote into the shoulder seam is shown on the busts of Henry VII and Henry VIII, and described on p. 18 of Chapter I and p. 155 of Chapter II.

The tubular vertically slit sleeves of Fig. 233 are also gathered into part of the shoulder seams. The black velvet bonet is of the shape described in Chapter I. The hosen are striped vertically in two colours, and square-toed shoes with narrow backs are worn.

The tunic with bases of a more supple nature worn by the French gentleman of the same period (Fig. 234) is of plain velvet.   It is open up the front
on the chest like the tunics worn by Figs. 8 and 9, but the line at the top of
the neck is extremely wide.   Width across the chest was the mode at this
time and to obtain this effect the top of the tunic was extended from armpit
to armpit.   The neck of the shirt follows much the same line.   Between the

Fig. 233. French Nobleman, 1500          Fig. 234. French, 1500–10

shirt and the tunic is seen part of the placard.   The ornamental pouch,
with its three tassels, and a dagger stuck through a slot at the back, is fastened
close up against the waistbelt.   The surcote is a development of the earlier
garment, and is made of velvet having a gold passement [1] border round its
edges, etc.   It is cut on the semicircle, with a deep collar: the sleeves,
fairly close at the armhole, widen out towards the wrists, and have a horizontal slit at the bend of the elbow.   The customary bonet and shoes are
worn, and in this instance the more usual plain hosen.

[1] In wardrobe accounts and inventories of the sixteenth century, the earlier spelling of the
medieval word 'passement' (gold or silver lace) is changed to PASSAMAYNE.

FRANCIS I

*King of France, 1494 until 1530 (see also pp. 185 and 188)*

Politics often influence fashions, as the following events illustrate.

Francis I, born at Cognac 12th September 1494, was the son of Charles, Comte d'Angoulême, who married in 1488 Louise (born 1476, died 1532), daughter of Philippe, Duke of Savoy, and Marguerite de Bourbon. Francis ascended the throne of France, 1st January 1515. He married first, 10th May 1514, the Princess Claude, daughter of Louis XII. She died 26th October 1524. The King married secondly in 1530 Eleanor, the widow of Emmanuel the Fortunate, King of Portugal, and daughter of Philippe le Beau and Joanna of Castile.

At the time of his accession Francis was considered a very handsome man, but his curious long-pointed nose must have marred his appearance very considerably. He 'had the largest nose of any man in France, except his jester,' Triboulet by name. He was a fearless and fascinating man, of great courtliness of manner, and unbounded liberality. His passionate admiration of feminine beauty was not conducive to a happy domestic life; he was a profligate; dissipation and extravagance were his dominant passions. Immediately on his accession he laid claim to the Duchy of Milan. This brought about his first Italian campaign, which ended in the 'Battle of the Giants' at Marignano, 1515. On the death of the Emperor Maximilian in 1519 both Francis and Charles I (V), King of Spain, became candidates for the Crown of the Holy Roman Empire. The electors' decision was in favour of Charles, and henceforth repeated ruptures—four in number—occurred between these two monarchs. On this account Francis sought an alliance with Henry VIII, and their meeting for its discussion took place at the historic Field of the Cloth of Gold, 1520.

The culmination of the antipathy between Charles and Francis led to the latter's second Italian campaign, ending in the Battle of Pavia, 1525. Francis fought for dear life, conspicuous in his splendid armour, over which he wore a tunic with bases of cloth of silver damask, the Collar of St. Michael, and a helmet surmounted by a huge panache of white ostrich plumes. (A very similar costume is depicted in a French Illum. MS., relating to the Battle of Marignano, 1515; and in this the bases are not striped and counterchanged, but plain pleated cloth of silver damask, with border of gold four inches deep embroidered with his motto.) At the Battle of Pavia Francis's horse was killed under him, and he received several wounds—one in his head, the blood covering his face so that he would have been unrecognized save for his magnificent equipment which gave him away, and he was taken prisoner.

Charles sent him to Madrid, where he spent a year in captivity. The resulting lull in the campaign had interesting results from the point of view of our subject, since Spanish influence in France was practically unchecked, and the fashions of Spain were introduced widely there. The popularity of these fashions grew steadily and spread throughout Europe, though they do not appear to have had any marked effect in England until the reign of Queen Mary.    After a twelvemonth, Francis bought his freedom by promising to relinquish Burgundy to Charles, but, as soon as he got back to France, he broke his word and launched his third Italian campaign.    In this enterprise Francis was aided by a number of the Italian Princes and by the Pope, in opposition to Charles, who raised the fear of God in them.    And not without cause!    The coalition ended in disaster.    The Imperial Army (if it may be so called, since Charles, although nominated as Holy Roman Emperor, had not yet been crowned by the Pope) sacked Rome, to the horror of Christendom; Pope Clement VII (a de' Medici), who refused to divorce Henry VIII, became a prisoner; the Italian League was dissolved: the French troops were expelled from Italy; and France was forced to enter into the Peace of Cambrai, leaving Charles master of Italy, 1529.

The Peace of Cambrai was referred to ironically as 'La Paix des Dames' because the concord of Europe was arranged by two women, Louise of Savoy, the French King's mother, and Marguerite of Austria, the Emperor Charles V's aunt.

Here are some further contemporary descriptions of costumes worn by Francis I.    At an entertainment at the French Court in 1518 Francis wore a surcote of cloth of silver with a raised pile in a design of very beautiful flowers, 'the lining being of Spanish heron's feathers, which are much used here, and very expensive; and his doublet was of very costly cloth of gold; he had no crown on his head or anything but his usual cloth cap' (bonet).

On another occasion Francis wore 'a cap of gold tissue, slashed [or cutte] all over, with knotts, and the lining was of silver brocade; his doublet being of the richest cloth of gold.'    This cap or bonet was evidently in the German style.

A description of some of his dresses in 1520 is given on pp. 185, 188, and 242.

TENYSE (*continued from p. 43*)

Sports kit, even in Tudor times, reached quite a high standard of perfection.

The somewhat unctuous Venetian Ambassador again extols his hero; and speaking of Henry in 1519 says that 'he is extremely fond of tenes, at which game it is the prettiest thing in the world to see him play, his fair skin glowing through a shert of the finest texture.'

In Fig. 235 Henry is seen playing his favourite game.    He wears a shirt, which is similar in style to that described on p. 21, and shorts, or, as they were then called, 'slops' (*see* vol. ii, p. 245)—little drawers, probably of silk or velvet ornamented with cuttes, the edges of which are outlined with gold cord. Shoes of the period complete his costume, for his legs are bare. Henry was very proud of his fine legs!

In a wardrobe account of the early years of Henry's reign, mention is made of two 'tenes cotes,' one of black velvet and the other of blue. This garment was a surcote, but of less ample proportions than usual, if one may judge by entries which specify the amount of the material used: 'Item. Delyuered by the Kinges commandement to Hilton iij yerds quarter of blacke Velwete for a Tenes Cote for the Kinges grace.' These 'tenes cotes' were used by Henry to wrap round him after the heat of a vigorous game.

In May 1527 Henry hurt his left foot while playing tennis, and in consequence was forced to wear for some time an easy slipper of black velvet.

The Racquet shown in Figs. 235 and 236 is the type in use during the first part of the sixteenth century. It is taken from a drawing, dating 1555, by Scaino de Salo who describes it thus: 'It should be like a guitar, the narrow part for the hand, and the rest gradually larger: it should be eleven inches wide at the widest, and one and a half feet in length from the end of the handle to the head; and the face like a small hoop of wood, the inside of which is perforated all round, to hold the strings, which are like the thickest that are put on a viola, along and across it, like a well-made net.'

Fig. 235. King Henry VIII at Tenyse

Rabelais informs us that 'the cords of the racquets are made of the guts of sheep or goats.'

A less expensive substitute was 'an instrument of wood [Fig. 237] called a "Palleta" or "Mescola," made either quite round, or square, in the part with which the stroke is played, about six inches in width, and measuring, with the handle, two feet in length.'

The game was played on a covered court, across which a cord,[1] with fringe or tassels hanging from it, was stretched.

Tennis balls were at first made of compressed wool, but by this time they were formed of 'good leather stuffed with good hair.' Such balls were distinctly hard, as in order to make them bounce they had to be packed very tightly.

The best tennis balls were made of white kid cut in two circles, each being slit half-way down and stitched so as to fit round the ball. The stuffing was of yellow hemp, sometimes human hair, wound round the core and hammered into shape in the 'cup' used by ball makers. Tennis balls of a somewhat later date were also of white kid, cut in four gores and stuffed with hair. In diameter they varied from $1\frac{3}{4}$ to $2\frac{1}{8}$ inches.

Fig. 236. Tenyse Racquet          Fig. 237. Palleta

Referring to tennis the courtly Castiglione (born 1478, died 1529) says: 'Also it is a noble exercise, and meete for one living in Court to play at Tenise, where the disposition of the bodie, the quicknes and nimbleness of everie member is much perceived, and almost whatsoever a man can see in all other exercises.'

(*Continued on p.* 686)

## ROYALTY AND NOBILITY—WOMEN: 1509–30

This part includes dress similar to that worn by ladies of Henry VII's reign, and also the contemporary Flemish, Franco-Flemish, French, and Spanish, both as worn in the respective countries, and as they influenced the English Court.

### KATHERINE OF ARAGON

*First Queen-Consort of Henry VIII, 1509 until 1530* (continued from p. 64)

Katherine of Aragon, Princess of Wales, who had been left a widow in 1502 after only five months of matrimony, married as her second husband the young King Henry VIII, 3rd June, 1509.

---

[1] The net of modern times did not appear until the seventeenth century.

PLATE X B. KING HENRY VIII,
1521 : Portrait by an unknown artist.   Private collection
By kind permission of A. L. Nicholson, Esq.

PLATE X A. THE PRINCESS KATHERINE OF ARAGON,
1501 : Portrait by an unknown artist.   Kunsthistorisches Museum, Vienna
Photo by Mansell

Her appearance has been described on p. 64.   A son was born to Henry and Katherine, 1st January 1510, at Richmond; he was named after his father, and became Duke of Cornwall.   To celebrate the birth of this Prince, a grand tournament was held at Westminster the following February (*see* p. 168).   In the Tournament Roll which commemorates this event, the Queen is shown seated in the Royal box, under a canopy of cloth of gold. In front of her is a parapet covered with a large-patterned scarlet and gold brocade, obscuring the lower part of the dress which was mounted, without doubt, over the Spanish farthingale.

Fig. 239 is a reconstructional drawing of Queen Katherine in 1510, wearing this dress of crimson and gold brocade.   The bodice and sleeves are of the usual fashion, shown in Fig. 241, but the skirt hangs quite plain in front over the farthingale, with the fullness concentrated at the back, where it falls

Fig. 238.
Badge of Queen Katherine

Fig. 239.
Katherine of Aragon, Queen of England, 1510

in a long train of many folds.   The headdress is described on p. 323. The baby Prince died seven weeks and three days later, after which Katherine began to realize that to keep her husband's allegiance was no easy task.   She did her best to ingratiate herself with Henry; and taking the advice of her Confessor, Friar Diego, abandoned all thoughts of working for her father's Spanish interests in the land of her adoption.

The spiritual side of her life Katherine took very seriously, fasting twice a week on all saints' days and during Lent.   When in State attire or in the privacy of her chamber she always wore beneath visible garments the rough serge gown of a Franciscan nun.

Her life with Henry was indifferently happy, but no seriously disturbing factor entered it until the advent of Anne Boleyn, about 1527. It was at this time that Henry resolved to put Katherine on one side and marry Anne.   Divorce proceedings were undertaken, and while these were pending Queen Katherine lived in a state of loneliness at Greenwich, while pressure was brought to bear upon her to obtain her consent to the divorce.

At last in May 1529 Henry could wait no longer for the sanction of Rome. At Blackfriars the Great Hall was made ready for the sittings of the Legatine Court which opened on 18th June. The Scribe stood forth and cried: 'Say,

Fig. 240.    Flemish Noble Ladies    Fig. 241.

Henry, King of England, come into the Court,' to be repeated by the Crier—but Henry was far away at Greenwich.

Then 'Say, Katherine, Queen of England, come into the Court' rang out twice, and into the crowded hall moved the Queen in rich black damask, satin, and sable, supported by John Fisher and three other bishops, followed by a great train of ladies.                    (Continued on p. 264)

The costumes illustrated in Figs. 240 and 241 are taken from Flemish tapestries, and show the fashionable garb worn by Noble ladies of Flanders from about 1500 to 1515.    It is permissible to surmise that both English and French ladies of quality adopted similar styles.

There is some resemblance between Figs. 240 and 63; in both cases the body and skirt are cut all in one; but in Fig. 240 the sleeves are the latest vogue, a revival of that in favour during the last reign: the shape is shown in diagram, Fig. 67.    The front of the body is treated in the usual way.    Sometimes it was edged with narrow fur; but in this instance it is outlined by a band of gold passamayne.    The belt is made on a curve so as to fit closely round the top of the hips and is fastened with a circular jewelled ornament.

This lady has caught up the decorated hem of her gown to reveal the skirt of the underdress, the close sleeves of which show also at the wrists.    A mantle could be worn with this toilet if occasion demanded.    The headdress is described on p. 109.

The lady in Fig. 241 is dressed in much the same type of gown, except that the bodice is closer fitting, and has a border of dark velvet.    The right arm partly obscures the small silk scarf which girdles the waist and is seen to better advantage in Plate IV.    The headdress is a fanciful arrangement of the early 'Gable.'

## THE SPANISH FARTHINGALE

The Spanish 'Farthingale,' Fig. 242, derived from the Spanish word 'verdugado,' French 'vertugale,' introduced into England by Katherine of Aragon in 1501, had its origin in Spain.

Fig. 242. The Spanish Farthingale     Fig. 243. The Wheel

It was a petticoat of linen or canvas, into which bands of cane, whalebone, or steel were inserted horizontally at intervals from the waist downwards, increasing in circumference as they approached the bottom edge. The characteristic feature of the Spanish farthingale was that it widened gradually from the waist to the hem. An ordinary underpetticoat was placed over this framework to mask the hard unsightly lines of the ribs; and the underdress (sometimes visible) and overskirt were arranged above it.

During the first decade of the sixteenth century the farthingale was not obtrusive; but at a later date it became much more distended as shown in Fig. 242, which is a drawing of the Spanish farthingale fashionable during the next decade.

(Continued on p. 503)

### The Lady Margaret Tudor

#### Queen-Dowager of Scotland, 1509–39 (continued from p. 69)

With a series of charming women at the head of Tudor society, it is reasonable to suppose that the fashion gossips of the day should be centred round them and their vagaries. Other Royal ladies, sisters of His Majesty, must not be overlooked.

Margaret, Queen of Scotland, was a woman of decided personality and charm. After she had lost her first husband (at Flodden Field, 9th September 1513) she became somewhat of a nuisance to her own family with her subsequent political and matrimonial troubles. The ten years she had spent in Scotland had by no means lessened her passion for rich and expensive 'gear.'[1]

One might imagine that up North gorgeous raiment was somewhat out of bounds. On the contrary we are told the Scots 'were not behind, but far above the English both in apparel and extensive jewellery.'

Like that of a queen of earlier days (see vol. ii, p. 85) Margaret's wardrobe was more than usually troublesome to her husband, for, when they were crossing the Firth of Forth on one of his expeditions, her baggage, contained in thirty-five wagons, had to be unloaded, ferried across, and reloaded while he, poor man, patiently waited!

Contemporary records mention: 'Item the 25 day of January 1512 to be the Queens, one nightgown 12 ells black fine satin, price per ell 28s. £6 16s.' This was a robe-de-chambre or dressing-gown, fairly ample to require 12 ells in its creation. Later the King presented her with 'a velvet riding dress.'

This first Tudor Princess worshipped fine clothes; and her secretary,

---

[1] 'Gear' was a regular word for any kind of equipment—apparel, armour, household goods. See Letter from Louis XII, p. 209.

Sir Christopher Garnish, in a letter to her brother, Henry VIII, dated 1515, gives an account of a prolonged attack of sciatica which had overtaken the Scottish Queen; and reports that by reason of her great feebleness she is unable to rise from her bed.   Alluding to the handsome present of dresses recently sent to her by the King, he says:

'It would pity any mans heart to hear the shrieks and cries that her Grace giveth, when she is removed or turned; and yet for all that, her Grace hath a marvellous mind upon her apparel for her body.   Her Grace hath caused the gown of cloth of gold and the gown cloth of tissue that your Grace did send unto her by me to be made against this time; and the fashion liketh her so well that she will send for them and have them holden before her Grace, once or twice a day, for to look on them, though that her Grace may not wear them; and her Grace hath within the said castle [Morpeth] twenty-two gowns of cloth of gold and silks, and that notwithstanding, her Grace hath sent for more silks in all haste to Edinburgh and thus the silks is this same day brought unto her.   And her Grace will have in all haste a gown of purple velvet lined with cloth of gold, a gown of right crimson velvet, to be furred with ermines, and three gowns more and three kirtles of satin, and this five or six days her Grace hath had none other mind but ever to see her apparel. I prey God that it may be all for the best.'

In the Royal collection at the Palace of Holyroodhouse there is a full-length portrait of Queen Margaret Tudor of Scotland.   This painting on canvas, seven feet ten inches by four feet six inches, is a copy, by Daniel Mytens, executed by order of King James I of England, from an original portrait which cannot be traced with certainty.   The copy bears a statement that the Queen's age was twenty-six, and thus the original painting was probably done in 1515. It is interesting in several ways.   First, it is one of the two earliest representations of the type of French dress exemplified in Fig. 255 and particularly of the French hood worn in England: the other is a portrait of her sister Mary, Duchess of Suffolk, referred to on p. 212.   Secondly, in spite of the minute and careful representation of the detail of Queen Margaret's costume, so exact that the portrait might well pass as contemporary work, the large size of its canvas, the technique, and the definitely seventeenth-century treatment of the background, assure the author that the copy must have been modified to some extent by Mytens to conform to the taste of his period.

The Queen of Scotland being thus portrayed in the very latest French fashion might strike the reader as unexpected, even if it be remembered that the Queen's grace was passionately fond of fine clothes; but it may be accounted for by the fact that in 1515 Margaret was in England on a visit to her brother, Henry VIII, and there met her younger sister, Mary, newly arrived from France, with a complete outfit of the latest creations.   Whether Margaret benefited by sisterly generosity or merely copied Mary's finery cannot be stated with any certainty, but the style of these portraits strongly suggests that one or the other was the case, although this particular fashion was very rarely adopted by any English lady at so early a date.

The dress shown in the portrait under discussion is carried out in crimson velvet, but despite its French origin a long train has been introduced in accordance with the English mode. The sleeves are lined and turned back with leopard skin, and the same fur edges the sides of the open front of the skirt. The underskirt and under-sleeves are of cloth of gold damask, and a girdle of two strands of gold beads, alternating with pearls and ending in a tassel, descends the front of the underskirt. The Queen wears the French hood exactly the same as that shown in Fig. 403.

A three-quarter portrait of Queen Margaret wearing an identical costume is in the possession of The Queen's College, Oxford. It is supposed by some to be the original from which Mytens made his copy.

The Queen-Dowager of Scotland died 1539.

Fig. 244. The Empress Eleanor, 1503 (*after Pintoricchio*)

## SPANISH STYLES: 1490–1530

A style of dress, illustrated in Fig. 244, was in vogue during the last decade of the fifteenth century and the first and second decades of the sixteenth. It is taken from one of the frescoes in the library at Siena, painted by 'Il Pintoricchio.' The subject is the betrothal of the Emperor Frederick III and Eleanor of Portugal, which took place at Siena in 1452—they were married at Rome in the same year—two years before the painter was born!

Records prove that Pintoricchio was at work on the series of frescoes, ten in number, illustrating the life of Pope Pius II (born 1405, Pope 1458, died 1464) of which this is one, between the years 1503 and 1508,[1] and he has shown the Empress Eleanor wearing the Spanish costume, tempered with Italian influence, in fashion between 1490 and 1510.

The dress in Fig. 244 has a close-fitting bodice cut square at the neck opening, which is filled in with gauze embroidered with gold in lines. The bodice is decorated with a border round the neck opening and down the front, and is composed of a fabric woven in black and gold squares or lines. The ample skirt is of the same material, but without ornament, and is worn over the Spanish farthingale.

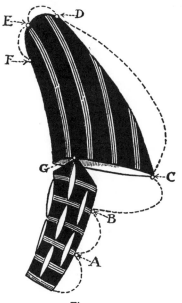

Fig. 245

The sleeves, made in two sections, of another colour, striped with gold, are formed as shown in diagram, Fig. 245, with slits on the part covering the forearm. This section is fixed to the upper part at two points only. The back seams of both sections are open from wrist to shoulder, but the edges are fastened together with jewelled ornaments at A, B, C, and D. Jewelled ornaments are used also to connect the two sections, about elbow level at G (and H inside), and at E and F securing the upper sleeve to the shoulder. Under this is a full white lawn sleeve, which puffs out as shown in dotted line between the various openings and slits.

A bordered mantle of gold damask, rather short in front but long and trailing behind, is worn according to the mode, over one shoulder (notice the turned-back portion), one arm passing through a vertical slit. On the opposite side the mantle is draped over the forearm.

The ornament at the shoulder, the kerchief carried in the hand, and the headdress (described on p. 334) are of much interest.

This type of costume was worn at the Court of Isabella the Catholic. Joanna of Castile probably wore one like Fig. 244 when she visited England in 1501 (see p. 43) and many such costumes must have been included in her sister Katherine's trousseau: but there is no evidence that this style was adopted by English ladies at this date; on the other hand, it influenced to a certain extent the fashions of a later period.

---

[1] This is an instance of the pitfalls which await the unwary student, if he assumes that the costume shown was necessarily in fashion at the date of the event depicted.

ELEANOR, ARCHDUCHESS OF AUSTRIA

*Queen-Consort of Emmanuel of Portugal, 1498 until 1530*

Eleanor of Austria (also known as Eleanor of Spain, of Portugal, and of France), great-granddaughter of the Empress Eleanor and eldest daughter of Philippe le Beau and Joanna of Castile, was born at Louvain in 1498. She is seen at the age of four in Fig. 72. The greater part of her youth was spent at Malines, Brussels, Ghent, and Antwerp under the guardianship of her aunt, the Archduchess Marguerite of Austria, Regent of the Netherlands.

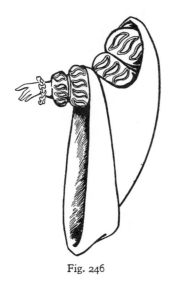

Fig. 246

Fig. 247 (*right*).
Doña Mentia Zenetta, 1529

She became the second wife of Emmanuel, King of Portugal, in 1518 and was left a widow in 1521.

Plate XI is a drawing made from a portrait of Eleanor of Austria, which dates about 1518. The bodice and skirt are made of a rich gold and red brocade. The bodice is cut square at the neck, with a rising curve over the chest, showing a white cambric tucker drawn in with a lacet. The sleeves are an innovation, being copied from a masculine fashion adopted from the Swiss style mentioned on p. 62. They are very full, composed of straps of dark velvet striped with gold, caught together at intervals by emeralds in gold mounts; and are worn over full white cambric (sometimes gold tissue) under-sleeves which puff between the straps, and also in a series of puffs round the arm-hole. Over these are curiously shaped sleeves of lynx, cut as shown in diagram,

Fig. 246. They are fixed at the back of the armhole, and open down the whole of the front, except at the bottom point where they are attached on the fore-arm with an emerald ornament to the strapped velvet sleeve. The entire sleeve is characteristically Spanish, but shows some Swiss influence in the straps (*see* Figs. 246 and 248). The skirt is displayed over the Spanish far-thingale, here seen at its full dimensions. It is open up the front revealing an underdress of patterned cloth of gold, and is bordered at edges and hem with a narrow band of lynx. The diagram (Fig. 258) illustrates the cut of this skirt: the headdress of gold tissue is arranged in the Spanish manner

Fig. 249. The Empress Isabella, 1532
(*after Titian*)

Fig. 248. A Lady of Seville, 1529

described under Fig. 158, fixed to a band of emeralds, pearls, and diamonds over hair dressed as described under Fig. 249. The girdle and other jewellery should be noticed.

Fig. 247 is from a drawing of a Spanish Grandee's lady, Doña Mentia Zenetta of the House of Mendoza, and dates 1529. It is the style of costume worn every day by Noble ladies of Spain during the second, third, and fourth decades of the sixteenth century and is interesting because it shows some details which eventually influenced English and French fashions. Such are the back of the sleeve with its lining turned back, and especially the manner in which the garded puffings start in front of the armpit encircling the arm-hole and descend the full length of the sleeve. The plastron front was some-times repeated at the back. The whole dress is carried out in a horizontal striped silk, and worn over the Spanish farthingale with the folds at the back forming a train. The curious headdress is described on p. 335.

Another Spanish lady, a native of Seville, is shown in Fig. 248, whose costume has many points in common with those already described in this section. The large earrings; the circular silk fan which opens and closes; the sash round the waist and tied in front; the skirt raised to show the chopines; and the headdress (described on p. 335) are interesting details.

A beautiful Spanish sleeve is worn by the Empress Isabella (Fig. 249). It is shaped like the diagram, Fig. 299, but the front seam is left open. The whole dress in the original portrait of the Empress, painted by Titian about 1537, is composed of rose-coloured velvet ornamented with rich gold braid three to four inches in width; down the sides of the bodice front it is narrowed by folding. The edges of the sleeves are caught together with jewels in gold mounts. Two gold cords fixed with pearls at intervals and arranged in lines decorate the white transparent lawn PARTLET and small under-sleeves.

Fig. 250. Spanish, first half of the sixteenth century

The upper, middle, and even the lower classes of Spaniards had by this time exceeded all bounds in extravagance in dress, although prohibited by earlier pragmatics; and in 1515 Joanna, Queen of Castile since 1504, issued a decree forbidding brocades, gold and silver embroideries, and trimmings to be worn at all, and strictly limiting the wearing of silk in any form. However, this pragmatic, like its predecessors, was entirely ignored. The Queen, who had in the hey-day of her married life been accustomed to rich and lavish display in dress, felt considerable sympathy for her Spanish subjects, was over-ruled by the Cortes though digressions from the law were overlooked. The same applies to the young Charles V, whose taste for magnificent apparel had never been checked; so whatever decrees he might issue for the limitation of costume in Spain, he and his Court, noted for their extravagance, were the first to disregard the letter and spirit of his precepts. Therefore it is not surprising that the pragmatics were not obeyed for long, or by any but the middle classes. When Charles left Spain in 1520 the Cortes became alarmed and petitioned him to order that the sumptuary laws with regard to silk, brocades, gold, embroideries, and gold and silver passamayne should be strictly enforced during his absence, since they saw that with such a splendid Court as his, they would not be enforced in his presence. The example of the Court had struck too deeply, and the craving for rich and beautiful clothes had really taken hold of Spaniards. But if he was sufficiently interested to make such an order, it is evident that it proved quite ineffective.

A pragmatic of the year 1537 decreed that the use of brocades and silks, and of gold and silver embroideries, was prohibited. These laws were generally evaded by making gold lace and ornaments separately, and then stitching them on to the garment, a process, it was discovered, which cost a great deal more than actual embroidery would have done. Eventually the making of such embellishments was prohibited altogether.

## THE LADY MARY TUDOR I

*Third Queen-Consort of Louis XII of France: Duchess of Suffolk,*
*1498–1533*

In the National Gallery, London, there is a head-and-shoulders portrait, No. 2615, of the Princess Mary Tudor I, born 1498—and this brings us to the first really interesting Princess amongst those named Mary. She is the fifth on the list of fourteen in the English Royal family, and the first in the present volume. The list is given below:

1. Mary, granddaughter of Henry III.
2. Mary, daughter of Edward I.
3. Mary, daughter of Edward III.
4. Mary, daughter of Edward IV.
5. Mary, daughter of Henry VII.
6. Mary I, daughter of Henry VIII.
7. Mary, daughter of James I.
8. Mary, daughter of Charles I.
9. Mary II, daughter of James II.
10. Mary, daughter of George II.
11. Mary, daughter of George III.
12. Mary, daughter of Duke of Cambridge.
13. Mary, Queen-Mother of Great Britain, Queen of George V.
14. Mary, daughter of George V.

The portrait under consideration, said on good authority to have been painted by Jehan Perréal, is reproduced in Plate XII. It represents the Princess Mary I at the time of her marriage to Louis XII of France in 1514. She is shown wearing a costume almost identical with that worn by Queen

Eleanor (Plate XI). It would be interesting to know which of the gowns included in her trousseau (*see* p. 209) she is wearing. There is no mention, in the official list, of gowns in the Spanish style; but it should be remembered that Royal ladies, even in Tudor times, adopted certain fashions according to the exigencies of their social engagements.

The square-necked bodice, piped with red velvet, is of red and gold brocade. The sleeves in this case are of the same brocade shaped in a similar manner to diagram, Fig. 245. They are wide at elbow level and open down the outside seams, through which the full lawn under-sleeves puff. These under-sleeves also form puffs and cascades at the wrists. A similar series of puffs appears round the armholes. The skirt worn by the Princess was constructed without doubt on the same lines as that shown in Fig. 244. For the study of jewellery of this period this portrait is invaluable. The hair-dressing is on the same lines as that in Plate XI, but without plaits, and a circlet of pearls and rubies is worn in place of the cap.

In the Fitzwilliam Museum, Cambridge, there is a three-quarter-length portrait of a lady wearing a Spanish dress of the type just described. Probably there are many other portraits of like nature scattered throughout the British Isles.

Fig. 251. The Princess Mary I, 1514

In an Illum. MS. dated 1514 there is a miniature depicting the Princess Mary Tudor being received by Louis XII in Paris. Fig. 251 is taken from this source. The Princess is dressed in the French fashion, supervised no doubt by Jehan Perréal. The gown is of cloth of gold; it consists of a tight-fitting body cut square at the neck, the sleeves close-fitting on the shoulders (*see* diagram, Fig. 67) but widening at the wrists, where they are edged with a border of ermine about four inches in width. A narrow edging of ermine about half an inch wide surrounds the neck, descends the front of the body part, and edges the hem of the ample skirt and train, which, however, is not worn over a farthingale. The posture assumed by the Princess prevents the girdle, if there is one, from being shown in the original miniature. It is more than likely that she wears one, as they were in fashion at this time. It would surround the waist loosely and be fastened in front with an ornament, the long

PLATE XII. THE PRINCESS MARY TUDOR, 1514: Portrait attributed to Jehan Perréal
National Gallery.   *By kind permission of the Directors*

end hanging down the front of the skirt. This girdle would be of gold-smith's work, formed like a chain, and set with pearls. The headdress surmounted by a Princess's coronet (*see* Fig. 427) is shown in diagram, Fig. 397.

Princess Mary's trousseau included many dresses of the most costly materials then known, designed in the French, English, and Milanese fashion under the direction of the artist Jehan Perréal 'of Paris' who was sent over by Louis XII to supervise their construction. The results of the artist's efforts so delighted the old King that he sent a letter by the Earl of Worcester thanking Jehan for 'devysing new collars and goodlie gear' for the Queen his bride. The wedding gown was of white cloth of silver, and six dresses were made in the Italian fashion (*see* Fig. 252) in compliment to Louis, who was titular Sovereign of Milan. This style is also well illustrated in the various portraits executed by Italian artists of this period. A further sixteen dresses were after the English mode, and on the lines of those described in the first part of this section. Her jewellery was wonderful, and some items are described on p. 355.

In the Princess's wardrobe accounts are mentioned smocks, night kerchiefs to wrap around the head while in bed if so desired, and, what is interesting at this date, RAILS. These garments were a kind of dressing jacket or 'tire-wrap' put on while the 'tire-woman' or lady's maid dressed her mistress's hair or adjusted other details of the toilet. Elizabeth Langton was the name of Princess Mary's 'wardrobe maid.'

Some excerpts taken from the Princess's inventory of robes, dated 1514, are here given.

### Robes in the French mode

1. Item one velvet robe of purple colour, lined with yellow cloth of gold on satin.

2. Item one robe of cloth of gold decorated with baudekyn damask and furred with ermine.

3. Item one robe of cloth of silver damask lined with crimson velvet embossed in gold.

4. Item one robe of figured cloth of gold in a kind of damask furred with pampilion.

5. Item one other robe of crimson cloth of gold damask of Italian work furred with mink.

6. Item one robe of purple cloth of gold tissue furred with sable.

7. Item one robe of crimson satin lined with green cloth of gold damask.

8. Item one robe of crimson satin embossed in gold and worked with birds' eyes, lined with purple two-pile velvet embossed in gold.

9. Item one robe of crimson double-pile velvet lined with crimson cloth of gold damask in a design of cuttes.

10. Item one black velvet robe lined with ermine.

11. Item one robe of purple satin lined with purple cloth of gold of damask.

12. Item one crimson satin robe embossed in gold of baudekyn furred with Romaine.

13. Item one robe of gray satin embossed in gold in the manner of birds' eyes, lined with crimson velvet.

14. Item one robe of yellow velvet lined with Romaine.

15. Item one robe of yellow velvet trimmed with the skins of black coneys.

### Cottes in the French mode

16. Item one gray satin cotte embossed in gold with birds' eyes.

17. Item one cotte of purple cloth of gold in the manner of camelot (*see* vol. ii, p. 463).

18. Item one other of crimson satin.

19. Item one other cotte of crinkled white cloth of gold, figured in white.

20. Item one cotte of silver cloth of Venetian baudekyn.

21. Item one cotte of gold satin broché on gold in the colour of green birds' eyes.

22. Item one cotte of crimson cloth of gold damask of baudekyn.

23. Item seven pairs of sleeves suitable for the said cottes.

### Robes in the English style

24. Item one crimson satin robe edged with cloth of silver damask lined with black taffeta.

25. Item one satin broché robe on silver baudekyn lined with lamb, i.e. bogy.

26. Item one robe of satin broché in crimson on gold in the new fashion, and bordered with velvet and lined with black taffeta.

27. Item one robe of black velvet bordered with black satin and lined with black taffeta.

28. Item one robe of black velvet lined with marten.

29. Item one robe of black velvet bordered with mink and lined with calaber.

30. Item one robe of yellow velvet bordered with figured cloth of gold in white and lined with taffeta.

31. Item one robe of cloth of gold figured in figures and white tissue, furred with ermine.

32. Item one robe of satin embossed with silver bordered with gold and lined with white taffeta.

### Cottes in the English style

33. Item one silver cotte in the manner of camelot bordered with crimson velvet.

34. Item one cotte of green satin bordered with cloth of gold.

35. Item one cotte of black satin tissue on gold bordered with crimson velvet.

36. Item one cotte of crimson satin bordered with cloth of gold.

37. Item one cotte of purple satin edged with cloth of gold.

38. Item one cotte of white satin edged with crimson velvet.

39. Item one cotte of yellow satin bordered with crimson velvet.

40. Item seven pairs of sleeves suitable for the said cottes.

41. Item one robe of silver cloth in a kind of damask of baudekyn, bordered with cloth of gold lined with white taffeta.

### Robes in the Milanese style

42. Item one robe of green satin lined with cloth of silver damask and bordered with cloth of silver damask.

43. Item one robe of cloth of gold embroidered in circles, lined with green velvet and green taffeta and bordered with crimson satin.

### Milanese 'bonets'

44. Item three bonets, the first of crimson velvet, another of black velvet, and the other of crimson satin.

### Aiglettes for robes in the Milanese style, without laces.   The aiglettes are attached to the robe

45. Item xxviii large aiglettes in Venetian gold and xii small.

46. Item xxviii large aiglettes made of gold and crimson silk and xii small.

47. Item xxviii large aiglettes of gold and green silk and twelve small.

### Mantle, capes

48. Item one scarlet mantle, two capes of black velvet.  Twelve pieces belonging to the capes.

Some of these combinations of colours may appear crude, but it must be remembered that the inventory was made by a mere man—Adam of Windsor —and his descriptions lack the artistic touch which would make the colour schemes seemingly more attractive.

Some notes on the carriages and horses owned by this Princess are given on p. 375.

The retinue of a Royal bride of Tudor times is set forth below and is of interest.

Two ladies-in-waiting, of which one was Mary Boleyn, elder sister of the renowned Anne; five gentlemen-in-waiting; three chamberers or chamber-maids; twelve other gentlemen; three chaplains; fifteen yeomen; twenty grooms; nine footmen; five pages; and thirty-six ordinary servants to attend the suite.

Mary's life as a Queen of France was not of long duration—just three months. In the short time she had at her disposal she managed to see a good deal of Charles Brandon, and, almost before the breath was out of Louis's body,

Fig. 252. The Princess Mary I, 1520

clandestinely married him (*see* p. 176). Their public marriage took place at Easter, 1515.

A half-length portrait of Mary and her husband, Charles Brandon, Duke of Suffolk, attributed to Jan van Mabuse, and said by an expert to have been painted at the time of their marriage, shows her wearing a costume suggestive of Fig. 255 with the French hood (*see also* Fig. 402). This picture is interesting as being one of the first two examples in England of the appearance of this hood (*see* pp. 201, 336 and p. 337).

From this date onwards Mary Tudor I, Queen-Dowager of France, is referred to as Mary, Duchess of Suffolk.

This fascinating duchess lived hereafter a peaceful social life, and on great occasions appeared sumptuously attired. She was present with the Court when Henry received the Emperor Charles V at Canterbury in May 1520, and the Venetian calendar briefly describes a dress worn by her. It was of the Italian fashion and Fig. 252 suggests what it might have been.   This is of silver tissue, having a plastron front to the bodice covered with a network of pearls and jewels; the Italian sleeves, constructed as described under Fig. 20, are also covered with the same network.   The trained skirt, worn *without* a farthingale, is composed of narrow panels of silver tissue bordered with gold passamayne, and laced together with gold cords, the ends being finished off with fine pearls in lieu of aiglettes.   An Italian cap, similar to that shown in Fig. 140, is worn, and an Italian fan is carried attached by pearls and jewels to the waistband.

The presence of the Lady Mary, Queen-Dowager of France, at the Field of the Cloth of Gold is recorded in the Venetian calendar, but unfortunately no mention is made of any of the costumes she wore there.

The Princess Mary I died 25th June 1533, and was buried in great state in the Abbey Church of St. Edmundsbury, but later removed to the Church of St. Mary.   The tomb unfortunately is without an effigy.

Her elder daughter, Frances, married Henry Grey, Marquess of Dorset, who in 1551 was created in right of his wife third Duke of Suffolk (beheaded 1554).   They were the parents of the Ladies Jane, Katherine, and Mary Grey.   Her younger daughter, Eleanor, married in 1537 Henry de Clifford (1517–70), second Earl of Cumberland, whose only daughter and heiress, Margaret, married Henry Stanley, Earl of Derby.

The title of Princess Mary Tudor devolves henceforth upon her niece, the elder daughter of King Henry VIII.

In May 1520 Queen Katherine met her nephew the Emperor Charles V for the first time, and the Venetian calendar gives some descriptions of the dresses worn by the Royal ladies who were present.

*Queen Katherine* was 'dressed in cloth of gold lined with ermine and beautiful strings of pearls round her neck.'   Her whole appearance was probably like that shown in Fig. 239.

On Whit Sunday at a service in Canterbury Cathedral the Queen wore 'an underskirt of silver tissue, and a gown of cloth of gold lined with violet velvet, with raised pile, on which the roses of England were wrought in gold. She wore a carcanet of very fine large pearls, from which hung a very valuable diamond cross.   Her headdress was of black velvet striped with gold, and ornamented with jewels and pearls.'   Here again the dress would resemble that in Fig. 239, but the skirt was open up the front to show the violet velvet lining.   The headdress was very similar to that shown in this drawing.

On the following day Queen Katherine 'wore an underskirt of cloth of gold with a black ground [brocade], cutte and laced with gold and black cords, at whose extremities, in lieu of aiglettes, there hung pearls and jewels, her gown being one half of cloth of gold and the other half of violet velvet with a raised pile, the flowers in relief being embroidered with gold thread and pearls.  Her headdress was in the Flemish fashion, with a long veil and no cap, which gave her additional grace.  Round her neck were five large strings of pearls, with a pendant St. George on horseback slaying the dragon, all in diamonds.'  Unusual, as Queens-Consort in Tudor times were not ladies of the Order of the Garter.

*The Lady Mary*, Queen-Dowager of France and Duchess of Suffolk, attending Mass on Whit Sunday with the rest of the Court, was 'dressed in silver tissue, in strips, after the Italian fashion, joined throughout with gold cords, at the extremities of which were fine pearls as aiglettes.'   (*See* Fig. 252.) At a State banquet on Whit Monday, the Lady Mary is stated to have worn silver tissue, no other details being given.  It might have been the same dress she wore the day before.

*Queen Germaine*, widow of Ferdinand V of Spain, was present at the banquet, and wore cloth of gold in the Flemish fashion.

At the second meeting at Gravelines in July of the same year the Emperor was accompanied by his aunt, the Archduchess Marguerite, who came 'in a covered litter of black velvet.  Behind her litter were forty Ladies and a waggon, and a litter in like manner black.  All the ladies were dressed in black velvet, and they were all young and handsome except one [the Mistress of the Maids] who seemed rather graceful notwithstanding her ugliness.'

### THE FIELD OF THE CLOTH OF GOLD

The costumes of the ladies who graced the meeting at the Field of the Cloth of Gold receive scant attention from Edward Hall, who does no more than mention 'the apparel of the Ladies, their riche attyres, their sumptuous Iuelles, their diversities of beauties, and the goodly behavior from day to day, sithe the first meeting, ten mennes wittes can scarce declare it.'  He also mentions that in one of the many masques which took place 'ten of the Ladies were apparrelled after the Genowayes fashion, the other X ladies were attired after the fashion of Myllayne.'

Information respecting the ladies at this meeting is recorded, however, by a French writer: 'The suites of the two Queens—Katherine of Aragon and Claude of France—were gorgeous in the extreme,' and the writer supplements Hall by stating that the 'English dames wore the richest and costlyest habits, but the French ones arranged theirs with more taste and elegance, so that their visitors soon began to adopt the mode of the country, by which they lost in modesty what they gained in comeliness.'

Little mention is made in the Venetian calendar of the costumes worn by the ladies: thus on one occasion 'the Queen and all her ladies were superbly dressed.'

One reference to *Queen Katherine*, dated 12th June, is as follows: 'The headdress of the English Queen was in the Spanish fashion, with a tress of hair over her shoulders and gown [most likely after the style shown in Fig. 399], which last was all of cloth of gold; and round her neck were most beautiful jewels and pearls. She was in a litter, covered completely with cloth of gold, embroidered with crimson satin foliage, which was also wrought with gold. The litter was open, with certain small gilt columns, like a triumphal car— a very beautiful sight. The horses and pages were all covered in like manner, as also the forty palfreys of her ladies, and the six waggons.'

It is stated that when *Queen Claude* attended a joust on 11th June, she 'was dressed in cloth of silver, the underskirt being of cloth of gold, and she wore a carcanet of precious stones.'

At the same joust, 'the Queens were present; first, came the English Queen in a beautiful litter covered with crimson satin, embroidered with gold in relief [no mention is made of her dress]. Next, Queen Mary in a litter of cloth of gold, wrought with lilies, and two letters, namely, an L and an M joined together and covered with porcupines, the emblems of King Louis (*see* Fig. 37). Three waggons followed, one covered with cloth of gold, one with cloth of gold on crimson, and the other with cloth of gold on azure, crowded with ladies, the rest of whom were on palfreys; they were handsome and well arrayed. . . . Then came the Queen of France in a litter of cloth of silver, wrought all over with gold knots, the horse coverings and furniture corresponding. Twelve ladies accompanied her, dressed in stiff brocade, with many jewels round their necks. . . . Then came "Madame" [the King's mother, Louise of Savoy], in her litter of black velvet, with an infinite number of ladies all dressed in crimson velvet, their sleeves lined with cloth of gold, a beautiful fashion.'

## The Lady Mary Tudor II

### 1516 *until* 1533

The Princess Mary, elder daughter of King Henry VIII, born 1516, now makes her début. In 1525, at the age of nine years, she was declared by her father heiress to the Crown and Princess of Wales. In August of the same year, 'the Princess went to her principality of Wales, with a suitable and honourable escort, and she will reside there until the time of her marriage.' Ludlow Castle was her usual residence.

The livery colours assigned to her are stated in a letter of Wolsey's to Sir Andrew Windsor, authorizing him to deliver to Dr. Butts, 'appointed physician to my Lady Princess, a livery of blue and green in damask, for himself, and in blue and green cloth for his two servants; also a cloth livery for the apothecary.'

The young Princess now bcame another pawn in her father's game of foreign politics, and it is from an illuminated treaty between Henry and Francis I, wherein the Princess Mary is betrothed to the Duc d'Orléans, that the costume shown in Fig. 253 is derived.    It dates 1527 and depicts another style of dress in vogue during the decade 1520–30.    The Princess wears a dress of a medium shade of blue, the bodice cut with a plastron front and outlined at the square neck with a band of gold set with precious stones.    Inside the neck opening

Fig. 253. The Princess Mary II, 1527

is set the tucker, drawn in close with a narrow black lacet.    The skirt, worn over the Spanish farthingale of moderate dimensions, is cut on the oval principle, the fullness at the back forming a long train.    At the waist a long silk scarf is loosely knotted, having tassels at its extremities; and a rosary is slung to the girdle.    The sleeves fit the shoulders, where they are decorated with a line of cuttes in the German manner.    Below this there is a puff with slits reaching to half-way below the elbows, where again the sleeve is close-fitting to the wrist with another line of cuttes and finishes with a band of passa-mayne.    The full white sleeves of the camise show between the cuttes and slits, and form a deep flounce or cuff hanging over the hand.    The treatment of the sleeve is not unlike that worn by the Spanish lady (Fig. 248).

It is curious to find the old-fashioned hood, described under Fig. 151, being worn by a girl of eleven years; but in those days childhood ended early.

Some of the items from a wardrobe account of dresses, materials, and quantities supplied to the Princess of Wales in 1531 are interesting.

'A gown of cloth of silver tissue, the same to be lined with plain cloth of silver; a gown of purple velvet, to be lined with the same; a gown of black tinsel, to be lined with the same; a gown of *right* crimson satin, to be lined with cloth of gold tissue; a gown of black *lukes* furred with ermines—every of the said gowns to contain eleven and a half yards; a nightgown of black velvet of ten yards, furred with coney; a kirtle of cloth of gold, with works and *sleeves* of the same; a kirtle of cloth of silver tissue and sleeves of the same; a kirtle of black tinsel with sleeves of the same, every of the kirtles with sleeves to contain seven and a half yards; six pieces of *pointing* RIBAND and for garters; eight ounces of lacing riband; one piece of broad riband for girdles; sixteen pair of velvet shoes; three French hoods; . . . a night bonet of ermines; ten thousand pins; one pound of thread; two hundred needles' (*see* p. 593).

The word 'right' denotes a pure crimson; and it should be noted that all kirtles or underskirts which are visible beneath the open overskirt, and the under-sleeves, nearly always match.

'Pointing ribands' were the same as points, laces, or FERRETS (*see* p. 442), but lacing riband was used to lace the bodice down the front or back.

After the birth of the Lady Elizabeth in 1533 Mary was deprived of her title and inheritance as Princess of Wales and styled simply 'Madam Mary.'

(*Continued on p. 271*)

## FRENCH FASHIONS

### The Princess Claude of France

*First Queen-Consort of Francis I of France, 1499–1524*

Claude, daughter of Louis XII and Anne of Brittany, was born 1499, and married 10th May 1514 Francis, Duc de Valois, later Francis I, King of France. Their family consisted of:

Francis, the Dauphin, born 1517, died 1536.

Henry, Duc d'Orléans, born 1518, afterwards Dauphin and later Henry II.

Charles, Duc d'Orléans, born 1521, died 1545.

Charlotte, born 1516, died young.

Magdalene, born 1520, married January 1537 James V of Scotland. Died July 1537.

Marguerite, born 1523, married 1559 Edmund Philibert, Duke of Savoy. Died 1574.

A meek and pious woman, conscious of her husband's marital infidelities, but uncomplaining and patient, Queen Claude maintained the tradition of her virtuous mother.

Brantôme says: 'Her circle was a paradise on earth, a school of honour and virtue, and the ornament of France, as foreigners were wont to declare when they were admitted within it; for they ever met a courteous reception; and when they were expected, it was the Queen's express command that her ladies should attire themselves richly, and exert all their talents for the entertainment of her guests, without absenting themselves in the pursuit of other amusements.'

Although these ladies took part in all the Court festivities, they were so guarded in their conduct and deportment, having been kept in austere restraint by the Queen, that they remained (for a while) unsullied by the Court impurities. Queen Claude's chaste example was nullified, before long, by her less estimable mother-in-law, Louise of Savoy, who urged her son, Francis I, to include the Queen's ladies-in-waiting at all amusements and pageantries. Finding themselves thus emancipated from the restraints of former Court etiquette, they speedily overstepped the limits of decorum.

Fig. 254. French, 1510–20

Queen Claude died 26th October 1524.

Fig. 254 shows the fashion in France which was in vogue from about 1510 to 1520. It is the style of costume seen in a series of tapestries depicting Biblical history, some pieces of which are in the Musée des Arts Décoratifs, Paris, and others in the Cathedral of Angers. The bodice is cut to fit the figure more closely than hitherto, and is fastened at the back by lacing. The neck opening is cut square, but it generally took a slight upward curve across the bust. It is edged with a band of gold passamayne or velvet in a darker colour than the dress. Inside the neck opening is seen the camise or chemisette of fine white lawn or cambric drawn up to lie close on the neck by a narrow lacet or twist, usually referred to as a 'corse of silk,' the ends being tied in front. The sleeves are very much off the shoulders, in fact, there is practically no portion of the usual shoulder-piece of the bodice crossing them, the top of the sleeve being fixed to the band which edges the neck opening. The sleeves shown in Fig. 254 are square at the ends like those in Fig. 63 and in diagram, Fig. 65, but the latest vogue was to turn the edges, which normally came at the wrist, right back, and pin the edges tightly round the upper arm

Fig. 255. FRENCH NOBLE LADY, 1515-35

revealing the rich lining and giving a pronounced square-cuff effect. The forearm is covered by a rather loose under-sleeve, terminating in a band edged with a narrow frill of cambric which closely encircles the wrist. These under-sleeves were often decorated with cuttes as seen in Fig. 69. The ample skirt, with long train, is divided up the front, and bordered with gold passamayne. At the waist a narrow scarf of silk is tied in a loop and two ends. The hang of the underdress suggests that a stiff underskirt, rather than the farthingale, is worn under it.

A further development of the costume shown in Fig. 254 is illustrated in Fig. 255. This is taken from a portrait of a lady of the Court of Francis I, and exemplifies the fashion in vogue approximately between 1515 and 1535.

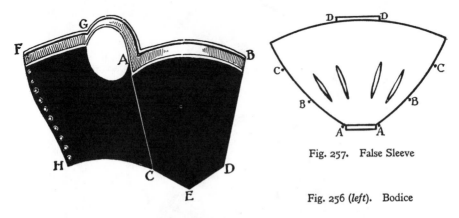

Fig. 257. False Sleeve

Fig. 256 (*left*). Bodice

It is the origin of the fashions worn at the English Court during the second half of Henry VIII's reign, and is portrayed in many portraits by Holbein. This fashion with modifications and variations continued during the reigns of Edward VI and Mary, and until the middle of the reign of Queen Elizabeth.

The velvet bodice is close-fitting, and the method of making it was to employ a plastron front, A, B, C, D, E, in Fig. 256, seamed to the side pieces, which were usually cut all in one with the back: this type of bodice is often seen in portraits of the time, with the difference that in place of the seam, the plastron has its edges turned over and attached to the bodice foundation by a series of French knots. The square neck opening, curved at the top as previously described, is filled in with a drawn-up lawn tucker or partlet. The sleeves are cut on the lines described for Fig. 254. They are turned back to show the lining of fur. Their shape is rectangular, and they are larger than before. The same method of attaching the top of the sleeve to the bodice, as described for Fig. 254, is adopted here, and, in fact, all sleeves of this type in fashion during the period under discussion were inserted in this manner. Refer to diagram, Fig. 256, where the portion GA is the under part of the armhole; the top of the sleeve is attached to the band. The under-sleeve is considerably more bulky and decorated with cuttes. This particular under-sleeve is a separate article of dress—a FALSE SLEEVE—which extended only to the elbow, where it was buttoned or tied round the arm. For the shape of a slightly later 'false sleeve' *see* Fig. 257. The full white cambric or lawn sleeves of the chemisette or smock are seen through the cuttes, and the wrists are edged with lawn frills worked with black silk.

The skirt is cut on the semicircular plan (*see* Fig. 258). The semicircle cut out at the top, which encircles the waist, is considerably larger than the circumference of the waist. This is gathered or pleated into a waistband, or

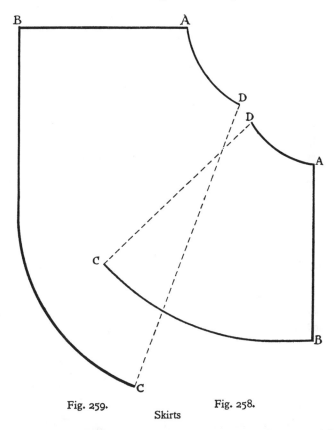

Fig. 259.

Skirts

Fig. 258.

attached to the edge of the bodice. The raw edge of the material of the top of the skirt is turned under like a hem, then folded into numerous pleats from one and a half inches to two inches in depth, the apex of each pleat being attached to the edge of the bodice (Fig. 260). The nearest approach to such a manner of attaching the skirt to the waistband or bodice is in the *organ-pleats* of modern dressmaking, only, in this case, the pleated-up top-edge of the skirt is turned over, inwards, and stitched from inside— thus throwing the skirt out at right angles. In Fig. 255 the skirt of velvet hangs in rather stiff folds. Previous to 1530 it was worn over many under-skirts as the Spanish farthingale was little known in France until that year, being introduced, it is said, by Eleanor of Austria on her marriage to Francis I.

This skirt is open up the front showing an underpetticote of silk, satin, or brocade, and the triangular effect of this is a very characteristic feature.

Fig. 260. Organ-pleats

Following the waist-line and hanging down the front is the rich girdle of goldsmith's work and jewels, with a large ornament at its extremity.

This type of costume was worn by Queen Claude, as seen in her portraits, and by all the fashionable ladies of the Court. The most conspicuous amongst these was the great beauty, Françoise de Foix. Born in 1495, she was married at the age of twelve to the Comte de Châteaubriand. She was enticed to Court by a subterfuge, where the King immediately fell for her, and she there and then became his mistress. The Comtesse de Châteaubriand reigned supreme during the 1520's, and was present at the Field of the Cloth of Gold, only to be ousted later by her rival, Mlle de Heilly.

Court ladies, infamous or famous, Mlle de Heilly or Diane de Poitiers, are shown in their portraits wearing costumes similar to Fig. 255.

(*Continued on p. 272*)

### The Corset

*(See also vol. i, p. 34, and vol. ii, pp. 37, 158, 205, 233)*

At various stages in the development of costume 'small middles' achieved by tight lacing were much in vogue.

The ladies of the Court of Francis I were the first to mould their waists into symmetrical and gradually decreasing lines by means of a low-necked bodice without sleeves, called a VASQUINE or 'basquine.' This was worn over the chemise, and was laced down the back and very tightly drawn in at the waist in order to give a slender appearance. It was made of stiffened material covered with camelot or other silk stuff and often embroidered. On the small basque which surrounded the waist-line was tied the cone-shaped Spanish farthingale (but lately introduced, see p. 199) and over it one or more petticotes, the top one being known as a GRUMEOUR.

Fig. 261. The Corset, c. 1530

During the second decade of the sixteenth century corsets were made of thin iron deliberately designed to constrict the figure. Fig. 261 is a drawing made from an existing corset of about 1530. It is somewhat clumsy, being constructed of iron. Such corsets (or cages) were in two parts, a front and back, and consisted of a series of perforated bands of metal, which could be covered with soft leather, silk, or other material. They were hinged at one side, and the other fastened by hooks, bolts, or sometimes slots for padlocking. These corsets, besides achieving a slender waist, had certain disciplinary advantages, for it was recommended that a husband should padlock his erring wife in her corset, and keep her locked up until she promised to behave herself. Disuse of such corsets in modern times is much regretted by some! Corsets of steel were first made by the Italians, and Catherine de' Medici brought some in her trousseau when she came to France in 1533, aged thirteen, as the bride of Henry, Duc d'Orléans, afterward King Henry II. These Italian corsets were similar in shape to that shown in Fig. 261, but by the use of supple steel the waist was greatly reduced. At once corsets of this kind sprang into favour, and during the greater part of the sixteenth century they formed the model on which the figures of the great ladies of Europe were moulded. The same type of corset was adopted in England about 1533, and continued in use until the 1580's.

Catherine de' Medici's waist is said to have measured sixteen inches in circumference; but that of her daughter-in-law, Mary Stuart, only fifteen.

(Continued on p. 504)

### The Fan (see vol. i, p. 41)

The origin of the fan is to be found in the Orient, Greece, and Rome, before the Christian era; it did not reach the West until the Roman conquests. With the decline of Roman power, the fan vanished into obscurity from these parts, to emerge again in Italy during the later Middle Ages. The Renaissance brought the Italian fan to the notice of western Europe, and it is at this time we find a few references to its use.

The characteristic Italian fan was of the banner type, called a 'ventarola,' as shown in Fig. 763, and was used by married and unmarried women of all classes from the highest to the lowest. This kind was made of different sorts of material. The best had the frame covered with silk and richly ornamented. Others were of finely embossed leather, and the common variety for general use was covered with linen or even paper. All kinds had rigid handles, and these were treated in many ways, from a plain stick to a highly ornamental appendage. The other kind of fan used by Italian ladies of the fifteenth century, and much more beautiful, was that composed of feathers—feathers of the ostrich and peacock preferably, whose quills were set in a long ornamental handle so as to imbricate the plumes in gradations of their natural growth.

An elegant Italian fan, set with a mirror surrounded with tips of ostrich feathers, is carried by the Empress Eleanor (1490–1510) (Fig. 244), and another is seen attached to the girdle of the Italian dress worn by Princess Mary I (1520) (Fig. 252).

At a later period we find the Queen of France, Catherine de' Medici (Fig. 525), with a fan made in her native land and consisting of a panache of ostrich feathers set in a very ornate handle. Oval or heart-shaped fans of ornamental leatherwork manufactured in the East are mentioned in an inventory of her wardrobe made in 1588; these were probably brought with her when she left Florence.

Peacocks' feathers took second place to those of the ostrich, and fans of lesser quality were frequently composed of pheasants' feathers. Fans were made in the West from about the middle of the century onwards.

Of quite a different type is the circular silk or paper fan carried by the Spanish lady (Fig. 248). The material is folded in many pleats, and is attached by a pin at the top of the handle, the 'leaf' itself hanging closed up on one side: by means of a string and ring, or tassel, it is pulled up to form a disc or circle as shown in the drawing. Another method was to fix the ends of the pleated material to two sticks hinged at the top like a pair of modern nutcrackers, but to shut the fan one stick had to be turned right over the top and brought down on the other side of the stationary stick. Fig. 669 shows one of these fans half shut.

(Continued on p. 505)

## UNDERCLOTHES

During the reign of Henry VIII mention is found in wardrobe accounts of smocks and shifts.

One description of a smock states that it was of Irish linen embroidered at the neck and wrists with gold and silk. Small frills appeared at the neck and at the wrists of the sleeves of smocks in general, which became fuller to allow them to puff out through the openings of the false sleeves of the over garment. These frills were decorated with Spanish work or cutwork. Smocks sometimes only reached to the waist. Such garments were worn for ornament, and were usually richly embroidered. They were put on over a long smock of simple design. The corset was adjusted over the undersmock. Petticotes or kyrtles became very rich, especially the outer ones. In the latter part of the reign, when the gown was open up the front, it is reasonable to conjecture that the part of the petticote visible to the eye was ornamented on the front breadth only, the remainder of the garment being made of less expensive material.

## EMBROIDERY  (continued from p. 50)

In the early sixteenth century the needlework of men, both monastic and lay, was as highly prized as that done by women. Pattern books of embroidery and lace, dated 1527, show men working at frames, and these books are stated to have been written 'for the profit of men as well as of women.'

At this time the use of rich and beautiful embroideries was stimulated by the influx into England of French broderers, and much of their time was occupied in the embellishment of ecclesiastical vestments. After the Reformation and the suppression of the monasteries (1537–40), the constant demand of the Church for beautiful embroideries came to an end. Skilled broderers, thus finding themselves suddenly stranded, turned their attention entirely to costume; and the fashion for embellishing the garments of ladies

Fig. 262

and gentlemen of Henry VIII's Court with this type of decoration was again revived, to a greater extent than hitherto.

Broderers' Hall was built in Cutter Lane in 1515, according to an indenture dated 23rd March of that year.

A Broderers' Company existed at Bristol at an earlier date.

Three of Henry's wives were good needlewomen. Anne of Cleves introduced the German Renaissance designs, and worked a good deal in the 'Opus Pulvinarium' style, and Catherine Parr has left specimens of her handiwork behind, which testify to her proficiency in the art.

Fig. 263

### SPANISH WORK (continued from p. 48)

During the reign of Henry VIII 'Spanish work' was the most fashionable form of decoration used at the neck and wrists of shirt, shift, smock, or partlet, both for men and women.

Fig. 262 gives an example, dating about 1530, worked in black floss-silk upon fine white lawn.

Another simple design, into which coral stitch has been introduced, is shown in Fig. 263; this is about the same date. The outlines are worked in close coral stitch, and the fillings in Spanish stitch and eyelet holes.

The beautiful Duchess of Milan (the lady whose response to Henry VIII's

Fig. 264

amorous advances was that she had 'only one head') is represented in her portrait by Holbein, in the National Gallery, London, very simply attired in black velvet, satin, and sable. Her neck and wrist frills of lawn are edged with a very narrow overcasting of black silk (*see* Fig. 264). The portrait was painted in 1538. The frills in Figs. 47 and 48 are treated in the same manner.

Fig. 265 gives an elaborate design, in which the spiral stems and outlines are worked in close coral stitch, the wide stems in square chain, and the veinings in back stitch, an English treatment of Spanish work. This dates about 1540.

Scrolls from which conventional flowers and fruit spring are characteristic of Spanish work between 1510 and 1560. By this time gold and silver thread was often introduced into it; carnations, roses, and other motifs spring from spiral stems.

Fig. 266 shows part of a panel worked in black silk and gold thread upon a

Fig. 265

fine white linen ground; the design is divided into lozenges or squares, each containing a quaint bird—herons, turkeys, eagles—alternating with conventional flowers or formal ornament. This is worked in Spanish stitch; the outlines in chain stitch, with pulled and lace stitches as fillings. The rounds are alternately in gold thread and black, and filling stitch.

(*Continued on p.* 585)

### Stumpwork (*continued from p.* 50)

After the Reformation the type of work later called 'Stumpwork' was revived; but its former ecclesiastical character was deliberately omitted or disguised. In place of saints and Biblical personages, historical and contemporary notabilities were represented. But it sometimes happened that figures of saints were surreptitiously introduced, under the protection of

Fig. 266

'modern' habiliments, as a manifestation that pre-Reformation doctrines were not entirely dead.

Various articles in daily use, such as book-covers, purses, caskets, armorial banners, wall hangings, etc. etc., were decorated in this manner. In contemporary inventories this stumpwork is described as 'embroidered with embosted worke of silver, gold, and coloured silks,' 'embroidered with highe embosted work' or 'Mosse-worke.'

(*Continued on p.* 586)

### Interlaced Work

A very effective style of embroidery is often seen on the doublets and surcoats in portraits of the nobility during the second half of Henry VIII's reign. It was worked in gold braid, cord, or both, in intricate interlaced patterns. Fig. 267 is an example, and is taken from a portrait of Henry VIII. It decorates the surcote of blue velvet. Each band of embroidery is framed with a narrow gold braid edged on both sides with loops of gold floss-silk.

Frequently jewels set in gold mounts were introduced into the interlacing, as seen in a portrait of Edward VI (Plate XX and Fig. 268).

Fig. 269 shows an interlaced design combined with leaf motifs worked in gold bullion.  Sometimes appliqué was used for similar embellishments.

Fig. 267

This design is taken from Holbein's portrait of Henry VIII in the National Gallery, Rome, and is embroidered on the doublet.  The white shirt puffs out through the cuttes in the centre of the design.

Fig. 268

Fig. 269

Fig. 270 is taken from a pattern painted on a beam recently discovered in a Tudor house.  It is given here as an excellent example of the type of design frequently used for embroidery. In the original the ground is a deep red, the scrolls and interlaced pattern are yellow ochre outlined with white, the latter having four green spots in the centre of each. The leaf motif A is also green. The portion at the end is a long white label whereon is a text in fifteenth-century black lettering.

The interlaced work of this period was obviously borrowed from Celtic and Anglo-Saxon sources (*see* vol. i, p. 254).

Costume of both sexes was lavishly decorated and richly embroidered in gold and silver during the reigns of Henry VIII and his successors.

Fig. 270

## Turkey Work

Embroidery worked in coloured wools on a strong foundation was much used in the sixteenth century for 'carpets' and covers of seats and cushions, cupboard cloths, etc. It was a coarse imitation of oriental embroidery known as 'Turkey work,' and akin to 'Opus Pulvinarium.'

In the papers relating to the preparations for the marriage in 1514 of the Princess Mary, daughter of Henry VII, the following is recorded:

'Item iiij longe and large carpetts to cover the flowre of the same chamber' (her bed-chamber).

'Wolle' carpets are mentioned in the same document, which also refers to 'Carpetts about her bedde of wolle and upon the cubbords and windowes of velvet.'

In an inventory dated 1547 mention is made of 'one Turkey carpett with borders at the ends with lions cont, in length vj yerdes iij qrts and in bredthe ij yerdes ij qrts.' From the given dimensions of this carpet it was obviously a floor covering. Carpets were just coming into use, but usually they were used at this time for covering tables, and are frequently seen in sixteenth-century portraits used in this manner. A 'foot-cloth' was really a small carpet, a rug, placed in front of a Chair of Estate, and is sometimes to be seen in portraits of this time.  The floors, even in Royal apartments, during the first half of the sixteenth century were strewed with 'grise' or dried meadow grass.

(*Continued on p.* 419)

## LACE

It is not intended to describe here every kind of lace and the formation of its delicate detail, but merely to enumerate the various sorts of lace in use at the different periods discussed in this volume.

Lace, made of fine threads intricately woven into patterns chiefly characterized by geometrical design, as we know lace to-day, was little used in England during the reign of Henry VIII.  It made its first appearance in this country after 1530.  It was obtained from abroad, and distributed chiefly through the medium of merchants who travelled about the country—the pedlars.

The art of lace-making was known to the English nuns before this time, but its use was entirely confined to Church vestments.

The art had been practised on the Continent at an earlier date, especially in Flanders.  Thread lace and pillow lace were made there as early as 1450; and contemporary paintings by Flemish artists show that it was worn, as an item of ecclesiastical and civil costume, during the latter part of the fifteenth century.  It is said that every country in Europe has learnt the art from the Flemings, but Italy also claims a share in the invention: Venice, Milan, and Genoa were the cities where lace was first made, chiefly by nuns; and there is evidence that Spain was not far behind.  Thread lace was known in the second half of the fifteenth century, but used exclusively for Church vestments.

The proper definition of lace is that it is finished with two edges: one purl (to purl is to fringe with a waved edge), picot (purl loops), couronne (a row of little points at equal distances), or some fancy edge; the other, the straight edge (engrêlure) or footing.

The ground work is one of two kinds: either a fine network (réseau) on which the pattern is worked, or a pattern worked separately and afterwards connected by threads (brides) ornamented and strengthened with button stitches to keep the whole design together.

Lace is made in two different ways:

*Pillow lace* is made on a cushion on which a parchment pattern is laid, the pattern being tricked out originally with small fishbones (hence 'bone-lace'), and afterwards with pins, round which the thread is plaited from a great number of small bobbins.  Pillow lace was made originally in Flanders and in Spain, certainly during the fifteenth century, and perhaps even earlier.

*Point lace* is fabricated entirely with the needle; and at the same period was made in Italy, and later in Spain.  *Italian point* or Needlepoint was also known as 'Punto in Aria.'

It is needless to state that, as generations of lace-makers succeeded one another, many different methods and designs were evolved.

The pillow- or bone-lace-making industry was started in England, it is said, by Katherine of Aragon, who inherited the gift of expert needlecraft from her mother. While awaiting the Pope's reply to her appeal against divorce, and while residing at Ampthill, Buckden, and Kimbolton (1532–6), she spent most of her time in making Spanish work, cutwork, and lace, assisted by her ladies-in-waiting. The Queen also instructed and encouraged the surrounding villagers in the art of lace - making, thus originating what is now known as Buckingham lace.

Fig. 271

After the Reformation the number of nuns—skilled lace-makers — greatly decreased; and, had they been allowed to die out entirely, there would have been few, if any, competent persons left to carry on the craft. Fortunately, some ladies of the great Catholic families, emulating Queen Katherine, saved the situation by taking into their households the few remaining exponents of the art, employing them to instruct their families and waiting-women.

Catherine de' Medici introduced the art of lace-making into France, from Italy, in 1533. This was chiefly the kind known as 'point lace' or 'needle-point,' and 'raised point.'

In Flanders the industry of lace-making was greatly encouraged by the Emperor Charles V, who made it compulsory that the craft should be taught in schools. Fig. 271 is a portion of Flemish lace. This same Emperor was responsible for lace-making being introduced to Arras.

By the end of Henry VIII's reign, lace, in all the varieties then known, both English-made and foreign, was used (somewhat sparingly) for the embellishment of garments worn by the nobility and wealthy classes.

(Continued on p. 420)

Fig. 272

# SECTION II: 1530-47

## ROYALTY AND NOBILITY—MEN

### KING HENRY VIII (*continued from p. 195*)

A Venetian touring England in August 1531 has left a description of King Henry. He says: 'He is tall of stature, very well formed, and of very handsome presence.' He was forty years old and in the prime of life. In view of this statement we may once again call attention to the common error of representing the King as bloated in countenance and stout in figure.

Attractive as Henry's character was in his early days, it became less and less creditable as he grew older. He became very like his contemporary, Francis I. 'Both were arbitrary, arrogant, and despotic; headstrong, ungovernable, and over-reaching; proud, intolerant, and faithless to their word; both tarnished their glory by profligacy.'

In 1536 Henry had a fall from his horse, a serious matter for a man of his bulk, and a year later he experienced the first *mal de jambe*, which became worse as time went on. At the age of fifty-five he became very corpulent, and this, together with his other infirmities, made him extremely irritable, though his troubles were mitigated somewhat by the attention of his 'Kate,' as he called the prudent and gentle Catherine Parr. He was brave, accomplished, learned, and on occasion generous; his conduct and manners were rendered grossly indelicate by his consciousness of being above censure. His magnificence and the estimation in which he was held by other European monarchs, helped to keep in awe the few who might have opposed his capricious and unconstitutional measures.

Although it was absolutely necessary for him (and, with him, the country) to break away from the rule of Rome in order to obtain his divorce from Katherine of Aragon, he died 28th January 1547 as he had lived, a Catholic. 'This man, who began a vain brilliant sensualist with the feelings of a gentleman, ended a repulsive blood-stained monster, the more dangerous because his evil was always held to be good by himself and those around him.'

Henry VIII at the age of forty-four (1535) can be seen at Hampton Court in a half-figure portrait by Joost van Cleve. This is known as the Scroll portrait, because of the piece of white paper held in the left hand, and is considered one of the truest likenesses. By this time His Majesty has begun to put on weight.

The doublet, cut square across the chest, is of gold brocade, cross-barred with pearls, having large pearl ornaments at the intersections; alternate lozenges being slashed in the German manner, the shirt puffing through the slashes. The full sleeves are treated in the same manner. The doublet, without doubt, has bases or a skirt of gold brocade, but how it is trimmed must be left to conjecture; possibly with bands in the usual way. The white shirt of soft cambric or silk is gathered into a narrow neckband of gold, set with rubies and pearls and headed by a small frill round the neck. The gold and jewelled neckband is continued doubly down the front of the shirt. The frills are repeated at the wrists. Over the shoulders is a surcote, but the material of which it is composed cannot be seen in the portrait, only the sable lining which is turned back to form revers.

On his head, now polled close, the King wears the new version of the French bonet cut with the brim and the crown both flat. On the underside of the brim pearls and jewels are set; and on the inside an ostrich plume is so arranged that its tip falls over the right ear. Similar plumes are sometimes found hanging over the left ear. In this portrait the bonet is of black velvet, and from this time onward it is worth noting that the bonet is always black. To its right side is fixed a medallion, bearing in coloured enamels figures representing Our Lady and the infant Jesus.

In all probability the hosen would be of white silk, with square-toed shoes to match.

In the *Household Book* of Sir Thomas L'Estrange of Hunstanton there is an item dated 1533 for payment of eight shillings for a pair of knit hosen for the King. These were probably of thread.

The head-and-shoulders portrait by Holbein at Althorp shows Henry at the age of forty-five (1536), and already his appearance is becoming bloated and especially is the neck becoming very thick. His dress is obviously in the same style as shown in Plate XIII.

In the fresco, partly described on p. 16, Henry VIII is shown wearing for the first time (1537) the familiar costume illustrated in Plate XIII. The doublet with skirt and sleeves is of cloth of gold damask, and the surcote is of crimson velvet lined and turned back with sable.

It is an interesting fact that this fresco, painted by Hans Holbein in 1537, was the model from which many portraits of the King were painted, notably those at St. James's Palace, Petworth, Chatsworth, Ditchley, and Trinity College, Cambridge. These are the most familiar representations of the King, and show him at the age of about forty-six.

Amongst the treasures of St. John's College, Cambridge, is one of the two known vellum copies, with coloured title-page, of the first edition of the Great Bible of Henry VIII; this formerly belonged to Thomas Cromwell, Vicar-General and Earl of Essex.    It was printed partly in Paris and partly in London in 1538-9, and published in 1539 by 'Poyntz & Grafton, Merchants & Printers.    Two Citizens & Grocers of London who suffered loss

Fig. 273. Thomas Cromwell, 1538                    Fig. 274. Noble

and incurred danger in common with Tyndal and Coverdale and Rogers in bringing out the Bible in the Vulgar tongue.'

On its title-page are many figures, including a portrait of Thomas Cromwell, born about 1485.   He became steward and councillor to Cardinal Wolsey, 1524; principal secretary to Henry VIII, 1534; Vicar-General, 1536; Earl of Essex and Great Chamberlain of England, 1540; but on 28th July of the same year he was beheaded.   Fig. 273, made from this portrait, depicts Cromwell wearing a full gown with wide tubular sleeves of rich black silk, bordered with narrow bands of gold, the fronts being edged with sable or marten.   The close-fitting sleeves of the underdress are in velvet of a shade known at this time as 'fig-brown.'   The underdress must be shaped like that worn by the gentleman in Fig. 275, and may be of the same colour as the sleeves.   However, in the original the hosen and shoes are black, so possibly the doublet and skirt are also black but with sleeves of fig colour. The skull cap, shown inset, is partly covered by a black hat similar to that shown in Fig. 371.

This 'lay vicegerent' should be of special interest to jam manufacturers, for he made a present 'to the King's grace at Eltham' in 1532 of some 'marmalado.'

Fig. 274 represents a gentleman in attendance on the Vicar-General, taken from the same title page. It illustrates the type of dress worn by the more serious members of the aristocracy during the last fifteen years of Henry VIII's reign.

The doublet in the original, probably made of silk, is a delicate pinkish-mauve in colour. This colour is frequently seen at this period in Illum. MSS. and in some paintings, and appears to have been a very fashionable shade. In this case it contrasts admirably with the much deeper tone of purple used to represent the velvet bands with which this garment is trimmed.

The close-fitting doublet has the same kind of skirt as that described under Fig. 232; its square neck opening is surrounded by a border of dark purple velvet. Four cuttes on the chest are piped with the same, and the waistbelt and two gards round the bottom of the skirt also consist of purple velvet. The white lawn shirt has narrow frills at the neck and wrists, and appears through the cuttes.

Fig. 275. Noble

The surcote, cut as shown in Fig. 278—longer than those worn by the 'smart set'—is of cloth of gold damask, lined and turned back with sable or marten, and edged with a double band of gold.

The sleeves, full at the top and tight-fitting on the lower arms, are cut as described under Fig. 35. They are of the same material as the surcote and form part of it.

The black velvet bonet has a gold medallion on the underside of the brim, which is also trimmed with a double row of tubular gold beads sewn at intervals. The plain hosen are grey-blue in colour; and the black square-toed shoes are decorated with cuttes.

From the same group of notabilities comes the young gentleman (Fig. 275), who gives an intelligible idea of the doublet and skirt so much the mode at this period; the latter shows the transition from the corrugated bases to the 'skirt' with softer folds. The doublet has full sleeves, and the complete costume, with hosen, is grey (russet) in the original illustration. The material is either silk or cloth, the neck and skirt being bound with a band of deep yellow velvet. The shoes and circular pouch are of black leather, the latter decorated with a gold edging, button, and leaf design.

We now return to the King at the age of fifty-one, represented in Plate XIII, made by permission from the portrait by Hans Eworth in the Dining Hall of Trinity College, Cambridge. The principal details of His Majesty's costume are as follows:

First, a shirt of very fine lawn or silk, embroidered at the neck and wrists with stitchery. Since Henry's neck was thick and short he nearly always

Fig. 276.   Vest and Skirt

Fig. 277 (*right*).   Tassel

wore a small turned-down collar attached to the neckband, but at the wrists there are narrow frills.

The TRUNKS or slops, seen to better advantage in Fig. 235, are drawn on over the ends of the shirt, and the hosen are tied to them by means of laces and points. These garments—two short cylinders fixed to a waistbelt—called 'sloppes' derive their name from slip, i.e. anything that can be *slipped* on easily (*see* vol. ii, p. 245). Hence the use of the word for more than one article of clothing. Towards the end of the fifteenth century the name was applied to mourning robes, and during the first part of the sixteenth century to a nightgown or dressing-gown.

A VEST—like a modern dress waistcoat, very open on the breast and without sleeves—is worn over the doublet. The skirt is attached to the waist of this garment; it is pleated and open up the front and shows a further and more flexible development of the bases (*see* Fig. 276). That worn by Henry is of deep steel-blue silk. The sleeved doublet is of the same material and colour, and braided with silver, set with rubies in gold mounts, and cutte to show puffings of an undergarment, shirt, or lining. The sleeves are treated in the same manner. At the waist-line a small white silk sash or scarf is worn tied in front with one loop and two ends, and a second carries the cord from which hang the elaborate dagger and tassel. One such tassel in silk and gold is shown in Fig. 277.

On top of this is worn the surcote of deep wallflower-red velvet embroidered with gold, an elaboration of the garment which first appeared in Richard III's reign, and which was in vogue under Henry VII (*see* Fig. 25). A diagram of the surcote is shown in Fig. 278. It descends to about knee level; is lined with sable and turned back as previously to form revers at C and D. At this time the revers continued round the back of the shoulders forming a square collar. The tubular sleeves of the surcote have lost their original simplicity in the process of pushing them up (*see* p. 26, Chap. I), and are now made with a large fixed puff on the shoulder, the lower tubular parts hanging behind the arm (*see* G) with the vertical slit treated in a fancy manner (*see* FF). The wide collar and the large puffed sleeves give the effect of very broad shoulders so characteristic a feature of all well-dressed men of this period. Half of this surcote is shown in the diagram of cut (Fig. 279) in which the lettering corresponds to that in Fig. 278. The measurements are suitable for a medium sized man. The half-front is set beside the half-back, and the edges to be seamed together are marked, leaving the armhole, E. The portion having broken lines is pleated into the shoulder seam, leaving sufficient material for the back of the neck. C is the left revers, and B the left bottom front corner; A is the right.

Around the King's neck hangs a rich gold chain suspending a jewelled medallion; and across the shoulders a collar of goldsmith's work and jewels is very widely set. The King frequently wore the Collar of the Garter. The bonet, as before, is of black velvet; but now the feather is little seen above the brim in front as the point of the quill is fixed well back on one side, the end only being conspicuous curling over the opposite side, generally the right.

The hosen are of white silk, favoured by the King as more becoming to the shapely leg of which he was justly proud. The garter is worn on the left leg; and square-toed white silk shoes complete this costume.

A full-length portrait at Hampton Court, painted by Gwillim Stretes, showing a young nobleman, once said to be Thomas Howard, Earl of Surrey

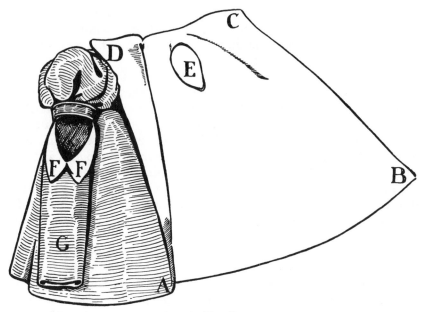

Fig. 278. THE SURCOTE

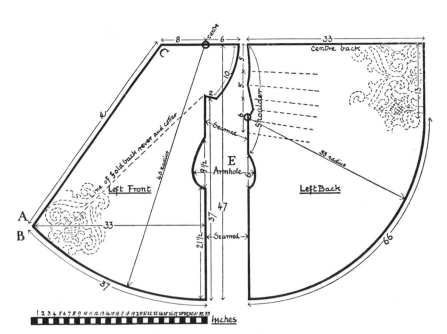

Fig. 279. DIAGRAM OF SURCOTE

(born about 1516, executed 1548), is now supposed to represent Henry Fitz Roy, Duke of Richmond (born 1519, died 1536), a natural son of Henry VIII.

The portrait depicts a costume in the height of fashion during the later years of the reign. The particular interest of this painting lies in its colour scheme — the whole costume is carried out in red velvet, silk, and satin: even the flat Tudor cap is in red velvet, which is unusual. The shirt of white lawn is beautifully embroidered in Spanish work round the *high* collar and down the fronts, and the neck frill assumes the appearance of a very small ruff. The shoes of red velvet follow the natural shape of the foot.

Fig. 280. Noble

Fig. 280—this drawing shows a nobleman of the period under discussion and is inspired by the portrait just described. The doublet which has lost its skirt in favour of a deep basque, is open up the front and reveals the black silk Spanish work on the collar and down the front of the shirt. There is a small frill round the neck. The sleeves of the doublet show on the lower arm, and finish at the wrists with Spanish work to match the shirt.

The surcote is of a trellis-work brocade with very large puffed sleeves which descend only to the elbows. This surcote is without the tubular part of the sleeves. It is lined with silk, displayed where it is turned back broadly on the shoulders, and the lining is edged with two rows of gold passamayne.

The drawing shows the new Tudor cap with the feather curling over the left ear, the well-fitting hosen, often made of silk or even velvet, and the shoes cutte to show the white lining.

Fig. 281. Poniard

This nobleman has an elaborate dagger slung by a cord and tassel to the waist sash. A dagger of the period, but much simpler in design, is given in Fig. 281. The anelace, dirk, misericorde, poniard, and the Italian stiletto are all varieties of the dagger.

Shirts worn at this time were similar in shape to those described earlier (*see* p. 21). In wardrobe accounts of the reign of Henry VIII the shirt (sometimes spelt 'shert,' *see* vol. i, p. 268) is frequently mentioned—'Sherts of Lynon cloth'—and many are described as made of fine Holland cloth garded with lace, and 'pynched,' that is tucked or pleated. It took three ells of material to make a shirt. Henry had 'playn sherts with high collars to wear under harness' [armour].

### Mourning Robes or 'Slops'

At funerals the mourners, both men and women, and the officials taking part, entirely covered their ordinary clothes with long black gowns reaching to the ground and having wide sleeves and often long trains. Over their heads, and above their headdress, they wore ample hoods coming well down over the shoulders.

## FRENCH FASHIONS

### Francis I (*continued from p. 194*)

#### King of France, 1530–47

After the mortification resulting from the Peace of Cambrai, Francis I, chastened abroad, had more leisure for affairs at home. A desire for splendour, ostentation, and show still possessed him, and his ambition, checked in the field, turned to the realm of fashion. He strove thus to outdo his enemy the Emperor Charles, and also that more showy monarch—our own Henry. From this time onward the Court of France excelled in magnificence that of any preceding French monarch. The King assembled around him the most learned, *artistic*, and supremely elegant men and women of the time, such as Leonardo da Vinci, Andrea del Sarto, Rosso, Primaticcio, and Benvenuto Cellini, together with those whose only claim to favour or distinction was the possession of a 'pretty wit.' Chivalry was dead, but gallantry of the new order, combining a satirical view of ordinary morality with licentious practice, reigned in its stead. Women, for the first time, took their place among the men in all the dissipations of the Court. 'King Francis,' wrote Brantôme, ' . . . considering that ladies were an ornament to the court, wished to fill it with them, contrary to old customs' (*see* p. 71). Pomp, sumptuous ceremonial, and extravagant entertainments were carried to the extreme: at the same time the minor arts were diligently cultivated and had an exquisite artificiality of their own. The orgy of luxury indulged in by courtiers and nobility of this King was an amplification of the splendour and formalities observed at the courts of the Italian princes who had lately flourished during the Renaissance. So much dissipation, no doubt, shortened the life of Francis I: 'The Lady-killer is going,' exclaimed the Comte d'Aumale a few minutes before the King expired on 31st March 1547.

The general tendencies of *la mode*, and the causes which were responsible for them, have been well expressed by the distinguished French authority, Ary Renan. The following is a translation of the relevant passages, which are quoted because of the extensive influence which French fashions exerted in England.

'The Court of Francis I was indeed a Court, in the vaguely legendary sense that one gives to the word. Spiritual culture, sentiments, morals, tastes, and fashions had a completely new attraction of novelty.

'One of the characteristic features of costume under this reign was the love of contrast; materials were mixed and slashed in profusion; braids and passements of all kinds weighted them down. The other chief characteristic was the taste for heavy regular folds, artificially obtained by means of a rigid apparatus known as the 'basquine'[1] and the 'vertugale.'[2] These broke the lines of the human body, which so far one had been able to perceive under clothing. The idea of narrowing the waist, and richly draping the lower part of the body in a kind of bell-shape, marks the transference from the old draping to the conventional form of later costume.

'At Court festivals, which were more numerous than they had ever been under the eyes of a King whose taste was all for elegance, women took their place among men for the first time: there was a growing movement towards luxury, which was encouraged by emulation. Sumptuary ordinances gave way more and more to display, for had not the King set the example and given his encouragement? Did not the King give to the ladies presents of complete toilettes for each ceremony, for balls, voyages, hunts? Was not the Field of the Cloth of Gold a ruinously dazzling spectacle?

'The Italians and Spaniards who overran France, and also the captivity of Francis I in the States of Charles V (1525), exercised a strong influence over fashion. The splendid exactitude of Rabelais gives his descriptions the value of a graphic document.'

### François Rabelais, 1495–1555

Amongst the personalities whose fame or notoriety still wakes a responsive chord to-day, is one of the most popular satirists of history: François Rabelais, born 1495, son of an apothecary and innkeeper at Chinon.

He first became a monk of the Order of Cordeliers, and subsequently, in 1523, a Benedictine. In 1530 he gave up Holy Orders and became a medical student. In 1532 he became a physician. He went to Rome in 1534 in the embassy of the Cardinal du Bellay, who interceded successfully with the Pope for Rabelais's absolution from his vows. His famous book, *Gargantua et*

---

[1] The corset.        [2] The farthingale.

*Pantagruel,* was begun in 1532; and in chapter viii, 'How they apparelled Gargantua,' will be found a graphic description of the costume worn at this period. Later, Rabelais was Canon of Saint-Maur and Curé of Meudon, dying in 1555.

The following from the above-mentioned book refers to the costumes worn by nobles at the Court of Francis I:

'Their chausses were of "Estamine" or "Tamine," a woollen material in scarlet ingraine, white or black. Their BREECHES were of velvet, of the same colour as their chausses, or very near, embroidered and cutte according to their fancy. The pourpoints were of cloth of gold, cloth of silver, velvet, satin, damask, taffeta of the same colours, cutte, embroidered, and suitably trimmed. The points or aiglettes were of enamelled gold, and the laces of silk in corresponding colours. The surcotes were of cloth of gold, or silver, tissue, velvet, and all embroidered. These robes or costumes were every whit as costly as those of the ladies. Their girdles were of silk of the colour of the pourpoints. Every one had a beautiful sword by his side, the hilt and handle whereof were gilt, and the scabbard of velvet, of the colour of the breeches, with the chape of gold and goldsmith's work. The dagger was the same. Their bonets were of black velvet, adorned with jewels and buttons of gold. Upon them they wore a white plume most prettily and Mignon-like, gracefully parted by so many rows of gold spangles [studded up the quill and flecked with spangles] at the end whereof hung dangling in a more sparkling resplendency fair rubies and emeralds. Take note of the bonets; some are smooth, some hairy, others are covered with velvet, others with taffeta, others with satin.

The portrait of Francis I by Jean Clouet in the Louvre, from which Plate VII B is drawn, shows the height of French fashion of the 1520's. This type of costume, made familiar by this artist's portraits, was not monopolized by the King, since it was worn, with numerous variations, by all noblemen and courtiers during the remainder of his reign.

It will be recognized that the slashings and puffings with which this costume is decorated have their origin in the eccentric styles adopted by the Swiss Landsknechten (Plate VII A). A full description is as follows:

The fine lawn shirt, the embroidered edge worked with much stitchery, is seen at the neck: covering the shirt is the pourpoint cut very low and wide at the neck, and composed of a striped material—white satin embroidered with gold, alternating with closely set black velvet bands edged and striped with gold. The very large puffed sleeves are of the same materials. Down the centre front of the pourpoint, and of the sleeves, there are openings through which the white taffeta lining is drawn out in puffs, kept in place by gold aiglettes at intervals. A close-fitting sleeveless vest very much open in front was often worn over the pourpoint and fastened only in front at the waist.[1]  This opening gave a very broad effect to the chest and was much in favour on that account.  In an alternative arrangement a pleated skirt was attached to the vest as shown in Fig. 276 and described under Plate XIII.

The word 'breeches' makes its first appearance in this work in vol. i, p. 157.  It occurs in Wycliff's translation (1378) of Genesis iii. 7, from which it passed into the famous 'Breeches Bible,' printed at Geneva in 1560. In earlier inventories the word is spelt 'brytches' or 'breche'; by this time it was passing into general use.  These breeches, or, as they were called in French, HAUTS-DE-CHAUSSES, were very elaborate.  They were known

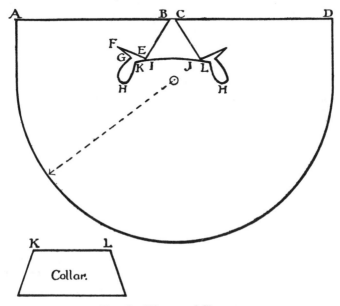

Fig. 282. Diagram of Chamarre

also as TONNELETS.  The Italian name CANNONI was given to breeches reaching from waist to knee, while very short ones were known in French as CULOT.

In Plate VII B the right thigh is encased in a tonnelet made up of horizontal bands of white silk edged with gold and decorated with a series of cuttes. Under these is a lining of purple taffeta which projects beneath the cuttes and puffs between the bands.  The left thigh is treated in much the same manner but the bands of gold are arranged spirally over the turquoise blue. Each of the tonnelets is joined to the hip portion of rose colour, which in this case matches the vest, and is decorated with cuttes pulled out with white.

Hauts-de-chausses were, without doubt, made up upon a foundation, with all these puffs and slashes arranged on it, and were drawn on in the same manner as a pair of close-fitting breeches.  The tops were fastened by hooks

[1] This vest evidently took the place of modern braces and helped to support the haut-de-chausses or skirt.

to the waist part of the vest or pourpoint, the junction being masked by a narrow belt.   The hosen of silk are different, the right being purple, the left striped black and white.   Garters of gold are bound round the leg below the knee, crossed and entwined at the back, brought round above the knee, one tied in front, the other behind.

Over this close-fitting body garment is placed the surcote of cloth of gold (or velvet) with an embroidered border and lined with turquoise-blue silk or satin.   This surcote is of almost the same shape as that worn by Fig. 234, except that the collar is a little different.   It was called in French a 'chamarre.' A diagram of this surcote is given in Fig. 282.   The distances AB–CD are the two fronts, and each measures about thirty-six inches.   The points B and C turn back and form the revers.   FE is gathered into FG.   HH are the armholes. I and J are on the back, where an external box-pleat is formed out of part of the material of the back, reducing it to the width of the top of the turned-back collar, shown at K and L.   The collar is joined to the surcote here.   The sleeves, shaped like that upon the right arm of the gentleman in Fig. 234, but without the horizontal slit, are inserted at the armholes HH.   The construction of the surcote is then complete.   In Plate VII B the edges of the sleeves are turned back to just beneath the shoulder, showing more of the lining than of the outside of the sleeve, and the border is also turned back to show the embroidery.

The bonet has its brim cut from a larger sector of a circle than hitherto, the effect of which is that it slopes outwards rather more than formerly from the head to the top edge (see Fig. 359 B).   The underside of the brim is decorated with jewels and pearls.   Between the flat crown and the brim a small ostrich feather is set so that its edge is just visible, the end of the feather dipping on the right side.   The quills of such plumes were frequently ornamented with gold spangles, pearls, or diamonds, and the plume itself flecked with gold.   A close-fitting cap, sometimes plain but more usually jewelled, follows the natural line of the head and is worn beneath the bonet.   A pendant is hung from a jewelled collar, and a sword is slung from the waistbelt. Fashionable square-toed shoes of gold, with strap over the instep, complete this costume.

In 1532 'the Frenche Kyng caused two gownes to be made of white velvet, pricked with gold of damaske, and the capes and vestes were of frettes of whipped gold of damaske very riche; whiche two gounes he sent to the Kyng of Englande, praying hym to choose the one, and to weare it for his sake, whiche gladly tooke it, and so that Tewesdaie, the twoo Kynges were both in one suite.'

In Plate XIV we see Francis on horseback in a costume very similar to that shown in Plate VII B.   The only real difference is, that in Plate XIV he is wearing a pleated skirt over his tonnelets.

This portrait is reproduced chiefly on account of the horse furniture, showing as it does the transition from the housing seen in Fig. 228, to the saddle-cloth.   This, as well as the reins, breastband, and breeching or crupper,

PLATE XIV. FRANCIS I, KING OF FRANCE: Portrait by an unknown artist
Chantilly.   *Photo by Mansell*

are of blue velvet powdered with golden fleurs-de-lys; all of these are profusely decorated with silken tassels of gold or blue. The method of tying up the tail, like a skein of wool, should be noticed.

Another equestrian portrait of Francis I, useful for the study of horse furniture, is No. 5962 in the Louvre. The King is in armour, with bases of rose-coloured velvet and gold: the trappings of the French hackney, cream with black points, are of the same coloured velvet in a very beautiful design of open work, with long pendent tassels.

In a miniature in a French Illum. MS. Francis I is represented enthroned, and surrounded by dignitaries of the realm. This is probably the earliest illustration to show a French King wearing a Royal mantle in the particular manner which it depicts. The garment is draped in exactly the same way as that shown in Fig. 553, vol. ii; namely, by fastening it on the right shoulder, so exposing the right side of the figure from shoulder to foot. On the left side the mass of material is draped over the shoulder, leaving the left arm free. The mantle is cut as a complete circle, or perhaps oval; and, in the miniature under discussion, it is of blue velvet (and sometimes purple velvet), powdered with gold fleurs-de-lys, and lined throughout with ermine. Over it is worn

Fig. 283. A French Noble

a cape of the same fur. Later portraits of kings of France [1] and of other European sovereigns show the royal mantle worn in this fashion.

The noble (Fig. 283) is in the fashion contemporary with Francis I (Plate VII B). The lines of the upper part of the underdress are the same, and the decoration is entirely Swiss in character. To the vest a skirt is attached, and is of the same material. The chief object of interest is the cloak, surcote, or 'chamarre,' a garment which at first sight might appear to be more elaborate than it is. Fig. 284 gives a diagram of its shape. It is a square, AD FG, measuring eighty-four inches approximately: and cut up the front, BC, and

[1] The State portraits of Louis XIV, XV, and XVI show these monarchs thus apparelled, and are familiar to most people.

again at right angles like a T, the front portions IJ forming revers. A box pleat is made in the back, and an oblong collar about twelve inches by thirty inches is attached along the full length of the opening as seen in the dotted

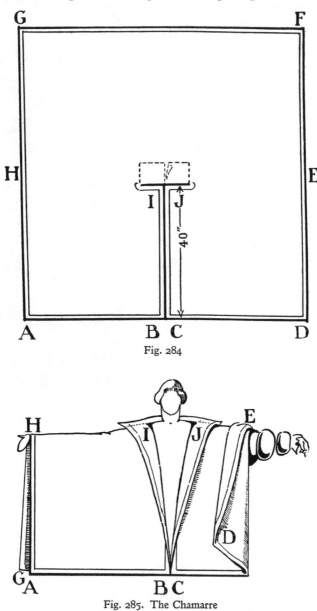

Fig. 284

Fig. 285. The Chamarre

line. When this was placed on the shoulders, the fronts, IJ, were turned back and worn open and wide, and with the collar gave breadth to the shoulders, an effect much desired by the well dressed throughout Europe. The manner in which the ends of the square E and H were turned back over the full sleeves of the pourpoint is best understood by referring to Fig. 285.

Very beautiful materials were used for this cloak and lining, and a rich passamayne surrounded all the edges *both inside and out.*

### THE EMPEROR CHARLES V, 1530 *until* 1547 *(continued from p. 182)*

On the 24th February 1530 Charles was crowned at Bologna by Pope Clement VII as the Emperor Charles V—the last Holy Roman Emperor to be crowned by a Pope.

His appearance in manhood, on his own admission, was by nature ugly. But as the artists who painted his likeness rarely flattered him, he once remarked that he agreeably disappointed those who, only knowing him from his portraits, expected to find a plainer man. His portraits show him with the same fair complexion, brown eyes, and hair, with wavy beards on the upper lip, and close curled on the chin. In bearing, Charles had a great sense of Imperial dignity despite the fact that he was a small man. He was, we are told, endowed with common sense and prudence. Modest and simple in his tastes, he had the greatest admiration for children, animals, and all the beautiful things of Nature. His economy with regard to his own person will be alluded to hereafter. He was a great reader, and as a connoisseur of painting he insisted on the pre-eminence of Titian's art

Fig. 286. Charles V in Coronation Robes, 1530

in portraiture. Music had been his passion since childhood. The Imperial choir was the best in Europe, and it accompanied him wherever he went,

Fig. 287. THE EMPEROR CHARLES V, 1533. After Titian

whether at state functions or on the battlefield.    In secular music his tastes were sentimental, his favourite song being *Mille Regrets*.    Charles is to be congratulated—he knew his faults and owned to them.    Obstinacy, waste of personal energy on unnecessary detail, and gluttony seem to have been his worst characteristics; yet despite these failings he was indefatigable in business, diplomatic, and far-sighted.    Of great military genius, he was never so happy, so well, or so genial, as when leading his armies.

For his coronation in 1530 Charles V made his public entry into Bologna wearing complete armour of steel, damascened with gold, and over it bases of gold brocade.    The Imperial eagle surmounted his helmet, and the Collar of the Golden Fleece was about his neck.    He was mounted upon a beautiful Spanish genet, a dark bay, caparisoned with gold, with the Imperial eagle in black embroidered on both sides of the front and back housings.  A canopy of gold was borne over him by four noblemen in complete armour, and by his stirrup went twenty-five boys of good family chosen as pages by the city of Bologna. He was followed by twenty-four young gentlemen of Bologna dressed in golden-yellow velvet and mounted on choice Turkish horses.

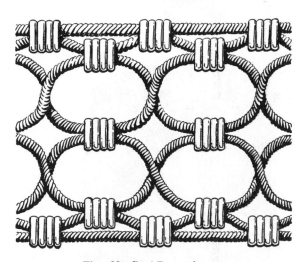

Fig. 288. Cord Decoration

The Emperor's coronation robes (Fig. 286) consisted of a dalmatic of heavy gold brocade in a large Renaissance pattern, over an alb of white silk.    Above the dalmatic was placed the lorum, which, seen from the front, forms an elongated X.    This effect was achieved by placing the lorum round the neck and shoulders like a stole and crossing the long ends at the waist, where they were secured by ties or pins.    It was composed of very rich material, usually cloth of gold or cloth of gold damask embellished with pearls and precious stones.    The Imperial eagle surrounded by jewels was an important feature of the decoration.    A semicircular mantle suspended over the shoulders was made of cloth of gold, the Imperial eagle being displayed over its whole surface: it was lined with silk, usually red.    Above the mantle was an ermine cape, fastened by an immense gold and jewelled brooch.    The Order of the Golden Fleece was worn, and an elaborate sceptre and orb with a high standing cross were carried.    The Imperial crown is described on p. 349.

Simon Bening of Bruges painted a miniature of the Emperor in full robes of the Golden Fleece in the 'Status de l'Ordre du Toison d'Or.'

Titian's first portrait of Charles V was painted at Bologna in 1533, and shows him in full armour. In the same year Titian painted another portrait of the Emperor, reproduced in Fig. 287, and considered 'one of Titian's triumphs; it ranks among the greatest portraits of the world.' He is wearing a dress of the French fashion as described under Plate VII B. His jerkin is of cloth of gold, with borders of interlaced design embroidered in gold. The high neck is finished with a small frill of white lawn. The Badge of the Golden Fleece is suspended from a double chain surrounding the neck. From a narrow waist-belt hangs a dagger, with a large tassel attached to it, the top part in filigree gold, the fringe in white silk.

Fig. 289. The Emperor Charles V, 1545
(*after Titian*)

The sleeves of the doublet, unseen except through the small opening in the front of the jerkin, are of white satin striped with narrow gold, made in a series of puffed panes which correspond in manner with the tonnelets. *Tall hosen* of white silk are drawn up over the latter and turned down at the top, and white shoes are worn. The surcote is not so fantastic in shape as that worn by Francis I (Plate VII B), being cut smaller than a semicircle. It is of white damask, lined and turned back with sable, and has large puffed sleeves banded with a novel ornamentation (Fig. 288) of gold cords passed through groups of four rings. A black velvet bonet with small white plume completes this dignified dress. A feature of this portrait, now in the Prado, Madrid, is the large hound who peers anxiously into his master's face. A greyhound seems to have been a very usual companion to a nobleman at this time according to Illum. MSS and portraits.

About twelve years later Titian painted the three-quarter portrait of the Emperor now in the Civic Museum, Verona. Fig. 289 is made from this portrait. It shows him wearing a surcote of black velvet with small puffed short sleeves, lined and turned back with black satin. Two bands of black velvet outline the edge. A black velvet doublet having a white turned-down collar is worn. Hosen and shoes were, in all probability, black. The cap, like Fig. 359 B, is undecorated, and brown leather gloves and a white tasselled handkerchief are carried. (*Continued on p.* 400)

## James V

### *King of Scotland, 1512–42*

Fig. 290 is drawn from a portrait of James V of Scotland, painted about 1540. He was born in 1512, and ascended the throne at the age of eighteen months. After Flodden, his mother ruled over the Scots in his name, and won over the country to the English side; but as he grew up he became a thorn in the side of his Uncle Henry. In 1537 he married Magdalene, daughter of the French King, who died the same year. His second wife was also a French lady, Mary, daughter of Claude, Duc de Guise, and widow of Louis d'Orléans, Duc de Longueville. Their daughter Mary was born in 1542 while the King was sulking in bed; six days later he died, it is said, of melancholy. Her mother and the Earl of Arran then acted as Regents for the little Queen Regnant.

James V left several natural sons, among them James, who proved to be his half-sister's most dangerous enemy. In 1562 the title of Earl of Moray was given him, and was confirmed in 1563 by the Queen in a new charter. On Mary's abdication in 1567 he acted as Regent for her little son, James VI, born 1566. Moray was murdered at Linlithgow in 1569, old style.

The costume (Fig. 290) worn by James V is more elaborate than one would expect. It has a decided French touch, which is accounted for by the fact that his sympathies and both his wives were French. The surcote with full sleeves is decorated with bands of gold passamayne, having large cuttes with brocade puffed through in a somewhat artificial manner: the turned-back revers are set with pearls: under this is a jerkin of white, cut vertically in five places, and worn over an undergarment of brocade. The narrow basque tapers to points in front, the corners overlapping; all the edges are bound with bullion. The nether garments match the sleeves, but little of them is seen in the original. The flat cap of black velvet, shaped like Fig. 359 B, has aiglettes underneath the brim, and a large black plume on the right side.

In 1534, James had received the Golden Fleece from the Emperor Charles V. Not to be outdone, Francis I conferred the Order of St. Michael upon him, and the following year Henry VIII created him a Knight of the Garter. So many coveted Orders must have turned the head, even of a Scot, as he soon conceived the idea of reviving the ancient Order of the Thistle or St. Andrew. This was in 1540; and he is evidently very proud of this achievement, since in his portrait he is fondly fingering the Badge hung from the Collar. As shown in Fig. 291, this is composed of thistles, sixteen in number, and leaves linked together:[1] they appear to be mounted on a shaped black velvet band. The Badge or Jewel is of gold enamelled with the figure of St.

[1] Later, bunches of rue sprigs alternated with the thistles.

Fig. 290. KING JAMES V OF SCOTLAND, 1540

Andrew holding the cross of his martyrdom in silver on a blue ground, surrounded by rays of gold, within a border bearing the motto. When the Badge was worn alone it was hung from a dark green riband.

It is interesting to find a record of HIGHLAND DRESS at this early date, 1538. When James V went hunting, we are told, he wore a short 'heland' coat of velvet in various colours lined with green taffeta; hose of 'heland tertane,' and 'heland sarkis' of Holland cloth. No further description is forthcoming so we must imagine the shape of the complete costume. The coat and hose, according to the national custom, were striped down and across—tarstin (*see* vol. i, p. 12 note), and the highland shirt or sarkis of Holland cloth were doubtless embroidered. A general practice was to dip or smear a shirt in wax, tallow, and even tar, to make it dampproof. The dress of a Scottish nobleman of a later date is given in Fig. 615. The ordinary highlander wore coats of skin, and his appearance would be something like Fig. 124 (vol. i), only in place of military equipment he would wear a skin coat over his striped tunic or shirt, with a bonet of fur or cloth.

Fig. 291. Collar & Badge of St. Andrew

For the state robes worn by Henry VIII in the later years of his reign miniatures in documents of the period furnish us with all details. The King in full state is also represented in the painting of the Barber-Surgeons. This picture was begun by Holbein and painted to commemorate the union of the Barbers' Company with the Guild of Surgeons in 1540. It was finished by Hans Eworth. In all these representations the King wears the same kind of doublet with sleeves and skirt as in most of his later portraits, but without the surcote. In place of the latter he wears an ample semicircular mantle. In some miniatures this is shown of velvet, in others of gold brocade. In each case the mantle is lined throughout with ermine, having a hood and cape part of the same fur. The usual bejewelled black velvet bonet is worn surmounted by the Royal crown with two arches.

Fig. 292 is a drawing composed of details taken from some of these miniatures, and shows the regal dress worn by Henry VIII during the period 1530 to 1547.

Fig. 292. KING HENRY VIII, 1543

The King is seated upon a chair similar in shape to that shown in Fig. 215, probably gilded and upholdered in cloth of gold or crimson velvet. The dorsal is of crimson velvet, with the Royal Arms of England, crowned and supported by a greyhound argent and a dragon gules, embroidered upon it. The canopy or 'sparver' is edged with a valence of the same coloured velvet outlined and tasselled with gold.

The robe worn by the King reaches to the feet and is of cloth of gold with sleeves measuring about twenty inches round and edged with ermine at the wrists. The caped hood is of the same material and fur. Over all is the Royal mantle of rich blue or purple velvet, made in a complete circle or oval, lined throughout with white silk or ermine, and draped across the knees in the orthodox manner.[1] The crown, sceptre, and orb are the usual regalia.

Onwards from 1540 Henry's costume changed but slightly. This cannot be said of his figure. In 1542, when he was fifty, it was written, 'he is already very stout and daily growing heavier, he seems very old and grey.' Henry's bulk eventually became enormous, so that 'three of the biggest men that could be found could get inside his doublet.'

The King is represented at a little earlier date in a portrait by Hoorenbault now at Warwick Castle. There was a similar portrait hanging over the door of the Cartoon Gallery at Knowle, and another is in the National Portrait Gallery, London (No. 496). In 1933 a portrait of Henry VIII was brought to light at Castle Howard. In all these paintings the King is shown decidedly stouter, and he grasps a staff, which he constantly used when in middle age. Fig. 293 is a composite drawing made from these portraits in which the costume answers the description given by Edward Hall in 1540. It is as follows:

'His persone was apparelled in a coate of purple velvet, somewhat made lyke a frocke, all over enbrodered with flat gold of damaske with small lace mixed betwene of the same gold, and other laces of the same so goyng trauerse wyse, that the ground lytle appered: about whyche garment was a rych garde very curiously enbrodered, the sleves and brest were cut lyned with cloth of golde, and tyed together with great buttons of Diamonds, Rubyes, and Orient Perle, his swoorde and swoorde gyrdle adorned with stones and especiall Emerodes, his night cappe garnished with stone, but his bonet was so ryche of Iuels that few men could value them. Besyde all this he ware in baudricke wyse a collar of such Balystes and Perle that few men ever saw the lyke.'

The collar of 'Balystes' or pink rubies was worn over one shoulder and under the opposite arm — baldrick-wise. The 'coate . . . somewhat made lyke a frocke' mentioned above was a straight loose garment cut slightly on the semicircular plan and fitted close on the shoulders, becoming wider as it descended: to what length is uncertain, as all these

---

[1] In miniatures of earlier Illum. MSS., kings seated in Royal robes nearly always have the mantle arranged over the knees in this manner.

Fig. 293. KING HENRY VIII, 1544

portraits show only three-quarters of the figure; however, one conjectures that it reached to mid-calf.    The narrow tubular sleeves were set in the armhole without the usual large puffs, which gave the effect of very sloping shoulders in definite contrast to the wide shoulders recently (p. 239) described.    These sleeves were slit horizontally at elbow level and through the openings the richly ornamented sleeves of the doublet, 'cut, lyned with cloth of golde, and tyed together with great buttons of Diamonds,' etc., protruded.    The whole garment was embroidered with rows of narrow gold cords
('rewed'), two or three in number, *transverse-
wise*.    Rich gardes or bands, ' curiously embroidered,' descended the front of the garment
and the upper part of the tubular sleeves;
the same pattern was used across the ends of
the tubes.    This pattern was often barred at
right angles with goldsmith's work set with
jewels.    Take, for example, the much-advertised
Castle Howard portrait of Henry VIII.    In
this the frock is of faintly figured crimson
velvet, covered with transverse rows of groups
of three gold cords.    The fronts are braided
in a *simple* pattern (Fig. 294), the same 'gardes'
descending the tops of the tubular sleeves and
appearing in horizontal bands round the tube
part.    These braided 'gardes' are crossed at
intervals by ornaments of goldsmith's work
each set with three rubies.    A V - shaped
ermine collar reveals a part of the doublet,
and there is a narrow piece of the same fur
at all edges.    In all these portraits the bejewelled black velvet bonet is without a
plume.

Fig. 294

In 1544 it was reported that the King
became so weak on his legs that he could
hardly stand, therefore he found his staff
most helpful.    Two years later we find him being carried from one room to another in a chair fixed between two shafts or poles, called 'trains,' and borne by two or more servants.    In view of these afflictions it seems incredible that such a decrepit old gentleman should be able to sit his horse; but it was remarked at the time that 'the King of England is always at the chase'!

The method of carrying a man in a chair is explained by a Venetian wood-cut, dating about 1530, wherein is shown Antonio da Leyva, Commander-in-Chief of the Emperor Charles V's troops, who 'caused himself to be carried in a chair of purple velvet by four men.'    The chair in question is after the same style as that shown in Fig. 215, but the rings through which the poles are passed are attached to the sides of the curved legs.   The four men are dressed in Landsknechten costume.

There is another document (Harleian, 1419) of sartorial interest in the British Museum.   It is an inventory of the costumes and household goods belonging to the King, and was compiled in the year 1547.   In it we learn that Sir Anthony Denny, Kt., was Keeper of the Great Wardrobe.   Amongst hundreds of other items this inventory mentions:

Full robes of the Orders of the Garter; Toison d'or; and St. Michael. Also thirty-nine gowns; 24 doublets; 23 pairs of hosen; 7 cloaks; 18 *cottes*; 13 *capes*; 16 *frocks*; 7 jerkyns; 4 partletts; 10 *cassocks*; numerous slops; 23 girdles, including swordbelts; 3 purses; many hats and bonets; shirts and gloves.

In tabulating this inventory the compiler has used names for some of the garments which were practically obsolete at the time and are somewhat misleading.   For instance, *cotte* refers not to the article described in vol. ii, but to the garment with skirt and bases worn by the fashionable in this reign. *Cape* means the surcote, and a *frock* was a loose coat, such as is worn by Henry VIII in the Castle Howard portrait.   *Cassock* does not refer to the clerical garment: it was a loose outer garment similar to a frock and is listed as follows: 'One long Cassock gowne with straight sleeves of black velvett rewed [rew =a row or line] with venice Silver, welted with velvet and lyned with satin.'

The *cloak*, which formed a comfortable wrap, became a favourite luxury during this reign.   It was shaped either as a complete circle or as a semi-circle, and made of cloth, often lined throughout with fur.   The King had 'A cloke of Sables lined with black Tapzat [figured] Damaske wrought with roses, with x rounde buttons set with little sparkes of counterfet Rubies and Saphiers.'   His Majesty was also the possessor of a cloke lined with elk skins.

Item:

'A short Spanyshe gown of a newe making of black Dammaske with Roses, and two narrow gardes and one brode garde of black velvett embroidered with black silk, lyned with sarcenet and faced with black satin.'

Item:

'A little purse of Spanishe Woorke and a Girdle with three tassels of silke.'

Further interesting details may be gathered from other sources — that Richard Cicyll was Groom of the Robes, and, in 1529, was paid forty-one shillings and eightpence for a yard and a quarter of purple velvet 'for Maistres Anne.' The following year he received five shillings and eightpence for four pieces of Venice gold passamayne 'for the Kings Grace.'

In 1532 six shillings and eightpence was paid to him 'for a payer of sloppes for the Kings Grace.'

'Paied to the wif of Willim Armerer for ij dousin of handekerchers and sherts for them of the Chambre being at the King's finding v li, xjs, iiijd.'

A kerchief worn by both men and women about their necks and cheeks was called a MOFELER or muffler, and must have added greatly to their comfort when out of doors. A hat with a plume cost the King fifteen shillings, and amongst a list of 'glasses to look in' is— 'a square lookinge steele glass set with purple velvet and a passement of Venice gold set square about the same.'

There was an account paid to Henry Arnold the Cordyner for shoes and buskins £4 18s., and hosen forty-one shillings and eight-pence for the use of Maister Henry Knevet.

Fig. 295. A Dog-collar

'3 payre of hawkes-gloves, with two lined with velvet'; '44 dog collars of sondrye makynge' [Fig. 295 shows one]; '138 hawkes hoods' are other interesting items.

A staff was a very useful accessory to the infirm King as stated on pp. 255 and 257. Several items under the heading Walking Staves appear in the inventory, and are as follows:

'A Staffe of unicornes horne garnished with golde having a Diall in the Toppe and at the nether ende a virall [ferrule] of gold.'

'A cane garnished with golde having a perfume at the Top, under that a diall, with a pair of twitchers [nippers or tweezers], and a pair of compasses of golde, and a footreule of gold; a knife and a file the haft of gold, with a whet-stone tipped with gold.' All these articles were fitted into a case forming the ornamental knob at the top of the stick.

'A cane garnished with silver and gilt, with astronomie upon it.'

A 'diall' could either mean a compass, a sundial, or a clock.

In 1532 a reward was given to 'the servant of Maister Cromewell' for bringing sucado and marmalado to 'the Kings Grace to Eltham.' 'Sucado' was candied oranges and was packed in barrels. 'Orengegs' were very scarce in Henry VIII's reign, so this was a noble gift. Orange pie is mentioned as a costly dish. This fruit was introduced into England in the latter part of the fifteenth century and was made more popular by the entourage of Katherine of Aragon. Mention of the fruit occurs in privy purse expenses: 'Oranges from Spayn to the Queen [Elysabeth] at Richmond. April 1502.'

### THE GLOVE (*continued from vol. ii, p.* 94)

The mention of gloves in wardrobe accounts is not so frequent as one would expect, considering the number of portraits of noblemen and ladies of this period who are shown carrying them. The fashionable way of holding gloves in the hand was to fold each in half, the wrist part held towards the front.

Gloves decorated with cuttes through which the wearer of either sex could display finger-rings were *the* thing amongst smart people of western Europe; this was a German fashion dating back to the fourteenth century (*see* vol. ii, p. 91). The fit of the glove as worn during the sixteenth century was little better than when they first appeared with separate fingers in the reign of Henry II. They were still rather large in size, but the decoration was much more elaborate.

Fig. 296.
A Glove of Henry VIII

In Fig. 296 is drawn one of a pair of gloves said to have belonged to Henry VIII. They are of soft buff leather, with cuffs or gauntlets of white satin divided into eight panels, each embroidered with flowers and leaves in coloured silks and gold thread. Each panel is edged with gold-spangled lace and lined with rose-coloured silk. Round the wrist is a ruching of the same coloured silk edged with gold lace. From finger-tip to the base of the gauntlet measures twelve and a half inches.

Gauntlets to gloves were not always quite so deep as this, at least, they appear not to be so because the base was sometimes cut up at right angles and folded over the middle of the cuttes to make loops. Fig. 305 carries a glove treated in this manner. This fashion of elaborately decorated gauntlets was carried to great lengths.

Henry VIII's hawking glove is in the possession of the Ashmolean Museum, Oxford. This is much less ornate, being made of plain buff leather with a short gauntlet, on which the only decoration is a number of circular discs worked in dull red thread and silver wire.

Ordinary plain gloves seem to have been inexpensive at this time as the King paid only 2s. 9d. for eleven pairs: 'for a dousin and a halfe of Spanysshe gloves' 7s. 6d. was paid to one Jacson, a hardwareman. The Princess Mary, in 1544, received as a gift from a Spanish duchess, 'ten pair of Spayneshe gloves.'

Perfumed gloves were known in the first half of the sixteenth century, for Henry VIII received a gift of a pair in 1541, but they came from Italy. Such gloves were rare and expensive, for they cost 3s. 4d.! Ordinary leather gloves could be bought for 4d. a pair.

There were some customs associated with the glove at this time in addition to those of an earlier date still in use (see vol. ii, p. 93): as a favour of one's lady-love, a memorial of a friend, and as a mark to be challenged by an enemy. These were worn in the hat.

(Continued on p. 551)

### THE HANDKERCHIEF

The use of the sudarium (see vol. i, pp. 125, 152, and 199) or handkerchief was a custom of Republican Rome from the second century B.C. For the first ten centuries of the Christian era this useful and sanitary adjunct continued to be at hand amongst a few highly cultured persons throughout Europe.

The handkerchief reappears in the fifteenth century first in Italy and afterwards in other countries of Europe. A few references to it occur in wardrobe accounts of royalty and the nobility at this time, in which they are usually reckoned by the dozen. In the early part of the sixteenth century this elegant accessory was known by the names of 'muck-rinder,' 'muckender,' 'muckiter,' 'mokador,' or 'mokedore' (the latter said to be derived from the French 'mouchoir'). It was often referred to as a napkin: 'A Napkyn see that thou hast in rediness thy nose to clense.' The more refined called it a 'handcouvrechef,' hence 'handkerchief.' Usually square in shape, for general practical use they were made of linen and plain, the ornamentation varying according to the taste and wealth of the user. The best were of Holland cloth, a superior kind of linen, embroidered with silk in colours, Venys gold or silver, and fringed. Tassels, about one and a half inches long, or small wooden acorns covered with white thread, were often attached to the corners (see Fig. 289). Sometimes handkerchiefs were edged with cutwork, Flanders work, or Spanish work. 'Vj doss hand kerchers of playne lynon cloth' is an item from a wardrobe account. Gentlemen carried the handkerchief in the hand or perhaps tucked into a part of their dress: sometimes it was attached by one corner to the waistbelt.

Ladies nearly always carried a handkerchief in the hand (see Fig. 244), or fastened to it their girdles, and there is no doubt that, when necessary, they used the folds of their voluminous sleeves as a convenient place of concealment. These handkerchiefs were somewhat smaller than those used by gentlemen, which latter were from fifteen to eighteen inches square.

(Continued on p. 549)

### NIGHTSHIRTS, NIGHTCAPS, AND NIGHTGOWNS

Until the close of the fifteenth century it was the custom for both men and women to go to bed in a state of nature. In Tudor times it became the fashion to wear a covering in the form of a NIGHTSHIRT, a mode no doubt prompted by the spirit of the Reformation.

This garment was shaped, according to meagre evidence, on the lines of the fashionable dayshirt described on p. 21, in fact, a dayshirt worn at night. The first mention of such a garment occurs in records of this reign where it is stated that Henry VIII *always* wore a nightshirt—though presumably with interludes. No bridegroom or bride wore a nightshirt, but it is not certain how long the abstention lasted. When Henry wished to repudiate his marriage with the Lady Anne of Cleves he declared he was never without one at night; in other words, the marriage was not consummated.

There is a miniature painted in 1534, said to be of Henry Fitz Roy, Duke of Richmond. Fig. 297, a drawing of it, shows this 'goodlie yong lord,' and from the little that is seen of the nightshirt, it is of white linen with a collar having three straps on each side for tying it close up to the throat. Enough of the top of the sleeve is visible to show that it was full and gathered into the armhole.

Fig. 297. Nightcap

A woman's night garment was now called a 'nightshift' or 'smock.'

*Nightcaps*, known also as 'night-bonets' or 'biggins' (a nightcap of coarser make), were sometimes worn. These were either shaped like the coif (first mentioned in vol. ii, p. 176), or were close-fitting skullcaps. They were occasionally worn in the day-time; and an engraving of King Henry by Cornelys Metsys, dated 1544, shows him wearing one. Night-caps were made of linen, silk, or fine cloth, chiefly in white, though sometimes in colours. The King had a 'nightbonet' in scarlet which cost four shillings: 'A nightcap of black velvet embroidered,' is another item from the King's wardrobe account.

Henry Fitz Roy (Fig. 297) wears a nightcap completely covering the hair. It is of fine linen worked with a design in black floss silk, the turned-back piece edged with small loops of silk.

A nightgown was a different garment from a nightshirt. It was the equivalent of the dressing-gown as used at the present day.

On the death of Cardinal Wolsey in 1530, George Cavendish hastened to Court to tell the news. To use his own words: 'The next day I was sent for to the King, conducted by Mr. Norris, where the King was in his nightgown of rochet [1] velvet, furred with sables, before whom I kneeled the space of an hour.' Its shape is described below.

The Earl of Northumberland (born 1489, died 1527) possessed a night-gown of russet furred with 'foyngs.' This was the fur of the polecat, the back of which was a very dark brown and underneath a pale yellow or cream. This nobleman used bedroom slippers, for an item in his wardrobe account runs: 'Night buskyns of rede leder and black cordwyn furred with black lambe.' It should be explained that 'cordwyn' was a fine quality Spanish leather.

In 1532 Henry ordered from John Malte as a gift: 'A nightgown for the Lady Anne' (Boleyn). As previously mentioned this was not a bed garment, as those knowing Henry's propensities might imagine, but a *robe de chambre* or 'dressing-gown.' Its details are interesting:

| | | |
|---|---|---|
| xiij yds blac satin at viijs the yard | v *li* iiijs | |
| Paied John Malte for making | | vjs viijd |
| viij yd blac taffata to lyne the goune at viijs the yd | iij *li* iiijs | |
| iij yd blac velvet for the border and edge of the the same gowne at xiijs iiijd the yarde | ij *li* | |
| ij yds Buckeram for to lyne the upper sleeves of the same gowne | | xijd |
| | x *li* xvs viijd | |

In shape this nightgown was a loose wrap-over garment reaching to the feet. Of black satin, it was lined throughout with black taffeta and had wide bands of velvet down the fronts and round the hem. Its sleeves were large, and as buckram was used to line the upper parts they must have been much puffed at the shoulders. There would be a deep turned-down collar, and cuffs of black velvet at the moderately wide wrists. The whole effect must have been somewhat sombre, especially when it is remembered that the Lady Anne is said to have had black hair (*see* p. 617).

Fig. 298

---

[1] Rochet here does not mean the ecclesiastical vestment, but the colour. The word can mean russet (reddish brown or grey); or 'rouget' (red).

### ROYALTY AND NOBILITY—WOMEN: 1530–47

### KATHERINE

#### First Queen-Consort of Henry VIII, 1530–6

In the autumn of 1531, the Queen was removed from Windsor to More House, Herts. She was parted from her beloved daughter, the Princess Mary, whom she never saw again. The indignation of the populace was high, and often Henry, when he appeared in public or was taking part in the chase, was approached by the people who entreated him to reinstate the Queen. It throws a radiant light on Katherine's character to learn from a Venetian visitor who saw her in August 1531, a time when she must have been suffering from extreme uneasiness of mind, that 'Her Majesty is not of tall stature, rather small; she is somewhat stout, and *has always a smile on her countenance.*' From More House Katherine was sent to reside at Ampthill in the summer of 1532, and in the following year Henry succeeded, through the instrumentality of Archbishop Cranmer, in obtaining a divorce on 23rd May.

In June the Queen took up her abode at the Palace of Buckden, and while in her retirement at this place she made a prolonged and stubborn fight against the decree. Katherine remained at Buckden until May 1535 when she moved to Kimbolton Castle, whence she made her final appeal to her nephew, the Emperor Charles V, in November. This having been ignored, Katherine lost all hope, and resigned herself to her fate. At Christmas of this year the Queen had a relapse and became seriously ill. The end came at the second hour after midnight, 8th January 1536. As a biographer relates, Katherine died unconquered as she had lived; a great lady to the last, sacrificed in death, as she had been in life, to the expediency of high politics. Her body was laid in Peterborough Cathedral.

### ANNE BOLEYN

#### Second Queen-Consort of Henry VIII, 1503–36

Anne Boleyn was the second daughter of Sir Thomas Boleyn and was born probably at Hever Castle in 1503. Carefully educated and trained in accomplishments befitting a young lady of her breeding, she began her social career at the age of eleven, when she accompanied the Princess Mary to France in 1514.[1] It is said that the Lady Anne was at one time lady-in-waiting to the Archduchess Marguerite.

---

[1] Some authorities argue that Anne did not go with her sister, Mary Boleyn, to France, but followed her some years later.

The Venetian Ambassador describes Anne Boleyn as 'of middle stature, swarthy complexion, long neck, wide mouth, eyes black and beautiful, hair black, wonderful long hair, but not one of the handsomest women in the world.' In bearing a very elegant creature, she occupies an important place in the history of costume. On the death of Louis XII and the return of Mary Tudor to England, Anne remained behind, and was 'received in a place of much honour with the other Queen'—Queen Claude.

It is doubtful whether Anne was present with the other members of her family at the Field of the Cloth of Gold in 1520. Her mother was in attendance on Queen Katherine, and Sir Thomas Boleyn in the suite of King Henry. During her sojourn at the French Court the Lady Anne learnt much, and became proficient in all the little niceties of politeness for which the French are famous, for we learn that 'Anne so improved her graces that you would never have judged her English in her fashions, but native French.' There are various conflicting opinions as to her character which we pass over, giving her credit for remarkable shrewdness and subtlety.

About 1522 Anne was recalled to England, and later, about 1525, entered upon her duties as lady-in-waiting to Queen Katherine.

All seems to have passed most agreeably for this young lady at the Court of the amorous Henry, for about a twelvemonth. In 1527, when the idea of divorcing his wife entered His Majesty's head, it is possible that Anne began to dream of herself as a successor. Encouragement came on 1st September 1532, when Henry created her Marchioness of Pembroke; and she was, according to one account, secretly married to the King on the 14th November 1532, six months before Henry obtained his divorce from Katherine of Aragon. On the other hand, the ever-vigilant Eustace Chapuys informed his master, the Emperor, that the marriage took place secretly on the Feast of the Conversion of St Paul, 25th January 1533.

An eyewitness at Court wrote, 'Madame Anne . . . has nothing but the king's great love.'

A description of Anne Boleyn as she appeared at her coronation is given below, 'by a person who lived at the time and was present thereat.'

'Then came the queen in a white litter of white cloth of gold, not covered or bailled,[1] which was led by two palfreis clad in white damask down to the ground head and all;[2] led by her footmen. Over her was borne a canopie of cloth of gold, with four gilt staves, and four silver bells. For the bearing of which canopie were appointed sixteen knights, foure to beare it one space on foot, and other foure another space. She had on a circot of white cloth of tissue and a mantle of the same, furred with ermine, hir haire hanging down, but on hir head she had a coif [3] with a circlet about it full of rich stones.' The ladies of her suite travelled in chariettes.

Another authority gives a slightly different account of this procession: 'At ten o'clock the Lady Anne left the Tower in an open litter, so that all

---

[1] See p. 135.                    [2] Housing, see vol. ii, Fig. 472.
[3] Like Fig. 139, but without the cap.   See also Fig. 140.

might see her, but before she came out all the cavalry preceded her, all in very fine order and richly bedight. Then came the gentlemen of rank, and then all the ladies and gentlemen on horseback and in chars, very brave. The Queen was dressed in a robe of crimson brocade covered with precious stones, and round her neck she wore a string of pearls larger than big chickpeas, and a jewel of diamonds of great value. On her head she bore a wreath in the fashion of a crown of immense worth, and in her hand she carried some flowers' — an interesting instance of the appearance of a 'bouquet.'

Amongst the numerous chariots which followed was one covered with cloth of gold in which sat 'divers ancient old ladies'—an eyewitness's rather unappreciative reference to the Dowager-Duchess of Norfolk and the Dowager-Marchioness of Dorset.

The crowd who witnessed this pageantry would not uncover their heads as the new Queen passed. Her jester, observing this slight paid to his mistress, cried out: 'I think you have all scurvy heads and dare not uncover.'

The coronation banquet in the Queen's honour was, as usual, a very magnificent affair. One detail which was noticed is worth recording: 'Two maids sat under the table at the Queen's feet during dinner, and two attendant countesses did hold a fine cloth before the Queen's face, when she list to spit, or do otherwise at her pleasure.'

In October 1534 Anne's hold over her husband's affections began to wane. Day by day her position became more and more precarious until the climax was reached on the 19th May, 1536.

Queen Anne's behaviour on the scaffold was all that could be desired. She certainly made a dignified exit, gowned to perfection, as she always had been, in a dress of grey brocade, the sleeves lined and turned back with grey squirrel, the same fur edging the fronts of her skirt, which opened to show an underskirt of rose-coloured satin. To the last she remained faithful to the French hood; it was of black velvet ornamented with pearls. For the general character of this costume see Fig. 255. Hardly had the sword fallen on Anne Boleyn than the wedding ring was on Jane Seymour's finger.

### ELIZABETH TUDOR, 1533 *until* 1547

Some particulars regarding Anne Boleyn's daughter, 'The Lady Elizabeth,' at the early age of three years are gleaned from a letter written by Margaret, wife of Sir Thomas Bryan, a kinsman of the Boleyns, to Cromwell. This lady was appointed governess (she had filled the same office to the Lady Mary) or 'the lady mistress' to the motherless Princess Elizabeth, and in her letter she expresses much anxiety for the well-being of her charge. Amongst other things she deplores the lack of raiment for the child, even for one of less important parentage. 'She hath,' so Lady Bryan points out, 'neither gown nor kertel, nor petecot, nor no maner of linnin for smokes, nor

PLATE XV. QUEEN JANE SEYMOUR, 1536: Portrait by Hans Holbein
Kunsthistorisches Museum, Vienna.  *Photo by Mansell*

cerchefes, nor sleves, nor rayls, nor body-stychets, nor handcerchers, nor mofelers, nor begens.'

'Goun nor kertel nor petecot' need no explanation, but it must be borne in mind that all these garments were in miniature—to be worn by a child of three years.   Details of 'smokes' (otherwise smocks) are to be found on p. 224, and 'rayles' on p. 209. BODY-STYCHETS were corsets, but this item represents binding cloths.  'Mofelers' (see p. 259) were wraps for the head and shoulders.  For 'begens' refer to p. 111.   The English name for the Flemish 'béguin' was 'biggin.' The misspelling 'begens' is applied to a close cap coming well over the ears and firmly binding the forehead (see Figs. 614 and 741). This was used for young children to assist nature in closing the serrated articulations of the skull.   All these eight items of baby garments should have been made of wool or linen of the finest texture. (Continued on p. 285)

JANE SEYMOUR (see also p. 287)

*Third Queen-Consort of Henry VIII, 1509–37*

Jane, daughter of Sir John Seymour, was born about 1509, and married Henry VIII as his third Queen, 20th May 1536.  'Of middle stature and no great beauty: so fair that one would call her rather pale than otherwise.'

It was Queen Jane's privilege to be the first of a long series of English ladies to sit to the great painter Hans Holbein.  She was Queen-Consort for only seventeen months, dying in 1537, and Holbein's portrait of her (now at Vienna and reproduced in Plate XV) was painted during the latter half of 1536.  It is a very valuable authority for the costume in fashion during the second half of Henry VIII's reign.  The bodice, sleeves, and skirt are of crimson velvet: the turned-back sleeve-linings appear to be silk of the same shade, entirely covered by a network of gold cord or perhaps bugle beads. The false sleeves and underskirt are of cloth of silver damask.   Notice should be taken of the beautiful pendant or pectoral on the bodice.

Upon this portrait the details of Plate XVI are based; it does not pretend to represent Jane Seymour herself, but any high-born lady of the Court. The style, which is the latest mode, is similar in some respects to the earlier fashion shown in Fig. 255.   The dress is composed of a rich plain velvet in a soft shade of purple, the sleeves turned back with miniver, and the false sleeves and underskirt of blue cloth of gold of damask.   The shape of the bodice remains the same as shown in diagram, Fig. 256.   The sleeves revert to the shape shown in Fig. 66 but are larger.   They are close-fitting at the arm-hole, but widely open at the wrist (see diagram, Fig. 67). An alternative pattern requiring only one seam, and that in front, is given in diagram, Fig. 299. The edge of the sleeve, which formerly fell upon the wrist, is turned back, and pinned closely round the upper arm, at a short distance from the shoulder, in the same manner as shown in diagram, Fig. 300. This arrangement gave that very angular effect which was considered so modish by the well-dressed women of the period. At the back of the arm the edges of the sleeve form a long loop (*see* diagram, Fig. 301). The lining of these sleeves was of all kinds of material, but chiefly furs of one of the varieties already mentioned—ermine, sable, miniver, leopard, squirrel, etc. (*see also* p. 273).

The false sleeve also assumed an angular shape and was cut as shown in diagram, Fig. 257. It was usually made of the same material as the underskirt, often, but not always, patterned and lined with a contrasting colour.

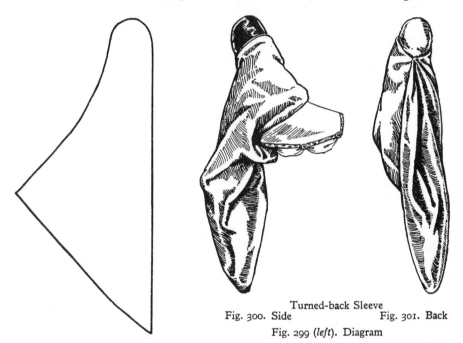

Turned-back Sleeve
Fig. 300. Side　　　　　　　　Fig. 301. Back
Fig. 299 (*left*). Diagram

Whether the material was plain or patterned it often had cuttes radiating from the wrist to the elbow. Its two side edges were clasped together at intervals at A, B, and C, with jewels set in elaborate gold mounts; and the very full sleeve of the camise or smock of white lawn puffed through the cuttes and between the jewelled clasps. A frill of needlework edged the smock sleeve and fell from the wrists. The Spanish work used for the purpose by Jane Seymour is reproduced in Fig. 262.

The skirt of this period, as worn by English ladies, had a long train and was cut as a semi-oval (*see* diagram, Fig. 259). Most of the gathers, or organ-pleats (*see* Fig. 260 and p. 221), were concentrated at the back of the waist, with only a few at the sides: this arrangement produced ample folds down the back which formed the train. The sides of the skirt were without folds, being kept flat and funnel-shaped over the Spanish farthingale (*see* Fig. 590). These skirts were open up the front, edged with gold passamayne or a narrow

border of fur: the sides sloping up to the waist giving the fashionable triangular effect to the rich underskirt.    Such skirts are worn by the ladies in
Plate XVI and Figs. 302 and 314.

A characteristic of the skirts of continental ladies at this time was that
they had no trains.

The materials of which these skirts were composed, and the bodice, too,
for they always matched, were of various kinds.    Most often one of those
marvellous patterned brocades or damasks for which Renaissance Italy was
renowned was used: or the material had a gold design upon a coloured velvet
or silk ground.    A plain velvet or a patterned velvet having one, two, or even
three piles was another variant.    Sometimes the dress was of plain cloth of
silver or gold, or coloured cloth of gold.    On occasion these rich fabrics were
embroidered with gold and coloured silks.

Usually these patterned materials were of a very large design; and in order
to display the pattern to full advantage it was necessary to dispense with any
folds at the sides of the skirt.

When the material was of sufficient width only one constructional seam
down the middle of the back was required; or if a narrow fabric was used the
selvedges were seamed together *before* the back seam was completed, great
care being taken to match up the pattern.    By this means the beautiful
design was unbroken and displayed complete down the front and sides (*see*
Fig. 302).    If the seam down the back was carefully mitred it formed a
symmetrical pattern.

Fig. 302 shows a lady costumed as described under Plate XVI, except that
the gown is carried out in a large-patterned damask, a cut velvet upon a silk
gold ground, or an embossed velvet.    Notice that the dressmakers of this
time always chose the most important motif in the pattern of their material
for the centre of the plastron front.

An item of deportment that should be observed by the student is that in
portraits of Tudor ladies they are nearly always posed with their hands
clasped at waist level.    This emphasized the desired angle of the turned-back
sleeve.

Another portrait of Queen Jane Seymour was contained in the fresco by
Hans Holbein (*see* p. 16); and the copy at Hampton Court shows her in the
costume of the year 1537.    It is made exactly as described under Plate XVI.
The dress—bodice, sleeves, skirt, and long train—is of gold brocade or embroidered with an interlaced pattern.    The sleeves are lined and turned back
with ermine, and the underskirt and false sleeves are of crimson velvet.
The Queen wears the gable headdress, with its black velvet hood turned up
in whelk-shell fashion.    A pearl lace twice surrounds the neck, and has a
tau-cross pendant of jewels.    An ornament similar to that shown in the Vienna
portrait is fastened to the front of the bodice; and six rows of pearls hang low
in a wide sweep from the edge of the shoulders.

Fig. 302. THE MODE OF THE 1530's

## THE LADY MARY TUDOR II, 1530 *until* 1544 *(continued from p. 217)*

In the Ashmolean Museum, Oxford, is a three-quarter-length portrait said to be the Princess Mary, attributed to Jean van Cleef, and painted (according to an expert) in the year 1537. The Princess has a pleasant expression, and is good looking with a girlish face displaying a charming personality. She is seated in one of the delightful chairs of the period (*see* Fig. 215), and is dressed in bodice, sleeves, and skirt of black velvet. The square neck opening is edged with pearls with cutwork set inside it resting on the neck. The sleeves are not so large as usual at this time; they are lined with crimson satin, and edged with a narrow band of ermine. The sleeves are turned back to just above the elbow level, revealing the false sleeves of gold brocade ornamented with cuttes and finished with frills of cutwork at the wrists. The underskirt is of the same gold brocade. Surrounding the waist is a girdle of two rows of pearls, three pearls in each row alternating with jewels set in rich gold mounts. It does not fall down the front as usual. On the bodice is a fine ornament of gold set with six pearls surrounding a jewel, and a large peardrop pearl hangs from it. A lace of pearls with pendant is wound twice round the neck.

The French hood is described on p. 338. *(Continued on p. 285)*

## PERFUMES AND POMANDERS

The arts of distilling exquisite-smelling perfumes and of preparing unguents long remained the monopoly of Italy. In the year 1533 Catherine de' Medici brought in her entourage a Florentine named René who was an expert in the manufacture of perfumery, cosmetics, *and* poisons. He established himself on the Pont au Change, Paris, and developed a lively trade. From that time the use of perfumes became general among the French and English of wealth and fashion.

Receipts for making perfumes used during the Tudor and Elizabethan periods are still extant, and can be utilized to-day. A simple and economical substitute for the elaborate concoction mentioned as being used by Cardinal Wolsey (p. 178), was an orange covered with cloves stuck close together into the rind. This pine-cone-looking ball maintained its delicious aroma for a very long time, and kept (it was believed) disease at bay.

Girdles composed of jewels in gold settings, beads of enamel, gold or silver, and pearls were worn round the waist at the edge of the bodice, with a long end descending in front. To its extremity was attached

## THE POMANDER *(continued from p. 45)*

During the reign of Henry VIII pomanders came into general use, and were made in many and various designs. They were usually hung at the end of

the long girdle. In size they were from one and a half to two and a half
inches in diameter, and often very elaborately decorated.

Fig. 303 illustrates an early sixteenth-century pomander, comprising an
upper and lower hemisphere of gold filigree hinged together and containing a
ball of perfume.

Fig. 304 shows one dating from the first half of the sixteenth century. It
is made in gold, enamel, and jewels, in a series of sectors, hinged at the bottom
and fastened with a catch at the top, each sector having two perforated lids
and containing different scents.

A pomander belonging to Katherine of Aragon is mentioned under date

Fig. 303. Pomander

Fig. 304 (right)

1530 as 'inscribed with H and K' and another with 'ostrich feathers and red
roses.' Also 'a pomander of gold w$^t$ Diall in yt' evidently containing a watch.

According to an inventory dated 1543 Princess Mary had 'iiij long girdles
of goldsmiths work with pomanders at the ends.' 'Geven to my Lady Elizabeth g'ce. Item a pomander of golde w$^t$ a Diall in yt.' The Countess of
Bath in 1549 had 'item a gerdyll of crown gold set out w$^t$ a great pearl and a
pomander.'

(Continued on p. 553)

## FRENCH FASHIONS (continued from p. 222)

### ELEANOR, ARCHDUCHESS OF AUSTRIA

#### Second Queen-Consort of Francis I of France, 1530 until 1547

Eleanor of Austria married, secondly, in 1530, Francis I of France. Her
married life was very unhappy owing to her husband's deep infatuation for
the beautiful Duchesse d'Étampes.

There is at Hampton Court a portrait head and shoulders of Eleanor as
Queen of France, by Joost van Cleve, in the style of dress described under

Plate XI, the approximate date of which is 1530.  This portrait is listed No. 2 in the inventory of Henry VIII's pictures, taken in 1547, and is described as follows: 'The Frinshe queene Elonora, in the Spanyshe arraie, and a cap on her headd, with an orange in her hand.'

This is proof beyond doubt that Plate XI depicts the Spanish mode, and also that Eleanor sometimes wore Spanish costume at the time she was the wife of the French King.

Rabelais has something to say about the costume Queen Eleanor wore when making her state entry into Bordeaux at the time of her marriage.

'The Queen was garbed in the Spanish style having on her head a coif or Crispine of twisted Clothe of gold, made with gold butterflies, within which was her hair, hanging behind as far as her heels, twisted with gold bands [see Fig. 399], and she had a bonet of crimson velvet on her head, covered with jewels, in which was a white feather curled in the same manner as the King was wearing that day [see Fig. 400].  Her gown was of crimson velvet, lined with white taffata, with which the sleeves were puffed, instead of with the chemise; the sleeves of the gown being covered with gold and silver embroideries.  Her surcote was of white satin all round, covered with beaten silver heavily jewelled.'

Many other interesting details of costume as worn by the ladies of France at this time are given by Rabelais:

'Next to their chemise they put on a beautiful vasquine of pure silk camelot: above that went the taffata or tabby farthingale of white, red, tawny, grey, or of any other colour.  Above a white taffata petti-cotte they had another of cloth of tissue, or brocade, embroidered with fine gold and interwoven with needlework, or it had an overrobe of satin, damask, or velvet, in orange, tawny, green, cendre, blue, yellow, bright red, crimson, white Clothe of gold or silver and *cannetille* embroidery, according to the auspicious occasion.

'Their gowns, according to the season, were either of Clothe of gold or silver frisure; of red satin covered with gold cannetille, of white taffata, blue, black, tanne, of serge de soie, camelot de soie, velvet, clothe of gold or silver tissue, velvet or satin pourfilé embroidered of gold in diverse designs.

'In summer, instead of the robes, they wore beautiful mantles, made of the aforesaid materials, or a Moorish mantle, a BERNOUS de velours violet à *frisure d'or* sur *canetille* d'argent, and gold girdles garnished with small Indian pearls at the intersections.  They always carried a beautiful *panache* of the colour of their sleeves well trimmed with spangles of gold.

'In winter they had their taffata gowns of all colours as above named, lined with hind-wolves or speckled lynxes, black spotted weasels, martens of Calabria, sables, and other costly furs of inestimable value.

'Their headdresses also varied with the season of the year.  In winter the French mode.  In spring the Spanish, in summer the fashions of Tuscany, except on Holydays and Sundays at which time they were of the French mode, because they accounted it more honourable, and better befitting the garb of grave purity.

'Their paternosters or rosaries, rings, bracelets, collars and carcanets were all of precious stones, such as carbuncles, balas rubies, diamonds, sapphires, emeralds, turquoises, garnets, agates, beryles, and marvellously matched pearls.

'They wore chausses [1] of scarlet, crimson, or purple ingrain, which reached just three fingers above the knee, have the edge beautified with exquisite embroideries, and rare incisions of the cutter's art. Their garters were of the colour of their bracelets, and circled the knee a little both over and under [as described under Plate VII B]. Their shoes, ESCARPINS and PAN-TOUFLES were either of red, violet, or crimson velvet, pinked and jagged like a crayfish's beard.'

Some of the foregoing items need explanation:

Vasquine (see p. 222).

Cannetille was gold or silver edging.

Frisure d'or. Gold or silver metal twisted into a pattern and laid on the fabric. It looked like heavy embroidery.

Panache (see vol. ii, p. 311). Here it refers to a fan usually composed of feathers.

Jaseran—a small gold chain.

Escarpins—slippers.

Pantoufles. Slippers without backs—mules.

No new modes in the costume of French ladies made their appearance during this time: the characteristic dress remained as noted in Section I of this chapter.

The leaders of fashion in the French Court, in order of their influence, were the unscrupulous Duchesse d'Étampes, Diane de Poitiers, and the Dauphine, Catherine de' Medici—the last of little account at this time, but later on . . .!

### Anne de Heilly

#### Duchesse d'Étampes, 1525–76

Most celebrated amongst the courtesans who disturbed the tranquillity of the Court was Anne de Heilly (born 1508), who appeared in 1525 at the age of seventeen as lady-in-waiting to Louise of Savoy, Madame d'Angoulême, and became the official mistress of Francis I in 1526. To mask this liaison she was given in marriage to Jean de Brosse, an unnecessary precaution perhaps in such a profligate Court. Brosse was rewarded for his services by being created Duc d'Étampes and Governor of Brittany. The Duchesse was 'the most beautiful of clever women and the most clever of beauties,' with a perfect complexion and golden chestnut hair; dignified and graceful, she was

---

[1] Clearly the word indicates what were later in the century known as stockings. See Chap. IV, p. 545.

as uncertain as a leopard and as relentless as a panther in disposition.   She was banished the Court before 1547 and died in 1576.

Corneille de Lyon painted a head-and-shoulders portrait of the Duchesse about 1548, in which she is wearing a dress and French hood, apparently like those shown in Fig. 255.

### Diane de Poitiers

*Duchesse de Valentinois, 1499–1566*

A lady of somewhat similar reputation was Diane de Poitiers, who was born 1499.   She was the daughter of Jehan de Poitiers, Comte de Saint-Vallier, and married in 1514 Louis de Brézé, Comte de Maulevrier, Grant Sénéchal of Normandy.   The Comtesse was lady-in-waiting to Queen Claude from 1515 to 1524, and in this capacity attended the infant Prince Henry, the Queen's second son.

The Comtesse was left a widow in 1531 with two daughters.   She did not, however, retire from Court, where she became a prominent figure: nor did she garb herself in the sombre robes of a widow known as the 'Grand Deuil' (deep mourning), but wore half-mourning, 'Petit Deuil,' instead. This authorized silk as well as velvet and might be in the latest fashion.   There is a three-quarter portrait at Versailles of 'Madame la Grante Sénéchale' from which Fig. 305 is taken.   It shows Diane in ceremonial mourning attire.   The dress is of plain black velvet with the bodice edged with pearls, and cut in an unusual manner on the chest revealing an undergarment of purple veiled with a transparent lawn chemisette.   This bodice is evidently only an under-bodice with the sleeves attached to it: an outer bodice covers it as far as the

Fig. 305. Diane de Poitiers, 1531

breast line.   The sleeves are cut square as shown in diagram, Fig. 65, but not quite so large, and are turned back over full under-sleeves of white lawn. Around the upper arms are three bars of miniver denoting the lady's rank of Comtesse de Saint-Vallier (1531–47).   The girdle (Fig. 305) and pendent pomander are of pearls and diamonds (no other jewels being worn) and she holds a magnifying glass in her right hand; her left is partly covered by one glove and holds the other.   The French hood of earlier shape (*see* Fig. 395) has a white lining, and a wire inserted in the front edge to give the correct bow line.    Inside this is a small ruching of white lawn.

Diane's complexion is said to have been faultless, even at the age of sixty, and her hair of a rich purple-black took a bronze tint in the sunshine.    No wonder the young Dauphin fell for this very lovely woman, who owed her peerless beauty, it was said, to the constant use of cold water for washing.[1] Before he ascended the throne as Henry II, she became his acknowledged mistress, and headed the Court party in opposition to the Duchesse d'Étampes. After the banishment of this lady, Diane reigned supreme.    She married her daughters, Françoise in 1538 to the Duc de Bouillon, Prince of Sedan, and Louise in 1547 to Claude of Lorraine, Duc d'Aumale.    By this marriage Diane became ancestress of Louis XV.

Of brilliant intellect, exquisite taste in all the arts, and great charm of mind, this lady was created Duchesse de Valentinois in 1548 and installed in the Château de Chenonceaux, where she kept a marvellous Court.    After the death of the King in 1559 she withdrew from public life, and lived at the Château d'Anet until her death in 1566.

## CATHERINE DE' MEDICI

### Dauphine and Queen-Consort of Henry II of France, 1519 until 1547

Catherine, only child of Lorenzo de' Medici, Duke of Urbino, and Madeleine de la Tour d'Auvergne,[2] was born at Florence, 13th April 1519.    She was the last of the elder branch of the Medici family, and was left an orphan three weeks after her birth.

During the first eight years of her life she resided at the Medici Palace. In 1527 she was placed under the guardianship of nuns at the Convent of Le Murate, in whose charge she remained until 1530, when she was sent to Rome.    She lived there until her marriage, which was arranged by her uncle, Julius de' Medici—Pope Clement VII—to Henry, the second son of Francis I of France, in 1533.

Catherine's appearance at the age of fourteen is described by the Venetian Ambassador at Rome.    He writes: 'She is small and slender, with fair hair; thin and not pretty in face, but with the fine eyes peculiar to all the de' Medici.    She has a remarkably kind, gentle, and cordial manner.'

The author, Brantôme, who was with the French Court at the time of Catherine's marriage, has left a description of her as a bride.    'Her appearance is dignified, but at the same time gracious; her expression is pleasing, and her taste in dress excellent; she has a fine figure, a white complexion, small feet, very well-shaped hands, and a particularly beautiful voice.'

[1] The portrait of Diane in her bath, painted by François Clouet and entitled 'La Dame au Bain,' is in the Cook collection, and must be familiar to all by reason of its numerous reproductions. (See Fig. 555.)
[2] Brantôme calls her Magdelaine de Boulogne.

When Catherine landed at Marseilles, 12th October 1533, she was robed in gold brocade in the Italian style.    In the procession through the town she rode by the side of her uncle, John Stuart, Duke of Albany, who had married her mother's sister.

The marriage of Catherine and Henry of Orleans was solemnized at Marseilles Cathedral, on the 28th October of the same year, the Pope himself officiating.    On this occasion Catherine was dressed in a similar style, but entirely in rich white silk, embroidered with gold and precious stones, set in Florentine gold filigree work.    Conspicuous among her jewels were seven wonderful pearls of unusual size—a present from her uncle, Pope Clement VII.

The children of Henry and Catherine were:

Francis, born 1543, married Mary Stuart in 1558, succeeded as Francis II 1559; d.s.p. 1560.

Elizabeth, born 1545, married Philip II of Spain 1559; died in 1568 leaving two daughters (*see* p. 574).

Claude, born 1547, married Charles II, Duke of Lorraine, in 1559. Died 1575.

Charles, born 1550, succeeded as Charles IX 1560; married in 1570 Elizabeth, daughter of the Emperor Maximilian II; d.s.p. 1574.

Henry, born 1551, Duc d'Anjou, elected King of Poland 1573, succeeded as Henry III in 1574, married Louise de Vaudémont, assassinated 1589; d.s.p.

Marguerite, born 1553, married in 1572 Henry, King of Navarre, afterward Henry IV of France, marriage dissolved 1590, died 1615.

Francis, born 1554, Duc d'Alençon 1576, Duke of Brabant, 1582; d.s.p. 1584.                            (*Continued on p. 433*)


## BRANTÔME, 1540–1614

Brantôme, from whose writings so many particulars of feminine costume are derived, deserves a place here amongst the ladies.

Pierre de Bourdeille, Seigneur de Brantôme, known as Brantôme the French historian, was born in Périgord in 1540.    He spent his early years at the Court of Marguerite de Valois, sister of Francis I, to whom his mother was lady-in-waiting.    Destined for the church, he was made Abbé of Brantôme in 1553, at the age of sixteen.    He afterwards spent some time at Genoa, Milan, Ferrara, and Rome.    He accompanied Mary Stuart back to Scotland in 1561, and in London he was most graciously received by Queen Elizabeth.    Soon after his return to France, Brantôme entered the household of the Duc d'Anjou as gentleman-in-waiting.    He visited Toledo, Lisbon, and Madrid, and was present at Malta during the attack on the island by the Turks in 1565.    In his official capacity Brantôme attended the obsequies of Charles IX and the coronation of Henry III, and in 1576 he accompanied the Queen-Mother to

Poitou.   Before the year 1584 he composed his *Discourses*, afterwards made into a book and called *Vies des Dames galantes* and *Vies des Dames illustres*, published in Leyden and sold by F. Foppons, Brussels, in 1665.   His appearance at Court ceased after the death of Catherine de' Medici in 1589.   He died 15th July 1614, and was interred in the chapel of his Château de Richmont.

Posterity has perhaps judged the French Court too extensively from the writings of Brantôme.   It may well be that he has allowed his personal preferences to colour his opinions, rendering them unduly flattering in some cases and needlessly scurrilous in others.

### The Lady Anne of Cleves

*Fourth Queen-Consort of Henry VIII, 1516–57*

The prevailing English fashions had no difficulty in holding their own against the Flemish styles which were brought over by Anne of Cleves when she came to England to be married to Henry VIII.   Anne, second daughter of John III, Duke of Cleves, was born 22nd September 1516, and married 6th January 1539.   She was an interesting, though somewhat brainless, personality, with an oval face, long nose, chestnut eyes, light complexion, and very pale lips.   She had 'rather nice long yellow hair.'   In France Anne was reported to be ugly; but Thomas Cromwell, Vicar-General who arranged the marriage between the Lutheran Princess and Henry, told the King that 'every one praised her beauty.'   Hans Holbein was sent to the Netherlands to paint the lady's portrait; and the following excerpt from a letter addressed to Henry refers to this matter: 'Your Grace's servante, Hanze Albein, hath taken the effigies of my Ladye Anne and the Lady Amelye, and hath expressed theyr imaiges verye lyvelye.'   Holbein was paid £53 6s. 8d. for this portrait. However, when Henry saw the original he was anything but satisfied.   The marriage was soon annulled, and Cromwell paid the penalty with his head. Queen Anne was awarded a goodly sum as compensation for the loss of 'so difficult a husband as Henry.'   Her divorce, dating 10th July 1540, left her with the title of The Lady Anne of Cleves, and the remainder of her frivolous life was spent in England, where she became a leader of Tudor society.

Fig. 306 is taken from the portrait of Anne of Cleves painted by Hans Wertinger before she came to England.[1]   Her Flemish dress is composed of

[1] A portrait of Anne's sister Sybilla, wife of John George, Elector of Saxony, with her son, painted by Lucas Cranach, can be seen at Warwick Castle.   The Electress wears an elaborate German costume.

a rich brown velvet, decorated with bands of gold brocade.    The bodice and skirt are similar to those described under Fig. 307, but the sleeves are cut somewhat on the leg-of-mutton principle, except that the widest parts are at elbow level.    They are not pleated full into the armhole.    The bands of gold brocade are sewn on spiral fashion, and cuttes appear in places.

The cap is constructed on the lines described under Fig. 410; but the portion that surrounds the head in this latter drawing is replaced by a gable frame, ornamented with jewelled buttons and gold embroidery, matching that which

Fig. 306. The Lady Anne of Cleves, 1537

Fig. 307. The Lady Anne of Cleves, 1538

surrounds the neck opening of the plastron.    Above this is placed a circular flat bonet, with the brim cut on the left side.    It is of yellow velvet with a leaf design worked out entirely in small pearls.    'A round bonet or cappe set full of Orient Perle of a very proper fassyon.'

When Anne of Cleves arrived in England she appeared in the costume affected by ladies of her father's duchy; which must have been a novelty at Henry's Court and in great contrast to the fashionable attire of the moment.

Fig. 307 represents the Lady Anne in the familiar type of Flemish dress. It is derived from the original portrait by Holbein now in the Louvre.    Several copies or variants of this same portrait are to be found in England.

The complete dress is made of a deep shade of old-rose velvet, and decorated with bands of gold passamayne in two widths.    The bodice is close-fitting, slightly high-waisted, and widely open in front down to the waist-line, revealing a moderately low cut under bodice or plastron. This is composed of gold brocade or embroidery: sometimes the bodice was laced across the plastron, as shown in Fig. 306. The neck opening of the plastron has a rich ornamental border of gold embroidery, edged with small pearls. In addition, jewelled buttons are set at equal distances; a band of the same ornamental border surrounds the throat. The neck opening is covered with a partlet of fine lawn, having horizontal bands of cutwork. A gold belt and buckle closely confine the waist. The sleeves are made up on a close-fitting foundation, and have large puffs on the upper part of the arms; they are caught in close to the arms below the puffs with bands of passamayne, and thence widen out enormously at the wrist openings, as shown in diagram, Fig. 67. The invisible under-sleeves would be of rich material, matching the plastron, and show a puff of the smock sleeve finished with Flemish cutwork at the wrists.

The skirt, perhaps worn over the Spanish farthingale, sets stiffly and in funnel shape; but it is without a train, 'after the Dutche fassion rownde.' The skirt overlaps up the front—a characteristic feature of the Flemish mode. The elaborate Flemish headdress is described under Fig. 391.

Attention is again called to the fact that at this time a skirt *without* a train was looked upon as a novelty, or rather a foreign fashion. The 'all round skirt' was in vogue in Spain, Portugal, France, Flanders (Dutch), and a part of Germany, but was not adopted in England until the end of the reign of Edward VI.

Edward Hall well describes this dress when he relates that Anne of Cleves, on the day she first met her future husband, 'issued out of her tent beyng apparelled in a ryche gowne of clothe of golde reised, made rounde without any trayne after the Dutche fassyon, and on her head a kall, and ouer that a round bonet or cappe set full of Orient perle of a very propre fassyon, and about her necke she had a partelet set full of riche stone which glystered all the felde.' A few days later 'after dyner she chaunged into a gowne of tissue with longe sleues gyrte to her, furred with ryche sables, her narrow sleeves were very costly, but on her head she had a cap as she ware on the Saturdai before with a cornet of laune [see Fig. 307], which cap was so ryche of Perle and Stone, that it was judged to be of great valew.'

A *cornet* was a cap worn rather far back on the head. In the fifteenth century 'cornet' was another name for the hennin. This diminished, first into a truncated cone, then flower-pot shape, and lastly a close-fitting coif (*see* vol. ii, p. 448).

On her wedding day the Lady Anne 'was apparelled in a gowne of ryche cloth of gold set full of large flowers of great and Orient Pearle, made after the Dutche fassion rownde, her here hangyng downe, whych was fayre, yelowe and long. On her head a Coronall of gold replenished with great stone, and set about full of branches of *rosemary*; about her necke and middle Iuelles of great valew and estimacion.' Rosemary 'for remembrance'!—but Anne's later memories must have been mainly of disillusion. It is likely that the custom of wearing rosemary by Tudor brides was introduced by this lady.

'Madame de Cleves so far from claiming to be married, is more joyous than ever, and wears new dresses every day,' writes the French Ambassador. Whether any of these were supplied by her ex-husband we do not know, except that there is an entry in one of Henry's wardrobe accounts for 'a gown of black wrought velvet, furred with pampilion,' for the Lady Anne. When she settled down to her ex-married life as a high society dame, she gave up Flemish dress and eagerly adopted English and French fashions.

'Solempne Iusts,' at which the Court was present, were holden 'Sonday' 1542, 'on whiche daie she [the Lady Anne of Cleves] was appareiled after the Englishe fassiõ, with a French whode, which so set furth her beautie and good visage, that every creature reioysed to behold her.'

In later life the Lady Anne turned to the Roman faith; and at her death, 17th July 1557, she was interred with the gracious consent of Queen Mary in Westminster Abbey, the monks under Feckenham being reinstated from November 1556 to July 1559.

## CATHERINE HOWARD

### Fifth Queen-Consort of Henry VIII, 1521–42

Henry's fifth venture, Catherine, daughter of Lord Edmund Howard, was born 1521. At the age of eighteen she became maid of honour to Queen Anne Boleyn. The date of her marriage with the King is unknown, but she was officially acknowledged Queen on 11th August 1540. In appearance Catherine is described as 'a very little girl.' She had pretensions to beauty, but the French Ambassador (a connoisseur in such matters, who has left numerous evidences of his judgment) considered it commonplace. She had a fair skin, hazel eyes, and auburn hair. Catherine Howard's half-figure portrait, No. 1119 in the National Portrait Gallery, London, painted in 1542 after Holbein, is interesting from the point of view of costume. Fig. 308 is a drawing made from it. It shows her wearing a sleeve which evidently follows a fashion set by Anne of Cleves. Although this was not generally adopted by ladies in the few remaining years of Henry VIII's reign, it is to be found on effigies dating the second half of the sixteenth century.

Fig. 308.
Catherine Howard, Queen of England, 1542

The sleeves in this portrait are very full, cut leg-of-mutton shape, gathered or pleated into the armhole. They are made of black velvet, widely open at the side from shoulder to wrist, and edged with gold embroidery (*see* Fig. 309) with aiglettes at intervals. The open space is filled in with black satin, gathered transversely. The wrist frills are of beautiful Spanish work (*see* Fig. 265).

The close-fitting bodice is of black satin, with a yoke of black velvet, all in one with an upstanding collar, lined with white satin, worn half opened and slightly turned back. This collar is a revival of a fashion, of Flemish origin, worn by ladies of Henry VII's reign (*see* Figs. 27 and 68). A pendant of goldsmith's work and jewels is worn below the collar opening (*see* Fig. 461), and a pearl and gold lace, with smaller pendant, at the throat. The skirt and train, although unseen in the portrait, would probably be of black satin, opening over an underskirt of black velvet. A girdle of pearls and gold with a large pendant of jewels at the end encircles the waist, and hangs down the front of the underskirt. A description of the French hood will be found on p. 338. During the period of her attainder 'for misdemeanour' in 1542, Queen Catherine resided at Syon House, unperturbed by the trend of events, for the Imperial Ambassador writes to his Sovereign that she is 'making good cheer, fatter and more beautiful than ever, taking great care to be well apparelled.' Her execution took place on 13th February 1542.

Fig. 309. Embroidery with Aiglette

## CATHERINE PARR

*Sixth and last Queen-Consort of Henry VIII, 1510–48*

Catherine, daughter of Sir Thomas Parr, relict of the Hon. Edward Borough, and of John Nevill, Lord Latimer, was born in 1512. Lady Latimer married King Henry 12th July 1543. 'Of small stature,' she made no impression by her appearance, but was a thoroughly good motherly soul. 'The queen is graceful and of cheerful countenance: and is praised for her virtue,' said a very punctilious Spaniard. She exercised a wholesome influence on Henry during his closing years, and nursed him with great devotion. She was tactful, and to some extent mitigated the violence of his temper. Queen Catherine often intervened to save victims from the penalties of the Act of Six Articles; she reconciled the Princess Elizabeth to her father, and was much loved by both his daughters. Catherine certainly had the advantage of her five predecessors, inasmuch as she had graduated for her very difficult task, through previous experiences of married life, partnered by two mature widowers with grown-up families.

There is a very beautiful portrait of a noble lady in the possession of the Boothe family at Glendon Hall, Northants. It dates from the last years of Henry VIII's reign and illustrates the costume which persisted during the reigns of Edward VI and Mary. The artist is as yet unknown. The picture is painted on a 'table' measuring seventy by thirty-four inches, and has been described as a portrait of Queen Catherine Parr [1] or even of the Princess Elizabeth. There is no authentic evidence that it represents either of these ladies. The fact remains, however, that it is an excellent illustration of the costume of a great lady of the period above mentioned, such as would certainly have been worn by the Queen.

Plate XVII reproduces a water-colour made from this portrait. In line it is similar to the costume shown in Fig. 255 and Plate XVI. The gown is composed of cloth of silver damask. The sleeves are exceptionally close-fitting at the shoulders—a characteristic detail of the fashion just coming into vogue—and widen out as usual (see Fig. 67). They

Fig. 310. Arabesque Pattern

are turned back, and fastened tightly round the upper arm, whence they fall in the still fashionable angular manner. The sleeves in this illustration are lined with squirrel.

The underskirt and false sleeves are of rose-coloured silk embroidered with a gold Arabesque pattern. This is founded on the circle and square design, prevalent in the East and introduced into Europe by the oriental metal workers of Venice. It was also employed by the Moors who brought it with them into Spain, in consequence of which it was known as Spanish Arabesque. The paintings of Raphael display a variety of Arabesque design which is also influenced by Greco-Roman art. The embroidery on this costume (Plate

---

[1] It is stated by experts that no portrait of Catherine Parr has survived, but many paintings, even to-day, bear her name. The head-and-shoulders portrait of this Queen at Lambeth Palace, in which she is wearing the gable headdress, is of doubtful authenticity.

XVII) is inspired by the work of this artist, and is reproduced on a larger scale in Fig. 310, the border in Fig. 311. Green laces with gold aiglettes tie the edges of the false sleeves together, and each sleeve has three puffs of white (one unseen) protruding through cuttes, in addition to the customary puffs below. The underdress also has an embroidered border. The girdle of emeralds surrounding the waist is fairly simple; and from it is slung a girdle, different in design, consisting of two rows of cameos alternating with green beads, finished with a green silk tassel. The French hood is mentioned on p. 339.

Fig. 311. Embroidered Border

A Spaniard who came to this country in the entourage of the Duke of Najera—a Spanish grandee who had been sent by the Emperor Charles V on a visit to Henry's Court in 1544—records a pleasant English custom of the time. When Queen Catherine Parr was about to retire to her chamber she offered the Duke her hand to kiss. 'He would likewise have kissed that of the Princess Mary, but she offered her lips; and so he saluted her and all the other ladies.' Such friendly salutations, though customary among the English aristocracy, greatly surprised foreign visitors. Some were delighted, but many, including the punctilious Spaniards, were shocked. Refer also to p. 410.

This same gentleman was present at one of the Court functions held in the Duke's honour, at which he says 'there was music and much beautiful dancing. The Queen danced first with her brother very gracefully, and then Princess Mary and the Princess of Scotland [the Lady Margaret Douglas, Queen Margaret's daughter] danced with other gentlemen, and many other ladies also danced; a Venetian of the King's household dancing some gaillards with such extraordinary activity that he seemed to have wings upon his feet; surely never was a man seen so agile.'

The Queen's costume which she wore on this occasion is next described:

'She wore an underskirt, showing in front, of cloth of gold, and a sleeved overdress of brocade lined with crimson satin, the sleeves themselves being lined with crimson velvet, and the train was two yards long. She wore hanging from the neck two crosses and a jewel of very magnificent diamonds, and she wore a great number of splendid diamonds in her headdress.'

Princess Mary's dress was even more splendid than that of the Queen, being entirely of cloth of gold and purple velvet.

The Queen-Dowager married as her fourth husband, Thomas, Lord Seymour of Sudeley. This much-married lady was the last of the six Queens of the much-married King Henry VIII.

A contemporary portrait of Queen Catherine Parr in painted glass is to be seen in the Chapel of Sudeley Castle.[1] Fig. 312 is a drawing made from this authority. The date is the last year of her life, 1548. Her gown of black velvet is quite plain, having a close-fitting bodice with a collar open at the throat. The sleeves are cut square from the elbow like Fig. 254 and diagram, Fig. 65, which represents a fashion of about twenty-five years earlier, and are turned back showing the sable lining, while the false sleeves are dull purple finished at the wrists with a frill of Spanish work. The skirt has a train, and is worn over a moderate sized farthingale. The headdress of black velvet is similar to that shown in Fig. 395. Her jewels consist of a brooch and a girdle with pomander.

Fig. 312. Catherine Parr, Queen of England, 1548

Queen Catherine Parr died of an ordinary puerperal fever, 5th September 1548, and is buried at Sudeley Castle.

### THE LADIES MARY AND ELIZABETH, 1544 until 1547 (continued from pp. 271, 267)

Contemporary with Plate XVII is the half-length portrait of the Princess Mary in the National Portrait Gallery, London, dated 1544.

In it she is shown wearing a costume made of red and gold brocade, the sleeves being lined and turned back with crimson velvet. The false sleeves appear to be of gold tissue, the cuttes being outlined with narrow black velvet. The French hood (see p. 338) with its pearl decoration, and the Princess's jewellery, should be a subject of careful study.

[1] The effigy of this Lady in the Lady-Chapel at Sudeley Castle, although dating from the middle of the nineteenth century, shows Catherine Parr in the correct costume this time.

Fig. 313. 'THE LADY ELIZABETH, HER GRACE,' 1546

We are fortunate in possessing a three-quarter-length Franco-Flemish portrait of the Princess Elizabeth of much the same date: it is now at Windsor, and is reproduced in Fig. 313 by gracious permission of H.M. the King. It was painted in 1546 when the Princess was aged thirteen, and is mentioned in the inventory of Henry VIII's pictures, dated 1547, as 'a Table of the Ladye Elizabeth, her Grace, with a book in her hande her goune like crimson clothe of golde, with woorkes.'

The gown, including the lining of the turned-back sleeves, is of crimson cloth of gold damask. Notice that the sleeves are cut very close-fitting at the top of the upper arm. The elongated false sleeves, ornamented with cuttes and jewels in gold mounts surrounded with pearls, and the underskirt, are both of silver-grey satin 'with woorks,' i.e. embroidered with a raised pattern in gold. The French hood similar to the Princess Mary's is shown in Fig. 406.

A very valuable authority for the costumes worn at the end of this reign is the picture at Hampton Court showing Henry VIII and his family. It consists of a central panel wherein Henry is seated with his Queen, and his son, Prince Edward, stands beside him. One of the side panels contains a portrait of the Princess Mary, and the other the Princess Elizabeth. This is a composite picture, made up for the sentimental satisfaction of the new King, Edward VI, probably by his Court painter, Gwillim Stretes: the age of Edward fixes the date about 1547. There is no doubt that the Queen is Edward's mother Jane Seymour (who died, it must be remembered, ten years previously).

She wears the gable or whelk-shell headdress, which was more favoured by this Queen than by any of her three successors. Another interesting point is that the Queen is dressed in almost the exact costume depicted in the copy of Holbein's original fresco, dating 1537 (*see* p. 269). Did Gwillim Stretes copy this dress from the fresco? Most probably he did!

Fig. 314. The Princess Elizabeth, 1547

In the Hampton Court picture the Queen is dressed in bodice, sleeves, skirt, and train of gold brocade, the sleeves lined and turned back with ermine; the underskirt and false sleeves are of crimson velvet. She holds in her hand either a pomander or a reliquary of gold, set with a large emerald, and attached to the end of the girdle.

The two Princesses, Mary and Elizabeth, are labelled with wrong names. The discrepancy of sixteen years between their ages is ignored. The Princess Elizabeth may be identified by her gold pendant, an A (Anne Boleyn), set with an emerald and having a pearl drop (*see* p. 363). The Princesses are dressed alike in slate-coloured damask, the skirts, mounted over Spanish farthingales, having very long trains after the English fashion. The underskirts and false sleeves of both are of deep red velvet. The sleeves, worn by the Princess Mary, are turned back with a lining of the same damask; but the Princess Elizabeth's sleeves are lined and turned back with grey fur. The headdresses are French hoods similar to that shown in Fig. 403. The drawing (Fig. 314) is made from this portrait of the Princess Elizabeth.

It is surprising to find that a composition containing so many demonstrable inaccuracies should yet be a faithful record. There are close resemblances between the costumes shown and other portraits of reliable dates; and the inference to be drawn is that costume varied but little between the years 1537 and 1547.

Fig. 315. The Countess of Oxford, 1537

An example of heraldic state dress as worn during this reign is to be seen on a brass of 1537 in Wivenhoe Church. This is to the memory of Elizabeth, Countess of Oxford, second wife of the thirteenth Earl and widow of William, Viscount Beaumont, and is shown in Fig. 315. The sideless gown is white, embroidered with heraldic ermine spots, and is worn over a dress in a similar style to that shown in Part I of this chapter. It is almost certain that the Spanish farthingale of moderate proportions was worn underneath, for it is unlikely that any lady living during the despotic reign of the farthingale would ever appear without it, even for state dress.[1]

Over this is worn the heraldic mantle, displaying Scrope, 'azure, a bend or,' quartering Tiptoft, 'argent, a saltire engrailed, gules,' and fastened with jewelled bosses at the neck.   This lady wears the gable headdress as shown in Fig. 152, but surmounted by a Viscountess's coronet.

## THE YEOMEN OF THE GUARD

### *Temp.* HENRY VIII (*continued from p. 52*)

Early in his reign Henry VIII increased the numbers of the Yeomen of the Guard from three to six hundred 'and, by God, they were all as big as Giants.'   Their annual salaries totalled £2,500, in money of that time. About 1518 their number was reduced to one hundred and fifty.

In addition to the corps of ordinary yeomen there were four 'Yeomen Ushers' who were, in fact, members of an earlier establishment, 'The Yeomen of the Crown,' a corps raised by Edward IV, and consisting of 'xxiiij most seemly persons, cleanly, and strongest archers, honest of condition and of behaviour, bold men, chosen and tried out of every Lord's house in England for their cunning and virtue.   Thereof one to be Yeoman of the Robes, another to be Yeoman of the Wardrobe of Beds in the Household: other two be Yeomen of the Chamber.'

Fig. 316

'The Yeomen Ushers' were on duty in pairs to guard the door of the Great Chamber, and to preserve order within.   The remainder of the Yeomen of the Guard formed a Royal bodyguard.

During the early part of his reign Henry VIII was in residence at the Tower for quite a long period, during which the Yeomen of the Guard were in constant attendance upon his person.   When the King was absent from the Tower, the fact that it remained a Royal residence was indicated by the installation of a detachment of twelve yeomen permanently stationed there. These were called 'Tower warders' to distinguish them from the remainder of the corps of Yeomen of the Guard: the distinction still holds good, and Tower warders take no part in the Court duties of the Yeomen of the Guard to-day.

In the first years of Henry VIII's reign the costume of the corps of the Yeomen of the Guard was the same as shown in Plate III A, except that the vine

---

[1] A parallel example occurred in the mid-nineteenth century when ladies were seldom seen outside their dressing-rooms without the crinoline.

branch or wreath disappeared about 1527, and the rose was now surmounted by a crown (*see* Fig. 316).

The year 1514 introduces the first scarlet livery, which eventually took the place of the green and white coats shown in Plate III A, as a state livery. The date of the change is authenticated by an account which mentions materials for the livery of the guard, including scarlet cloth, white fustian, and black velvet. The first was for coats, the fustian for the doublets worn under the coats, and the black velvet for garding, and in some instances for the doublets.

In the Sanuto Diaries, 21st May to 14th July 1520, it is definitely stated that the Yeomen of the Guard who attended Henry VIII at the Field of the

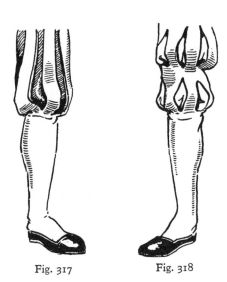

Fig. 317          Fig. 318

Cloth of Gold were dressed in doublets of white and green velvet in chequers, with the Royal badge of the rose embroidered on their breasts, and with halberts in their hands. With the alteration in their doublets, as above, they are illustrated in Plate III A. Evidently the scarlet liveries were not ready, but nevertheless the yeomen are so represented in the painting at Hampton Court, executed between 1538 and 1540, as shown in Plate III B.

This drawing, made from this painting, represents a Yeoman of the Guard as he appeared during the period 1530–50. All members of the guard are shown in coats or tunics fitting the breast, shoulders, and back, whereon is embroidered both back and front a network of gold cords and metal bosses or spangles, in the centre of which is set the rose, now quarterly red and white, and the 'Crowne Imperiall' bordered by gold embroidered gards. The wide neck opening is also edged with a band of gold embroidery. The sleeves consist of one large puff, with a single wide gard of black velvet between two narrow gards of the same. The skirt or base is widely pleated, having gards of black velvet, one at the bottom edge and the other half-way up, each between two narrow gards.

Some of the doublets visible at neck and forearm are of black velvet, others are of white fustian. Some bonets are depicted of black velvet, others red, being flat in shape as described under Fig. 359 C. The leg coverings or hosen are wide at the top and slashed in three different ways as Plate III B, Figs. 317 and 318 show. The linings pulled through are in four variations of colour as follows:

White hose, cutte, with black lining.
White hose, cutte, with yellow lining.
White hose, cutte, with green lining.
Red hose, cutte, with black lining.

A sword with black scabbard is slung from a black waistbelt, and the design of the halbert is slightly different from that used at an earlier date.

Some time about the middle of the reign the order was that the doublet, hosen, and bonet were to be of the same colour.

The Ordinary livery was the same as described in the last reign, and this remained in use until 1530. After this date it was of scarlet, cut on similar lines to the State coat; but the sleeves were smaller and lacked the horizontal gard of black velvet. The front had the rose and crown only, and was bordered or strapped like braces with black velvet, in place of the gold embroidery of the State livery.

The skirts or bases had only two bands or gards toward the lower edge. The bonets of black were the same as worn with the State livery, but the colour of the rest of the dress seems to have varied according to the fancy of the wearer.

The Watching livery of russet was severely plain, as hitherto, and references to the garment itself are found mentioning 'jacketts' and 'gowns.'

## GENTLEMEN PENSIONERS

In 1509 Henry VIII established a new Royal Bodyguard for the better protection of his august person, the idea originating from the French kings' bodyguard, founded in 1474 by Louis XI, and known as 'Gentils hommes de l'Hôtel du Roy, ou Pensionnaires.'

The corps was recruited from 'gentlemen of blood,' men of gentle birth but little fortune, and was, on all state and public occasions and at Court, in closer attendance upon the King than the Yeomen of the Guard.

There were different names for this corps on its first formation: 'A Retineue of Speers or Men at Arms,' 'Men of the Spears,' 'Gentlemen of the Speres,' 'The Kings Spears of Honour,' and 'Gentlemen Pensioners,' which last they retained during the sixteenth century and onwards. At first they were cavalry, wearing armour and carrying long spears; but after a short time the corps was employed on foot inside the Royal residences, and in consequence the battle-axe on a long staff—a pole-axe—was added to their equipment.

These gentlemen were fifty in number and every one had three horses and three attendants: an archer, a demi-lance, and a servant known as a 'custrell,' who was armed with a long sword, sharp from guard to point, and having three edges. The first captain (1509) was Henry Bourchier, Earl of Essex, K.G. (born 1472, died 1540), and the first lieutenant, Sir John Pechie.

In 1526 the corps was augmented by the addition of a standard bearer, a clerk of the cheque (who kept the roll and extracted fines from absentees), and a harbinger of second grade. This means that the harbinger was a gentleman, the first grade being a knight, the third a yeoman. It was his duty to arrange quarters for the corps when attending the King on any progress.

The costume of the Gentlemen Pensioners, as evidenced by the meagre illustrations available, was a gentleman's rich dress, in one of the various styles then in fashion. Edward Hall saw them dressed in cloth of gold. They all carried halberts after the same pattern as those used by the Yeomen of the Guard. The trappings of their horses were of the same expensive material 'and their servants richly apparelled also.'

In 1544 we hear that their dress was of one suit of red and yellow damask —the Royal colours. They were mounted on barded horses, the head-feathers and trappings being of the same colours.

(Continued on p. 420)

# SECTION III: 1509–47

## MIDDLE AND LOWER CLASSES

The old order of social standing was now completely changed. Wealth superseded noble blood and rank was judged by the amount of income.

A new aristocracy had arisen— 'Novi Homines' was the derisive term applied to them by Thomas Howard (1473–1554), Earl of Surrey and third Duke of Norfolk, and echoed by the few remaining families of ancient lineage —ancient but in some cases impoverished by civil war and ruined by the extravagance demanded of all courtiers, especially those attending Henry VIII. Bankruptcy resulted and estates passed to the opulent merchant, or land was divided up and sold piecemeal to tenants and small farmers.

Fig. 319. Thomas Linacre, M.D.

The erstwhile so-called middle class has now risen considerably in the social scale. Even some professional men were honoured with knighthoods, and, further, mere artists were dubbed, Sir Antonio Moro being the first. And as for woolstaplers—they were positively created peers of the realm! The latter now find a place in the section dealing with the nobility while the former still remain middle class.

### PROFESSIONAL

At the commencement of the sixteenth century the robes of Doctors of Medicine underwent a further change. Portraits of eminent physicians of this period are to be found in many collections.

Thomas Linacre, M.D. (born about 1460, died 1524), studied medicine in Italy 1485–92, was appointed tutor to Arthur, Prince of Wales, and became a pioneer of the New Learning. He founded the College of Physicians in 1518, and was Court physician to Henry VIII. Fig. 319 is made from a drawing of a portrait.  His gown appears to be long, black, and ungirded, lined and turned back with brown fur and having tubular sleeves slit at elbow level. For an earlier example of this gown *see* vol. ii, Fig. 561.  The underdress is a tunic buttoned up the front having a small frill of white at the neck.  Ordinary hosen and shoes would be worn.

Fig. 320. Sixteenth-century Rose

A note of horticultural interest is worthy of insertion here.  The type of rose with five petals grown in medieval times is shown in Fig. 320.  A later variety is shown in Fig. 54, taken from an Illum. MS. of the late fifteenth century.  Not long before his death in 1524 Dr. Linacre introduced the cultivated damask rose into England: such roses from abroad were expensive at the beginning of the sixteenth century, as much as two shillings being paid for a single red rose.

Dr. John Chambre (born 1470, died 1549) is seen on the right of Henry VIII in the picture by Holbein commemorating the Union of the Barbers' Company with the Guild of Chirurgeons as the surgeons were called in Tudor times. He received his M.D. at Padua in 1506, and was physician to Henry VII and Henry VIII, and Oxford conferred an M.D. degree upon him in 1531.

Fig. 322.
Sir William Butts, M.D., 1543

Fig. 321 (*left*). John Chambre, M.D.

The doctor wears an underrobe of black velvet and over it a long gown of black cloth with wide open sleeves lined and edged with brown fur.  The collar is high at the back and rolled over to show the lining (*see* Fig. 321).

In the National Portrait Gallery, London, there is a head-and-shoulders portrait (No. 210) of Sir William Butts, M.D. (born 1485, died 1545), physician to the King and 'a considerable man of affairs.'  It was painted about 1543, and shows him in a black gown with fur-lined hood attached and a gold chain about his neck (*see* Fig. 322). The caps worn by both are described under Headgear.

Physicians sometimes wore the livery colours of the Royal or noble personages to whose household they were attached (*see* p. 215).

A Doctor of Law (Fig. 323) is represented in the person of Bryan Roos, 'doctor of Lawe, sometime p'son of this Church,' whose brass is at Childrey, Berks. He is wearing a gown of the conventional shape, first seen in Fig. 220, vol. ii, and over it a fur-lined hood turned well down on the shoulders, the

Fig. 323. Doctor of Law    Fig. 324. Merchant            Fig. 325

cape-part almost reaching to the elbows. He is without his legal coif, but wears a pileus with a small point. We have it on the authority of the Venetian calendar that lawyers did not 'doff their white coifs even in the King's presence.'

## GENTRY

During the first half of this reign gentlemen wore the style of clothes illustrated in the first section of this chapter, but in a modified form and less ornate. Old gentlemen still retained the long gowns and fashions as worn by them in early life when Henry VII was on the throne.

About 1520 a slight change is noticeable in the costume of the gentry and the merchant as depicted in brasses commemorating these worthy people. Fig. 324 represents a wealthy merchant whose long gown of cloth, or even velvet, lined and turned back with fur, is open and ungirded. The long tubular sleeves are now mere panels, long and often flat, the arm passing through an opening cut like an inverted T. The back view of a similar gown is seen in Fig. 325, which shows the shape adopted by the clergy of the Reformed Church at a later date. Under this gown the merchant wears a skirted doublet with loose sleeves, and a pouch and rosary, though unseen, are suspended from the waistbelt. An undervest, the descendant of the plastron, is seen in Fig. 324 rising beneath the top of the doublet, and under it is the shirt. Hosen of cloth, yarn, or worsted, shoes of leather with round or square toes, and a bonet of velvet, cloth, or fur complete this typical costume of the opulent commoner.

Fig. 326. Flemish Gentleman

Fig. 326 is a drawing made from an incised slab in Stalhill churchyard, near Bruges, Flanders. It shows the costume of a well-to-do young man, and although Flemish it is the general style of dress worn by an Englishman or Frenchman of the first quarter of the sixteenth century. In detail it is similar to some of the illustrations in the preceding chapter, with the exception of the high neck of the under-tunic which is finished at the top with a narrow frill of fine linen, perhaps simply embroidered at the edge. The long hanging sleeves belong to the surcote. The full sleeves of the tunic are gathered at the armholes and into the deep cuffs on the forearms and fasten with one button.

Fig. 327 shows a curiously shaped hood worn by a burgess of some importance. It is fastened around the neck under the deep turned-down collar of the cloth gown. Another burgess (Fig. 328) has placed a short cape over his wide gown, most of the folds being gathered at the back.

The consequential person (Fig. 329) belongs to the period 1540–60. Of good standing, he was probably something influential in the city, or a private gentleman. His clothes were of the best quality; the skirted doublet buttoned up the front showing a turned-down collar to the shirt was of cloth, so was his gown which hung at the back like that in Fig. 325 and was lined throughout with marten. Short hosen were sewn to the slops above the knee, being gartered above and below. A flat cap of black velvet, a dagger slung from the waistbelt, brown leather gloves, and black leather shoes add the necessary distinction to his appearance.

Fig. 330 is typical of the English gentleman of the latter part of Henry VIII's reign. His costume is modelled on that worn by the nobility, but less ostentatious and of moderate proportions. It consists of a tunic with skirt: the sleeves could be of the same material and colour or different as shown.

Fig. 327.    Fig. 328.    Fig. 329. A Personage
Burgesses

This is worn over a shirt with a turned-down collar tied at the throat. The surcote in this instance matches the tunic and forms a 'suit' (1495). This would be carried out in a dark-coloured cloth edged with bands of velvet and braid, or with braid alone. It was not essential, however, that tunic and surcote should be alike, and frequently one sees in illustrations the tunic worn without a surcote. A flat cap of velvet or cloth was the usual head-covering, and long top-boots with square toes were worn over the hosen when required.

The young gentleman about to engage in sword and buckler play (Fig. 331) wears only a tunic with skirt open up the front. On occasion he would don a surcote. The decoration of the tunic comprises bands of dark-coloured velvet, and cuttes which reveal the linen shirt. The large sleeves finish at the elbow, or they could reach to the wrists. Notice that the belt and sword carriage have been added for the occasion. The exercise gained by the practice with sword and buckler was greatly encouraged, in fact, enjoined by the authorities as a means of keeping the youth and manhood of England fit. A buckler (front and back inset) was a small round shield about twelve inches in diameter, often made of steel, with a handle across the back by which it was held out at arm's length to ward off the sword thrusts of the adversary: at the back there was a hook to suspend it from the belt above the sword. The noise made by these two arms when the wearer strutted, or the striking of

Fig. 330. English Gentleman      Fig. 331. Sword and Buckler

his sword on his own buckler or his opponent's, originated the appellation, 'a swashbuckler.' Bucklers were also made of wood or wickerwork covered with leather and reinforced with brass or steel studs.

'Henchmen' was a term applied at this time to pages of honour  They were the sons of gentlemen and always walked near the King's horse in public processions.

The pages who attended the King and nobility at the Westminster tournament, 1511, were dressed as shown in Fig. 332 in tunics parti-per-pale russet and yellow with golden chains baldric-wise. Their hosen were scarlet, and shoes and bonets of black. An upstanding white plume decorated each of the latter, and the brim was tied up with a white lacet. A baton of the Tudor livery colours, white and green, was carried.

A surprising fellow to meet in Tudor times is to be seen in Fig. 333. He is a necessary adjunct to the sport of kings—a jockey in the Royal employ. His costume has been referred to on p. 157, and supplementary details have been extracted from that mine of information, the Tournament Roll. His parti-coloured doublet is of green Bruges satin and white fustian, with the Tudor rose and crown embroidered on the chest. It is cut square at the neck,

Fig. 332. Royal Page          Fig. 333. A Tudor Jockey

showing the gathered shirt and belted at the waist. The under-sleeves are close-fitting, with wide cylindrical upper-sleeves to elbow length and pleated into the armholes. The headgear is of black velvet with a gold button. The parti-hosen are counterchanged, and broad-toed black shoes with double straps complete the outfit.

The 'music' of the pipe and tabor, otherwise the drum, was very popular with the masses during the whole of the sixteenth century; even the Royal Consort included these instruments, but in that case the performer was, of course, a skilled musician.

This young man (Fig. 334), whose dress is that of the ordinary middle class, is engaged in amusing himself—and others—with a delectable tune on pipe and tabor; they were generally used together and played by one and the same person. The tabor is slung on the left wrist and kept in position by the left knee.

Fig. 335 is a drawing of a 'Patch,' the name applied generally to a domestic fool, originating from his patched or motley garments or the Italian 'pazzo,' a fool. On the other hand, James IV's Court fool retained his own name, John Magilrie.

The costume in Fig. 335, taken from a *Psalterium cum Cantis,* is coloured in blue with gold spots and scarlet with gold stripes. The tunic, cut tabard

Fig. 334. Pipe and Tabor

Fig. 335 (*right*). 'Patch'

fashion, is parti-coloured quarterly, the sleeves, hood with earpieces, long slops, and hosen following the same arrangement. Spherical bells were often dispersed profusely over the dress of a fool, chiefly at the points of the garments. In the original illumination one bell is on the main point of the hood and a row of bells on a band is worn just above the knee. The bauble varied in detail: sometimes the baton was surmounted by a jester's head, or a bladder on a string; at other times by long streamers of different colours. In Henry VIII's wardrobe account appears the 'item, 2 hose for Patch and 4 parti-hose 18s.'

Dancing was a pastime much indulged in by the people of Merrie England from the King down to the meanest peasant. The many annual festivals gave opportunities for merry-making and one of the most general holiday amusements was Morris dancing. This was originally derived from the Moors of

Spain ('Moresco,' a Moorish dancer), and found its way through France and Flanders into England in early Tudor days.    Included in the Morris were certain characters: Robin Hood, Maid Marian, Friar Tuck, a jester, a hobby-horse, and a dragon, but chief among them were the dancers.    They wore costumes, fantastic yet with an element of period as shown in Fig. 336, which represents a typical Morris dancer in gay colours.    The most important features were the long streamers attached to the shoulders and the bells

Fig. 336. Morris Dancer

round the wrists, knees, and often ankles.    The short jacket, say of green, very open on the chest, showing a placard striped black and white, had a fancy white collar, short basque, and dagged shoulder-pieces of green alternating with long streamers, two or three inches wide and lined with yellow.    The evolutions of the dancer created a whirlpool of dazzling lines and curves as these streamers floated in the air,[1] and to complete the effect brilliant-coloured caps with long feathered quills were worn.

For a team of Morris dancers engaged by the churchwardens of Thame

---

[1] At a later period when streamers became obsolete, multi-coloured ribbons took their place. Other innovations crept in from time to time.

when the Church Ales were revived under Queen Mary, were bought the
following:

|  | s. | d. |
|---|---|---|
| Item pay<sup>d</sup> for xiij yards of grene for men's cottes | xiij | |
| pd for ij yards and half of yelow cotton | | xx |
| pd for v pear of say [hosen] | iij | iiij |
| pd for coloured thread | | iiij |
| pd for makynge of the cottes | vj | x |
| pd for ix dorsn daunchyng bells | iij | vj |

Important members of the community at this time, especially in London,
were the *apprentices* (*see* vol. ii, p. 189). Their recognized dress (Fig. 338),
which was more or less regulated by custom, consisted of a tunic of blue
cloth reaching to about the thigh, with moderately close sleeves worn over
the ordinary shirt. Hosen attached to short slops (unseen) were 'sewed up
close thereto, as they were all in one piece.' This was their usual summer
attire; but in winter their shirts, hosen, and tunics were supplemented by a
blue cloth cloak (Fig. 337). A blue coat was the distinctive garb of a menial,
and was the habit of serving-men and boys during the whole of the sixteenth

Figs. 337, 338. Apprentices

Fig. 339 (*right*). An Adventurous Young Man, 1511

and the early part of the seventeenth century. A servant was frequently
referred to as a 'bluecoat,' and to be 'blue-coated' or 'blue-bottled' was a
term of scorn. Even the official coat of a beadle was blue.

London apprentices in the time of Henry VIII wore round black caps with flat brims (*see* Fig. 359 C), like those in general use at the time.

Because they were worn by this class of unfledged tradesmen, 'flatcap' became a snobbish appellation for an apprentice. 'Goodman' was a term of contemptuous familiarity and to greet any one with 'goodman flatcap' was to ensure for oneself a sound box on the ear or something worse.

Fig. 339 is an honest young man of no particular breeding —the sort one would meet at any time on any day (though, perhaps, excepting holidays) in town or country. His tunic is similar in shape to those appearing in this chapter, and was that which was generally worn. It is fastened only by laces and a belt round the waist secured by a buckle. A similar buckle used for this purpose was unearthed in the City of London, and is shown in Fig. 340; it is of iron, and the leather belt is ingeniously fastened round it by a thong

Fig. 340. Buckle

inserted twice through a hole, the splayed ends being welted over each other. A felt cap, coarse hosen, leather pouch and shoes are worn. The date of the

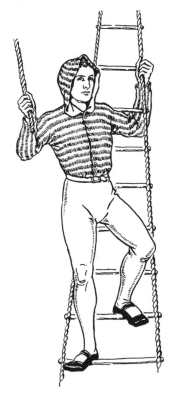

Fig. 342. A Spanish Shipowner

Fig. 341 (*left*). An English 'Sailer'

print from which Fig. 339 is taken is 1511. Possibly this young man has a sense for adventure, or a liking for the sea, and, as there was much talk at this time of galleons being built for His Majesty, the 'Father of the British Navy,' he might volunteer for service as a 'sailer.' The rig was very attractive, as Fig. 341 shows: practical, if a trifle fantastic, consisting of a jacket combined with close sleeves and a hood, of a strong blue and white material in horizontal stripes. The scarlet hosen, which fasten round the waist, are of a stout fabric, and the black shoes are of leather. For full dress the hood would be thrown back and a black bonnet worn.

Fig. 343. Sailor or Wharfman of Barcelona, c. 1529          Fig. 344. A Farmer

Medieval sailors had a distich rolled in wax and fastened to their wrists for identification purposes.

A Spanish *shipowner* is seen in Fig. 342, and his costume has some points similar to the dress worn by English seamen at a later date. His jacket of dark cloth has sleeves of the fashionable shape, the sleeves of the shirt coming out below them. The skirts of this garment hang from beneath the jacket over wide slops of blue and white or red and white coarse linen. To the close cap, worn in stormy weather, was added a black blocked felt cap when dallying on the quay. A cutlass with black scabbard and belt, black shoes, and coarse worsted leg coverings, complete this nautical outfit.

A Spanish seaman of lower grade is seen in Fig. 343, hauling in a boat by a leather belt over his shoulder attached to a rope with a disc at the end. These discs were twisted round the main haulage robe (*see* on his right) to obtain extra power. The short jacket piped with colour is dark, the puffs of the sleeves white, and the lower part of the sleeves dark. Short white slops leave the legs bare, and when on shore the feet are shod in rope or straw shoes. Probably the smart French bonet in black was a gift or possibly looted.

## COUNTRYMEN

Perhaps the most interesting of the middle classes is the yeoman, who now gradually begins to fill the gap between a gentleman and a peasant.

Fig. 345. A Peasant

Fig. 346 (*right*). A Looby

Towards the end of the fifteenth century there originated a difference with little distinction in the social grade of the countryman. Those who had acquired sufficient means to enable them to purchase the land which they cultivated became freeholders and were known as 'yeomen,' a title of one who had 'freeland of forty shillings by the year.' He ranked next below an esquire, and these small landowners or yeomen increased to such an extent in both numbers and prosperity that their position was fully recognized by the time of Henry VIII.

Inferior to the yeoman was the 'farmer,' who cultivated land not his own but for which he paid rent.

The *farmer* (Fig. 344), respectfully touching his cap, is about to pay his rent. He has donned for the occasion his best tunic, now sadly out of date, having seen service through more than one generation. The same applies to his cap, hosen, and shoes.

The *peasant* (Fig. 345) fingering his old felt cap, in the act of offering his eggs for sale, wears a very quaint jacket, short, and with close sleeves, the neck covered with a piece of cloth the same as the jacket, which at first sight suggests a hood thrown back. The pleated portion at the back let into the jacket is also curious. A pouch would be attached to the girdle and the somewhat ragged hosen extend over the tops of the rough boots.

The cheery young countryman (Fig. 346) comes from an Illum. MS. dated 1527. His tunic is of simple cut, open at the throat, and worn over a shirt

Fig. 347. A Cornemuse          Fig. 348. Dame Drury, 1533

unseen. The arrangement of the pouch is described under Fig. 91. The hosen of coarse material are ill-fitting, and are kept close to the knee by a strap bound round the leg. The hat and shoes are of the usual shape.

The cornemuse (Fig. 347) continued to be much used by peasants to entertain their helpmates and the village community.

## MIDDLE-CLASS WOMEN

### GENTRY

The *gentlewoman* (Fig. 348) is Dame Drury, wife of Sir Robert Drury, who died in 1533. The drawing is made from her effigy in St. Mary's Church, St. Edmundsbury. Her cloth gown is cut all in one, fitting the figure and forming many folds in the skirt, being cut on the old-fashioned plan. The wide sleeves are turned back showing the silk lining, like those worn by noble ladies; but they are not draped in such a stiff manner, and display the fashionable false sleeve with a frill falling over the hand. A rich chain passes twice round the neck over the partlet, which is fastened by a brooch. The belt, worn low, carries some useful articles as well as an ornament. The mantle denotes that she is an important person, the wife of a country knight. The gable headdress of black velvet is quite simple, having flaps at the side of the face, pinned to the forehead pad so that they fall in a slight curve inwards on the cheek. Behind is a small curtain falling to the back of the shoulders.

Fig. 349. A Flemish Gentlewoman

In the National Gallery, London, are two panels (No. 657) of a triptych painted by Jacob Cornelissen (1470?–1533). They contain portraits of a Dutch or Flemish gentleman and lady. The latter is shown in Fig. 349. She is gowned in black velvet, having wide open sleeves lined and turned back with white fur. The neck is outlined with a narrow band of gold which also descends the front of the dress. From the gold girdle is hung a rosary of scarlet beads ending in a gold cross. A béguin, shaped like that shown in Figs. 388 and 389, is worn, but as the lady is not a widow the barbe is omitted.

The gentlewoman (Fig. 350) belongs to the middle part of Henry VIII's reign, clad in a simple gown of silk or cloth with a band of velvet at the edge of the neck opening revealing the lawn partlet, with high neckband and small

Fig. 350. An English Gentlewoman, 1530

frill. The sleeves are square, like Fig. 65, and turned back showing the silk lining over close-fitting sleeves with a frill at the wrist. A velvet waistband is fastened in front with an ornament and to it would be slung a rosary, pouch, book, or reliquary. Her headdress is described under Fig. 407.

In the Illum. MS. from which Fig. 251 is taken there is a seated figure (Fig. 351) representing France. She is dressed as a woman of the upper class, and in the original miniature the gown is of fine blue cloth with a border of black velvet at the neck. The sleeves are turned back with ermine, but this is because she is an emblematic figure—no woman of the people would be

Fig. 351. A French Gentlewoman, 1514          Fig. 352. A Merchant's Wife, 1538

allowed to use such regal fur for the embellishment of her garments. Her headdress is of plain black velvet, shaped like that worn by Princess Mary (Fig. 251) and shown in diagram, Fig. 397. The ornaments are a gold medallion hung by two chains around the neck, and a gold girdle. The seat is an interesting item.

The agitated old lady (Fig. 352) comes from the title-page of the Bible mentioned on p. 234. In the original she is crying out: 'Vivat Rex.' Her dress is of grey cloth with bands of black, and has a full skirt gathered to the waist-line of the bodice; a narrow white band is tied over the seam. The full sleeves are gathered into the armholes and into cuffs at the wrists, where they are turned back and bound with yellow cord, so as to form a loop at the point: the sleeves of the smock show beneath. Over her shoulders and passing *under* her arms, a square kerchief is tied behind by its corners. This method of covering the shoulders was very usual with women of all classes when attired in homely dress.   The white cap is characteristic of the time, and the belt carrying a pouch and other accessories (unseen) including a needlecase was indispensable to the good housewife.

Fig. 353. A Spinster

### LOWER CLASSES, WOMEN

A woman of the people (Fig. 353) is engaged in the usual pursuit of spinning, an occupation thoroughly recommended, as 'it stoppeth a gap, it saveth a woman from being idle and the product was needful.'  The distaff is fixed to a stand and kept firm by the right foot.   On top the flax is bound by a small cylinder.   The spinster drags the threads of flax and twists them with her right-hand thumb and first finger, and with the left twirls the bobbin.   As the yarn increases in length it is wound on the bobbin : already she has filled five, and these are placed in a circular box beside her.   The spinning chair is three-legged, and the seat, covered with a cushion, is triangular.   She's an industrious little woman and a careful soul—she does not sit on her skirt, you notice, though the student of costume may regret that no underclothes are visible.

A chamberer or chambermaid wore nothing very distinctive in Tudor times, as Fig. 354 shows.   An ordinary gown with close sleeves that could be rolled up when at work, a kerchief tied round the neck, a rectangular piece of linen pinned round the head to keep the hair clean, similar to the head-covering worn by peasants, and an apron constituted her 'uniform,' according to illustrations of the period.   The apron was oblong, the waistband being attached to its narrow end for only a short distance, the corners hanging at the sides.   The besom, made of twigs, usually of the broom plant or heather,

Fig. 354. A Chamberer

tied round a long handle, was a superior household implement. A more common example with short handle is inset.

The two young countrywomen (Figs. 355 and 356), who work on the land, are dressed more or less alike: one in a dark gown with a fancy white and coloured apron, the other in a light one banded with dark cloth, and a plain

Figs. 355, 356. Countrywomen　　　　　Fig. 357. To Market

white apron. The bodices of both have plain fronts and are laced up the back: the smocks under these are gathered into neckbands, and the full sleeves into wristbands.

The old woman on her way to market (Fig. 357) is garbed in much the same manner in a gown of dark homespun with the bodice bordered with black. Her smock is of linen which she has woven on her own loom, and is of substantial make. The same linen supplies her cap and her ill-fitting hosen, and her large square-toed shoes are of thick black leather.

# SECTION IV: 1509–47

## HAIRDRESSING

Henry VIII's styles of hairdressing changed during the course of his reign as referred to on pp. 155 and 318, and shown in Fig. 211, Plate IX, Figs. 231 and 235, Plates X B and XIII, and Figs. 292 and 293.

Where hair is described as being bobbed and waved level with the ears, the effect is that given in Fig. 107.

Hairdressing and games do not appear at first to be closely connected, but the following incident is a curious case of cause and effect.

The custom of cutting the 'King cake' on Twelfth Night was observed in France as well as in England. This cake contained a bean; and whoever was fortunate enough to find it concealed in his portion was elected 'king.' Great sport ensued, and for the rest of the evening the pseudo-monarch was treated with mock reverence and mimic ceremonies, and all his commands were implicitly obeyed.

While this pastime was in progress at the hotel of the Comte de Saint-Pol at Paris in 1521, Francis I arrived from Romorentin when the January snow laid deep upon the ground. Always eager for a 'rag,' Francis notified to the Count his intention of attacking the hotel and chastising the 'usurper.' Barricades of heaped snow were quickly erected. The guests were supplied with ammunition such as huge snowballs, eggs, apples, etc., and the assailants were armed with the same missiles. Everything went gaily until the attacking party were about to force an entrance, when a guest (Jacques de Lorges, Comte de Montgoméry, afterwards Duc d'Aubigny, died 1559, aged eighty-one), snatched a burning log from the hearth, threw it from a window above, and struck Francis on the head, inflicting a deep and severe wound.

Francis was badly hurt, and for several days his life was in the balance. In order to treat the wound satisfactorily all his beautiful hair had to be cut off. Amid the consternation of the Court Francis alone remained calm, remarking that if a sovereign engaged in the pastimes of a child, like a child he must be content to pay the penalty of his folly. From this time onward Francis I always wore his hair clipped close, and the courtiers followed his example.

When Henry heard what had happened, he also adopted the new style, and his Court followed the Royal example, and had their heads 'polled.' All England imitated the Court, and for a few years short hair remained fashionable. By 1526, however, Henry, and presumably his Court, had indulged once more in bobbed hair, and he is so represented in a miniature of that date. Tonsorial fashions in England for the next nine years are uncertain, but it is recorded by Stow the historian that 'the 8th of May [1535] the King commanded all about his Court to poll their heads, and to give them example hee caused his own head to bee polled, and from henceforth his beard to be notted and no more shaven.'

All portraits of Henry VIII after 1536 depict him wearing his hair 'polled,' or cut close to the head, and with a soft curly beard upon his upper lip and chin.

As regards German fashions in hairdressing it is recorded by Sandoval that the Emperor Charles V cut his hair short in August 1529 'as a vow' for his safe passage from Barcelona to Genoa, 'or, as others have it, for a pain in the head,' and thereafter wore it in this way.

Fig. 358. Charles Brandon, Duke of Suffolk
(*after Holbein*)

*Beards.* Some portraits show Henry VIII in early life with a beard, and some clean shaven. Taken together with documentary evidence these pictures suggest that between the years 1519 and 1535 he wore a beard, or was without one, just as the fancy took him. As mentioned earlier he had a beard in 1519; but in the following year, at the time of the Field of the Cloth of Gold, he was clean shaven and wore bobbed hair.

The following excerpt gives an example of the sporadic appearance and disappearance of Royal beards. 'At the conclusion of the Treaty with France, 8th October 1518, it was agreed betwixt both princes [Henry and Francis] that there should be an interview in July 1519, which yet took not effect, because of the death of Maximilian. . . . Therefore it was put off till 1520; both kings in the meanwhile agreeing not to cut off their beards till they saw each other.'

In 1535, after a prolonged series of alterations, Henry VIII commanded his beard to be 'notted' (bunched) and 'no more shaven.'

Many of Holbein's portraits, painted in England between 1536 and 1543, some of which appear under Headgear in Figs. 361, 362, 363, 365, show that the beard was worn in a variety of ways by certain persons of rank.

In Germany, the Emperor Charles V, clean shaven in youth, wore at the age of twenty-five (Plate VIII B) a short soft fluffy beard, slightly pointed on the upper lip and round the jaw, not covering the front of the chin; in later life he is portrayed by Titian wearing a stiffer beard, covering the upper lip and chin, cut short and rounded.

The typical German beard of his time was a short stiff growth, cut wide either square or fan-shape, and allowed to grow only to the level of the point of the chin. This is seen in Plate VIII A and seems to have been a popular mode in military circles. It was seldom encountered in England, although a recently discovered Holbein portrait of Charles Brandon, Duke of Suffolk, shows this type of beard, which suggests a thick fringe (*see* Fig. 358). A bushy beard is worn by the German gentleman (Fig. 371).

A method adopted by many gentlemen on the Continent was to dress the beard with warm wax to stiffen and thicken it and make it spread out broad at the bottom. This treatment remained the vogue with some until the end of the century.

## HEADGEAR, 1509–47

During the first part of the reign the French bonet was in general use as shown in the various illustrations in Part I of this chapter, and of the same shape as described in Chapter I (*see* Fig. 359 A). Those worn by Henry VIII

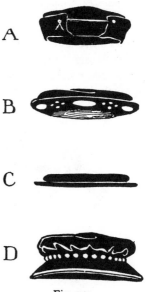

Fig. 359

(Fig. 211), James IV (Fig. 226), Maximilian (Fig. 110), Charles Brandon (Fig. 358), and the Frenchmen (Figs. 233 and 234) are more or less of the same style. Towards the end of the second decade of the century bonets were more decorated. Plate IX and Fig. 274 are examples. Besides the medallion, tubular beads of goldsmith's work, sometimes with jewels and pearls in addition, were set at all angles on the brim. Ornamentation increased owing to Italian influence as may be seen in Fig. 219, who is wearing one such cap and known in western Europe as a 'Myllan cap,' a style of headgear fashionable in Milan, a city much within the focus of all Europe at this time. It was made of rich material, velvet, silk, cloth of gold or silver and decorated in a fancy manner with cuttes, aiglettes, and other finery. This gentleman has added two ostrich plumes with peardrop pearls hanging from the quills. The cap has also gold cords or chains suspended from it so that it could be pushed back on to the shoulders as described on p. 94. It is worn over a network and jewelled coif. Feathers in caps and bonets were worn in 1510.

Fig. 360 is another example of a Myllan cap composed of deep red velvet, the upstanding brim edged with gold passamayne. Gold tissue is puffed over the top and each piece secured by a ruby set in gold, with a peardrop pearl attached to it. A double gold cord encircles the brim chain-wise.

'Item, a bonet of black velvet, with a brooch and a naket woman with xviij pair agglettes and xviij buttons, and a small cheyne about thedge of the same' is from the inventory dated 1527 of Henry Fitz Roy, Duke of Richmond. This is obviously a Myllan cap.

The cap worn by the noble (Fig. 8) was probably a Myllan cap.

Fig. 360. Myllan cap

The Italian (Fig. 218) has adopted the German style of hat of black velvet, rather large, having an embattled edge to the brim. It is worn very much on one side over a turban-coif of gold network on coloured silk and tilted at the opposite angle from the hat.

The mode of wearing the coif or small cap very much on one side of the head was, as mentioned on p. 95, an Italian fashion which, according to the following account taken from the Venetian calendar for 1520, was still in vogue. When Charles V visited England in that year he was attended by many Spanish grandees, amongst them the Duke of Alba. At a banquet on Whit Monday evening: 'The viands were so numerous that the banquet lasted four hours, after which the tables being removed, dancing commenced and the ball was opened by the Duke of Alba, a sexagenarian, but still amorous. He danced with a Spanish lady, his favourite, not handsome, but beyond measure graceful. The dance throughout was "The Gloves of Spain" with a very gay finale to

Fig. 361. 'Simon George, de Cornwall'
(after Holbein)

Fig. 362. Sir Thomas Wyat
(after Holbein)

the sound of the fife. The dress of the Duke's lady would be long to describe, but the Duke himself wore a small cap of tawny cloth, with a green silk tassel across the cap which he cocked to the left, in the Ghibelline fashion.'

At the same time the nobility introduced a simplified form of the French bonet which became very popular for ordinary wear. Its shape is shown in Fig. 359 C. The brim, like the rim of a plate, is almost circular and measures about two and a half inches in width, and the crown, a disc, about eighteen inches in diameter. The edges of the latter were pleated or gathered into the head opening of the brim, and when off the head it was possible to lay it

Fig. 364. John More (*after Holbein*)

Fig. 363 (*left*). Lord Vaux
(*after Holbein*)

down quite flat like a plate, hence its name 'flat cap.' Velvet, beaver, or cloth were the materials of which this cap was made and without any decoration, a single feather being exceptional. Several of Holbein's drawings show this

Fig. 365. The Marquess of Northampton, 1547 (*after Holbein*)

type of flat cap worn very much on one side, the brim suggesting a halo when viewed sideways. Fig. 361 (made from Holbein's drawing of 'Sir George of Cornwall,' 1528) shows one made of black beaver; this *has* a short feather, the quill end tucked into the very narrow cap-band. Another made of cloth, and without a feather, is seen in Fig. 362. Similar caps are shown in Figs. 363 and 364, the latter having the brim made in two sections, the ends overlapping.

The flat cap in its original aspect held its own for a comparatively short time; because it was a useful head-covering for ordinary wear it soon found its way on to the heads of the masses. For this reason the fashionable added expensive ornaments to the underside of the brim. Fig. 365, made from Holbein's drawing of William Parr (1513–71), created Marquess of Northampton 1547, shows him at the age of thirty-four and illustrates the latest treatment. The edge of the brim is indented and many beads and buttons are

Fig. 366. French, 1547          Fig. 367. French, 1543

distributed over the underside. A medallion and feather are also added. In Holbein's original sketch detail drawings of these ornaments are made by the side of the cap. They, the medallion, three enamel beads, and a button are reproduced in Fig. 365 behind the head.

Two examples of the flat cap are given in Fig. 367 taken from a portrait of a Frenchman dated 1543, and in Fig 366 from another dated 1547.

In Fig. 359 B one sees the newest form of cap. The crown part was still cut circular and gathered or pleated into the headband, but the brim was made to slant slightly upward—an alteration necessary to show off the handsome ornaments to better advantage. It was still shaped like a plate-rim, a small section being cut from it and joined up; this gave the desired upward turn.

On the inside of the brim an ostrich plume was laid and so arranged that the fronds on one side of the quill showed above the edge of the brim, the end drooping over the side either the right or the left, filling in the cavity between the brim and the top of the ear. The cap was always worn tilted either to the left or the right.

Velvet was the principal material used and generally black. Red was sometimes favoured, but other colours very seldom. This type of cap is made familiar by the later portraits of Henry VIII. It is seen in Plate XIII.

The cap worn by Francis I (Plate VII B), worn over a coif, and Charles V (Fig. 287) are variants of this headgear.

Fig. 280 shows the same shaped cap, except that the latest mode was to turn the brim down irregularly especially on one side of the front. Ornaments on the underside of the brim were therefore dispensed with.

Fig. 368. The Emperor Maximilian in 1519 (*after Albrecht Dürer*)

A characteristic hat was worn by the Flemish aristocracy—large, round, and flat. That shown in Fig. 368 is typical. The crown is soft and cut circular; probably it is made in four sections like Fig. 369. The brim is wide and stiff, divided in two or more places; the ends which overlap have very acute-angled corners. Its sole decoration is a small gold ouche. Although Dürer's work, from which this drawing is taken, dates 1519, the hat worn by Maximilian is the shape he frequently used in earlier years.

The portrait bust of Charles V in the Gruuthuse, Bruges, shows him at about the age of eighteen (1518). At this time he was styled Comte de Flandre. His tastes and sentiments were thoroughly Flemish, therefore it is safe to designate his headgear as characteristic of that country. Fig. 369 is made from this bust. The crown of the hat is circular and constructed of four pieces; the brim, almost flat, is in two sections, the ends overlapping each other, and underneath it is set a medallion on one side. That these hats were stiff is obvious from the way in which Francis I raises it from his head as seen in Fig. 228.   This hat is of the Flemish fashion, but two ostrich plumes have been added to it.   Velvet, beaver, cloth, or felt were the materials used in the making of these Flemish hats, and they were usually black.

Fig. 370 is from the portrait of Henry VIII painted in 1521 (Plate X B) and described on p. 190.   The King is depicted wearing bobbed hair, a close beard, and a black hat of definite Flemish character, similar to those illustrated in Figs. 368 and 369.   In the original portrait the hat is painted solid black, obviously felt, and circular and flat in shape with a crown like Fig. 369.   The brim is cut at the sides and the edges

Fig. 369. The Comte de Flandre, 1514

tied together by gold laces and aiglettes.   A gold ornament is fixed on the left side.   The shirt is very finely gathered into a narrow embroidered neckband, and the stomacher or placard is decorated with two double rows of pearls framing an embroidered band of pleasing design in gold on black.   A small portion of the doublet of white and gold brocade is seen bordered with embroidery in gold on black.   The pale yellow lining of the crimson velvet surcote gathered at the revers is quite a usual fancy.

A portrait dated 1526 of Ferdinand, the second son of Philippe le Beau, is reproduced in Fig. 2.   His black velvet hat having an enseigne on the left front and rows of three buttons at the sides is typically Flemish.   His black velvet robe with collar, lined with sable, is worn over a doublet of green velvet.   The gold border to this is embroidered with a Latin inscription (illegible, unfortunately), and round the neck is a black band carrying the Toison d'or under the doublet.   His Hapsburg features are pronounced.

Already in 1521 he had married Anne of Hungary and Bohemia and succeeded his brother as Emperor, being crowned at Frankfort in 1558 as Ferdinand I. He died in 1564.

The large beaver hat of Flemish origin referred to in the last chapter went entirely out of fashion among the nobility of England soon after Henry VIII's accession. It is, however, frequently seen in representations of men-at-arms, etc. In Germany this large hat in various designs and materials became very general (*see* Plate VII A), and is an essential part of the recognized German national costume of the first half of the

Fig. 370. King Henry VIII, 1521

sixteenth century. A modified form of the same hat was worn in Italy and is seen in Fig. 218.

The German hat shown in Fig. 371 has an individuality entirely of its own. The crown is circular, soft, and flat, and the brim so wide that, being cut up at right angles, the outside edges can be folded over and fixed to the base of the crown to form heavy loops. To keep them fairly rigid these loops were

Fig. 371. German

often tied together here and there. Sometimes a medallion was fixed in a prominent position. Fig. 372 shows the back view of these large hats, which were always worn very much on one side, and usually over a coif. A similar hat is worn by the Landsknecht (Plate VII A), and a description of it is given on p. 174. Fig. 373 shows a specimen of a cutte coif as worn by Germans of various denominations, often under the large hat. The loops round the edge are constructed in the same manner as described under Fig. 371, but the ends are turned under. The crown is decorated with five radiating cuttes.

Fig. 374 is a blocked felt cap modelled on the lines of Fig. 125. It is black and the brim, void in front, is tied up by bands across the top. This cap is worn by a private gentleman, therefore the type could not be a recognized part of an official dress. Neither could that worn by Sir Thomas More

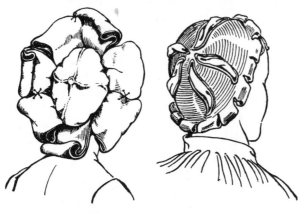

Figs. 372 (*left*) and 373 (*centre*)
Fig. 374 (*above*). Blocked Felt

(born 1480 and beheaded 1535). This cap (Fig. 375) is in the fashion of the last reign, in spite of the fact that the portrait from which the figure is taken was painted in 1528. Although forty-eight at the time, the Saint still retains the headgear of his youth. The portrait is of interest chiefly because it shows him wearing 'gazings,' otherwise spectacles. The material of which the earliest spectacle frames were made was cuir-bouilli, later of bone or horn; the wealthy had them of gold or silver. At this time the manufacture of spectacles was monopolized by the Germans, but the lenses, cut from rock crystal, came from Venice. Another form of frame, riveted at the nose, was also in use.

The cap worn by Dr. Linacre (Fig. 319) is influenced in shape by the universal bonet with the brims curiously tied together by laces or cords.

Hats and caps of blocked felt were considered the distinctive headgear of the clergy and professional classes.

Fig. 375. Sir Thomas More, 1528

They were, however, worn by other persons who would scarcely come within this category—for instance, Figs. 124, 127, and 212.

Fig. 321 is from a portrait of Dr. John Chambre. His black blocked felt cap is worn over a skull cap of black velvet in shape like that shown in Fig. 273 inset. From a contemporary source we learn that a *velvet* cap was the distinctive headgear of a physician and known as a 'physick cap.'

A skull cap is absent in the portrait of Dr. Linacre, who died in 1524, therefore the portrait of Dr. Chambre (Fig. 333), painted at about the age of fifty-five (1525), is probably the first to show the physick cap. This suggests that it came into use about this time. Dr. Butts (Fig. 322) wears a blocked felt cap not unlike Fig. 374. His physick cap has two ends for tying under the chin.

On a newel of one of the stalls in the Chapel of Jesus College, Cambridge, is carved the figure of some academic personage. The head and shoulders are reproduced in Fig. 376. This little man wears a blocked felt hat, but the interesting point about him is that one can examine his back—unlike most effigies that are nearly always lying on their backs. It shows the *fall* of the

Fig. 376. Academic

hood when thrown back off the head, and the exceptionally wide opening, seen front and back, which originally surrounded the face. In it one sees the transitional stage between the old official hood and the modern apology for one. This is referred to in vol. ii, p. 213.

The 'biretta,' Italian 'berretta,' Spanish 'birreta,' was a square cap worn by clerics of the Roman Catholic Church. Cardinals wore it of red, bishops purple, and priests black. The biretta was originally a round cap in use among the laity as early as the thirteenth century (*see* Fig. 223, vol. ii). It was ordained in 1311 that priests should wear a skull cap if to be bareheaded in choir was inconvenient. The round or skull cap, being made in four sections, gradually evolved into a square. It had a button on top at the point where the seams met—a useful adjunct when removing it. In Fig. 227 is seen a biretta of the early sixteenth century. See pp. 690 and 733 for further developments.

The flat cap was in very general use among the middle classes, both men and boys, during the reigns of Henry VIII, Edward VI, and Mary. It was made of velvet when worn by men of importance, and of cloth, knitted wool, or felt when worn by the commoner. Its appearance is shown in Figs. 363 and 364, and on some of the figures in the middle-class section.

Fig. 377 gives a sectional diagram with the approximate measurements, and it will be seen that the brim is double and extends part of the way up the sides of the crown to C. From A, down the *inside* of the brim and over the crown to B, it measures nineteen and a half inches from side to side, and twenty-three from front to back.

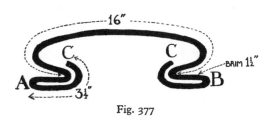

Fig. 377

John Stow has something to say about the flat caps worn by Londoners which is worth quoting.

'The youthful citizens took them to the new fashion of flat caps, knit of woollen yarn black, but so light that they were obliged to tie them under their chins, for else the wind would be master over them. The use of these flat round caps so far increased (being of less price than the French bonet) that in short time young aldermen took the wearing of them; Sir John White wore it in his mayoralty, and was the first that left example to his followers; but now the Spanish felt,[1] or the like counterfeit, is most commonly of all men both spiritual and temporal taken to use, so that the French bonet or square cap, and also the round or flat cap, have for the most part given place to the Spanish felt, but yet in London amongst the graver sort (I mean the liveries of companies), remaineth a memory of the hoods of old time worn by their predecessors; these hoods were worn, the roundlets upon their heads, the skirts to hang behind in their necks to keep them warm, the tippet to lie on their shoulder, or to wind about their necks, these hoods were of old time made in colours according to their gowns, which were of two colours, as red and blue, or red and purple, murrey, or as it pleased their masters and wardens to appoint to the companies; but now of late time, they have used their gowns to be all of one colour, and those of the saddest, but their hoods being made

Fig. 378. A Spanish 'Sailer'

---

[1] Spanish felt was of a superior quality and much in demand by the upper classes, which encouraged some Spanish and Flemish feltmakers to come to England.

of one half of the same cloth their gowns be of, the other half remaineth red as of old time.'

Sir John White, grocer, was mayor in 1563, so that the latter part of the above description belongs to Chapter IV. It is interesting to note that Stow is perhaps the first writer to refer to the roll of the chaperon as a 'roundlet,' and to call the hanging cape part of the hood 'the skirts,' and the liripipe 'the tippet.' The description of the livery gowns belongs to the 1580's.

For the cap worn by a Doctor of Law see Fig. 323, and of Medicine, see Figs. 319, 321, and 322.

The sailor hat of Nelson's and modern times has its origin in the headgear worn by the 'sailers' of Barcelona at the beginning of the sixteenth century. Fig. 378, from a contemporary drawing, shows a typical Spanish salt wearing a hat, most likely made of leather, and of a blue colour, though they are found also in a shade of violet. Most Spanish 'sailers' were dressed like Fig. 342, but often minus the jacket, and in their shirts with the sleeves rolled up.

Nightcaps are described on p. 262.

## HEADDRESSES

### THE GABLE HEADDRESS (*continued from p. 108*)

The gable headdress, as worn by noble ladies in the time of Henry VII, was in vogue during the first ten years of Henry VIII's reign. From its earliest form, shown in Fig. 150, to the latest (Fig. 381), it is mainly associated with England. Margaret Tudor introduced it into Scotland, but it was not very generally adopted in that country. In its early form it was sometimes worn in Flanders, but rarely (if ever) in France or Germany.

Its very newest shape, as worn by Queen Katherine of Aragon in 1510, is seen in Fig. 239. The rigid front of the gable, called the frontlet and labelled E in the last chapter, is still a stiffened flat frame, but considerably wider than before. It is of crimson, cross-barred and bordered with gold, set with jewels—rubies, diamonds, and pearls. A white linen coif, covering the hair, is unseen under the solidly constructed box-like back portion of the headdress itself, and is referred to in Fig. 151, p. 107. The top and sides of this framework are all in one and sewn to the back, which is shaped so that its top edge follows the line of the gable front as at T in Fig. 381. To the horizontal bottom edge of the back is fixed the curtain, shaped as a truncated sector of a circle, rather like the half of a simple lampshade. This headdress is composed entirely of crimson velvet, which is rather unusual.

A slight modification in the shape of the headdress described under Fig. 152 took place at a date between 1520 and 1526. It is seen in Fig. 379, taken from the portrait of Queen Katherine of Aragon, now in the National Portrait

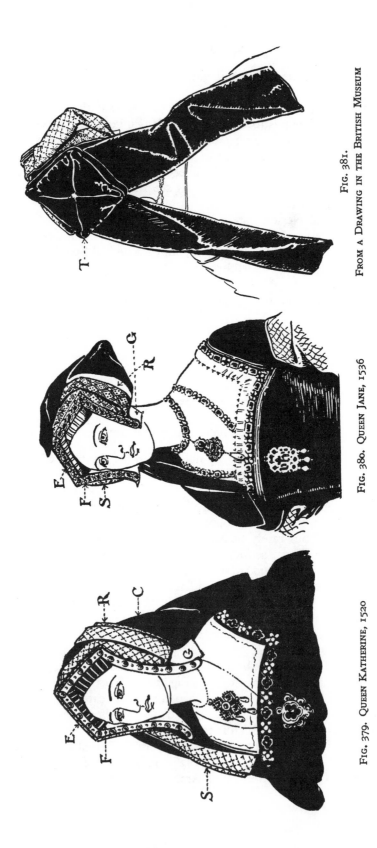

FIG. 381.

FROM A DRAWING IN THE BRITISH MUSEUM

FIG. 380. QUEEN JANE, 1536

FIG. 379. QUEEN KATHERINE, 1520

Gallery. This is said to have been painted by Johannes Corvus, who came to England from France on one or two occasions between 1510 and 1520 to execute commissions. It shows Queen Katherine at the age of about thirty-five, thus dating the portrait at 1520.

In Fig. 379 the linen coif is retained as a foundation for the whole, underneath the box-like structure with its lappets, G. The first narrow band, E, of gold and jewels, is quite rigid, the long ends having now a more definite inward curve. The usual bandage of striped silk, F, is used as a padding on the forehead. The semicircular hood of black velvet, C (Fig. 153), is now slit up the centre of the back only; it is laid on top of the coif with its straight edge fixed just behind the band of jewels, E, and falls down the back. On top of this again is fixed a development of the band, RS, formed of a piece of folded cloth of gold or brocade, slightly padded. This lies behind the frontlet of jewels, E, with the long ends hanging down on each side of the face. It had become the vogue to turn up one end and pin it to the side of the headdress, as seen in the drawing.

The final arrangement of this headdress, so characteristic of the later years of Henry VIII's reign, and immortalized by Holbein, is seen in Fig. 380. This is reproduced from the portrait of Queen Jane Seymour painted by this artist in 1536. Similar headdresses may be seen in portraits of other great ladies of this time. The narrow band of jewels or frontlet, E, is shorter, about level with the mouth; the lappets of the cap, G, are consequently shorter, being attached as before to the frontlet, E. The bandage, F, is still retained in place of the pad, except when the hair is worn waved on the forehead. The back hair would be bound closely round the head, more or less after the method shown in Fig. 409, to take up as little room as possible under the headdress. The latest arrangement of the hood, C, slit only in the centre of the back, was achieved as follows: The right half was turned up across the back of the head and dexterously folded or twisted into the shape of a whelk-shell (this headdress is often referred to as the 'whelk-shell headdress'), projecting on the left side, the end being pinned up flat on top; several small ornamental pins were used to set the folds of the whelk-shell into suitable shapes. The remaining (left) half of the hood, C, was brought round the back of the neck to the right side and draped over that shoulder. To complete the effect, both ends of the padded band of gold brocade, RS, were pinned up to the sides of the headdress.

A simplification of the hood part used with this headdress took place about this date, probably owing to the bulkiness and weight of material used in the semicircle (Fig. 381). The box-like head part was retained, as described under Fig. 151, and to the edges of the sloping back roof were fixed, in place of the earlier hood, long flat tubes of black velvet, crossing each other and together forming a 'set-square,' with a diamond of black velvet, T, at the back of the box. The ends or tubes, taking far less material than before, were worn flowing, or were pinned up in various ways on top of the headdress. The front remained the same, as shown in Fig. 380.

The Lady Mary.

Fig. 382

Fig. 382 is from an original drawing of the Princess Mary II made by Holbein, presumably in 1536 when the Princess had been reinstated in her father's affections, and when she was summoned by him to come to Court at Richmond to take part in the Christmas festivities. She wears the gable headdress, but it is not easy to determine whether the black velvet takes the form of the hood (Figs. 138 and 153) or of flat tubes (Fig. 381). Whichever form is used, the two hanging portions are most effectively treated—raised, folded back, and draped on top. There is no clear indication of how this is actually arrived at. It is only possible to achieve a satisfactory arrangement by placing a headdress on a block, and carefully and artistically folding the black velvet oneself, fixing it with tiny gold ornamental pins. It should be observed that a little hair is seen at the sides of the head.

These last two versions of the gable, diamond, or whelk-shell headdress remained in fashion until the end of Henry VIII's reign, when they were entirely superseded in the wardrobe of a fashionable woman by the 'French hood.' Old ladies retained this style of headdress well into the reign of Queen Elizabeth, but it vanished altogether about 1570.

An unusual arrangement of the gable headdress, worn by a lady of sixty-six, is shown in Fig. 383 and illustrates in its use the variety of individual fancy. This one is taken from the head-and-shoulders portrait of Margaret Plantagenet, Countess of Salisbury (the lady referred to on p. 417, vol. ii), painted in 1535, and now in the National Portrait Gallery, London. The portrait is interesting for many reasons, especially because it shows the gable without a frontlet,

Fig. 383. Margaret Plantagenet, Countess of Salisbury, 1535

back semicircular black velvet drapery, or the usual band of gold brocade. The gable frame or kennel is covered with white lawn, the edges stitched with black silk, and the ends folded under. Ermine is laid over this, although originally it was miniver—a fact revealed by an X-ray photograph of the portrait, which showed that the black spots had been added at a later date.

For further study of the gable headdress reference should be made to the various portraits by Holbein and other contemporary artists, especially to Holbein's drawings preserved at Windsor.[1] It is, however, difficult to determine the exact variant portrayed even by these authorities; since there were many ways of arranging the folds, it is only occasionally that a twist or turn will decide whether the semicircular hood is depicted (Fig. 153) or the tubular extensions described in Fig. 381.

The method of binding the head under the various types of gable headdress was probably the same as is described under Fig. 409.

### THE BÉGUIN—FLEMISH AND GERMAN HEADDRESSES

The headdress shown in Figs. 384 and 385, worn by a Flemish woman of middle class, shows a later arrangement of the béguin referred to on p. 111. In shape it is as simple as its predecessor, but the folding is a little more

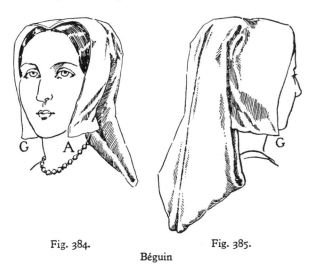

Fig. 384.                    Fig. 385.

Béguin

complicated. Diagram, Fig. 386, shows the position of the foldings, dotted, and diagram, Fig. 387 (illustrating one half), explains the direction of the folds. The crosses marked R and S in Fig. 386 give the points where the linen is pinned together at the nape. The bottom edges I to P are turned up, passing

[1] These studies for portraits were executed between the years 1528 and 1543. Collotypes of them can be obtained.

underneath the portion H R S Q, and attached to the inside of the headdress about crown level.

Great ladies much favoured the simple béguin for the ordinary routine of everyday life; it could be easily washed.

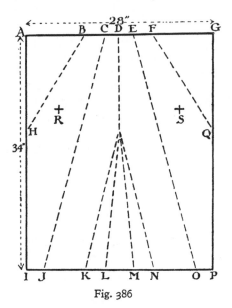

Fig. 386

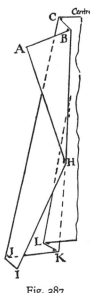

Fig. 387

Fig. 388, showing a simple-shaped béguin worn by a widow (*see* diagram, Fig. 389), is a drawing made from a portrait of the Archduchess Marguerite of Austria painted by van Orley about 1520 and in the Musée des Beaux Arts, Brussels.

To achieve the result shown in Fig. 388 the procedure was as follows:

First, a close-fitting white linen cap covers the hair, with the exception of a small wave on the temples. The widow's barbe (*see* vol. ii, p. 191, and vol. iii, Fig. 149) is then fixed in place. *Above* this is a piece of transparent gauze, fastened close round the head and covering the forehead and eyebrows. Surmounting all this is the béguin of white stiffened linen, the front edge creased to dip in the centre, and the sides pinned to the barbe so as to bow outwards at the

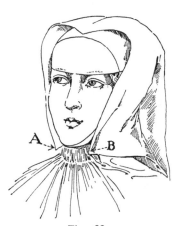

Fig. 388.
The Archduchess Marguerite, 1520

temples. It is pinned together also at the nape, at a point set back from the edges, which gives the folds shown in the drawing. Refer to Fig. 164 and diagram, Fig. 165.

In the National Gallery, London, there is a beautifully painted portrait (No. 1652) of the Dutch School which was for many years described as repre-

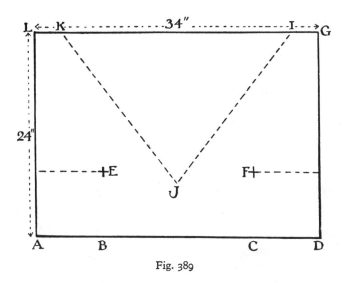

Fig. 389

senting Queen Catherine Parr. This has been identified as a portrait, dating 1543, of Madame Van der Goes, a Flemish lady, who wears the head-dress particularly associated with her country.

A drawing of it is given in Fig. 390. First a stiffened linen coif, something like that in Fig. 134, but deeper from back to front, is put on, and tied with a tape under the chin. The rectangular piece of stiffened lawn or veil (*see* diagram, Fig. 389) is then placed on top; it follows the shape of the coif beneath. The letters in Fig. 390 correspond with those in diagram, Fig. 389, and explain the arrangement of the veil. Small button-holes are worked at E and F, through which a fine tape is passed and tied tightly behind, effecting the folds seen in the drawing. The veil is then pinned to the tape of the coif, below the ears, and its stiffening produces the angular appear-ance at the sides.

Fig. 390. Madame Van der Goes, 1543

The decoration of the fine lawn smock is shown in Fig. 395. The neck is edged with a line, headed by loops, of fine gold cord. Below are roses in gold repoussé, alternating with frettes worked in black silk. The border is finished with a second row of fine gold cord, and the opening on the breast is fastened with two hooks and eyes of gold.

A headdress (Fig. 391) worn by Anne of Cleves at the time of her marriage is mentioned under the description of her costume (Fig. 306). It is definitely Flemish and, although comment was made upon it when first seen in England on her arrival in 1539, it was not adopted in this country. Its shape is similar to that described under Fig. 157, and it is composed of a melon-shaped frame constructed of some stiffened material. It is cut out in front to fit the head, and at the back descends in a curve to the nape. Caps such as this, made of silk or velvet, were decorated in an elaborate manner, often cross-barred in gold with pearls or jewels at the intersections, and jewels set

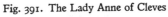

Fig. 391. The Lady Anne of Cleves                Fig. 392. German

in the spaces between—'so ryche of Perle and Stone.' Under this cap are two preliminary items. The first to be donned is a close-fitting cap made of gold tissue or soft metal, plain or figured, and edged with small pearls. Above this is placed a rectangular piece of fine lawn, about six to eight inches in width. The principal cap is then put on and secured to the head by a kind of clip—a band of flexible gold, set with jewels. To the left side of the cap an elaborate tassel was sometimes attached. As a last touch to this beautiful headdress the rectangular pieces of lawn hanging at the sides of the face are pinned to the back part of the cap, giving them a right-angle effect on both sides. This much resembles the béguin in line. Similar headdresses are to be found in portraits of foreign noble ladies by German artists.

A definitely German headdress is shown in Fig. 392, taken from a portrait by Antonio Moro. It illustrates convincingly the melon-shaped undercap mentioned under Fig. 391, and although bulging at the back defines the shape of the head. A thin veil covers this and projects over the brows, and over it is fixed a band of embroidery or goldsmith's work.

If the word were not taboo in the history of costume the characteristically

German headdress worn by the lady (Fig. 393) would certainly be described as 'becoming'! The drawing of the hat is taken from a portrait, painted, it is said, by Hans Holbein, and was in a private collection in Switzerland. The

Fig. 393. Anne, Queen of Hungary, 1530 (*after Holbein*)

original has 'Anne Regina,' aged twenty-seven, 1530, inscribed above the head; but this is of no value for identification purposes as twentieth-century experts place no reliance on painted titles. These were usually added later by the owner, who inserted the name of any suitable person he thought interesting; a prevalent but irritating vice, widely practised on portraits by eighteenth- and nine-teenth-century historical enthusiasts. Until recently the portrait was supposed to represent Anne Boleyn, and many engravings of it bear her name; but that theory has been abandoned. It is conclusively proved to be Anne, daughter of 'His Apostolic Majesty,' Wladislav II, King of Hungary and Bohemia, and sister of King Louis II. This Princess married the Archduke Ferdinand of Austria in 1521, and after the tragic death of her brother, Louis II, at the Battle of

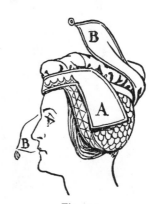

Fig. 394

Mohács in 1526, the crowns of Hungary and Bohemia were ultimately secured by her husband, who in 1558 became the Emperor Ferdinand I.

The headdress (Fig. 393 and diagram, Fig. 394) is a hat worn over, first,

hairdressing as shown in Fig. 141.   Secondly a caul of what appears to be a network in a scale design having a woven gold border edged with pearls which rests on the hair at the sides of the face.   Above this is placed the hat of black velvet.   It has a front portion cut in a peculiar shape to give the modish square effect (see A in diagram).   This is attached to the front of the brim of the bag-shaped crown.   A band, shown B in the diagram, is fixed to the brim at the back and is brought round, the points being fastened together with a jewel in front.   The decoration consists of an edging of gold, five or more ornaments of goldsmith's work set with jewels and pearls, groups of three bars of large and small pearls, and an upstanding plume.

The dress with large puffed and cutte sleeves is of cloth of gold with a pattern outlined in red silk.   Notice should be taken of the jewelled carcanet, the ornament hung by a black ferret, the embroidery in gold on the chemisette, and the knots of gold which fasten the cuttes together.   The usual gold chain over the shoulders holds up the front of the bodice.

Fig. 395

### A FRENCH VERSION OF THE BÉGUIN

Fig. 396
Louise of Savoy, Duchesse d'Angoulême

A headdress similar in shape to the béguin, but made of black velvet and lined with silk, was much in use for ordinary wear among Royal and Noble ladies and matrons.   It was popular during the first half of the sixteenth century in France and England, although its origin is even earlier; it is seen worn by a woman in Fig. 602 and in diagram, Fig. 618, of vol. ii.   The first example of the French hood worn by Anne of Brittany (1507) (Fig. 162) bears a striking resemblance.

This black velvet headdress is shaped as shown in diagram, Fig. 163, except that the front AB is straight, as indicated by the broken line; and it is depicted in a miniature portrait of Louise of Savoy, Duchesse d'Angoulême, mother of Francis I (Fig. 396).

Among other ladies of Royal and Noble birth who are shown in their portraits wearing the same kind of headdress are: Katherine of Aragon in her later years; Catherine Parr (Fig. 312); Marguerite of Angoulême, sister of Francis I, who married Henry II, King of Navarre; and Aimée Motier de la Fayette.

In a portrait, dating about 1519–21, in the National Portrait Gallery, London, Margaret, Queen of Scotland, wears the same type of headdress as that shown in Fig. 396, but with this difference—the black velvet béguin or hood, lined with white satin, is slightly turned back, and under it a white lawn cap, with a narrow pleated frill at its edge, rests on the hair. The portrait is repro-

Fig. 397. Margaret Tudor, Queen of Scotland, 1520

duced in Fig. 397. The dress worn by Queen Margaret is of black silk with a velvet pattern. The sleeves are turned back, probably in the manner described under Fig. 254, and lined with black velvet. The full skirt could be open up the front or closed; either would be correct. The arrangements of the heavy carcanet of interlaced goldsmith's work is very characteristic of the time.

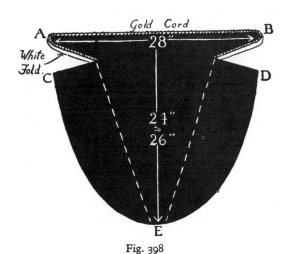

Fig. 398

The hood worn by Princess Mary I depicted in an Illum. MS. dating 1514 is another and somewhat rare version of this headdress. It is shown in Fig. 251 and in diagram, Fig. 398. It is made of black velvet lined with white silk. The front part and side pieces AB are edged with gold cord. A lining of white lawn is fixed inside this part. The side portions CD are folded under at the dotted lines, the edges seamed together, and slightly gathered at E. This forms a bag which falls behind the shoulders.

### THE SPANISH RETICULATED CAUL

This Spanish headdress is obviously of Italian origin and was adopted by the Spaniards. Reference should be made in this connection to the drawing of Beatrice d' Este (Fig. 140).

Under Fig. 244 is given a description of the costume worn by the Empress Eleanor, wife of Frederick III. Fig. 399 is a profile drawing of the same lady's headdress.[1] The upper end of this long tapering network is wide enough to go round the head, and is edged with a row of pearls; it is made of gold network, with pearls or jewels at the intersections. This network caul sometimes reached the heels, and from the nape downwards it was usually bound and cross-plaited with narrow gold bands, their ends forming a tassel, sometimes elaborately ornamented with pearls, jewels, beads, etc. The hair was visible inside the net, and it is obvious that the wearer, like the fashionable twelfth-century ladies of England and France, added false hair. Alternatively a tube of silk stuffed with tow was sometimes enclosed in the network. With this headdress it was usual to wear a gold fillet, set with jewels (notice the correct level of this fillet), to keep the caul more firmly in position. Frequently these network cauls were made entirely of strung pearls.

Rabelais describes the caul worn by Queen Eleanor when she arrived in France in 1530. He says it was 'made with gold butterflies.' These were worked in very fine gold gauze or gold filigree, probably set with diamonds or other jewels poised at the intersections of the network.

Rabelais also states that the Queen 'had a bonet of crimson velvet on her head, covered with jewels, in which was a white feather curled.' This bonet, somewhat German in character, is illustrated in the drawing, Fig. 400, and is described as a 'bonet à la *coquarde*,' a term used to denote any headdress coquettishly perched on one side. Fig. 401 shows the caul worn by the Princess Marie of Portugal, stepdaughter of Queen Eleanor. Her caul covers the back of the head, but does not appear to be continued in a long tube down the back. It seems to be secured on the forehead by an ornament which passes backwards over the top of the head, probably to the nape. Two jewelled ornaments fix the caul on each side of the head, and below them the hair

Fig. 399.
Reticulated
Caul

---

[1] This headdress is given here because the dress of the Empress is described in this chapter (*see* p. 203), but it must be borne in mind that they are both of the fashion of 1490–1510 which lasted until 1530 and even later. (*See also* Figs. 411, 412, and 413).

puffs out over the waved pieces which lie next the cheeks. The end of the caul is seen beneath all this hair at the side of the neck. This headdress shows Moorish influence. One of the portraits of Queen Eleanor illustrates a caul exactly like this.

Another character-istic style of Spanish hairdressing is seen in the portrait of the Empress Isabella by Titian. Plaits of hair are wound round the head and secured on top by a jewelled or-nament as shown in Fig. 249. At the sides, the hair is curled or waved, and puffed out behind the plaits sur-rounding the face. This is much the same style of hairdressing as the coiffure shown in Plate XI and Figs. 400 and 401.

A headdress, typi-cally Spanish, is worn by the lady in Fig. 247 and is a development of that shown in Fig. 399. A veil of lawn, silk, or gauze, which is passed through a ring of goldsmith's work, is placed on the hair; the long end, or pigtail, is encased in the fabric and bound with bands of gold ending in an orna-

Fig. 401.
The Princess Marie
of Portugal

Fig. 400.
Eleanor, Queen of
France, 1530

Fig. 402. Spanish

ment to which coins are attached (a Moorish fancy). The edge of the veil is pinked, and the front part, folded back off the forehead, passes through the ring, the latter giving a halo effect.

Fig. 248 is wearing a similar headdress, but the arrangement of the veil on the head indicates that the edge is gathered into a band, the whole suggesting a mob-cap.

Fig. 402 is not unlike the last, except that the turned-back front portion of the veil is stiffened and stands up from the head like a coronet. It is possible that this is a separate piece. The lady who wore this headdress was a native of Valencia, and the sleeve (Fig. 246) is also hers.

FRENCH HEADDRESSES

*(Continued from p. 111)*

The headdress worn by Fig. 254 (1510–20) shows a near approach towards that known later in England as the 'French hood.' The black velvet back part is cut as shown in diagram, Fig. 163, having the *straight* edge AB as indicated by a broken line. This is turned back to the *solid* line, AB of the same diagram, thus forming a curve. The hood is worn over a small close-fitting cap placed very much on the back of the head.

In a Flemish calendar painted in 1530 by Simon Binninc (Add. MS. 24098 British Museum, under February, fol. 19B, and April, fol. 21B) there are two ladies wearing hoods like Fig. 254, the turned-back portion being lined with red.

In Figs. 403 (three-quarter view) and 404 (side view) is seen the French hood in fashion at the Court of France from about 1515 to 1535. It is taken from a drawing of Diane de Poitiers in the Bibliothèque Nationale, Paris. A drawing of Queen Claude (died 1524) in the same library shows her wearing a headdress exactly similar.

First, a close-fitting cap, white or coloured and edged with pearls, is placed on the head and tied, almost invisibly, under the chin. Pearls edge the cap and continue along the string. Beneath the front edge of this cap appears a goffered frill of double gold gauze, which rests upon the hair, waved, and parted in the centre. To the front edge of the black velvet hood (shaped as shown in diagram, Fig. 163) is fixed a wire, stiff enough to preserve the desired shape, yet flexible. Sometimes the wire is simply covered with black velvet—a piping; but in this case (Fig. 403) it is masked or replaced by a plain band of gold or goldsmith's work. This semi-rigid edge forms a graceful curve of crescent shape, fitting close to the cheeks before and below the ears, widening and sloping backward at the temples and above the crown. The coloured or white lining is folded forward to show between the gold band and the close-fitting cap; and the remainder of the black velvet tube falls down the back.

The headdress worn by Margaret Tudor in her portrait, dating 1515 (?), in Holyroodhouse Palace is modelled on that shown in Fig. 403. In place of the band of goldsmith's work there illustrated, a row of gold filigree beads, finishing in a very pronounced outward curve, edges the front of the black velvet hood. It is turned back, showing the white satin lining over a red cap which has a band of gold embroidery on its edge. A narrow goffering of gold gauze rests upon the hair.

The portrait of this same Queen in the National Portrait Gallery, Edinburgh, attributed to Jan van Mabuse, suggests that it was painted when she was younger than in the portrait at Holyroodhouse Palace. In it the Queen

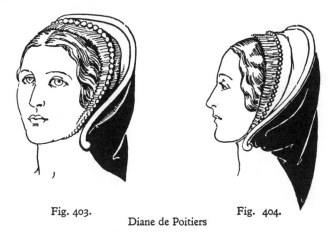

Fig. 403.

Diane de Poitiers

Fig. 404.

wears the black velvet hood, the front of which is decorated with a row of gold embossed beads, alternately circular and tubular in shape, giving a very rich effect. Only a small portion of the coloured lining of the hood is seen, and under this is a white cap with an ornamental band of lozenge design in gold. Very little of the finely pleated gold gauze is seen resting on the hair.

### THE FRENCH HOOD COMES TO ENGLAND

If we may credit the date allocated to the famous portrait by Jan van Mabuse showing Mary Tudor, Queen - Dowager of France, with her second husband, Charles Brandon, Duke of Suffolk, we must accept the early date of 1515 as that of the first appearance in England of the French hood, for she wears it in this picture. She thus has the distinction of introducing it into England, anticipating by seven years its appearance in Anne Boleyn's wardrobe.[1]

The hood worn by Mary, Duchess of Suffolk, is very similar to that shown in Fig. 403, except that the wired upstanding edge

Fig. 405. Anne Boleyn, Queen of England, 1532

[1] Anne Boleyn has been held hitherto to be the sponsor of the French hood in England.

to the black velvet hood is masked by more elaborate goldsmith's work, and set with some jewels.

Anne Boleyn returned to England from France in 1522. Her portrait in the National Portrait Gallery, London, said to have been painted between the years 1532 and 1536, shows her wearing a French hood and is shown in Fig. 405 (*refer to* Fig. 411). The front of it is composed of a piece of stiffened material, probably buckram, covered with black velvet and shaped rather like a horseshoe. This is edged, top and bottom, with a row of pearls. From the back of this fell the hood in its new shape, a simple tube of black velvet, cut rectangular, the two long edges being seamed together. Resting on the hair is a goffering of doubled gold gauze.

Fig. 406.
Queen Catherine Howard, 1542

A similar headdress to that shown in Fig. 405 is worn by Princess Mary, elder daughter of Henry VIII, in a portrait in the Ashmolean Museum, painted in 1537 (*see* p. 271). The horseshoe piece is of crimson silk, its forward edge decorated with a row of large pearls, and the back edge with clusters of pearls, alternating with jewels. The black velvet tube hangs behind. Under the headdress, and lying on the hair, is a border of cutwork, probably the edge of a cap. Peardrop pearl earrings are worn—rather an exceptional accessory.

Fig. 406 is a drawing of the French hood worn by Queen Catherine Howard in her portrait of the Holbein School dating 1542 in the National Portrait Gallery, London. The white cap has changed in shape: it is cut back much further behind the temples, but curves forward on the cheek in front of the ears. To this part the narrow chin-strap is attached. The cap is edged round the top curve only by a band of passamayne, and a goffering of double gold gauze underneath it rests on the hair. The wire edging of the black velvet hood is masked by gold beads alternately spherical and cylindrical in shape.

Fig. 407.
The Lady Elizabeth, 1546

The next example of the French hood may be seen in the portrait of the Princess Mary, painted in 1544, and exhibited in the same gallery. The Princess wears a white cap of almost the same shape as that shown in Fig. 406; it is edged on the top curve only by a row of pearls, with small gold beads.

between each. The turned-back portion (lining) of the black velvet hood is red, and has a more solid appearance than the previous example—in fact, it resembles the horseshoe front referred to under Fig. 405, save that it is now shaped like a crescent. The top edge of this portion is decorated with rubies in gold mounts alternating with groups of five pearls, giving the effect of an upstanding coronet.

The French hood worn by the Princess Elizabeth (1546) (Fig. 313) is seen side view in Fig. 407. It is somewhat similar to Princess Mary's, but the vermilion 'turn-back' has now become a false piece, separate from the hood and almost kidney-shaped. The back part descends in a sweep forward, continuing to the level of the chin and edged with jewels (*see at* B). The front part sweeps backward and curves up to the eye level, and is edged with pearls (*see at* A). A goffering of gold gauze appears from under this. The 'coronet' effect, B, is composed of rubies set in gold mounts alternating with groups of four pearls.

Fig. 408. A Gentlewoman

The French hood illustrated in Plate XVII is modelled on the same lines as that of the Princess Elizabeth.

The French hood worn by the gentlewoman (Fig. 350) is reproduced in Fig. 408. The black velvet hood is clearly shown gathered at the top and meeting the band of beads which slope from the top-back to well forward on the cheek. The front part resting on the hair is in folded coloured silk, although it was usual to have it also in folded black velvet; even then the third fold-back could be of a colour.

Fig. 409. Queen Anne Boleyn
(*after Holbein*)

The arrangement of the cap with its binding and safety-pins shown in Fig. 409, taken from the drawing of 'Anna Bollein Queen' by Holbein, suggests that it was utilized as a secure foundation for fixing the French hood. First a band or fold of white is bound round the head. (On top of this would be fixed the forehead pad F of striped silk when wearing the gable headdress (*see* p. 325). The cap, wired along its front edge, is placed above it and secured by a piece of soft material tied round. Notice the safety-pin through the first band and the hair, thus keeping the lappet close to the cheek.

Fig. 410 gives five varieties of beads such as were used on the 'coronet' of French hoods. They were made of gold, often embellished with coloured enamels in varying patterns which sometimes included jewels.  Beads often alternated with jewels set in elaborate mounts.

After the 1530's the French hood superseded the gable headdress, and was universally worn by great and noble ladies in western Europe for upwards of seventy years.

(*Continued on p.* 450)

Fig. 410

### THE BAG-BACK HOOD

#### (*A variant of the French hood*)

Another version of the headdress worn in France is seen in the drawing, Fig. 411.   It is taken from a portrait by Jean Clouet of the Princess Charlotte, daughter of Francis I (born 1516, died 1524), and although this headdress is worn by a child of eight it is identical with those in fashion among noble ladies of this time.

It consists of a curved front piece, horseshoe shape, covered with gold tissue, banded with gold and set with pearls.   The back part is formed like a bag, also of gold tissue, passamayne, and pearls.  To the end of the bag a tassel of silk or gold was sometimes fixed.   Under this and resting on the smooth hair is a cap of fine folded lawn, the headdress and cap being secured by a very narrow band under the chin. Other Royal ladies whose portraits show them wearing headdresses resembling Fig. 411 are Queen Eleanor of France, 1530; Magdalene, daughter of Francis I and Queen of James V of Scotland, 1537; Jeanne d'Albert, daughter of Henry II, King of Navarre, and mother of Henry IV, King of France.   In a portrait attributed to Jean Clouet the last of these ladies is represented at the age of ten (1525), and the front of her headdress has a band of gold set with jewels, with the bag part made of black velvet.

Fig. 411.
The Princess Charlotte of France, 1524

The little lady Jacqueline de Bourgogne (?) in her portrait by Jan van of Mabuse (No. 2211 in the National Gallery, London) wears the same type of headdress as illustrated in Fig. 411. The bag hanging behind is of white satin embroidered with a design of interlacing circles in dull green silk, each circle and interspace containing a group of pearls. The part which covers the head is of black velvet, and in front of it is the curved horseshoe piece like that shown in Fig. 411. It is covered with gold tissue and edged top and bottom with a row of pearls, and is worn over a little cap of fine gold embroidery or rucked gold gauze. The headdress is tied under the chin by a fine cord.

## FANCY HEADDRESSES

There are half-figure portraits of Diane de Poitiers, one at Cambridge and another at Eton, and both are alike. They are erroneously said to be of Jane Shore, which is impossible as they illustrate French fancy Classic headdresses of the later years of Francis I.

Fig. 412 is a drawing of the portrait owned by King's College, Cambridge.[1] The side hair is done into small plaits, twisted and taken up over the top of the

Fig. 412. Diane de Poitiers
*(By kind permission of the Provost and Fellows of King's College, Cambridge)*

Fig. 413.
Pseudo Classic Greek

head; the front hair is treated in the same way, and also taken back over the head. A series of jewels in beautiful gold mounts (*see* Fig. 434) encircles the head, and behind this the hair is curled in true 1938 fashion. Two strings of pearls and a rich carcanet, composed of ornaments matching those in the hair, are presumably the only items of costume worn.

The reclining nude figure of Diane, sculptured by Jean Goujon as an ornament for a fountain at Anet, of which Fig. 413 is a drawing of the head, shows the mid-sixteenth-century idea of a Classic Greek coiffure as worn by the goddess Diana. The hair is parted in the centre, waved at the sides, and looped over a stephane;[2] and above this are two plaits of hair bound with

[1] At the time vol. ii was written this portrait was supposed to represent Jane Shore; it has since been definitely identified.
[2] See vol. i, p. 61.

riband, the top ones coiled round spirally like rams' horns.  Only the sculptor knew where the smaller plaits, connected by a loop supporting a small vase, come from.  However, it is a good example of a sixteenth-century fancy headdress.

### MIDDLE CLASSES

Fig. 414. Mrs. Pemberton

The miniature of Mrs. Pemberton by Holbein,[1] now in the Victoria and Albert Museum, gives an excellent example of a headdress worn by a country gentlewoman of Northants in the latter part of the reign of Henry VIII.  It is reproduced in Fig. 414.  Over her hair she wears a close-fitting cap of white linen.  The cap of the same material worn over this has a square bag-crown fixed to the curve of the front piece shaped as shown in diagram, Fig. 415 A; the edges C and D are sewn together, forming a frill, and the inside curve is joined to the nine-inch square bag-crown.  When the cap is put on the head, EF is folded outward along the broken line, and the ends turned up *inside* and pinned level with the ears.  B shows the cap when arranged in this way.  The folding of the kerchief is described under Fig. 352.

A characteristic cap of the sixteenth century is worn by the woman, Fig. 352. A circular piece of linen or even lawn is gathered into a narrow front band,

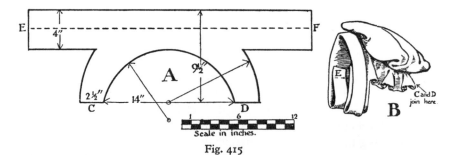

Fig. 415

the ends of which are turned-up-under, just below the lobe of the ears.  A string or strip ties under the chin.

The headdress of the spinster (Fig. 353) is but a rectangle of linen tied round the head, the ends falling well below the neck.

[1] Sold in 1904 for £2,750.

The caps worn by the two peasant women (Figs. 355 and 356) are rectangular pieces of linen gathered in at the nape of the neck and bound round the head by a piece of the same or different material. The nice-looking girl (Fig. 355) has turned the front part back to show more of her face, but her companion has not done so.

The cap worn by the old woman (Fig. 357) is shaped on much the same lines as the preceding, except that the front part is longer and is worn turned back.

When indoors, unmarried women as a rule had no head-covering, but wore their hair in plaits, or knotted at the back of the head, forming tussocks. The hair was almost concealed under a headdress of some kind after marriage.

## FOOTGEAR: 1509–47

The round-toed shoes something like a bear's paw, well padded, the spatula shape being exaggerated, continued to be the vogue during the early years of Henry VIII's reign. (*See* the last sole plan, Fig. 167). These are illustrated in the figures dealt with in the first part of this chapter and under Footgear, Chapter I.

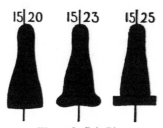

Fig. 416. Sole Plans

Fig. 417 is a drawing made from an original round-toed shoe worn during the second and third decades of the century. It is of black leather stitched round the edge, and has three darts on the low-cut instep. The back (Fig. 418) rises higher than previously, and the shoe fastens with a strap and buckle. Square-toed shoes were, however, the fashion in France at an earlier date as depicted in Figs. 233 and 234. The drawings of Henry VIII (Plate IX (1520) and Fig. 232 (1527)) show the transition in the toe part from the round to the square.

Fig. 417

Fig. 419 is a specimen of the first shoe with a definite square toe, and dates approximately from 1520. It is drawn from an original unearthed from the City ditch. Of black leather it has three cuttes on the instep, and the upper is composed of two pieces, front and back. Henry VIII in later life is shown in all his full-length portraits wearing square-toed shoes like Fig. 420, very low in the heel and well up over the instep. They are always white to match the hosen and made of velvet, silk, or satin. The decoration usually consists of

Fig. 418

cuttes, but at least one portrait of the King shows white silk shoes embroidered with pearls in a scroll and floral design on the instep, and a band of the same embroidery at the instep and toe.

Fig. 419

In Fig. 421 is seen the first of the square-toed shoes with warts at the corners which came into fashion in the twenties. The original is of brown leather with the sole coloured red. The back (see Fig. 422) has increased in height and is cutte in four places. The sole plan (Fig. 423) shows that extra pieces of leather were fixed at the toe and heel, the latter being the first appearance of any pretensions to a 'heel' which developed later.

Fig. 424 shows a slightly different treatment of the wart; the toe is slightly rounded and the warts project at the back at right angles to the main sole. The edge over the instep is decorated with loops. Ladies did not despise these curious toed shoes, as is shown in Fig. 425. This is taken from the effigy of one of the wives of George Talbot, fourth Earl of Shrewsbury, who died in 1528 and lies in Sheffield Cathedral.

Fig. 420

Some authorities attribute the fashion for square-toed shoes to Henry VIII, on the ground that he suffered from gout. This was not until he was middle-aged, so it could not have been the cause of their origin, as already in 1500 or earlier round and later square toes were in fashion.

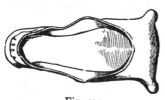

Fig. 421

Toes to shoes reached such absurd proportions that a sumptuary law was passed by Henry VIII to prohibit excessive breadth.

Footgear at this time appears to have been very inexpensive. A pair of leather shoes were valued at 8d. Velvet shoes cost 12d., white velvet, such as the King usually wore, were 20d. the pair, and black velvet 18d. '3 paire of velvet shoes of sundry colors for the King's use,' appear in a wardrobe account. 'To Henry Arnolde the Cordyner for shoes and buskyns for Maister Henry Knevet £4 18s. Hosen 41s. 8d.'

Fig. 422

It is an interesting fact that through the ages mankind with any personal pride, rich or poor, has always been careful to be well shod even if garments were shabby. It was an unwritten law with the Greeks (see vol. i, p. 51), and it must have been so with the Tudors if the quantities of boots and shoes in a single wardrobe are any proof.   Numerous entries appear in Henry VIII's inventories, and the Emperor Charles V acquired 163 pairs of shoes and slippers in twelve months between 1519 and 1520.   He also ordered 53 pairs of hosen at the same time.   Nor were these sovereigns the exception!

The attractiveness of a woman's neat leg and shoe obviously appealed to Count Castiglione, for when referring to the women of France and Italy he says:

Fig. 423

'Have ye not had an eye otherwhile, when either in the streetes going to Church, or in any other place, or in sporting, or by any other chaunce it happeneth that a woman lifteth up her clothes so high, that she sheweth her foote, and sometimes a litle of her pretie legge unwittingly?'

And again:

'And seemth she not to you to have a verie good grace, if ye behold her

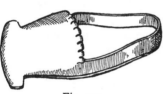

Fig. 424

then with a certaine womanly disposition, cleanely and precise [dainty] with her shoes of velvet, and her hose setting cleane to her legge?'

During the reign of Henry VIII the upper part of the garment which clothed the leg was occasionally referred to as *hosen*, the lower part was sometimes called 'stocks.'  That they were at times separate is evident from the following excerpt from the King's wardrobe account: 'A yarde and a quarter of green velvet for stocks to a payr of hose for the Kings Grace.'    Stocks of green velvet seem a little unusual, as all full-length portraits of Henry show him wearing these garments of white silk, and the same applies to his shoes.

Slippers, escarpins, very like modern men's leather bedroom slippers, were worn by both ladies and gentlemen indoors, and were made of various materials and often embroidered.  'Seevyn paire slippers of the Spanysshe fasshion, corked and garnysshid with golde' are mentioned in an inventory as belonging to Katherine of Aragon.

Rabelais has had something to say about escarpins and also about pantoufles on p. 274. These were slippers without back, in fact, mules.

Fig. 425

Cork was much used for the soles of shoes and slippers.   A pad of cork was sometimes placed between the uppers and the leather sole, and it was quite usual for the entire sole to be of cork.

The rather extraordinary shoes worn by the gentleman (Fig. 326) have an exaggerated edition of the round and pointed toe as shown in the third sole plan (Fig. 167) and are of Flemish type.

The man who took his business seriously wore shoes and boots of normal shape, high in the instep, with sufficient covering for the heel and made of substantial leather (Fig. 426). Such shoes are worn by the apprentices (Figs. 337 and 338).

The shape of the footgear usually worn by the lower middle classes varied. In some cases the round-toed shoe is favoured, most likely from the fact that they have been presented to the wearer by a superior; otherwise any other shoes and boots that happened to be available would serve their purpose.

Fig. 426

Long boots worn for riding had toes which followed the dictates of fashion; round at first and square later. They were elaborately decorated with cuttes when worn by fashionable men, and Plate IX and Fig. 228 show excellent examples. The colours of the leather were usually black, brown, fawn, or yellow ochre.

The boots worn by the gentleman (Fig. 330) were strong and substantial leather, made for use and not ornament. They reached well up the thigh and were chiefly in black, brown, and fawn. The necks of spurs were much reduced in length at this time, and were set close upon the heel: the rowel became larger, resembling an eight-pointed star or the petals of a flower (*see* Fig. 909).

## JEWELLERY: 1509–47

Henry VIII had a great passion for jewels and jewellery, and this naturally inspired the wealthy nobles, especially the 'Novi Homines,' to indulge in great display. More frequent interchange of commerce with the Continent was responsible for this love of jewellery. To-day we might call it a vulgar show of opulence, but to give the Tudors due credit they really admired precious stones set in masterpieces of the goldsmith's art, not only for their intrinsic value, but, above all, for their beauty.

Henry's own expenditure in this direction was enormous: in three years (1529–32) he spent no less than £10,801 on jewellery, besides £1,517 on plate.

A great deal of the most finished jewellery worn by both sexes of the nobility was created by master-craftsmen in Italy followed by those of France, southern Germany, and Flanders. Many of these came to England, and were employed by the King and his courtiers. Native craftsmen were not far behind their Continental rivals in the excellence of their work, but it continued on the old lines until some time after the Reformation. In nearly all cases, artists of repute supplied the goldsmiths with designs for jewellery, and several books on the subject were published and are still in existence. Amongst these artists, all of whom were of German nationality, must be mentioned Albrecht Dürer, Hans Brosamer (1480–1554), Vigil Solis (1514–62), and Hans Holbein; the work of the last can be studied in a portfolio in the Print Room of the British Museum. This contains one hundred and seventy-nine pen-and-ink designs for all kinds of jewellery, most of them to be carried out by the goldsmith, Hans of Antwerp, known as 'John Anwarpe,' although his family name was Van der Goes. He was nominated to the post of the King's Goldsmith by Thomas Cromwell, 'Master of the King's Jewel House,' and was made a Freeman of the Goldsmiths' Company. The jewellers of Augsburg, it is said, were among the first in Europe, and jewellery from the studios and workshops of this city and of Nuremberg was highly esteemed not only all over Germany, but also in France, England, the Low Countries, and Spain. Of the Italian school of jewellers, Benvenuto Cellini stands out prominently. Born in 1500 at Florence, he was apprenticed as a gold worker in 1515. Later, from 1540 to 1545, he lived in Paris, during which time his influence wrought considerable changes in the style of French jewellery. After an exciting existence he died in 1571. His principles of craftsmanship, and many practical hints, are to be found in his autobiography. According to Cellini, much inspiration for fanciful and *grotesque* treatment in some of his work was gained from the antique designs in the frescoes, such as were discovered, 1506, in the Baths of Petus, Rome, the so-called Grottoes.

With the destruction of the shrines, and the scattering of Church vessels and other accumulated treasures after the Reformation, quantities of jewels fell into the hands of foreign financiers and merchants, to be sold by them to the sovereigns and nobility of Europe at a huge profit. Chief amongst these foreign financiers was the House of Fugger of Augsburg, at this time represented by Raymund (1489–1535) and his brother Anton (1493–1560), both of whom were created Counts of Kirchberg of the Holy Roman Empire. It is owing to the energies of this family, and its far-reaching money-lending business, that Emperors and Kings were able to indulge in such magnificence of costume, furniture, pomp, court ceremonial—and war. Of course, our Henry was one of the Fugger clients, and amongst other purchases procured the celebrated jewel long known as the 'Three Brothers.' The chief glory of this jewel, and the origin of its name, lay in *three* oblong balas rubies about one and a quarter inches long. Originally belonging to Charles le Téméraire, and worn by him 'on every exalted occasion with great ostentation,' these magnificent rubies were looted from his pavilion by a common Swiss soldier after the Battle of Granson in 1475, who parted with them for a small sum to the Magistrates of Berne. They were eventually bought by Jacob Fugger (1459–1525) about 1505 for 47,000 Swiss florins, in the hope that they would one day return to the House of Austria.

To these three jewels, now set clear owing to their transcendent quality, were added a great diamond [1] about an inch square in an open setting with an enormous oriental pearl pendant, and three other large oriental pearls of varying shapes composing an ornament as seen in Fig. 427.

Some thirty years later search was made throughout the world for precious gems to decorate the diadem of the Sultan of Turkey, Solyman II 'the Magnificent' (born 1495, reigned 1520–66); but Count Jacob Fugger, at great pecuniary loss, and despite strong entreaties, would not dispose of the jewel to any but a Christian. The 'Three Brothers' therefore remained the property of the Fugger brothers for forty years, until it was sold to the *most*

Fig. 427.
'The Three Brothers'

Christian King Henry VIII a year or so before he died, for a sum not stated, but—one would imagine—sufficiently high. The transaction was not concluded, however, until the reign of his son Edward VI.

After the Conquest of Mexico in 1521 by Hernando Cortes (1485–1547), and the discovery of the rich mines there, gold and silver became more plentiful. The price of gold and silver rose very considerably, and there was a great demand for these precious metals by the goldsmiths and jewellers of Europe. The gold mines of Mexico were only surpassed by those of Peru, discovered and conquered in 1529–30 by Francisco Pizarro, born 1478, married the Inca's daughter, and murdered 1541.

Of jewels the ruby seems to have been most in favour, followed by the emerald and sapphire, for setting in ornaments for personal adornment and the decoration of special objects. Lesser precious stones, such as the amethyst, topaz, carbuncle, jacinth, and crystal, were used for the same purpose for less expensive work.

Until about the first quarter of the sixteenth century, all these stones, precious and semi-precious, were set 'en cabochon,' that is polished, but not cut into regular shapes. After this period, they were mostly cut or faceted, but the most valuable were 'table-cut,' i.e. rectangular with bevelled edges, the underside shaped like a pyramid. In inventories, jewels are frequently mentioned as being 'pointed, tabled, *rocked*, or round.' The diamond in previous centuries was much prized, though rare, and, of course, used 'en cabochon,' whereby it was deprived of the brilliancy which it attained in the sixteenth century. The new mode of cutting it in facets became more general since Louis van Berghem of Bruges introduced it in 1475. The most valued diamond was table cut.

---

[1] Philippe de Comines (1455–1519) in his *Memoirs* states that Charles's 'great Diamond (perhaps the largest and finest Jewel in *Europe*) with a large Oriental Pearl fix'd to it, was taken up, view'd, put up again into the Case, thrown under a Waggon, taken up again by the same Soldier, and after all offer'd to a Priest for a Florin, who bought it, and sent it to the Chief Magistrate of that Country, who return'd him three Franks as a sufficient Reward.'

Peru yielded immense quantities of emeralds, besides rubies, yellow topaz, blue and white sapphires, and amethysts.

Pearls were almost as lavishly used as in the days of the Byzantine Empire. New fisheries were now discovered off the coast of Central America, such as the Pearl Islands in the Gulf of Panama.

The styles of enamelling previously mentioned were now augmented by that in the round or relief, which was largely employed in the creation of lovely objects of jewellery. Niello work was also much used. For painted enamels, colours were mixed with fluxes applied to a copper plate, and then covered with a translucent flux: upon this the design was outlined with a black enamel, round which the other colours were filled in.

### CROWNS AND CORONETS

The crown as used by Henry VIII is seen in Fig. 292, taken from an Illum. MS. dated 1543. It is the usual jewelled circlet supporting four crosses patée and as many fleurs-de-lys, and has two arches. The crown surmounting the Royal coat of arms in the same drawing has but four fleurs-de-lys, curiously enough, rising from the circlet.

In Fig. 231 Henry VIII is seen at an earlier date (1527) wearing the arched crown with the circlet set inside the brim of his bonet. The Crown of Scotland, shown in Fig. 528, was remodelled by James V about 1540, using some of the gold and jewels from the crown of Robert Bruce. The circlet is set with carbuncles, jacinths, amethysts, topaz, crystal, and pearls. Above this rise ten crosses fleurie alternating with as many fleurs-de-lys; between each pair is a single raised pearl. The arches of gold have oak leaves in red and gold enamel as crockets, and support the mound of blue enamel powdered with golden stars; this holds the cross of black and gold

Fig. 428.
A Princess's Coronet

enamel, set in the centre with an amethyst, and bearing seven pearls on the arms. The cap was originally of purple velvet costing 32s. 6d. per yard. According to the contemporary accounts, the weight of the crown was 56 ounces and the cost £52 7s. 6d.

For the Imperial crown of the emperors of the Holy Roman Empire at this period, see Fig. 286, taken from a contemporary woodcut. This crown contains, within its single arched circlet of gold and jewels, a golden mitre symbolical of the semi-ecclesiastical attributes of the Head of the Holy Roman Empire. It was, however, worn in a different manner from the episcopal mitre, its openings showing over the forehead and back of the head instead of over the ears. Like all mitres, it has at the back two pearled and fringed pendent lappets, called 'infulae.'

The Illum. MS. from which Fig. 251 is taken also supplies us with details

of a princess's coronet, reproduced in Fig. 428.    The circlet is engraved with
ovals and lozenges, and above it rise eight leaf motifs—not fleurs-de-lys—with
trefoils between.

## COLLARS

The fact that the Order of St. Michael of France had possessed a collar since
1469 (*see* vol. ii, Fig. 565) most likely prompted Henry VIII to institute one
for the Order of the Garter.    This was decreed in 1510, and consisted of
alternating garters and knots, the former enclosing roses.    In so doing he
was but adapting an existing collar for the purpose, as is proved by the draw-

Fig. 429. Portion of Collar

ings, Figs. 182, 183, 184.    The collar thus instituted is shown in Fig. 339,
vol. ii; and in the same volume is given the Lesser George (Fig. 340), introduced in 1521.

One of the best representations of the collar with the pendent George is
to be seen in Holbein's portrait of the Duke of Norfolk at Windsor Castle.

Fig. 430. Jewelled Medallion

Fig. 431. Lord Mayor's Collar

At the decease of a Knight of the Garter, the collar was not always returned
to the sovereign in its original condition; at least, the will of Charles Brandon,
Duke of Suffolk, dated 1545, directs: 'I will, that a cup of gold be made out
of my Collar of the Garter, and given to the King.'    Collars of no Order, but
worn as ornaments, were particularly rich.    In several of his portraits, the
King wears a wide jewelled collar arranged broadly over the shoulders; and to

achieve the desired *wide* effect it must have been fastened with a hook on the shoulders. Fig. 429 is a drawing of a part of one of these collars, of rich gold work set with rubies and pearls. In addition to this, he frequently wore a large medallion (Fig. 430) suspended either by a chain or, as shown, by two kinds of gold beads, or by a narrow ribbon. This medallion is set with four emeralds on a mount of embossed gold, and might once have contained a relic.

Henry VIII is shown wearing rich collars in Plates IX (1520) and XIII (1542), Figs. 211 (1512) and 293 (1545); also a nobleman (Fig. 280).

At his death in 1544, Sir John Alleyn — mercer, Lord Mayor, 1535, and a member of Henry VIII's council, 'a man of great wisdom and also of great charity' — presented the City of London with a collar to be worn by his successors.

Fig. 432. Section of Collar

This is illustrated in Fig. 431, and displays 'Knots between the SS, and each end finished with an ornament in the shape of a portcullis': to the central union rose in enamel between the two portcullises is attached a pendant.

For an illustration of the Collar of St. Andrew, or the Thistle, see Fig. 291.

The Collar of the Golden Fleece worn by Charles, Archduke and Emperor, in Figs. 286, 369, and Plate VIII, vary slightly. The usual design of the collar is shown more clearly in Fig. 552, vol. ii.

Portions of two less ornate collars are given in Figs. 432 and 433. The former, worn by Francis I in one of his portraits, has rubies in circular gold mounts connected by jointed bars terminating in fleurs-de-lys. The latter, from a portrait of Frederick I of Denmark, has definite roses of gold set with rubies from which spring oak leaves of gold with large pearls in the centres.

Fig. 433. Section of Collar

### CHAINS, CARCANETS

As in the last reign, gold chains were very popular, and their massiness was carried to great excess. The King naturally had many, and an entry in a wardrobe account states that in 1511 he paid £199 for one weighing 98 ounces. Later we find another entry: 'Item to the Italian jeweller for a cheyne of golde weying V oz and di xiiij *li* iijs iiijd' (£14 3s. 4d.).

By his will made in 1517, Sir Thomas Parr, Knight, left to his son William, brother of Queen Katherine Parr and later created Marquis of Northampton, 'my great chain of gold which is worth cxll that the King's grace gave me.'

Margaret, widow of Sir William Capell, leaves in her will, proved 1522, 'To my son, Sir Giles Capell, King Edward the Fifths chain.'

It is recorded that at the Dissolution (1538–9) much of the goldsmith's work purloined from the abbeys and monasteries got into the hands of commercial men, who melted it down, refashioned it into ostentatious 'massy' chains, and sold these to wealthy upstarts.

Chains with immense links were worn in Germany by both men and women at this period. Almost any portrait by a German painter, especially by Lucas Cranach, shows one of these heavy chains.

Carcanets and chains, such as are mentioned in Chapter I, were still much

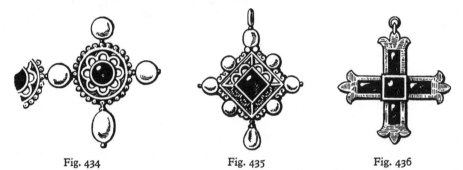

Fig. 434                    Fig. 435                    Fig. 436

worn by ladies, as seen in Figs. 240, 241, 254, and 397. Amongst the jewellery worn by Diane de Poitiers, in the head-and-shoulders portrait referred to under Fig. 412, is a very elaborate and beautiful carcanet, one member of which is shown in Fig. 434—a circular pierced motif with a small ruby in the centre, a pearl at the top and a larger one at the bottom; and joined to its neighbours by single pearls. Above, a string—or as it was called at this time a 'lace'— of pearls is wound twice round the neck; and from the carcanet hangs a rectangular pendant (Fig. 435), set with a ruby and eight pearls. The coiffure (see Fig. 412) combines a band of many rectangular jewels like Fig. 435, but the eight pearls are all the same size and shape. A circular jewel is suspended over the forehead.

The carcanet worn by Anne of Cleves in her portrait by Holbein (Fig. 307) is shown in detail in Fig. 437. It is formed of floral motifs separated by leaf-like scrolls in gold: the flowers are in white enamel on gold, each set with a ruby and flanked with four pearls. A gold cross fleurie (Fig. 436) is attached to this carcanet; it has a ruby set in the centre and emeralds on each limb.

Fig. 437.   Section of Carcanet

### ENSEIGNES AND BONET ORNAMENTS

Enseignes and medallions for headgear became even more ornate, and in nearly all instances bore some figured design. 'It was the custom at that epoch to wear little golden medals, upon which every nobleman or man of quality had some device or fancy of his own engraved; and these were worn in the cap.' This statement was made by Cellini in 1525. Backgrounds were formed of a variety of different styles of enamel, and semi-precious stones such as lapis lazuli, agate, and sardonyx. Even more popular were cameos, which (like the precious stones just mentioned) were usu-

Fig. 438. Enseigne

ally surrounded by jewel-studded gold rims, and frequently by frames of wire and filigree in floral forms. The subjects of the cameos were as a rule inspired by the antique, and by contemporary paintings and engravings. There were many gem engravers in the sixteenth century whose names have been handed down to us. Most famous of them was Matteo del Nassaro who died in 1546, much patronized by Francis I and his Court; the work of this cameo artist always found a place on the costume of the exquisitely dressed courtier.

Fig. 439

Fig. 438 shows an enseigne worn by Charles V. The background is of enamel, the design in gold; the letters C and D—Carolus Dominus—are flanked by knots, and between them is a fire steel—a motif from the Collar of the Golden Fleece—below is a pomegranate between two lambs, all surmounted by a coronet. The medallion is edged with pearls fixed on by gold pins.

An enseigne showing a warrior saint in enamel and gold is worn by the Marquess of Northampton (Fig. 365). Inset are shown the small ornaments which are sewn to the underside of the brim.

Fig. 440

The introduction of ornaments of goldsmith's work on the brim of the bonet is referred to on p. 316, and in the portrait of Charles, Comte de Flandres, 1506, Plate VIII A, these ornaments appear for the first time and may be plainly seen. Fig. 439 is a more detailed illustration. In Fig. 440 another specimen is given; and both kinds are sprinkled at all angles over the wide brim of two different hats worn by him. These drawings are not in perspective—the ornaments are triangular in section and taper towards one end, and are carried out in gold on enamel, and one is embellished with gold globules; pearls and jewels were often introduced. Although the broad brims of German and Flemish hats gave ample scope for the display of such decorations, the idea was, nevertheless, applied to the under part of the narrower flat brim of English bonets at a later date.

This treatment is shown for the first time in the portrait of 'Sir George de Cornwall,' painted by Holbein in 1539, and reproduced in Fig. 441. The flat brim of the bonet is decorated on the underside with vase-shaped beads in gold, Fig. 442, dotted about indiscriminately, interspersed with small buttons and golden fish per saltire (Fig. 443). On the left side is a largegn enseie of a saint in enamel and gold: and behind it a group of gold and enamel violas (Fig. 444).

Fig. 445 is part of the underside of the brim of one of Henry VIII's flat bonets worn from the 1530's. In Plate XIII he is wearing a similar bonet. Jewels in rose-mounts alternate all round the brim with triangular groups of five pearls and gold cord. In some other portraits the pearls and cord form semicircles which alternate with jewels set in mounts of varying designs. The nobleman (1539) (Fig. 274) has two rows of narrow ornaments or gold filigree beads round the brim of his bonet.

Fig. 441.
'Sir George de Cornwall,' 1539

Fig. 442

Fig. 443

Fig. 444

A more bizarre arrangement of such ornaments has already been mentioned under Fig. 365.

In England, where the gable headdress and later the French hood reigned supreme, there was little use for hat ornaments among ladies. However, Fig. 446 is given as being a beautiful specimen of German-made jewellery. It would be worn on a headdress similar to that shown in Fig. 393, perched on one side. The stone is a finely faceted diamond framed with honeysuckle petals in gold. The figure is of gold or silver, and sometimes such figures were carved in ivory or some semi-precious stone.

The pendant (Fig. 447) is also of German design but cumbersome: of gold and enamel, it is set with two jewels, and a pear pearl is fixed at the base.

The pendant (Fig. 448) worn by Anne of Cleves in one of her portraits is most certainly of German design. The three circles enclosing rubies in four semicircles, and the two smaller circles, are surrounded by gold globules.

Fig. 393 shows other types of German jewellery.

The list of the jewellery owned by the Princess Mary Tudor I at the time of her first marriage is a long one, and only a small selection can be given here. This inventory has been chosen from the large number available, because it gives a fair sample of the lady's jewel casket as well as because she was an

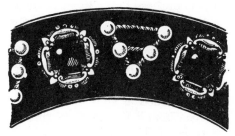

Fig. 445. Bonet Brim

interesting woman. There were carcanets of diamonds and rubies, many girdles of goldsmith's work and jewels, finger-rings, and aiglettes for tie-laces. Brooches of pearls, diamonds, rubies, and emeralds, and some shaped like fleurs-de-lys and roses. Twenty diamonds set in a border of gold for ornamenting the latest thing in headdresses—the French hood. Eight large pearls set as false-sleeve clasps; and eight others for a carcanet. Eighteen

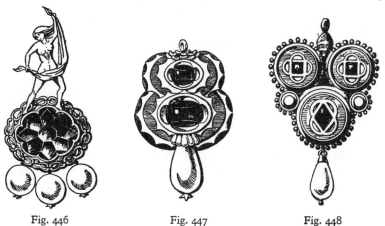

Fig. 446      Fig. 447      Fig. 448

large pearls valued at 10,000 crowns for another carcanet. A large emerald, and a large ruby and two diamonds set in gold mounts in a ring. Also a pendant in the form of the letter M, set with diamonds and having pearl drops.

A few other items from the same inventory are added:

'First a cronell for her head of golde and stone in the day of her mariage.

'Item a goodlie devise for her neke set with stone and perle.

'Item a goodlie gurdill of golde of as goodlie facion as may be devised.

'Item ii braseletts of golde set with stone and perle.

'Item on the nexte day for her change a Riche Juell of golde with a cheyne of golde for her nekke.

'Item a goodlie gurdill of golde.

'Item a goodlie Crosse gilte poisaunt xiij<sup>xx</sup> unc.

'Item a faire coffer of silver to lay in her Juellis.'

Many of these formed part of the crown jewels of France, and were sent to the Princess by King Louis previous to their marriage. Among them was the celebrated diamond called 'Le Miroir de Naples.' This interesting jewel has been described by a contemporary as being very large, as broad as a full-sized finger, and having a pear-shaped pearl as big as a pigeon's egg suspended from it. This was worn by Mary on the front of her bodice as a pectoral, and was valued at 60,000 crowns.

When Francis I came to the throne of France, he was much concerned that the widowed Queen Mary should have carried off to England this much prized French crown jewel. Queen Claude asked for it—nay, demanded it, as belonging by right to the Queens-Consort of France. Henry VIII, into whose possession the 'Mirror of Naples,' together with other items of the French crown jewels, had found its way (see p. 176), refused to restore it to France, although Francis offered him a trifling 30,000 crowns for the whole. After this nothing more appears to have been heard of it. Some authorities suggest that it is masquerading under another name; but this does not appear possible, in view of the fact that the 'Mirror of Naples' was such an unusual size, unless, of course, it has been recut.

The jewellery worn by the Princess Mary I in Plate XII is very lovely, and every item is worthy of special attention: one wonders if any of it, perhaps the 'cronell' of rubies, each surrounded by small pearls, is included in the above lists. She wears besides a lace of pearls round her neck with a pendant of emeralds and a drop pearl, an elaborate carcanet of emeralds and pearls: four brooches on the shoulders and sleeves, also of emeralds, rubies, and pearls; and a bracelet of oval rubies and diamonds. It was rather unusual for a lady to wear a bracelet, but in this case she is in Spanish dress. Two rings are on the fingers of her right hand, and perhaps more than one on her left. She clasps a crystal-covered cup with both hands, thus emulating Mary Magdalene and her alabaster cruse of precious ointment. In the portrait alluded to on p. 101, she also holds a cup, but of silver; and Isabella, Queen of Denmark, in her portrait by Mabuse dated 1513, clasps a crystal cup in like manner.

The jewelled ornaments worn at the Court of Francis I were as valuable for their exquisite settings as for the gems they contained. A large proportion of these masterpieces of the jeweller's art was created by such men as Leonardo da Vinci, Cellini, and the great decorative artist Francesco Primaticcio (1504–70), and their pupils. A munificent patron of the jeweller was the Cardinal d'Amboise (1460–1510), archbishop and statesman, a great admirer of the Italian style, who had previously imported from Milan and Genoa many examples of exquisitely wrought jewellery: he had also invited some

Italian craftsmen to France, by whose influence much of the Italian character was infused into French-made articles of jewellery and goldsmith's work. Francis I bedizened himself with many ornaments purchased for large sums of money from an orfèvre of Paris named Robert Rousset. Another gold-smith employed by Francis was Jean Duvet, who was born at Langres in 1485 and died about 1562. It was at the Court of France that the fancy originated for initial pendants and trinkets engraved with mottoes and devices. There was great rivalry amongst the courtiers in exercising their brains and ingenuity in inventing mottoes to express the assumed state of mind of the wearer, the donor, or the recipient.

Fig. 449. Sleeve Clasp

The introduction of the 'False sleeve' brought into use another piece of jewellery, the *sleeve-clasp*. Fig. 449 is an example of one in which the curved edges were fastened together (*see under* Fig. 257); usually three were used, one at the wrist, and the other two at intervals along the lower edges. Others were placed on the false sleeve itself, at the ends of the long cuttes which decorated it. Later, when cuttes were superseded by small pads, these ornaments were placed in the same positions. Such clasps, ornamental as well as useful, contained nearly always square or round jewels set in ornate gold mounts, and either fastened with a pin underneath like a brooch, or had rings by which they were sewn on.

Fig. 450
Jewelled Motif

*Ornaments*, not necessarily brooches, were used in great numbers dispersed about the costume of both ladies and gentlemen. They could be pinned on, but were more generally sewn, and nearly always took the form of a square or circular jewel in a gold setting. Fig. 450 is a specimen of an oblong jewel, and the placing of the angles in curved or scroll motifs is characteristic. When a mount of this kind contained a circular jewel, or a square one set square or lozenge-wise, the ornament resembled a rose as shown in Fig. 451. A survey of portraits of the period will show that this type of setting was almost universal.

Fig. 451. Rose Setting

## GIRDLES

During the reign of Henry VIII the girdle became more and more elaborate in design, and richer in jewels and pearls.

The drawings of ladies dispersed throughout this chapter show such girdles, but on a very small scale: therefore Fig. 452 is given as an example. It dates about 1530, and consists of engraved spherical ornaments in gold, which might be also enamelled, alternating with table-cut rubies in ornate settings linked by pearls.

A very lovely girdle is worn by Jane Seymour in her portrait (1536) (Plate XV). A detail of it is given in Fig. 453. It consists of two strands, quite a usual thing with the richest girdles: each is composed of vase-shaped ornaments in gold and black enamel, alternating with cubical ornaments of the same, splayed at the top and bottom edges. On each side is set a ruby in a gold mount, and joining this to the vase there is a pearl. As the end of the girdle is unseen in the portrait, one surmises that either a reliquary or a pomander is attached to it. Plates XI, XVI, and XVII, and Figs. 255 and 302,

Fig. 452.　　Fig. 453.

Girdles

show the girdle complete in itself; and in Fig. 253 the rosary is slung from the sash or girdle.

## FINGER RINGS

Two great chests, filled with gold and jewels of inestimable value, were taken from the shrine of St. Thomas of Canterbury at the looting of the cathedral's treasures. Two magnificent jewels at least fell into Henry VIII's hands; one a great ruby, and the other the great diamond given by Louis VII of France in 1179. Both were set in separate rings for the impious fingers of this sacrilegeous monarch.

Fig. 454 is a drawing of a ruby ring worn by Henry VIII in the Castle Howard portrait. Is it the Canterbury jewel? It is set in a rose mount,

Fig. 454. Ring

leaf-like motifs forming the shank or shoulder, which often received as much attention from the goldsmith as the setting of the stone itself. When not in use, and for display upon the tire table or casket, or the jeweller's shop-window, rings were kept on short wooden rods or rolls of parchment. Thus, an inventory of Henry VIII of 1527 reads:

'Upon a finger stall seven rings, one a ruby, another an emerald, and a turquoise, another a table diamond, another a triangular diamond, another a *rocky* [*see* p. 360] diamond.'

Rings with jewels set in rose mounts are to be found in many portraits of noblemen and noblewomen of the sixteenth century.

A very simple ring set with a jewel is worn by the Duchess of Milan, seen in Fig. 264.

Elizabeth, Countess of Oxford, 1537, leaves many items of jewellery in her will. 'My largest ring with a sharp diamond, my ring with the five roses, my ring of gold with a sapphire of divers squares,' which, of course, means *faceted*. Included also are a book of gold, 'my Jesus of diamonds set in gold, and four basins and ewers.' See Fig. 217.

One learns little of the use of the turquoise in jewellery, although this semi-precious stone had been known at an earlier date, and is referred to by Chaucer. This seems rather extraordinary, as the turquoise was supposed to have the quality of taking away all enmity, and also of reconciling a man to his wife. However, we sometimes find it mentioned as in the above will, and also in the will of Robert Fabyan (*see* p. 144), citizen and draper of London, who leaves to his daughter Mary 'a ryng of gold, sett with a Turques, a dyamaunt, and a ruby.' He also leaves mourning 'ryngs of gold, wheryn ys graven Momento.'

Fig. 455.
Aiglette

*Aiglettes* of gold, and often set with jewels and pearls, make a decorative effect to the costumes of both ladies and gentlemen of this period. They were not always used as a means of fastening, but as ornaments usually in pairs. Their purpose can best be judged by their position on the dress. They are often specified in inventories as being in sets; for instance: 'Itm pd to Mabell the goldesmythe for the fasciõ of xj payr of Agletts xs,' appears in the accounts of the Princess Mary II, which also contain: 'xxxij^ti payr of Agletts Itm v sorts of Agletts of golde, eñÿ sorte xij payr.'

An ornamental aiglette is shown in Fig. 455, and one at the end of the embroidery in Fig. 309. Fig. 456 gives an aiglette, circular in section, of gold decorated with niello and a pearl set in a band of black enamel top and bottom. Fig. 457 is another, square or hexagonal in section, floriated at the top, and set with jewels.

Below are given a few items from the same inventory dating from 1542 to 1547:

'Itm ooñ Rubie set in a ℔, and ooñ ple [pearl] pendũnte at the same.'
'Itm a litle chayne of golde wᵗ xvj litle ples and xxxij small diamonds '
'Itm a Ciphre of Diamonds.'
'Itm a Cyfer set wᵗ x Diamonds.'

'Itm a Boke of golde w^t the Kings face and hir gracs mothers.'

A book of this kind, about four by three inches, was sometimes suspended at the end of the girdle.

'Item a lace for her to goo once a bought her gracs necke conteyning xxvj greate perle.'

'Item a carckanet for her gracs necke with iiij^xx and iiij great perle laced w^t the xxj Rubies afore namyed augmentyd to the same.'

'Item ij fayr lacs of golde for the necke set w^t Diamonds Rubies and Ples.'

'Item a Crosse of golde set w^t v Diamonds iiij Rubies w^t an Emaurawde in the mydds and iij perles pendant at the same.'

Numerous brooches 'showing stories' from Biblical history are mentioned.

'Itm a payr of Braceletts of golde set w^t Diamonds and Rubies and in ayther of them one Emaurawde, geuen by the Quenes g̃ce shortly aft hir mariage.'

'Itm a girdle w^t xix diamonds set in golde laced w^t iiij^xx xx great ples.'

Many other girdles of like nature are included.

'Itm ooñ vpper Abillement of goldesmyth w^rke set w^t xx^ti fayr table Diamonds and laced w^t lvij great perles.'

'Itm ooñ nether Abillement of goldesmyth w^rke set w^t xiij table and square Diamonds and laced w^t xlij meane [small] ples.'

Fig. 456.    Fig. 457.
Aiglettes

There are several such items.

'Abillement' or 'billement' means attire or array. Upper abillements refer to the bands of jewels set round the front of the gable headdress or over the 'coronet' of the French hood. A nether abillement was the band of jewels which surrounded the neck of the bodice.

Rocked, rok, rocky was a term usually applied to a species of ruby and sometimes to a diamond.

### PENDANTS AND JEWELS

One of the most important items of jewellery, and very popular during this and the two following reigns, was the pendant, with its subsidiaries the pectoral ornament and the cross. The designs show a great variety, both of pattern and of material, the result being beautiful specimens of the goldsmith's and jeweller's art.

The pendant (Fig. 459) is taken from Mabuse's portrait, painted in 1513, of Isabella of Austria, daughter of Philippe le Beau and Joanna of Castile, born in 1501 and the wife of Christian II of Denmark. The five motifs

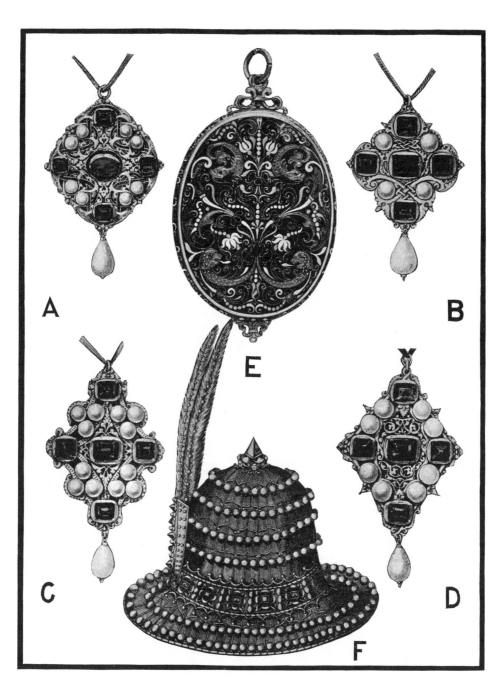

PLATE XVIII. ARTICLES OF JEWELLERY

which compose the cross are all alike of gold, set with rubies and three drop pearls.

Fig. 465 is a pendant of a ruby set in a gold scroll and leaf mount with four pearls, and three pearls, two round and one peardrop, suspended from it. It is a reproduction of a design by Albrecht Dürer, dated 1515.

Fig. 460 is a pendant in the shape of a cross, about four inches long, worn by Katherine of Aragon in her portrait, said to have been painted by Corvus in 1526. It consists of an emerald, four rubies, and three pear pearls: it is hung from a very small gold chain, and doubtless contains a relic.

Fig. 458 is a pectoral ornament about three inches in width, also worn by Katherine, consisting of a large emerald mounted in gold scroll work. Both of these are shown in the drawing, Fig. 379.

Fig. 458. Pectoral

In the drawing of the Empress Isabella, dating about 1526 (Fig. 249), is seen a pectoral, and Fig. 464 gives it on a larger scale. Two rubies are set in the gold work, with a lace of pearls attached to its extremity and a peardrop pearl in the centre.

Jane Seymour, in her portrait at Vienna (Plate XV), wears a pendant on her neck (Fig. 461): this consists of a square ruby below an oval emerald in a mount of goldsmith's work, with a pendent pearl. A similar example is shown in Fig. 463, in which a small pearl replaces the emerald.

Four pendants, reproductions of Holbein's designs executed between 1536 and 1543, are shown in Figs. A, B, C, and D, Plate XVIII. As the drawings are in pen and ink and no colour introduced except in Fig. A—this has a ruby in the centre—one must imagine the kind of jewel. The mounts of these pendants are decorated in the spaces between the jewels with chased or enamelled designs of scroll or leaf work. A noticeable point about the jewels one sees painted in portraits is that they are nearly always shown as *black*. The deep rich colour of the stone, whether ruby, emerald, or sapphire, might appear to the artist's eye dark enough to account for this treatment. Considering the variety of jewels enumerated in wills and inventories when referring to pendants or any other items of jewellery, it is quite unreasonable to suppose that only black enamel or jet was used.

In Fig. 462 we have a pendant worn by Catherine Howard (1542), combining the rose of the Tudors and the lion of the Howards, and supporting a table-cut ruby with a small diamond set above.

The pendant attached to the Lord Mayor's collar (Fig. 431) is composed of square rubies enclosed in circles around a square emerald. Between the four rubies are leaf-shaped motifs in gold. A pear pearl hangs from it.

Pendants or pectoral ornaments consisting mainly of monograms became very popular during the latter part of Henry VIII's reign. The initial B is worn by Anne Boleyn (Fig. 405), and a more ornate specimen is given in

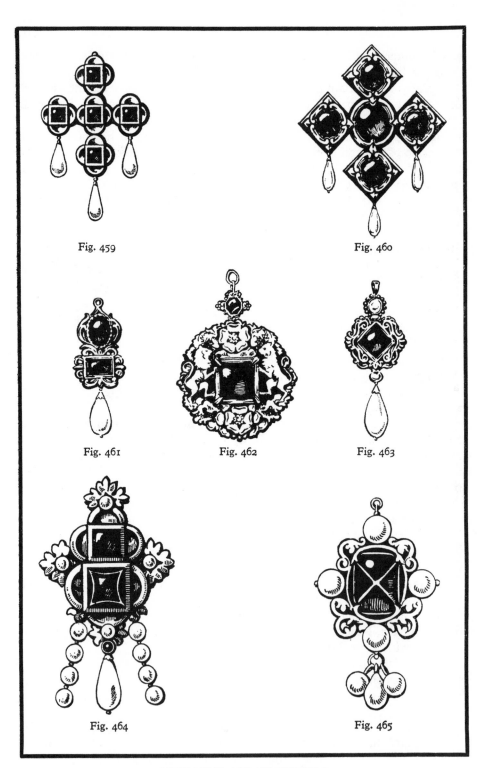

Fig. 459

Fig. 460

Fig. 461

Fig. 462

Fig. 463

Fig. 464

Fig. 465

PENDANTS AND PECTORALS

Fig. 466—a reproduction of one of Holbein's designs, the pierced gold initials HA—obviously Henry and Anne—have a large table diamond set in the centre. Another pendant designed by Holbein (Fig. 467) is more decorative in treatment, and shows an emerald mounted upon HI, for Henry and Jane. This has three pear pearls suspended from the bases of the letters. Queen Jane (Plate XV) is wearing an elaborate example of a 'Jesus' in which the IHS is in black enamel surrounded by goldsmith's work, with smaller pieces of enamel set above and below the letters.

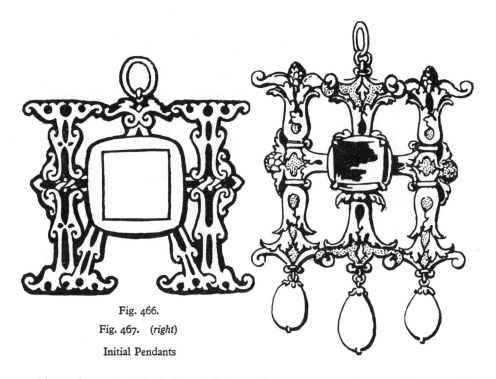

Fig. 466.

Fig. 467. (right)

Initial Pendants

The Princess Elizabeth (1547) (Fig. 314) wears one pendant pearl suspended from an emerald set in the centre of the initial A (Fig. 468), most likely her mother's jewel.

A definitely cruciform pendant is shown in Fig. 469. A pearl finishes the corners of the table-cut ruby, and from the sides spring leaf motifs in gold.

Holbein gives a design (Fig. 470) for a cross in gold and niello work with pearls set in the angles. At the bottom is a ring for suspending a large pearl. Anne of Cleves (Fig. 307) wears one something like this.

The tau cross (see vol. ii, Fig. 664) was much in favour with ladies, who sometimes wore it in plain gold, or engraved or decorated with niello; more frequently it was set with pearls and jewels.

Gentlemen also wore very rich pendants, and in many portraits of Henry VIII and noblemen one sees a circular pendant attached to a small chain or

cord hung round the neck, usually in addition to an ornate collar.   Fig. 430
shows one of these pendants of gold set with four rubies and a small diamond

Fig. 468

Fig. 469

Fig. 470

in the centre; the ring by which it is suspended rises from an ornament of
scrolls.   This pendant might once have been used as a reliquary.

An elaborate whistle pendant in gold,
designed by Hans Brosamer for some
great admiral, is shown in Fig. 471.   The
sound is produced by blowing down the
mouthpiece in the figure's head, through
the trunk into the hole of the hollow ball.

Miniatures set in jewelled frames and
used as pendants are mentioned on p. 152.

The 'Table of the Ladye Elizabeth,
her Grace' at Windsor Castle might be
considered to exhibit a lavish display
of jewellery for so young a maiden.

Fig. 471. Whistle

The four drawings of jewellery here shown are made from this portrait,
and are of gold, enamel, diamonds, and pearls.   The pectoral (Fig. 472) is a

very lovely piece in gold, having a double cross crosslet in black enamel with diamonds and pearls. The 'upper abillement' around the French hood and the 'nether abillement' at the neck of the bodice have ornaments (Fig. 473) alternating with groups of six pearls; the girdle is fashioned in the same manner, except that only two large pearls separate every two ornaments. On the false sleeves, the puffs, which have now taken the place of cuttes, are finished top and bottom with ornaments, as shown in Fig. 475.

A pendant to be worn at the neck is given in Fig. 474.

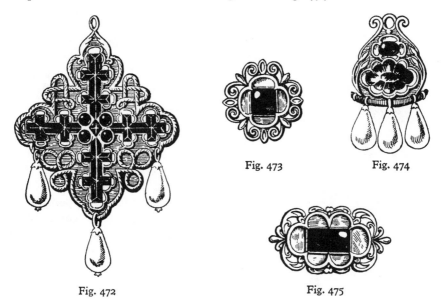

Fig. 473

Fig. 474

Fig. 472

Fig. 475

## CLOCKS

Clocks had been known since the ninth century, and these sounded the hours by a mechanical bell. The addition of a dial and hand is as early in England as 1344: the hours and quarters were marked by long and short rays as in a star. The mainspring was first employed by a clockmaker of Nuremburg at the beginning of the sixteenth century: this enabled the working to be confined in quite a small case.

The first table clocks were circular or square boxes (Fig. 476), with the dial and one hand set on the top. They were made of metal or wood, beautifully decorated, and sometimes set with jewels.

Fig. 476. Table Clock

Standing clocks were considered a very great luxury in the time of Henry VIII. £30 is a price mentioned as having been paid for one, which was a

large sum in those days.    There were others which cost a great deal more.
A characteristic standing clock of the sixteenth century is shown in Fig. 477,
taken from a painting dated 1540.    It is of bronze or gold and black enamel,
and about twelve inches in height.    The internal works of a gilt bronze
standing clock, now at Windsor, are said to have been presented by Henry VIII
to Anne Boleyn.    Holbein designed one, if not more, for the King in 1543.
A reproduction of one of his designs can be seen in the *Connoisseur*, vol.
xxxvii, p. 139.    At Henry's death seventeen clocks of various kinds were in
the Royal collection.    The descriptions of
seven clocks taken from the King's inventory,
1547, and given below, may appeal to those
interested:

Fig. 477. Standing Clock

'Item one clocke of Iron within a case of
glasse the frame of the case beinge of iron
guilte with three plommettes [weights] of lead
and twooe belles whiche stryke the quarter and
halfe of an howre.'

'Item one round clocke of Iron with sondrye
doores of copper graved showinge howe the
Sea doth ebbe and flowe with a case of glasse
sette in Iron guilte standinge upon a foot or
case of wode with iij greate counterpayses
[counterpoises] and twooe smalle of copper and
the third smalle one beinge of leade.'

'Item one Larumme or watche of Iron the
case beinge likewise Iron guilte with twooe
plommettes of leade.'

'Item one clocke of copper and guilte with
a chyme to the same showinge all the dayes
in the yere and the planettes with three
movinge Dialls to the same, one of them beinge silver enamelid blewe and
the twelve signs guilte with three greate counterpaises of copper and guilte
and three verye smalle counterpeases of the like copper guilte.'

'Item one clocke of Iron with a chyme to the same having leaves of copper
and a garnyture above of like copper with a roose on each side and before
one smalle schutchyon with the kynges armes enamyled with three counterpaises of copper and three litle counterpaises of leade.'

'Item a Larome of copper garnished with siluer enameled with dyvers
coollers having in the toppe a boye of siluer standing uppon a grene molehyll
and undre the mollehill a flower of siluer the same Larome standing uppon
three pomegranettes of siluer.'

## GUILDS AND TRADE (*continued from p. 134*)

The attempts to reach the Indies southward and westward now began to bear fruit. The voyages of Columbus and of the Cabots showed that between the Atlantic and their goal lay the huge continent of North America: the Portuguese had been more successful, since Vasco da Gama (1469–1524) reached India by the Cape route in 1498.

These discoveries opened out tremendous possibilities for trade, or perhaps it should be termed 'barter,' or exchange of commodities. This change of locale in commerce upset the working of the Hanseatic League, whose strength had already been weakened by dissensions and embroilments, and by the Treaty of Assen it received such a blow that its power never recovered.

Early in this reign the Staple of the Merchant Adventurers was moved to Antwerp, and their trade was still mainly with the Netherlands.

The gowns of the City Livery Companies remained as described in the last chapter until the year 1525. Again Stow is helpful, and explains the transition of the livery gown thus:

1525. 'More, in the 16th of Henry VIII, Sir William Bayly, then being mayor, made a request, for that clothes of ray (as he alleged) were evil wrought, his officers might be permitted (contrary to custom) for that year to wear gowns of one colour; to the which, in a common council, one answered and said, "Yea, it might be permitted," and no man said, "Nay," and so it passed. Thus much for party coloured and ray gowns have I read: but for benevolence to the mayor, I find that of later time that each man giving forty shillings towards his charges, received four yards of broad cloth to make him a gown, for Thomas White performed it in the 1st of Queen Mary; but Sir Thomas Lodge gave instead of four yards of broad cloth, three yards of satin to make them doublets, and since that the three yards of satin is turned into a silver spoon, and so it holdeth.'

Now Sir William Bayly, who was elected Lord Mayor, 1524, was a draper; and he probably had a large stock of black cloth on his hands. He therefore chose this sombre hue, and four yards of black broadcloth was allowed for each gown. The hood remained as before, made in the livery colours. Later, in Elizabeth's reign, Sir Thomas Lodge, grocer and Lord Mayor in 1562, upset things by substituting a doublet, and the livery men then had to find their own gowns. Later still, the doublet had to give place to a silver spoon. No illustration of this new black livery gown of this date (1524) appears to exist. Whether the doctors, in the painting of Henry VIII presenting a charter to the Barber-Surgeons (1540–3), are wearing livery gowns or not is uncertain. These gowns are of black damask made with the fashionable large, puffed sleeves over fairly close under-sleeves of puce-pink satin, and carry parti-coloured crimson and black hoods by the liripipe over their left shoulders.

The nearest approach to the gown in use at this time, although dated 1566, is that shown in Fig. 798.

Sweeping changes took place in 1545, when by Act of Parliament the property of all guilds throughout England was confiscated. The ostensible reason given at the time was the imputation that guild money had been spent on matters which did not meet with the Government's approval; but in truth it was to replenish the coffers of the spendthrift King and his extravagant courtiers.

Although the guilds had outlived their purpose and were a hopeless hindrance to trade, those of London escaped total extinction by adopting drastic modifications in their antiquated system.

## WEAVING AND MATERIALS

A change had now come over the weaving industry. By this time the power of the 'master-clothier' had developed, and continued up to the end of the eighteenth century. He employed a great number of men, bought wool in large quantities, caused it to be spun, dyed, and finished. Each craftsman was obliged to co-operate in the one business concern controlled by this capitalist clothier, who sold the article complete to the merchants and drapers, who, in their turn, retailed it to the public.

The following fourteen craftsmen were employed in the manufacture of the finished cloth:

The *parter* sorted the wool.
The *dyer* dyed the requisite colour.
The *oiler* sprinkled the cloth with oil.
The *mixer* spread it and rubbed it in.
The *stock-carder* carded the wool.
The *knee-carder* transferred it to smaller rolls on quills.
The *spinster* span.
The *weaver* wove with the help of a small boy.
The *brayer* cleaned the weave from oil and dirt.
The *burler* removed knots, loose ends, etc.
The *fuller* washed the cloth. Originally a *walker* trampled it in a trough of water: this process was known as 'walking.'
The *rower* used teazles to draw up loose fibres from the body of the cloth.
The *shearman* turned the cloth and levelled the nap.
The *drawer* or *tenter* stretched the finished cloth.

A famous master-clothier of this time was John Smalwoode alias Winchecombe, known as 'Jack of Newbury' from the place where he resided and had his works. A pioneer of the clothing trade, he amassed great wealth, employing five hundred craftsmen and one hundred looms. In 1513 he led one hundred of his own journeymen at his own expense to Flodden Field, and later entertained King Henry and Queen Katherine most sumptuously at his house in Newbury. For these two reasons he was offered a knighthood but, curiously enough to a modern commercial mind, refused it. The 'most considerable clothier England ever beheld' died in 1520.

Another master-clothier, in his prime when Henry VIII ascended the throne, was Maister Thomas Spring (1456–1523) of Lavenham, Suffolk: 'Clothmaker alias yoman, alias Gentleman, alias Merchant,' a very important person and very rich. One has only to visit the little town of Lavenham and see the beautiful church erected by his grandfather, father, and especially himself in association with John de Vere (1443–1513), thirteenth Earl of Oxford; the delightful guildhall of Corpus Christi; and the numerous half-timbered houses, to realize what the cloth industry of those days meant. Kersey, which is close by, was once a cloth-making centre, and is a particularly charming village with only one blemish—a bungalow (1930).

Henry VIII greatly encouraged the weaving industry, and, for example, granted Crosby Hall, Chelsea, to Anthonio Bonorica, an Italian merchant. The King very much favoured the merchants of Italy, because they brought 'magnificent silks, velvets, tissues of gold, jewels, and other luxuries for the pleasure of us, and our dearest wyeff, the Queen.'

The King therefore directed that cloth of gold and tissue should only adorn dukes and marquesses; purple should be reserved for the Royal family; silks and velvets might be worn by the opulent commoner, but none inferior to an earl in dignity might use embroidery.

## LIST OF MATERIALS

*Amen*, see *Lasting*.

*Blanket*, a soft and loosely woven woollen material of *superior* make, used for bed covers and chiefly made at Witney. The material cost 12*d.* an ell, and 'two pair of blanketts' were valued at 5*s.* 4*d.*

*Boratoes, boratto*, a light material woven of silk and wool. A similar stuff was called *bombazine* and *bombassins*.

*Brocade*, silken material woven with a pattern in gold, silver, or contrasting colours. The patterns were usually floral or geometrical, and were sometimes raised.

*Brocatel*, a large patterned silk brocade. The equivalent is used to-day for furnishing.

*Brussel clothe, bryssell tykes*, perhaps a kind of cloth made in Brussels.

*Bustyans*, another name for fustian.

*Chambletts*, sixteenth-century name for camelot (*see* vol. ii, p. 188).

*Chanévaz, canevaz*, canvas.

*Cogware* (*see* vol. ii, p. 282). A coarse common cloth like frieze much used by cogmen who manned cogges, i.e. small boats which waited on larger vessels.

*Cloth of gold of Damask* had one of the fashionable large patterns woven upon it, and all gold.

*Crimson* (or other colour) *cloth of gold of Damask* was like the preceding, only the ground and pattern were shot. On the other hand, it might have a shot ground and a coloured pattern, or vice versa. Sometimes, especially in the case of velvet, the ground was of gold and the pattern in a colour, or the pattern gold on a coloured velvet ground.

So great was the demand for these expensive materials that in 1513 three to four thousand pieces, each containing twenty-five yards, were imported from Italy. The cost of these materials was £7 4s. 7d. per yard, and a payment was made to John Cavalcant, obviously a shrewd business man who used false arguments and hypocritical talk, of £144 10s. for twenty yards. In the Princess Mary II's privy purse expenses we find cloth of gold and of silver costing 40s. and a little later 38s. per yard. Cloth of silver cost 40s. per yard in 1538. There were considerable restrictions to the use of cloth of gold and of silver.

*Damask cloth of gold* or *silver*, see *Gold, cloth of.*

*Denmark satin*, see *Lasting.*

*Dowlas,* a coarse linen chiefly used during the sixteenth century by the lower classes.

*Draft,* see *Lasting.*

*Durance,* 'Durance of Duretty with Thread,' 'Durance of Duretty with Silk,' probably denotes any enduring fabric. At first it was only a name for buff leather, hence a stuff of that colour made in imitation of it.

*Estamine,* see *Tamette.*

*Frisadoe, frisadue, frizado,* a woollen material of which little is known; evidently expensive, and in colour usually red. A kind of frieze.

*Galonner,* to lace, to adorn with gold or silver, hence used for lace or passamayne.

*Gold, cloth of,* also *cloth of silver.* Cloth of gold and silver as described on p. 129 continued to be very much used.

*Grograine,* woven with large woof and a rough pile in linen and wool, linen and silk, or wool and silk. A coarse grain or texture.

*Jenet,* the fur of a horse in black and in grey.

*Kersey (see* vol. ii, p. 282). Kersey of exceptionally fine make was used by the nobility and upper classes for hosen. A kersey cloth of very fine quality was also used by them for other garments.

In records of Henry VIII's reign mention is made of several kinds of kersey: 'checkarseys' kerseys called 'dossens,' and kerseys called 'straits,' 'Devonshire kersies' called 'washers,' or 'washwhites,' 'ordinarie kersies,' 'sortinge kersies,' which all varied according to texture, length, and weight. The usual measurements were eighteen yards long and one yard and a nail wide.

*Lasting (amen, draft),* a contraction of 'everlasting.' A stout, closely woven worsted, dyed black or colours. It was woven either with a double twill or with satin twill, in which latter case it was called 'Denmark satin.' It was also figured, and when used in good quality for church furniture was called 'amen' or 'draft.'

*Linsey woolsey,* cloth woven from linen and wool in equal parts.

*Lockram,* a linen cloth originally woven at Locronan in Brittany.

*Musers*, see *Spangles*.

*Normandie cloth.* The same as Holland cloth, but made in Normandy.

*Pampilion*, a kind of fur. Gowns were 'furred with pampilion,' and twenty-five skins cost £60. It is suggested that the name is derived from Pamplona, and that the fur came from Navarre.

*Paper.* During the reign of Henry VIII all paper required for correspondence was made in Flanders. The watermark was often a hand, whose middle finger was connected by a straight line with a star.

*Passement.* During the first quarter of the sixteenth century it is spelt *passamayne*.

*Penniston*, a coarse frieze regulated in length, *being wet*, between twelve and thirteen yards of thirty-seven inches to the yard, and in breadth fifty-seven inches. Made at Penistone, Yorks.

*Perpicuana*, see Perpetuana, p. 790.

*Rashes*, material made from inferior silk, or silk and wool; also of combing and carding wool mixed together.

*Rugges*, a rough hairy shaggy material, much worn by the poorer classes.

*Russells*, a wool satin, a worsted calendered or hot-pressed in the finishing to give it a lustrous, sheeny surface.

*Russet.* The word 'russet' was from early times applied to homespun cloth (*see* vol. ii, p. 65), but in the early Tudor period this term was also applied to the *colour*. Hall refers to the costumes of the Royal household as yellow and russet, and the drawings in the Tournament Roll show these colours, which proves that the term was applied to either grey or brown.

*Sassanette*, same as sarcenet.

*Satin* was most profusely used for the costumes of the great, although it cost but 8s. per yard. All of it was imported.

'*Satten of Bruges*,' an imitation satin with thread weft.

*Say, saye, sayes*, a coarse woollen cloth made in Flanders. In early Tudor times this name was also given to a thin kind of silken material.

'*Silkes of newe making*,' i.e. of the most recent fashion, whatever that may have been.

*Spangles* or *musers* became more generally used in the reign of Henry VIII. It is doubtful if they were stamped with facets as early as this time.

*Stamine*, a worsted cloth now made in a better quality, and frequently used for backing panels of valuable tapestry.

*Taffeta*, a very much used thin silk.

*Tamette, tamy, tammis*, a woollen material also known as stamine.

*Tinsel, tilsent, tilson*, a material having a sparkling, glistening, and shining surface made in all colours. It was also made by overlaying the material with a thin coating of gold or silver.

*Velvet.* Plain velvets were used to a very great extent during the reign of Henry VIII. There was also a vogue for figured velvets. These were woven in two colours with two and sometimes three piles; for instance, one part of the pattern in a pile of, say, blue, the other part of the pattern and second pile in crimson, and the third pile or background producing an amalgamation of the two colours—purple. With two piles the ground was sometimes gold or silver. The price of velvet at this time was 41s. 8d. per yard.

## PATTERNS

It must be borne in mind that the design of patterns remained in vogue for many years. It would be quite consistent with the mode for a lady or gentleman of the fashionable Court of Henry VIII to appear in a brocade of,

Fig. 478. Black and Silver Brocade

say, mid-fifteenth-century design. The shape of the dress, especially with the ladies, was the cause of this. As long as skirts were made without folds large patterns persisted. The pomegranate, the badge of Queen Katherine (Fig. 238), was much in evidence upon the woven fabrics imported from Italy and especially from Venice. Its shape was well adapted to the requirements of the Renaissance style, and this also applies to the ogival panel.

Fig. 478 represents a brocade in black and silver, and dates the first thirty years of the sixteenth century. The design of its chief motif is, of course, inspired by the oleander of the previous period.

Fig. 479 gives a Venetian velvet of the second quarter of the sixteenth century. It is woven in at least two piles and in three colours. The pattern comprises ogival bands connected by coronets, and enclosing a motif which still retains traces of the pomegranate and the pine. Pomegranate buds, plentiful in this design, are frequent after this time.

Fig. 479. Venetian Velvet

The conventionalized acanthus branch and leaf made its appearance about the middle of the reign, and at the same time the central portion of the ogival panel was occupied by a vase-shaped motif which, more or less, suggested the line of the pomegranate fruit. From this sprang all kinds of conventional flowers, chiefly the rose, and leaves.

The lady (Fig. 302) has a much favoured new pattern on her dress. The ground would be of silk or velvet, or velvet upon velvet, and includes pomegranates, flowers, and leaves. The floral motif, as just stated, would most likely be springing from a vase with curved handles. A similar pattern in green velvet upon gold is worn by Lady Jane Grey in Plate XXIV.

The acanthus pattern is familiar to every one to-day by reason of its being much used in damasks for furniture and hangings.

## COLOURS

Although brown, blue, pink, tawny, and violet are the only colours enumerated in an Act of 1534 relating to English dyers, it does not follow that all shades of red were excluded. For the more delicate and intricate shades, and numerous tones, England had to depend upon materials imported from abroad. To the above must be added two new colours—names of a red hue:

*Incarnadine, incarnet,* flesh colour, a light pink or light crimson.
*Migraine,* a shade of scarlet or red, the colour of the pips of the pomegranate.

*Yellow* was a colour which denoted joy, and to dress oneself in yellow was an outward sign of rejoicing.

(*Continued on p.* 463)

## VEHICLES (*continued from p.* 140)

### *Chariot, charrette, char, litter*

Henry VIII, a great traveller, realized that good roads considerably added to his comfort; and during the early part of his reign laws were passed for the improvement of old roads, and several new ones were made. This state of things was the cause of a few more wheeled vehicles being used, but the horse-borne litter was still retained for ceremonial occasions.

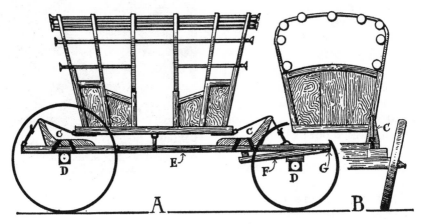

Fig. 480. A Chariot

Fig. 480 shows a chariot or char of the early years of the sixteenth century. The drawing is made from the remains of an existing one. A is a side view and B the front and back. The body part is no more than that of a litter transformed. An entrance is made between the wheels (a step was often provided); the single seats are placed opposite each other front and back. As already stated, the method of suspending the body on leather straps to obviate the discomfort of bumping and jolting was known earlier. In Fig. 480 we have an illustration of it. Each leather strap is attached to an iron loop on the under-framing of the body, passes over an upright shown at C, and is buckled through a loop fixed to the end of the axle-tree frame, D. A strap fixed to the middle of the body was attached to the 'perch,' E, or centre pole, to prevent too much swaying.

Turning was made more practicable, though to a limited extent, by the introduction of a triangular under-frame or swivel, F, to the foremost axle-tree. The shaft, for dividing a pair of horses and to bear the splinter bar and swingle-trees for the traces, was slotted in at G.

Fig. 481 is made from a photograph of the body part of a chariot used by the Elector John Frederick of Saxony in 1527, and preserved in the castle at Coburg. It would also answer the purpose of a litter, but was suspended by leather straps as described under Fig. 480, and the uprights fixed to the chassis were probably higher. A door closed the entrance between the wheels, and the panels at the sides, front, and back were decorated with an elaborate design of scrolls and figures. These two types (Figs. 480 and 481) illustrate the descriptions of chariots given in the text of Chapter II, and could be used with or without the bail and covering. The first to be seen in England was apparently that used by the ladies-in-waiting to Queen Katherine at her coronation, June 1509. The Queen herself was 'sitting in her litter borne by two white palfreys,[1] the litter covered and richlie appareled and the palfries trapped [2] in white cloth of gold; hir person apparelled in white satin

imbrodered, hir haire hanging downe to hir backe of very great length, beautifull and goodlie to behold, and on hir head a coronall set with manie rich orient stones. Next after six honorable personages on white palfries all apparelled in cloth of gold, and then a *chariot* covered and the ladies therein all apparelled in cloth of gold. And another sort of ladies, and then another chariot, and so in

Fig. 481. Body of a Chariot

order, everie one after their degrees in cloth of gold, cloth of silver, tinsels, and velvet, with imbroderies. Everie couplement of the said chariots and the draught harnesses were powdered with ermins in-mixed with cloth of gold: and so with much joy and honor they came to Westminster.'

Some excerpts from the inventory of the Princess Mary Tudor I give interesting particulars of the equipage of a Royal lady.

'A beautiful litter, covered with cloth of gold embroidered with fleurs-de-lys, and carried by two large horses equipped with both saddles and harness all complete and covered with similar cloth; inside the litter there are four large cushions covered with the same cloth of gold, and on the outside this litter is covered with a scarlet English cloth.'

There is mention of a second litter, complete with harness, all of cloth of gold.

'Then a fine suspended (or slung) chariot covered with cloth of gold, with a fringe of gold all round the said chariot, and, inside, four large cushions

---

[1] Palfreys were sometimes called footcloth horses in contradistinction to war horses or destriers.
[2] For a trapper or housing see vol. ii, Fig. 472.

covered with the same cloth, and a scarlet cover for putting outside the sai chariot.

'To draw this chariot there is a full accoutrement of six horses, of which three have saddles. The whole covered with the same cloth of gold and trappings.

'Item a beautiful chariot covered with embroidered fleurs-de-lys, fringed with gold all round, and inside there are four cushions covered with similar cloth, with a scarlet cover for the outside, like the previous one.

'To draw this chariot there are a further six accoutred horses, three of which likewise have saddles, the whole covered with similar cloth and trappings.

'Item also another chariot covered with crimson velvet fringed all round with gold fringe, and inside four cushions covered with similar crimson velvet; for the outside there is only waxed cloth as a cover.

'To draw which chariot there is the accoutrement of six other horses all complete, three of which have saddles all covered with the same crimson velvet and similar trappings.

'Made at Abbeville this 12th day of October 1514.

(*Signed*) FILLEUL.'

Besides these there were three other chariots for the ladies and gentlemen in attendance. One was covered in cloth of gold, the other two with crimson velvet, with horse furniture to match.

'Item a closed char for her wardrobe of the robes and ij chariotts for the wardrobe of the robes. ij Large cannavas [canvas] and ij borehidis [boar hides] for the said chariotts to save the stuf drie.'

### HORSES

'There are seventeen hackneys for the service of the same lady, all covered with cloths, of which fifteen are all white and two of dark gray, which have been brought from England.

'Item a pack [or sumpter] horse of similar skin, which the groom of the said lady says is for carrying various accoutrements connected with the affairs of the stable.

'Item there are also eighteen young horses, both large and small, which serve to draw the three suspended chariots.

'Item six other young horses which are intended to draw the covered char carrying the wardrobe of the said lady.

'Item there are also thirteen intended to draw the covered char for the garrison and officers or for tapestry or anything else they may be wanted for, all of which horses are not well harnessed at present, several pieces being missing.

'Item there are two large fine and young horses which are intended to carry the litter of the said lady.

'Made as below at Abbeville the 12th day of October 1514.

(Signed) FILLEUL.'

Then there were eight 'large and goodlie palfrais for the said Ladie princess to ride,' furnished with rich harness and side-saddles of cloth of gold, velvet, and goldsmith's work, for her own use and for travelling. Besides these were 'a bottell horse for her flagons: a sompter horse for her trussing bedde . . . a nother for her cofres.'

'Item a change for the said palfries, that is to say as well pilions, saddles, and harness, and also coverings for the said litter and chariotts to cover them when it is foule wedder, and a change of harness for every of the horses of the said litter and ladies charriotts.'

Some accessories needful when on a journey, taken from the same inventory, are amusing:

'Item a trussing bedde to carry with her by the ways with *celor, testor,* and *counterpoint* of velvet or of damaske, *purpale of her colors,* with bedd, bolster, pillowes, *fustians,* shets and other necessaries there for.'

'Celors' or 'celours' were the ceilings of beds; a 'counterpoint' the bedspread; a 'testor' was the head-board of a bed, and 'fustians' were blankets. A sumpter-horse was provided for carrying the trussing-bed. Other items were—two coffers for her jewels, three for her plate, and 'iij large cofres for her wardrobe for bedds, shetis and fustians.' 'Then iij cloth sackes at the lest, and cases for trussing bedde.'

'Item a stole [stool] covered with crimson velvet, naylled with gilt nails, and a small canape with curteyns of crymsyne double sarcenet to hange a bowte the same stole.'

'Item a basyn for the said stole of silver'—and they say the Tudors were unsanitary!

The liveries of the nine footmen come within this list. These footmen were dressed in 'jaketts' or cottes bearing the family cognizance, hosen, long boots and bonets, in sets of three. One set had jackets of 'white cloth of gold quilted with scales, and crimson velvet [divided] per pale with cloth of gold embroidered with a porcapin and a rose.' A porcupine was the badge of Louis XII, and is shown in Fig. 37. The second set were dressed in 'jaketts of tawny cloth of gold of damaske, and blew velvet embroidered with the fleurs-de-lys and a Rose'; the third set in green velvet jackets, embroidered with red roses and the sun in splendour.

The litter used by Anne Boleyn at her coronation is described on p. 265.

'Charriottes à bras,' or 'chars,' were wagons almost as richly decorated as chariots and used in processions or in journeys for the conveyance of baggage —and ladies-in-waiting (see p. 375).

(Continued on p. 465)

END OF BOOK I

# TUDOR COSTUME
# AND FASHION

## BOOK II

# CHAPTER III

## THE REIGN OF KING EDWARD VI
### 1547–53

## THE REIGN OF QUEEN MARY
### 1553–8

## CONTEMPORARY SOVEREIGNS

| | ENGLAND | SCOTLAND | FRANCE | GERMANY | | SPAIN | SWEDEN | DENMARK |
|---|---|---|---|---|---|---|---|---|
| 1547 | Edward VI | Mary Stuart<br>Francis II of France | Henry II<br>1547–59<br>Catherine de' Medici | Charles V | = | Charles I | Gustavus Vasa | Christian III |
| 1553 | Mary | | | | | | | |
| 1556 | | | | | | →Philip II<br>1556–98<br>1. Maria of Portugal<br>2. Mary Tudor<br>3. Elizabeth de Valois<br>4. Anne of Austria | | |
| 1558 | | | | →Ferdinand I<br>1558–64<br>Anne of Hungary<br>and Bohemia | | | | |

383

# HISTORICAL DATA, 1547–1558

1547. Accession of Edward VI and the establishment of Protestantism.
Protectorate of the Duke of Somerset, until 1549.

1548. First Act of Uniformity.
French alliance with Scotland.

1549. The first Prayer Book published.
The new Pilgrimage of Grace in the south-west.
Robert Ket's rebellion in Norfolk and Suffolk, August.

1550. Treaty of Peace between England, Scotland, and France.

1551. William Camden born in the Old Bailey, son of a painter-stainer of Lichfield. Wrote *Britannia*, published in 1586, the first systematic survey of antiquities of England, partly based on John Leland. First English version 1610. Head master of Westminster 1593. Clarenceux King of Arms. Died at Chislehurst 1623.
War between France and Germany, until 1554.

1552. The second Prayer Book published; second Act of Uniformity.

1553. Richard Chancellor reaches Moscow and opens up trade with Russia.
John Lyly born. Wrote many plays, chiefly upon classic subjects, founder of the popular style called 'euphuism,' the type in literature and polite conversation much used in the sixteenth century. Died 1606.

Death of Edward VI, 6th July.
Lady Jane Grey. Queen from 8th July to the 19th.
Accession of Mary and the beginning of the Romanist reaction.

1554. 'England returns to the bosom of the Roman Church,' November.
Insurrection of Kent, headed by Sir Thomas Wyatt, to dethrone Queen Mary and replace Lady Jane Grey on the throne.

1555. The old laws against heresy revived and enforced with great severity.
Diet of Augsburg, in which 'a complete liberty of conscience was granted to those States and Princes in the Empire who had embraced Protestant opinions.'

1555-6. Charles V resigned the Netherlands, the Spanish possessions in 1556 and, formally, the Empire in 1558.
The era of the Protestant martyrs. Bishop Hooper, 9th February. Bishops Ridley and Latimer, 16th October. Archbishop Cranmer, 21st March.

1557. War with France, until 1559.

1558. Surrender of Calais to the French. Mary of Scotland marries the Dauphin.
George Peele born. Wrote comedies and tragedies, and devised the Lord Mayor's pageant in 1585 and in 1591. Died 1597/8.
Death of Queen Mary and accession of Queen Elizabeth.

# THE ARTS, 1547–58

### SCULPTURE: MONUMENTAL EFFIGIES (*continued from p.* 145)

THE years covered by the reigns of Edward VI and Mary were not propitious for the craft of the monumental masons. A period of transition had arrived: the reckless destruction of many monumental effigies dating from the earlier centuries has deprived us of much detail of value and interest. Craftsmen of the Gothic tradition were dying out, and, when new monuments were required, the younger generation sought inspiration from Italy and from the Classic style which was just beginning to reach England.

At the same time, the conservative Englishman was not too eager to have the memory of his children, parents, and grandparents surrounded with the trappings of a foreigner. However, by degrees a compromise was achieved between the old and the new, and one notices the introduction of some Classic feature here and there into what at first appears to be the work of an earlier generation.

(*Continued on p.* 472)

### MEMORIAL BRASSES (*continued from p.* 145)

During this period, the reigns of Edward VI and Mary, very few (if any) brasses were laid down: and this was a direct consequence of the religious controversies and political dissensions of the times.

(*Continued on p.* 472)

### TAPESTRY (*continued from p.* 145)

### *Temp. Edward VI and Queen Mary*

As a matter of course Edward VI and Queen Mary inherited most, if not all, the sets of tapestry previously possessed by their father. The subject of at least one set in use at this time is known, 'The Siege of Antioch.' It was hung in the Audience Chamber at Hatfield, while the Princess Elizabeth was in residence there in 1557.

During the period between 1547 and 1558, little of importance occurred in the history of tapestry, but some interesting details are at hand regarding the production of a masterpiece of the time. Detailed instructions issued to the famous Flemish tapestry weaver, William Pannemaker, are still extant in the 'Imperial Command' received by him in 1548 from the Emperor Charles V. These instructions had been revised and elaborated by the Emperor's business-like sister Marie, Queen of Hungary, widow of Louis II, who edited a stringent contract by which Pannemaker was bound to supply the very best materials, etc. The silk used was to come from Granada, the gold from Milan. Eighty-three different tints of colour, each subdivided into twenty-two series, each of which again comprised from two to five tones, making altogether something like eight thousand shades of colour, are specified. The subject was to commemorate 'The Conquest of Tunis.'[1] In the year 1535, the Emperor had taken the artist, Jan Vermeyen, with him on this expedition as a member of his retinue, to enable him to design with strict truthfulness the cartoons representing various events in the campaign.

The execution of Vermeyen's cartoons occupied Pannemaker and eighty-four picked weavers for five years. The set was completed early in 1554.

The tapestries were justly prized by their owner, for they are reckoned among the most beautiful in existence. They consist of twelve panels, and are extremely useful for the study of military equipment, ships, and the costume of the Turks in the sixteenth century.

These twelve panels were sent on their completion to England for the marriage festivities of Queen Mary and Philip II. They were hung from pillar to pillar in the nave of Winchester Cathedral; the iron hooks which held the supporting rods are still in position. After the wedding the tapestries were returned to Spain with the utmost care, and thereafter were constantly used at Spanish Court functions. They used to ornament the palace of King Alphonso XIII in Madrid.

A reference to these tapestries in John Elder's letter is of sufficient interest to be inserted here:

'Where [Whitehall] in the mean season two princely presents came to Their Majesties. The one from the Emperor, which is XII pieces of Arras work, so richly wrought with gold, silver, and silk, as none in the world may excel them. In which pieces be so excellently wrought and set out all the Emperor's Majesties procedings and Victories against the Turks as Apelles were not able (if he were alive) to mend any parcel thereof with his pencil.'

(Continued on p. 473)

---

[1] The campaign in Tunis took place in 1535, and was undertaken to quell the invasion of northern Africa by the Turks. Charles V dispatched a fleet under the command of Doria, who achieved the conquest of Tunis.

Andrea Doria was born at Oneglia, near Genoa, in 1468. After having been in the service of the Genoese as Captain-General, he had sided with Francis I against the Emperor; but upon his native place being attacked by the French, he joined the Emperor Charles, and drove the French out of Genoa in 1528. This hero of the conquest of Tunis lived in great state in Genoa, and even at the age of ninety continued to command his galleys. He died in his bed in 1560.

PORTRAITS AND PAINTERS (*continued from p. 153*)

*Temp. Edward VI and Mary*, 1547 *to* 1558

In addition to Hans Eworth and Corneille de Lyon, both of whom lived until 1574, the most important Flemish painters whose works are useful for the study of costume in fashion during the reigns of Edward VI and Queen Mary are the following:

The family POURBUS, father, son, and grandson, were artists to whom we owe much information on costume. PIETER POURBUS, the father, born at Gouda in 1510, was specially a painter of portraits. He died at Bruges in 1584.

ANTONIO MORO, born at Utrecht in 1517. The dates of his itinerary are useful:

| | | | |
|---|---|---|---|
| In Italy | 1550–1 | In Madrid | 1559 |
| In Madrid | 1552 | In Utrecht | 1564 |
| In England | 1553 | In Antwerp | 1568 |
| In Utrecht | 1555 | | |

He was sent to England by Marie, Queen of Hungary, to paint for her nephew, Prince Philip of Spain, a portrait of Queen Mary. The exact date of his receiving the honour of knighthood is not known, but since it was for services rendered to Queen Mary, the year must have been 1553. Sir Antonio died about 1576.

GWILLIM STRETES, STREETES, or STREATE, born in Holland. He flourished 1546–56, and was one of the successors to Holbein. His first portrait of any importance is that of the Earl of Surrey, at Hampton Court (considered by some to represent the Duke of Richmond, natural son of Henry VIII). He became painter to the King.

LUCAS DE HEERE, born at Ghent in 1534, did not come to England until 1568. He died in Paris in 1584.

HANS EWORTH came into prominence about 1550 and remained a fashionable portrait painter until 1575. During this period he signed himself HE. Up to quite recently (1912) some of his works were attributed to Antonio Moro and Lucas de Heere. His paintings are characterized by the truthful, yet perhaps unflattering, portraiture of his sitters, the detail of accessories, and the introduction of armorial bearings into the general design of his composition. He died about 1575–6.

ALONZO SANCHEZ COELLO, born at Bonifacio near Valencia in 1515, though of Portuguese nationality, is known as a Spanish painter. He studied in Italy for many years and returned to Spain in 1541, settling in Madrid where he was appointed Court painter to Philip II. Although religious themes were his chief interest, there are portraits by him of the Infante Don Carlos and the Infanta Isabella in the Prado.

The paynter-stayners who flourished during these two reigns were:

NICHOLAS DE MODENA, an Italian who supervised the ornaments for Henry VIII's funeral obsequies, and became later 'art decorator' of the various 'dysguisings,' masques, and revels which took place at Court. He died 1571.

BARTOLOMMEO PENNI was another Italian, born at Florence, who became paynter-decorator to Edward VI.

JOHN BOSSAM flourished from 1550: 'that most rare English drawer of story works in black and white.'

NICHOLAS LYZARD continued in the office of paynter-stayner during Edward VI's reign, and was appointed serjeant-paynter by Queen Mary.

(*Continued on p. 476*)

# SECTION I: 1547–58

## ROYALTY AND NOBILITY—MEN: 1547–58

### KING EDWARD VI, 1537–53

Edward VI, fifth child of Henry VIII, was born at Hampton Court, 12th October 1537. His mother was Queen Jane Seymour who died twelve days later, a victim to bad judgment on the part of her physicians. The third of our bachelor kings, he was crowned 25th February 1547 at Westminster by Thomas Cranmer, Archbishop of Canterbury. In appearance Edward was fragile, moderately good looking with grey eyes, delicate complexion, and fair hair worn cut close to the head. His health was always precarious; at fourteen he writes in his *Journal* (2nd April 1551): 'I fell sick of the Measels and Small Pox.' His early portraits show him with a round pleasant face, but in those painted towards the end of his reign the face is long and rather narrow with a pointed chin. A celebrated Milanese physician who visited him in 1552 said: 'His stature was below the medium . . . his general appearance dignified and formal.'

Fig. 482. A Badge of King Edward VI

The early education forced upon him at the age of six, and a slight deafness, somewhat tempered the exuberance of youth. He was eager to acquire knowledge, but at the same time, despite his serious outlook on life, he was as fond of fun and games as any other boy. His tutors were selected with great discernment: Dr. John Cheke, born at Cambridge 1514, and Professor of Greek at St. John's College, taught him classics; Dr. Christopher Tye instructed the Prince in the art of music, Philip van Wilder being specially engaged to teach him to play the lute.

Very religious by nature, he was an ardent student of the Scriptures, and took exceptional pleasure in listening to sermons; so it is not to be wondered at that from his early years he was an enthusiastic religious reformer. Somewhat later he showed signs of developing many of the better traits of his father's character.

Edward was never created Prince of Wales, although preparations for the ceremony of his crowning were in progress when his father died. Nor was he created a Knight of the Garter, though on his accession to the throne he automatically became sovereign of that Most Noble Order.

Henry VIII had planned a carefully balanced Council of Regency in the event of his death during Edward's minority, but on Henry's demise this council was set aside, and the Earl of Hertford, a moving spirit of the Reforming Party, became Lord Protector, assuming the title of Duke of Somerset. He remained in office until October 1549, and was followed by the self-seeking John Dudley, Earl of Warwick, created Duke of Northumberland by Edward VI in 1551. Dudley was a son of Henry VII's infamous lawyer (*see* Chapter I, p. 14) and eventually died on the scaffold 22nd August 1553, after a shameful apostasy from the faith for which he had plunged England into bloodshed.

As early as 1542, Henry VIII endeavoured to arrange a marriage between his son, aged five years, and Mary Queen of Scotland—then only a few weeks old. During the following year the betrothal became an actuality by treaty concluded at Greenwich on 1st July 1543. But the Scottish Catholics favoured an alliance with France, and at the end of the same year Scotland repudiated the Greenwich agreement, with dire results to herself. In 1548 the infant Queen was sent to France to be educated as the destined bride of a future King—Francis II. At this juncture certain persons of high standing in the English Government were occupied in arranging a suitable marriage among the nobility of England for Edward, who had become King the year before. On 21st May 1550 Edward refers to the subject himself in his *Journal*. He writes: 'My Lord Marquess of Northampton had Commission . . . to treat of all things, and chiefly of Marriage for Me to the Lady Elizabeth his Daughter.' On the 26th of October the same year this entry occurs: 'The Lord Strange confessed how the Duke [of Suffolk] willed him to stir me to marry his third Daughter, the Lady Jane.' This was the Lady Jane Grey to whom he left in his will the crown of England, although he had no legal power to do so.

On 19th February 1547 the coronation festivities began. Mounted on a white horse *before* a canopy of gold, the boy King must have made an imposing figure as he rode from the Tower through London to the Palace of Westminster. He inherited much of his father's splendid dignity of bearing, and his costume, described by a contemporary, proves that on occasion he was thoroughly well dressed:

'The kynges Royall Maj^tie walking a lytell before his canopy, because the people might the better see his grace, his highness being richly apparelled with a riche gowne of cloth of silver all over embrodered with damaske golde, with a girkyn of white velvett, wrought with Venyce silver, garnished with precious stones, as rubies and diamonds, with true-loves of pearles, a doblet of white velvet according to the same, with like precious stones and pearls, a white velvet cappe garneshed with lyke stones, and perles, and a pere of buskenes of white velvet. His horse caparison of crymoysyn sattyn, imbrodered with perles and damaske gold.'

A painting of the procession existed at Cowdray House (*see* p. 420).

Another interesting feature in this cavalcade was the presence of the Lady Elizabeth and the Lady Anne of Cleves, both dressed in the latest French fashion all in silver. They were seated side by side in a chariot covered with cloth of silver. Unfortunately this is not shown in the painting above mentioned.

According to custom special robes were prepared for King Edward's coronation ceremonies. The first set was of the usual crimson velvet, the mantle 'with a longe trayne,' the surcote and hood all furred with powdered ermine throughout. These 'were called his parliament robes, wering on his hede a cappe of black velvett.' After the crowning and the hearing of Mass he changed into robes of purple, velvet, and ermine. Altogether the King's appearance was like the drawing, Fig. 211, which shows his father as a young man wearing similar robes.

It is interesting to know what garments King Edward wore under these regal trappings. Fortunately a list of them is extant:

'ij shertes, oone of Lawne, the other crymesyn sarsenet wyde in the collers.

'A breche of camerycke to the myd thighe, gathered together before and behynde, and a breche belt of crymesyn velvet sette the same.

'A payr of hosen of crymesyn sarsenet, Vaumpes and all.

'A payre of Sabetynes [shoes] of clothe of bawkekyn.'

A painting by Stretes showing Edward VI in state robes is in the possession of the Bridewell Royal Free Hospital. In this he wears over his doublet only the Royal mantle lined with ermine and a cape with hood of the same. The crown appears to be set on the bonet. The Garter Collar and the sceptre are the only other emblems of sovereignty.

On 12th June 1550 King Edward writes in his *Journal*: 'I was elected of the Company of St. Michael in France by the French King and his Order.' And on 20th of the same month the following information is given: 'The French King was invested with the Order of the Garter in his Bed-Chamber, where he gave a Chain to the Garter worth 200*l* and his Gown dressed with Auglets worth 25*l*, the Bishop of Ely making an Oration, and the Cardinal of Lorrain making him Answer.' Edward did not receive the French Order until 17th July. On that day 'Monsieur le Mareschal . . . came to present the Order of Monseigneur Michael; whereafter with Ceremonies accustomed, he had put on the Garments, he, and Monsieur Gye likewise of the Order, came one at my right Hand, the other at my left to the Chappel, whereafter the Communion celebrated, each of them kissed my cheek. After that they dined with Me, and talked after Dinner, and saw some Pastime and so went home again.' Monsieur le Mareschal Saint-André seems to have been popular with the King, for we read: 'The next Morning he came to Me to mine Arraying, and saw my Bed-Chamber, and went a hunting with Hounds; and saw Me shoot, and saw all my Guards shoot together. He dined with Me, heard Me play on the Lute, Ride; came to Me to my study, supped with Me, and so departed to Richmond.' The King was then in residence at Hampton Court.

Edward VI has received much undeserved credit as an extensive founder of grammar schools.[1]   He did, however, use part of the vast sums accumulated by his father from the suppressed ecclesiastical institutions to endow some such schools, including the famous Christ's Hospital (1553) (*see* p. 424), together with three other foundations for three classes of indigent poor.

St. Bartholomew's and St. Thomas's Hospitals, founded in 1102 and 1228 respectively, were endowed, and the Royal Palace of Bridewell was given up as a home for the reform of vagrants and disorderly persons.   Besides the grammar schools which owed their origin to Edward's initiative, the Royal example inspired similar foundations in various parts of the country, and other schools were started in certain towns, by petition and help of the burgesses.

The Puritans made their first appearance in this reign.   This fact may have influenced some writers [2] to suggest that the Court of Edward VI was sombre and funereal.   This view seems to be far from the truth, for Edward's own journal makes frequent references to the gaieties and splendid entertainments which took place.   As for dress, examination of the portraits of the time shows apparel fully as gorgeous as ever was worn in the last reign.

Plate XIX is taken from a portrait of King Edward VI at Christ's Hospital painted about 1548.   There is another almost identical at Windsor Castle. It will be seen that the costume worn by Edward is similar in most details to that of his father.   The surcote is of vermilion velvet, garded with gold passamayne and lined with ermine.   A feature to be noticed is that the collar, or turned-back lining of ermine, surrounds the neck, and does not, as previously, fall back wide on the shoulders.   This gives a view of the way the full sleeve is pleated, or gathered, into the armhole.   The King's slender figure appears somewhat overwhelmed in this ample garment.   The doublet, with sleeves of white cloth of silver of damask bordered with a wide design in squares of silver embroidery, is slightly different from the earlier vogue.   It is closed higher at the throat, with a stand-up collar; a narrow collar of white lawn is inside, and turns down over it.   The skirt part (originally the bases, and later a pleated skirt) is shorter, and forms a deep basque.   In consequence the slops are more conspicuous.   They are of silver embroidery worn over white silk hosen.   Edward VI was the first English monarch to wear knitted hose of silk.   A pair of long silk STOCKINGS was presented to him by Sir Thomas Gresham.   Sir Thomas had procured them from some Spanish merchants and this unusual gift greatly pleased his youthful majesty.   About this same time Diane de Poitiers made a present of some knitted silk stockings manufactured in Italy to Henry II of France and Catherine de' Medici. Shoes had now become more normal in the toe, though somewhat rounded, and followed the shape of the foot.

A noticeable feature of this costume is the bonet.   At this time it was

---

[1] The name 'grammar school' was given to schools before the grammar of the English language was written or taught, and when all grammatical knowledge was obtained by the study of ancient languages.   Latin was the chief subject of instruction in the early grammar schools, and the language in which teaching was given.

[2] For example, the ambassador, Antoine de Noailles, and Henri Griffet (1698–1771), who wrote *A New Light on the History of Mary, Queen of England*, which influenced David Hume (1711–76) and Dr. Lingard (1771–1851).

PLATE XX. KING EDWARD VI: Portrait by Gwillim Stretes
Hampton Court Palace. *By gracious permission of H.M. the King.*
*Photo by Mansell*

not so flat as hitherto and the band of jewels was placed round the crown
on top of the brim; the white feather drooping over the left side, with a
fancy gold tassel hanging from it; a gold dagger in a black sheath, slung
from a narrow white and silver waistbelt, and ornamented with a large black
silk tassel. The background shows a repetition of the Vol, the armorial
bearings of the Seymours. Birds on the wing see more than beings and
beasts.

Another portrait of King Edward shows a handkerchief attached by one
corner to the waistbelt. It is of fine white lawn, with the hem embroidered
in red silk. It measures about fifteen inches
square. '6 handkerchers edged with passamayne
of gold and silk' is an item which appears in one
of the lists of New Year's gifts to the King.

Fig. 483

A pleasing design, embroidered in black silk on
a linen neck-frill, is seen in a portrait of Edward
VI at Packwood House (Figs. 483 and 484). The
edge of the frill is worked in double blanket-
stitch, and on top of each fold is a quatre-foil
with fleur-de-lys motifs at the corners. This frill is particularly interesting
because it shows for the first time a method, much used at a later period,
of catching the edges together to form what was known in heraldry as
nebulée and dovetail.

Plate XX reproduces a later portrait of Edward VI by Gwillim Stretes at
Hampton Court. The costume is carried out entirely in black satin, elaborately braided in gold, with emeralds in gold settings placed thereon at intervals
(see Fig. 268). The surcote is not so ample as that shown in Plate XIX,
and the turn-back sets wide on the shoulders, a return to the mode characteristic of the latter part of Henry VIII's reign. The slops are even more
conspicuous below the basque and have vertical bands of the same braiding
as on the doublet and the surcote.

Fig. 484

For centuries it had been, and was still, the privilege of all gentlemen when
wearing civil full dress to carry swords unless fashion during certain periods
dictated otherwise. Attention is called to the sword. A drawing of one of
this period is shown in Fig. 485; the hilt is of the cross type. The tapering
*grip* is bound with wire, and finished with an ornamental pointed *pommel*;

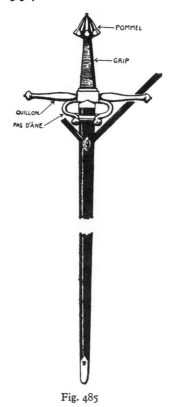

Fig. 485

the *quillons* are straight with circular ornaments at the ends, and the *pas-d'âne* are seen below them. The scabbard of plain velvet, ending in a metal *chape*, encloses the steel blade which is probably richly damascened. This sword is slung from the waistbelt by two straps fixed to the scabbard by circular ornaments. One strap is hooked to the waistbelt in front, the other on the left side towards the back. The waistbelt (Fig. 486) fastens low down in front, the ends of the belt having metal ornaments, one with a ring, the other with a hook at A.

A more elaborate sword handle with part of the scabbard of the same date is shown in Fig. 563.

Edward VI's Lord Chamberlain of the Household was Thomas, first Baron Wentworth (born 1501, died 1551). 'The Lord Wentworth Lord Chamberlain, died about ten of the Clock at Night, leaving behind him sixteen Children,' writes Edward in his *Journal* under date 3rd March 1550–1. Fig. 487 is made from his portrait by Hans Eworth dating 1547, and in it is seen the latest development of the style of dress worn in Henry VIII's time. The doublet is of black silk, braided at the edge with black and buttoned down the front. From the high collar falls a white turn-back collar. Over the doublet is worn the surcote of black velvet, lined and turned back with ermine. The sleeves are made loose enough on the lower arm to allow for the sleeve of the doublet underneath, and there are large puffs on the shoulders. When the sleeve was raised high above the shoulder it was said to be MAHOITERED, viz. stuffed with wadding (French *maheutre* or *mahoitre*, a wadded sleeve). It appears for the first time in this drawing (for the cut, reference should be made to Fig. 522 C). The sleeves in Fig. 487 are decorated with three narrow bands of ermine, the centre one descending the full length of the arm. These bands are fixed at intervals with pairs of gold aiglettes. A pocket like that shown in Fig. 495 would be attached to the narrow waistbelt. The slops

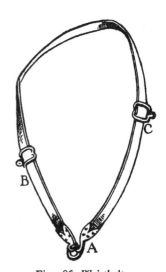

Fig. 486. Waistbelt

are of black velvet gathered or pleated into a narrow band which surrounds the thigh. The black velvet bonet has a turned-down brim, with a flat crown, and is without ornament or feather.

An excerpt from Edward VI's *Journal*, under date 4th November 1550, when the King received Mary of Guise, Queen-Dowager of Scotland, is given below as an example of Court ceremonial:

The '*Duke of Suffolk*, the Lord Fitzwater, the Lord Bray, and divers other Lords and Gentlemen, accompanied with his wife the *Lady Francis*, the *Lady Margaret*, the Dutchesses of Richmond and of Northumberland, the Lady Jane daughter to the Duke of Suffolk; the Marquess of Northampton and Winchester; the Countesses of Arundel, Bedford, and Huntingdon, and Rutland; with 100 other Ladies and Gentlewomen went to her, and brought her through London to Westminster. At the Gate there received her the Duke of Northumberland, Great Master, and the Treasurer, and Comptroller, and the Earl of Pembrook, with all the Sewers, and Carvers, and Cup-bearers, to the number of thirty. In the Hall I met her, with all the rest of the Lords of my Council, as the Lord Treasurer, the Marquis of Northampton, etc., and from the outer-Gate up to the Presence-Chamber, on both sides, stood the *Guard*. The Court, the Hall, and the Stairs, were full of Servingmen; the Presence-Chamber, Great-Chamber, and her Presence-Chamber, of Gentlemen. And so having brought her to her Chamber, I retired to Mine.

Fig. 487. The first Baron Wentworth, 1547. After Hans Eworth
(*National Portrait Gallery*)

'I went to her to Dinner; she dined under the same Cloth of State, at my Left Hand; at her *rereward* dined my Cousin Francis, and my Cousin Margaret; at Mine sat the French Ambassadour. We were served by two Services, two Sewers, Cupbearers, Carvers, and Gentlemen. Her *Master-Hostel* came before her Service, and my Officers before Mine. There were two Cupboards, one of Gold four Stages high, another of massy Silver six Stages: In her great Chamber dined at three Boards the Ladies only. After Dinner, when she had heard some Musick, I brought her to the Hall, and so she went away.'

One or two notes on the above may be helpful. The 'Duke of Suffolk' was Henry Grey, who married the Lady Frances Brandon, second daughter of Charles Brandon, Duke of Suffolk, see pp. 176 and 213.

'My cousin Margaret' was the Lady Margaret Douglas, the mother of Lord Darnley. The 'Guard,' of course, means the Yeomen of the Guard. The King does not mention the Gentlemen Pensioners, but doubtless they also were present.

'At her rereward' must mean, according to the usual precedence at banquets, that the 'cousins' sat on the Queen's left, and the 'French Ambassadour' —invited doubtless out of compliment to the Queen—on the King's right.

The 'Master-Hostel' was the Queen's Chamberlain, or Comptroller of her household.

At the premature age of sixteen, the young King, who had been ailing for most of his short life, died of lung trouble at Greenwich, 6th July 1553. The nostrums of the female quack, to whose tender care he was committed after the physicians had pronounced his case hopeless, probably hastened his end.

## FRENCH FASHIONS

### HENRY II

#### King of France, 1518–59

In the portrait of Henry II of France, painted by François Clouet and now in the Musée Condé at Chantilly, is seen the characteristic French fashion of this period. Fig. 488 is a drawing made from this portrait.

Henry, the second son of Francis I and Queen Claude, was born in 1518. He married Catherine de' Medici in 1533, and was father of three successive kings of France. On the death of his elder brother Francis in 1536, he became Dauphin and ascended the throne of France in 1547 as Henry II. In appearance he was tall with broad shoulders and short neck; of dark complexion with sharp black eyes, large nose, black hair, and at the age of thirty-two a 'beard coming to a point, two fingers long.' He was extremely active, possessing abnormal muscular strength combined with great dignity, which served him in good stead as a great sportsman, keen tennis player, and expert tilter. At the age of thirty-six, however, he became rather corpulent, and his hair turned grey.

When the time came to make the arrangements for his crowning, the King surveyed the robes and consecration ornaments which had been used by his predecessors. Finding them unsatisfactory and somewhat impaired by time, he had very gorgeous new ones made for his own coronation.

The costume worn by Henry II in the portrait referred to above is carried out entirely in black and white. The doublet is close-fitting (JUSTAU-CORPS) and has a high collar, short puffed sleeves, and basque. It is constructed of *bands* of white silk, ornamented with cuttes and attached at the

PLATE XXI. HENRY II, KING OF FRANCE, 1558: Portrait by Francis Clouet
Private collection.   *Photo by Fleming*

edges by heavy black silk stitchery. The separate sleeves are white decorated with very small cuttes between transversal groups of three rows of black silk stitches. The treatment of garments with these minute cuttes was called 'pinking.' The slops are composed of bands called PANES of white silk worked with black, between which the white silk puffed foundation is seen. The bonet is black velvet with a white ostrich tip. It is said that Henry II usually wore a suit of black and white out of compliment to Diane de Poitiers, who favoured this combination. Some of his doublets were embroidered with 'three crescents intertwined and carrying the cipher of the double D linked and joined with an H.' A portrait of this King at the age of thirty-seven (1556) in the Musée du Puy (Fig. 489) shows him in a doublet of white soft leather treated in the same manner as the JERKIN described under Fig. 495. Over it he has a black velvet surcote lined and turned back with white fur through the short sleeve of which his left arm passes, his forearm resting on the chair, with his hand on the hilt of his sword; the right arm is outside the surcote sleeve and gloves are held in the hand. The usual black velvet flat cap with white feather is worn.

Plate XXI is a reproduction from a private collection of a very fine equestrian portrait of Henry II painted by François Clouet about 1558. The black velvet doublet is ornamented with very beautiful gold embroidery at the front, sides, and edges, while lines of gold cord converge to the waist and spread out over the rather deep basque. The sleeves, which are treated in the same way,

Fig. 488. Henry II, King of France (after Clouet)

are not worn, but hang from the back of the shoulder. The close sleeves and slops are of white satin having bands of gold with pinking between. The most interesting details are the elaborately embroidered white tops of the BOOT HOSE and the JACK BOOTS. The horse furniture, too, is of exceptional interest. The saddle, saddle-cloth, and well-padded front bate are white embroidered with gold. The rest of the trappings are of gold with coloured silk tassels in a beautiful design, incorporating the cipher D and D reversed with H. The first, of course, refers to Diane de Poitiers, but in the opinion of the author there is some doubt if both initials are D's; the right one *could* pass for a C, in which case the Queen has not been overlooked. The King carries a long riding-rod in his right hand, and wears the fashionable gloves cutte at the wrist and folded over to form loops (*see* Fig. 645).

Fig. 489. HENRY II, KING OF FRANCE, 1555

A Venetian gentleman, who saw him at the age of thirty-six playing tennis with a racquet (Fig. 490), describes this costume thus:

'He is clad all in white, with white shoes, too, and a straw hat of the finest on his head. He played in his doublet.' Unfortunately the shape of the straw hat is not mentioned. In all probability it had a basin crown fitting close to the head, and a wide brim. His death, which created a sensation in sporting circles throughout Europe, was caused by a fatal wound in the eye inflicted by his opponent, the Comte de Montgoméry,[1] at a Royal wedding tournament in 1559.

Fig. 367 shows another decorative treatment of a black velvet jerkin worn by a Frenchman in 1543. Lines of fine gold cord are sewn horizontally across it, and the manner in which they join the arm openings demonstrates that the latter are cut at right angles to the jerkin with shoulder seams.

Fig. 490. Racquet

Fig. 491. William West, Esq., 1551.
National Gallery

There is a three-quarter portrait, No. 4252, in the National Gallery, London, of 'William West, Esq.,' born 1519 and created Baron de la Warr in 1570. It was painted about 1551, and depicts the ordinary attire of a young gentleman of Edward VI's reign (Fig. 491). The doublet of fine black cloth has vertical cuttes below the chest and a long basque edged with strands of bullion like the cloak. It is worn over crimson silk, and the sleeves, moderately full at the shoulders and close at the wrists, are of the same colour and material. At the neck and wrists are frills embroidered with Spanish work. The slops are of more ample proportions, and are composed of panes of black velvet with the black satin lining very much pulled through. A full and rather deep cloak of cloth without lining, bound with flat gold bullion with loops of

[1] Gabriel de Montgoméry (1533–74) was a captain in the French King's Scottish Bodyguard and son of James de Lorge, a Scottish gentleman who purchased, in Normandy, the Seignory of Montgoméry, which conferred upon him the title of Count.

the same at the edge (*see* inset), hangs from the shoulders; and the cap of black velvet with a narrow brim is decorated with groups of three gold buttons and a long white drooping plume.

Fig. 492 is taken from a portrait dating about 1550, and shows the black velvet jerkin, now decorated with narrow vertical lines of gold closely worked with bullion strands. Notice the way the lines are arranged, particularly those from shoulder to waist and continuing on the basque. The shape of the collar is very characteristic; it is very straight, close under the chin in front and high at the back. Observe also the shoulder pieces in the form of epaulets obviously derived from the wide shoulders of Fig. 504. The epaulet or narrow piece of material formed on the shoulder of the armhole was known as a 'welt' or 'pinion.' The basque is cut in one piece with the body part, and is edged with a row of indentations.

Fig. 492. Jerkin, 1549     Fig. 493. Jerkin, 1555

## THE EMPEROR CHARLES V, 1548–58 (*continued from p. 250*)

In later life the Emperor was painted by Titian in 1548 as he appeared at the Battle of Mühlberg, in full steel armour inlaid with gold,[1] mounted upon a chestnut Andalusian charger. The scarf and feathers in the helmet are scarlet. The horse furniture is scarlet and gold. When Charles reached middle life he appears to have lost interest in his personal appearance. Bernardo Navagero, the Venetian envoy, writes in 1548: 'His personal tastes were simple, his clothes, his table, his kennel and his stables were those of a modest prince rather than a mighty Emperor.'

It has been suggested that His Imperial Majesty adopted this course on purpose to counteract the insensate passion for dress among the gentry. In Germany he would wear a fustian cap and a woollen costume not worth a crown, all of one colour, and so the great nobles did likewise.

[1] Several of Charles V's suits of armour, including this one, are preserved in the Royal Armoury of Madrid.

Another portrait by Titian (1548) in the Pinakothek, Munich, displays simple richness combined with great dignity. Charles is seated in a purple velvet chair in front of a dorsal of orange damask. He is dressed entirely in black velvet without any decoration, a short sable-lined cloak is drawn closely around him, and he wears a plain flat black velvet bonet. The severity of this costume is relieved only by the turned-down white collar, the Golden Fleece, and dark brown leather gloves. Another Venetian, Alvise Mocenigo, states that the Emperor 'was most economical in his person, thinking it folly to give more than two hundred crowns for a fur; he often had his clothes mended, knew every detail, and missed a straying shirt or handkerchief.' During his last ten years he was possessed by a mania for frugality, and it was not beneath his dignity to wear threadbare clothes, old hats, and patched boots. On one occasion when about to make his entry into Nuremberg, for fear of his new cap being spoilt by the rain he sent forward into the town for an old one, and carried the new one under his arm.

We have a pathetic description of this great man in 1551 given by the English ambassador. He writes: 'I . . . found the Emperor at a bare table, without a carpet [1] or anything else upon it, saving his cloak, his brush, his spectacles, and his picktooth. Here His Majesty received the King's Highness's [Edward VI] letters very gently putting his hand to his bonet and uncovering the upper part of his head . . . he was newly rid of his gout and fever, and therefore his nether lip was in two places broken out, and he forced to keep a green leaf within his mouth at his tongue's end—a remedy, as I took it, against such his dryness as in his talk did increase upon him.'

The Emperor resigned the Empire to his brother Ferdinand,[2] 25th October 1558, and the crown of Spain to his son Philip, 15th January 1556; and, as a consequence, the Grand Mastership of the Order of the Golden Fleece became divided between Austria and Spain (see vol. ii, p. 402).

Charles retired to the monastery of S. Yuste, near Placentia, Estremadura, and died 21st September 1558. 'Not quite a great man nor quite a good man, but an honourable Christian gentleman,' says a biographer.

To him his son Philip erected an elaborate monument in his newly finished Escorial shortly after 1584. It stands on the north side of the high altar, and contains the kneeling effigies of Charles V and his wife Isabella, their daughter the Empress Maria, and his sisters, Queens Eleanor of France and Marie of Hungary. The figures are full size, in bronze, and with armorial mantles in colour. The artist, Pompeo Leoni, also executed Philip's own monument.

---

[1] Very rich carpets were frequently used as table covers.
[2] The Emperor Ferdinand I was educated by Spanish Dominicans, and spoke Spanish only, even when he had already long been ruling in German lands.

### SPANISH STYLES: 1547–58

For the contemporary Spanish fashion, Fig. 494, reproducing a three-quarter portrait of a Spanish gentleman by the Italian artist, Moroni (by courtesy of the Earl of Warwick), is chosen as an example. Although it is dated 1560 the style was in vogue quite ten years earlier. The drawing shows

a Spanish jerkin. This garment was worn over the doublet, and had no sleeves to be worn on the arm; but at this time it often had short sleeves, and sometimes short puffed sleeves reaching half-way down the upper arms. 'The jerkin was merely an outside coat worn generally over the doublet which it greatly resembled.' The jerkin in Fig. 494 has a short basque and cutte shoulder sleeves of black velvet, without any other decoration. It has a high collar, and from the top of it falls a square-shaped collar of cut-work, mounted on rose-coloured satin, having tiny tassels at the corners (a similar collar is shown in Fig. 688). The cuffs match the collar. The sleeves of the doublet are of deep rose satin, decorated with pinking in the manner described under Fig. 488. The slops have wide panes of crimson velvet edged and braided diagonally with rose silk cord, with deep rose satin linings pulled through. The pattern of the braid is shown below the picture.

Fig. 494. A Spanish Gentleman
(*after Moroni*)

The bonet is black velvet without jewel or feather. The hosen, the tops of which are just visible in the original painting, are of rose-coloured silk.

Jerkins similar in shape to the one described above are depicted in several portraits of Spanish and Italian gentlemen painted by Italian artists about the same date.

## MAXIMILIAN

### *Archduke of Austria, 1522 until 1558*

The Archduke Maximilian of Austria, later Maximilian II, Holy Roman Emperor (1564–75), is shown in Fig. 495, taken from a portrait in the Prado, Madrid, painted in 1551 by Antonio Moro. Maximilian was the son of the Emperor Ferdinand I, and a nephew of Charles V. He was born about 1522 and married his cousin the Archduchess Maria.

Although a German his costume is regulated by French fashion as regards all details except the jerkin, which is of Spanish type. The jerkin and shoulder sleeves in Fig. 495 are of soft white leather. After the garment was made up, the body part from high breast level to waist-line was cut vertically in narrow strips half an inch in width, finishing in a row of scallops 'lired' or bound with gold thread. A second similar row of scallops was fixed at the waist under the first. The doublet and sleeves are of white silk, also cut vertically in strips and banded transversely with gold braid, the body part being occasionally visible between the strips of the jerkin. The white panes

Fig. 495. The Archduke Maximilian, 1551
*(after Moro)*

of the slops are heavily braided with gold, with the lining of white taffety 'pulled out' between them. Panes were fixed to a hip-yoke which descended from waist-line to hip-bone level, and fitted close to the figure (*refer to* Fig. 496), the lower part of the slops gradually bulging out. A black velvet bonet is worn and the Toison d'or encircles the neck. The pocket or pouch is a fine example of those in use among fashionable people of this period. Variants of the jerkin described above are

Fig. 496. Slops

to be seen in several portraits, chiefly foreign, dating about this time (*see* Fig. 489).

## PHILIP OF SPAIN

### *King of Naples and Jerusalem, 1527 until 1558*

Philip of Spain, only son of the Emperor Charles V and Isabella of Portugal, was born at Valladolid, 21st May 1527. In his early years he was surrounded by strict and narrow-minded devotees, and not until the termination of hostilities with Italy, and the subsequent return of the Emperor in 1533, did he see his father for the first time. Heir to the largest empire in the world, he was educated with great care by a Professor of Salamanca called Siliceo, whom Philip afterwards made Archbishop of Toledo and Primate of Spain, and Don Juan Zuniga, who taught the young Prince the various accomplishments necessary for one in so exalted a position. At the age of fourteen the Emperor took charge of his son's education in politics.

The various portraits of Philip show him as a good-looking young man of fair complexion with yellow hair, grey eyes, and a pleasant expression. Another description refers to 'a fine broad brow, large blue eyes, dense fair eyebrows very close together, a nose well formed, a large mouth with a thick and pendent under-lip which rather spoiled his appearance. His skin was white and his hair flaxen.' He was a little below the average height, graceful, erect, and dapper of person. Grave and reserved, he relaxed when occasion required, and could become most courteous and affable. Dancing was, in fact, the one frivolity that this solemn Prince allowed himself.

An eyewitness of Philip's entry into London on the occasion of his visit in 1554, describes him in these words:

'Of visage he is well favoured, with a broad forehead, and grey eyes, straight nosed, and manly countenance. From the forehead to the point of his chin, his face groweth small. His pace is princely, and gate so straight and upright, as he loseth no inch of his height; with a yellow head and a yellow beard. And thus to conclude, he is so well proportioned of body, arm, leg, and every other limb to the same, as nature cannot work a more perfect pattern; and, as I have learned, of the age of xxviij years; whose Majesty I judge to be of a stout stomach, pregnant witted, and of most gentle nature.'

The chief points of Philip of Spain's character were that he was by nature a kind man, a loyal and dutiful son, a loving husband and father. From birth he firmly believed that he had a semi-divine mission, and was himself God's instrument to fight His battles and wipe out heresy. Towards middle age a hereditary gloom, deepened by fanaticism, took possession of him, and he became distrustful, secret, crafty, and over-cautious. No disaster thwarted him; it was God's will, that was enough.

Biased historians have hitherto held Philip responsible for the drastic extirpation of heresy in this country. As a matter of fact, his energies were directed against the rash zeal of the Catholic party, and the era of martyrs did not begin until six months after he left England for the first time. During

Fig. 497. PRINCE PHILIP OF SPAIN, 1548.  After Titian

his second visit in 1557 he was the means of saving many victims from the flames by his active intercessions.

Philip's titles were many. Those proclaimed in conjunction with Queen Mary's at their marriage were: 'Philip and Mary, by the Grace of God King and Queen of England, France, Naples, Jerusalem, and Ireland, Defenders of the Faith, Princes of Spain and Sicily, Archdukes of Austria, Dukes of Milan, Burgundy, and Brabant, Counts of Hapsburg, Flanders, and Tyrol.'

On the day of Prince Philip's marriage in 1554 with Mary Tudor, the Emperor equalized his son's rank with that of Queen Mary by making him King of Naples and of Jerusalem. The crowns of Spain were also transferred to Philip on the abdication of his father, together with the sovereignty of the New World, 16th January 1556. Henceforth he was known as King Philip II.[1]

Prince Philip had previously married (15th November 1542) the Princess Maria, daughter of Joam III, King of Portugal, and Catalina, youngest daughter of Philippe le Beau. Don Carlos (died 1568) was their only son. The Princess died November 1543.

One of the Emperor Charles V's schemes, evolved in 1548, for centralizing the government of Spain, was to form an entourage around his son Philip, consisting of members of the most powerful Spanish noble families; and he also introduced into the Royal household the punctilious formulae of the Court [2] of his ancestor, the magnificent Philippe le Bon, Duke of Burgundy (see vol. ii, p. 400).

This change in the regime was not altogether congenial to Prince Philip, whose personal tastes were of the simplest. He disliked the pomp, glamour, and flattery inevitable to the life of Royal personages under such a system, and from early manhood preferred the domestic circle of his own family. In dress he was moderate and his usual attire was plain though rich. Nevertheless on all necessary occasions he would appear garbed in the superb raiment befitting his exalted position. Of this type Fig. 497 is a good example.

It is made from the portrait of Prince Philip in the Royal Pitti Gallery, Florence. The original was painted by Titian from a sketch made either in 1548 at Milan, or in 1550 at Augsburg, and was presented to Duke Cosimo I. It has been suggested that this is a copy of another portrait of Philip, in the Gallery at Naples. The Naples portrait is exactly the same, but the background is slightly different.

In Fig. 497 the doublet, sleeves, and slops (now still more pronounced) are composed of bands of pale yellow satin edged with passamayne, having pairs of aiglettes, called in Spanish 'puntas,' set at intervals. One such aiglette is shown in Fig. 455. The bands are embroidered with a design

---

[1] Philip's grandfather, Philippe le Beau, is known as Philip I, King of Spain.

[2] The elaborate ceremonial and etiquette of the Burgundian Court, adopted by that of Spain in the middle of the sixteenth century, retained its hold until the end of the Spanish monarchy in April 1931.

shown again in Fig. 498. The floral motifs are worked in silver thread, and the stems are silver chainlets. The collar and wrists are edged with a series of loops like Fig. 499. A plain white lawn collar surrounds the neck, and the Toison d'or is worn.

The doublet is now slightly padded from below chest level to the sloping waist. The surcote is of rich brown satin, the fronts turned back with sable; it has large sleeves with bands in the same design as those on the doublet; the sleeves are sufficiently short to show those of the doublet worn beneath it at the wrists. The hosen are of pale yellow silk, and the cutte shoes, of the same shade in velvet, have a series of very small loops at the edge. The Prince holds his dagger in the right hand with the hilt pointing downwards.

The portrait of Philip, painted by Titian at Augsburg in 1550–1 and now in the Prado, Madrid, shows him wearing a beautiful suit of damascened armour, over slops, hosen, and shoes of white silk. This portrait, one of the finest in the world, was sent to Queen Mary at the time the Spanish marriage was arranged.

Fig. 498.
Embroidery

An inventory of his costumes, besides other items for his personal use, to be worn during his sojourn in England, was compiled by a certain Andres Muñoz, valet to his young son, Don Carlos. It is of exceptional interest, as it gives numerous details of the costumes worn not only by Philip himself, but by many of his courtiers,

Fig. 499

attendants, servants, and military escort. It appears that this wonderful masculine trousseau, chiefly prepared in the city of Valladolid, caused a great sensation throughout Spain. Previous to this date, 1554, lavish display and ostentation in the dress of the middle classes, as has been already noted, was strictly prohibited. Gradually these laws had been applied with less and less stringency, but now the opportunity for release seemed to have been reached. The Cortes of Castile boldly presented a petition to the Emperor, asking that these sumptuary laws should be repealed. The petition, however, was not granted, because both the Emperor and his son realized that instead of the wealth of the country flowing into their own coffers, it would probably be 'used in decking the undistinguished persons of private citizens.'

Philip's portrait, painted by Antonio Moro in 1554 (Plate XXII), shows him in a jerkin composed of wide bands of velvet each edged with passamayne, the centre portion of the velvet being cutte to show the doublet underneath. These bands are held together at intervals by fancy buttons (Fig. 500), often very elaborate and set with jewels. The jerkin is long enough to form a

Fig. 500. Button

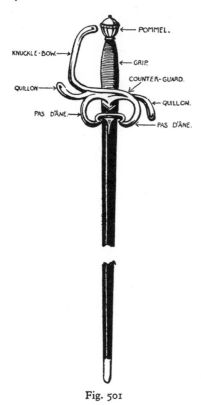

POMMEL.

KNUCKLE-BOW.

GRIP.

COUNTER-GUARD.

QUILLON.

QUILLON.

PAS D'ANE.

PAS D'ÂNE.

Fig. 501

basque shorter than that previously worn, and has a moderately high collar. Underneath the jerkin is worn the doublet of white satin, and banded with silver and pearls, having close sleeves to the wrist. The slops, now appearing much larger owing to the reduction of the basque, match the doublet in treatment of decoration and material. These three garments, the jerkin, the doublet, and the slops, together with hose and shoes of white silk, comprise a 'suit.'

Fig. 501 shows the type of sword-hilt with spherical pommel, used during the second half of the sixteenth century. It is the type carried by Englishmen, Frenchmen, and Spaniards. A curved guard for the hand, or knuckle-bow, appears at this time fixed to the top of the 'grip' and in a line with one of the *quillons*. The *pas-d'âne*, formed of two rings curving below the quillons on each side of the base of the hilt, was a further addition. The whole of the hilt was often decorated with chasing, and was sometimes much jewelled. Fig. 502 shows the sword carriage, or HANGER, of the second half of the sixteenth century. It is made of two pieces

of leather fixed at the top with a hook, E, which is hooked to the waist-belt on the left side at C (*refer to* Fig. 486). The ends of each are cut into three straps—F is one of them— and these are buckled back to form loops through which the scabbard of the sword is passed. A belt, having a hook, or toggle, D, is attached to the carriage, and hooks across the front into the ring, B (*see* Fig. 486), on the right side of the waistbelt, *not* to the centre fastening, A, as hitherto. The Archduke Maximilian, Fig. 495, carries a sword, the hilt of which is shown in Fig. 503.

For a jewelled sword-handle, see Fig. 563.

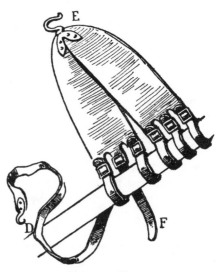

E

D

F

Fig. 502. Hanger

PLATE XXII. PRINCE PHILIP OF SPAIN, 1554: Portrait by Antonio Moro
Prado, Madrid.  *Photo by Mansell*

When Philip disembarked from his galleon at Southampton, 19th July 1554, and proceeded along the High Street, he presented a very gracious and attractive appearance, his slight dapper figure sitting erect upon the beautiful white charger, caparisoned in crimson velvet embroidered in gold, which Sir Anthony Browne, Master of the Horse, presented to him in the Queen's name.[1]   He then made his way to the Church of the Holy Rood, and there returned thanks for his safe voyage.   Afterwards the Prince was conducted to a house prepared for his reception near the Watergate, and not far from the church. The rooms occupied by Philip had been specially garnished, by order of the Queen, the walls being covered with gold embroidered damask hangings from the Royal collection.   The furniture, as was usual at this period, consisted of exceptional pieces of a most sumptuous nature.   The English household servitors were dressed in the red and yellow liveries of Aragon by special direction of the Queen.

He was dressed on this occasion more or less as shown in Plate XXII, in black velvet and silver, with massive gold chains and jewels around his neck.   His black velvet bonet, worn at the correct rakish angle, was decorated with jewels, and a white plume fell in graceful lines over the left ear—a costume well suited to set off his pink and white complexion, close-cropped yellow hair and close-cut beard.   The Earl of Arundel had been sent by the Queen to invest him with the Order of the Garter on his landing. The Order of the Golden Fleece, hung from a gold chain, was doubtless also worn.

Fig. 503

Having stayed four days in Southampton [2] His Highness proceeded to Winchester.   The journey of twelve miles was made in torrents of rain; and despite the scarlet felt cloak and black sombrero—substitutes for a modern mackintosh and umbrella — Philip's magnificent black velvet surcote, smothered with silver and diamond embroidery, and worn over doublet and slops of white satin embroidered in gold, was soaked through and

---

[1] Horses for Philip's use had been shipped to England, and in addition to these he brought six hundred Andalusian jennets to improve the English breed of horses.

[2] In Speed's *History of Southampton*, 1909, occurs the statement that Philip 'remained three days in the town, during which time he appears to have done little but hear mass at Holy Rood and drink beer.   He made a very unfavourable impression on the townspeople by his ungracious manners.'   This criticism ignores contemporary evidence which emphatically contradicts these accusations.

through.  He was quite unperturbed by these somewhat trying conditions, which necessitated a call at the Hospital of St. Cross to change into an equally gorgeous costume.  This consisted of a black velvet surcote covered with gold BUGLES, and a suit of white silk-velvet trimmed in similar fashion. Thus fortified Philip continued on his way to Winchester, where, on arrival, he and his numerous train of nobles entered the cathedral to hear Mass, and then on to the deanery where he was housed.

After supper that evening, the clock chiming the hour of ten, Prince Philip was summoned to the Bishop's palace where the Queen awaited him.  For their first meeting he chose a suit of white silk and white kid embroidered in gold, and a French surcote embroidered in gold and silver, 'and very gallant he looked' we are told.  At any rate, it is known that he made a great impression on his ten-years-senior bride.  In due course the Queen presented each of her ladies-in-waiting [1] to the Prince, who, 'so as not to break the custom of the country, which is a very good one,' kissed them all 'in his way.'  Evidently Her Majesty was not displeased, for it is on record that she was in high spirits during that evening, 'chatting gaily, and although she is a little elderly she displays the grace befitting a Queen.'  When the time came for the Prince and his attendants to take their leave, the Queen instructed Philip in that seemingly modern salutation, which may mean so much or so little—'Good night.'[2]  Approving thereof, Philip approached the ladies-in-waiting to repeat it to them; but as he confronted them the words slipped his memory and he had to appeal to the Queen for help, 'whereat she was well pleased.'  Returning to the ladies with more assurance, he made another attempt, and, whatever his success with the language, he did not neglect the very good 'custom of the country.'

A public reception was held by the Queen on the following day in the great hall of the Bishop's palace.  'The Hall, which is beautifully hung with cloth of gold and silk, measures forty of my paces long and twenty wide,' says a member of Philip's entourage.  For the ceremony the Prince was attired in purple velvet and gold.  His wedding suit on 25th July was of white satin covered with jewelled embroidery, and over it a long mantle of cloth of gold and ermine ornamented with pearls and precious stones surmounted by the Collar of the Garter.  The mantle was a present from the Queen, who wore one like it.  Simon Renard, the Emperor's representative, reports to his master that 'the Queen has had a collar [of the Garter] made, which cost seven or eight thousand crowns, besides several rich dresses for His Highness.'  It is not stated in which style these rich dresses were fashioned, neither do we learn where they were made—whether in London or ordered from Valladolid.

These descriptions of other costumes in Philip's wardrobe are taken from the inventory by Andres Muñoz, to which reference has already been made. They are more or less literal translations from the original Spanish, and are

[1] One was the Lady Jane Dormer, who afterwards became the wife of the Duke of Feria.

[2] This phrase has been in use since mediæval times.

valuable here for the reason that Philip and his attendant nobles influenced the English fashions, and introduced many details into the costume of the people during the reign of Queen Mary.

Here are eight suits worn by His Imperial and Royal Highness:

(1) A costume of crimson velvet completely covered with embroidery of an heraldic pattern of large flowers in seed pearls, the leaves formed of *half-braids* of silver, the interstices being filled with silver bullion. The lining of the short cloak or MUCETA was of flat [dull] cloth of silver embroidered in the same manner. The hosen were of silk.

(2) Another very pretty costume was a brown satin cloak with trimmings of *chainlets* formed of silk twist in gold and pipings of silver. The linings were of a lighter shade encrusted with silver. The doublet and slops were of white silk-velvet embroidered in the same manner.

(3) A very handsome costume made in the French fashion had a cloak of black velvet with two different designs of embroideries of pipings in gold and silver twist. The jerkin and hosen were of crimson velvet, and the doublet was of satin with the same embroidery of very beautiful workmanship.

(4) A second very rich French costume had very gorgeous and costly embroidery of narrow trimmings of gold and silver, lined with a light material of *frizzed silver*. The jerkin, doublet, slops, and hosen were of white silk-velvet.

(5) A very pretty surcote was of black velvet embroidered with *quills* of gold and twists of silver in a manner that showed some silver slashings and unfinished weaving (cuttes) with a ground of embroidery of leaves formed of twists of gold thread enclosing narrow strands of silver bullion. The suit worn underneath was of white silk-velvet embroidered with gold and silver.

(6) A beautiful costume had a surcote of grey satin covered with alternate stripes of applied gold chains and silver bugles, and lined with embossed cloth of silver. The suit was of white satin ornamented in the same way.

(7) Another suit consisted entirely of white silk-velvet covered with costly gold embroidery and gold *filigree*.

(8) One of the most elaborate costumes in Philip's wardrobe included a surcote of black velvet, with a border of gold bugles and heavy twisted silver cord worked into a design similar to that in fashion during Henry VIII's reign (*see* Fig. 267). The garment itself was almost hidden under closely embroidered sprigs in gold, the leaves being filled in with silver filigree. The spaces between the sprigs were cutte showing the white satin lining. With this surcote was worn a suit of white silk-velvet and gold embroideries.

Costumes (1), (2), (3), (4), (7) are well represented in Plate XXII and (5), (6), (8) in Fig. 497.

It is interesting to notice that many of Philip's costumes were carried out in schemes of black and white, gold and silver.

Space will permit only of a few of the costumes made for the members of Philip's suite as described by Andres Muñoz.

The Admiral of Castile, Don Antonio de Toledo, amongst other costumes had one suit of white silk-velvet and satin trimmed with gold passamayne, very fine, that was made with consummate workmanship. His muceta was of black velvet embroidered with a marvellous plated ornamentation of gold, half a yard in breadth, with a stitching of silver spirals and a border of embroidery of thick tendrils of gold. This cape was lined with cloth of silver. The admiral's pages wore liveries of purple velvet lined with yellow satin. Over their jackets they had mantles of the same garnished with loops of cloth of gold. The other attendants were several lackeys, six servants, four trumpeters, and three kettle-drummers all dressed in the same livery.

The Marqués de los Valles appeared in a suit of purple velvet and satin. The gold embroidery embodied a scale design with pearl-drop pendants. The muceta worn with it was also of purple velvet, decorated with the same embroidery and lined with cloth of silver. His lackeys wore jackets and hosen of black velvet and doublets of satin, garnished with *welts* of the same velvet, and on top of them two backstitches of brown silk; over this dress they had capes of black cloth with the same garniture. The pages wore GALDRESES of the same cloth and braiding, and capes of velvet.

A black velvet muceta embroidered with quills of silver about eight inches in width showed many a graceful difference of working, and was very lucent and costly. This was worn by the Duke of Alba over a suit of white satin of the same workmanship. The Duke of Medina Celi had a French costume in purple and white velvet, with two trimmings of gold and silver quills embroidered with YY and with interlaced letters which spelt 'Juana Manuel.' This [says Muñoz] was a satisfactory garment to see.

The costume made for the Marquis de Pescara was also in the French style, carried out in black velvet and crimson satin. The cape of black velvet was trellissed with silver and loops of gold, showing a gold rose in each square of trellissing. The lackeys attending this nobleman wore capes of black cloth with two gards of black velvet, slashed in the centre, on both sides of which there was a design embroidered in brown silk flanked by two rows of gold passamayne. The jackets were of the same velvet garnished in like manner; the pages were similarly attired but wore gold chains. Five gentlemen of the household were garbed in the same style.

The Marqués de Aguillara had a costume of brown velvet, the muceta embroidered with large raised roses and crossings, in a manner that formed several squares of graceful outline. The embroidery required twenty-seven marks' weight of gold. The lackeys wore jackets, doublets, and hosen of scarlet velvet garnished with black and white embroidery; sufficiently costly and handsome to see. The pages wore under-dresses and galdreses of scarlet velvet with ornamentations called *entranzado*.

The costume made for the Duke of Saldanha had a cape and suit all of worked gold on black velvet, with an embroidery of quills of gold using twenty-two marks' weight of bullion. The Duke had another costume of brown velvet and a muceta of crimson velvet, also a jerkin of Cordoban leather dressed with amber, with an embroidery of quills of gold; very costly. Further he had a collar of gold with thick stems enchased with emeralds, rubies, and diamonds of great value, the intermediate pieces being studded with large pearls. More than this, he possessed a great number of jewels, medals, and buttons of great worth.

The costume of the guards who accompanied Philip to England, as noted by Muñoz, was exceptionally rich. This display turned out to be a prodigious waste of good material, as the guards were allowed no part in the show. Neither bodyguard nor men-at-arms were allowed to land, on pain of death; and they remained, perforce, cooped up on board the Spanish galleons. The reason for this was that it was believed that Spanish troops, if brought ashore, might create a feeling of distrust among the English people. Eventually the fleet was sent to Portsmouth to revictual, before sailing to Flanders to join the Emperor's forces.

The hundred halberdiers of the Spanish guard were very well clad and a very good set of men. Among them were their sergeants and lieutenants, chiefs of squadrons. These wore doublets of red and yellow (the livery colours of Aragon) garnished with sashes of crimson velvet, one-sixth of a yard in width, with others of the same width of white velvet; the crimson sash had slashes formed in a kind of square with thick cordons of silk for edging of the braid; these were of white, scarlet, and yellow, the colours of His Highness's livery. The caps, shoon, hosen, scabbards, and sword-belts were of yellow velvet with the same braid. The Count de Feria was their captain and Hernando de Sayavedre their lieutenant.

A hundred German halberdiers, all well-disciplined men, and garbed similarly to the Landsknechten (Fig. 224), were in the same device and costume, except that all the silk of their dress was doubled, because it was their custom and habit to carry themselves with bravura, in the German fashion. Their captain was Christopher, a German. A hundred German mounted archers were dressed in the same device and uniform, except that they wore cloaks of yellow velvet, with frocks of velvet of the same colour and braiding. Their captain was the Count de Hornes, and their ensign Monsieur Turlon.

The following explanations of the various terms used in describing the decoration of these costumes may be of interest:

*Bugle*, a glass bead. The Venetians were the first to manufacture bugles, and from them most countries of Europe derived their supplies. In the sixteenth century bugles were of gold or silver. *Jet* bugles were also very fashionable, the mineral being found at this period chiefly at Whitby, in Aude (France), and Asturia (Spain).

*Half-braids* were very narrow braids.

*Muceta, or museta*, a short cloak. For details see under diagram, Fig. 507.

*Chains* or *chainlets* were either small chains of metal in gold or silver sewn on to the garment, or embroidery in a chain pattern.

Material of *frizzed silver* was a fabric woven with very fine silver or gold thread upon a coloured silk, satin, velvet, or cloth of silver or gold ground, so giving the appearance of silver or gold hair.

*Quills* or *quilling* were plaits or pipings of folded or quilled material, somewhat resembling cords. These quills were sewn on in straight lines and curves, and wrought into patterns, in the same manner as cord or braid: designs were frequently of the interlaced type (*see* p. 227).

*Filigree*, small motifs of metal in gold or silver, sewn on and embodied in the design of the embroidery.

*Welt*, a narrow strip of material put on the edge of a garment as a border, binding, or hem; also a narrow ridge or raised stripe.

*Galdres*, a gown worn by men and women. Gowns or robes such as were worn by gentlemen in Henry VII's reign. Galdreses, when applied to women, meant any fashionable gowns or dresses.

*Entranzado*, garniture, decoration, usually plaited gold, silver, or silk braid.

## NOBILITY: MEN, 1553–8

'The nobility are by nature very courteous, especially to foreigners . . . they, save such as are employed at Court, do not habitually reside in the cities but in their own country mansions, where they keep up very grand establishments.'—VENETIAN CALENDAR.

### EDWARD COURTENAY

*Earl of Devonshire, Baron Courtenay of Okehampton and Plympton, 1526–56*

It is obvious that the black velvet jerkin worn by the English gentleman in Fig. 504 is influenced by the Spanish mode. The drawing is made from a portrait by Hans Eworth of Edward Courtenay, who was born about 1526, and at the age of thirteen was confined by Henry VIII to the Tower, chiefly because he was unfortunate enough to be a great-grandson of King Edward IV. He was released by Queen Mary and created Earl of Devonshire in 1553. He bore the Sword of State at her coronation, and for this office he had intended to appear in a very splendid suit of blue velvet embroidered with gold, but the Queen, being desirous of wearing the same shade, instantly commanded this young man of twenty-seven to set aside such fine array for more sober attire. By common consent the earl was chosen as a husband for the Princess Elizabeth, but becoming implicated in Wyatt's rebellion he was again sent to the Tower for a year in 1554. In 1555 he was sent abroad out of the way and died of fever at Padua, 1556.

Courtenay is described by his contemporaries as one of the handsomest and most agreeable young noblemen of his age.

The jerkin in Fig. 504 has a high upstanding collar supporting a pleated linen frill, and the shoulders are cut wide. It is tied by laces and aiglettes down the front. The sleeves of the doublet and the paned slops are of white silk. The increased size of the latter should be noticed.

Lord Guyldeford Dudley is described as a very tall strong youth with light hair. On one occasion it is stated that he wore a suit of white silk embroidered with gold. On the scaffold his costume was of black velvet cutte over satin white and would have been made like that shown in Fig. 504.

In the group (Fig. 531) of Philip and Mary, the original of which was painted by Hans Eworth in 1558, Philip is in a black velvet jerkin ornamented with silk braid and bugles. It is cut sloping to a point at the waist with deep basques. The sleeves of the doublet, and the slops, are of cutte pale yellow satin. A short Spanish cloak—the muceta—made of black velvet and lined with black silk, hangs from his shoulders. The bonet is of black velvet with a small white plume, and the blue and gold garter is buckled on his yellow behosed left leg.

Fig. 493 shows a characteristic jerkin worn during the later part of Queen Mary's reign and the early part of Elizabeth's. It is taken from a portrait by Antonio Moro, dating about 1555, and is made of black velvet braided with narrow gold, either cord or braid. The epaulets are composed of a

Fig. 504.
Edward Courtenay, Earl of Devonshire, 1553

series of braided loops; and the basque is divided into tabs, the front ones cut in one with the front widths of the body part, and the tabs next to these joined on to the body part at the waist-line and overlapping each other to the centre of the back. The bulging over the waist is due to padding. One of the gold buttons is inset.

Fig. 505 shows the type of costume worn by a fashionable young English nobleman towards the close of Queen Mary's reign. The illustration is adapted from a three-quarter-length portrait of Henry FitzAlan, Lord Maltravers, a youth of nineteen, who died in Brussels in 1556. The portrait was almost certainly painted by Hans Eworth. The jerkin is of a material, probably thick white silk, woven or embroidered with a design (Fig. 506) in gold; the converging cuttes down the centre and sides are edged

Fig. 505. LORD MALTRAVERS, 1556. After Hans Eworth

with gold passamayne which also decorates the collar and basque. The edge of the basque is finished with escallopes or indentations (heraldic term: engrailed). The high collar is surmounted by a small close frill, or RUFF. The doublet closely fits the figure and the jerkin is cut to fit over it. The sleeves and paned slops are of white damask.

Over the shoulders his lordship wears the newest thing—the muceta — just introduced from Spain. The diagram (Fig. 507) gives the shape — three-fourths of a circle—which produces many voluminous folds in wear. It often had ornaments down the front for fastening with buttons, cords, loops and buttons, or, in place of buttons, small tassels, sometimes both. This Spanish cloak is distinguished by a long hood rounded or pointed at the top

Fig. 506

and usually fastened down the front in the manner described above. Fig. 508 shows the shape of the hood, the portion AA being sewn to the neck opening of the cloak. The projecting ends, BB, form lapels on both sides of the

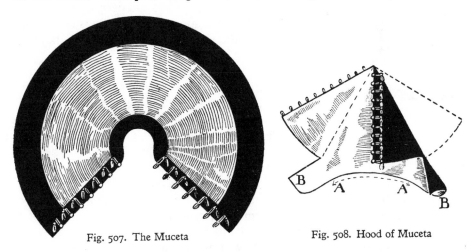

Fig. 507. The Muceta

Fig. 508. Hood of Muceta

neck. The muceta worn by Lord Maltravers is of black silk or satin, having a hood of black velvet studded with gold buttons. In fact, the enormous number of buttons worn by English gentlemen at this time was commented upon by the Spaniards in Philip's retinue.

The cloak is lined and turned back with ermine, forming revers and a deep collar. With a practical hood this collar would be superfluous; hence the hood, in this case, is flat,[1] and merely ornamental—quite a usual fancy.

The black velvet bonet is decorated with gold buttons round the crown, and a small white ostrich tip droops on the left side.

Legs have been added to the drawing (Fig. 505) and these are clothed in white silk hosen and long black leather boots.

In the Prado, Madrid, there is a portrait of Don Carlos, son of Philip II, painted by Sanchez Coello. The boy's age cannot be less than eleven years, which dates the portrait at 1556, and makes it contemporary with the portrait of Lord Maltravers. On comparing the two portraits it is seen that the Prince's doublet and slops are of different material and decoration, but the same shape. The bonet is identical, and the muceta, which stands out from the shoulders in large radiating folds, is of black satin with a six-inch border of black velvet, and is lined and turned back with ermine. The portrait of Don Carlos is a front view; but it is probable that there is a similar hood arrangement at the back.

Fig. 509. Henry Lee, Esq., 1555

There is another portrait of Don Carlos by Coello in the Kunsthistorisches Museum, Vienna. In it the details of the Infante's dress are the same, but the materials and decoration are different. The flat hood of the muceta is plainly seen. Hosen and shoes take the place of boots, as shown in Fig. 505.

This young man (Fig 509) is of considerable importance, for he is seen sitting on the left of Lord Williams of Thame amongst the commissioners at the burning of Bishops Latimer and Ridley 'in the ditch over against Balliol College,'[2] Oxford, 16th October 1555. It seems probable that he is Sir Henry Lee (born 1530, died 1610), to whom Ridley gave a new groat as a memento; the two on Lord Williams's right are presumably the Vice-Chancellor and the Mayor. The drawing is taken from Foxe's *Acts and Monuments*, published in 1563, but the costume is distinctly that in vogue during the reigns of Edward VI and Mary.

It is the everyday dress of the upper classes, and consists of a doublet with a deep basque and close-fitting sleeves raised on the shoulders. On top of

---

[1] Flat unpractical hoods of this kind can be seen to-day on the backs of ecclesiastical copes.

[2] The cross, commemorating the burning of Latimer and Ridley, is to be seen in the centre of the road in Broad Street immediately opposite Messrs Lindsey & Sons, opticians. It is a Greek cross in plain stone. Originally it was placed nearer St Michael's Church.

this is draped a cloak with a high collar braided deeply round the shoulders. Over his hosen he has drawn boot hose to protect them from the slush— practical though unusual, as they were generally worn inside boots; these he has probably used when on the road but left behind at his lodging.   A flat cap with feather, a gold chain wound twice round his neck, sword, stout leather shoes, and gloves complete this young aristocrat's outfit.

We are informed that on this occasion the Mayor of Oxford, Richard Whit- tington, entertained the commissioners very lavishly.   In the City accounts appear the following:

'Item. For wine to my Lord Williams and his retinue at the burning of the Bishops, 3s. 4d.   Item. For 2 pair of gloves double garnished for my Lord and Lady Williams 4s.

'Item [the next morning] a bottle of Malmsey 14d.'

## EMBROIDERY (*continued from p.* 230)

After the abbeys and monasteries had been ruthlessly looted of their sacred belongings, it became the fashion, about 1550, to use embroidered vestments and Church hangings as decorations in the rooms of private houses.

Fig. 510. Gold Braiding

During the reigns of Edward VI and Queen Mary, Spanish work was very much in favour.   Queen Mary had inherited her Spanish mother's taste in needlework.

(*Continued on p.* 583)

Fig. 511. Gold Embroidery

## LACE (*continued from p. 231*)

Lace now seems to be called indifferently purle, passamayne, or bone lace (1556).

Frequent mention of lace is made in wardrobe accounts during this time, and bone lace constantly appears in the same records.

Bobbin lace is of less frequent occurrence. It is made of coarser thread than bone lace.

Ruffles made or wrought out of England, commonly called cutwork, were forbidden to any one under the degree of a baron.

(*Continued on p. 589*)

## THE YEOMEN OF THE GUARD (*continued from p. 292*)

### *Temp.* EDWARD VI

In the reign of Edward VI the full corps of the Yeomen of the Guard numbered sixty-six 'Yeoman in Ordinary,' who were on duty on ordinary occasions, 141 'Yeomen Extraordinary,' in reserve for ceremonial and state

functions, and 15 'Tower Warders' permanently stationed at the Tower in readiness to guard the King when he was lodged there.

The livery worn by the Yeomen of the Guard during this reign was practically the same as that of Henry VIII's time. The only remaining representation of the guard of this period was in a picture of the coronation procession of Edward VI at Cowdray House, but unfortunately this was destroyed in the disastrous fire which occurred there in 1793. The existing reproduction[1] of this picture is not too satisfactory, but in it the hat worn appears to be rather larger than before, and the bases of the tunics are sufficiently long to obscure the small slops fashionable in Edward VI's reign. At one time during this reign hats were scarlet, but more usually they were of black velvet or cloth.

### *Temp.* QUEEN MARY

At the accession of Mary the corps numbered 207 picked men. This number was immediately increased by another 200, an augmentation deemed necessary in view of the disturbances which had arisen from the ferment of controversy as to whether the Princess Mary or the Lady Jane Grey was the rightful successor to the crown.

[1] *Archaeologia*, vol. viii, 1787, p. 406.

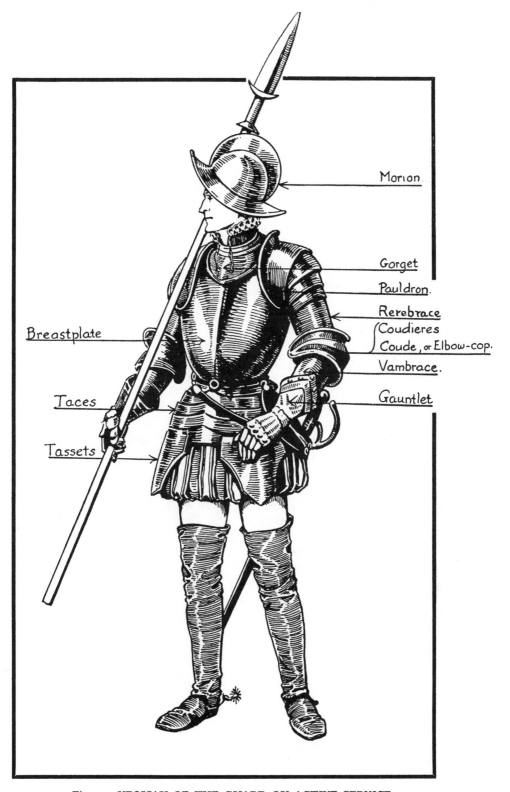

Morion.

Gorget

Pauldron.

Rerebrace

Coudieres

Coude, or Elbow-cop.

Vambrace.

Gauntlet

Breastplate

Taces

Tassets

Fig. 512. YEOMAN OF THE GUARD ON ACTIVE SERVICE

Until about 1550 the Yeomen of the Guard were dressed as described under Plate III B. Plate XXIII A shows a yeoman in the livery in use about 1550–75: it is taken from an Illum. MS. dated 1568.

The tunic of scarlet cloth smartly fits the figure, and the bases have disappeared and given place to a shorter unpleated basque cut on the semicircular plan, opening up the front. The neck opening is higher and shows the upstanding collar of the doublet, which is finished off with the ruff or band about an inch and a half wide. The sleeves of the tunic finish above the elbow, and are puffed as of old. It should be noticed that the garding on the basque is slightly different from that shown in Plate III B. Trellis-work embroidery in gold in a closer pattern is retained; but the rose is now the 'union rose,' that is, one of gold superimposed with a second rose of silver. It is an interesting fact that at this time, and for some time later, the union rose is shown on all contemporary drawings. The doublet, of which only the high collar and close-fitting sleeves are seen, is of a dull liver-coloured purple. The slops are purple, and the panes and hose are of a dull yellow colour that could be termed ochre. The hat, now for the first time adorned with a small white feather, is black, so are the waist and sword belts, the scabbard, and the shoes.

Fig. 513.
Archer of the Yeomen of the Guard

The Yeomen of the Guard frequently went on active service, and were then equipped with MORIONS and demi-suits of armour. These details are shown in Fig. 512 with the different parts of the armour named in the margin; the man shown is a horseman. As it was usual for part of the guard to be mounted, he wears high boots over the ordinary hose and carries a javelin; when serving on foot, the halberd was always used.

The *Morion* was a basin-shaped helmet surmounted by a semicircular comb. The brim was circular, extending back and front into very pronounced points. It was of Spanish origin and appeared about the middle of the sixteenth century.

The CABASSET is very like the morion, but is distinguished from it by the pointed apex in place of the comb.

Archers of the Yeomen of the Guard wore leather tunics, the sleeves of which were sometimes of chain-mail over slops and hose. Above the tunic was placed the BRIGANDINE, and upon the head the morion or SALADE. The arms carried were large bows and long arrows (*see* Fig. 513).

The *brigandine* was a jacket composed of some strong material—canvas or linen—on the inside, with an outer covering of velvet or silk when worn by important people, and of linen or leather in the case of the rank and file of the army. Between these layers of material were small strips of thin iron, disposed like taces, or the slats of a Venetian blind, kept in place by rivets set close together, the metal heads being visible externally. Brigandines sometimes had sleeves, and usually descended to the hips; they were fastened down the front or sides by hooks, laces, or buttons. They formed a useful item of war equipment, being less expensive than plate armour, serviceable, pliable to the movement of the body, and at the same time resisting sword, dagger, and spear thrusts.

The *salade* was a shallow loose-fitting helmet, the rear peak prolonged over the back of the neck. It had usually a vision-slit in front, but sometimes this was cut in a pivoted visor, which could be thrown back.

## GENTLEMEN PENSIONERS

The corps, 'all in red damask with pole-axes in hand,' attended Edward VI at his coronation. They 'went on either side the way on foot.' By this arrangement they were placed longitudinally, at proper distances, so that the King was as nearly as possible in the centre of the band. In the procession to the Abbey they followed the peers in the rear, immediately before the Yeomen of the Guard. Shortly afterwards they are described as riding five in a row and clad in white and black and 'in harness [1] from top to toe, and goodly bases of cotes, and their men in like colours of cloth.'

The first great opportunity of proving their worth occurred during the attack on Whitehall Palace by the rebels under Sir Thomas Wyatt. On this occasion the corps were equipped in full armour.

Queen Mary behaved with great courage, and refused to leave the palace by the Watergate as Her Majesty's dependence on her loyal bodyguard in the time of danger was absolute, and her gratitude was most gracious and sincere. The full corps was in attendance on the Queen during her marriage celebrations at Winchester; they were her own special guard, her bridegroom having his own corps of 'Allemains and Spaniards,' and Swiss and some English gentlemen.

In 1556 we have the earliest description of the banner of the corps: this was

[1] 'Harness' means armour.

red and yellow, and bore, on one side, a white hart, and on the other a black eagle with gilded legs, the former being one of the cognizances of Queen Mary and the black eagle part of the armorial bearings of King Philip.

The colour of the costume was now changed to the Tudor livery colours of white and green, and the attendants were dressed in the same but of less rich material.

(*Continued on p.* 686)

## MIDDLE CLASSES

The period covered by these two reigns was too short for any notable changes to take place in the dress worn by the middle and lower classes of both sexes. Men and women of the upper class followed the prevailing

fashions with moderation as their means and social position allowed, the general style of their clothes being as a rule some years behind that of their betters. Much the same applies to the burgesses and lower classes, who continued to dress in the same manner as described under Chapter II.

There is an exception, however, and this definitely falls within the scope of this chapter—the costume worn by

### The Boys of Christ's Hospital

At their first appearance after the foundation of Christ's Hospital, when they lined the streets for the procession of the Lord Mayor and aldermen to St. Paul's on Christmas Day, 1552, the children, numbering three hundred and forty, were clothed in a livery of russet cotton. When they attended the Spittal Sermon at the Easter following they were dressed in blue, 'and so have continued ever since,' says Stow.

Edward VI received the Hospital Corporation and presented them with their Charter, June 1553. This event is commemorated in the picture at Christ's Hospital, Horsham, and on this occasion the boys were dressed in their new livery as shown in Fig. 514.

Fig. 514.
Christ's Hospital Boy, 1553

It consisted of a long dark blue cloth gown reaching to the ankles and fastened up the front with pewter buttons having thereon a bust of Edward VI and the inscription 'EDWARDUS VI D G REX F.' It was girt about the waist by a red leather belt, and had an upstanding collar about one and a half or two inches wide, finishing with a white gathered neckband.[1] Under the gown was

[1] This neckband gave place to the Geneva band in the reign of Charles II, and buckles were added to the shoes early in the eighteenth century.

worn a long russet kersey cassock, with russet worsted hosen and black leather shoes. A flat black felt cap and brown leather or white cotton gloves completed the livery. It should be pointed out that a blue coat was not entirely the distinctive or monopolized livery of Christ's Hospital (*see* Apprentices, p. 302).

## ROYALTY AND NOBILITY—WOMEN: 1547-58

### THE LADY JANE GREY, 1537-54

Of the women, other than the Royal Princesses, the Lady Mary, the Lady Elizabeth, and the vacuous Anne of Cleves, who occupied important positions during Edward VI's reign, the most prominent was the Lady Jane. She was the eldest daughter of the Lady Frances Brandon who married Henry Grey, Marquess of Dorset, later (1551) Duke of Suffolk, and great-great-grand-daughter of Queen Elizabeth Wydeville. The Lady Jane was born at Bradgate in 1537.

In appearance she was petite : her face was what we should call to-day pretty, with small features, well-shaped nose, light hazel eyes, and auburn hair. She possessed firmness, capacity, and knowledge of affairs. Her learning in divinity and religious controversial subjects acquired under her tutors, Roger Ascham and John Aylmer, Bishop of London, was profound. Gentle, affectionate, firm as a rock where any principle was concerned, she would have made an ideal queen-consort and a perfect queen-regnant.

Fig. 515. The Lady Jane Grey
(*from a contemporary portrait*)

In adversity she displayed great nobility and beauty of character. Lady Jane's first appearance in public was made at the age of fourteen when she

Fig. 516. The Lady Jane Grey

accompanied her mother, the Duchess of Suffolk, on the occasion of the visit of Mary of Guise, the Dowager-Queen of Scotland, to Greenwich Palace. She afterwards became the guest of the Princess Mary. On 21st May 1553 the Lady Jane married Guyldeford, fourth son of John Dudley, created Earl of Warwick in 1547, and Duke of Northumberland in 1551. She was proclaimed Queen in London, 10th July 1553, but nine days later her reign was at an end; after imprisonment in the Tower, both she and her husband were executed 12th February 1554.

In dress the Lady Jane displayed great taste, so Ascham considered, as he suggested that her 'seemly apparelling' should form the model for the Princess Elizabeth.

The drawing (Fig. 515) is made from an original portrait of this lady. Her dress is of nasturtium-red velvet with sleeves turned back showing a deep peacock-blue lining. The yoke and false sleeves are of the same blue in satin with a cornflower design worked in gold. Spanish work decorates the inside of the open collar to match the wrist-frills, and above it is a second collar of white gauze embroidered with red silk. (*Refer to* Fig. 541 for details of the French hood.)

A costume worn by the Lady Jane in July 1553 has been described by a Genoese, Baptist Spinola, and Plate XXIV is a drawing made from these details. The dress is of cloth of gold woven with a raised Renaissance pattern in green velvet: the shoulder yoke, underskirt, and turned-back part of the sleeves are of plain green velvet, and the false sleeves of cloth of gold. The collar is turned back as in Fig. 515, lined with gold, and a second collar inside is of fine lawn decorated with Spanish work to match the wrist-frills. The French hood is described under Fig. 541. It is said that the lady wore many

Fig. 517

jewels about her person. Sometimes, especially on state occasions, she was mounted on CHOPINS to make her look taller (*see* Fig. 560).

There is a portrait of Lady Jane at Melton Constable showing her in a costume similar to Plate XXIV, and carried out in white damask, with false sleeves and underskirt in cream and gold brocade. The painting has suffered a great deal from restoration, but from a costume point of view it is interesting. (See *Country Life*, 22nd September 1928.)

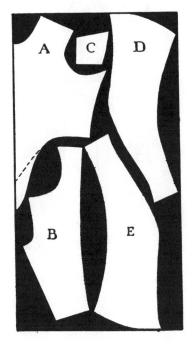

Fig. 518. Bodice

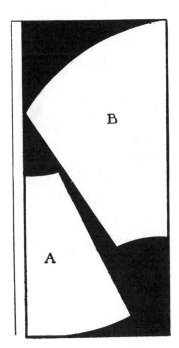

Fig. 519. Skirt

The head-and-shoulders portrait of Lady Jane, by Eworth, in the National Portrait Gallery, London (No. 764), is the latest, if one may judge by the headdress. The only visible part of her dress suggests a black velvet surcote, with a double row of narrow miniver edging on the moderately mahoitered sleeves, collar, and down the front. This surcote is influenced by Spanish fashions, and its style was known as 'à l'Espagnolle.' (See Fig. 521 which shows it in detail.)

The headdress is the flat-fronted, rather wide French hood of black velvet, without the slightest ornamentation.

The costume is a simple dress as Fig. 516 shows, and one that would be worn on ordinary occasions by great ladies, at home or out of doors. A similar costume is depicted in a portrait dated as early as 1551.

On the day of her execution, 13th November 1553, amongst those led out of the Tower on foot was 'The Lady Jane in a blacke gown of cloth, turned down; the Cape lined with fese velvet, and edged about with the same, in a French hood, all black, with a black byllyment, a black velvet book hanging before her, and another book in her hand open.'

Fig. 520. A Noble Lady

Fig. 521. The Spanish Surcote

This contemporary description is a little perplexing—the 'gown of cloth, turned down' and the 'fese velvet' are not easy to explain. The 'black byllyment' refers to the under-cap of the French hood and to the partlet: the 'black velvet book hanging before her' was suspended from her girdle.

In Fig. 517 is seen a lady's simple dress. The close-fitting bodice, high collar, sleeves pleated into the armhole, and skirt without a train worn over the Spanish farthingale, are the foundations on which much ornamentation was lavished during the following fifty years.

Fig. 518 gives the pattern of this bodice and sleeve, shown white, laid upon a piece of silk or cloth, shown black. The material is folded double.

A is half the front, the dotted line showing where the point of the waist finished in this its earliest version; B the half back; C the half-collar; and D and E the over and under part of the sleeve.[1]   Fig. 519 gives on a smaller scale the cut of the skirt.   A is half the front, and B half the back without a train.   Under the all-round surcote a train would have been incongruous. These diagrams are taken from a sixteenth-century pattern book.

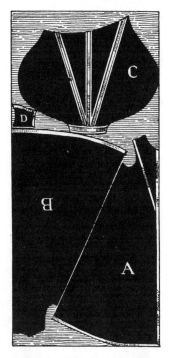

A noble lady of the reign of Edward VI is given in Fig. 520.   She wears definitely English dress, in contradistinction to the French with its mahoitered sleeves (*see* Fig. 524) and the Spanish surcote (*see* Fig. 521).   The costume is carried out in plain dark velvet, and the sleeves, cut as described under Plate XVI and diagram, Fig. 67, are very tight-fitting on the upper arm, also very much off the shoulders, and are turned back showing the lining of the same velvet as the outer sleeve.   Delicate filigree gold beads, set tubular and spherical alternately, are headed by an edging of cutwork round the square neck of the very *décolleté* bodice; this edging is drawn in by a black silk lace.   The low-cut neck-line is of the older fashion, as seen in Plate XVII. The false sleeves are of the same material as the underskirt, and on them are placed, *not* cuttes as usual, but raised pads having pairs of aiglettes at the ends of each.   The skirt has a slight train

Fig. 522. Diagram of Surcote

without folds over the Spanish farthingale, and opens out over an underskirt of silk woven with a large pattern in velvet.   The French hood is wide, and the gauze pleating lies only across the top of the hair.

## SPANISH STYLES

The surcote, introduced from Spain and worn by the lady in Fig. 521, is of dark coloured velvet edged with a passamayne of gold.   Notice the lines from the shoulders, which meet the centre lines a little below waist level, forming a W.   The garment is cut to hang from the shoulders, front and back, in a straight line.   In front it is open, being fastened only at the throat, revealing the under-dress of a different colour and material such as is shown worn by the lady in Fig. 517.   Sometimes the surcote and under-dress were

[1] It is curious that there is no curved-out cut at the top of the under-sleeve; also that the lay-out of these patterns does not permit of the same planning in the case of velvet or figured material.

of the same colour and fabric. The short mahoitered sleeves are decorated with wider passamayne. Inside the high collar of the surcote there is another of white lawn: often such collars were embroidered with black silk Spanish work. For the cut of this surcote refer to Fig. 522. A is half the front; B half the back; C one of the mahoitered sleeves, and D half the collar.

This surcote has already been noted under Fig. 516; the differences in the latter are (a) the vertical slits on the chest, and (b) that the fronts meet all the way down. The under-dress is shaped as shown in Fig. 517. It might be of light coloured silk, with lines of braid on the bodice converging to the point at the waist. The sleeves are braided diagonally, and braid decorates the skirt. From the girdle hangs a pomander.

Fig. 523. The Princess Mary II, 1553

## THE LADY MARY II

*(continued from p. 288)*

Fig. 523 is drawn from a three-quarter portrait of the Princess Mary dating about 1551–3. The dress worn by the Princess is of black velvet trimmed with narrow bands of miniver. The arrangement of lines of fur on the mahoitered sleeves is pleasing; the close-fitting braided sleeves and underskirt or kirtle are of white satin braided with black and silver lace, and the embroidered lawn partlet with high turned-down-in-front collar is braided with similar but narrower braid.

The headdress, worn over hair arranged in a double wave around the head, is an amalgamation of the jewelled network cap as seen in Fig. 547, with a wired front edged with pearls. A heart-shaped pomander or purse, attached to a tiny box perhaps containing some relic, is carried in the right hand. The purse, on a larger scale, is inset. The original measures about four inches in width.

*(Continued on p. 438)*

## FRENCH FASHIONS

ELEANOR, ARCHDUCHESS OF AUSTRIA

*Queen-Dowager of France, 1547–58*

*(continued from p. 273)*

Eleanor, Queen of Portugal and France, was left a widow for the second time in 1547, and withdrew to Spain where, with her sister Marie, Queen of Hungary, she devoted the rest of her life to her brother the Emperor Charles V.

Roger Ascham, Latin tutor to the Princess Elizabeth, wrote from Augsburg to his friend Mr. Raven an amusing letter which enlightens us on the subject of widows' mourning, dress, manners, etc. Ascham was among those, including Queen Eleanor, Francis I's widow, who attended Mass on the 5th October 1550. He writes:

' . . . the French Queen, the Emperor's sister, was there: she came to Mass clad very solemnly all in white cambric, a robe gathered in plaits [1] wrought very fair as need be with needle white work, as white as a dove. A train of ladies followed her, as black and evil as she was white. Her Mass was sung in prick song by Frenchmen very cunningly, and a gentleman played at the organs excellently. A French Whipit, Sir John, bestirred himself so at the altar as I wished Patrick by to have learned some of his knacks. . . . The Queen sat in a closet above; her ladies kneeled all abroad in the chapel among us. The Regent of Flanders had left at Bruxelles a sort of fair lusty young ladies; they came not out, but were kept in mew [see p. 157] for fear of gosshawks of Spain and France; yet they came to [view] and stood above in windows, as well content to show themselves as we to see them.

'They had on French gowns of black velvet, garded down right from the collar with broad gards, one with another, some of cloth of gold, some of cloth of silver, great chains arranged with precious jewels. On their heads they had glistering cauls of goldsmith work, and black velvet caps above with frills of great agletts of gold, with white feathers round about the compass of their caps. They seemed boys rather than ladies, excellent to have played in tragedies. There was not one well-favoured among them, save one young lady, fair and well-favoured. The Queen went from Mass to dinner; I followed her; and because we were gentlemen of England, I and another was admitted to come into her chamber where she sat at dinner. She is served with no women, as great states are there in England; but altogether with men, having their caps on their heads whilst they come into the chamber where she sits, and there one takes off all their caps. I stood very near the table and saw all.

'Men, as I said, served; only two women stood by the fire-side not far from the table, for the chamber was little, and talked very loud and lewdly with whom they would as methought.

---

[1] Presumably pleats, but a mere man does not know the difference (*see also under* Fig. 554).

'This Queen's service, compared with my Lady Elizabeth's my mistress, is not so prince-like nor honourably handled. Her first course was apples, pears, plums, grapes, nuts: and this meat she began. Then she had bacon and chickens almost covered with *sale* [1] onions, that all the chamber smelled of it. She had a roast caponet, and a pasty of wild-boar; and I, thus marking all the behaviour, was content to lose the second course, lest I should have lost mine own dinner at home.'

Fig. 524. French Noble Lady

In wearing white for mourning, Queen Eleanor was reversing the tradition set by Anne of Brittany (*see* p. 71).

There is at Hampton Court a three-quarter-length portrait of Eleanor in widow's weeds by an unknown artist, from which Fig. 551 showing the headdress has been taken (*see* p. 455). The dress and the wide sleeves are entirely in black, with white under-sleeves and goffered frills at the wrists. The pleated part of the widow's barbe covers the entire front to below the waist, the plain portion passing over the shoulders. She appears to have placed a long black silk scarf, stole-wise, over this.

Eleanor, Archduchess of Austria, Queen of Portugal, and subsequently of France, died in 1558.

Several illustrations of Catherine de' Medici in her widow's weeds are extant, and answer to Ascham's descriptions of Eleanor's except that they are entirely in black; they are of a later date, since Catherine did not become a widow until 1559. Fig. 661 is derived from these illustrations, and should be referred to for comparison with the description on p. 566.

Of Queen Eleanor's maids of honour, 'one young lady, fair and well-favoured,' is shown in Fig. 524. Ascham describes her dress so well that there remains nothing more to explain, except the black velvet cap. This is worn over a gold caul, and is decorated round the crown with laces and golden aiglettes. White plumes rest on the brim on the left side. The costume is of the French fashion, and a little in advance of that worn in England at this time (1550). It shows the latest vogue of sleeve raised on the shoulder. A detail of a rather exaggerated mahoitered sleeve is given in Fig. 820 showing very plainly its humped padding on top and in front of the armpit; it fits close round the arm just above the elbow.

[1] 'Sale' in this case obviously means stale or fermented—considered rather a tasty dish.

CATHERINE DE' MEDICI

*Queen-Mother of France, 1547 until 1558*

(*continued from p. 277*)

From the moment it was announced that Catherine de' Medici was to become the wife of the French King's son, the French people manifested their dislike of her, on account of what they regarded as her *bourgeois* extraction. This dislike steadily increased, growing from prejudice to hatred. During her life as Queen, and later Queen-Regent, of France, her every action was misrepresented, and nothing credited save that which defamed her character. Few historical personalities have been so extravagantly vilified as this amiable lady—she has been accused of every conceivable crime it is possible to commit. Modern historians and biographers, however, have had the advantage of a much wider field of research than that open to earlier writers; and during the twentieth century much information has been gleaned, which shows the falsity of previous judgments, and throws a very different light upon the true disposition of 'the Italian woman.' Catherine was a woman of strong character, of pleasing and agreeable manners, and a great stickler for convention. Never at any time during her life did she show a revengeful spirit, or a natural tendency to cruelty. Wise and chaste in the midst of a licentious Court, she was 'an indefatigable peace-maker,' showing great toleration of Protestants and Catholics alike—thus perhaps earning the bigots' accusation of duplicity.

Brantôme, who knew Queen Catherine well, and has always been considered her great admirer, writes of her with some enthusiasm as follows:

'She was of rich and very fine presence; of great majesty, but very gentle when need was; of noble appearance and good grace, her visage handsome and agreeable, her bosom very beautiful, the skin smooth, as I have heard from several of her ladies; of a fine plumpness also, the leg and thigh very beautiful—as I have heard from the same ladies; and she took great pleasure in being well shod, and in having her stockings well and tightly drawn up. Besides all this, the most beautiful hand that was ever seen, as I believe. She always clothed herself well and superbly, often with some pretty and new invention.'

A portrait of Catherine, by Corneille de Lyon, painted about 1549, may be still in existence. It is recorded that in this portrait the Queen is shown 'attired in the French mode [*see* Fig. 255] with a little cap [the French hood] edged with pearls, and a dress with large sleeves of cloth of silver, the latter turned back with lynx.'

While staying at Lyons, in 1574, the Queen-Regent visited this artist in his studio, and there she saw the portrait painted twenty-five years before. It revived memories of the days when, almost a nonentity, she shared the throne of France with her dear, yet not too faithful, husband.

Fig. 525. CATHERINE DE' MEDICI, QUEEN OF FRANCE, c. 1555

In the Uffizi Gallery at Florence is a full-length portrait of Catherine de'
Medici, by Pourbus. In it she is shown wearing the fashionable dress
of this period. Fig. 525 is a drawing made from this portrait. The dress
is of black velvet, entirely covered with a trellis-work of pearls, with sapphires
in gold mounts set at the intersections; the spaces between are embroidered
with a design in gold (Fig. 526).[1] The full-busted bodice is close-fitting at
the sixteen-inch waist, and cut very wide at the neck opening, which is
filled in at the sides with a quilted partlet of gauze set with sapphires and pearls.
A small upstanding collar of gauze, partly goffered and edged with lace, surrounds the sides and back of the neck, leaving the throat bare. The sleeves
are turned back with ermine and have the square effect shown in Fig. 255.
The false sleeves are of pale pink satin, treated in the same manner as the
underskirt, or kirtle, which is of the same colour and material, and decorated

Fig. 526                     Fig. 527

with a trellis-work similar to the over-dress, but enclosing embroidery of
silver in a different design (Fig. 527). The kirtle is widely distended over
the Spanish farthingale. A girdle of pearls and sapphires is continued down
the front, emphasizing the decided long point to the waist-line of the bodice,
and terminating in a beautiful cross-ornament of gold set with sapphires and
pearls.

The French hood, decorated with the same gems, but *without* the tubular
part, is worn, and the Queen holds in her right hand a large fan of ostrich
tips, fixed to a rigid handle of gold set with jewels to match her dress.

It is said that this Queen invented the side-saddle, but this is not correct
(*see* vol. ii, Fig. 215). Nevertheless, according to Brantôme, Catherine 'was
very good on horseback, and bold, sitting with ease, and being the first to
put the leg around a pommel, which was far more graceful and becoming than
sitting with the feet upon a plank.[2] Till she was sixty years of age and over
she liked to ride on horseback, and after her weakness prevented her she
pined for it. She was fond of seeing comedies and tragedies; but after
*Sophonisbe*, a tragedy composed by M. de Saint-Gélais, was very well represented by her daughters and other ladies and damoiselles and gentlemen of

---

[1] Figs. 526 and 527 are not indicated in Fig. 255.          [2] Refer to p. 604.

her Court at Blois, for the marriages of M. du Cypière and the Marquise d'Elbœuf, she took an opinion that it was harmful to the affairs of the king-dom, and would never have tragedies played again. But she listened readily to comedies and tragi-comedies, and even those of Zani and Pantalon, taking great pleasure in them, and laughing with all her heart like any other.'

(*Continued on p.* 566)

## MARY STUART

### *Queen of Scotland, Dauphine of France, 1542 until 1558*

During the course of the period covered by this chapter there was a young girl living at the French Court who was destined to play a prominent part in the politics and affairs of Europe—the Queen of Scotland, Mary Stewart. Born at Linlithgow, 8th December 1542, the only child of James V and Mary, daughter of Claude, Duc de Guise, she succeeded her father at the tender age of six days. The babe was crowned Queen of Scotland by Cardinal Beaton in the chapel of Stirling Castle, 11th September 1543, 'with such solemnity as they do use in this country, which is not very costly.'

At the age of six years Queen Mary was sent to France [1] to be educated as the betrothed wife of Francis the Dauphin, whom she married at Notre-Dame, 24th April 1558. Her husband received the title of King of Scotland, while Mary was created Reine-Dauphine. On the death of Mary, Queen of Eng-land, in the following November 'the title of Queen of England was taken by the Court of France for Queen Mary in a quiet off-hand way.' This was but in accordance with Roman Catholic principles, as Elizabeth Tudor was looked upon as illegitimate, and Mary Stuart was next heiress to the crown, therefore Francis and Mary were styled 'King and Queen of England, Scot-land, and Ireland.' They also quartered the Royal Arms of England with their own.

Of the multitude of portraits of Mary Stuart only about fifteen are genuine. From these, numerous copies and versions have been made during the course of the four following centuries. Apart from these, all others alleged to represent Mary Queen of Scots are spurious.

In appearance Mary Stuart possessed a graceful figure, tall and slender. She had a brilliant complexion, hazel eyes, the upper eyelids rather thick, with arched eyebrows faintly defined; a long straight nose, and a thin mouth with full underlip. Her forehead was high and round, surmounted by yellowish auburn hair in youth: 'si blonds et cendrés' (that hair so beautiful, so fair and *grey*) so much admired by Brantôme. The cheek-bones were somewhat pronounced and her ears unusually large.[2] Her hands were beauti-fully white with long taper fingers. After the death of her first husband she lost her bright colouring and her skin became an alabaster white.

---

[1] According to French orthography the name of her house was now spelt 'Stuart.'
[2] See Plate XXXIII.

MARIA    SCOTIÆ    REGINA.

Fig. 528. 1558

Fig. 528 represents Mary Stuart at the age of sixteen. The figure above the waist is taken from François Clouet's two drawings, one in the Musée Condé at Chantilly, the other in the Bibliothèque Nationale, Paris. They only show down to the waist, but enough is seen to construct the skirt. The costume was of white satin, the bodice and skirt decorated with wide bands of gold embroidery. The design is shown in Fig. 529. The bodice, rounded at the neck opening, was worn over a partlet of embroidered gauze with an upstanding collar finished in gofferings. The fifteen-inch waist was moulded by a steel corset. The skirt was of moderate proportions compared with that shown in Fig. 525. The sleeves, with puff 'à la ballonnoise' at the

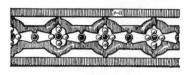

Fig. 529.
Gold Embroidery set with Jewels

shoulders, were ornamented with lines of gold cord caught together with pearls or small gold and jewelled buttons. Her earrings, necklaces, girdle, and pomander were of pearls set with gold. The coif set far back on the head was of gold embroidery, pearls, and jewels (see Fig. 548). This may have been the Queen's wedding gown, for it is recorded that when Henry II led his future daughter-in-law to the altar she was wearing white satin, with a mantle of blue velvet embroidered with lilies in silver. Her coronet was of diamonds valued at half a million crowns, and her whole person glistened with gems.

(Continued on p. 511)

## QUEEN MARY, 1553–8 (continued from p. 430)

Mary, the second child of Henry VIII and Katherine of Aragon, was born at Greenwich, 8th February 1516. Her appearance as a young woman has been set forth on p. 271.

In the year 1553 Queen Mary is described as 'a faded little woman, with a white face, no eyebrows, and russet hair. At thirty-seven an old maid, disillusioned and wearied by years of cruel injustice.'

'She has no eyebrows, is a perfect saint, and dresses very badly,' is an unfair opinion of a Spaniard.

A more favourable pen-portrait of Mary Tudor is given by Soranzo in his report to the Venetian Senate: 'She is of low stature, with a red and white complexion, and very thin; her eyes are light-coloured and large, and her hair reddish; her face is round, with a nose rather low and wide; and were not her

PLATE XXV. QUEEN MARY, 1553: Portrait by Antonio Moro
Prado, Madrid. *Photo by Mansell*

age on the decline she might be called handsome rather than the contrary.'
The kindly disposed Venetian Ambassador also states that 'Her Majesty's
countenance indicates great benignity and clemency, which are not belied
by her conduct.'

From other sources we learn that Mary's complexion was invariably sallow.
During the latter part of her life the Queen was never free from headaches
and palpitation of the heart. She was also a great sufferer from melancholy
and so short-sighted that she could not read or
study anything clearly without placing her eyes
quite close to the object.

Giovanni Michiel, Venetian Ambassador
Extraordinary 1553, has some pleasant and
unbiased things to say about Queen Mary:

'Besides feminine accomplishments, such as
needlework and every sort of embroidery, she
is very proficient in music, playing especially
on the clavichord and lute so excellently, that
when she attended to this, which she does but
little, she surprised good performers both by
the rapidity of her execution and method of
playing.'

Of 'Bloody Mary' much that is libellous has
been written by champions of the Reformation
and others. According to contemporary and
unbiased opinion she was 'a most amiable Princess.' Her zeal for the orthodox religion, her
implicit faith in her husband's high sense of
duty, made her the tool of circumstance. If

Fig. 530.
A Badge of Queen Mary

Mary had not wedded a man whose lifelong obsession was the conversion
of heretic Europe, posterity might have remembered her name with greater
charity.

On the 30th September 1553 Queen Mary made her triumphal progress
from the Tower to the Palace of Westminster, enthroned in a chariot open on
all sides save for the canopy, entirely covered with gold tissue; and the
trappings of the six horses which drew it were of red velvet and gold. The
Queen 'sat in a gown of blew velvet, furred with powdered ermine, having on
her head a caul of cloth of tissue beset with pearl and stone, and about the
same upon her head a round circlet of gold, much like a hooped garland
beset so richly with many precious stones that the value thereof was inestimable.

'After the Queen's chariot came another chariot having the canopy all of
one covering, with cloth of silver all white, and vj horses betrapped with the
same, bearing the said chariot; and therein sat at the end, with her face
forward, the Lady Elizabeth; and at the other end, with her back forward,
the Lady Anne of Cleves.' It is obvious from this statement that the Princess
Elizabeth had precedence over her stepmother—an interesting point.

The coronation took place the following day at Westminster Abbey, the ceremony being conducted by Stephen Gardiner, Bishop of Winchester. This ceremony is of unusual interest, being the first coronation of a queen-regnant in English history. The procedure adopted was almost identical with that used when a king is crowned.

In her robes of crimson velvet and ermine the Queen entered the Abbey, and was first led by Stephen Gardiner round all four sides of a platform so that all the company might see her, the Bishop crying in a loud voice that all might hear him: 'Sirs, here present is Mary, rightful and undoubted inheritrix by the Laws of God and man to the Crown and Royal Dignity of this realm of England, France, and Ireland, whereupon you shall understand that this day is appointed by all the Peers of this land for the consecration, inunction, and coronation of the said most excellent Princess Mary; will you serve at this time, and give your wills and assent to the same consecration, inunction, and coronation?' All the company shouted joyfully, 'Yea, Yea!' After this Her Majesty went to the altar to hear a sermon preached by George Day, Bishop of Chichester,[1] the subject being obedience due to monarchs from their subjects. At the end the Queen prostrated herself on the ground and received benediction with many prayers. Retiring to the robing chamber, she had her robes removed and returning 'in her corset'[2] she prostrated herself again. At this stage the Queen was anointed with the Holy Oil on her breast, shoulders, forehead, and temples. After this she was clad in the Alb of white taffeta, with the Dalmatic of very rich material over it. Shoes of gold were then put on, and over them golden spurs were strapped. Next came the girding of the Sword, after which the State Mantle of crimson velvet furred with ermine was fastened across the shoulders. This mantle had been specially consecrated; it was not the one Queen Mary was wearing when she arrived at the Abbey.

The Sceptres of the Cross and the Dove were placed in the right and left hands respectively, the Queen changing the Dove over to the right hand in order to receive the Orb. Finally, she was crowned with three crowns, one for England, one for France, and one for Ireland. Thus arrayed, Queen Mary, seated upon the throne, received the homage of all the lords spiritual and temporal. Mass was then performed 'with much solemnity, the Queen kneeling throughout with great devotion and great tokens of religion, which being ended, she entered the aforesaid retired apartment, and speedily came forth with the Orb in her hand and the Royal Sceptre, clad in a mantle of *purple* velvet furred with tufts of ermine, and with the round cap, as monarchs are wont to wear'—the Cap of Maintenance. Thus arrayed, Queen Mary I was acclaimed by the people.

All illustrations of Queen Mary in State robes show that she wore the Royal mantle of velvet with a cape of ermine over a surcote (*see* Fig. 292 and

---

[1] George Day (1501–56) was Master of St. John's College, 1537, and Provost of King's College, Cambridge, 1538. Made Bishop of Chichester, 1543.
[2] A petticoat and bodice.

Plate XLIV). Sometimes the surcote was omitted, as when the mantle was worn over fashionable dress of some very rich material. In full state the Royal crown only was worn: on less formal occasions the crown would surmount the French hood, or the latter would be worn without it.

A portrait of Queen Mary was painted by Antonio Moro about the end of 1553 (Plate XXV) and sent to Prince Philip of Spain. It hung in the gallery of the Prado. There is a copy in the dining hall at Trinity College, Cambridge. In it the Queen wears the usual style of costume in a deep grey-blue velvet, the sleeves turned back with the same velvet; the false sleeves and underskirt are of silk brocade, the large pattern in a lighter shade of the same grey-blue upon a deeper toned ground. The inside of the collar and the wrist-frills are decorated with Spanish work. The girdle, without the customary long end, is a beautiful example of goldsmith's work and jewels (see Fig. 565). From it is suspended by a riband, a jewelled pomander, or reliquary (see Fig. 564). The French hood is reproduced in Fig. 531.

We have a further account of Queen Mary's dresses from Giacomo Soranzo, the Venetian Ambassador, in which he reports that:

'She seems to delight above all in arraying herself elegantly and magnificently, and her garments are of two sorts: the one a *gown such as men wear*, but fitting very close, with an under-petticoat, which has a very long train, and this is her ordinary costume, being also that of the gentlewomen of England. *The other garment* is a gown and bodice with wide hanging sleeves in the French fashion, which she wears on State occasions, and she also wears much embroidery, and gowns and mantles of cloth of gold, and cloth of silver of great value, and changes every day. She also makes great use of jewels, wearing them both on her *chaperon*, and round her neck, and as trimming for her gowns.'

The 'gown such as men wear' refers to the Spanish surcote worn by the lady (Fig. 521). When this was made 'fitting very close,' it formed a bodice and skirt combined and is shown in Fig. 523. 'The other garment' is illustrated in Plate XXVI and Fig. 531. The 'chaperon,' of course, means the French hood.

For her first meeting with Philip of Spain (see p. 410) the Queen was gowned in black velvet over an underskirt of frosted silver. The jewels she wore were magnificent. On the day of her marriage (25th July 1554—the Feast day of St. James the Patron Saint of Spain) Her Majesty 'blazed with jewels to an extent that dazzled those who gazed upon her' as she swept up the nave of Winchester Cathedral (see p. 386) to her chair [1] before the high altar. Her long mantle was of brocaded cloth of gold bordered with pearls and diamonds of great size, and lined with ermine. Her dress, in shape like Fig. 520, was also of gold smothered with the same precious stones, and the underskirt of white satin was embroidered with silver. The French hood in black velvet was surmounted by a double row of large diamonds. On her breast the

---

[1] Still preserved there. It is said that this chair, originally covered with blue velvet, was blessed and sent to Queen Mary by the Pope.

Queen wore a remarkable ornament—the gift sent to her by her bridegroom. It was a large table diamond mounted in a superb gold setting and valued at 50,000 ducats: from this hung an immense peardrop pearl (*see* p. 461).

Andres Muñoz thus describes two costumes worn by Queen Mary:

'The Queen was clad in a galdres [1] of black velvet, high in the neck, according to the custom over there, without any ornament whatsoever, with a front [2] of frosted silver embroidery, and a chapiron [3] of black velvet with its gold pieces, of great value, gracefully set; and a narrow girdle of very marvellous stones and a collar of the same sort.' Again: 'The Queen came dressed in purple velvet, and the galdres lined with brocade [4] and a front of embroidered frosted gold with very rich precious stones and pearls from the Orient and seed pearls; with chapiron, girdle, and collar of the same stone work.'

It will be interesting to have the opinion of another Spaniard regarding the dresses of English ladies. 'They wear farthingales of coloured cloth without silk,' he says, emphasizing the contrast between these and the more highly decorated and embroidered farthingales of his own country; 'the gowns they wear over them are of damask, satin, or velvet of various colours, but very badly made.'

Another portrait of Queen Mary, painted in 1554 by Hans Eworth, belongs to the Society of Antiquaries of London. The costume is reproduced in Plate XXVI by kind permission of the committee of the society. In it the Queen is seen wearing a very rich dress of yellow cloth of gold of damask over the Spanish farthingale of large size. Here one realizes the great advantage gained by the very wide farthingale in showing off the intricate design of the embroidery on the underskirt. The sleeves illustrate the prevailing fashion for narrow shoulders and tight-fitting tops, the turned-back part being lined with sable. The false sleeves and underskirt appear to be of a pale rose-coloured satin embroidered with two shades of bullion, a gold and a red gold. The design is in the elaborate arabesque style. The large false sleeves, on which the raised-pad effect is well in evidence, help to make the sable turned-back stand out at an angle, an effect aided also by the position of the arms (*see* p. 269). Details to notice are the jewelled collar with the tau cross round the neck; the outer collar of the bodice with an inner one embroidered with Spanish work; the reliquary at the end of a loop of 'ferret' suspended from the waist girdle; and the wide French hood.

In medieval times the term 'ferret' [5] was sometimes applied to the 'lacet' finished at the end with an aiglette. In the sixteenth century it meant a narrow stout band of silk or cotton—a 'riban.' [6] 'Black rybens for lassys.'

In the portrait group (Fig. 531), painted in 1558, the Queen is wearing a dress shaped like that in Plate XXVI, composed of dark blue velvet, with sleeves turned back with squirrel. The false sleeves and underskirt are of gold brocade.

---

[1] The robe or gown.     [2] Refers to the underskirt.     [3] 'Chapiron' means the French hood.
[4] The turned-back sleeves were lined with brocade.
[5] Compare the modern use of the word 'ferret,' which is applied to the narrow green ribbon used by the legal fraternity for lacing together the sheets of deeds and other legal documents.
[6] Called in the middle of the sixteenth century a 'ribbon.'

Fig. 531. KING PHILIP II AND QUEEN MARY, 1558

Queen Mary died in London, 17th November 1558. On 13th December the corpse of the late Queen was brought from St. James's to Westminster 'in a chariot with a painted effigy adorned in crimson velvet and her crown on her head, her sceptre in her hand and many goodly rings on her fingers, lying on cloth of gold with a cross of silver. xiiij day her grace was buried.'

### JANE GUYLDEFORD

*Duchess of Northumberland, 1551-5*

Fig. 532.
Jane, Duchess of Northumberland, 1555

Probably the latest example, on a brass, of a noble lady wearing an heraldic mantle is on that to the memory of Jane, sister and heiress of Sir Henry Guyldeford, in St. Luke's, Chelsea. This lady married John Dudley who was created Duke of Northumberland in 1551, and who is notorious for his attempt to place his daughter-in-law, Lady Jane Grey, upon the throne, in consequence of which he was beheaded in 1553. The Duchess was the mother of three famous sons—Ambrose, Guyldeford, and Robert Dudley, and died in 1555. She is reproduced in Fig. 532, her dress and headdress being of the style fashionable in these reigns; her heraldic mantle of state, lined with ermine, is charged with the armorial bearings of the families of Guyldeford, Halden, West, La Warr, Cantelupe, Mortimer, and Grelle.

The brass to the memory of a gentlewoman, Mistress D'Arcy, at Tolleshunt D'Arcy, Essex, is the authority for the costume shown in Fig. 533, which is a style affected by some of this class from, approximately, 1554. The dress shows the French and Spanish influences.

The surcote with deep collar and

Fig. 533. Mistress D'Arcy, 1555

cutte mahoitered shoulder sleeves ties down the front, and is worn over an under-dress with close-fitting sleeves. A front view of the headdress is shown in Fig. 542 from which the design of the cutwork edging to the inside collar, which is repeated on the cuffs, may be seen. A book with an elaborate cover hangs by a narrow riband looped to the girdle underneath the surcote.

The dress of the lady shown in Fig. 534 is of the same period. The drawing is from the brass to the memory of Dame Drury, at Hawstead, Suffolk. Her bodice and sash are similar to those last described, but she has an all-round skirt; the collar of the bodice turns down displaying the frill of cutwork

Fig. 534. Dame Drury, 1557

Fig. 535. Dame Brydges, 1558

round the neck. From the mahoitered sleeves hang long tubular ones, and the under-sleeves are banded cambric or lawn with frills of the same cutwork at the wrists. The headdress is an interesting feature and is described on p. 450.

Fig. 535 is a drawing made from the effigy at Ludgershall, Wilts, of Dame Brydges, who died in 1558. The costume is that in fashion during the previous decade and in the true English style. The bodice and sleeves are those which have been described under Figs. 67, 256, and 261, except that the turned-back portions of the sleeves are of soft material and therefore hang in folds. The false sleeves vary slightly in shape from the diagram, Fig. 257. Those in Fig. 535 are decorated with three cuttes and bead ornaments (*see* inset). The square collar is turned back and shows the pleated neckband of lawn. A moderate-sized farthingale distends the trained skirt, and down the front of the underskirt hangs a girdle, terminating in a pomander and fastened at the waist to the narrow sash which is tied in front. The French hood is in its simplest form and of black velvet. The whole figure is interesting as an example of modified fashions worn by an aristocrat.

# SECTION II: 1547–58

## HAIRDRESSING

Hair close cut to the head was now universal in spite of the fact that the first coronation medal ever struck shows Edward VI wearing longer hair than usual, which might almost be termed bobbed. In all his portraits as King he is nevertheless shown with close-cropped hair. Such a portrait is in the Library of Canterbury Cathedral from which Fig. 536 is drawn. It

Fig. 536. King Edward VI, 1551          Fig. 537. William Parr, c. 1559

represents the King as a boy of about fourteen with hair cut close to the head. This is also seen in Plates XIX and XX.

The hairdressing affected by Philip II in Fig. 497 illustrates the Spanish fashion of this period. The hair is straight, and brushed back off the forehead and temples.

As far as can be seen from the portrait (Fig. 505) young Lord Maltravers wore his in the same style. After the death of Queen Mary this mode of hairdressing appears to have sunk into oblivion for a time.

Beards of various lengths and shapes were worn by those of mature manhood, and full beards upon the upper lip. In 1551 this growth of hair was dignified by a special name first referred to in English as 'mowchatowes.' This word derives originally from the Greek 'mustax,' the upper lip:

the modern English form, MOUSTACHE, comes from the French 'moustache,' the alternative MUSTACHIO partly from the Spanish 'mostacho' and partly from the Italian 'mostaccio.'

Very seldom, if ever, was a beard worn without moustaches.

Fig. 538.
Embroidered pattern from doublet of Edward VI, Canterbury

Fig. 537, taken from a drawing of William Parr, Marquess of Northampton, at the age of about forty-five, is an example of the general facial adornment of a middle-aged nobleman.

As mentioned in Chap. II, beards were sometimes worn stiffened with wax. Henry II in the portrait, Fig. 489, clearly does so.

## HEADGEAR, 1547–58

There was very little new in the style of headgear fashionable during the eleven years covered by this chapter. Fig. 359 D gives the most up-to-date shape, which was liable to variation in width of brim and its ornamentations.

Fig. 539. Henry II, King of France

Plates XIX and XX show a moderately wide brim turned up or down according to the taste of the wearer. The crowns are flat, and a feather droops over one ear. The hat worn by Edward VI (Fig. 536) is an exceptionally flat bonet of black velvet with a very shallow brim ornamented with pearls and gold-enamelled beads covering the narrow hatband. A curled feather droops from the left side, and to the quill is fixed a gold ornament. The design down the front of the King's doublet is shown on a larger scale in Fig. 538. It would be carried out in gold embroidery.

The hat worn by the King in Plate XIX is higher in the crown with a gold curled tassel hanging from the quill. Small gold beads are set on the hatband. It was, however, more general to wear a hat with the brim turned down, a fancy first mentioned on page 317. As a consequence, the join of the crown and brim was visible, so a narrow hatband was added to make it tidy. Hatbands were very often decorated with a series of ornaments, buttons, studs, etc., set at intervals. Brooches and aiglettes were frequently used, and these were set with jewels, pearls, and enamels. The nobility wore continuous strands of various jewels and ornaments around their hats. The upturned brim as shown in Fig. 365 was still considered smart, and caps without any brim as worn by Henry II (Fig. 488) were much favoured in France. The King did not limit himself to this style of hat; in fact, that shown in Fig. 539 is the shape he usually wore. Of black velvet, it has rows of three gold buttons on the under-side of the crown, which probably stiffened it and helped to keep it from sinking down and becoming too flat. The same arrangement of buttons, of smaller size, is used on the top side of the brim, and an ostrich tip curls over on the right. Around the King's neck is a double string of gold filigree beads. The whole suit is of black velvet, closely sewn with small gold cord, and the black silk embroidery on the collar is worthy of notice.

At the middle of this period the crown of the hat was made fuller and larger (*see* Figs. 494 and 505).

## HAIRDRESSING—WOMEN: 1547–58

The style of hairdressing favoured by the ladies of this period is shown in Fig. 540. Most of them parted their hair in the middle, a few drew it back off the forehead, and all puffed or waved it at the sides, so filling the cavity left by the bow of the French hood; and made the remainder into a coil at the back of the head. This coil formed a substantial foundation on which to fix the French hood or other headdress: frequently it was confined in a caul, which might be made of pearls or goldsmith's work set with jewels (Fig. 549).

Fig. 540

Another method of arranging the hair at the sides of the face is described under Fig. 544. This style can be traced back to the hairdressing of Joanna of Castile (Plate V). Fig. 545 shows a slightly different treatment which can also be seen in Fig. 242. Catherine de' Medici wore her hair at the side closely crimped horizontally (*see* Fig. 543).

## HEADDRESSES: 1547–58

### THE FRENCH HOOD (*continued from p. 340*)

The latest version of the French hood, in vogue during the six years Edward VI was on the throne, is exemplified in Fig. 515 and in profile, Fig. 541. The front piece of black velvet is curved and finishes *behind* the

ear, and the edge is decorated with a band of gold set with emeralds faceted in points between groups of three pearls. Behind this is a second curved piece of white satin edged with a flat roll of velvet, on which are set groups of three pearls and single rubies in gold mounts giving a decided 'coronet' effect. The points of these crescent-shaped pieces all radiate from behind the ears. The black velvet hood itself is fixed behind the second crescent, and the part that falls down the back (*see* Fig. 590) is now definitely a flat tube, as first mentioned under Fig. 405, but without the folds in the nape of the neck as seen in Fig. 407, these being now obsolete.

The headdress of Dame Drury (Fig. 534) is but the French hood in its original form, like that of Dame Brydges (Fig. 535), but the former has achieved the fashionable line by adding a roll of material bound with gold cords over the front. This style could also

Fig. 541. Lady Jane Grey

be carried out in white linen, as is shown in Fig. 542, or in black velvet: it is of the usual shape as seen in the diagram, Fig. 163. The front is wired to give the bow effect, and a piece of silk, placed at the nape *under* the tube, is tied round the head with a knot on top.

The French hood worn by Catherine de' Medici is mentioned under Fig. 525. A narrow goffering of gold gauze edges the front of the hood, and is here used to break the hard line between the hood and the much crimped hair. It is the first example of a French hood without the tube at the back; this was often dispensed with as it was found somewhat inconvenient when worn with a

Fig. 542. Mistress D'Arcy, 1555

stand-up collar. Nevertheless, Catherine sometimes appeared with the tubular attachment in spite of the fact that she has at the same time a stand-up collar. She is wearing such a hood in a miniature of Clouet's now in the Uffizi, reproduced in Fig. 543. In this portrait the front is of pale pink silk or satin studded with pearls; both the front edge and the ridge are outlined with rubies in gold mounts separated by groups of three pearls.

The French hood as worn in Queen Mary's reign made its appearance just before she came to the throne, as proved by the portrait of Lady Jane Grey from which Fig. 516 is taken. Fig. 544 gives a three-quarter view of Mary herself wearing it. The ridge of jewels or coronet marked B now takes a different line (compare with Fig. 407). It is almost flat and wider at the top, and descends in a slight curve *inward*, finishing behind the ears. The black velvet front part,

Fig. 543. Catherine de' Medici, 1547
(*after Clouet*)

which lies on the hair, also becomes flatter and wider. Particular notice should be taken of the dip over the forehead and of the big curves at the sides which are rectangular at the bottom (*see at* A).

Queen Mary

Fig. 544. 1553          Fig. 545. 1555

What was originally the turned-back lining is now represented by a shaped piece of white or coloured silk or satin (*see at* C), a further development of that seen in Fig. 541. The tube is fixed to the back part of the ridge by pleats—a single box-pleat or sometimes a double one. The front part of the hood is severely plain, the only portion ornamented being the ridge: the jewels seen in Fig. 544 are three pearls, two with one on top, alternating with an enamel and gold ornament set with a ruby or diamond in the centre. The hair, like that in Figs. 515 and 541, is parted in the middle and lies smooth on the forehead, a portion being brought round from the back to form a puff which fills the cavity left by the side curves of the hood. This portion is carried backwards under the hood over the top of the head.

Fig. 546. The Attifet

The profile portrait of Queen Mary, from a medallion struck in 1555, reproduced in Fig. 545, explains the side construction of a somewhat similar French hood. It is wide and flat across the top like Fig. 544, but the piece of silk or satin, C, is reduced in size. The tube is pleated into the back with a piping, the superfluous material being arranged in folds to form a bag which contains the back hair, the tube itself falling over it. In front, braided plaits in place of puffs fill the cavities of the side curves.

The French hood worn by Lady Jane Grey (Fig. 516) has neither ridge nor ornamentation. This also applies to the headdress in Fig. 521, which, however, shows the dip on the forehead.

The price of a French 'whood,' according to the Princess Elizabeth's household accounts for 1553, was perhaps exorbitant. Two of them cost £2 8s. 9d, which sum, of course, does not include the gold and jewels; but as one had to pay in those days 20s. to 30s. per yard for velvet, not much was left for the lining or the making.

Shortly after the middle of the century a contrivance called an ATTIFET came into vogue (*see* Fig. 546). This was a wire of brass inserted in the edge of the front part of the hood or headdress and formed a curve on each side of the temples with a point on the forehead—in fact, it gave a bow or top-of-a-heart shape to the front.

Fig. 546 illustrates the use of the attifet with the French hood. The back portion comprises a roll from which the flat tube hangs down the back.

A suggestion of a wire is visible in the headdress of the lady (Fig. 521). The Princess Mary (Fig. 523) wears a very up-to-date headdress. It is the

ESCOFFION (*see* Fig. 547) to which an attifet front, edged with pearls, has been added. This style of headdress was quite popular with the ladies of both England and France.

Wire is definitely used in the cap worn by Queen Eleanor (Figs. 551 and 554).

Milan had long been celebrated for its wonderful headgear (*see* p. 313), besides fancy goods such as ferrets or ribands, gloves and pouches; and the vendors of Milanese wares began to be known as 'milliners.' A *fashion note*, recommended by French milliners in order to achieve the fashionable curve of the headdress, was to insert a wire of brass at the edge—the attifet, in fact.

### OTHER FRENCH HEADDRESSES
(*continued from p. 337*)

Fig. 547 is made from a portrait of Jeanne d'Albret, born 1528 at Fontainebleau

Fig. 547.
Jeanne d'Albret, Queen of Navarre

and only child of Henry II, King of Navarre. In 1548 she married Antoine, Duc de Bourbon, known as 'l'Échangeur,' because he could not be true to any faith. Her son Henry was born in 1553, and on the death of her father in 1555 she became Queen of Navarre in her own right. The headdress shown in Fig. 547 is known as an 'escoffion,' and was fashionable in France for a decade or so. It was a round cap of gold network and jewels mounted on a foundation of gold or silk. This particular one is shaped like a low hassock, cross-barred at the sides, and edged with a band of jewels. The back is plain with a row of pearls down the centre. The hair is brushed back off the forehead, slightly puffed over the ears, and confined by a band of gold round the head, having a jewel in a gold mount set on top. The cap is worn over this right off the back of the head, and encloses the remainder of the hair. The Queen of Navarre was left a widow in 1562, and in a drawing by François Clouet dated 1570

Fig. 548. Mary Stuart, 1559

she wears widow's weeds in exactly the same style as those shown in Fig. 884. Queen Jeanne died suddenly in Paris, to which city she had come to attend the marriage of her son with Marguerite de Valois, 1572.

The escoffion worn by Mary Queen of Scots in Fig. 528 is reproduced in

Fig. 548. In shape it is similar to the last, except that it is wider on top of the head than at the sides. The front part is of gold tissue, cross-barred with gold and having pearls at the intersections and centres. On the front and back edges are set jewels in gold quatrefoil mounts alternating with pearls. Where the front rests on the hair there is a narrow goffering of gold gauze. The oval-shaped back, either of plain gold tissue or coloured silk, has a band of the same jewels down the centre. The hair is waved off the temples with a puff over the ears, the remainder being confined within the cap. The large jewel on the forehead, perhaps, serves the purpose of securing the cap more firmly on the head.

Fig. 549

A network caul was often used to cover the coil of hair dressed at the back of the head, and was much favoured by English and French ladies. It is seen worn by the ladies in Figs. 550, 524, 549, and many others. It has its origin in the network caps worn in Italy.

Up to this time ladies had no hats of their own to use as an extra head covering, so during the reign of Henry II they adopted the velvet cap worn by gentlemen as described under Headgear of this chapter. Fig. 550 is one of the earliest examples, worn over a caul of gold and pearls. The lady is dressed in a Spanish surcote like Figs. 516 and 575.

Another such hat or cap is worn by the lady (Fig. 524) and, together with the caul, was known as a 'chapeau à l'Italienne,' and is often referred to in writings of the period. It is distinctly Italian in character (*refer to* Fig. 662), and is usually carried out in black velvet, although coloured velvets or silks were sometimes used. The brim resembles that of a man's hat, the whole effect

Fig. 550. A French Hat

being, in fact, decidedly masculine. The full crown is pleated into the brim, the join being covered by a narrow band to which are fixed aiglettes at all angles. Several small plumes are coquettishly set at the back on one side. The hair is rolled off the forehead, and confined at the back under a caul of gold network.

The widow's headdress as worn by Eleanor, Queen-Dowager of France, is shown in Fig. 551. First of all the widow's barbe is placed under the chin and tied up to the coil of hair fixed just below the cranium. Over her hair she wears a gauze cap finely gathered to a wire edging covered with white stitchery. This wire, the attifet, is bent to bow down on the forehead and curve round at the temples to the level of the mouth. At this point the wiring is bent into goffered or nebulée folds which continue up the side of the face. On top a lawn veil twenty-four by eighty inches, but folded in two as shown

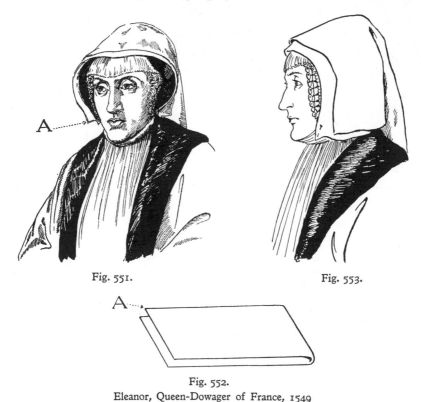

Fig. 551.

Fig. 553.

Fig. 552.
Eleanor, Queen-Dowager of France, 1549

in diagram, Fig. 552, is placed round the head as described under Fig. 164; a corner of the outer fold is marked A, and the inner corner is pinned to the band of the barbe. The folds are then pinned together in the nape of the neck and the remainder hangs down the back. A black silk scarf is placed round the neck over the barbe, the plain part of the latter falling over the arms as far as the elbows. A side view of this headdress is given in Fig. 553.

A similar type of widow's headdress is to be seen in the sculptured portrait bust of Queen Eleanor in the Prado. In the drawing (Fig. 554) the pleated under-cap is clearly shown, as are also the second cap with attifet front and the lawn veil, and these more distinctly than in Fig. 551. The barbe hangs from beneath the collar, which is possibly part of the barbe itself.

LA REINE ELEANOR.

Fig. 554

The interest of the sculpture lies not merely in its representation of the Queen-Dowager in advanced years, but more particularly in the robe she is wearing, which is of white *pleated* material, such as is referred to by Roger Ascham (*see* p. 431). The sculpture definitely portrays narrow tucks, about half an inch deep and about an inch apart, and arranged horizontally. The fronts of the robe are folded over to form stole-effects on both sides of the barbe.

To the readers of a book on costume the description of a lady in her bath can have no interest, nevertheless the accompanying drawing, Fig. 555, is inserted. It is from the portrait of Diane de Poitiers in her bath, clothed only in a small headdress of gauze ruchings, which is the equivalent of the boudoir cap of to-day.

Some authorities doubt if this is Diane, because when Clouet painted the portrait, in 1549, she was in her fifty-first year, a fact which the painting in no way reveals. They forget that contemporaries state that she retained her beauty and youthful appearance almost to the end of her life, and she lived to be sixty-seven.

At Chantilly there is a painting identical with this in the main composition, but the head is that of Gabrielle d'Estrées.

Fig. 555. Diane de Poitiers
(*after Clouet*)

## FOOTGEAR, 1547–58

By the time Edward VI ascended the throne footgear had begun to assume a more natural shape in the toes. This shape is first seen in Fig. 280 and in the first sole plan, Fig. 556. These show that the toe is rounded but somewhat clumsy in appearance. Fig. 504 illustrates a modification, and in it one sees that eventually the toe not only became quite natural, but at the same time elegant (*see also* the second sole plan, Fig. 556).

Cuttes on shoes were reintroduced from the Continent, and they are first seen worn by Prince Philip (Fig. 497). Although the sole follows the outline of the foot the cuttes, intended as ornaments, give an ugly bulging appearance.

Fig. 556    Fig. 557    Fig. 558

Shoes treated in this manner are said to be 'razed.' Fig. 557 is the shoe in question. Over the joints of the toes on the uppers are three long cuttes, and a series of small ones surrounds the heel. Across the instep are three rows of ornamental stitching, and all round the edge of the shoe are very small loops. These shoes nearly always matched the hosen in colour if not in material, which was either velvet, silk, or satin.

Fig. 558 gives a shoe cut higher at the heel and on the instep; from the centre of the latter a V-shaped piece has been cut, although a round-topped upper was also in vogue. The decoration consists of a series of very small cuttes which greatly improves the appearance of the shoe as compared with that in Fig. 557.

Nothing new in long boots is noticeable in England at this period: the shape of the toe becomes natural as with the shoe. The boots worn by Lord Maltravers (Fig. 505) are good examples.

Fig. 559

The 'botte à genouillère' or 'jack-boot' made its appearance in France at the end of this period, as seen in the portrait of Henry II (Plate XXI). The latter name is perhaps due to the leather being 'jacked,' i.e. beaten or pommelled hard. This boot is reproduced in Fig. 559. The narrowness at the ankle would be found inconvenient for passing the foot through, although it must be more pliable in this part than at the top because creases or folds are shown. The ridge at the top is triangular in section; the toe is rounded and the heel rather square.

Common sense forewarned the careful, well-dressed man that to put his legs, clothed in silk hosen, into the rough interior of long leather boots would ultimately ruin delicate leg wear. A lining of linen, shaped like a stocking,

Fig. 560. Chopine

was therefore devised, and drawn up over the hosen for protection before pulling on the boots. These linen stockings were called 'boot-hose,' but at this early period were unseen.

CHOPINES were clogs of cork covered with plain or decorated leather in various colours; these could be slipped on and off, but were usually all in one with the shoe (Fig. 560). They were used in Turkey and Persia, adopted in Italy, and found their way, via Venice, into England. Ladies of quality and fashion used chopines to give them height; and, as they were awkward to walk in, it was necessary for the wearer to be supported by a man or woman, usually by the arm, 'to the end that they may not fall.' The Spanish lady (Fig. 248) is wearing chopines.

It was in 1557 that the cordwainers received their second charter from Philip and Mary.

## JEWELLERY, 1547–58

Edward VI naturally inherited most of his father's enormous store of personal jewels and articles of jewellery and, of course, the English Crown Jewels. The juvenile King was not too young to realize the advantages gained by these inestimable assets, and appears to have followed the example set by his grandfather as a means of speculation. Like other monarchs and persons of great wealth, he not only locked up money in jewels, but also found them a universally accepted security when he wished to raise a loan. In his journal we have several memoranda bearing on this subject, and the following is a very good specimen:

25th April 1550. 'A bargain made with the Foulcare [the Fuggers] for about 60,000*l.*, that in May and August should be payed for the defraying of it. (1) That the Foulcare should be put off for 10 in the 100. (2) That I should buy 12,000 Marks weight, at 6*s.* the ounce, to be delivered at Antwerp, and so conveyed over. (3) I should pay 100,000 Crowns for a very fair Jewel of his, four Rubies marvelous big, one Orient and great Diamond, and one great Pearl.'

And again:

29th February 1551. 'Paiment was made of 63500*l.* Flemish to the Foulcare, all saving 6000*l.* which he borrowed in French Crowns by Sir Philip Hobbey.' His allusion to the Fuggers as Foul-care is not without a certain exquisite appropriateness.

### COLLARS

It is an interesting point that no sovereign of the House of Tudor was painted showing the Collar of the Order of the Garter.[1] Queen Mary was spared the embarrassment experienced by a much later Queen-Regnant

[1] If one is in existence the author would be glad to know of it.

because she wedded shortly after she ascended the throne. As King Philip
was joint sovereign, it was ordained that he had the right to wear the full
Insignia as Sovereign of the Order, so that it was not essential for the Queen
to do so.[1]

The collar of four petalled roses and rectangular links, worn by Edward VI
in Fig. 536, is not that of the Order of the Garter and, it should be noticed, it
carries the pendent Lesser George.

In the same drawing is seen a new mode, copied from abroad, of suspending
a jewelled ornament like a tassel over the quill of the feather in the bonet.
This is seen also in Plate XIX. Whether these new ornaments were native
made or not, it is a fact that from this time onwards new kinds of jewellery
were produced in England.

## PENDANTS

The decoration of pendants and pectoral ornaments consisted, as previously,
mainly of enamel; sometimes they were entirely without jewels, in which case
jewels were introduced into the frame. The pendant, with part of the chain
by which it is suspended, worn by the King in Plate XIX is reproduced in
Fig. 561. It is quite small,
not more than three inches in
length; the ruby, enclosed in
an acanthus leaf of gold, supports a 'proof' set in a coronet,
and from the pendant hangs a
pearl. The ornaments which
make up the chain are of gold
studded with pearls, and in
the centres of the connecting
chains are single ball-shaped
motifs of goldsmith's work.

Plate XX shows how lavishly
King Edward spread emeralds
set in beautiful gold mounts
over his whole costume of black
satin braided with gold. There
was an idea prevailing until
quite recently in the minds of

Fig. 561.
Pendant of Edward VI

Fig. 562.
Pendant of Henry II

most people that the Court of this godly young King of the Reformed Faith
was devoid of Tudor magnificence, but, as stated earlier, portraits of both
men and women and inventories of the period prove the contrary.

The two drawings of Henry II of France (Figs. 489 and 539) show some
articles of jewellery worth noticing. The pendant hung from the collar
is typically Franco-Italian in design. The cartouche framing has a grotesque

[1] See vol. vi, p. 99.

head at the top and a smaller one at the bottom, and encloses a figure of St. Michael in enamel (Fig. 562). The collar is crescent-shaped, and composed of pearls set close together like corn on the cob, bound with bands of gold, and suspended round the neck by linked golden balls. In Fig. 539 the neck-chain is entirely of filigree gold balls, and is wound twice round the neck, hanging half-way down the front of the doublet. The *upper* side of the bonet brim is now besprinkled with tiny flower-shaped gold ornaments, which are repeated in groups of three on the under-side of the crown.

The *enseigne* continued to hold its place in bonet or hat in England because it was the mode in France, where, according to an inventory of Henry II, Cellini made most of the jewellery worn by this monarch. Below are given some items as an example of the elaborate nature of such headgear ornaments:

Fig. 563. Sword of Edward VI

'A golden enseigne, representing several figures, garnished all around with small rose-diamonds; an enseigne of gold, the ground of lapis lazuli, the figure representing a Lucretia; an enseigne with a gold setting, the figure being a Ceres on an agate, the body of silver, the dress of gold; an enseigne of a David and a Goliath, the head, arms, and legs of agate.'

Jewels were extensively introduced into the decoration of the sword, especially on the handle. Fig. 563 is a fair specimen, taken from the drawing of Edward VI referred to under Fig. 536. The design is carried out in gold and jewels, the grip and scabbard having a background of velvet. At the side is shown one of the hooks by which the waist and sword belts are fastened.

The jewellery worn by Royal and noble ladies was as splendid as that of the previous reign.

The drawing of Lady Jane Grey (Fig. 515) shows her dressed in a sumptuous manner, and with jewels which can compare with those worn by the ladies of Henry VIII's Court. In Plate XXIV her upper abillement is of pearls and diamonds. Both Figs. 515 and 541 show a pendant of similar design to that in 463. She wears a girdle of engraved gold beads, and many jewels round her neck and on her French hood. In Figs. 544 and 545 we see the type of pendant so familiar in the portraits of Queen Mary. From early days, Princess and Queen, she was fond of beautiful jewels, and had a large number, among them 'The Three Brothers,' inherited from her father. The history of this jewel up to this date is obtained from the Latin work of Peter

Lambeck,[1] a grandson of Johann Jacob Fugger, Count Kirchberg (1516–75). Lambeck used as his authority the written description of it made about 1555 by his grandfather. In the Count's description he expresses the pious hope that 'The Three Brothers' might 'by the will of Providence' return into the possession of the House of Austria through the marriage of Queen Mary with Philip of Spain. However, the Count's desire was not realized.

Before his marriage, that is early in 1554, Prince Philip sent the Queen, by the Marqués de las Navas, a present of some wonderful jewels, including a remarkable diamond. This is described as ' a great table diamond mounted in a superb gold setting, and valued at 50,000 ducats; a necklace of eighteen brilliants worth 32,000 ducats; a great diamond, with a *fine pearl* pendant from it, worth 25,000 ducats, and other jewels, pearls, diamonds, emeralds, and rubies of inestimable value, for the Queen and her ladies' (19th June 1554).

The 'fine pearl' has an interesting history which is worth relating here. It was found by a slave in the Pearl Islands in 1513. Vasco Nuñez de Balboa (1475–1517), the discoverer of the Pacific Ocean, annexed this great pear-shaped pearl, and in return gave the slave his freedom. Having fallen out of favour with his sovereign, Ferdinand V, Balboa endeavoured to propitiate the King by sending this pearl amongst other presents. Its beauty was at

Fig. 564.
Pendant worn by
Queen Mary

once recognized, and the pearl became one of the most prized of the Spanish crown jewels. After Ferdinand's death it came into the possession of the Emperor Charles V, who handed it over to his son Philip, and the portrait of Queen Mary (Plate XXV), which hung in the Prado, shows her wearing this pearl and pendant. At the Queen's death the pearl was returned to Spain, where it remained for two hundred and fifty years.[2] Fig. 564 is a drawing of this historic jewel. The pendant of gold is set with a table

---

[1] Peter Lambeck was born in Hamburg in 1628 and died in 1680 in Vienna, where he had been librarian to the Emperor. During this time he made a comprehensive catalogue of a number of documents in the Imperial archives. This was published in 1669. From the same source comes the description of Charles le Téméraire's famous ceremonial hat shown in Plate XVIII F. Details are given on p. 121.

[2] Its subsequent history is of even greater interest, and at a later date this celebrated pearl received the name of 'La Pelegrina'—the Wanderer: it was worn by all the queens-consort until 1808, when Napoleon took Spain and placed his brother Joseph on the throne. When the latter fled, he took La Pelegrina with him amongst other treasures, and at his death left it to his nephew, Prince Charles Louis Napoleon, afterward Napoleon III. Being in somewhat distressed circumstances while in exile in England, Prince Napoleon took La Pelegrina to the 2nd Marquess of Abercorn and asked his advice about a purchaser. Without any hesitation, and without asking the price required, he wrote a cheque for a sum which has not been divulged. The pearl had always been set in a socket, and being very heavy frequently fell from its setting. Twice the Duchess lost this peerless pearl: once at a drawing-room at Buckingham Palace, where three hours later it was recovered riding upon a lady's velvet court train, and again at Windsor, much to the consternation of Queen Victoria *and* the Duchess, where, after three weeks, it was found in the squabbing of a sofa. The second Duke had it bored to make it more secure, but this impaired its value. However, succeeding duchesses have enjoyed its possession, and the last the author heard of it was in March 1931 when it was seen worn by the Duchess of Abercorn.

Fig. 565.
Portion of
Girdle

diamond, surrounded by scrolls in goldsmith's work and flanked by satyrs in white enamel; it is hung from a smaller diamond set in gold.

The girdle (Fig. 565) in the same portrait is of a beautiful design of sapphires in gold mounts alternating with leafy scrolls and pairs of pearls. At the end hangs a circular reliquary of gold (Fig. 566). The ground-work is dark enamel, and the gold cross of sapphires and diamonds has figures in white enamel seated between the limbs. The hinge and clasp for opening it can be seen in the drawing. The Queen's jeweller was named Robert Raynes.

When Philip came to England he brought 'a chest upholdered with red velvet six spans long, two spans high and three spans broad . . . filled with precious stones and other regal gold finery, jewels and neckchains.'

Another pearl, a beautiful white Indian and a perfect sphere in shape, twenty-eight carats in weight, is in the Museum of Zosima, Moscow. This is also known as 'La Pellegrina.'

The drawing (Fig. 525) shows Catherine de' Medici wearing a large pectoral cross set with large sapphires, with round and peardrop pearls hanging from its limbs. To this is attached a chain, composed of clusters of pearls something like large mulberries alternating with sapphires in gold mounts. The chain is draped over the shoulders in the approved manner. Round the throat is a small carcanet of rows of pearls with sapphires in gold mounts at intervals; pear-shaped pearls hang from the sap-

Fig. 566. Reliquary

Fig. 567. Reliquary

phires. The girdle, and the cruciform ornament hanging from it, are likewise in sapphires and pearls. The dress is covered with a close trellis-work of pearls: Catherine had an insatiable mania for pearls of great price—one wonders if the thousands used on her dress were of this kind.

The carcanet worn by Catherine in Fig. 543 has jewels set in rose mounts linked by what appear to be a D and a D reversed, joined together. This is the monogram of Diane de Poitiers. It is seen again on her stomacher, which gives the impression that this lady friend of the King was very much esteemed by the Queen.

A handsome carcanet is worn by the French lady (Fig. 550), and another by Queen Jeanne (Fig. 547), with a pendant in the form of the head and shoulders of a woman in enamels holding a pear-pearl. The lace of pearls round the shoulders is looped up on the front of the bodice, which clearly shows this recently introduced fashion. The jewels on the headdress are lozenge shape, with pearls on the sides alternating with circular stones in goldsmith's work, all set close together on a band of gold—a billement.

Mary Stuart's pendant and lace of pearls should be noticed, Fig. 548.

Fig. 567 shows a rather unusual cruciform *reliquary* displaying the five wounds of Our Lord. The Heart, a ruby surrounded by a Crown of Thorns in white enamel and gold, covers some small but precious relic, most likely a particle of the Blood of Our Lord, and is surmounted by a scroll inscribed 'I.N.R.I.' The wounded Hands and Feet are in white and red enamel and the cross is of gold with guttée de sang in red enamel. Pearls are set in the four angles, and a larger one hangs from the base.

The revival of Catholicism under Queen Mary may have brought such *objets de piété* again into favour; the actual example comes from a portrait by Holbein, and may very well be of his own design.

## RINGS

Edward VI refers to one of his finger rings in his *Journal* as follows: 'Monsieur le Mareschal dined with me. After dinner saw the strength of the English Archers. After he had so done, at his departure I gave him a Diamond from my finger, worth, by estimation, 150*l.*, both for Pains, and also for my Memory' (26th July 1550).

When the Venetian Ambassador saw Queen Mary in 1554, she was wearing two rings which attracted his attention. 'On her finger the Queen has two rings, with which she was espoused twice, first on her accession when she was crowned and confirmed the Treaty with France, and secondly when she became the wife of the present King of Spain.' During this period the wedding ring was changed from the right hand to the third finger of the left.

## GUILDS AND TRADE *(continued from p. 374)*

The governorship of the Merchant Adventurers was, in 1553, under Sebastian Cabot, and trade with rediscovered Muscovy began that year through the energies of Richard Chancellor, who was received at Moscow in a very friendly manner by the Tsar Ivan IV (1530–84) known as 'the Terrible.' The Tsar, eager for the 'search of new trades and countries,' wrote to Edward VI declaring that he was 'willing that you send unto us ships and vessels. And if you send one of your Majesties Council to treat with us, whereby your merchants may with all kinds of wares, and where they will, make their markets, they shall have their free mart with all liberties through my whole dominions, to come and go at their pleasure.'

This letter was received by Queen Mary on Chancellor's return in 1554, and commerce with Russia began under favourable conditions. This same year the Russia Company received its first charter, and two years later the first ambassador from the Tsar was honourably received in England. This agreement was not at all approved of by the merchants of the Hanseatic League, who were already established at Novgorod, 'the chiefest mart in all Muscovy,' but who were not held in very high esteem by the Russians.

## WEAVING, COLOURS

During the short reign of Edward VI an Act was passed for preventing frauds in the woollen manufacture in England, wherein was set forth that 'some for lack of knowledge and experience, and some of extreame covetousnes do daylie more and more studdye rather to make monye then to make good clothes,' and many restrictions were made.

According to another Act of the same reign, English dyers were limited in the variety of colours to the following: scarlet, red, crimson, murrey, pink, brown, blue, black, green, yellow, orange, tawny, russet, marble grey, sad new colour (a dark tone), azure, watchet (light blue), sheep's colour, motley, and iron grey.

The general reader may have the impression that the colours used for costume in the past were crude, but if he will turn to p. 386, and read and digest the quantities of shades of colour used in the weaving of tapestry, he will realize that the art of the dyer, if not in England, certainly in foreign lands, had reached an exceedingly high standard. If numerous shades, delicate tints, subtle hues and gradations of tone could be dyed for the use of tapestries, they must also have been used in dyeing velvets, satins, silks, and cloths.

## PATTERNS

Nothing new in patterns or designs is noticeable during this short period, except that known as the arabesque. This is to be seen on the underskirts worn by the lady (Plate XVI), and Queen Mary (Plate XXVI).

(*Continued on p. 787*)

## VEHICLES (*continued from p. 377*)

### *Coach, Char*

By Act of Parliament, 1555, two surveyors of roads were appointed in each parish to repair and maintain in good order the most important highways of England. Their energies (or lack of them) could only have been crowned with a minimum amount of success, for roads in general continued in a very bad state throughout the sixteenth century.

The origin of the word 'coach' is not absolutely certain. One authority suggests that the French first applied the word 'coche' to the char; others that it is derived from the town of Kocs in Hungary where coaches were first made. Charles VII of France received a coche from Hungary as a present in 1457. However, the name means a conveyance with a roof forming part of the frame of the body. The Queen of Francis I, Diane de Poitiers, and a corpulent nobleman, René de Laval, were the only people who then owned 'coches' in France.

The first Englishman to be called a coachbuilder was one Walter Rippon, who is said to have built the first coach in England for the Earl of Rutland in 1555, but what this was like is uncertain. He also built one for Queen Mary in 1556. A few particulars of Queen Mary's coach are given on p. 439.

There is extant a letter of the privy seal to the clerk of the Queen's stables, dated 1557, which gives some particulars relating to a char or wagon. This is inserted as it may interest the practical mind:

'By the Queen
'Marye the Queen,
'We will and commaunde you forthwithe uppon the sight hereof ye deliuer or cause to be deliuered to our trustie and well beloved servaunte Edmonde Standen Clarke of our Stable, one Wagon of tymbre work for Ladies and Gentlewomen of our Prevye Chamber with wheeles and axeltrees, stakes, nayles, clouts, and all maner of work thertoo apperteyninge; fine red cloths to kever and line the same wagon, fringed with redde sylke and lyned with redde buckeram paynted with redde colours; collars, drawghts of red lether, hamer clothes with our arms and badges in our colours; and all other things apperteininge unto the same Wagon.

'xxviiiᵗʰ daye of Aprill in the Thirde and fourthe Years of our Reign.'

A 'charriot'[1] or decorated wagon, such as has just been described, is illustrated in the book of drawings referred to on p. 485, and is reproduced in Fig. 568. Although the book dates 1559, the design of the three charriots shown is as old as the early days of the Tudors. All three are unoccupied, but were for the use of maids of honour or ladies-in-waiting who followed the Royal litter in the coronation procession of Queen Elizabeth. The ladies

---

[1] This spelling is used by the official of the College of Arms, who describes the figures in the procession of which he was an eye-witness.

themselves ride behind these charriots on palfreys, sitting side-saddle with their legs at right angles to the animals' bodies with their feet on planks. Obviously it was considered more dignified to appear on horseback than in a carriage, so that the ladies in question would ride in the charriot during a journey from one town to another, and transfer to their palfreys for the state entry. On this occasion, the presence of the empty charriots is purely formal.

Fig. 568. A 'Charriot'

The canopy of some rich material is supported by ornamental columns, which in the case of the front charriot have plumes at the top. The original pen-and-ink drawing is not coloured, but quite possibly the frame-work was entirely covered with gold, and lined inside with some colour, or it may have been decorated as set forth in the above letter, which possibly describes this very charriot.

Each vehicle is drawn by six horses, tandem-wise; the teams have no drivers, but footmen walk at the sides. The shaft horse of each is saddled, as shown in Fig. 568; the others have a saddle or hammer-cloths only. The leading horse alone carries plumes on his head.

(Continued on p. 796)

# CHAPTER IV

## THE REIGN OF QUEEN ELIZABETH

### 1558—1603

# CONTEMPORARY SOVEREIGNS

| | ENGLAND | SCOTLAND | FRANCE | GERMANY | SPAIN | SWEDEN | DENMARK |
|---|---|---|---|---|---|---|---|
| 1558 | Elizabeth | Mary | Henry II | Ferdinand I | Philip II | Gustavas Vasa | Christian III |
| 1559 | | | →Francis II 1559–60 Mary Stuart | | | | →Frederick II 1559–88 Sophia of Mecklenburg |
| 1560 | | | →Charles IX 1560–74 Elizabeth of Austria | | | →Eric XIV 1560, deposed 1568 Karren Mannsdatter | |
| 1564 | | | | →Maximilian II 1564–76 Maria of Austria | | | |
| 1567 | | →James VI 1567–1625 Anne of Denmark | | | | | |
| 1568 | | | | | | →John III 1568–92 1. Catherine of Poland 2. Guinilla Bulk | |
| 1574 | | | →Henry III 1574–89 Louise de Vaudemont | | | | |
| 1576 | | | | →Rudolph I 1576–1612 | | | |
| 1588 | | | | | | | →Christian IV 1588–1648 Anne Catherine of Brandenburg |
| 1589 | | | →Henry IV 1589–1610 1. Marguerite de Valois 2. Marie de' Medici | | | | |
| 1592 | | | | | | →Sigismund of Poland | |
| 1598 | | | | | →Philip III 1598–1621 Margaret of Austria | | |

1558. Accession of Elizabeth and the Reformation Settlement in England and Scotland.

1559. Peace between England, France, and Spain, at Congress of Cateau-Cambrésis.

The Third Act of Uniformity restores the second Prayer Book, and another Act of Supremacy severs the connection with Rome.

1560(?). Robert Greene born. 'An author of plays and penner of love pamphlets.' Died 1592.

1562. Religious wars in France, lasting until 1598.

First religious war in France. The Huguenots.

Second religious war followed in 1567–8, and a third in 1569–70.

1563. Sir Robert Naunton born at Alderton, Suffolk. Educated at Trinity College, Cambridge. Author of *Fragmenta Regalia*, Secretary of State to James I. Died 1635.

1564. Christopher Marlowe born. Poet and dramatist. Died 1593.

William Shakespeare born at Stratford-on-Avon. Died 1616.

Queen Elizabeth visits Cambridge, and witnesses three plays given by the students in King's College Chapel.

1567. The Duke of Alba sent to quell the insurrection in Flanders. Established the 'Bloody Council' 1568.

1568. The persecutions of the Protestants in the Netherlands under the Duke of Alba (1567–73) drove many refugees into England.

1570. Queen Elizabeth excommunicated by Pope Pius V.

Henry Clifford born. Writer in service of Lady Jane Dormer who was born in 1538.

Richard Tarlton (born at Condover, Salop), had made a reputation as a comic actor by 1570. One of Queen Elizabeth's actor-servants, with whom he remained until his death. He is credited with the power of diverting the Queen when her mood was least amiable. Died 1588.

1571. The Ridolfi Plot discovered, and execution of the Duke of Norfolk in 1572.

1572. Peaceful times for England, until 1577.

An alliance formed between England and France. Philip II schemes to restore Mary Queen of Scots.

Massacre of St. Bartholomew, 24th August.

1573. Inigo Jones born in London. Architect. Studied in Italy. Returned to England in 1605. Designed many settings and costumes for the Court masques of James I. Died 1652.

Ben Jonson born. Poet and dramatist. Poet Laureate 1619. Died 1637.

1574. Patent granted to James Burbage authorizing the Earl of Leicester's players. Date of birth unknown: actor, and first builder of theatres in England—Shoreditch and Blackfriars. Died 1597.

His son, Richard, born 1562, also an actor of repute, built the Globe Theatre, Southwark, 1599. Died 1619.

1576. Formation of the Holy League for the defence of the Holy Catholic Church in France.

*Commedia dell' arte* first given in England at Kenilworth.

1577. Thomas Coryate born at Odcombe, Somersetshire. A great traveller and author of *Coryats Crudities*. Died 1617.

Francis Drake's voyage round the world began; returned in 1580.

Raphael Holinshed's *Chronicles* published. Born about the beginning of the sixteenth century, wrote the *Chronicles of England, Scotland, and Ireland*, which furnished Shakespeare with materials for his historical plays. Died about 1580.

1579. John Fletcher, poet and dramatist, born. Died 1625.

1580. The Jesuits come to England.

John Taylor born in Gloucester, who later styled himself 'The King's Majesty's Water Poet.'

1582. Pope Gregory XIII (1572–85) reformed the calendar. Adopted by Italy, Spain, and Portugal immediately; France and the Catholic parts of Switzerland, Germany, and the Netherlands soon followed. Not used in England until 1752.

1583. The Throckmorton conspiracy.

*The Anatomie of Abuses* by Philip Stubbes published.

Sir Humphrey Gilbert, the pioneer of English colonization, endeavoured to establish a settlement in Newfoundland.

1584. Francis Beaumont, poet and dramatist, born. Died 1616.

1585. Sack of Antwerp by the Duke of Parma; many Flemings sought refuge in England. More craftsmen arrived.

Sir Walter Raleigh and Sir Richard Grenville settled Virginia.

1586. The Babington conspiracy.

Expedition under the Earl of Leicester to the Netherlands to assist the Dutch. Battle of Zutphen. Death of Sir Philip Sidney (born 1554).

1587. 'The Tragedy of Fotheringay.'

1588. The Armada, sent to invade England, shattered in the English Channel and destroyed by a gale in the North Sea and Atlantic. Death of the Earl of Leicester.

1592. *Henry VI* written by William Shakespeare. There is no authentic proof which definitely shows in what order his plays were written or produced.

1596. The Cadiz expedition.

1598. Edict of Nantes: Henry IV of France granted perfect toleration to all Protestants.

*Love's Labour's Lost* published. The first play with Shakespeare's name attached, 'may reasonably be assigned priority in point of time of all Shakespeare's dramatic productions.'

1601. Rebellion and execution of the Earl of Essex.

1603. Death of Queen Elizabeth. Accession of James VI of Scotland as James I of England.

# THE ARTS, 1558–1603

SCULPTURE, MONUMENTAL EFFIGIES (*continued from p. 385*)

WITH the influx of Protestant refugees from the Low Countries came architects and sculptors who had achieved a reputation throughout the Continent as tomb designers.   All the same, the Gothic touch in their work executed in this country was not entirely eliminated.   Figures are now found in reclining positions, lying on one hip with the head resting on hand and elbow.   Rush matting now covers the table tomb, being rolled up to form a pillow when the figure is recumbent.

Noble ladies, and sometimes their husbands, when lying on their backs, often have one corner of the mantle arranged in graceful drapery across the lower part of the body.

Kneeling figures make their appearance, usually with a faldstool in front of them, or, if there are two figures—husband and wife—they face each other with the stool between them: their prodigious family is ranged behind them, the boys after their father, the girls after their mother.   Or the family might be arranged in rows below their parents, still maintaining their order of precedence.

Into the decoration of the altar tomb, which is of no special interest to us except for its weepers and heraldic devices, are introduced, during the latter part of the century, various coloured marbles.

Decadence in the treatment of portrait sculpture in effigies is noticeable at the end of the century, in such points as globular eyeballs, receding chins, elbows stiffly bent, and legs weak-kneed and long.   Another blemish, useful as a detail of identification of the period: towards the end of the century the alabaster used for the figures is often discoloured by red veins.

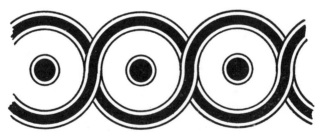

Fig. 569. Guilloche Ornament

MEMORIAL BRASSES (*continued from p. 385*)

Many more brasses were laid down during Queen Elizabeth's reign, and there was a decided improvement, both in technique and in the style of engraving employed.

During the early years of this reign, attempts were made to produce at home the necessary supplies for the growing trade in material for memorial brasses;

472

and, for the first time, plates of brass—'latten' or 'laton'—were manufactured in England. A 'copper and brasse myll near Thistleworth' (or Isleworth) is mentioned in a description of Middlesex at this time. The earliest English-made laton was inferior in quality to the imported material; it was thinner, and consequently wore out quicker by constant traffic.

Mural brasses now came into fashion. They were usually rectangular in shape; simple in style in the early examples, although by degrees the backgrounds of the figures were filled in with classical architectural details and heraldic designs.

Brasses executed during this reign often depicted the deceased kneeling at a prie-dieu or litany stool, which was sometimes covered with drapery. Also, a man and his wife were sometimes shown facing each other, and kneeling at such stools, and accompanied by representations of their family—the sons and daughters grouped on either side according to sex, behind or beneath their parents.

Inscriptions were engraved in English or Latin, with Roman or Gothic lettering.

### TAPESTRY (*continued from p. 386*)

The Renaissance period in tapestry continues during this reign, but the year 1570 marks the date of the commencement of its subdivision known as 'Late Renaissance.'

The figures representing gods and goddesses, Biblical characters, Classic heroes and heroines, and early historical personages which are found in tapestries of the second half of the sixteenth century, are nearly always garbed in costume of a fanciful nature. This being so, they are useless for the study of period costume. They do suggest, however, the type of dress worn in stage plays, disguisings, and masques of the sixteenth century, and represent almost the first intentional use of what we term to-day 'fancy dress.'

The skill of the Flemish weavers held first place among tapissers all through the sixteenth century, and Flanders continued to be the centre of manufacture until the troublous times of the Spanish oppression under the Duke of Alba. After this period many Flemish tapissers sought their fortunes in foreign countries. Many masterpieces of the tapisser's art decorated the walls of the English aristocracy. At Chawton Manor, the home of the Lewkenor family, there hung some tapestries made in 1564.

Robert Dudley, Earl of Leicester, has left some panels at Drayton House, Northamptonshire, and there were many beautiful pieces hung upon the walls of Kenilworth previous to the visit of Queen Elizabeth in 1575. (The earl's expenses incurred on that memorable occasion amounted to £60,000.)

William Cecil, Lord Burleigh, acquired much fine tapestry, which ultimately ornamented Hatfield House, though this was not actually completed until the early years of the seventeenth century.

Queen Elizabeth was not a monarch to be outdone by her subjects, or even by contemporary sovereigns. She possessed many beautiful examples of tapestry weaving, and we are told that the apartments of the Royal palaces shone with tapestries of gold, silver, and silk of different colours. Her private chapel at Hampton Court was hung with rich tapestries. In her bedchamber she had some very fine pieces, and many of the rooms in Hampton Court were adorned with tapestry of gold, silver, and velvet, some representing historical events. In other rooms oriental subjects were portrayed, and special mention is made of tapestry depicting Turkish and American scenes, 'all extremely natural.' 'In one chamber are several excessively rich tapestries which are hung up when the Queen gives audience to foreign ambassadors.'

A visitor to this country writing in 1589 mentions tapestry of silver cloth, on which various animals were embroidered in gold. 'This tapestry is suspended on the wall behind the Queen.' The presence chamber at Greenwich where 'she generally resides, particularly in summer, for the delightfulness of its situation' was hung with rich tapestry; and, as late as 1598, the floor, 'after the English fashion,' was strewed with rushes.

### English Tapestry

Practically all tapestries used in England, including those enumerated in the various household and wardrobe accounts of Queen Elizabeth, and of the nobility, were woven in the Netherlands.

The first tapestry-weaving factory was established in England as a result of the great interest in the art taken by a Warwickshire gentleman, William Sheldon. He sent a certain Richard Hyckes, of Barcheston, to the Netherlands in order to study the craft, and, on Hyckes's return to England, looms were set up at Barcheston and at Sheldon's country seat at Western, about the year 1558.[1] Some tapestries were woven at these places, but there is to-day no evidence of their existence.

In the year 1567 some Flemish weavers settled in Canterbury, Maidstone, Sandwich, Norwich, and Colchester. Two Dutch arras-weavers followed in 1570, and took up their abode in York. The amount of work turned out by these tapissers during the sixteenth century is unknown, neither does any undoubted specimen of their work exist to-day.

### French Tapestries

Tapestry produced in France during this time does not compare with the Flemish, although Francis I and Henry II made great efforts to establish a factory at Fontainebleau. Whatever success this factory achieved, the ultra-discriminating Catherine de' Medici did not deign to place an order with a firm in her adopted country, or even in her native land, but commissioned the tapissers of Brussels.

---

[1] A hundred years later, this factory became famous for its tapestries representing maps of the English counties.

The set she requisitioned took five years to complete, and was woven to commemorate the reception of the Polish Ambassadors at the Tuileries in 1573 and the departure of Henry, Duc d'Anjou, to assume the crown of Poland. These tapestries, finished by 1580, are now in the Museum of Florence, and are most useful for the study of French costume and other details of the Court of Charles IX (1560–74) and Henry III (1574–89).

## Italian Tapestries

Tapestry was made in Italy about the middle of the fifteenth century, but it is not of any appreciable importance.

About 1536, two Flemings, the brothers Hans and Nicolas Karcher, emigrated to Italy and were employed at a tapestry factory at Ferrara, presumably to raise the prestige of the business.

In 1546, a tapestry factory was established at Florence by Cosimo I, later Grand Duke of Tuscany, and in this year Nicolas Karcher left his brother in Ferrara to supervise it. He was joined in 1553 by a tapisser named Stoadamus, a native of Bruges, who designed cartoons and supervised the weaving. His work, however, was typically Flemish, characterized by burly Flemings of the middle and lower orders in *Italian* dress engaged in various pursuits, such as hunting, husbandry, etc.

This factory developed into what was known as the 'Arazzeria Medicae'; Jean van Roost was another Flemish tapisser in the firm.

Angelo Bronzino (1502–72) and afterwards Salviati, Italian artists, became designers of cartoons in this establishment which flourished until Cosimo's death in 1574.[1]

## ILLUMINATED MANUSCRIPTS (continued from p. 148)

Some of the Illum. MSS. produced in the reign of Elizabeth are of first-rate workmanship, and in the early part followed the traditional style. For instance, the miniature of the Queen at prayer, mentioned on p. 493, in the library at Lambeth, is a very beautiful and finished painting.

Later Illum MSS. lose the decorative treatment which was the great charm of those of earlier times; the figures now become simply water-colour drawings, such as were in vogue until the beginning of the twentieth century.

Documents still retained the method of showing a portrait in the initial letter, as in earlier works. There are many showing Queen Mary, some alone and some with Philip of Spain, and many more of Queen Elizabeth.

Later, the manuscript artist turned his attention to painting portraits on a small scale. Now that the printing press was in general use the demand for Illum. MSS. became less and less until the end of the century, when it may be said that the art of the manuscript writer and illuminator had almost completely died out.

[1] After this date its fame gradually diminished, and can be said to have ended when the House de' Medici became extinct in 1737. Many specimens of these Medici tapestries are to be seen to-day in the Royal collection at Florence.

PORTRAITS AND PAINTERS (*continued from p. 388*)

During the reign of Queen Elizabeth portrait painting became more general, as evidenced by the number of portraits of all kinds still extant.

FRANÇOIS CLOUET (or JANET) held the office of painter to the Court of France, 1541–72, and his works depict very accurately the French modes of his period.

FRANS POURBUS, son of Pieter Pourbus, was born at Bruges in 1545, and died at Antwerp in 1581. His son FRANS POURBUS II, born at Antwerp in 1569, was an eminent portrait painter who spent the best part of his life in portraying crowned heads. In 1610 he became painter at the French Court. He died in Paris in 1622.

NICHOLAS HILLIARD, born at Exeter in 1537, son of Richard Hilliard, who was High Sheriff of Exeter in 1560. Nicholas was the first Englishman to attain fame as a painter of portraits in miniature. It is not known whose pupil he was, but he says himself that he took Holbein's work as his model, though his own is very different from that of Holbein. He was also a goldsmith and jeweller. Queen Elizabeth appointed him her goldsmith, carver, and limner—'a painter in little.' He died in 1619, leaving a son, Laurence, who was also a miniature painter.

FEDERIGO ZUCCARO, an Italian born in 1542, was an eminent portrait painter who worked in England between 1574 and 1582. He died in 1609.

One of the most important portrait painters of this era, whose portraits of the nobility are numerous, is MARCUS GHEERAERTS THE YOUNGER, born at Bruges in 1561, son of Marcus Gheeraerts the Elder (born Bruges, 1525), who came to England with his father in 1568. He is also known as MARK GARRARD. His portraits can often be recognized by his habit of concealing one of the sitter's hands; evidently he found difficulty in painting these, and having laboured over one, shirked the other. He died in London in 1635–6.

PETER PAUL RUBENS, born at Siegen in Nassau 1577, son of Jan Rubens, an eminent man of law. In 1588 the family removed to Antwerp, where young Rubens received his education. He learned his craft from 1591 to 1600 under Tobias Verhaeght, Adam van Noort, and Otto van Veen. It was during this time that he received kind and appreciative support from the Archduke Albert and his wife, the Archduchess Isabella Clara Eugenia, Governess of the Netherlands.

Rubens went to Italy to study art in 1600, and to Spain in 1603.

JUAN PANTOJA DE LA CRUZ, born in Madrid in 1551, was a disciple of Sanchez Coello whom he succeeded as Court painter to Philip II. As such he painted numerous Royal portraits, some of which are mentioned in this book. 'All that he did is of admirable composition, being very definite and finished.' He died in his native city in 1610.

DON DIEGO RODRIGUEZ DE SILVA Y VELAZQUEZ, of supreme importance in the next century, was born in 1599.

EL GRECO—DOMINICO THEOTOCOPULI. Painter, architect, and sculptor. Born in Crete between 1545 and 1550. He studied first in Venice, then in Rome (1570). His first portrait, of Giulio Clovio, was painted between 1570 and 1578. In 1577 he went to Spain and settled at Toledo and became painter to Philip II from 1590. He painted thirty-two portraits besides other works. He died 7th April 1614.

Canvas was used for large portraits about this time much more generally than hitherto. Examples are the portraits of Charles IX by Clouet (Janet), 1569, at Vienna, and nearly all the works of Marcus Gheeraerts.

By the middle of Elizabeth's reign picture frames were carved and gilded, and towards the end of the century a vogue for painting them in addition came into use.

Among English *miniature painters* the two OLIVERS, father and son, were the most important. ISAAC OLIVER, born about 1566, was the son of a French refugee named Pierre Olivier, and was a pupil of Nicholas Hilliard. He died in 1617, leaving a son, PETER OLIVER, who became miniature painter to Charles I.

*Serjeant-paynters* working during the reign of Queen Elizabeth were: NICHOLAS LYZARD, who died in 1570.

GEORGE GOWER, who flourished 1575–85, was appointed to the office of serjeant-paynter to the Queen in 1584. He was granted the monopoly of making portraits of Queen Elizabeth, in oil, on boards, canvas, copper, and in woodcut.

LEONARD FRYER held the same office from 1598 to 1605.

The first Englishman who is known to have practised copperplate engraving was WILLIAM ROGERS. Plate XXXIX reproduces an example of his craft. He came into prominence about 1580 and worked until his death in 1610.

AUGUSTIN RYTHER was another engraver of repute. He was a native of Leeds, Yorkshire, and died in 1590.

CRISPIN VAN DE PASS THE ELDER, born at Armuyden about 1560, was an eminent draughtsman and engraver. There is no English print by him dated later than 1635.

CRISPIN VAN DE PASS THE YOUNGER, born at Utrecht in 1585, flourished during the first half of the seventeenth century.

In the eighteenth and nineteenth centuries any portrait of an elderly lady, painted with ruff, long stomacher, and farthingale, was inevitably labelled 'Queen Elizabeth,' quite irrespective of the lack of corroborative evidence, and frequently in the absence of any details for the identification of the period.

Many such portraits have been recognized in recent years as representing other well-known ladies; but unfortunately the false attributions are still so numerous that they have misled many students and others, and even to-day it is only too easy to be deceived into thinking one is contemplating the features of Queen Elizabeth instead of some lady of the Court, a noble lady, or a parvenu of the later part of the sixteenth century or of the reign of James I.

As early as 1563 it was found expedient to check the circulation of spurious portraits of Her Majesty, and a proclamation was issued forbidding ' . . . all paynters and gravers from drawing the picture of the Queen, till some cunning person meet therefor shall make a natural representation of Her Majesty's person, as a pattern for other persons to copy.'

In 1584 a licence grants the monopoly of making 'all maner of purtraictes and pictures of our person . . . in oyle cullers upon bourdes or canvas, or to grave the same on copper,' to 'George Gower our officer, maker, paynter . . . and we doe strictly forbydd and prohibit . . . all and every other persone or persons whatsoever, Englishmen or straingers . . . to entermeddle with the making, paynting or pryntinge . . . except only one Nichas Hilliard.'

It has been suggested that there was in the sixteenth century a factory for the reproduction of portraits of eminent people. This probably accounts for the existence of the large number of spurious portraits which is encountered to-day.

To enable the student to visualize the appearance of Queen Elizabeth at different periods, so far as she is represented by portraits and figures in this book, the following chronological list is inserted.

# SECTION I: 1558–80

## QUEEN ELIZABETH, 1549–80

'Elizabeth, Queen of England, France, and Ireland, Sovereign of the Most Noble Order of the Garter. She was the Delight of her own subjects, the Terror of Europe.' [1]

### INTRODUCTION

Queen Elizabeth is one of the best-known characters in history, so any description of her in these pages may be considered superfluous. The few remarks given here, however, may include some new details of interest to readers.

Appalling misrepresentations of 'Gloriana' have appeared frequently, upon the stage, in pageants, and at 'fancy-dress balls,' to say nothing of 'period' pictures and films—as defective in their lack of discrimination and accuracy as many of her so-called 'portraits'—sufficient, indeed, to grieve her departed spirit beyond endurance.

The recent controversy about her sex and parentage need not concern us; the odds favour a Tudor and a woman.

Elizabeth was born at Greenwich, 7th September 1533; the only child of Henry VIII and Anne Boleyn.

This Princess was named after her grandmother and her great-grandmother.

Fig. 570.
A Badge of Queen Elizabeth

There have been ten Princesses in the English Royal family bearing the name of Elizabeth. Elizabeth Tudor was the fifth, the others being:

1. Elizabeth, daughter of Edward I.
2. Elizabeth, daughter of Thomas of Brotherton.
3. Elizabeth, daughter of John of Gaunt.
4. Elizabeth, daughter of Edward IV, afterwards queen.
6. Elizabeth, daughter of James I.
7. Elizabeth, daughter of James II.
8. Elizabeth, daughter of George III.
9. Elizabeth, daughter of William IV.
10. Elizabeth, daughter of George VI.

[1] From a cartouche on an engraving of the Queen.

The following notes are intended as supplementary to those given with the various portraits of the Queen reproduced here.

### APPEARANCE

Some interesting descriptions of Elizabeth's appearance, at various times, are given below—some extracts from contemporary writings, and others by eminent historians:

1549　(16).　Frederick Chamberlin describes the picture referred to on p. 287 (Fig. 313), '. . . full rounded wide forehead, eyes full and wide, long nose, long oval face.'

Fig. 571. Queen Elizabeth, 1559.　After an engraving by Cock
(*British Museum*)

1558　(25).　Queen Elizabeth was twenty-five years old at the time of her accession. A description of her appearance at this time is as follows:

'She was of a commanding personality, her forehead was high and open, her nose aquiline, her complexion pale, and her hair a deep yellow, verging to red. Her features were good, but the length and narrowness of her face prevented her from having any just pretensions to beauty.'

1559　(26).　The accuracy of this description may be judged from the contemporary engraving dated 1559 from which Fig. 571 is made.

1564 (31). Referring to a series of portraits of about this date, Chamberlin summarizes his conclusions as follows:

'Nose long, almost straight, just a suspicion of aquiline, long face, complexion that of a dark brunette, with pale white skin, destitute of any ruddiness.'

The Scottish Ambassador of this date, Sir James Melville, tells us:

'Elizabeth had hair reder than yellow, curlit apparently of nature.' A sceptical gentleman!

1565 (32). When Elizabeth was thirty-two, an emissary from the Emperor Maximilian II, in conversation, quoted to her that the French Ambassador had 'pronounced Mary Stuart a very beautiful woman'; but Elizabeth of England retorted that she was 'superior to the Queen of Scotland.'

The remark contrasts oddly with another, made at the age of sixty-four, to another holder of the Ambassadorship of France: 'I was never beautiful, but I had the reputation of it thirty years ago.'

(Continued on p. 595)

## CHARACTER

Of her character much has been written. She possessed many faults; she was but human. She loved her England and passionately maintained its interests. She was majestic and dignified, but without the arrogance of upstarts, while her affable disposition is well known. Bishop Aylmer (tutor to Lady Jane Grey) affirms on the authority of Elizabeth's Italian tutor that she possessed in her youth two qualities, 'a singular wit and a marvellous meek stomach.'

William Thomas, Clerk of the Closet to Edward VI, who wrote in 1546, says that 'the Lady Elizabeth, which is at this time of the age of fourteen years, or thereabouts, is a very wittye and gentyll yonge lady.'

Stubbes,[1] whose virulent prejudice against sartorial magnificence predisposed him to anything but kindly criticism of so magnificent a person as the Queen, yet says: 'Yea, so affable, so lowly and humble is her Grace, as she will not disdaine to talk familiarlie to the meanest or poorest of her Grace's subjects upon special occasions.'

Elizabeth was always easy of access by her people of all classes, and would give personal attention to the complaints or petitions presented in the most informal manner to her. Her frequent promises of attention to affairs brought, however uncouthly, to her notice were always fulfilled. This kindly and good-natured accessibility won all hearts and endeared her, perhaps more than any other attribute, to her people.

[1] Author of *The Anatomie of Abuses*, 1583.

This is not the place to deal with Elizabeth's love affairs, most of which had some ulterior motive of statecraft behind them. 'She is a princess who can act any part she pleases,' said the French Ambassador, and the only men for whom she appears to have had any real regard were Leicester, Alençon, and Essex. While the matrimonial speculations of her unfortunate rival, Mary Stuart, terminated in lamentable tragedies, those of Elizabeth degenerated into farce.

As a modern schoolboy once said: 'Queen Elizabeth refused to marry anybody. She was one of the wisest queens that ever reigned.'

Although Queen Elizabeth's passion for dress is proverbial, as a young woman, and at the time she ascended the throne, her dress was quite normal. Roger Ascham, her tutor, tells us in 1549 that: 'In adornment she is elegant rather than showy.' She was then aged sixteen, and in 1557 Bishop Aylmer exhorts his pupil, the Lady Jane Grey, to emulate her kinswoman, the Lady Elizabeth, 'who goes clad in every respect as becomes a young maiden. And yet, no one is induced by the example of so illustrious a lady, and in so much gospel light, to lay aside, much less look down upon gold, jewels, and braidings of the hair.'

(Continued on p. 599)

### ACCOMPLISHMENTS

Like her father, Elizabeth was a great lover of music; in fact, a modern author [1] informs us that 'a tune on the virginals had always been more to Elizabeth's mind than a prayer.'

The envoy of the Emperor Maximilian II, writing to his sovereign in 1565, states that 'I had also seen her dancing in her apartments, some Italian dances, half Pavanne and half Galliard, and she also played very beautifully upon the clavichord [Fig. 572] and the lute [Fig. 573].'

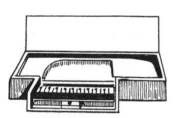

Fig. 572. Clavichord

Queen Elizabeth retained on her Royal establishments four sets of singing boys who belonged to the Cathedral of St. Paul, Westminster, St. George's Chapel, and the Household Chapel. She formed these boys of the Royal Chapel into a company of theatrical performers under the superintendence of Richard Edwards, the poet and musician. Shortly after this date she formed a second society of players, 'Children of the Revels,' and by these two companies all Lyly's plays, and many by Shakespeare and Ben Jonson, were first performed.

It is interesting to know Queen Elizabeth's favourite tune, and we have it definitely stated in a letter dated 10th July 1564 from the Spanish Ambassador. At a supper party we hear that 'the meal was attended with the usual cere-

[1] Lytton Strachey.

monies. Nothing could be more handsome than the entertainment. She [the Queen] made the band play *The Battle of Pavia*,[1] and declared it was the music that she liked best in the world.'

An amusing story was current at this time concerning Dr. Tye (*see* p. 156), a peevish and humoursome old man, especially in his latter days, who died in 1572. It shows how punctilious Elizabeth could be in the matter of music. On one occasion the doctor was playing to the Queen on the organ in the Chapel Royal. Much music was there, but it contained little to delight the ear. Elizabeth sent the verger to tell him that he played out of tune: whereupon he sent word that her ears were out of tune.

Thomas Tallis (*see* p. 156), died 1585, and William Byrd (1538–1623) were pre-eminent musicians and composers who received a special grant from Queen Elizabeth in 1575 for the monopoly of music printing.

The supreme master of Catholic Church music was Giovanni Pierluigi da Palestrina (1525–94). Many of his Masses were dedicated to Philip II.

Elizabeth was an unusually proficient linguist in both senses of the word. In her girlhood she was taught Greek, Latin, French, Italian, and Spanish. To speak six languages fluently would be a remarkable achievement for any one, and is doubly so in the case of a young woman who must have had hitherto scant opportunity for airing these accomplishments. So apt a pupil must have been a great joy to her tutors.

As to the oaths she was in the habit of using when she wished to assert herself very emphatically, they

Fig. 573. Lute

were numerous and well known, and probably caused less sensation to her contemporaries than they would have done in the nineteenth century.

As a needlewoman and embroideress Elizabeth's work was of the highest order. At an early age she made garments of excellent workmanship for her small brother.

In 1555 when Queen Mary had hopes of an heir, Elizabeth showed her sympathy in her sister's happiness by working, while a guest at Ashridge, a full set of baby garments. These were never required, and remained in the Brownlow family until a few years ago when they came under the hammer.

After she came to the throne her time was occupied with more important matters which left little for needlework. She found time, however, for a gamble at cards, as there are records of her winnings at play amounting to anything from £25 to £100.

The Queen was a good horsewoman at a time when all women could ride,

---

[1] *The Battle of Pavia* was a polyphonic vocal composition written by Clément Jannequin, and published in Paris in 1528. Curiously enough, Jannequin was in the service of Francis I, but the piece was composed to commemorate the victory of the Emperor Charles V over Francis I in 1525.

having been taught the manage by that master of the art, Claudio Corte. She was also a good hunter and spent many joyous days in her early woman-hood at this sport.   On occasion she was driven in her coach, a luxury which was fast finding favour with the aristocracy, and it is on record that once, having been driven too fast in her coach over the appalling roads, she was so knocked about that she suffered many aching pains and bruises as the result and had to retire for several days.   As the historian aptly remarks: 'No wonder that the Great Queen used her coach only when occasions of State demanded.'    (*Continued on p.* 600)

As the occupant of the throne of England is a woman and, moreover, a woman of strong personality, the costume of women is described first in this chapter.

### Queen Elizabeth's Wardrobe, 1558–80

Queen Elizabeth was so fond of her clothes that she would never part with any of them, and it is said that at her death there were three thousand dresses and 'head-attires' in her wardrobe.   It is not possible to describe them all because a complete record of them is not extant.   The following chrono-logical accounts must therefore suffice; they are based on portraits, miniatures, engravings (many of which are from portraits now unknown), and con-temporary descriptions.

With regard to the portraits, reference should be made to the paragraph on p. 477.   In the case of portraits of Elizabeth which are definitely dated, no difficulty arises; but the others have necessitated much consideration of points such as the circumstances under which they were painted, some special reference in the painting, or some item about the costume or other details.   By such methods the author has been able in most cases to allocate the period within a space of about five years.

For the costumes worn by Elizabeth as Princess see Figs. 313 and 314.

#### STATE ROBES

For her progress through London to the Tower on 28th November 1558 it is recorded that Queen Elizabeth's robes were of purple velvet and ermine. They would consist of a close-fitting bodice, with sleeves and a skirt bordered with ermine shaped like Fig. 517, and over them a mantle cut on the oval plan and lined with ermine, and a cape of the same fur. Although the fact is not mentioned, it is more than probable she wore a black velvet French hood like that in Fig. 544.

The College of Arms possesses a very interesting book of pen and ink drawings made by one of the officials of the College who was an eyewitness of the coronation procession on its way back from Westminster Abbey, 15th January 1559. Death had overtaken the Archbishop of Canterbury, and Dr. Heath, Archbishop of York, positively refused to crown Elizabeth as Supreme Head of the Church. Five Roman Catholic bishops declined for the same reason, but Dr. Owen Oglethorpe, Bishop of Carlisle, was prevailed upon at the last moment. He wore his own mitre and borrowed more splendid vestments than his own from Edmund Bonner, Bishop of London. The ceremony was almost the same as described for Queen Mary.

Part of this drawing is reproduced in Fig. 956, and shows the Queen borne in her litter. The drawing, crude though it is, accurately delineates the dress, crown, and sceptre, but *without* the Royal mantle as described below.

Two gentlemen selected from the large number in attendance on the Queen are shown in Figs. 609 and 610.

By kind permission of the Earl of Warwick the portrait of Queen Elizabeth in coronation robes, said to be by Gwillim Steetes, is reproduced in Plate XXVII. The bodice, sleeves, and full skirt are of a golden yellow silk ground, the Renaissance pattern being worked in dull silver and seed pearls. The point of the stomacher is very long and outlined by a girdle of gold set with rubies, sapphires, pearls, and diamonds. A narrow band of ermine edges the cuffs of the close sleeves, and there is, no doubt, a deep border of the same fur surrounding the hem of the skirt. A small goffered ruff edged with gold, high at the back and narrow in front, encircles the face. The State mantle is very gorgeous. It is of cloth of gold covered with embroidery in coloured silks incorporating red roses, grey-green leaves, and *silver* fleurs-de-lys and lined throughout with ermine; a deep collar or cape of the same fur is attached at the throat by long cords and tassels of gold. This cape is a substitute for the official hood, the latter being dispensed with on account of its bulk at the back of the neck; though it may be represented by a false hood lying flat on the back (*see* p. 418). The neck collar, shoulder collar or carcanet, girdle, orb, sceptre, and very beautiful arched crown worn over her flowing hair, are set with rubies, sapphires, pearls, and diamonds.

In nearly all illustrations of Elizabeth in State dress dating the first half of her reign her hair is worn parted in the middle, slightly waved on the temples, and flowing over the shoulders.

In an inventory of the Queen's wardrobe taken in 1600, her coronation robes are stated to have consisted of a dress with a long train of gold tissue lined with white sarcenet and bordered with ermine, and worn over the Spanish farthingale. The mantle was of cloth of gold tissued with gold and silver, furred and powdered with ermine. The veil of fine transparent silk was interwoven with gold threads, and had cutwork superimposed upon it.

Fig. 574. QUEEN ELIZABETH IN STATE DRESS (*see* Plate XXVIII)

PLATE XXVIII. QUEEN ELIZABETH WITH GODDESSES, 1560: Painting by Hans Eworth
Hampton Court Palace.   *By gracious permission of H.M. the King*

The border was composed of small gold buttons and tassels at intervals. The foregoing description suggests that these coronation robes might be the same as those shown in Plate XXVII.

The parliamentary robes worn by Queen Elizabeth were of the same shape and colour as worn by previous sovereigns, and are entered in one of the Royal wardrobe accounts thus:

'Item, one mantle of crimson velvet, furred throughout with powdered ermines, the mantle lace [cord] of silk and gold, with buttons and tassels to the same.

'Item, one kirtle and surcote of the same crimson velvet, the train and skirts furred with powdered ermines, the rest lined with [white] sarcenet, with a Cap of Maintenance (see vol. ii, Fig. 390) to the same, striped down-right with passamayne lace of gold, with a tassel of gold to the same furred with powdered ermines' (see Plate XLIII).

The robes of estate were the same as the above in detail but in purple velvet.

The picture painted by Hans Eworth in 1569, now at Hampton Court (Plate XXVIII), represents Queen Elizabeth greeted by Juno, Minerva, and Venus with Cupid. It is, of course, allegorical, but the costumes worn by the Queen and her two ladies-in-waiting are of the fashion of the early years of her reign. The Queen is wearing full state dress, which is reproduced in Fig. 574. The whole costume is in black velvet, with a tight-fitting long pointed bodice edged at the waist-line with small tabs and cut square at the neck. The skirt, open up the front, is edged with gold embroidery and rubies in gold mounts, the surface of the skirt being cutte in a set pattern to show silver underneath. The under-bodice, with high collar and close-fitting sleeves, and the underdress are of silver tissue covered with gold embroidery and pearls. The surcote, with a long train and short puffed sleeves, is of black velvet having a pattern in gold all over it and a gold embroidered border. A close ruff and wristlets, a ruby and gold carcanet, and a jewelled girdle complete this rich and dignified dress. The Royal Crown is worn over hairdressing as seen in the portrait (Fig. 571), and the Sceptre and Orb are carried.

The ladies-in-waiting are dressed, one in black velvet and gold, the other in scarlet velvet, and both wear French hoods.

It is interesting to note the costumes of the Goddesses Juno and Minerva, as they are excellent examples of the Elizabethan idea of the classic Greek. The coiffure of Venus is noted under Headdresses (p. 737).

Many illustrations of Queen Elizabeth in robes of state are to be found attached to statutes and documents. In all of them these robes consist of a close-fitting long stomachered bodice with close-fitting sleeves on the fore-arm; a full skirt over the Spanish farthingale; and ermine-lined mantle fastened by long cords and tassels, and having an ermine cape which represents the official hood. A close ruff and a jewelled collar, the Crown, Sceptre and Orb, complete this Royal outfit.

ELISABETH DEI GRATIA REGINA ANGLIÆ.

Fig. 575. 1559. From engraving by Cock. (*By courtesy of the British Museum*)

## OTHER COSTUMES, FULL DRESS, AND EVERYDAY DRESS

In Fig. 575 we see the new Queen ready to receive some Ambassador in private audience. Her Majesty wears a surcote of a dark-coloured damask similar in shape to that in Figs. 516 and 521, and cut as shown in diagram, Fig. 522. This garment, known as a costume à l'Espagnole, is made to be worn closed over a dress for extra warmth. It is lined throughout with fur, ermine or miniver, of which edgings show round the collar, down the front (where it is fastened with laces and aiglettes), round the hem, slits on the breast, and openings and bottom of the very short mahoitered sleeves. A narrow gold passamayne edges the openings of the garment. A small band, or ruff, of lawn is mounted on the upstanding collar of the under-dress and encircles the face. A diagram of the cut of the bodice and skirt of the dress worn underneath the surcote is given in Fig. 518. A jewelled carcanet with pendant is worn, and the French hood completes the everyday costume. This surcote, of Spanish origin, was very popular with great ladies in England and on the Continent, and it appears in varying forms and methods of decoration in many portraits of the time. The French hood is referred to on p. 741.

The costume illustrated in Plate XXIX is derived from a three-quarter-length portrait formerly at Clopton House, Stratford-on-Avon, and said to be Queen Elizabeth. Whether it is the Queen or some other lady of the period—1560–70—is immaterial; the costume depicted is that which was worn at this time by noble ladies of the realm for everyday use, in fact, such as Her Majesty would wear on ordinary occasions both indoors and out. The surcote is of black velvet, open up the front and edged with a band of ermine. The long sleeves attached to it are slightly raised upon the shoulders—the mahoitered sleeve is now going out of fashion with smartly dressed women—trimmed vertically with narrow bands of ermine with aiglettes set at intervals. A similar band edges the opening at elbow level, and these cross the hanging part. The underdress, made like that shown in Fig. 517, is of black silk or satin; the lines of the bodice being defined by narrow gold passamayne which also edges the opening of the skirt and the hem. A gold-edged escallope surrounds the pointed waist-line. The cloth of gold underskirt edged with gold embroidery is worn over the Spanish farthingale, and a gold girdle, with pomander, hangs down the front. The ruff of lawn is edged with fine lines of gold, and a carcanet of rubies, pearls, and diamonds is worn *under* the surcote encircling the neck twice and terminating with a large pendant. The French hood is worn and brown leather gloves are carried.

Fig. 576 is a drawing of the Queen as she appeared when she visited Cambridge in 1564. She stayed the night of 4th August at the house of Mr. Worthington at Haslingfield. The next afternoon, accompanied by divers ladies and gentlemen and her Gentlemen Pensioners, she set out for Cambridge, passing through Grantchester and arriving at Newnham about five o'clock. Robert Lane, Mayor of Cambridge, supported by the aldermen

Fig. 576. QUEEN ELIZABETH AS SHE APPEARED WHEN ENTERING CAMBRIDGE,
SATURDAY, 5TH AUGUST 1564

and all the burgesses, with the recorder, Robert Shute (afterwards one of the barons of the exchequer), all on horseback, met Her Majesty, a little above Newnham. Here the Mayor, according to custom, delivered the mace to the Queen together with 'a fair standing cup,' and Her Majesty returned the mace to him.

When she came to Newnham Mills she dismounted in the yard, and retired for a space into the miller's house—to titivate, we presume. After a while she remounted her horse, and entered Cambridge by Newnham Bridge. The Queen stayed at King's College, the best chambers and galleries being devoted to her use.

The drawing of Elizabeth's riding costume (Fig. 576) worn on this occasion is founded on contemporary descriptions. It was of black velvet, pounced or cutte all over in a design, and worn over an underdress of white satin. The bodice and sleeves were braided with narrow gold. Her hair was rolled off the face, the knob being enclosed in a gold network caul set with precious stones and pearls, and over it the Queen wore a flat cap of black velvet—the bonet—with gold embroidery round the brim and crown: a white ostrich-tip drooped over the left side. A touch of colour was supplied by a sky-blue silk suspending the Lesser George in enamels set with diamonds. A 'riding-rod,' or whip, might be carried, but it was not necessary as a groom would be in attendance. If one was used by the Queen, the handle would be covered with crimson velvet and studded with jewels.

The rich horse furniture of the period was of vermilion velvet embroidered and embrossed with gold.

Queen Elizabeth is following the example set by Catherine de' Medici of riding side-saddle with a pommel, although on full State occasions it was customary for the Queen to use a plank or footboard as evidenced by her seal, 1586 (see Fig. 705). Elizabeth was, like her father, a good judge of horse-flesh and her mount was a thorough-bred Arab.

The next day being Sunday, the Queen went in great state to King's College Chapel. 'Then Mr. William, Master of King's College, orator, making his three curtesies, kneeled down upon the first greece [1] of the West door.' The Queen entered during the Litany under a canopy [2] carried over her head by four Doctors of Divinity, 'and going into her travys [3] . . . and marvellously revising at the beauty of the Chappel, greatly praised it above all other in her realme.' [4]

This same Sunday evening Her Majesty witnessed a play, the *Aulularia* of Plautus, acted by certain selected persons chosen out of the colleges. On Monday at nine o'clock the play *Dido*, written by Edward Halliwell, Fellow of King's College, was presented before the Queen. Thomas Preston,

---

[1] A step.

[2] According to custom . . . 'which the footmen as their fee claimed: and it was redeemed for £3–6–8.' This canopy may be the one in the possession of the Fitzwilliam Museum.

[3] Travys, the specially erected chair of state, with dais, and dorsal, probably similar to those shown in Fig. 292.

[4] Other actual words used by Queen Elizabeth were 'O domus antiqua et religiosa.'

later Fellow of King's College and afterwards Master of Trinity Hall, played so well in this tragedy, and 'did so genteely and gracefully disporte before her' that the Queen gave him a pension of £20 a year.   On Tuesday, the 8th, the play called *Ezechias* by Nicholas Udall was performed by the King's College.

Elizabeth left Cambridge for Ely on Wednesday, 9th August, two days earlier than was anticipated.   Frankly, Her Majesty was rather bored by the innumerable Greek and Latin orations made to her.   One delivered by Mr. Dodington, a Greek professor of Trinity College, occupied 'the space of a quarter of an hour, and was considered very short.'   However, on her departure she remarked to the university professors with all her usual charm and graciousness that, if a larger provision of beer and ale had been made, she would have stayed until Friday.   We are not told if the day was wet or fine. Queen Elizabeth was habitually indifferent to the weather.   'A most extreme rain' would not prevent her mounting her horse, or ordering her coach to be ready at the appointed time.

In September 1564 the Queen in order to impress Sir James Melville—

Fig. 577

that Franco-Scot with his courtly foreign graces—wore a different dress every day, one day English, another French, and a third Italian; and was delighted when he announced that the Italian style suited her best, as it showed off her golden hair to advantage wearing a caul and bonet 'as they do in Italy.'   At Christmas in the following year, spent at Westminster Palace, Elizabeth was very richly apparelled in a gown of purple velvet, embroidered with silver very richly set with jewels.   She wore a carcanet of gold and many precious stones.

On 31st August 1566 Queen Elizabeth visited Oxford and stayed at Christ Church.   The preparations for the event were not so elaborate as at Cambridge, and the reception itself was far less imposing.   The Queen travelled 'in a rich chariot' to Wolvercote, and three miles on the Woodstock Road she was met by the heads of the houses in their gowns and hoods. The days of her stay were spent, as at Cambridge, in hearing orations and plays, or in attending the exercises of the university.

On 6th September after dinner Her Majesty mounted her horse and set out for Rycote.

A full-length portrait said to be of Queen Elizabeth is in the possession of the Earl of Buckinghamshire at Hampden House.   It has been attributed to Zuccaro, but it is more probable that Hans Eworth was the artist.   The features, especially the nose, are not those of Elizabeth; but the presence of the Royal armorial bearings, embroidered upon the dorsal, favour the likelihood of its being by Eworth's hand.   The costume dates 1565–73, and is similar in style to that shown in Fig. 579.   It is reproduced by kind permission of the Earl in Plate XXX.   The bodice, sleeves, and circular skirt, worn over the Spanish farthingale, are of deep rose velvet decorated with two bands of gold embroidery designed in two rows of leaves on a central stalk (*see* Fig. 577) having a heavy edging of gold passamayne top and bottom. The moderately mahoitered sleeves are decorated with bands of the same embroidery on a smaller scale, between which are puffs fixed with rubies in gold mounts; there are also puffs or cuttes set at an angle on the plain part of the sleeves between the groups of bands. Short sleeves mahoitered on the shoulders are now giving place to slightly tapering sleeves still padded on the shoulders and pleated or gathered into the armholes. The neck of the bodice is rounded upwards in front, and is filled in with a partlet of gauze banded with narrow gold and open at the throat; a stand-up collar supports a small gold-edged ruff.

A small detail to be noticed is that the skirt of velvet is woven or embroidered with small gold Greek crosses per saltire having tiny cuttes between them, whereas the bodice is of plain velvet embroidered.

A handsome jewelled carcanet is draped around the shoulders and suspends a square ruby and pendent pearl. A mirror in a gold frame hangs at the end of the twisted pearl girdle. The headdress consists of a front piece surrounded by two rows of pearls and a roll of rose and gold tissue, but there is no tube hanging therefrom. An exotic flower is fastened on the left side.

In the original painting the background is very ornate, the dorsal and chair being covered with elaborate embroidery, but in Plate XXX both are shown in purple velvet.

It should be noticed that the Queen grasps the knob of the chair and her forearm rests on a cushion *placed over the arms*. This is a little unusual, for the method of posing the arm in this manner was not adopted by painters until a later period and is referred to under Fig. 731.

The library at Lambeth Palace possesses a book of *Christian Prayers* printed in London in 1569. In it is a miniature of Queen Elizabeth at prayer, and she wears a dress almost identical with that shown in Plate XXX. It is of crimson velvet, the bodice and sleeves being decorated in the same manner; but the skirt is divided, by bands of gold embroidery or passamayne in which are set rubies, emeralds, and pearls, into tapering panels of gold scroll work upon crimson velvet.

A painted panel was discovered at Little Gaddesden House, Hertfordshire, depicting Lord William Howard and other gentlemen about to arrest the Princess Elizabeth at Ashridge House for suspected implication in Wyatt's rebellion, 1554. Elizabeth's costume (Fig. 578), and those of the gentlemen, date about 1570, a positive proof that the panel was painted at this date or even later. The dress in Fig. 578 is simple in shape. It consists of a tight short-waisted bodice open and turned back at the throat forming revers and lined with a contasting colour: close-fitting sleeves raised on the shoulders: and a semicircular skirt worn over the Spanish farthingale. It is made of a red material having two lines of narrow fancy braid which form horizontal stripes. A zigzag border of braid surrounds the skirt and descends the sides of the open front.  The underskirt of white is elaborately ornamented with rows of braid and embroidered motifs on alternate bands.   A small ruff attached to the top of the high collar of the under-garment closely encircles the face.   The hat is either of black velvet or blocked felt, and is of a new shape modelled on the lines of those worn by gentlemen at this time.   This type of costume was worn by the Queen, noble ladies, and gentlewomen as a smart out-of-door everyday dress, and, so it appears, when mounted.

In George Turbervile's *The Noble Arte of Venerie*, published in 1575,

Fig. 578. Queen Elizabeth, 1570

there are woodcuts of Queen Elizabeth wearing a very similar dress.   The only differences are that the bodice, rounded at the top, shows the partlet and close ruff; and that the sleeves are open up the front and tied in three places.   Although she has been riding to the hunt, her all-round skirt is distended by the Spanish farthingale.   The high hat with ostrich feathers is shown in Fig. 873.

Other illustrations in the same work show the Queen hawking and mounted, and also on foot; in each case she wears a dress almost identical in shape, but not decoration, with the portrait, No. 190, in the National Portrait Gallery (*see* Plate XXXI B).

The 'Darnley' three-quarter-length portrait of Queen Elizabeth (Plate XXXI A), now in the National Portrait Gallery, No. 2082, has been dated at 1570.   The name of the artist is uncertain.   The dress worn by the Queen consists of a close-fitting bodice with a normal waist-line edged with small tabs.   The neck is high with a stand-up collar to which the ruff, a little larger than hitherto, is fixed goffered into deep nebulée sets.   The sleeves are leg-of-mutton shape, with a small roll and puffs on the shoulders.   The same decoration is placed on the lower part of the sleeves about four inches from the wrists, and suggests cuffs.   The full all-round skirt is worn over the Spanish farthingale.   The whole dress is composed of white silk brocaded in a floral scroll design in gold.   The front of the bodice is frogged with gold passamayne intermixed with rose-coloured floss silk which is fluffed at the extremities forming tiny tassels.   Pearls and rubies set in gold encircle the waist, but there is no pendant end.   On the right side a jewel, set in a very beautiful mount composed of six human figures and scroll work in gold, is suspended by a black ferret from the waist-belt.   Two rows of pearls hang round the neck and are looped to form a circle on the right side.   A fan of

A  B

C D

PLATE XXXI. QUEEN ELIZABETH

A. The 'Darnley,' 1570.   B. and C. *c.* 1575: Portraits by unknown artists
National Portrait Gallery.   *By kind permission of the Directors*

D. The 'Pelican,' 1575: Portrait by an unknown artist
*By kind permission of E. Peter Jones, Esq.*

natural-tinted ostrich tips set in a gold mount and handle is carried in the right hand. The headdress is a network cap of jewels and pearls set at the back of the head like the ridge on the French hood: a gauze veil arranged behind as shown in Fig. 579 hangs from it.

Fig. 579 gives the outline of the garments worn by Queen Elizabeth between the years 1570 and 1580. It is photographed from a crayon drawing made in London by Zuccaro in 1575. This dress is shaped on the same lines as that shown in the 'Darnley' portrait, in fact, in a whole series of portraits, obviously painted about this time because the lines of the dress and headdress are very similar in all of them. There are very slight differences, such as the method of filling in the neck and the decorative treatment of the whole costume, but in general style all these dresses are identical. Other examples may be seen in Plate XXX, the Lambeth Palace Prayer Book, Nos. 190 and 200 in the National Portrait Gallery (Plate XXXI B and C), one of Turbervile's woodcuts, and the 'Pelican' and 'Portland' portraits. In Fig. 579 the bodice is short-waisted and the sleeves fit moderately close and are raised on the shoulders. The skirt is worn over the Spanish farthingale. The headdress shown is of special interest because a back view of it is also drawn. It is an embroidered veil, and the edge goffered where it is attached to the head. At the back the lines of the goffering suggest an escallop shell; in front a series of loops or 8's surrounds the head behind a cap or band of jewels like a coronet.

To this period—1575—must be assigned the two head-and-shoulder portraits of Queen Elizabeth in the National Portrait Gallery, London, just referred to. In the former Elizabeth wears a dress of the same shape as that shown in Fig. 579, carried out in black velvet elaborately embroidered with a leaf design in gold, cross-barred, and set with pearls. The sleeves, however, are in the older fashion as seen in Plate XXX. The skirt is open up the front showing a white satin underskirt worn over the Spanish farthingale. The Queen holds a red rose in her right hand and a white feather fan in her left.

In the second portrait, No. 200 (Plate XXXI C), the Queen wears a dress of white satin decorated with bands of gold embroidery with cuttes outlined with gold, and jewels in gold mounts between them. The sleeves are not so much raised on the shoulders and are finished round the armholes with cutte rolls. A bunch of pansies, Elizabeth's favourite flower, is held in the right hand. The Lesser George is suspended by a black riband surrounding the neck. The ruffs and headdresses in both portraits are similar to those described under Fig. 579.

In the 'Pelican' portrait (Plate XXX D) dating the same period Elizabeth is wearing a similar shaped dress in deep red velvet. The rolls over the shoulders are very pronounced, and the sleeves and partlet are embroidered with Spanish work. Two red roses are tucked into the side of the bodice, and the whole dress is much bejewelled. The pelican in enamels worn as a pendant has given its name to the portrait.

There is a drawing in the British Museum of a procession of the Knights

Fig. 579. ZUCCARO'S DRAWING OF QUEEN ELIZABETH, 1575
(*By courtesy of the British Museum*)

of the Garter, dated 1576, in which the Queen is the principal figure. As Sovereign of the Order, she wears the crimson velvet surcote over her farthingaled dress. The mantle is, according to this drawing, of white, which contradicts a former statement made in vol. ii, p. 241, to the effect that the mantle was of purple velvet. The Collar of the Order encircles the shoulders rather low down, and the hood is omitted. Neither does the Queen wear the headdress, which at this time was nothing more than a gentleman's fashionable hat (*see* Fig. 623); this remained the official headgear of the Order during the course of the sixteenth century.[1]

In place of a hat the Queen is wearing a veil arranged as described under Fig. 579. Other innovations are the large ostrich fan carried in the hand, and the omission of the hood, sword, and garter. It is curious that Elizabeth, so punctilious with regard to official ceremony and tradition, should not have dressed the part correctly. Later queens have, however, been guilty of the same offence.

The portrait in the Accademia delle Belle Arti, Siena, by Cornelius Ketel was painted in 1578 (Plate XXXII A). The dress is made on similar lines to that shown in the 'Darnley' portrait, but is of black velvet. The Queen holds a colander in her left hand and as in the 'Portland' portrait a group of courtiers is seen standing in the background; one of these is Sir Christopher Hatton.

A three-quarter portrait dating about 1579 or 1580 finds its place here. It is No. 2471 in the National Portrait Gallery, bequeathed by Sir Aston Webb (Plate XXXII B). There are other portraits very similar; one in the National Maritime Museum, another at Arbury Park. They all show the Queen in everyday dress, consisting of black velvet with a band of gold embroidery set with jewels in gold mounts down the front. In the Arbury portrait the girdle of pearls and jewels is very rich. The full sleeves in all three are of white linen heavily embroidered with black silk; a detailed drawing of the Arbury sleeve is given in Fig. 686. The circular ruff edged with cutwork is *supported* by a wide circular collar of black velvet. The veil, put on the head as described under Fig. 579, is very voluminous and is decorated with bands of cutwork. A fan of ostrich feathers in a rigid jewelled handle is seen in both the Arbury and the National Portrait Gallery portraits, though there are slight differences in the decoration. In the Maritime she holds a sceptre.

The full-length portrait of Queen Elizabeth painted by Gheeraerts and owned by the Duke of Portland was exhibited at the Queen Elizabeth Exhibition, 1933 (Plate XXXII C). On the modern label was the date 1580. The dress in this portrait is shaped like that shown in Fig. 579; it has rolls, set with jewels round the armholes of the sleeves, but at the waist there are no tabs and the dress appears to be fastened down the front of the bodice and skirt with frogs of gold set with jewels. The material of which this

---

[1] In the seventeenth century it became more elaborate, with a higher crown of black velvet pleated into the brim and surmounted by numerous white ostrich plumes, exactly like that worn by Queen Elizabeth for riding (*see* Fig. 623).

dress is made is rich white silk embroidered in colours and gold, with groups of flowers and leaves on stalks diaper-wise with a conventional design in gold. A very fine carcanet of jewels with a pendant surrounds the shoulders, and a double row of pearls is draped round the neck in the same manner as shown in the 'Darnley' portrait; except that it hangs towards the left, and a pendent jewel hangs from the waist on the right. The large circular ruff is of starched lawn edged with deep cutwork. A voluminous green mantle, bordered and covered with gold embroidery and lined with white silk, hangs from the shoulders, but without a cord fastening. The headdress is elaborate; it is in the form of a French hood and covered in pearls, surmounted by an upstanding coronet of goldsmith's work, jewels, and pearls. A fan hangs from the girdle on the left side, while gloves are carried in the left hand, a branch of myrtle in the right. The Sword of State lies at her feet accompanied by a small dog of the spaniel breed. Three courtiers stand in the background.

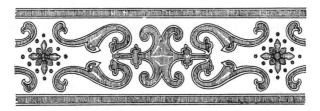

Fig. 580

### FURNITURE

The surroundings of a great personage always excite the interest of the public, and the beauty and lavishness of Queen Elizabeth's homes—Windsor, Whitehall, Greenwich, Hampton Court, etc.—were household words all over Europe. Foreigners who visited Elizabeth's Court were greatly impressed by the magnificence they beheld, and many have, fortunately, written detailed descriptions.

'I have seen,' says a German, writing home in 1559, 'several very fine summer residences that belong to her, in two of which I have been myself, and I may say that there are none in the world so richly garnished with costly furniture of silk adorned with gold, pearls, and precious stones. Then she has some twenty other houses, all of which might justly be called Royal summer residences.'

As this description was written in the first year of her reign it is clear that she inherited these numerous palaces from her father with the Crown.

The following details are taken from other written descriptions:

At Windsor the Royal apartments consisted of magnificent halls, chambers, bedchambers, and bathrooms. The banqueting hall was said to be seventy-eight yards long by thirty yards wide. The bedchambers contained the four-

A       B

C       D

PLATE XXXII. QUEEN ELIZABETH
A. The 'Siena,' 1578: Portrait by Cornelius Ketel
Accademia delle Belle Arti, Siena.  *By kind permission of the Director*
B. 1579–80: Portrait by an unknown artist.   National Portrait Gallery
*By kind permission of the Directors*
C. The 'Portland,' 1580: Portrait by Marcus Gheeraerts
Welbeck Abbey.  *By kind permission of the Duke of Portland*
D. The 'Ermine,' 1585: Portrait by Nicholas Hilliard
Hatfield House.  *By kind permission of the Marquess of Salisbury*

post beds used by Henry VII, Henry VIII, and Edward VI, all of them eleven feet square, with hangings of silks glistening with gold and silver.

Elizabeth's own bedchamber was hung with tapestry taken from a palace of the French King during the English occupation early in the fifteenth century. The bed, not so gigantic as that of her forbears, had curious coverings of embroidery, and the cushions were 'curiously wrought' by Elizabeth's own hands. A table of red and white marble occupied an important position. Two bathrooms were close at hand, so there is no reason why the glorious 'Gloriana' should be accused of having a bath *only* when her physician commanded it. These had the walls and ceiling covered with looking-glass.

Fig. 581. Draw-table

Bathrooms leading out of bedrooms began to be built in all the best houses towards the end of the sixteenth century. One for the Countess of Northumberland cost the Earl £400. He protested, and gave vent to his opinion that a bathroom 'this 15 yeare before was never miste nor wanting.'

Fig. 582. Oak Chair

Queen Elizabeth caused the Terrace Walk to be made on the north side of the castle, from which there was a pleasant view of the surrounding country. It was her favourite promenade.

Furniture in general consisted of draw-tables which had portions to draw out at both ends, with bulbous legs joined at the base by a footrail; also tables of other kinds.

The Court cupboard was also important; and coffers, as before mentioned, were common. 'Chests with drawers,' just coming into use, were composite pieces of furniture, the top being a coffer with a hinged lid as of old; the lower portion contained two or more drawers.

Seats comprised square oak chairs, with solid backs and arm-rests, on which cushions were placed, besides types of chair already described under Fig. 215, chairs of the later style as shown in Figs. 674 and 731, and innumerable stools such as that shown in Fig. 756. All these seats would be upholdered in velvet, silk, damask, or embroidery. The decoration of the wood-work consisted of elaborate carving of polished oak, and towards the end of the century marquetry was first introduced. Often the carved oak was painted with the patterns picked out in colours, the more raised motifs being gilded.

The following are some items from an inventory of furniture dated 1590.

> 'Bed steads of walnuttre and Markatre
> Chares of walnuttre and Markatre
> Stools of walnuttre and Markatre
> Fourmes of walnuttre
> Tables of walnuttre and Markatre
> Tables of marble
> Stooles of nedlewoorke cruell.'

With what joy one would have attended a sale of furniture in Tudor times when items fetched such convenient prices for small purses:

'Item two damask chaires iii low stooles of damask & two long quishions of damask priced and valued 1ˢ.'

'Item two long drawinge tables of Walnottree one folding table of wainscott and a little table of wainscott price Vˡⁱ.'

'Item two fyne merketree cupbords & two liverey cupbords price XIIIˡⁱ.'

'Item 6 wallnottree formes & 24 stooles of wallnottree price Lˢ.'

'Item 6 walnottree chaires price xxxˢ.'

'Item three other pictures vidzᵗ Quene Maries. Queene Elizabeths & Constantynes the Great. price xˢ.'

The floors of rooms in palaces, where a great deal of company was admitted, were strewn with rushes or hay, a method which continued until the end of the reign. Even in the Presence Chambers this was done. 'Only where the Queen was to come out and up to her seat were carpets laid down worked in Turkish knot.' Towards the end of the century, however, carpets were more generally used in the private apartments of Royalty and the nobility.

In the palace of Whitehall the Presence Chamber was a large lofty room with a gilded ceiling on which were painted important battle scenes. A very beautiful fireplace adorned the Council Chamber; on this the Royal Arms, supported by two lions, were cut in the stone 'as clear as crystal.'

Among the many paintings which hung upon the walls of the numerous rooms were portraits of Henry VI, Richard III, Edward IV, the Emperor Charles V, the Duke of Saxony, Katherine of Aragon, Philip of Spain—and of Zwingli and many other divines. Two of special interest were the portrait of Elizabeth at the age of sixteen, now at Windsor (a drawing of it is given in Fig. 313), and in the corridor overlooking the tilt yard 'a picture of King Edward VI, representing at first sight something quite deformed till, by looking through a small hole in the cover which is put over it, you see it in its true proportions.' This painting now hangs in the National Portrait Gallery, No. 1299.

Along the walls of the corridor leading to the River Gate were hung the armorial shields with mottoes of those knights who solicited Her Majesty's permission to take part in the tournaments. If the Queen accorded permission, the bearers of these shields presented them to her, and they made a very imposing array.

The ceiling of the Queen's bedchamber was entirely gilded, but the room had only one window. The Royal bed was ingeniously composed of woods of different colours. One sometimes sees in national museums these Tudor beds with the cornice, back, posts, etc., elaborately inlaid with all kinds of woods. The coverlids or quilts were of silk, velvet, gold, silver, and embroidery.

Elizabeth kept all her jewellery and other things of special value and sentiment in a little chest ornamented all over with pearls, and her writing table consisted of two pedestal cabinets of exquisite silversmith's work. Another was of ebony inlaid with silver, and had two boxes of silver—one for ink and the other for dust or sand. The writing board lifted up and formed the lid of a receptacle for papers, etc., and had a mirror set inside it.

In this room was 'a piece of clockwork, an Ethiop riding upon a rhinoceros, with four attendants, who all make their obeisance when it strikes the hour.'

The palace at Greenwich dates back to the reign of Edward I, and successive kings resided there occasionally until Henry V granted the manor to Thomas Beaufort, Duke of Exeter, and later to Humphrey, Duke of Gloucester. This Duke rebuilt the palace and called it 'Placentia' or a 'Manor of Pleasaunce.' He enclosed the park and erected within it a tower on the spot where the Observatory now stands, and at his death the domain reverted to the Crown. Edward IV bestowed much cost in finishing and enlarging the palace, and granted it to his Queen Elizabeth Wydeville for life. Henry VII often resided at this place, and beautified the palace by the addition of a brick front toward the water-side; Henry VIII spent much money to make Greenwich 'a pleasant, perfect, and princely palace.' During his reign it became one of the principal scenes of those festivities for which his Court was celebrated. Here Edward VI died, and Mary and Elizabeth were born, the latter spending a great deal of her time at her favourite summer residence.

In the palace we learn that the Presence Chamber overlooked the river, and here was set the usual Chair of Estate on a dais under a canopy with plumes at the corners, 'where the Queen sits in her magnificence.' It also contained a positive organ.

Most of the rooms at Greenwich were hung with tapestries wrought in gold and silver (see p. 474).

The Chapel Royal was hung with cloth of gold; the font of silver was raised three steps high, and the pulpit was covered with gold-embroidered red velvet. Almost half of the chapel was taken up by a large high altar of gold; and there, divided off from the rest, was a recess entirely of cloth of gold out of which the Queen came when she was about to receive the Sacrament.

In 1598 we get some details of Hampton Court from Paul Hentzner, a German, who, unfortunately, is not quite correct in some of his descriptions.

He writes: 'We were led into two chambers, called the Presence, or Chamber of Audience, which shone with tapestry of gold, and silver, and silk of different colours, and a small chapel, richly hung with tapestry, where the Queen performs her devotions.'    The windows are said to have been glazed with crystal.

In the Great Hall hung many portraits, those of Henry VIII, Edward VI, Charles V, Philip II, and Mary Queen of Scots, and a painting of the Battle of Pavia, being the most conspicuous.    Several musical instruments were noticed, made entirely of glass except the strings, and a great number of cushions were lying about all elaborately embroidered with gold and silver.

Fig. 583.            Fig. 584.            Fig. 585.
Tassels used on Chairs and Cushions

'All the other rooms, being very numerous, were adorned with tapestries of gold, silver, and velvet'—in short, the whole palace shone with precious metal.

In the Royal Chamber the bed 'costers' or hangings, the 'sparver' (top of tester), and the 'stranets' or curtains were of very costly silk; and in another chamber, not far distant, was a bed the tester of which was embroidered by Anne Boleyn and presented by her to Henry VIII.    Even the warming-pan was of gold garnished with small diamonds and rubies, with two ragged pearl pendants.

Many of the counterpoynts and coverlids were of rich silk or velvet, and lined with ermine.

Nonesuch Palace, a wonderful fairylike place according to contemporary prints, was begun by Henry VIII near Cheam, Surrey, but he did not live to see it finished.    Queen Mary sold it to the fourteenth Earl of Arundel, and Queen Elizabeth bought it back from the then possessor, Lord Lumley.

In an inventory made at this time is set forth a wealth of magnificent furniture of English and foreign manufacture, including some special beds.    The 'counter-poynte' of one was of velvet, embroidered with two horses and a man riding upon one of them. Another had a 'cieler' on top of the four posts, and 'tester' (back) of white Turkey silk, a counterpane of white sarcenet, the whole embroidered with popinjays. Another bed was hung with purple Nimeguen [1] silk embroidered with dolphins. The tapestries enumerated in this inventory were very numerous and of great beauty.

In this same inventory there is mention of chairs being upholdered in purple velvet fringed with purple silk; of cloth of gold having a raised pattern of crimson velvet; and some with a pattern in black velvet. One set was covered in cloth of gold with a pattern of wreaths and flowers in cloth of silver and crimson velvet.

So vast a concourse accompanied Elizabeth on the elaborate progresses which to the end of her life she insisted on making that even the long cavalcade of coaches, chariots, and waggons was sometimes insufficient. Such progresses entailed the conveyance of the whole Court and officers of the household and all their servants, and, in addition, a large staff of menials to minister to their wants. The Queen's wardrobe of personal necessities alone sometimes occupied as many as three hundred baggage waggons, and on one occasion, when she was visiting 'The Vine,' near Basingstoke, in September 1601, not only was much furniture brought from Hampton Court, but 'the willing and obedient people of the County of Southampton' brought, at two days' warning, seven score beds and the furniture (i.e. bedding) thereof —so great was their love for the Queen.

Those who wish to know more about domestic matters will find a great deal of useful information in *Elizabethan Life in Town and Country*, by M. St. Clare Byrne.

## NOBILITY—WOMEN: 1558–80

Having reviewed the current fashions as exemplified in the descriptions of Queen Elizabeth's costumes, an explanation of the details and other items is necessary.

### THE FARTHINGALE (*continued from p.* 199)

The farthingale as first described in Chapter II, p. 65, continued to be worn during the periods covered by Chapter III and this section of Chapter IV.

---

[1] The name of the town in Guelderland, Flanders, where this silk was made.

As worn by French Royal ladies and the nobility its circumference at the hem was often abnormal as seen in Fig. 525. Queen Elizabeth varied the size of her farthingale according to circumstances, as evinced in her costumes illustrated in this section; and ladies of fashion followed her example.

(*Continued on p.* 618)

## THE CORSET (*continued from p.* 223)

The type of corset worn by fashionable women during this period was the same as described on p. 222, and shown in Figs. 242 and 261.

(*Continued on p.* 622)

## THE RUFF OR BAND

In Chapter II it has been pointed out that cutwork or lace edging decorated the neckbands of gentlemen's shirts. Next, a small frill appeared on the top of the neckband, as noted on p. 167; and by the time of Edward VI this neck frill had developed into a small ruff. The process of development can be traced in the illustrations throughout Chapter III.

The ladies of Edward VI and Mary's reigns adopted this frill to finish off the collars of their partlets. It became more pronounced during the early years of this reign and was worn by both sexes. It was but a mere frill about an inch to an inch and a half wide, and became what we know as the 'ruff'; but the more correct name is the 'band,' so called because it was made as a *band* or long strip of linen or lawn, varying in width according to the period of its development; its length might be anything from one and a half to six yards. It was hemmed on both edges, one edge being ornamented with stitchery, gold-thread, or cutwork. A string was inserted in the other edge, by means of which it was all drawn up tight into many folds. This string was also used to tie it round the neck, and its tasselled ends hung down in front.

Fig. 862 illustrates this method of forming a small ruff. On the lady's neck, left, the ruff is seen correctly set, the inside edges being tacked to the top of the high collar of the bodice. On the right side, the ruff is purposely left unattached to the corner of the collar, which is turned down: and the band is shown drawn out along part of the length of the band string. At first these bands were narrow, as it was not possible to stiffen them: but the introduction of starch paved the way for astounding changes.

Starch, called by the Puritans 'the Devil's liquor,' was known and manufactured in Flanders; but the practice of clear-starching did not reach England until 1560. In this year William Boonen, a Dutchman, was appointed as Queen Elizabeth's coachman, and his wife monopolized in England the knowledge of clear-starching. The Queen availed herself of Mistress Boonen's services until 1564, when a rival artist appeared upon the scene in the person of one Mistress Dingham van der Plasse, a Fleming. This lady became a professional starcher of ruffs and cuffs—a service for which she charged high prices. The flutes of the goffering were called the 'set,' generally nebulée, and to accomplish them the laundresses used setting-sticks of wood, later of bone, which were heated and then thrust into the folds of the linen or lawn. This somewhat primitive method could only produce ruffs of a minimum size, but in 1573 'began the making of steel poking-sticks,' and with the use of these implements work was made easier and the result more satisfactory.

Cuffs at the wrist usually matched the ruff and a 'suit of ruffs' means a ruff and a pair of cuffs.

(*Continued on p.* 623)

### THE VEIL

The first appearance in England during the sixteenth century of gauze drapery hanging from the back and fixed to the headdress is seen in the 'Darnley' portrait of Queen Elizabeth, 1570. This veil is of plain transparent material. In Zuccaro's drawing, 1575 (Fig. 579), the gauze is patterned all over with needlework, *not* lace, and the edge is goffered over the top of the head. The veil now becomes a more important item of costume and, according to the drawing, is worn enveloping the sides of the figure as well as the back.

In the National Portrait Gallery, No. 190 (Plate XXXI B), the veil is again of transparent gauze with smaller yet higher gofferings around the head; but it is more elaborate in No. 200 (Plate XXXI C) in the same gallery. It is composed of black net or gauze, cross-barred with narrow black velvet having large pearls at the intersections and at the apex of each goffering. This veil is somewhat similar to one described in a Royal wardrobe account: 'One vale of blacke networke, florished with Venice silver like flagon worke, and embrodered all over with roses of Venice gold, silver, and silk, of colours of silk-woman's worke.'

The 'Siena' portrait, 1578, shows the veil arranged in a different way, as described under Fig. 721, Section II.

(*Continued on p.* 626)

### THE FAN (*continued from p.* 224)

The Italian banner-shaped fan continued in general use during the remainder of the sixteenth century, but chiefly among the women of Italy and especially the ladies of Venice. They were sarcastically termed 'fly whisks' by Westerners.

A beautiful Italian feather fan is shown in Fig. 586, composed of five straight and uncurled ostrich feathers rising from a group of curled tips, with a rigid handle of ivory and gold. Such a fan formed the model of those used by the great ladies of Europe during the second half of the sixteenth century, and in England throughout Queen Elizabeth's reign.

On the Queen's accession, she artlessly let it be known that the most acceptable gift that she could receive from her subjects was a fan—although she did
not decline presents of other kinds.    The City Fathers did not need a second
hint: on every New Year's Day they brought their Royal mistress, with becoming humility, a rich and beautiful fan.    In such gifts they wisely did not
stint themselves.

In many portraits of the Queen she is seen holding a feather fan in her hand,

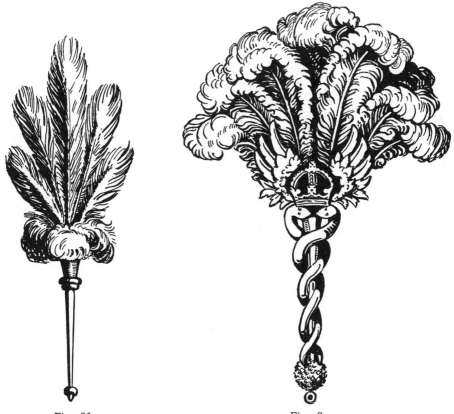

Fig. 586                                      Fig. 587

attached by a narrow ferret or riband to the girdle at her waist.    Her wardrobe
contained many such fans, and a few are described below.    A fan belonging
to the Queen in 1577 was of 'flowers of sylke of sundry colours, the handill
of an inbrawdry worke set with small sede perle.'    A fan presented to Her
Majesty for a ''Newyers-tyde' gift had the handle studded with diamonds.
'A fanne of white feathers, with a handle of gold, having two snakes wyndinge
about it, garnished with a ball of diamonds at the ende, and a crowne on each
side within a paire of wings garnished with diamonds' was in the Queen's
possession in 1600.    This description has inspired Fig. 587.

'One fanne of feathers of divers colours, the handle of golde, with a bare and a ragged staffe on both sides [obviously a gift from some member of the Dudley family] and a looking glasse on thone side' proves that, contrary to report, Elizabeth actually *carried* a mirror.

Another example had 'one handle of golde enameled, set with small rubies and emerodes, with a Shipp under saile on thone side.'

In the inventory of her wardrobe made in 1603, no fewer than thirty-one beautiful fans of great worth are enumerated. Some of these were of feathers and others of the new folding type. As much as £40 was sometimes given for a fan in Elizabeth's time. (*Continued on p.* 628)

Fig. 588. Embroidery on Cushion of the Period

Elizabeth set the standard in her realm of a thoroughly well-dressed woman, so that it was natural for the ladies of the Court and other ladies of quality to follow her lead. A general similarity therefore exists between the wardrobes of these ladies and those of their Royal mistress. Thus the noble lady in Fig. 589 is wearing a costume which, although fashionable under Henry VIII and Mary, continued to be popular during the first half of Elizabeth's reign, especially with the more sedate women of the aristocracy. It should be noticed that the turned-back sleeves no longer assume the angular effect which was so modish in Henry VIII's time. The partlet of fine lawn entirely covers the shoulders and is high round the throat, finishing in a small ruff. Also the overskirt is divided down the front and folded back on itself, being held by laces sewn to the skirt beneath the folded portions; the tagged ends pass through holes in the latter, and tie in bows of one loop and two ends.

Fig. 589. A Noble Lady, 1560
(Lady Maud Vernon, Bakewell)

The back view of the lady (Fig. 590) explains three important features of sixteenth-century costume: first the effect produced by the wide turned-back sleeves in vogue for many years, and first seen in Plate XVI; secondly, the definite English mode of the Spanish farthingale worn under a *trained* skirt, with the bulk of the material arranged at the back; and thirdly the regulation tube hanging at the back of the French hood.

The dress just described will serve as a type of those worn by the ladies of the Court on most occasions during the earlier part of Elizabeth's reign; and William Harrison, with his usual disarming frankness, has much to say about the occupations of these same ladies when not in attendance. Thus: 'Ancient ladies of the Court do shun and avoid idleness, some of them exercising their fingers with the needle, others in caulwork, divers in spinning of silk, some in continual reading either of the Holy Scriptures, or histories of our own or foreign nations about us, and divers in writing volumes of their own, or translating of other mens into our English and Latin tongues.' Again: 'Many of the eldest sort also are skilful in surgery and distillation of waters, besides sundry other artificial practises pertaining to the ornature and commendations of their bodies.' The 'younger sort,' however, engaged in mere amusement instead of such useful employment: who 'in the mean time apply their lutes, citharnes, pricksong, and all kind of music; which they use only for recreation sake, when they have leisure, and are free from attendance upon the Queen's Majesty, or such as they belong unto.'

Fig. 590. La Mode, 1550–80

The beauty of Englishwomen always attracted the admiration of foreign visitors. Such a one was Herr Johann Jacob Breuning von Buchenbach, who spent some time in England between 1592 and 1595. 'At no other Court,' he writes—and he had been at many, including the Imperial, 'have I ever seen so much splendour and such fine clothes. This holds good both of the men and of the Countesses and other Noble Ladies, who were of rare surpassing beauty and for the main part in Italian costume with breasts bared. In their hands they held large black plumes or other fans wherewith to cool themselves.'

Fig. 591. Gold embroidered Border

The Spanish surcote, fashionable during the first twenty years of this reign, is shown in Fig. 592. The only differences from those already illustrated are the sleeves and the treatment of the back: this is cut wide enough across the shoulders to form pleats from twelve to fifteen inches long. It has buttons and loops of fine cord part of the way down the front, and the collar is high and upstanding at the back. The sleeves, cut on the leg of mutton plan, hang behind the arm, but they could be worn over the arm since buttons and loops are provided for that purpose.

A similar garment (an original one) was shown at the Elizabethan Exhibition of 1933. It is made of deep claret-coloured velvet decorated down the open fronts, round the hem, up the side-seams, and on the shoulder rolls with a design worked with very small white opaque beads. Fig 593 gives two of the chief motifs of the design, which measures four inches from the lowest line to the highest point. The buttons (Fig. 594) are of claret velvet mounted on metal shanks, bound with fine white silk and studded with white beads.

Fig. 592. The Spanish Surcote

The dimensions of this surcote are of interest. The two fronts are forty-four inches each at the hem; at the back the hem is eighty inches; the fronts are

Fig. 593. Pattern in Beadwork

fifty-four, and the centre back fifty-eight inches long. It is made up of twenty-one-inch velvet, all the widths being joined with a straight seam—

*selvage to selvage.*  The leg-of-mutton-shaped hanging sleeves are twenty-nine inches at the front seam and thirty-two at the back; they widen from ten round the wrist to eighteen at elbow level; the shoulder rolls are formed of loops.

Fig. 594. Button

The garment in the condition when examined had no lining; this originally must have been of silk in the same or contrasting colour.

The effigy in Hereford Cathedral, to the memory of the wife of Sir Richard Denton, who died in 1566 at the age of eighteen, is excellent study for the costume worn by the provincial aristocracy in the early years of this reign (*see* Fig. 595).  The dress with bodice and skirt, which appear to be cut all in one, is of black velvet: the high collar and mahoitered sleeves with long hanging panels behind are banded with gold passamayne.  The skirt is short in front, an arrangement sometimes seen in illustrations of this period, and falls over an underskirt of vermilion silk mounted on the farthingale.  The tight sleeves are of the same material, having gold embroidery down both seams. White lawn is used for the partlet with high collar, and for the small ruffs and cuffs.  The carcanet and girdle are gold chains; and the pendent waist ornament and pomander are in goldsmith's work.  This effigy affords a good side view of the French hood, which is referred to on p. 743.  A cloak of crimson with a high collar spreads its ample folds over the altar tomb upon which Lady Denton rests.

Fig. 595. Lady Denton, 1566

## Margaret Douglas

### Countess of Lennox, 1515–78

The everyday outdoor dress of a great lady of the 1560's is depicted in Fig. 596.  It is taken from a three-quarter portrait of Margaret Douglas, Countess of Lennox (born 1515), daughter of Margaret Tudor, Queen-Dowager of Scotland, and her second husband, Archibald Douglas, Earl of Angus.  She married in 1544 Matthew Stewart, fourth Earl of Lennox,

Regent of Scotland, and was the mother of Henry Stewart Lord Darnley, and Charles Stewart. Although of Scottish nationality this lady spent a great deal of time at the English Court. The historian, Camden, has some-something interesting to say about her. 'She was,' he says, 'a matron of singular piety, patience, and modesty; who was thrice cast into the Tower (as I have heard her say herself) not for any crime of treason, but for love matters; first, when Thomas Howard, son of Thos.

Howard the first Duke of Norfolk of that name, falling in love with her, died in the Tower of London [1536]; then for the love of Henry, Lord Darnley, her son to Mary Queen of Scots; and lastly for the love of Charles, her younger son, to Elizabeth Cavendish, mother of the Lady Arabella.'

Lady Lennox's costume is representative of the fashion worn at this time.

The velvet gown is woven or embroidered with a gold spot (compare with Plate XXX), and is made in the prevailing style of close-fitting bodice, with rolls on the shoulders and moderately full sleeves of mottled cloth of gold. The high collar supports a small ruff, and the skirt opens over an underskirt which matches the sleeves, mounted over the Spanish farthingale. The Countess wears a hat over a network caul (compare with Figs. 576 and 597), and carries a beautiful fan of the usual design,

Fig. 596. The Countess of Lennox, 1560

and a large lawn handkerchief with a deep border of lace and insertion in reticella.

Margaret appears to have been a bit troublesome to her kinswoman, Queen Elizabeth. She suffered from ill-health owing to the severity of her imprisonments. She died at Hackney in 1578, having survived her eight children and left her affairs so involved that Elizabeth had to pay her funeral expenses.

### MARY STUART

*Queen of Scotland and Queen-Dowager of France, 1559 until 1580*

(*continued from p. 438*)

For a portrait of Mary Stuart as Queen-Consort of France, from July 1559 to December 1560, reference must be made to the miniature now in the Uffizi, Florence. This miniature is framed with those of other members

Fig. 597. Mary Stuart, 1560

of the French Royal family, which are said to have been sent by Catherine de' Medici to her relatives at home.[1]

In the National Portrait Gallery, London, is a head-and-shoulders portrait (eight by eleven inches), No. 1766, of Mary, precisely similar to this miniature. Undoubtedly this is a close copy, on a larger scale, of the miniature: probably made in France after she had become a widow, and perhaps before she returned to Scotland.

Fig. 597 is made from the painting in the National Portrait Gallery. The style of the dress would be like that shown in Fig. 596, but perhaps more elaborate. The bodice is black velvet with pointed oblong cuttes in two lines radiating from the shoulders to the waist: narrow shoulder-pieces surround the armholes: the undergarment seen through the cuttes is white, probably linen, embroidered with Spanish work.

Plate XXXIII is a reproduction of a portrait of Mary Stuart in the Victoria and Albert Museum, itself an enlarged copy of a miniature painting in the Royal Library at Windsor, and dates 1560–1. Experts pronounce it to be an excellent likeness. The dress is of incarnadine satin—a satin which goes

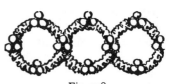

Fig. 598

almost crimson in the shadows and a faint lilac-pink in the high lights—made on simple lines as shown in Fig. 517. The whole dress is covered with perpendicular double rows of fancy silver braid, with groups of three tiny silver ball buttons set closely in the intermediate spaces. The sleeves are slightly gathered at the shoulders and fit the forearm close, ending in lace cuffs. No ruff is worn; and the very high collar, edged with silver thread from which oval spangles of jet hang, is turned back with white showing a bare throat. Round the neck, knotted and hanging in front, is a cordon of some of Mary's famous black pearls 'like black muscades'; the earrings, being pear-shaped white pearls, do not match, which seems rather

Fig. 599. Mary Stuart, 1560

[1] Marie de' Medici may have sent them to Florence at a later date.

PLATE XXXIII. MARY STUART, QUEEN OF SCOTLAND AND FRANCE, 1560–1
Victoria and Albert Museum. *By kind permission of the Directors*

unusual. The coif or escoffion is of a dull black mesh, perhaps very narrow black velvet network; it has a border of silver loops containing groups of three minute granules of white (*see* Fig. 598) and there is a row of white pearls at the front edge. A richly jewelled escoffion worn by the Queen of Scotland, Fig. 599, is described on p. 751.

There is reason to believe, according to the following excerpt from Brantôme, that on some occasion while Mary Stuart was in France she must have appeared in the costume of her native country. He says: 'See what virtue there was in such beauty and grace that they could turn coarse barbarism into sweet civility and social grace. We must not be surprised, therefore, that being dressed (as I have seen her) in the barbarous costume of the uncivilized people of her country, she appeared, in mortal body and coarse ungainly clothing, a true goddess. Those who have seen her thus dressed will admit this truth; and those who did not see her can look at her *portrait, in which she is thus attired.* I have heard the Queen-Mother, and the King, too, say that she looked more beautiful, more agreeable, more desirable in that picture than in any of the others.'

The portrait mentioned, depicting the Queen in Scottish dress, has not yet been discovered, if still in existence. Should it come to light in the future, perhaps in some secluded country manor, the find could not fail to prove a discovery of the utmost importance.

The only description we have of Mary Stuart's Scottish costume concerns the long loose cloak of damask worn over the under-

Fig. 600. A Highland Gentlewoman

dress. The Queen had three more of these Highland mantles, one of black frise trimmed with gold and lined with black taffeta, another of blue and a third white.

'The Queen, the Parliament now ended, hath made her Highland apparel for her journey into Argile,' 1563.

Fig. 600 is given to help the reader to visualize the rest of the dress, based upon that generally worn by a Scottish gentlewoman. Her rectangular cloak was less rich, and striped in colours, in fact, a tartan; two corners were fastened on the breast by a brooch or buckle, the material behind forming a kind of burnous. The brooch was of silver or brass according to the quality of the person, and had a crystal or some other semi-precious stone in the centre surrounded by smaller ones. This mantle, cloak, or PLAID

Fig. 601. Mary Stuart, 1561

(*see* vol. i, p. 88) was gathered high in the waist by a leather belt ornamented with silver, and having a mordant some eight inches long engraved in a characteristic Celtic design, often intermixed with stones or coral. The underdress was a close descendant of the gwn (*see* vol. i, p. 18), of some bright coloured cloth, with close sleeves perhaps having gold buttons at the wrist and down the front of the body part. The headdress was a kerchief of white linen, folded corner-wise and tied under the chin over hair worn loose and long, but bound by a snood. Shoes were of old Celtic pattern, as worn by the woman in Fig. 40 (vol. i).

Mary Stuart-Valois was left a widow at the age of eighteen, 5th December 1560.

There are several portraits of her by Clouet and his school known as the 'Deuil Blanc' portraits. One of these, not a good example, is in the National Portrait Gallery (No. 555). Another is in the Wallace Collection. The most authentic is the drawing in the Bibliothèque Nationale, Paris. Fig. 601 is made from this. The black velvet dress worn with this headdress is made like that shown in Fig. 517.

If the drawing in the Musée Condé, Chantilly, of the school of Clouet, is really Mary Stuart, then we have a portrait of her at the age of nineteen, made in 1561 before she left France. The costume is very simple and rather austere, as can be seen from Fig. 602, and consists of a dark underdress, showing a lawn partlet and small frill, and having a girdle at the waist. Over this is a light-coloured robe turned back with lynx: the full sleeves are pleated and slightly padded on the shoulders (*see also* Fig. 823). The coif of white lawn is without the peak, and round the back of it is set in horseshoe shape a band of jewels.

Fig. 602. Mary Stuart, 1561

Having been a widowed queen nine months, Mary left France and landed at Leith, 19th August 1561, and took up her residence at the 'Palace of Halyrudhous.'

The next seven years of her reign as Queen of Scotland were crowded with incident—her marriage with Lord Darnley in 1565, the murder of Rizzio and the birth of her son James in 1566. The tragedy of Kirk-o'-Field, her marriage with James Hepburn, Earl of Bothwell (born c. 1536, died 1577), the defeat at Carberry Hill, her captivity at Loch Leven, and abdication 24th July, kept her busy during 1567. In May 1568, after two previous attempts, she escaped from Loch Leven, and was recaptured at Carlisle, all within a space of sixteen days. Henceforth, Mary Stuart was the State prisoner of the English Government, being shifted from one place of residence to another—eight in number.

Of her wardrobe during this hectic time there is plenty of information contained in the inventory made in 1562. This includes sixty dresses, chiefly of cloth of gold, of silver, velvet, satin, and silk: five cloaks in the Spanish fashion, and nine others, and two Royal mantles of velvet and ermine. Thirty-four corsets known as vasquines (see p. 222); sixteen foreparts, which might mean stomachers and under-skirts, chiefly of cloth of gold, cloth of silver, and satin; and a 'vertugade' or farthingale 'expanded by girdles of whalebone.' It is a foregone conclusion that her apparel, regulated by State functions and the routine of everyday life, was of the French fashion, simple but rich, and mainly of white silk or satin, or black velvet.

One entry in the above inventory is of special interest—a sunshade. 'Item a little canopy of crimson satin of three quarter long, furnished with fringes and tassels made of gold and crimson silk, many little painted buttons, all serving to bear, to make shadow for the Queen.' Surely this is the first mention of a sunshade since Greek and Roman days (see vol. i, p. 41).

During her later years Queen Mary wore widow's weeds on only two occasions.

Both her marriages, with Darnley, 29th July 1565, as with Bothwell, 15th May 1567, were celebrated in the old chapel at Holyroodhouse, and for both of them she wore widow's deep mourning robes. To have worn mourning as a bridal dress must have been a decidedly unusual experience, and in the second case at least definitely superfluous.

On ordinary occasions she probably wore a dress under an outer robe with large sleeves, like Fig. 602 or 823, such garments being worn by great ladies in their homes. The Queen is seen gowned in this fashion in the Blairs College painting.

As early as 1561 Mary wore PERUKES according to an inventory of that date. Her hair gave her much concern; perhaps it was getting thin, although at the age of nineteen this seems very improbable. It is much more likely that these perukes were only fashionable additions. An important piece of information on the subject is given by Claude Nau, the Queen's French secretary, who states that in her flight from Langside (May 1568) she had her head shaved; no doubt for purposes of disguise. Consequently there was every excuse for her to use as many perukes as she liked from that time onwards. We know she possessed such a number of changes of wig, chiefly dark auburn, that her favourite lady-in-waiting, Mary Seaton, could deck the head of her Royal mistress with a different one every day. She was the finest 'busker,' as Mary admitted, and Sir Francis Knollys, writing to Sir William Cecil in 1568, mentions the art in which Mary Seaton was so proficient—'whereof we have seen divers experiences since her coming hither; and among other pretty devices, yesterday and this day, she did set such a curled hair upon the Queen, that was said to be a PEREWYKE—that showed very delicately, and every other day she hath a new device of headdressing without any cost, and yet setteth forth a woman gaily well.' Nicholas White, who had an interview with Mary Stuart at Tutbury in February 1569, says with unsophisticated surprise that 'her hair of itself is black, and yet Mr. Knollys told me that she wears hair of sundry colours.'

On top of her coiffure the Queen usually wore a white coif (Fig. 875) with an attifet front edged with lace, and over it a fine transparent veil also edged with lace—a headdress evidently inspired by her widow's weeds.

The four Marys—Mary Livingston, Mary Beton, Mary Fleming, and Mary Seton—who had accompanied the young Queen to France and had returned to Scotland with her would, like their mistress, be much influenced in their attire by French fashions of the 1550's. The costume worn by the Queen's ladies-in-waiting was undoubtedly similar to that shown in Fig. 589, which exemplifies the dress worn by the ladies of the Scottish aristocracy of the 1550's and 1560's.

An excellent horsewoman, Queen Mary possessed suitable garments for riding. Plate XXXIV is a suggestion of what she would wear when entering Edinburgh in state, or on some similar occasion. The riding costume is of fine white silk or cloth braided with gold, the bodice and sleeves being almost covered with braid set in oblique and perpendicular lines. There are four cuttes on the front, and groups of three loops surround the armholes; a green ribbon suspends the Badge of the Thistle.

The cut of the skirt is that generally adopted for ordinary wear—half or two-thirds of a circle; skirts were not specially shaped for saddle and pommel like a riding-habit of the nineteenth century. A blue velvet cloak with a border of gold embroidery hangs from the shoulders, and a blue bonet, decorated with jewels and a small white feather, might be worn over a network caul. The mount is a cream French hackney with black points.

Although the Queen of Scotland owned a litter, covered with crimson velvet and fringed with silk and gold, 'and two little chairs in it,' with harnessing thereto, besides a coach, she seldom used either, much preferring the saddle. Besides, she showed to great advantage on horseback, loving horses as much as she did dogs.

At Carberry Hill 'she gathered an army of those whom she thought her most faithful adherents, leading it herself—at its head, mounted on a good horse, dressed in a simple petticote of white taffetas, with a coif of crêpe on her head.' 'Petticote' means the riding dress, and was obviously untrimmed: the taffeta must have been of a substantial texture for hard wear on horseback. The coif of crêpe with veil was like that shown in Fig. 875.

It is also recorded that in time of war Mary Stuart wore a 'steel bonet,' but more likely the morion, and carried a pistol at her saddle-bow. Randolph writing to Cecil in 1562 reports that the Queen, during the siege of Lord Gordon's

Fig. 602A.          Fig. 603.          Fig. 604.
Three Society Ladies, 1578

castle in Inverness, expressed the regret that 'she was not a man to know what life it was to lie all night in the fields, or to walk upon the Causeway with a jack [coat of mail], and a knapscull, a Glasgow buckler, and a broadsword.'

On 14th April 1568 the Queen attempted an escape from Loch Leven disguised as her laundress, but heavily veiled; however, her beautiful white hands, such as no washerwoman ever had, betrayed her identity. The costume of a laundress, though not very different in shape from the dress worn by others of the lower classes, is seen in Fig. 719.

(Continued on p. 634)

The three ladies of the English aristocracy (Figs. 602A, 603, and 604) are attending a funeral in 1578. They are not mourners, otherwise they would be wearing mourning robes: they are 'Diuers other gentlewoemen not in black cloth'—just smart Society people who like an interment and have come out of pure curiosity.   The lady (Fig. 602A) wears a walking dress of black silk trimmed with black velvet and golden crowsfeet.   The bodice, with full leg-of-mutton sleeves, is cutte six times on the chest; it buttons down the front and has shoulder pieces of black velvet.   A gold chain is wound round the neck, across the front, and under the left arm.   At the waistbelt a chain suspends a bag.   The black hat with high crown, worn at a jauntish angle, is decorated round the band with gold, and two black ostrich feathers set with gold crows-feet cover the crown at one side.   The lady with her (Fig. 603) wears a dress of brown velvet with partlet and sleeves of lighter brown silk covered with a trellis-work of narrow brown velvet.   The shoulder pieces and skirt are braided with grey, and the latter opens over a black satin underskirt having black velvet bows and tiny roses up the front.

The third lady (Fig. 604) wears cinnamon-brown cloth or silk banded at different angles on the bodice, sleeves, and skirts with velvet of a deeper shade. Down the entire fronts of the overskirt a wider band of velvet is criss-crossed with fine gold.   The last two ladies wear the French hood, and all three have the Spanish farthingale, but of moderate proportions.


### The Baldachin, Sunshade, Umbrella

Sunshades were used by the Greeks and Romans as described in vol. i, page 41.

The ecclesiastic *baldachin* was a canopy over an altar or bishop's throne, and was usually made of very rich material such as baudekyn; a portable baldachin was carried on four rods over a monarch in coronation processions.

In the second half of the sixteenth century a small baldachin supported on a single rod—a sunshade, PARASOL, UMBRELLA—was used by persons of rank in Italy and Spain as a protection from sun or rain.   Henri Estienne is the first to make reference to the use of such a sunshade in his *Dialogues* (1578).

That Mary Stuart should have possessed 'a little canopy' (*see* page 515) as early as 1562, or even earlier, is remarkable.

It is true that Daniel Defoe, writing one hundred and fifty years later, states that Queen Elizabeth used an umbrella to keep the rain off when walking on the terrace at Windsor; but we have only his authority for this!

Possibly the earliest representation in England of a sixteenth-century sunshade or umbrella is to be seen in the portrait of Sir Henry Unton, No. 710 in the National Portrait Gallery, which was painted after his death in 1596. He is shown surrounded by pictures of episodes in his life; and in Italy, when mounted on horseback, he carried an all-white sunshade, including the stick.   The frame is obviously constructed on the same principle as the Greek sunshade shown in Fig. 17, vol. i.

## MOURNING ROBES

The Countess of Surrey officiated as chief mourner at the funeral of Lady Lumley, 1578, and Fig. 605 shows her in mourning robes of heavy black. The underdress is of the prevailing fashion as shown by the lady (Fig. 604), but plain and of black cloth. The up-to-date *barbe* takes the form of a pleated white lawn front tied round the neck and waist; and over her head is a black

Fig. 605.          Fig. 606.
Mourning Robes

hood, cut semicircular and bordered and lined with white. From the shoulders hangs a mantle with a train, the length of which was regulated. The train-bearer in this instance was 'Mrs Coote the Queen's woman' (Fig. 606), lent for this occasion by Her Majesty as a special favour. She wears the usual dress of a gentlewoman in black cloth with a barbe, a white lawn close-fitting cap gathered into a band round her face, and over this a starched lawn veil fastened V.A.D. fashion.

## FRANCES SIDNEY

### Countess of Sussex, 1531–89

Frances, the daughter of Sir William Sidney of Penshurst, was born 1531. In 1555 she married, as his second wife, Thomas Ratcliffe (born 1525), 'a goodly gentleman,' who succeeded as third Earl of Sussex in 1557. He was invested a K.G. the same year, and held many official posts, among them that of Lord Chamberlain of the Household, 1572. He died 1583. The Countess of Sussex (Fig. 607) was the foundress, under her will, of Sidney Sussex College, Cambridge (1596). This drawing is adapted from her full-length portrait by Hans Eworth in the dining hall of the college, by kind permission of the Master and Fellows. It shows the full dress of a noble lady

Fig. 607. THE COUNTESS OF SUSSEX.   After Hans Eworth
(*Sidney Sussex College, Cambridge*)

of the 1570's. It is carried out entirely in black velvet, embroidered all over with gold quatrefoils (*see* one inset below heraldic lozenge). In the original portrait these are about one inch in diameter, and set two and a half inches apart.

The costume consists of an underdress with bodice worn over the Spanish farthingale which slopes outward at the hem. The overdress fits at the waist, and is edged up the fronts with white fur—ermine or lynx. Narrow bands of the same fur outline the back seams of the sleeves and the edge of the shoulder pieces; these are decorated with three patches of fur and the sleeves with five. Narrow fur also edges the hem of the skirt and train. It appears to be the mode at this time for the turn-back of the fronts of the over-robe to widen considerably where it passes over the shoulders, and so form a high upstanding collar round the back of the head. This is seen in Figs. 607 and 867. The effect of this collar was to minimize the combined length of the head and neck, which had been artificially increased by the height of this headdress, contrary to the vogue at the end of the following period. The wearer thus appears to have neither neck nor shoulders. The ruff and cuffs are of goffered cambric, having a narrow black satin binding set with pearls at intervals along the edge.

A rich jewelled carcanet with pendant is partly hidden by the long fur, and a jewelled girdle worn *underneath* the overdress has an elaborate pomander at the end. The French hood is small and close-fitting, and in her left hand she holds a sable skin. The armorial bearings are displayed on a lozenge, Ratcliffe impaling Sidney, surmounted by a countess's coronet.

The Countess-Dowager died 9th March 1589; her effigy in St. Paul's Chapel, Westminster Abbey, shows her in robes of estate and wearing a rather large circular ruff and a coronet over a headdress something like Fig. 879. Many portraits of ladies of the 1560's and 1570's show them wearing an overdress similar to that described above.

Fig. 608. Gold Embroidery

Sumptuary laws regulating feminine dress did not affect the maids of honour or the ladies of the Court, who were granted exemption.

So much attention did women pay to raiment at this time that their vanities provoked the wrath of their ecclesiastical advisers. Things were rather worse in France than in England: so much so as to rouse the anger of a Franciscan friar, who in 1570 published an entertaining work entitled, *A Charitable Remonstrance to the Dames and Damoyselles of France touching their dissolute Adornments*. Such wholehearted condemnation was nothing new: as long ago as the eighth century B.C. Isaiah (iii. 18–24) had complained of much the same excess amongst the Jewish women.  Listen then to the pious father giving vent to his indignation:

'Look you, then, I pray you, whether there be no harm; and, first of all, let us consider what are your habiliments.  In brief, they are: false hair, wigs, curls, plaits, earrings, attifets, hair-nets, chaplets of jewels, masks, wirings, low-cut and open bodices garnished with fringes and braids, and others that are called burnouses; chains, jewels, bracelets, collars of diverse kinds and shapes, panaches, fans, busks, mahoitered sleeves with robes of velvet, satin, damaske, and taffata, altogether shameless and deeply cut back and front, as well as being cut square even below the armpits; peliçons and petticotes enriched with excessive embroideries, passamaynes, outrageous farthingales, hauts de chausses, shoes, and vests; stockings of silk and estamet of divers colours, with openwork seams, clocks and garters of the same; high-heeled Venetian slippers and pantoufles, and an infinity of other vanities.'

For denunciation of eccentricity of dress in England we turn again and again to *The Anatomie of Abuses*, published in 1583.  The author, Philip Stubbes, was born about 1555, and though educated at both universities graduated at neither.  His interest lay in people rather than in books; and so we find him travelling all over the country 'to see fashions, to acquaint myselfe with natures, qualities, properties, and conditions of all men.'  By the time his great work appeared he had developed pronounced Puritan sympathies, and to him all ordinary items of attire were extravagant and to be condemned.  His book thus throws interesting light on the manners of the times, though some of his statements must be gross exaggerations and require the proverbial grain of salt.  His *Anatomie* was virulent enough to provoke a reply (*The Anatomie of Absurditie*), and of his other considerable work, *A Christal Glasse for Christian Women*, published in 1591, no fewer than seven editions were called for.  Philip Stubbes, who must not be confused with his reputed brother John, the Puritan pamphleteer, died about 1610.

The Franciscan friar and Puritan fanatic, disagreeing violently on most matters, agreed on at least one, for Stubbes is no whit behind in his disapproval of women painting, or rather 'trimming,' their faces and dyeing their hair.  Thus he complains that 'the women of England use to colour their faces with certain oils, liquors, ungents and waters made to that end, whereby they think their beauty is greatly decorated.'  Further: 'In a man three ounces of lust, in a woman nine: for what meaneth else their outward tricking and dainty trimming of their heads, the laying out of their hairs, the painting and washing [with coloured water or dye] of their faces, the opening of their breasts, and discovering them to their waists, their bents [shapes] of whalebone [1] to bear out their bumes, their great sleeves and bumbasted shoulders, squared in breadth to make their waists small, their coloured hose, their variable shoes?'  Amongst special names for such preparations in use at this period we may mention 'fard,' white paint for the face, and 'slibbersawces,' washes and unguents kept in small boxes.  The same

---

[1] Probably their corsets or perhaps farthingales.

pernicious habit of painting the face and wearing false hair by fashionable women of London, good and bad alike, surprised and disgusted gentlefolk up from the country.

It is only fair to mention the contrary opinion of Samuel Kiechel in 1586–9, who refers to the resplendently fair and beautiful women of England, who did *not* paint, and who saluted all stranger-guests with a kiss and an embrace, 'for this is their custom and ettiquette, and any demur in conforming to it would be misconstrued as a sign of ill-breeding and a want of sense.'

Thomas Nashe in 1593 gibes at the effects of the elderly to restore their youth:

'Gorgeous ladies of the Court, never was I admitted so near any of you, as to see how you torture poor old Time with sponging, pinning, and pouncing; but they say his sickle you have burst in twain, to make your periwigs more elevated arches of . . . Why dye they and diet their faces with so many drugs as they do, as it were to correct God's workmanship, and reprove Him as a bungler, and one that is not his craftsmaster? Why ensparkle they their eyes with spiritualized distillations? Why tip they their tongues with *aurum potabile*? Why fill they age's frets with fresh colours? Even as roses and flowers in winter are preserved in close houses under earth, so preserve they their beauties by continual lying in bed.'

Many were the devices adopted to revive the complexion: and to soften wrinkles, night-masks 'well plastered within' were worn in bed.

## MASKS

'When they use to ride abroad they have invisories made of velvet, wherewith they cover their faces, having holes made in them against their eyes, where out they look.' Some masks had glass inserted in them. Queen Elizabeth often wore a mask while riding in her coach or on horseback, and even while hunting. This she sometimes removed, especially when addressing any one. Ladies wore masks also when walking and when attending the play.

In France ladies wore them to preserve their complexions and when they rode or walked. In fact a mask was considered so important an item of outdoor costume that to be seen without one was decidedly *en déshabillé*.

Gentlemen wore masks chiefly to conceal their identity during escapades and in the gaming houses.

'Masks of Medyoxes' were used chiefly in masques. They were divided down the centre, usually into good and bad halves, such as one side the human face, the other a skeleton, or an angel impaled with a devil.

## NOBILITY—MEN: 1558–80

The differences in social grade during the Elizabethan era are so clearly expressed by William Harrison that his own words are better than any modern description. Thus he writes: 'We in England divide our people commonly into four sorts, as gentlemen, citizens or burgesses, yeomen, and artificers or labourers.

Fig. 609.        Fig. 610.
Noblemen, 1559

Of gentlemen the first and chief (next the King) be the prince, dukes, marquesses, earls, viscounts, and barons, and these are called gentlemen of the greater sort, or (as our common usage of speech is) lords and noblemen: and next unto them be knights, esquires, and last of all they that are simply called Gentlemen.' He disapproves, however, of young men going abroad to sow their wild oats. 'Noblemen's and mean gentlemen's sons are foolishly sent to Italy, from whence they bring home nothing but mere Atheism, infidelity, vicious conversation, and ambitions and proud behaviour, whereby it commeth to pass that they return far worse men than they went out.' No wonder that when later on some of them became courtiers, although they were most learned knowing many languages and writing well, they had the reputation of being the biggest liars out.

From another source we learn that 'the nobles and yeomen willingly intermarry, and so do the burghers and nobility according to their wealth and rank.'

Many nobles and gentlemen attending on Her Majesty are shown in the drawings of Queen Elizabeth's coronation procession referred to on p. 485. Two are given in Figs. 609 and 610 as being examples of the style fashionable at this time. The costume worn by the gentleman (Fig. 609) is, in many respects, similar to that shown in Fig. 505, and can be said to be contemporary with it. The decoration of the doublet consists of six cuttes of varying length on the chest and three on each of the four tabs which form the basque: the large puffs on the shoulders are also decorated with them. The close-fitting sleeves are similarly treated with rows of very small cuttes.   An upstanding collar is now an essential part of the doublet.

In the last chapter it was noticed that slops were gradually increasing in size; they first appear in Plate XIX, and are noticeably larger in Fig. 487. Those worn by young Courteney (Fig. 504) are much more in evidence, and the latest (Fig. 505) are even more pronounced.   In Fig. 609 they are equally large, but the panes are narrower and consequently more numerous.   The fashionable contour of slops is a slope from the waist to their widest at the base, where they turn up under, and surround the thigh.

Fig. 496 illustrates the shape of a pair of slops of this period.   The full material and panes are fixed to a hip-yoke, which is covered by a basque, to ensure a sloping line on the hips.

When the full material which formed slops was covered with panes, they were said to be 'pansid.'

The other gentleman (Fig. 610) wears the same kind of suit underneath a short coat cut on the semicircle plan.   The coat has a wide open collar and puffed sleeves with rectangular false sleeves hanging from under the arm, the complete garment fastening with one button at the throat.   Both gentlemen wear the same kind of hat as described under Fig. 359 D, as also hosen, shoes, and swords slung by hangers from the waist-belt.

## HENRY STEWART

### Lord Darnley, 1545–67

Henry 'Stewarde,' by courtesy Lord Darnley, son of the Earl of Lennox and grandson of Margaret Tudor, Queen-Dowager of Scotland, was born in 1545.   Tall of stature with a graceful bearing, he had the youthful attraction of a fair smooth face, broad forehead, and auburn hair.   By nature he was arrogant, petulant, and self-willed, and had a weak sense of moral responsibility.   His mother very carefully educated him in England, though only in accomplishments and seeming good manners, in the hope that he would some day occupy an important position.   This was thrust upon him at the age of nineteen, but he entirely failed to justify expectations.

Fig. 611 is taken from a portrait of Lord Darnley painted by Hans Eworth in 1563.   He was just eighteen at the time, and as he was a very dressy young gentleman we may be sure that his clothes were of the latest and best English cut.

In the original portrait at Holyroodhouse Palace, the entire suit is painted in a very dark warm grey to suggest black silk braided with plaited black silk braid.   This descends the doublet and side-seams both front and back (see Fig. 612) and both the seams of the sleeves, with a double row of cuttes on the outside.   The edges of the panes of his slops are also outlined with braid.

Fig. 611.
Henry, Lord Darnley, 1563

Darnley made his exit from this world on the night of the tragedy of Kirk-o'-Field, amid exquisite surroundings befitting an ancestor of Great Britain's Royal family.

The house consisted of a hall built over an arched crypt, a cabinet and a chamber on the ground floor, with another built above it. These were all sumptuously furnished for the occasion, the hall with a set of beautiful tapestries (looted from the Gordons, by the way!), a chair of estate covered with leather, on a dais in front of a dorsal, both of black velvet fringed with black silk. In the chamber on the ground floor occupied by the Queen was placed a new bed of black figured velvet, enriched with passamaynes of gold and silver and fringed with the same. It had lately come into the Queen's possession with other spoils from Strathbogie.

In Darnley's room, the upper one, also hung with tapestry (of inferior quality we presume), a bath was provided, and a wondrous state bed erected, with hangings of violet-brown velvet ornamented with cloth of gold and silver and embroidered with ciphers and flowers in needlework of gold and silk. There were three coverlets, the uppermost of quilted blue taffeta. On the floor was a Turkey carpet, and the furniture included a high chair covered with purple velvet and fringed, three or four red velvet cushions, and a little table with a cover of green velvet.

During the evening of 10th February, some valuable tapestry, a fur coverlet, and the Queen's bed were removed, the latter being replaced by another of meaner sort hung with seedy purple velvet; and beside it were stacked quantities of gunpowder ready for the fatal moment.

Having sung Psalm V, and drunk a cup of wine to his servants, one of whom only, Taylor, slept in his chamber, Darnley retired to his velvet-hung bed wrapped in a velvet and sable nightgown or dressing-gown, and all was ready for the tragedy—two of the clock, Monday, 11th February 1567.

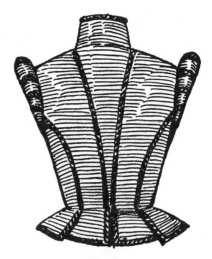

Fig. 612

Darnley's small brother, Charles, aged six, is shown in Fig. 613 taken from the same painting before mentioned. Most small boys of all periods were dressed like their fathers or big brothers, but in miniature; however, young Charles wears a distinctive costume of black silk braided with black, and consisting of a long gown with close-fitting sleeves raised on the shoulders, a 'suit of ruffs' edged with black stitchery or Spanish work, a gold girdle, and a flat black velvet cap with white ostrich feather. A gold key and ring are suspended by a black ferret from his neck. Lord Charles married in 1574

Fig. 613.
Lord Charles Stuart, 1563

Fig. 614.
Lord Edward Seymour, 1563

Elizabeth, daughter of Sir William Cavendish and his wife Elizabeth, better known as Bess of Hardwick. He died in 1576 leaving an only child, the Lady Arabella Stuart, who was born in 1575.

### LORD EDWARD SEYMOUR, 1561–3

Lord Edward Seymour at the age of two is shown in Fig. 614. He is taken from the three-quarter-length portrait of himself and mother (Katherine Grey) painted by Hans Eworth in 1563. She was the second daughter of Henry Grey, Duke of Suffolk, and his Duchess, Frances Brandon, daughter of Mary Tudor I, and therefore, like her sister Lady Jane Grey, in close succession to the throne. Contrary to regulations concerning persons of Royal blood she secretly married in 1560 Edward Seymour, Earl of Hertford, which offence so angered the Queen that both Lady Katherine and her husband were confined as State prisoners in the Tower.    There, in 1561, was born her son Edward, who one day might have been King Edward VII.    Her second son, Thomas, was also born there in 1562-3.

His young lordship wears a black velvet gown braided with fine gold.    It has a long skirt attached and the sleeves are puffed in the fashionable manner on the shoulders, whence hang long tubular sleeves.    The underdress with

Fig. 615.
Scottish Nobleman, 1567

Fig. 616.          Fig. 617.
Noblemen, 1570

close-fitting sleeves is of white silk.    Under his chin is pinned an embroidered bib, and a biggen is worn under a bonet of black velvet studded with gold and jewelled buttons, a white ostrich tip curling over the right side.

Fig. 615 is from a portrait, dated 1567, of a member of the Lennox family. It is interesting because the style fashionable in the previous reigns is at this time worn by a nobleman of Scotland.    The black velvet jerkin edged with strands of gold bullion worked at right angles to the edges is caught at the throat by a jewelled ornament, showing that the jerkin is worn immediately above the embroidered shirt.    The sleeves of rose-coloured satin are fixed to the outer garment and, with the slops of the same colour, are decorated with cuttes bound with gold showing white underneath; the slight padded ridge at the shoulders simulating the roll is somewhat unusual.    The hosen and cap feather are also rose-colour, the cap and shoes black; the sword is carried in a hanger of simple construction.

Figs. 616 and 617 are taken from the painted panel referred to on p. 493. The figures of Lord William Howard (Fig. 616) and Sir Edward Hastings in the original are extremely crude, but the shape and decoration of their costumes are sufficiently clear to enable them to be reproduced in black and white.

The fashions depicted are of the period 1570–5. Fig. 616 wears a PEASCOD DOUBLET with moderately full sleeves and a deep basque, also the new kind of breeches, lately introduced from Venice, called VENETIANS. Both doublet and venetians are profusely decorated with braids and cuttes: so also are the garments worn by Sir Edward (Fig. 617). His doublet is of the older shape, with larged puffed sleeves; and to the paned slops are attached canions tied at the knee. The hats of both gentlemen have high crowns and moderately wide brims, and one has an ostrich tip drooping over the left side. It should be noticed that these gentlemen are carrying staves and not swords. Courtesy apparently demanded that the latter should not be used when arresting a lady, above all, the Lady Elizabeth.

Fig. 618.          Fig. 619.
Gentlemen, 1575

Two gentlemen from Turbervile's work are shown in Figs. 618 and 619. They represent the fashions of the 1570's. The elder is wearing a plain suit of velvet, silk, or cloth, consisting of a doublet with no basques, shoulder pieces, plain sleeves, and the latest thing in breeches known as GALLYHOSEN. At each knee is a row of small tabs, and down the front of the doublet are buttons with worked button-holes—the sole decoration.

The younger man has chosen a suit of cloth banded with a silk braid. The slops, when compared with those of Fig. 611, slope more from the hips to their lowest extremities, a feature which is gradually prevailing.

## James VI

### *King of Scotland, 1566 until 1580*

Lord Darnley's son now makes his appearance on the scene. Born in Edinburgh Castle, 19th June 1566, he, James Stuart, became King of Scotland on his mother's abdication, 24th July 1567, and was crowned on the 29th of the same month. The drawing (Fig. 620), made from the portrait in the National Portrait Gallery, No. 63, shows King James VI, at the age of eight, in 1574; and like all other children, Royal or otherwise, he is dressed like a

Fig. 620. James VI,
King of Scotland, 1574

Fig. 621. La Mode, 1576

grown-up man. He wears a peascod doublet of soft pale-ochre leather, stitched up the front and round the sleeves. Small WINGS surround the armholes, and the collar is high to support the band. The doublet fastens with three gold buttons only, and around the waist is a narrow crimson velvet belt carrying the dagger, sword-belt, and sword all covered with the same velvet. The wide, full gallyhosen in moss-green velvet with loops at the knee are worn over pink stockings and pale buff shoes. The bonet of black velvet has several ostrich tips in natural colourings, and the hatband is composed of a string of pearls. His Small Majesty has at this early age already developed a love of falconry, and upon his gauntleted wrist he carries a favourite bird, with jess and bell attached to its leg. Later he became a very keen hunter, although a remarkably poor horseman.

The fashionable line has not changed much during this period, as may be seen by comparing Fig. 621 with either 611 or 619; the only appreciable difference is in the shape of the slops, which have become less pumpkin-shape than those in Figs. 609, 611, and 617.

The nobleman (Fig. 621) carried the Sword of State immediately in front of the Queen when walking in procession with the Knights of the Garter (1576). On all occasions of State or semi-State the Sword-bearer preceded the Sovereign. The suit is of light colouring and covered with stitchery in black silk. The puffs on the shoulders are obviously dispensed with because

Fig. 622. German Cloak, 1576

they would produce bulkiness in the Spanish cloak, whereas it hangs in radiating folds from the shoulders. It is made of satin or silk, has bands of black velvet of varying width, and is lined with brocade.

Fig. 623. A Knight of the Garter, 1576

Fig. 622 shows a cloak of German fashion worn by a nobleman in the same procession. It is made of silk cut on the circular plan, having sleeves that *could* be worn, but which usually hung empty outside. The cloak is bordered with bands of black velvet diminishing in width as they ascend. Two bands of black velvet border the lining, which is turned back forming revers, and having a step where the flat false hood meets them.

A Knight of the Garter taking part in the procession before mentioned is shown in Fig. 623. Additions and alterations to the Insignia of the Order are to be found in vol. ii, pp. 238 and 241. As there stated the original hood gave place to the chaperon in the reign of Edward IV. In Fig. 623

it should be noticed that the chaperon is still laid over the right shoulder, and that the circular roll is much reduced in size, the diameter measuring not more than six or seven inches.   The chaperon in turn was superseded in the reign of Henry VIII by the flat black velvet bonet with one small feather.   This knight (Fig. 623), dating 1576, is wearing the fashionable hat.   The mantle of the Order in 1515 was of violet velvet (*see* p. 161), but at this date was of white cloth with the Garter embroidered as usual upon the left shoulder. Later Elizabeth changed the white mantle back again to purple velvet.   The surcote, worn over a suit like that shown in Fig. 621, and the chaperon were of crimson velvet, the latter placed very low down on the back under the Collar, with the cape part spread out as shown in the back view.

## PERSONAGES OF DISTINCTION ABOUT THE COURT

### WILLIAM CECIL

#### *Lord Burleigh, 1520 until 1580*

The most important man in the kingdom at the beginning and during the

Fig. 624. William Cecil
Lord Burleigh, 1579

greater part of the reign was William Cecil.   He was born at Bourne, Lincolnshire, 1520, and served both Edward VI and Mary.   On her accession, Elizabeth made him Secretary of State, which post he held until 1572 when he was made Lord Treasurer of England—'a person of most subtle and active spirit . . . wholly intent on Her Majesty's service.'   William Cecil married in 1541 Mary, sister of Sir John Cheke (tutor of Edward VI), and mother of Thomas Cecil, born 1542 and created Earl of Exeter in 1605. Secondly, in 1546, he married Mildred, daughter of Sir Anthony Coke, and they were the parents of Robert, born 1563, who, in 1605, became the first Earl of Salisbury of the Cecil family.

William Cecil was raised to the peerage as Baron Burleigh in 1571 and received the Garter in 1572.   Twelve times Lord Burleigh entertained Queen Elizabeth in his home, each time for several weeks together, and each visit cost him approximately £3,000.   Burleigh House in the Strand was his town residence.

A portrait in the National Portrait Gallery, No. 604, shows Sir William Cecil at about the age of forty.   Many other portraits exist showing him at different ages; and Fig. 624, made from some of these, represents him at the end of this period when he was Lord Treasurer and K.G.   As befitting the dignity of his position Burleigh always dressed soberly but richly.   His suit is of black silk banded with black velvet, over it being a black velvet gown reminiscent of the Middle Ages, lined with sable.   He wears the Collar of the Garter, and in his official capacity a black velvet 'coif,' dating from Henry III's reign (*see* vol. ii, p. 176), under his black velvet hat.

(*Continued on p.* 642)

### Robert Dudley

*Earl of Leicester,* 1532–88

Most famous among the ostentatious courtiers who surrounded the Queen was Robert Dudley.   He was born about 1532, the fifth son of John, Duke of Northumberland.   His chief assets were his goodly person (which won Elizabeth's admiration), showy dress, and skill in the tactics of the courtier.   His paternal grandfather was Edmund Dudley, the extortioner favoured by Henry VII, who came to the block in 1510.   Of Robert's antecedents the uncharitable said that 'he was the son of a duke, the brother of a king, the grandson of an esquire, and the great-grandson of a carpenter, that the carpenter was the only honest man in the family, and the only one who died in his bed.'

Fig. 625. Robert Dudley, Earl of Leicester, 1578

Lord Robert Dudley, as he was known during 1551–3 and 1558–64, was gentleman to the Privy Chamber to Edward VI.   He married in 1549 Amy or Anne, heiress of Sir John Robsart, Kt., of Cumnor Place.   This lady died in 1560, under somewhat suspicious circumstances.   His rise in the Royal favour was nevertheless rapid; in 1559 the Garter was conferred upon him; in 1564 he was created Earl of Leicester; and he entertained the Queen most lavishly at Kenilworth in 1575. His portrait, No. 447 in the National Portrait Gallery, dates about this time (1560–70), and No. 105 in the same gallery shows him at a later date.   The Queen's strong attachment to Dudley is notorious, and there was some anxiety at the time lest she should marry him. Having abandoned in course of time all expectations of becoming King-Consort, he secretly married the Dowager Lady Sheffield, but in the end (1578) married bigamously Lettice Knollys, widow of Walter, Earl of Essex, much to the Queen's displeasure.   The Earl was appointed Lieutenant- and Captain-General of the Queen's armies and companies, 24th July 1588.

Fig. 625 is drawn from a portrait taken at the end of his life, though he is wearing a costume fashionable in the 1570's.   His peascod doublet is of white silk banded with gold; and in place of the ruff a turned-down linen collar edged with reticella is worn and matches the cuffs; the venetians are of grey and gold brocade; over them is placed a padded roll of white silk as described under Fig. 634, the panes decorated with a black velvet pattern (Fig. 626).   White openwork stockings are drawn up over the venetians at the knee.   This fancy treatment of the netherstocks, much the mode at this time, is the shocking indecency complained of by the puritanical Mr. Stubbes. A new fashion in shoes is worn.   They are of white satin and have narrow upstanding tongues.   The short surcote of black velvet lined with sable has full sleeves of black and gold brocade, with a row of gold ornaments set with jewels down the sides.   The hat is black velvet with an osprey and jewel.   The Earl carries his white rod of office in his right hand.   To the great regret of every one, especially the Queen, Lord Leicester died 3rd September 1588 at the age of fifty-four.

Fig. 626. Pattern on Panes

Ambrose Dudley, born about 1528, was Robert's elder brother and known as Lord Ambrose Dudley, 1551–4; he was restored in blood 1558, and became Earl of Warwick in 1561.   He married three times: first, Anne, daughter and co-heiress of William Whorewood; secondly, Elizabeth, daughter of Gilbert, Lord Talboys, before 1553; and thirdly, Lady Anne Russell, eldest daughter of Francis, second Earl of Bedford, in 1565.

In 1576 Lord Warwick fitted out two ships of twenty-five tons burden, and sent Frobisher to search out the North-west Passage.   This is all that is worth recording of him, except that his portrait painted about 1560 in the Wallace Collection, No. 534, shows him wearing a very elaborate doublet with high collar; the shape of the 'wings' is shown to good advantage.   His jewels are also worth noting.

The Earl of Warwick died in 1590; and his effigy, unaccompanied by any of his three wives, is to be seen in St. Mary's, Warwick.   His lordship is dressed in full armour and wears an earl's coronet.

### SIR CHRISTOPHER HATTON, 1540 *until* 1580

Another courtier and 'a man of real capacity' was Christopher Hatton, the youngest son of William Hatton, Esq., of Holdenby, Northants. Born in 1540, he went to Oxford in 1555, but took no degree. On his admission to the Inner Temple in 1559 he became 'the first great exampler of England's Barristers.' It was in 1561 that he attracted the attention of the Queen while dancing a galliard in a masque in which Lord Robert Dudley also took part. 'He came . . . to the Court in a mask [masque] where the Queen first took notice of him, loving him well for his handsome dancing, better for his proper person, and best of all for his great abilities.'

Fig. 627. Sir Christopher Hatton, 1589

In 1564 the Queen took him into her band of fifty Gentlemen Pensioners, and 'for his modest sweetness of condition . . . made him Captain of the Guard' in 1572. Hatton was Member of Parliament for Higham Ferrers in 1571, and for Northants the year following. Knighthood was conferred upon him in 1577.

Sir Christopher's costume, as shown in his portraits, was smart and of the latest fashion. Fig. 627 is reconstructed from these portraits and depicts him as he appeared between 1570 and 1580. There is a head-and-shoulders portrait of him in the National Portrait Gallery wearing the same dress, but dated 1589: the portrait is, however, a little earlier than this. The doublet is white with braidings of red and gold, and gold buttons down the front: between the braidings is a row of perpendicular pinkings. The venetians are red and gold brocade, with white fancy-woven stockings and French pantoufles. The cloak and hip-roll are of black velvet, diapered with pearls set in three leaves of gold.

The Italian bonet is of the same material; it has a row of gold jewelled ornaments round the hatband, a brooch, and tuft of feathers. Sometimes Hatton is shown wearing a goffered ruff, and sometimes a lawn collar of Spanish work edged with lace which matches that on his cuffs, as shown in Fig. 627.

The courtier standing in the background of the painting (Plate XXXII C) is said to be Sir Christopher. (*Continued on p.* 643)

The insertion of a note from Harrison on the subject of knighthood is opportune here:

'When a man is made a knight, he kneeling down is striken of the King, or his substitute with his sword naked upon the back or shoulder, the Prince saying, "Soyes Cheualier au nom de Dieu," and when he riseth up the King saith: "Aduances bon Cheualier." This is the manner of dubbing knights at this present time, and the term *dubbing* is the old term for that purpose and not *creation*, howbeit in our time the word *making* is most in use among the common sort.'

### Edward de Vere

#### *Earl of Oxford, 1550–1604*

A very dashing and fashionable young man of this era was Edward de Vere, born at Castle Hedingham, 1550, and the son of the sixteenth Earl of Oxford. Precocious in youth, he matriculated at Cambridge at the age of eight—an effort never equalled before or since. Young Edward succeeded to the title and the office of Great Chamberlain of England in 1562, and took his M.A. degree in 1564. In 1571 he married Anne Cecil (who died in 1588), daughter of Lord Burleigh. Naturally the seventeenth of a long line of earls of the de Vere family, dating back to 1155, was a great Society catch, as the following excerpt from a letter written by Lord St. John shows. He says:

'The Earl of Oxenforde hath gotten him a wyffe, or at the least a wyffe hath caught him. This is Mistress Anne Cycille, whereunto the Queen hath given her consent, the which hath caused great weeping, wailing, and sorrowful chere of those that hoped to have had that golden daye.' No long time after his wedding, he toured the Continent, like most young men of the nobility, without his wife we may assume. On his return in 1574, it was noted that: 'My Ld of Oxforth is lately growne into great credite; for the Q. Ma*tie* delitithe more in his parsonage & his dauncing & valientnes then any other . . . if it were not for his fyckle hed, he would passe any of them shortly.'

In 1575 he sat for his portrait—a head and shoulders, from which Fig. 846 has been drawn.

Yet Lord Oxford was by no means a mere Court gallant. 'At his own charge and in pure love of his country, he hired ships and joined the Grand Fleet sent to oppose the Spanish Armada.' He was, moreover, a poet and a wit of no mean order; but in spite of these admirable qualities, he was already a spendthrift, and in later life dissipated the greater part of his fortune. His second Countess was Elizabeth, daughter of Thomas Trentham, Esq., whom he married about 1591. His death took place in 1604; he was buried at Hackney, and Castle Hedingham passed into the hands of Lord Burleigh.

## Sir Philip Sidney, 1554–86

Philip Sidney, the pattern of chivalry, was born at Penshurst, 29th November 1554, son of Sir Henry Sidney, Lord Deputy of Ireland and President of Wales. The child was named after the husband of Queen Mary. To Shrewsbury he was sent to school so that he might be under the charge of Thomas Ashton, equally renowned as courtier and schoolmaster. He left Oxford in 1571 without taking a degree, and at eighteen, the usual age, obtained the requisite licence, dated 1572, to travel abroad, witnessing in Paris the massacre of St. Bartholomew. On his return to England he joined the Court at Kenilworth in 1575. An excellent portrait of him as a young man of twenty-three is in the National Portrait Gallery, No. 2096, and in this he wears a suit of the same cut as that shown in Fig. 655.

At Shottesbrooke Park is a very beautiful full-length portrait of Sir Philip Sidney painted about 1580 by Pantoja de la Cruz (1551–1610). He is shown at the age of twenty-six, wearing demi-armour, i.e. cuirass, armpieces, and tassets, of steel damascened with gold. The remainder of his equipment is of a pale buff colour; the slops are of soft leather with panes decorated with cuttes, and long round-tied boots turned down at the top are attached to the slops by inverted V-shaped straps (see Fig. 908).

A later portrait, dated 1585, will be found in the National Portrait Gallery, No. 1862. It is referred to on p. 547.

Although he was in temporary disgrace with the Queen for airing his opinions on her proposed French marriage, as also for quarrelling with the Earl of Oxford, he soon recovered the Royal favour and was knighted in 1583, and in the same year married Frances, daughter of Sir Francis Walsingham. So attached did Elizabeth become to her handsome young courtier that she prevented him from accompanying Sir Francis Drake to America, and even, it is said, disappointed him of the Polish throne. Sir Philip Sidney, 'a person of great parts,' 'a noble and matchless Gentleman,' was mortally wounded at Zutphen, 1586, and is buried in St. Paul's. For many months after his death it was counted indecent for any gentleman of quality to appear, at Court or in the city, in light or gaudy apparel.

## Sir John Hawkyns, 1532 *until* 1580

John Hawkyns was born at Plymouth in 1532. Chief of the 'Sea Lions' of the Elizabethan era he was knighted by Queen Elizabeth the year she ascended the throne. His seafaring expeditions were important; but what is more so to most men and women of to-day, he has the credit for introducing tobacco into England in 1565. 'Tabaco' was the native name for a leaf of the plant, rolled like a tube, through which the Indians inhaled the smoke. The name was adopted by the Spaniards for the leaf. In 1573 we have a statement made by Harrison the chronicler to this effect: 'In these daies, the taking-in of the smoke of the Indian herbe called "tabaco" by an instrument formed like a litle ladell, wherby it passeth from the mouth into the hed and stomach, is gretlie taken-up and used in England, against Rewmes and some other diseases ingendred in the longes and inward parts, and not without effect.'   Of his slave-trading activities the less said the better.

Sir John was elected Member of Parliament for his native city in 1572, and became Treasurer and Controller of the Navy from 1573 onwards.   Fig.

Fig. 628. A Young Gentleman, 1581

Fig. 629. An Overcoat, 1580

851 is taken from his portrait in the Plymouth City Museum.   In it, a three-quarter, he wears a peascod doublet with narrow hip-roll, venetians, and an embroidered cloak all in black.

The gentleman (Fig. 628) is taking the air at Brightstowe,[1] for the drawing is taken from a map of that place dated 1581.   The costume is of the type worn by the aristocracy in ordinary life.   It is a bright dress according to the original, the doublet being red cloth and the slops yellow braided with red. The cloak is of black cloth bound with black velvet, the hat also of black velvet, the hose yellow, shoes black, and gloves brown.   Should the weather be cold or stormy, he would don the very comfortable overcoat shown in Fig. 629.   This would be made of cloth, the best being of velvet faced with fur and often lined throughout with the same.   Its hanging sleeves could be

[1] Bristol, 'the place of the bridge.'

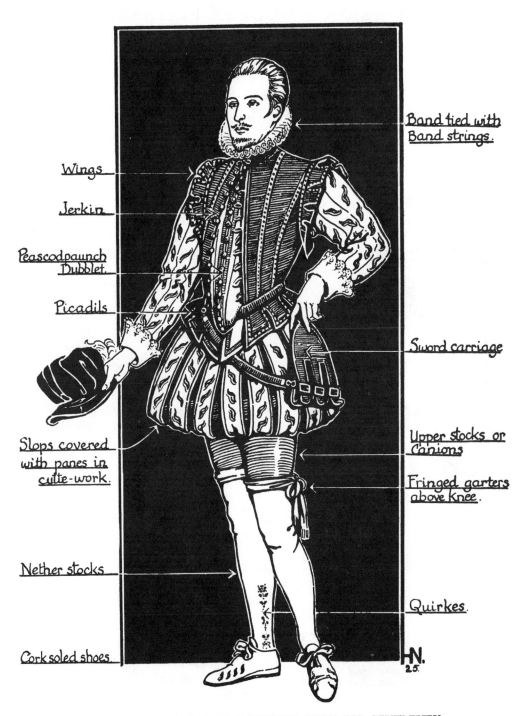

Band tied with Band strings.

Wings

Jerkin

Peascodpaunch Dubblet.

Picadils

Sword carriage

Slops covered with panes in cutte-work.

Upper stocks or Canions

Fringed garters above Knee.

Nether stocks

Quirkes.

Cork soled shoes.

HN. 25.

Fig. 630. GENERALIZED ELIZABETHAN MODE FOR GENTLEMEN

worn if required, the tabs at the wrists forming a protection for the hands even though gloves are carried. The hat is of velvet, cloth, or blocked felt, with a small plume.

The general survey of men's costume which follows applies not only to the period covered by Section I, but also to that of Section II. The subject has been concentrated in this place instead of being divided as has been done for women, because gentlemen's costume was not so varied during the Elizabethan era as that of the ladies.

Fig. 630 gives a practical illustration of all items of dress which, with slight differences, constituted fashionable attire during the whole period of Elizabeth's reign. The young man himself actually dates about 1580. The details of his costume which show affinities with both earlier and later styles are now described.

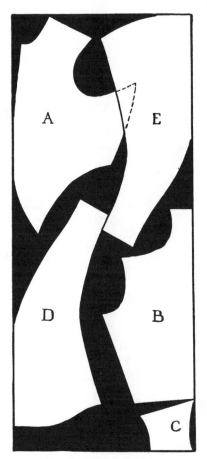

Fig. 631. Man's Doublet

### THE DOUBLET

The doublet was a close-fitting body garment cut in four sections as shown in the diagram, Fig. 631. A is half the front, B half the back, C half the high upstanding collar, and D and E are the outer and inner parts of a sleeve. It has been noted in describing the drawings in the previous chapter that a little padding was inserted in the front of the doublet just above the waist-line. By the year 1577 this padding, known as 'bombast,' became very pronounced. The doublet was generally fastened with buttons, and the centre line down the front, where it opened, gradually protruded from the chest into a curve at the waist suggesting a peascod in shape. This was known as a 'peascod paunch.' Later, whalebone busks were inserted behind the seams, or parchment glued together in layers was used as a foundation to make the fronts of the doublet stiff and stick out.

The peascod paunch appeared about 1574 and assumed its largest proportions between 1580 and 1590.

Fig. 632 shows a military gambeson of canvas covering diamond-shaped steel plates mounted on a lining of canvas. It has a peascod paunch and undoubtedly is constructed in much the same manner as the peascod-paunched doublet. A is half the front, which laces down the centre, and to it is attached a hip piece, D. B is half the back. The projecting portion C passes round the back under the arms, where it is laced to the corresponding part.

To the waist-line of the doublet a row of tabs was sewn, but when the front of it was cut in two, sometimes three, sections, these sections continued below the waist-line and formed one tab to each section, the seams being usually overlaid with braid or embroidery. This braiding of the seams is to be seen in several earlier drawings, for instance Figs. 492, 493, and a back view, Fig. 612. Loops or scallops sometimes took the place of tabs.

Any decoration of this kind acquired the name of PICADILS, derived from the Spanish 'pica,' a spear, diminutive 'picadilla,' meaning a *little spear-head*. At first the name was applied to the pointed edgings of

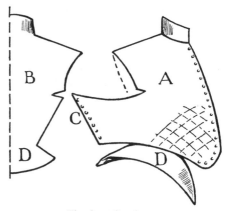

Fig. 632. Gambeson

the ruff (*see* p. 632) which suggested spear-points. Later—during the second half of this reign—it was given to any fancy-shaped edging. Those surrounding the armholes were generally termed 'wings.' Collars were finished off in this manner to help support the ruff or 'neck whisk.' Picadils reached their greatest development about the year 1595. Master Higgins, the tailor, who introduced the fashion of picadils into England, made a small fortune, and owned quite a large estate north of St. James's Palace. It is said that the road leading to his house was, in compliment to him, called 'Piccadilly.'

Stubbes, in a long rigmarole, gives some interesting details of the doublets as worn in the 1580's: 'They are no less monstrous than the rest of their garments; for now the fashion is to have them hang down to the middest of their theighs, being so hard-quilted, and stuffed with four, five, or six pounds of bombast at the least, and sewed, as they can neither work, nor yet will play in them, through the excessive heat; therefore they are forced to wear them loose about them.' This accounts for the doublet being often seen in portraits unfastened up the front, otherwise they could hardly stoop to the ground or give a gracious low bow. Some doublets were made of 'satin, taffeta, silk, grogram, chamlet, gold, silver, and what not.    Slashed, jagged, cutte, carned [tabbed] pincked and laced with all kinds of costly lace of divers and sundry colours.'

## THE JERKIN

The jerkin, cut to fit closely over the doublet, was very popular, and was made of leather, velvet, satin, or silk.    The waist-line and arm-holes were finished off with picadils.    It had no sleeves to be worn on the arm, but sometimes had long hanging ones, whence emerged the sleeves of the doublet underneath.

## CORSETS

Corsets were worn by fashionable men as well as by women.    Confining the waist helped considerably to accentuate the size of the slops.

The following is a further quotation from Stubbes:

'Their shirts, which all in a manner do wear (for if the Nobility or Gentry only did wear them, it were somedeal [somewhat] more tollerable) are either of cambrick, Holland [cloth], Lawn, or else of the finest cloth that may be got.    And of these kind of shirts every one now doth wear alike. . . . and wrought throughout with needle work of silk, and such like, and curiously stitched with open seam, and many other knackes besides.    Shirts cost ten, twenty, forty shillings; some five pounds, some twenty nobles, and some ten pound a piece.'

## TRUNKS OR SLOPS, AND HOSEN

Slops gradually increased in size between 1565 and 1575, often reaching vast proportions, and were in shape like a pumpkin with the greatest width in the middle, each leg being separate from the fork downwards.    These later slops sprang from a narrow waistband, the hip yoke being omitted. Panes elaborately embroidered and decorated, and often with many cuttes, were still the fashion.    The under part or lining was 'pulled through' in a manner which verged on the eccentric.    Shakespeare refers to these cutte slops as 'short blistered breeches' in *Henry VIII*, Act I, Sc. III, where Sir Thomas Lovel remarks: 'They must either (for so run the conditions) leave those remnants of fool and feather, that they got in France [meaning the German fashion of slashes, and long feathers in their hats, which were so fashionable at the Field of the Cloth of Gold] . . . renouncing clean the faith they have in tennis, and tall stockings, short blister'd breeches. . . .'

To make these slops stand out, busks of whalebone were used by the fashionable and wealthy; the less expensive alternative being bombast, i.e. a padding of wool, cotton, flock, horse-hair, bran, sawdust, or even rags. Slops were no longer attached to the lower edge of the doublet, in the manner shown in vol. ii, Fig. 314, but to the doublet lining or a canvas inner belt; eyelet holes and laces were, however, still employed.

The following directions from Richard Onslowe's letter to Sir William Cecil, Kt., February 1565, may be useful in the making of slops:

'. . . lyne a sloppe-hose not cut in panes with a lynyng of cotton stytched to the sloppe, over and besides the lynnen lynyng, and the other lynyng straight to the leg: and that any loose lynyng not straytt to the leg was not permytted, but for the lynyng of panes only: and that the hole upperstock being in our sloppe uncutt, could not be sayd to be in panes.'

The stages in the development of the proportions of slops and TRUNK-HOSE worn during the reign of Elizabeth have been so excellently summarized by Mr. Francis M. Kelly, that we cannot do better than reproduce his own words from the *Connoisseur*:

'1555–60. Reaching to about mid-thigh (the normal length) and moderately wide.

1560–5. Gradually swelling, length about same.

1565–75. Often of vast circumference, without appreciable lengthening.

1575–95. The older forms still seen, but the modish world either prefers venetians, or curtails the trunks till they are often no more than a padded roll barely covering the buttocks. (Trunk-hose are either worn with long cloth stockings sewn to them, or—from about 1570—they are equipped with canions.) For a while they appear to have lost favour with fashionable folk.

1595–1600. Revival of their vogue.'

Spanish trunk-hose broadened downwards to a square base.

Long hose, covering the leg from thigh to foot, continued in use, but about the 1560's an alternative divided form came into fashion. The upper portions covering the thigh were called UPPER STOCKS or CANIONS (a revival of tonnelets), and Fig. 633 is a drawing of one. It has a point in front attached to a strap and buckled above or below the knee. Canions appeared about 1570. The lower portions were called NETHER STOCKS or stockings, and were usually secured above the knee by garters with fringed ends. The following method of cross-gartering the knee was also adopted. The band of silk was placed first *above* the knee, crossed behind, and brought round and tied at the side *below* the knee. This method of tying could be reversed. Another way is shown in Fig. 793. Here the band of silk is first placed under the knee-cap, crossed behind, brought up above the knee, and tied in a loop and two ends on top.

Fig. 633. Canion

Nether stocks were 'curiously knitte with open seam down the leg, with "quirks" and CLOCKS about the ankles and sometimes interlaced with gold and silver threads as is wonderful to behold.'

> 'These worsted stocks of bravest dye,
> And silken garters fringed with gold,
> These corkēd shoes[1] to bear them high.'

[1] *See* p. 758.     [*Poem dated* 1595.]

Other materials besides worsted were used for making stocks (*see* p. 545).

'Venetians' was another name for canions which originated in Venice; they were really peg-top breeches.  Some were moderately padded on the hips, others outrageously so.  In Fig. 616, among others, the gentleman is wearing venetians.  Sometimes they were very rich and ornate, and Stubbes says that some cost as much as £100 per pair.  On top of venetians or canions a roll, or pansid slop on a smaller scale, was often worn (*see* Fig. 658).  Fig. 634 shows half of one of these rolls and is drawn from one in the London Museum. The original measures thirteen inches round the thigh.  The panes are composed of blue silk with a pattern in pale raw-sienna velvet; the under padding is covered with white silk woven with lines of gold and silver and a pine design.  A patch of white silk brocaded with sprigs of light and dark blue flowers and green leaves was inserted in the eighteenth century.

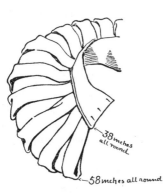

Fig. 634.
Half a Roll or Pansid Slop

Again the informative yet carping Stubbes is useful: 'Then they have hosen, which as they be of divers fashions so are they of sundry names.  Some be called French hose, some gally hose, and some Venetians.  The French hose are of two divers makings, for the common French hose containeth length, breadth, and sidenes sufficient, and is made very round. The other containeth neither length, breadth, nor sidenes, being not past a quarter of a yard wide, whereof some be paned, cutte, and drawn out with costly ornaments, with canions annexed reaching down beneath their knees.'

Gallyhosen, GALLIGASKINS, or galliegascoignes were large, wide breeches gathered or pleated at the waist and reaching down to the knees (*see* Figs. 620 and 807).  They were introduced from Gascony.

'The gallyhosen are made very large and wide, reaching down to their knees only, with three or four gards a piece laid down along either hose.

'The Venetian hosen, they reach beneath the knee to the gartering place of the leg, where they are tied finely with silk points, or some such like, and laid on also with rows of lace or gards as the other before.  And yet not withstanding all this is not sufficent, except they be made of silk, velvet, satin, damask, and other such precious things besides.  Yea, every one serving men and other inferior to them, in every condition will not stick to flaunt it out in these kind of hosen, with all their other apparel suitable thereunto.'

## STOCKINGS (*Chausses*): WOMEN AND MEN

At 'Newyers-tyde,' 1561, Mrs. Mountague, one of Queen Elizabeth's gentlewomen, presented Her Majesty with a pair of knitted silk stockings. It had taken quite ten years to discover the secret of making them, even with Edward VI's cast-off silk stockings as a model.

Mrs. Mountague told the Queen that she had had them made on purpose, and would set some more in hand at once if they pleased her. 'Do so,' said the Queen, 'for indeed I like silk stockings so well because they are pleasant, fine, and delicate, that henceforth I will wear no more cloth stockings.'

The stockings shown at Hatfield House (Fig. 635), said to have been worn by Queen Elizabeth, are knitted by hand, but look much more like crochet, in a silk thread almost as coarse as string. The stitch is plain-stitch, and over the whole surface are lozenges with open-work borders. These stockings are of a deep sulphur yellow, and bands of silk of the same shade two and a half inches wide are sewn to the tops, most likely to roll round the garters.

In a wardrobe account of about this time the following entry appears:

'To Alice Mountague, the Quene's Majestie's silk-woman, for sondryie nescesaries by her dilivered to her Majestie's use—£702 11s. 0¾d.'

It is not clear if the whole of this vast sum was spent on stockings. The salary of Henry Herne, the Queen's hosier, was only £11 7s. 10d. per annum.

Silk stockings formed an acceptable present to Elizabeth, e.g.: 'One peire of silk stockings and a peire of garters of white sypres, by Mrs. Vaughan.'

Fig. 635

Of course, the news of Her Majesty's latest acquisition of attractive silk hosiery gradually leaked out—or was it given voluntarily? Most certainly her ladies-in-waiting had every opportunity of a close inspection, and who knows but that many gentlemen-in-waiting may have been treated to a more distant view?

It was not long, however, before the ultra-fashionable of both sexes wore hand-knitted silk stockings, and the reputation of English-made hosiery attained a high standard. A stocking-maker of the time was known as a gordner or gradner. The ordinary person, and even the best-dressed, still used worsted, as silk stockings were very expensive. In 1564 an acute London apprentice named William Rider chanced to see a pair of knit worsted stockings in the lodgings of an Italian merchant from Mantua. He borrowed them—most likely without permission—and caused others to be made like them. These were the first hand-knitted stockings made in England since early medieval days.

Fancy knitted stockings are seen worn by gentlemen in Figs. 625 and 627.

(*Continued on p.* 630)

### Cloaks

Cloaks were circular, or shaped like that shown in diagram, Fig. 507. Some were short; others reached to the feet, and being ample resembled mantles.

Collars were usual, but a few cloaks were without them. The German cloak (*see* Figs. 622 and 654) was in reality a large jacket, with sleeves not intended to be worn but hanging, so giving width to the figure.

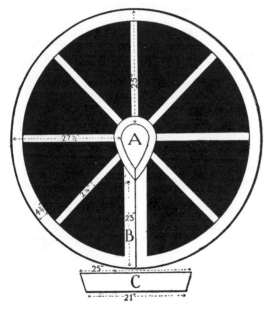

Fig. 636.
Diagram of Cloak

Fig. 637.
Embroidery on Cloak

The diagram (Fig. 636) is drawn from a cloak in the London Museum: A is the hole for the head, B the front, and C the collar. It is of crimson velvet having gold embroidery in a scroll design round the circumference and along the radii, shown white in the diagram. This design is reproduced in Fig. 637, and forms part of the four-and-a-half-inch border: the main scrolls are in gold silk appliqué edged with gold cord or twisted bullion, as are also the minor decorations. The edge is finished with a looped fringe of crimson silk and gold thread, and the cloak is lined throughout with a small patterned crimson and gold brocade.

A later version of the Spanish hooded cloak or muceta, described and figured in Chapter III, p. 417, is shown in Fig. 638. This muceta dates at the end of the century. The patterns, cut for a bishop by an eminent Spanish tailor of the period, are laid out on a length of cloth doubled. The reader should be able to puzzle out the construction for himself.

A hood of different shape, to be attached to a cloak, is given in Fig. 639, in which AB is the opening for the face, and BC surrounds the neck.

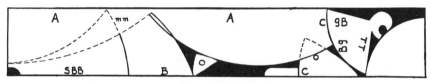

Manteo y museta de paño para obispo.

Fig. 638

A cross between a cloak and a jerkin, known as a MANDILION, was worn towards the end of the period covered by Part I. It was a loose short coat similar in shape to the journade (*see* vol. ii, Fig. 564), but sometimes slit up the sides. It was made of all kinds of material and often richly braided. It had sleeves which were seldom worn, the coat itself being used as a cape, or more frequently draped around the shoulders. The manner of wearing the mandilion askew, or 'Collie - Westonward' as this mode was termed by Harrison, is to be seen in the portrait of Sir Philip Sidney, No. 1862 in the National Portrait Gallery.

Stubbes tells us that the fashionable of the 80's and 90's 'have clokes . . . of diverse and sundry colours, white, red, taunie, black, green, yellow, russet, purple, violet, and infinite other colours: some of cloth, silk, velvet, taffata, and such like, whereof some be of the Spanish, French, and Dutch fashions. Some short scarcly reaching to the girdlestead, or waist, some to the knee, and othersome trayling upon the ground (almost) liker gowns than clokes. Then they are garded with velvet gardes, or else laced with costly lace either

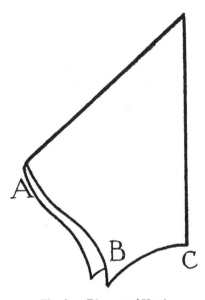

Fig. 639. Diagram of Hood

of gold, silver, or at least of silk three or four fingers broad down the back, about the skirts and everywhere else. And now of late they use to gard their clokes round about the skirts with bables, I should say bugles, and other kinds of glass, and all to shine to the eye. They are sometimes so lined as the inner side standeth almost in as much as the outside: some have sleeves, othersome have none, some have hoods to pull over the head, some have none; some are hanged with points and tassels of gold, silver, or silk, some without all this.'

He also mentions that 'some be made with collars and some without; some close to the body, some loose, which they call mandilians, covering the whole of the body down to the thighs, like bags or sacks that were drawn over them, hiding the demensions and lineaments of the same.'

### SWORDS AND DAGGERS

Fig. 640. Rapier

The sword was slung on the left hip by belts and a hanger, as described under Figs. 486, 501, and 502, and types of hilt can be seen in many of the previous drawings in vol. iii, especially Fig. 503. In the reign of the Emperor Charles V, the RAPIER was introduced from Italy into Spain, and brought to England in the entourage of Prince Philip. The rapier was also known in France and Germany, and became a fashionable weapon in England during the early years of Elizabeth's reign.

Stow in 1578 tells us that 'shortly after the thirteenth year [1571] of Elizabeth began long tucks [swords] and long rapiers, and he was held the greatest gallant that had the deepest ruffe and longest rapier.' This type of sword (Fig. 640) had a long thin narrow blade, generally four-sided, the best being forged at Toledo, with a basket or cup-hilt either solid or perforated with a pattern, the smartest being of silver or silver gilt 'damasked, varnished, and engraven marvellous goodly.' The quillons were straight or curved, and the handle long.

The rapier was expressly designed for thrusting. Gentlemen rivalled each other in the length of their rapiers, so that Queen Elizabeth was forced to issue a proclamation in 1580 limiting the length of the blade to thirty-six inches. The scabbards were as ornate as the hilts, being often covered with velvet decorated with gold or silver, and sometimes set with jewels.

In the Italian mode of fighting, the rapier was held in the right hand to attack, and the dagger in the left to defend, and divert the thrusts of the adversary.

The dagger, originally stuck through the pouch and later (in the reign of Henry VIII) slung by a cord from the waist sash, was during the Elizabethan era passed through the waist-belt on the right side, the handle or dudgeon projecting in front so as to be readily grasped. This fashion of

Fig. 641. Dagger

carrying the dagger was introduced by the Spaniards in the last reign, and in this volume Lord Darnley is the first to be shown wearing it (Fig. 611). The top of the hilt is just visible. Probably the first Englishman's portrait to show the dagger stuck through the waist-belt is that of Ambrose Dudley (1560) in the Wallace Collection.

Fig. 641 shows an ordinary dagger of this period. When carried by the nobility, the handle was often elaborately decorated. The length of the blade varied, and daggers are usually referred to as long or short; but in 1562 the length of blade was limited to twelve inches.

The term 'bilbo' meant a sword blade made in Bilbao, and noted for the fine temper of its blade. It is frequently used humorously for the sword of a braggart.

### THE HANDKERCHIEF (continued from p. 261)

During the reign of Elizabeth, handkerchiefs were universally used by ladies and gentlemen, and generally carried in the hand. They were made of very fine linen, lawn, cambric, or silk, about twelve or fifteen inches square—very large by modern standards—and edged with embroidery or lace of various widths, and sometimes both.

The useful yet dainty handkerchief often had a picot edging, and ornaments worked in white thread are sometimes seen hanging from the corners in portraits. Fig. 642 shows one kind in use.

Fig. 642

The estimation in which handkerchiefs were held is evidenced by the mention of them in wills and bequests, and many details are found in wardrobe

Fig. 643. Embroidered Border in Handkerchief

accounts. A set of six handkerchiefs edged with passamayne of gold and silk was a New Year's gift to Queen Mary, and Queen Elizabeth frequently received such gifts.  The following is a typical entry of 1578: 'Six faire handkerches of camerike of black Spanish worke edged with a brode bone lace of gold and silver.'  A handkerchief belonging to Queen Elizabeth was left behind after one of her visits to Warwick Castle, and can be seen there for the asking.  It is of deep cream linen (possibly with age) having a border two inches wide embroidered with red roses and green leaves in silks and gold thread.  Fig. 643 is a drawing of the border.  The handkerchief measures thirteen inches square.

Borders embroidered with blue thread of Coventry—a very vivid blue— were fashionable during the later part of the reign.  At this time also handkerchiefs were often made of tiffany.

The historian Stow tells us that 'maydes and gentlewomen gave to their favourites, as tokens of their love, little handkerchiefs of about three or four inches square, wrought round about, with buttons at each corner.'  The best were edged with gold and silver lace.  The fortunate recipient wore these favours tucked into the band of his hat, and on this account they were of diminutive size.

A few lines from a poem of this time proves the handkerchief to be a very important item of dress even among the lower classes:

'Nor imitate with Socrates,
  to wipe thy snivelled nose
Vpon thy cap, as he would doe,
  nor yet upon thy clothes.

But keepe it cleane with handkerchiffe,
  provided for the same,
Not with thy fingers or thy sleeve,
  therein thou art too blame.'

The handkerchief was the most general item of dress for the medium of perfumery.  When used by fashionable men and women it was scented with some delicious perfume.  Certain scents had disinfecting properties, which none the less had a pleasant smell and were very necessary.

The modern handkerchief sachet had its prototype in the 'sweete bagges' of Elizabethan days, which were dainty accessories much appreciated by both ladies and gentlemen.  Such articles were often presented to the Queen: 'A sweete bagge all over ymbrodered, and six handkerchers'; '24 small sweete bagges of sarsenett of sundry cullors, and six handkerchers of camberick wrought with black silk, and edged with a passamayne of gold, given by Mrs. Huggens.'

## THE GLOVE (*continued from p. 261*)

Gloves used by ladies and gentlemen of this period had cuffs or gauntlets larger than before and richly embroidered in silks, bullion, and often spangles. Silk fringe, sometimes mixed with gold thread, finished off the bottom edge. A characteristic feature of Elizabethan gloves was the two, or perhaps three, loops also embroidered, which connected loosely the two edges of the gauntlet. Those of the very best quality were imported from Venice.

Fig. 644 shows one of these embroidered gloves as worn by the fashionable. It is made of light buff leather. The embroidery consists of roses in silk of two shades of pink and blue, with green trees linked by half-circles of silver wire gimp. A fanciful bird appears twice in the border. Below the gauntlet is a narrow binding of pink silk finished with silver fringe. The loops are also of pink silk embroidered with silver. This glove once belonged to Mary Queen of Scots, and is now in the Saffron Walden Museum. It measures fourteen and a half inches from finger-tip to base of fringe.

Fig. 644. Glove of Mary Stuart

Shakespeare's gloves can be seen in the museum at Stratford - on - Avon. They are about the same length, but cut in one with the cuff. Fancy braids and a narrow fringe finish off the edge, and on the back is a braided design. Several Elizabethan gloves are to be found in museums. A beautiful pair, of white embroidered kid, was presented to Queen Elizabeth by the University of Oxford, but inadvertently left behind; they now repose in the Ashmolean. On the occasion of another visit to Oxford: '6th Sept. 1566. This day, the Commissary and Proctors in the name of the whole University, presented unto the Queen's Majesty six pairs of gloves, that were very fine; and to divers of the Noblemen, and to the Officers of the Queen's House, some two pair, some one; which were accepted thankfully.'

Fig. 645. Cutte Glove

The man of fashion was very fastidious about his gloves; so that the author of *A Briefe Conceipte of English Pollicys* writes in 1581: 'There is no man can be contented now with any other gloves than is made in France or in Spain nor Kersey, but it must be of Flanders dye.'   However, Duke Frederick of Württemberg considered English-made gloves good enough for him, as he commissions his secretary while travelling in this country to purchase some. 'Six pair English gloves, of equal quality at 8*s*., making 48*s*. = 12 Gulden 12 Batzen,' are included in his account for goods bought.

Fig. 646. Mitten

Gloves with a series of cuttes round the fingers to show the rings were still fashionable, and an excellent example is to be seen in the portrait of the Empress Maria by Antonio Moro in the Prado.   Fig. 645 is a drawing of them. Holes in gloves were made also to prevent any ill effects from confined perspiration: 'White prick seamed gloves of kid.'   It is stated that on more than one occasion Queen Elizabeth wore gloves of kid having five air-holes, rather larger than melon seeds, stamped in the palms. Gloves were also made of chicken-skin, not necessarily of a chicken but the prepared skin of a very young animal, and ornamented in various ways.

Perfumed gloves were very little used during the first years of the reign of Elizabeth.   In 1573 the young Earl of Oxford, returning from his travels on the Continent, brought some from Italy, including many other 'pleasant things' such as 'sweet-bags,' and perfumed leather jerkins.  He presented Her Majesty with 'a payre of perfumed gloves, trimmed onlie with foure tuftes of roses in culler'd silk.  The queene took such pleasure in those gloves that she was pictured with those gloves upon her hands.'   So deliciously smelling were they that she christened the scent 'The Earl of Oxford's perfume.'   Gloves of this odour came to be known as 'Oxford gloves'—'two pairs of Oxford gloves' cost 2*s*. 4*d*.—although they were not necessarily made in Oxford.

In 1578 when the Queen again visited Cambridge the Vice-Chancellor presented her with 'a pair of perfumed gloves garnished with embroiderie and goldsmiths-wourke.'   These cost the University 60*s*.   '15 paires of perfumed gloves' were given by different people to the Queen as New Year's gifts in 1599.

White gloves were worn at weddings—'innocent white wedding gloves'—

and the custom of winning a pair of gloves by kissing a person when caught sleeping originated in the sixteenth century.

*Mittens* (*see* vol. ii, p. 93). In the sixteenth century this term is applied not only to a bag for the fingers and a separate compartment for the thumb, but also to *warm* gloves with separate fingers. They were made of many kinds of material: leather, linen, or velvet mittens with stitched or fancy ornament, or knitted wool.

Fig. 646 gives one of a pair of mittens which belonged to Queen Elizabeth. They measure sixteen inches in length, and are of crimson velvet embroidered on the backs with a design (*see* inset) in gold, and edged with gold cord. The cuffs are covered with white satin cut in panels at the bottom, and worked in a design of flowers, leaves, etc., in various coloured silks, gold and silver thread and spangles; the whole background is besprinkled with tiny beads.

According to Shakespeare (*Winter's Tale*) gloves [1] were sold by milliners: 'No milliner can so fit his customers with gloves' (*see* p. 453).

### Perfumes and Pomanders and Roses (*continued from p. 272*)

Edmund Howes tells us that perfumes were not made in England until the early years of Elizabeth's reign. At this time very strong aromatics, such as musk and civet, formed the basis of most preparations. Sweet-smelling waters were distilled from roses, lavender, rosemary, and juniper, and were used to scent handkerchiefs, clothes, and bed-linen.

Floors were perfumed with sweet-smelling rushes or sprinkled with scented waters. For fumigating the atmosphere of stuffy rooms, perfumed bellows were brought into use. 'The smoke of juniper is in great request with us to sweeten our chambers.'

A pomander of the time of Elizabeth is shown in Fig. 647. It takes the form of a vase two inches in diameter, and is of gold and enamels. There are six sections, each containing space for one kind of perfume; these are hinged at the bottom and fall when the catch at the top is released, like the pomander shown in Fig. 304. The ladies (Figs. 679 and 595) are carrying pomanders at the ends of their girdles.

Fig. 647. Pomander

'Perfumes of sundry kyndes bought and provided by John Wynyarde and John Doden £68 7s. 11d.' is a heavy item which occurs in the Queen's accounts for 1568.

That gentlemen used pomanders is not certain, but most likely. It was,

[1] The Glovers' Company was not incorporated until 1638.

however, the correct thing for both ladies and gentlemen to carry on their persons a 'casting-bottle' with a perforated top and containing scent.

The scent of flowers was also much appreciated, especially by the ladies, for we are informed that they 'will carry in their hands nosegays and posies of flowers to smell at, and which is more, two or three nosegays sticked in their breasts before.'

That Queen Elizabeth was passionately fond of flowers is well known. As before mentioned, pansies were much in the Royal favour, even perhaps taking precedence over roses; though in some of her portraits the Queen is shown with one in her hand, and in others she wears a full-blown rose, such as are familiar to us to-day, fastened to her ruff. She liked also to be surrounded by flowers, and her chambers were made cheerful with the presence of cut blooms in large bowls and vases. Even in her progresses through the country she indulged in her love of flowers: so that as much as £182 5s. 5d. was so spent by Francis Cornwalles, groom-porter, for the privy chamber of presence 'for flowers and bowes [bowers].'

The cult of the rose had now developed since Dr. Linacre's introduction (see p. 294) owing to the perseverance and skill of John Gerard, the celebrated English herbalist and surgeon. He was born at Nantwich in 1545 and lived in Holborn, where he had a garden in which he devoted a great deal of his time to the cultivation of rare plants, especially those for medicinal use, and nine different varieties of roses. He also became an expert in the laying out of gardens, including those of Lord Burleigh's house in the Strand and at Theobalds, Hertfordshire. He died in 1611, and is buried in St. Andrew's, Holborn, but no monument is erected to his memory.

Fig. 648. Embroidered Border

It will have become apparent to the reader of the foregoing descriptions that the garments clothing English men and women were a medley drawn from many nations: thus the same man might one day appear dressed entirely as a Spaniard, and on the next in a variety of garments each characteristic of a different country. Harrison makes a strong point of this foible of his countrymen, saying that it is very difficult to describe pure English dress as the numerous fanciful follies, culled from all over the known world, displayed in gentlemen's attire are astonishing. To-day it is the Spanish style and to-morrow the French fashion or the German guise. 'By and by the Turkish manner is generally best liked of, otherwise the Morisco gowns and the Barbarian sleeves, the mandilion worn to Collie weston ward (*see* p. 547) and the short French breeches (*see* Figs. 658 and 751).'

This was even more obvious to foreigners: a Dutchman visiting England during this period remarks that 'the English dress in elegant, light, and costly garments, but are very inconsistent and desirous of novelties, changing their costumes every year both men and women.'

The sartorial mind of the average Englishman of Tudor times is well expressed in the woodcut (Fig. 649). Here is the story: 'Yea, many men are become so effeminate, that they care not what they spend in disguising themselves, ever desiring new toys, and inventing new fashions. Therefore, a certain man, that would picture every countryman in his accustomed apparel, when he had painted other nations, he pictured the Englishman all naked,

Fig. 649. He 's an Englishman

unto whom he gave a pair of sheares in the one hand, and a piece of cloth in the other, to the end he should shape his apparel after such fashion as himselfe liked, sith he could find no kind of garment that could please him any while together.'

Underneath the picture is written this soliloquy:

'I am an Englishman, and naked I stand here,
Musing in my mynde what rayment I shal were;
For now I wyll were thys, and now I wyl were that;
Now I wyl were I cannot tel what.
All new fashyons be plesaunt to me;
I wyl haue them, whether I thryue or thee.'

ANDREW BOORDE.

The authors of the *Church Homilies*, published in 1562, eagerly seized upon such an attractive weakness for their fulminations. In the homily *Against Excess of Apparel* they refer with approval to the Israelites who 'were contented with such apparel as God gave them, although it were base and simple. And God so blessed them that their shoes and clothes lasted fortie years.'

The Elizabethans were not so well favoured by the Almighty, nor were they by any means so careful and contented. 'Most commonly he that ruffleth in his sables, in his fine furred gown, corked slippers, trim buskins, and warm mittens is more ready to chill for cold, than the poor labouring man, which can abide in the field all the day long, when the north wind blows, with a few beggarly clouts about him.   We were loth to wear such as our fathers have left us; we think not that sufficient or good enough for us.   We must have one gown for the day, another for the night; one long, another short, one for winter, another for summer; one through furred, another but faced; one for the working day, another for the holy-day; one of this colour, another of that colour; one of cloth, another of silk or damask.   We must have change of apparel, one afore dinner, and another after; one of the Spanish fashion, another Turkey; and to be brief, never content with sufficient.'

It is to be regretted that such excellent advice fell upon deaf ears, and the sermons evidently had little effect.   For at the beginning of the seventeenth century the good work was continued by Thomas Dekker, who, in his *Seuen Deadly Sinnes of London*, hurls further caustic remarks at the fashionable Englishman.   His suit, he says, 'is like a traitors body that hath been hanged, drawn, and quartered, and is set up in several places; his codpiece is in Denmark, the collar of his doublet and the belly in France: the short waist hangs over a Dutch Botchers [a mender, a patcher] stall vtrich: his huge slopps speaks Spanish: Poland gives him boots: the block for his head alters faster than the feltmaker can fit him, and thereupon we are called in scorn "blockheads."'

One of many examples of cosmopolitan fashion can be illustrated by Figs. 655, 664, 673, 737, and description of Fig. 665; the same gentleman might wear any of the slops there shown, be they English, French, German, Italian, or Spanish.


## FRENCH FASHIONS, 1558–80

The special reason for treating the costume of English women before that of men does not apply to foreign countries, so that in dealing with France, Italy, and Spain, we shall return to the normal order, and give precedence to the gentlemen.


### KING CHARLES IX, 1550–74

An excellent example of the height of fashion in France is illustrated in Plate XXXVI.   This is taken from the full-length portrait group of Catherine de' Medici with her three surviving sons and daughter (Plate XXXV), which has been reproduced by kind permission of the owner, Miss Oswald-Smith, from the original at Shottesbrooke Park.   Of the school of François Clouet, it was painted in 1561 when Charles IX (the subject of Plate XXXVI) was eleven years of age, in spite of which his costume is that of a full-grown man. The three brothers are dressed alike in suits of amber satin decorated with silver passamayne in perpendicular and oblique lines.   The doublet is slightly padded at the waist, the lines of decoration converging from shoulders to the waist and surrounding the tabs.   The left wing is clearly defined in

ANNO A IA SVÆ XI

PLATE XXXV. CATHERINE DE' MEDICI AND HER FAMILY, 1561
Shottesbrooke Park. *By kind permission of Miss Oswald-Smith*

shape, and is finished back and front in points like that shown in Fig. 630. The sleeves are close-fitting and the slops are decorated in the same manner as the doublet, as is also the velvet cloak. This and the hosen and shoes match the dress in colour; a pendant hangs from a blue cordon, while waist and sword belt, and scabbard, are of amber velvet. The hat, of amber velvet, is decorated with triangles of clustered pearls, and carries a natural-coloured ostrich feather. Brown gloves turned back at the wrist to show the grey lining are carried. Charles, Duc d'Orléans, second son of Henry II and Catherine, was born 27th June 1550 at Saint-Germain-en-Laye. He ascended the throne of France in 1560, on the death of his brother Francis II, as Charles IX.

In appearance as a young man he was tall and slim like his younger brother Henry, but feeble and sickly, his demeanour being spoiled by a habit of

Fig. 650. Charles IX, 1569 (*after François Clouet*

stooping and an awkward way of holding his head on one side. His complexion was fair and pale, his hair dark brown, his countenance haggard and unpleasing, his eyes glassy and listless except when he became excited, when they flashed like fire. In disposition he was indolent and without moral courage, and easily influenced by his dominating mother. Poetry and hunting were his chief amusements, and he was particularly fond of dogs, which swarmed all over his apartments, an Italian greyhound being his constant companion. Fig. 844 is made from a drawing of this King at the age of nineteen in the Bibliothèque Nationale, Paris.

A year later we have the well-known portrait (Fig. 650) of Charles IX at the age of twenty. The original is by François Clouet and is in the Kunsthistorisches Museum, Vienna. The King has now grown a small moustache,

Fig. 651         Fig. 652

and his costume consists of a black velvet jerkin with basques which are in the fashion of twenty years earlier.  It is banded with wide bands of gold embroidery of a delightful and complicated pattern.  The black velvet cloak has two bands of embroidery all round the edge.  The design of this is not shown in Fig. 650, but Fig. 651 is a detailed drawing of it.  A duplicate portrait by the same artist is in the Louvre; it is identical except for the embroidery, the different pattern of which is shown in Fig. 652.

The underdress is of white silk or satin, thereby carrying out the same scheme as was adopted by his father.  The chair upholdered in crimson

Fig. 653. François de Lorraine,
Duc de Guise, 1560

Fig. 654.
Odet de Coligny, 1569

velvet is a typical French one of the period.  Many portraits of Charles IX in later life are extant.

Death struck terror into the heart of this young king.  Overcome with remorse for the reluctant consent he was made to give under moral pressure to the Massacre of St. Bartholomew (1572) and the murder of Coligny, he died, 30th May 1574.

The French nobleman (Fig. 653) is dressed entirely in white except the hat and cloak which are of black velvet, the latter edged with wide gold lace. The edgings of the bands of white on the doublet and slops are of a narrow fancy gold braid.

Fig. 654 is made from a drawing of the three brothers Coligny, all of whom met with violent deaths—two being poisoned and one a victim of the massacre of St. Bartholomew. The figure represents the eldest, Odet (1517–69), Cardinal de Chastillon. Although French he wears a German fashion in cloaks. It has practical sleeves with wings or shoulder pieces, but these were not usually worn on the arm but hung from the shoulders, giving an effect of breadth to the figure. The garment itself is cut as a semicircle like an ordinary cloak; sometimes it was much less than a semicircle. It is elaborately braided, having cuttes or pinking between braids, and fastens down the front, if desired, by buttons and frogs. Another German cloak is seen in Fig. 622. The dress worn underneath the cloak in Fig. 654 is a doublet with trunk hose, not paned, but decorated with horizontal bands of braid.

Fig. 655. A French Gentleman, 1568

The three-quarter-length drawing (Fig. 655) is made from a portrait in the Louvre of a French gentleman dating about 1568. The very attractive suit is carried out in soft buff leather, most probably chamois; the peascod doublet is elaborately pinked, and the decoration of the pansid slops is a cut steel braid outlined with vermilion silk. The venetians are of plain leather. Cut steel buttons fasten the doublet, and a line of steel braid overlies the seams. A black waist- and sword-belt, scabbard, and dagger tucked in the waist-belt at the left back, buff nether stocks, and shoes complete this very smart costume.

## Henry, Duc d'Anjou, 1551 until 1580

Henry, Duc d'Anjou, third son of Henry II and Catherine, was born 19th September 1551 at Fontainebleau. He is seen at the age of ten in the portrait group (Plate XXXV) standing on the right, dressed in the same manner as his brother Charles.

When he reached manhood Henry is described as tall, slim, and elegant, although it was said he looked like a walking spectre. His eyes were sunken, his mouth always twitching, and his gaze unsteady. He wore a small satanic moustache and a narrow pointed beard.

When the Polish Ambassadors came to Paris in 1573 to offer the Crown of Poland to Henry, the fêtes given in their honour were most lavish and magnificent; and to commemorate this auspicious event the Queen-Mother commanded several panels of tapestry to be made by Flemish tapissers. Fig. 656 is reconstructed from the portrait of the Duc d'Anjou depicted in one of the panels.

His dress appears to consist of a peascod-paunched doublet of light-coloured silk, braided and pinked, with venetians of the same material but untrimmed; a moderate-sized ruff, a short black velvet cloak draped over the left shoulder, and a very characteristic Italian hat. His stockings and shoes

Fig. 656. Duc d'Anjou, 1573

Fig. 657. Duc d'Alençon

match the rest of this dress. A black ribbon surrounds his neck, and he is fingering some jewel or the badge of St. Michael suspended therefrom. Henry is credited by some with being intensely effeminate, 'weaker than woman and worse than harlot,' nevertheless, a man of keen intelligence and cultivated mind, who during his command in the religious wars showed great courage, for which he won golden opinions.

The Duc d'Anjou succeeded to the Crown of France as Henry III on the death of his brother Charles in 1574. (*Continued on p.* 654)

### FRANÇOIS, DUC D'ALENÇON, 1554 *until* 1580

The small figure in the left-hand corner of the group (Plate XXXV) is François, Duc d'Alençon, at the age of eleven, the youngest son of Henry II and Catherine, who was born in 1554. He was not a normal child; rather deformed, he had smallpox while still young which left his not-too-beautiful face deeply pitted. However, in some of his later portraits he is depicted as a quite good-looking young man. In 1572 the Queen-Mother suggested François as a suitable husband for Queen Elizabeth—he was just eighteen while she was thirty-nine.

Elizabeth was full of admiration for her young lover—from hearsay only, most likely through his Ambassador Jean de Simier, Baron de Saint-Marc, whom he sent over in 1579 to do his wooing for him. Always astute, the Queen did suggest 'the absurdity that in the general opinion of the world might grow' if she married this ill-favoured, pock-marked boy after refusing so many suitors of great worthiness. At the end of this year François rushed over to England, heavily disguised, to see the Queen. She then admitted to him that 'he had been represented to her as hideous, hump-back, and deformed, but she found him the reverse and most handsome in her eyes.' Love is blind, they say! England was much opposed to this marriage of their Queen and Alençon, since (1576) Duc d'Anjou, but the matrimonial negotiations and the courtship of the young couple waxed and waned at intervals.

Fig. 658.
A Nobleman, 1570

A miniature of Alençon, painted about 1574, and showing the whole figure, can be seen in the Victoria and Albert Museum. Fig. 657 is made from it. The slightly peascod doublet, with straight basque and full sleeves, and the short slops are of white silk covered with delicate gold embroidery. An ample cloak of black velvet, banded with a fancy jet trimming and lined with black fur, swings from the shoulders. The black velvet Italian hat has diamond ornaments around the brim, with a large ruby surrounded by diamonds and surmounted by black fronds. A small ruff, white and gold sword-belt, white hosen, and black shoes with red ties are worn. In his right hand, resting upon a green velvet gold-fringed table-cloth, Alençon holds a portrait of Queen Elizabeth.

A nobleman of the 1570's is shown in Fig. 658. The usual peascod doublet is cutte in six places, and has sleeves with spiral bands of cuttes: a paned hip-roll and venetians ornamented up the fronts with embroidery are worn under a long cloak. This is of fine material, cut on the semicircle, and gathered in groups to a deep band which looks like a collar. The garment is tied by cords and tassels over the left shoulder and under the right arm.

Fig. 659. ELIZABETH OF AUSTRIA, QUEEN OF FRANCE

## NOBLE LADIES, 1558–80

### ELIZABETH OF AUSTRIA

#### *Queen of France, 1557–92*

The First Lady in the Land—at least, the most important leader of feminine fashion—was Elizabeth or Isabella of Austria, second daughter of the Emperor Maximilian II and his cousin Maria, daughter of the Emperor Charles V. This Archduchess, who was born in 1557, married Charles IX of France in 1572.

'She was very beautiful, having the complexion of her face as fine and delicate as any lady of her Court, and very agreeable. Her figure was beautiful also, though it was of only medium height,' thought Brantôme; very devout, she always had a 'night-lamp filled with wax which she kept lighted on her bed to read and pray to God, though other Queens and Princesses kept theirs upon their sideboards.'

The Queen's costume, shown in Fig. 659, is similar in many respects to that worn by Mary Stuart (Fig. 528). The sleeves have the same character, and are trimmed with spiral puffings fixed with jewels. The bodice and skirt are of a delicate patterned brocade edged with embroidery; and the skirt is open up the front to show an under-skirt of plain silk. A profusion of jewels ornaments the coif, neck, bodice, waist, and sleeves.

Elizabeth was so devoted a wife that when Charles IX died in 1574, she could 'not forget her husband in a second marriage . . . Such was the great constancy and noble firmness of this virtuous Queen, which she kept to the end of her days, towards the venerated bones of the King her husband, which she honoured incessantly with regrets and tears.' Fig. 884 is made from a drawing by François Quesnel and shows Elizabeth of Austria in widow's weeds.

On her death-bed the Queen 'felt especial longing for a sight of His Majesty, her most beloved brother [the Emperor Rudolph II]. His Majesty had arrived the previous night by *mail-coach* with but a few horses. His arrival caused the Queen no little joy in her great suffering before the end.' She died in January 1592 at the age of thirty-five.

### LOUISE OF LORRAINE

#### *Queen of France, 1575 until 1580*

At the time Henry, Duc d'Anjou, was on his way to Poland, 'he saw at Balmont in Lorraine, Mademoiselle de Vaudemont, Louise de Lorraine, one of the handsomest, best, and most accomplished princesses in Christendom, on whom he cast his eyes so ardently that he was soon in love.' On his return to France, and soon after his accession, he sent for the lady, and married her in 1575.    She is described by Brantôme as 'wise, chaste, and virtuous,' and 'delicate and loveable'; but she did not have a very happy time as Queen-Consort of France, owing to her very decadent husband and strong-minded mother-in-law.

Nearly all the portraits of Louise of Lorraine show her wearing the same style of dress and coiffure.    In Fig. 660 the Queen wears a robe of deep-toned velvet that recalls the style fashionable during Francis I's reign; indeed, it is entirely so except for the up-standing ruff and the hairdressing.    The presence of bands of jewels on the upper arms above the white fur suggests that these sleeves of old-fashioned shape are faked and are *not* turned back as described under Fig. 254: while the under-sleeves are not nearly so large as their predecessors.    The skirt is edged with fur up the fronts and at the hem, and the under-skirt is of a light colour with an embroidered border in gold.    From the bejewelled girdle hangs a handsome ornament ending in a peardrop pearl.

Fig. 660. Louise de Vaudemont, Queen of France

The chief feature of this costume, however, is the ruff, which is distinctly French, and is a development of that worn by Catherine de' Medici (Fig. 543), but simpler.    The shaped plain transparent collar part fits into the décolletage of the bodice and folds back in crescent form around the neck.    To the edge is fixed a pleated frill of the same lawn, in this particular case doubled; although lace and insertion might be used, pleated or put on plain.    Similar examples of this kind of ruff are seen in Figs. 755 and 757.

(Continued on p. 662)

## MARGUERITE DE VALOIS [1]

### Queen of Navarre, 1553 until 1580

The costume of a young girl of this period is seen in Plate XXXV.    This is Marguerite de Valois, the third daughter of Henry II and Catherine.    She was born in 1553 and therefore aged eight in the painting.    Her gown is of

---

[1] It should be borne in mind that there were two other princesses bearing the same name—Marguerite de Valois—of note in the sixteenth century: (1) The authoress of the *Heptameron* and of many poems was Marguerite, daughter of Charles, Duc d'Orléans and Comte d'Angoulême, and sister of Francis I.    Born in 1492, she married first, in 1509, Charles, Duc d'Alençon, who died

grey-blue velvet, and has a wide band of gold passamayne round the neck of the bodice and up the fronts and at the hem of the all-round skirt. The underdress is of cloth of silver, and a beautiful network cap—an escoffion —is worn composed of bands of jewels—rubies, diamonds, emeralds, and pearls. The collar and girdle are composed of the same jewels, the pendant being a pomander in the form of a gold vase.

She was considered a great beauty. Pierre de Ronsard (1524–85), whose prolific poems delighted all Europe, describes her features thus: 'Waving hair more dark than blond' (her hair was very black, having been derived from her father, so Brantôme tells us, though the painting (Plate XXXV) shows it as dark chestnut), her eyebrows like 'ebony bows,' brown eyes, tilted nose, and shell-like ears, 'teeth like rows of pearls,' slim, tender hands, and little feet.

Her future mother-in-law, Queen Jeanne of Navarre, was sceptical about her charms, for she admits, 'as for her beauty, I confess that she is well made, but she laces extravagantly; her face is arranged with so much art that it angers me, but at this [French] Court paint and powder are almost as common as in Spain.' Later on, the Queen states that 'she is fair to see, and well instructed, and of happy manner, but brought up in the most abandoned and loose company.'

Marguerite was very learned, and had some claims to be considered an authoress; and it is not surprising to learn from the aforesaid statement that she was also famous for her licentious manners, even in those days. She lived before her time: her place is the twentieth century.

Her ambitious mother evolved many plans for her daughter's marriage, and would be satisfied by nothing short of a Royal diadem. Don Carlos of Spain, Rudolph of Austria, and the King of Portugal were all approached without success; so, after a liaison with Henry, Duc de Guise, Marguerite eventually wedded Henry of Navarre, 18th August 1572. Thus she secured an insignificant crown, little dreaming that it would lead to the crown matrimonial of France.

Her wedding dress is described by Marguerite herself: 'I myself was in Royal splendour, with crown and mantle of ermine, all ablaze with jewels, and with my great blue train four ells long, borne by three princesses.'[1]

Another report of her wedding costume mentions that it was of cloth of gold, the bodice so closely covered with pearls as to look like a cuirass; over this was a blue velvet mantle nearly five yards long embroidered with fleurs-de-lys. Her dark hair was loose and flowing, and studded with diamond stars. After the marriage ceremony she heard Mass alone without her husband—he was a Huguenot. As a wedding present from her family and her bridegroom, quantities of jewels were given her amounting to £100,000.

in 1525. Her second husband, married in 1527, was Henry d'Albret, titular King of Navarre. Their only child, Jeanne d'Albret, later Queen-Regnant of Navarre, was the mother of Henry IV. Marguerite de Valois I died 1549. (2) A second Marguerite de Valois (II), niece of the above and daughter of Francis I, was born in 1523. She married in 1559 Emmanuel Philibert, Duke of Savoy, and died 1574.

Marguerite de Valois III, described in the text, was niece of No. (2) and great-niece of No. (1)

[1] Is this the first appearance of bridesmaids?

The five following days were devoted to splendid entertainments, until the 23rd—the eve of St. Bartholomew.

As Queen of Navarre Marguerite spent much time at the French Court where 'La Reine Margot' was a supreme leader of fashion. Whatever she appeared in she was the envy of all the Grandes Dames who desired to be a *à la mode*. At the suggestion of her mother, whom she greatly feared, she arrayed herself one day while at Cognac most gorgeously in the fine and superb apparel that she was accustomed to wear at Court for great and magnificent pomps and festivals. If her desire was to give pleasure to the noble ladies of the district, she succeeded beyond her utmost expectations, so great was their amazement when she appeared in a gown of silver tissue of dove colour, à la Bolonnoise, and hanging sleeves, and a rich headdress with a white veil.

'The Queen-Mother said to her: "My daughter, you look well." To which she answered: "Madame, I begin early to wear and to wear out my gowns and the fashions I have brought from Court, because when I return I shall bring nothing with me, only scissors and stuffs to dress me then according to current fashions." The Queen-Mother asked her: "What do you mean by that, my daughter? Is it not you yourself who invent and produce these fashions of dress? Wherever you go the Court will take them from you, not you from the Court." Which was true; for after she returned she was always in advance of the Court, so well did she know how to invent in her dainty mind all sorts of charming things.' [1]

From the same author we learn that at the fête at the Tuileries for the Polish nobles in 1573 'she was robed in a gown of rose-coloured Spanish velvet covered with spangles, with a bonet of the same adorned with plumes and jewels.' He says that she was painted in this dress: but where is the picture? He also tells us of another splendid costume worn by Queen Marguerite: 'I have seen her dressed in a robe of white satin that shimmered much, a trifle of rose-colour mingling in it [et un peu d'incarnadin meslé] . . . her head was adorned with quantities of pearls and jewels, especially brilliant diamonds, worn in the form of stars. . . . Her beautiful body, with its full, tall form, was robed in a gown of crinkled cloth of gold, the richest and most beautiful ever seen in France.' This material was a gift specially manufactured at Constantinople, and was fifteen ells long, costing one hundred crowns per ell.                                                    (Continued on p. 665)

### CATHERINE DE' MEDICI

#### Queen-Mother of France, 1558–89

(continued from p. 436)

On Queen Catherine's widowhood, in 1559, she set aside her rich attire, and wore heavy mourning, modelled on the prevailing fashionable lines, with a black veil attached to the front of her 'attifet'—the wired-out front of the headdress referred to on p. 452.

[1] Translated from Brantôme.

After an interval of ten years, however, her costume became more elaborate and rich, but always black.

There are several well-known portraits of her in widow's weeds. Fig. 661 is made from a contemporary drawing of the Queen-Mother a few months after she had become a widow. The dress is probably made of black silk, the bodice plain, very pointed in the stomacher, and buttoned up the front. A plain hemstitched white cambric collar surrounds the throat on top of the high collar of the bodice.

In most portraits the skirt is plain, but in others it is very finely pleated, almost like modern accordion pleating: it has a short train, and is worn over the Spanish farthingale of moderate dimensions.

The close-fitting cap of black gauze has an attifet front, and to this and the sides of the cap is gathered a portion of one corner of a voluminous square black veil. The veil is gathered again into the nape of the neck and wired out in curves over the shoulders, being fixed to the bodice just in front of the sleeve seam, thence falling in small pleats down the back and over the arms (see diagram, Fig. 721).

The figure of Catherine in the portrait group (Plate XXXV) is not very discernible, the dress being all in black against an almost black background. She

Fig. 661.

Catherine de' Medici, Queen-Mother of France

is represented at the age of fifty-two with chestnut-brown hair, looking many years older than in either the portrait by Pourbus at fifty (Fig. 525), or the original from which Fig. 661 is taken showing her in her fifty-first year. In Plate XXXV the dress of black silk is severely plain. The bodice, pointed at the waist, is fastened up the front with small silk buttons: the collar is high, and the pointed white collar is worn inside the ruff. The sleeves are moderately close-fitting, and of leg-of-mutton shape. The skirt is gathered into the waistband, and no farthingale is worn. The headdress is rounded, not pointed, on the forehead, the veil hanging straight from it: both are of black crêpe, a new kind of transparent material produced in Italy chiefly at Bologna. The veil was not always pleated, and there were other ways of attaching it to the cap (see Fig. 883).

Brantôme, still an invaluable source of information, writes:

'The Queen-Mother wished and commanded her ladies always to appear in grand and superb apparel, though she herself during her widowhood never clothed herself in worldly silks, unless they were lugubrious, but always properly and so well fitting that she looked the Queen above all else. It is true that on the days of the weddings of her two sons, Charles and Henry, she wore gowns of black velvet, wishing, she said, to solemnize the event by

Fig. 662.        Fig. 663.
Italian Gentlemen (*after Moroni*)

so signal an act. While she was married she always dressed very richly and superbly, and looked what she was.'

When Catherine reached middle age she became somewhat corpulent; but still, at sixty, 'her complexion was fresh, and she had not a wrinkle on her full round face.'

In 1581, Catherine, at the age of sixty-two, appears in the painting of the ball given in honour of the marriage of the Duc de Joyeuse, wearing widow's weeds of black satin. A head-and-shoulders portrait at the Louvre is interesting as showing how the depth of the attifet point varied. In this case it extends almost to the top of the nose.

Catherine de' Medici died at the Castle of Blois, 5th January 1589, at the age of seventy.

A few details relative to widows' weeds as worn by noble ladies in France are found in the writings of Brantôme. Colours, we are not surprised to learn, were forbidden to widows, 'though their skirts and petticoats, and also their hosen they may wear of a tan-gray, violet, or blue. Some that I see emancipate themselves in flesh - coloured red and chamois colour, as in times past, when as I have heard said, all colours could be worn in petticoats and stockings, but not in gowns. . . . Our widows of to-day dare not wear precious stones, except on their fingers, on some mirrors, on some Book of Hours, and on their belts; but never on their heads or bodies, unless a few pearls on their neck and arms. But I swear to you I have seen widows as dainty as could be in their black and white gowns, who attracted quite as many and as much as the bedizened brides and maidens.'

## ITALIAN INFLUENCES, 1558–80

### NOBILITY: MEN

The description of characteristic costumes of Italy is made difficult by the fact that the country was divided into numerous principalities and dukedoms. Their styles differ somewhat, so that although portraits are fairly plentiful, it is not easy to select representative examples. Venice was the chief of the Italian states, and it was a common thing for Venetians to visit France and England during the whole of the sixteenth century.

An attempt has been made to interpret the costume in the portraits of the two Italian gentlemen (Figs. 662 and 663) by Moroni, at Bergamo, in the most explicit manner possible. As they are both garbed entirely in black it is not an easy task.

Doublets with moderately close sleeves, padded pumpkin-shaped slops, and, in Fig. 662, venetians, hosen, and shoes are of the fashion which was general throughout Europe during the 1570's and 1580's. The hats are definitely Italian, with bag crowns pleated into a brim

Fig. 664. (after Moroni), 1560–70

or a rouleau. The most important detail is the manner in which these gentlemen wear their cloaks.

Fig. 662 has taken the right corner and draped it over the right shoulder, and it should be noticed that the edge of the cloak is finished with tiny black buttons.    Fig. 663 has caught the right-hand corner and holds it with the forearm, grasping the left side of the cloak with his right hand.    The cloak is bordered with bands of black satin.

Fig. 665

To prove that Italian gentlemen did not always wear sombre black, the portrait of Gian Girolamo Crumelli, by Moroni, is reproduced in Fig. 664.    This was painted about 1565–70, and the costume is entirely in rose colour.    The doublet, sleeves, and venetians have a pattern woven in silver in the material, the edgings being a very narrow loop fringe. The panes of the slops are embroidered with silver, and besides the silk knots at the knee are garters edged with silver and ending in silver tassels.    A black velvet bonet, black sword hanger and scabbard throw up the whole colour scheme.

For further reference, use may be made of three portraits in the National Gallery, London, Nos. 1022, 1316, and 2094.

An exceptionally fine three-quarter-length portrait of an Italian nobleman is to be seen at Shottesbrooke Park.    It represents a member of the Medici family and was painted by Bronzino about 1565.    The costume worn by this nobleman is in shape and colour exactly the same as that of the French gentleman (Fig. 655) except the decoration of the slops.    These are of white satin; the panes, about two and a half inches wide, are set close together, and are of brick-orange velvet or cloth cut out in a pattern of which Fig. 665 is a drawing, and outlined with a very small cord of a golden yellow colour.    The waist- and sword-belts are of black edged with gold, the latter being passed under three panes in the same manner as shown in Fig. 673.    A glimpse of this appears through the openwork design, which is very effective.

This portrait is but another example of the similarity of fashion prevalent throughout Europe at this time, and referred to by many contemporary writers.

Fig. 666.
Dr. Jerome Capivacio

Fig. 666 is taken from a portrait of Dr. Jerome Capivacio, who died at Padua in 1589.    His black velvet hat is full in the crown and pleated into the band, and the brim is fairly wide.[1]    Similar hats were worn in England, and may be seen in many of the drawings in Chapters II, III, and IV (Part I).

---

[1] This type of hat formed the model for the headgear worn by later doctors of various arts and sciences; especially it will be recognized as that worn by doctors of music.

The doctor is wearing *spectacles* of the latest type. The frames of these are made of bone, though copper, lead, iron, and even wood were in use for this purpose: the best qualities were of gold or silver. In Fig. 666 the frame is attached by leather straps round the ears. Spectacle lenses were still made in Venice, though in Queen Elizabeth's time this craft was practised in London, where it had already reached a high standard. Coloured glasses to protect the eyes had come into use during the last century, when they were made in Germany; for the best quality lenses beryl was used.

Fig. 667.
An Italian Lady (*after Moroni*)

### NOBLE LADIES

In England, as in France, the Italian vogue became that most sought after. Queen Elizabeth herself, on her own confession (*see* p. 492) favoured Italian fashions, and her ladies made haste to follow her example. It will, therefore, be useful to show a few examples of the costume worn by Italian noble ladies.

After minute investigation, the conclusion is reached that there is really very little difference between the costume of the leading nations of Europe, Germany, perhaps, excepted. Here and there one finds a detail or two which are decidedly national: otherwise the similarity is more or less general.

The chief distinctions are that Italian ladies, as a rule, ignored the farthingale, both Spanish (Fig. 242) and wheel (Fig. 243), but distended their skirts, possibly by the aid of the bolster (Fig. 713), to give the line of a modified farthingale.

The Italian ruff was small compared with the English, French, and Spanish, being either close to the neck and circular, or standing up from the shoulders in the Venetian (*see* Fig. 764) or the Florentine fashion (*see* Fig. 763).

Fig. 668

The international exchange of headgear and headdresses is complicated, but it will be found that when a headdress of foreign origin is shown in any of the drawings the fact is mentioned.

The Italian lady (Fig. 667) is taken from the seated portrait in the National Gallery, No. 1023, painted by Moroni in the 1570's. She is said to be one of the Fenaroli family. The dress is of rose-red satin with all edges of the cuttes and the garment rolled and bound over by a sort of blanket stitch in fine gold metal.   The inside turned-back collar and small close cuffs are of transparent lawn, having a charming yet simple pattern (Fig. 668) embroidered round the hem in red silk.   The underdress with sleeves is of gold-coloured satin or perhaps one of those exquisite materials woven by the expert Italian craftsmen: gold high lights with red - gold shadows, secured by a mixture of metal and silk, yet soft in texture, the prototype of which was woven at Constantinople centuries before, and originally known as baudekyn (see vol. ii, p. 123).

Fig. 669. A Lady of Pisa, 1580

Without doubt the shape of this distinctive Italian costume formed the model for the wardrobes of the western nobility—the high collar seen in England in Queen Mary's reign, stiff corsage, sleeves puffed on the shoulders and close on the arm, as seen in the drawings of Mary Stuart (Fig. 528) and Elizabeth of Austria (Fig. 659), the full trailing skirt open up the front and hanging in graceful folds from the waist, and, in this example, undistorted by the solid farthingale.   The flat fan of five sticks is plaited with ochre-coloured straw and has a rigid handle.

Quite a different style of dress is worn by the Italian lady (Fig. 669), taken from a plan of the city of Pisa and dated 1580.   The original is coloured, showing that the short over-robe with hanging sleeves is red and banded with gold.   The robe worn under this is blue, with bands of black having cuttes between them, as also round the sleeves and at the hem.   The under-robe is a pinkish mauve, forming an artistic combination with the red and blue.   The Italian fan opens and closes, but is fixed to a rigid handle.

## SPANISH STYLES: 1558–80

### NOBILITY: MEN

After the death of Queen Mary, there was no longer a vogue in England for new fashions of Spanish origin.   During her reign such styles had become incorporated in the fashionable attire of both men and women.   Under Queen Elizabeth their place was taken, both in England and France, by those of Italy.

Most of the Spaniards who had come to England were very unpopular there.   Many of the middle class, tradesmen and artisans, had settled in England, thinking that the marriage of their Prince ensured complete domination of the kingdom.   There were numerous conflicts between the shopkeepers of both nationalities, compelling the English authorities to take stringent measures by ordering all shops kept by Spanish tradesmen to close down.  Nothing remained for their disgusted proprietors but to return to their native land.

Despite the restrictions issued in the pragmatic of 1537 ingenious tailors devised a method of ornamenting the clothes of the upper classes by cutting out patterns in coloured cloth, and sewing them on to garments and overlaying them with delicate lace-like snippet work of applied cloth.   In face of this abuse, the Cortes of Valladolid begged the Emperor Charles V to forbid the use of any and every sort of trimming, lace, or adornment on garments both of men and women, which might give excuse for the scheming tailors to charge exorbitant prices.

Fig. 670. Philip II, 1559

Charles thought this too drastic; but in 1552 he issued a further pragmatic prohibiting this applied work, as well as the manufacture of gold and silver lace and ornaments, and also rigidly limiting the weaving and making of velvets, silks, and satins.   A ruinous policy!


### PHILIP II

#### King of Spain, 1558 until 1580

Philip as a young man was as splendid in his dress as his father, and for his forthcoming marriage with the Queen of England great preparations were made as described in Chapter III; but still a severe check was kept upon the clothes worn by the people in general.   Such were the conditions existing in Spain during the years 1552 to 1560.

Fig. 670 is taken from a portrait of 'His Catholic Majesty' at the age of thirty-two in 1559, shortly after he had become a widower for the second time, and was in consequence particularly amiably disposed towards Elizabeth. Through his Ambassador he proffered his assurances of friendship and good-will, having, indeed, intentions of marrying her.

Fig. 671 is an example of the costume affected by the nobles, including the hidalgos,[1] of the period covered by Part I.   It is entirely of black; the jerkin with high collar and the wings are of velvet, and the sleeves, paned slops, and hosen of black silk.   The shoes are of black Spanish leather.   A new feature is seen in the sleeves: they are slightly gathered along the front seam, producing folds around the arm.   This Spanish fashion will be observed in some of the later English and French figures.   It is mentioned in the introduction to Part II that the English ignored Spanish fashions.   Rucked sleeves must therefore have come to England via France.

Fig. 671. Spanish Noble
(after Antonio Moro)

Philip II married for the third time in 1559 his gifted and amiable bride, Isabel or Elizabeth de Valois, eldest daughter of Henry II and Catherine, who was the mother of two daughters, Isabella Clara Eugenia and Catherine Michela (see pp. 678, 680).   A drawing of Philip, taken from a miniature painted about this time, is given in Fig. 835.

Owing to the influence of the new Queen, who introduced some French ideas, Spanish costume became richer, more ornate and colourful; but by 1563 it was thought advisable to issue another pragmatic, ostensibly re-enforcing that of 1537 but really relaxing the regulations for the benefit of the upper classes only.   Silk weaving was revived, and great extravagance in dress and living followed during this period: in fact, weavers, tailors, dressmakers, and embroiderers were allowed a free hand in all their departments.

Noteworthy amongst tailors, these very important craftsmen of both ladies and gentlemen's apparel, was Juan de Alcega, who is represented in Fig. 672. He was a smart little citizen of Madrid, and published in 1589 a very useful and interesting book on patterns of garments and the best methods of cutting them out.   Presumably he always worked in his pinked and cutte doublet, which shows the style worn by the middle classes during the period about

[1] In Spain 'hidalgo' signifies a member of the class immediately below the highest in the land. The title 'don' gave the necessary distinction.

1565–89, and reminds us at once of Moroni's portrait of an Italian tailor, No. 697 in the National Gallery, London. His scissors and dividing compasses are much the same as are used to-day.

In the nine years of his married life with Elizabeth de Valois, Philip perhaps for the first time experienced anything like real happiness. Much of it was occupied in the erection of the Escorial in fulfilment of a vow to commemorate St. Lawrence in gratitude for his victory gained at St. Quentin on that saint's day, 10th August 1557. The first stone of this palace-monastery was laid in 1563, and here is the best opportunity for introducing an excerpt from Martin A. S. Hume's *Philip II of Spain*, which gives an entirely different idea of Philip from that usually held.

'Even in his home life his care for detail was as minute as it was in public affairs. The most unimportant trifle in the dress, management, studies, or play of his children came within his purview. The minutiae of the management of his flower-gardens, the little maladies of his servants, the good or ill temper of his dwarfs and jesters did not escape his vigilance. The furnishing and decoration of his rooms had to be done under his personal supervision, and the vast task of building the stupendous piles of the Escorial on an arid mountainside, and adorning it with triumphs of art from the

Fig. 672. Juan de Alcega, 1588

master hands of all Christendom, was performed down to the smallest particulars under his unwearied guidance.

'His favourite place for work was at the Escorial, where, said the Prior, four times as many dispatches were written as in Madrid. As soon as a portion of the edifice could be temporarily roofed in, the monks were installed, and thenceforward Philip passed his happiest moments in the keen, pure air of the Guadarramas, superintending the erection of the mighty monument which forms a fitting emblem of his genius—stupendous in its ambition, gloomy, rigid, and overweighted in its consummation. Here he loved to wander with his wife and children, overlooking the army of workmen who for twenty years were busy at their tasks, to watch the deft hands of the painters and sculptors—Sanchez Coello, the Carducci, Juan de Juanes, the Mudo, Giacomo Trezzo, and a host of others—whom he delighted to honour.

'As a patron of art in all its forms Philip was a very Maecenas. He followed his great father in his friendship for Titian, but he went far beyond the Emperor in his protection of other artists. Illuminators, miniaturists, and portrait painters were liberally paid and splendidly entertained. The masterpieces of religious art, the cunning workmanship of the Florentine goldsmiths and lapidaries, the marvels of penmanship of the medieval monks, the sculptures of the ancients, were all prized and understood by Philip, as they were by few men of his time.'

When the King became a widower for the third time in 1568, his grief was such that he retired from the world into the monastery of St. Jerome, and his hair and beard became quite white.   But 'his task in the world was greater to him even than his sorrow or his love.'   His gloom, deepened by fanaticism, influenced the whole Court and Society, and henceforth he and his attendant nobles dressed simply, and wholly in black: even the middle and lower classes followed the example set by the nobility.   It must, however, be remembered that the King kept most of the nobles aloof, surrounding himself only with his personal attendants.   The usual costume of the King was a suit fashioned on modified prevailing lines in black velvet or silk, and in his most sombre moods without any ornamentation.   When he was in a more cheerful vein, jet or black bugles edged the cuttes and panes of his dress.   On all occasions he wore the Badge of the Golden Fleece suspended on a gold chain.

In 1570, at the age of forty-three, Philip took as his fourth wife, Anne, daughter of the Emperor Ferdinand I, who was the mother of Philip III of Spain.   These ten years of domestic life gave Philip a second period of happiness, and Queen Anne's death in 1580 caused him the deepest grief, from which he never recovered although he lived another eighteen years. Costume and social life relapsed into their former austerity and dreariness.

(*Continued on p.* 673)

### THE IDOL OF EUROPE

Don Juan of Austria, the natural son of the Emperor Charles V and Barbara Blomberg of a Flemish noble family, was born 24th February 1546.   There is a three-quarter portrait by Coello[1] in which he appears about twelve years of age wearing a doublet like that in Fig. 768 with moderate-sized paned slops. After his father's death he was acknowledged by his half-brother Philip II, who sent him, at the age of sixteen, with his son, Don Carlos, and his nephew, Alexander Farnese, to the university at Alcalá.   He was given the Golden Fleece in 1566, and took up his first naval command (1566–8) in defence of the coast against African pirates; in 1570 he crushed the Morisco rebellion at Granada.   When only twenty-five, he reached the summit of his remarkable naval and military career, by inflicting so crushing a defeat upon the Turks that their naval power in the Mediterranean was completely destroyed.   As 'Captain-General of the Holy League,' he had under his command no fewer than three hundred galleys and eighty thousand men, the combined fleets of Spain, Venice, Genoa, Malta, and the Papacy; and this victory at Lepanto, near Corinth, on Sunday, 7th October 1571, won him the praise, gratitude, and affection of the Christian world.

He excelled in all manly sports, had no rival in the management of horses

---

[1] Reproduced in the *Connoisseur*, vol. 102, p. 62.

or in jousting, and often played 'tennis five or six hours together . . . and in the pursuit of these exercises he is unwearied.'

This brilliant illegitimate Hapsburg with golden hair and without the family jaw is described in 1575 as follows: 'He is of middle stature, well made, of a most beautiful countenance, and of admirable grace. He has little beard, but large moustache of a pale colour; he wears his hair long and turned upward, which becomes him greatly; he dresses sumptuously, and with such nicety that it is a marvel to see him.'

Unfortunately he is painted in all his portraits wearing a steel cuirass or a leather doublet over richly embroidered slops. Fig. 673 is made from the portrait by Antonio Moro in the Prado, in which the panes of the slops are somewhat narrow; a noticeable feature is the method of carrying the dagger slung by a chain from the waistbelt and passed behind three of the panes. The swordbelt also passes behind the panes on the opposite side. There is, however, one record of his appearing in ordinary clothes. This was when he was reviewing his fleet before Lepanto when he made a most picturesque figure, 'saluted by volleys of musketry. The

Fig. 673. 'Pansid Slops' of Don Juan

young Prince, gallant in white velvet and gold, stood erect in the stern castle of his gilded barge, with the sacred banner of the Pope fluttering over him.' During the battle he was in complete armour.

His later successes were the siege of Tunis in 1573, the Stadholdership of the Netherlands in 1575, and the victory of Gemblours in 1578. Scarcely had Queen Elizabeth offered him the crown matrimonial of England, when fever cut short his life at the siege of Namur, 1st October 1578. The hero of Lepanto is introduced here mainly because the method of dressing his beautiful golden hair became the rage of masculine Europe. His portrait showing this fashion is reproduced in Fig. 843.

### Elizabeth de Valois

#### *Queen of Spain, 1545–68*

The Queen of Peace and Kindness—'la reyna de la paz y de la bondad.'

Elizabeth de Valois, Queen of Spain, sometimes referred to as Isabel or Isabella,[1] was the eldest daughter of Henry II and Catherine, and was born in 1545. A political marriage with Philip II was arranged for by her father, and took place at Notre-Dame, 21st June 1559, the Duke of Alba acting as proxy

---

[1] The name of Elizabeth was Hispanicized into Isabella.

Fig. 674. Elizabeth de Valois, Queen of Spain

for the bridegroom. Her wedding dress is described as being of cloth of gold interwoven with pearls, and her mantle of blue velvet with a border of gold bullion twelve inches wide was borne by her sister Claude, and her sister-in-law, Mary Stuart. A much-bejewelled imperial crown 'cast a halo of light around her as she walked,' and from her neck were suspended Philip's portrait and a great pear - shaped pearl, the most prized treasure of the crown jewels of Spain—La Pelegrina.

It is said that this French Princess adopted Spanish dress after her marriage, and that she had no patience with the rigid puritanism and petty interference of stern authority which had prevailed in former times. She also introduced French fashions among her Court ladies so that the mixture of styles — Spanish and French — seen in portraits of many of them is explained.

Fig. 674 is made from a painting of Queen Elizabeth by Pantoja de la Cruz (1551–1610). If this portrait is the work of the artist to whom it is attributed, it must have been painted at the end of her life, since he was only seventeen when she died. The dress is in black velvet or some deep rich colour, having the bodice cut to fit the normal figure well in at the waist and finishing in a point in front. There are three rolls on the shoulders, and three rows of jewels in gold mounts descend from neck and shoulders and converge to the point of the waist where the belt of jewels encircles it. The hanging sleeves are in true Spanish type and are first illustrated in Fig. 592; they are a little more shaped on the curve at the back, and are caught together at the wrist and finished with small tabs. On these sleeves and down the front of the skirt distended by the Spanish farthingale are set loops of silk with two elaborate jewelled aiglettes on each (Fig. 675 and also Fig. 936). This type of decoration became most popular during the second half of the sixteenth century and is seen in many portraits of all nationalities. The close-fitting under-sleeves are of light-coloured satin, probably matching the silk loop decorations, and have small cuttes alternating with groups of pearls. At the

Fig. 675.
An Aiglette

LA REINE ELIZABETH DE VALOIS.

Fig. 676.　After Antonio Moro

wrist the sleeve is cut into a series of small tabs. Attention is drawn to the sable skin with head and feet garnished with goldsmith's work and jewels carried on the right forearm ready to place round the shoulders. A ring is passed through the golden nose of the animal to which is attached a gold and often jewelled chain (*see* Fig. 709). The chair is similar in shape to that shown in Fig. 650.

Elizabeth de Valois was pronounced a very beautiful and gifted princess,

Fig. 677

though judging by our modern standards of beauty her sister-in-law, Elizabeth of Austria, was decidedly the prettier. Brantôme, who knew her intimately, thus describes her: 'Her face was handsome, her hair and eyes so shaded her complexion and made it the more attractive. . . . Although she had had the smallpox after being grown-up and married, they had so well preserved her face with poultices of fresh eggs (a very proper thing for that purpose) that no marks appeared. . . . Her figure was very fine, taller than that of her sisters, which made her much admired in Spain, where such tall women are rare, and for that the more esteemed. And with this figure she had a bearing, a majesty, a gesture, a gait, and grace that intermingled the Frenchwoman with the Spaniard in sweetness and gravity.'

Extremely well dressed, this young Queen-Consort was the model for the great ladies of the Spanish Court.

'She never wore her gowns a second time, but gave them to her ladies and maids; and God knows,' remarks Brantôme, 'what gowns they were, so rich and so superb that the least was reckoned at three or four hundred crowns; for the King, her husband, kept her most superbly in such matters; so that every day she had a new one, as I was told by her tailor, who from being a very poor man became so rich that nothing exceeded him, as I saw myself. She dressed well, and very pompously, and her habiliments became her much; among other things her sleeves were slashed,

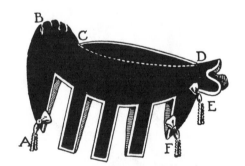

Fig. 678. Cut of sleeve

with scallops which they call, in Spanish, *puntas*; her headdress the same, where nothing lacked. Those who see her thus in painting admire her; I therefore leave you to think what pleasure they had who saw her face to face, with all her gestures and good graces. As for pearls and jewels in great quantity, she never lacked them, for the King, her husband, ordered a great estate for her and for her household.'

Extravagant young woman! Yet, ignorant of the tricks of tailors and dressmakers, a mere man may have been deceived, and her dresses were most likely altered and refurbished beyond recognition. And although those who now look at her portraits may not share Brantôme's opinion of her beauty, they cannot fail to notice the quantities of marvellous pearls and jewels that she habitually wore. The slashes to which he refers may be seen in Fig. 676. There are several versions of this dress shown in her portraits. Some are in black or rose velvet, others in white satin or brocade, and one, in the Fitz-william Museum, Cambridge, in rose-coloured satin. In Fig. 676, taken from a three-quarter portrait by Sir Antonio Moro, the whole dress is of white satin with a gold-embroidered border (Fig. 677) down the front and round the hem. The bodice finishes with tabs at the normal waist-line, and there are slashes on the breasts surrounded by groups of pearls. A diagram of the delightful sleeves with 'puntas' is given in Fig. 678. They are cut in two separate semicircles joined to-gether at AB and EF. BC is gathered or pleated into the armhole, and the length CD is folded back to the broken line when worn, to show a lining of contrasting colour. DE is the wrist, and from F to A the sleeves are cut as shown, forming straps which hang in a most attractive manner from behind the arm. As seen in the drawing, either arm might be passed through the wrist opening, or the whole sleeve might hang behind; the most chic manner was to have only one arm through the wrist opening.

Fig. 679.
A Spanish Lady, 1560 (*after Antonio Moro*)

The close-fitting under-sleeves were braided, often in zigzag lines. The surface of the skirt is cutte, and the usual ornaments of loops and jewelled aiglettes are placed in various positions about the dress. The headdress, something like the jewelled coif shown in Fig. 599, collier, and girdle are set with very fine jewels and pearls. A plain handkerchief is held in the right hand; the left, wearing one glove and holding the other, rests on a pedestal table covered with a velvet cloth buttoned up the edges.

To the great regret of the whole nation, Elizabeth de Valois died 1568.

Fig. 679 is from a three-quarter portrait by Antonio Moro of a noble lady, dating from 1550 to 1570. The dress is in a medium shade of velvet, with bands of very narrow white fur set on the mahoitered sleeves, at the divisions of the small tabs at the waist, and down the front openings of the skirt.    The close-fitting sleeves and under-skirt are of silk, or they could be of a damask or brocade.    The partlet is white lawn, embroidered with fine gold in a trellis-work design.    The cap is similar in shape to that shown in Fig. 548, but this lady has puffed out her hair at the sides.    She wears a ruff at the throat and small cuffs to match, with jewelled bracelets, a fine carcanet with pendant, girdle, and pomander.    This lady carries a sable skin in her right hand.

### Anne of Austria

#### Queen of Spain, 1549–80

Anne, daughter of the Emperor Ferdinand I, and fourth wife of Philip II, was born in 1549: a very homely soul, a great needlewoman, and rather over-whelmed by the 'vastness and majesty of the mission confided by Heaven to its chief.'  She had five children, all of whom died in infancy except her fourth son, who succeeded as Philip III. This drawing (Fig. 680) is made from the portrait of Queen Anne by Coello. The original is at Vienna.  The velvet dress has two rows of gold embroidery (a detail of which is inset as a heading to the drawing) down the front of the normally shaped bodice and skirt, along the hem of the skirt, and also round the new-shaped long hanging sleeves. These are cut on a similar plan to dia-gram, Fig. 67, but much longer from wrist to point; and the front seam is left open, the edges being caught together on the forearm.   The close under-sleeves are of a light-coloured satin embroidered with bands of gold.   Loops of silk with jewelled aiglettes are everywhere in evidence. (*See* Fig. 936.)

This Queen died at the age of thirty-one in 1580.

Fig. 680.
Anne of Austria, Queen of Spain

For some particulars of widow's weeds worn by Spanish ladies of noble birth we have Brantôme's authority. On one occasion he met Jeanne of Austria, the widow of the Infante Jean of Portugal: 'I approached the prin-cess,' he says, 'and kissed her gown in the Spanish manner. . . . I thought her very beautiful according to my taste, very well attired, and wearing on her head a Spanish coif of white crêpe coming low in a point upon her nose, and dressed as a Spanish widow, who wears silk usually.'

Fig. 681. Arms of the Broderers' Company

## EMBROIDERY (*continued from p. 419*)

Queen Elizabeth greatly encouraged the art of embroidery, and in the year of her accession the Broderers' Company of London were granted a coat of arms. The Company bore: Paly of six argent and azure, on a fesse gules, between three lions passant guardant or, two broches in saltier, between two trundles or. Crest, on a wreath, a dove displayed argent, encircled with gold all proper. Supporters, two lions or, guttée de sang (drops of blood). Motto: 'Omnia de Super.' (Fig. 681.)

Fig. 682 shows two kinds of broches. These were instruments used by embroiderers. An empty trundle, or quill, is shown in Fig. 683. Trundles

were used for winding silk, wool, or gold thread. A full trundle is seen in Fig. 684.

In 1561 the Broderers' Company of London received their first charter from Queen Elizabeth, and in her reign domestic embroidery began to flourish.

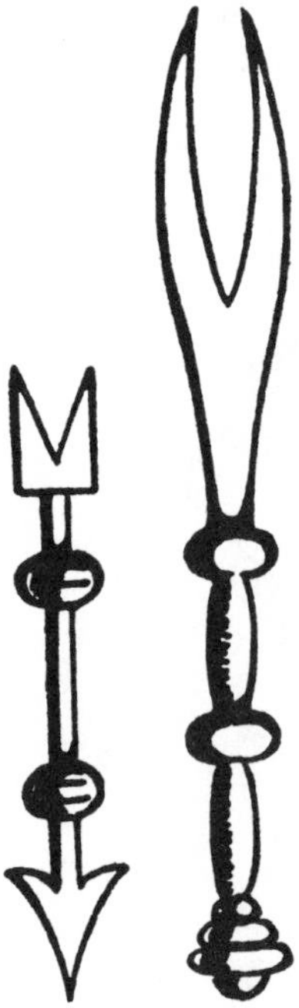

During the second half of the reign broderers introduced a variety of quaint conceits into their work—humorous animals, insects, reptiles, even certain species of vermin, and other curious objects which it is surprising to find interwoven in embroidery for costume — equalled only, perhaps, by the comic decorative detail used by illuminators of fourteenth-century manuscripts.

The following list of objects suitable for embroidery is taken from a contemporary work:

Fig. 682.
Broches

Fig. 683.

Fig. 684.
Trundles

Birds' eyes; divers personages; esses (ss); pomegranettes; roses; honiesocles; acorns; wild fernbrakes; pillars; essefirmes; wormes of silk of sondrie colours; like a dead tree; artichokes; caltroppes (a four-pointed iron instrument used in war to maim horses); antiques (figures in *ancient* dress); flies; snails; rainbows, clouds, and droppes and flames of fire; spiders; birdes of Arabia (birds of paradise); sondrie beasts and fowle; allover verie fair like seas, with divers devyses of rocks, shippes, and fishes; fountains; frutidge (clusters of fruit); butterflies; dogges of silver; birds in a cage.

All flowers then cultivated were employed, usually treated in the most naturalistic manner (*see* Fig. 685).

In a well-known portrait of Queen Elizabeth her dress is embroidered with eyes, ears,

Fig. 685. Coloured Embroidery upon Linen

and serpents—the first two, no doubt, symbolized her vigilance, the last, her subtilty. (Plate XLI D.)

Rows of obelisks flank the front and hem of one of her white satin gowns (Plate XL). The surface of this dress is embroidered all over with interlaced knots and scrolls in gold, and small pearls, intermixed with leaves, carnations, lilies, pansies (her favourite flower), butterflies, and worms.

Suns in splendour, made up in diamonds set in embroidery, cover the front of a petticoat, and Jove's thunderbolts and flames, in gold and rubies, decorate an apricot satin skirt (Plate XLII).

In the Hardwick portrait by Gheeraerts (Plate XLI C) of Her Majesty the white satin petticoat has, besides

Fig. 686

ordinary flowers, frogs, serpents, swans, ostriches, sea-horses, rabbits, and whales. The Queen stands upon a Turkey carpet.

Fig. 686 is a drawing of part of a design embroidered in black silk upon a white linen sleeve worn by Queen Elizabeth in a portrait at Arbury Park dating about 1590.

The Queen possessed many pairs of gloves. One pair was embroidered with frogs and flies.

Fig. 687

SPANISH WORK (*continued from p. 226*)

The chief characteristics of Spanish work of the time of Elizabeth are first, that the surface of the linen ground was decorated, as previously, with scrolls; these were in silk, but now worked in knot stitch, producing a thicker line than that used in the rest of the design. These scrolls or stems were frequently worked in gold thread instead of silk.

Secondly, all kinds of flowers, chiefly roses, carnations and honeysuckle, and fruits—less conventional in form than the patterns used earlier — sprang from these scrolls: birds, beasts, fishes, and other objects were encircled by them.

As the sixteenth century proceeded, stems and scrolls became less prominent, and the flowers, fruit, and objects more realistic (Fig. 687).

In addition to its use for the decoration of various items of costume, Spanish work was employed on bed hangings, coverlets, sheets, and 'pillow-beers,' [1] and, for such purposes, usually embroidered in black silk upon linen, or, as is sometimes specified in inventories, 'fine Holland cloth.'

Spanish work remained popular throughout the sixteenth century, but gradually disappeared from use during the reign of James I.

In modern times the type of needlework known in Tudor days as 'Spanish work' is generally referred to as 'Old English work.'   It is still made; but,

Fig. 688. Half an Embroidered Collar

while the designs used for it to-day are very similar to the patterns of Elizabeth's period, a variety of additional stitches has been incorporated.

A good pattern embroidered in black silk upon a linen collar edged with lace of simple design is reproduced in Fig. 688, which shows one side of it. It is taken from a head-and-shoulders portrait (in the Music School, Oxford) of Dr. John Bull.   This musician and composer was born in 1563, became Mus.Bac., Oxon, in 1586 and Mus.Doc. in 1592.   He died in 1628 at Antwerp where he was organist at the cathedral.   In the portrait is seen the upper part of a black robe and over it a white hood edged with white fur, with the head-part thrown back, leaving the head bare.   The collar, of course, is worn outside the hood.

### STUMPWORK (*continued from p. 227*)

Stumpwork was not extensively carried on in England during the reign of Elizabeth; it was much more popular upon the Continent.   In England, however, occasional references are found, which prove that some ladies occupied themselves with this kind of embroidery.

[1] A cover spread over the pillow during the daytime.

## PETIT POINT

A type of needlework which became very popular during the seventeenth and eighteenth centuries, and is commonly associated with that period, really made its first appearance in England during the reign of Elizabeth. It is known as 'petit point' (Fig. 689), and resembled tapestry, but was worked on a very much smaller scale, upon canvas, in coloured silks, or silks and wool, the whole surface being covered with needlework. Sometimes the work on the canvas ground was cut out and mounted on some plain material, chiefly velvet. It was used generally for wall panels, cushions, and the coverings of stools and chairs.

Fig. 689. Petit Point

## HALLINGS

For late sixteenth-century 'hallings' an embroidery which comes under the heading of 'Opus Consutum' was much used.

Fig. 690. Wall Hanging

Figures, flowers, patterns, and arabesques, etc., on a large scale, were worked in silks, wools, and gold thread, on backgrounds of velvet, silk, or brocade, probably with a linen or close canvas foundation. These were cut out and sewn to a ground of velvet, silk, or cloth, with every known variety of stitch. Subjects such as allegorical figures, standing under arches ornamented in the favourite Renaissance manner; shields of arms, sometimes surrounded by conventional wreaths of flowers and leaves; the whole design often framed with pilasters supporting a frieze of elaborate design — all this was appliquéd or worked with the needle on a dark-coloured velvet background or curtain.

In some of the great houses of the land this type of decorative needlework was much prized, and examples are still extant.

Fig. 690 shows a part of a hanging. It is composed of deep red velvet and golden yellow silk appliqué. The parts of each material cut away for the ground are used in the next row for the pattern, and vice versa. Silk

Fig. 691. Part of a Dorsal

gold cord, used double, covers the lines of the patterns where velvet and silk join.

A section, to be repeated, of gold embroidery upon a dark velvet ground is shown in Fig. 691. This design is a development of the interlaced work mentioned in Chapter II, p. 228. It is used as a dorsal, or hanging, in a portrait of Queen Elizabeth dating about 1590.

## FLOOR COVERINGS

References to carpets have been made on p. 229.

By the year 1575 'Turkey' carpets (i.e. Oriental, Persian, etc.) were used in the houses of the nobility and wealthy. The unenterprising and more conservative middle classes, although in some cases they might have been able to afford carpets, still retained the old custom of strewing the floors with rushes or 'grise.'

At the end of the sixteenth century carpets were in general use in the households of the wealthy.

Matting coverings for floors were quite usual after the middle of the century. At first this material was imported from Holland, but later on matting was made in Bedfordshire. A household account dated 1578 mentions: 'Item. Matting 3 Chambers with Bedfordshire mats, v*d*. a yard.'

It is useful to remember that in most portraits painted during the latter part of Queen Elizabeth's reign the figure stands upon an oriental carpet. By the dawn of the seventeenth century men are usually depicted standing on matting and women on carpets.

## LACE (*continued from p. 420*)

The art of the lace-maker had already made considerable progress at the time of Queen Elizabeth's accession, and thereafter thrived as a modest industry. It was not until many Flemish lace-makers had settled in the Midlands, after the Duke of Alba's persecutions in the Netherlands (1567),

Fig. 692. Lace—first half of reign

that lace was made, with their co-operation, in sufficient quantities to become an article of commerce. Since that time pillow lace-making has been practised continuously by women in the counties of Buckingham, Bedford, and Northampton.

During the first twenty-five years of her reign, Queen Elizabeth and the great ladies of her Court used a number of different kinds of lace as the edging to their narrow lawn bands or ruffs, and to cuffs, as seen in many contemporary portraits.   These included the following:

*Cutwork* and *Spanish work*.   These have been already described.

*Venys gold* or *passament*.   Fine threads of gold, woven in imitation of white thread lace.

*Italian point, needlepoint,* or *punto in aria,* as already stated, was worked on a pillow with the needle—made in Italy.

*Bone lace*.   The original name for fish-bone, and, later, pin-made lace.

Fig. 693.
Cutwork worn by Queen
Elizabeth in the 'Ermine'
Portrait.  Plate XXXII D

Fig. 694.
Cutwork worn by
Marguerite de Valois

When made with slightly coarser thread it was often called *bobbin lace*. *Gimp* was a heavier bobbin lace.   Price of bone lace varied between 40s. per dozen yards and 11s. 6d. per yard.

Fig. 692 gives an example of the design in lace used to edge the small band or ruff worn during the first part of Queen Elizabeth's reign.   It is taken from an effigy dating about 1565–70 and measures one and a half inches in width.

It was not until the 1580's that lace was used on a lavish scale.   By this time the band or ruff had greatly increased in size, owing to the introduction of starch and poking-sticks.

The laces used to border these bands were of great variety; among others were:

*Billement*.   The exact type of lace called billement has not yet been determined.

*Bone* or *bobbin.* Already described.

*Buckingham lace,* made of extremely fine thread, the ground and pattern being worked simultaneously.

*Crown lace* had the pattern worked on a succession of crowns, sometimes intermixed with acorns and roses.

*Cutwork,* of Flanders, Italy, and Spain; was much used by Queen Elizabeth on her ruffs, cuffs, foreparts, veils, smocks, nightcaps, cushions, and tooth cloths. See Figs. 693, 694.

*Diamond lace.* A lace woven of silver in lozenge design.

Fig. 695. Reticella worn by Queen Elizabeth in the 1580's.
Plate XLII

*Genoa lace.* Needlepoint, sometimes referred to as 'lace of Jeane.' Very rare, but used by Queen Elizabeth.

*Parchment lace* had the thick raised pattern formed of small pieces of parchment or vellum, called cartisane, cut out to the required shape, and worked over with thread. This same method applies to *guipure.*

*Point lace.* Needlepoint, of Genoa, Venice, Flanders, and England. Price, 6s. 8d. to 50s. per yard.

*Point coupé.* Another name for cutwork.

*Point tresse.* Lace made of human hair, with the needle.

*Reticella.* Another name for cutwork (*see* Fig. 693).

*Spanish chain.*   This explains itself.

*Spanish black point lace.*   Used occasionally for edging ruffs and cuffs.

*Venys gold, passament,* or *passamayne.*   Already noted.

Fig. 694 shows a pointed edging and an insertion of the same kind of lace. The edging measures two and a half inches and the insertion two inches in width.

Fig. 693 is a detail of one section of the lace which edges the band or ruff and cuffs worn by Queen Elizabeth in her portrait (*see* Plate XLII) by Marcus

Fig. 696. Reticella edging and insertion—second half of
sixteenth century

Gheeraerts.   It measures about four inches in depth and is of Italian workmanship known as reticella.

Some interesting items from wardrobe accounts of the period are here given:

'1 yd. of double Italian cutwork, ¼ yd. wide.     55s. 4d.

'1 yd. of double Flanders, worked with Italian purl.     33s. 4d.

'3 suits (ruffs and cuffs) of good lawn cutwork, ruffs edged with good bone lace, at 70s.     £10 10s.

'3 yards broad needlework lace of Italy, with the purl of similar work, at 50s. per yd.     £7 10s.

'A veil of white cutwork, trimmed with needlepoint lace. . . .'

## NEEDLES AND PINS

As the art of the broderer has now reached such a high standard of efficiency one may inquire what sort of needles were used.

The needle is of great antiquity, as proved by its discovery in burial places all the world over. Those used by the Egyptians were of bronze or gold. These metals, as well as polished iron, were used for making needles during the early periods in Europe. In the earlier Middle Ages steel needles were made in Antioch, Damascus, and Adrianople, and the Moors introduced them into Europe. The industry was being carried on in Nuremburg by the middle of the fourteenth century and at Cordova and Milan during the sixteenth. Steel needles were first produced in England in 1545, by a native of India whose daughter married an Englishman named Greening. Their son, Christopher, established a workshop in 1560 at Long Crendon, Bucks, which existed there as a needle factory until the middle of the nineteenth century, when most of the workers emigrated to Redditch.

Fig. 697. Needle-case

The cases in which these needles were kept usually hung from the girdle by a cord. The cover was flat and rectangular, and made of stiff embroidery, wood, metal, or even ivory or crystal: the ornamentation was often very rich. The actual booklet which carried the needles could be pulled down out of the case on a cord. Here is a sixteenth-century needle-case (Fig. 697) made of embroidered velvet, the booklet being covered with a piece of brocade.

Before the sixteenth century the case was lozenge-shaped. 'A nedell case of cristall garnysshed with silver gilt, with twoo thymbles in it' was a New Year's gift to Queen Elizabeth.

Thimbles of metal, bone, or leather were used as early as the twelfth century; in the thirteenth they were made of latten and later of silver.

Pins of bronze were made at Nuremburg as early as 1365. Those made in England during the fourteenth century were of brass and highly esteemed, and in the following century their manufacture became so extensive that import was prohibited in 1483. In the sixteenth century France also manufactured them. Pins have always been a very important item of costume and dressmaking, and an order of the late-fifteenth century is still extant, in which the following items occur: '6,000 large white pins, 6,000 lesser, 3,000 neete or polished, 1,000 great white, and 1,000 black,' while in an account for a trousseau dated 1494, 8,000 needles, 9,000 pins, and 6 silver thimbles are mentioned.

In a statute passed in 1543, entitled 'An Act for the True Making of Pynnes,' the price was fixed not to exceed 6s. 8d. per 1,000.

In Elizabeth's reign, the value of the annual importation of pins amounted to nearly £4,000.

Brass pins discovered during recent excavations at Baginton Castle, near Coventry, are unique, in that they are enclosed in protective sheaths, and must therefore be large ornamental pins.

A 'minikin' was a very small pin.

# SECTION II: 1580–1603

## QUEEN ELIZABETH, 1580–1603

APPEARANCE (*continued from p. 481*)

Queen Elizabeth's pride in her appearance lasted throughout her life, and at sixty she might easily have passed for twenty years younger—at a short distance.

1581 (48). Even at forty-eight 'she still retained a measure of her good looks. . . . If silver threads glistened among her once auburn locks, only tirewomen were wiser, for a periwig covered all deficiencies.'

1588 (55). The head-and-shoulders portrait of Queen Elizabeth by Marcus Gheeraerts, in the University Library, Cambridge (Plate XXXVII), shows her at about the age of fifty-five; it is pronounced by authorities to give the most accurate idea of the Queen's appearance. The complexion is pale, the shadows being painted in a cold grey; the eyes are brown, and the hair a dark auburn tinged with gold. This portrait, painted on a panel twenty-four inches by nineteen inches, was presented to the library by Vincent Skinner in 1588. The method of painting the face adopted in this portrait had the full approbation of Her Majesty, and it was used in many other likenesses of the Queen; hence the lack of modelling apparent in most of them. As Elizabeth matured in years her features became more pronounced and, conscious of this, she would not permit those who painted her to add *shade* to her portraits. 'Shade,' she said, 'was an accident, and not naturally existent in the face.' Pursuing the same theory, she preferred to give audience by daylight, and frequently in the open air, as the shades had then less force.

An onlooker, Samuel Kiechel, writing of a visit to England at the time of the Armada, said: 'The Queen sitting all alone in her splendid coach appeared like a goddess such as painters are wont to depict.'

1585 (52)    Writing some years after her death, Sir Robert Naunton,
to    Secretary of State to James I, describes the appearance of
1590 (57).    Queen Elizabeth between these dates: 'She was of person tall,
of haire and complexion faire, and therewith all well favoured,
but high nosed; of limbs and feature neate, and, which added
to the lustre of these externall graces, of a stately and majestick
comportment.'

Fig. 698 is a drawing made from a cameo representing the
Queen about 1590.

Fig. 698. Queen Elizabeth, c. 1590

1595 (62).    At sixty-two, a German visitor, Jacob Ratgeb, with a gallantry
borrowed from his Gallic neighbours, recorded that 'the Queen,
despite her age, can in grace and beauty vie with a maiden of
sixteen years.'

1598 (65).    Another German, Paul Hentzner, writing of a journey into
England in this year, gives a graphic account: 'Next came the
Queen, in the 65th year of her age (so we are told), very majestic;
her face oblong, fair but wrinkled; her eyes small, yet black [1]

---

[1] An error for 'brown.'

PLATE XXXVII. QUEEN ELIZABETH, 1587: Portrait by Marcus Gheeraerts
University Library, Cambridge. *By kind permission of the Syndics*

and pleasant; her nose a little hooked, her lips narrow, and her teeth black (a defect the English seem subject to, from their too great use of sugar). She had in her ears two pearls with very rich drops; her hair was of an auburn colour but false; upon her head she had a small crown, reported to be made of some of the gold of the celebrated Luneberg [1] table; her bosom was uncovered, as all the English ladies have it till they marry; and she had on a necklace of exceeding fine jewels; her hands were slender, her fingers rather long, and her stature neither tall nor low; her air was stately, her manner of speaking mild and obliging. That day she was dressed in white silk bordered with pearls of the size of beans, and over it a veil of black silk shot with silver threads; her train was very long, and the end of it borne by a marchioness; instead of a chain she had an oblong collar of gold and pearls.'

1599 (66). Elizabeth was very proud of her small, beautifully shaped hands, with long, delicate, nervous fingers. When giving audience, especially to any foreign potentate or ambassador, she would call attention to them by *unconsciously* drawing on and off her gloves and toying with her finger-rings. De Maurier, in his *Memoirs of Holland*, says: 'I heard from my father, who had been sent to her Court, that, at every audience he had with her, she pulled off her gloves more than a hundred times to display her hands, which were indeed very white and beautiful.'

1600 (67). 'It was commonly observed this Christmas [1600] that Her Majesty, when she came to be seen, was continuously painted not only all over her face, but her very neck and breast also, and that the same was in some places near half an inch thick.'

1602 (69). Sir John Harington, a godson of Elizabeth, writes: 'There is almost none that waited in Queen Elizabeth's Court and observed anything, but can tell, that it pleased her very much to seem, to be thought, and to be told that she looked young. The majesty and gravity of a sceptre borne 44 years could not alter that nature of a woman in her.'

In connection with the above the following story, although of an earlier date, may not be out of place.

Dr. Rudde, Bishop of St. David's, preached before her in Lent, 1596, and 'wishing in a goodly zeal, as well became him, that she should think sometimes of Mortality, being then sixty-three years of age, he took this text fit for that purpose out of the Psalms: "O teach us to remember our days, that

---

[1] The famous Luneberg table served as an altar in the Church of St. Michael at Luneberg. Whatever may have been the basis of the writer's comment (in 1598), it is an odd coincidence that, in 1598, a great part of the golden ornament and of the jewels which adorned the altar were stolen by a notorious robber, Nickel List, who was brought to justice early in 1599. The remains of the altar are now in the Provincial Museum, Hanover.

we may incline our hearts unto wisdom," [1] which text he handled so well, so learnedly, and so respectfully, as I dare undertake, and so should I if I had not been somewhat better acquainted with the humour, that it would have well pleased her, or at least no way offended her.    But when he had spoken a while of some sacred and mystical numbers . . . she perceiving whereto it tended began to be troubled with it.    The Bishop discovering all was not well, for the Pulpit stands there *vis-à-vis* to the Closet,[2] he fell to treat of some more plausible numbers, as of the number 666 making Latinus,[3] with which he said he could prove the Pope to be anti-Christ, also of the fatal number of 88 [the year of the Armada] which being so long before spoken of for a dangerous year, yet it hath pleased God that year not only to preserve her, but to give her a famous victory against the united forces of Rome and Spain; and so he said there was no doubt but she should pass this year also and many more, if she would in her meditations and soliloquies with God, as he doubted not she often did, and would say thus and thus.    So making indeed an excellent prayer by way of Prosopopoeia [4] in her Majestie's person acknowledging God's great graces and benefits and praying devoutly for the continuance of them, but withal interlarding it with some passages of Scripture that touch on the infirmities of age, as that of Ecclesiastes xii. 3, "When the grinders shall be few in number, and they wax dark that look out of the windows, etc., and the daughters of singing shall be abased," [5] and more to like purpose, he concluded his sermon.    The Queen, as the manner was, opened the window [of her pew], but she was so far from giving him thanks or good countenance, that she said plainly he should have kept his arithmetic for himself, but I see, said she, the greatest Clerks are not the wisest men, and so went away for the time discontented.'

'The Queen [March 1602] is still . . . frolicly and merry, only her face showeth some decay, which to conceal when she cometh in public she putteth many fine cloths into her mouth to bear out her cheeks, and sometimes as she is walking she will put off her petticote, as seeming too hot when others shake with cold.'

1603 (70).    The effigy of Queen Elizabeth in Westminster Abbey is considered to be an excellent portrait of her in old age.    It is taken from a death mask.

See also section on Portraits and Painters, p. 477.

---

[1] In a Bible dated 1569 this excerpt reads thus: 'Make us to know so our days that we number them: and we will frame a heart unto wisdom.'—Psalm xc. 12.

[2] The Royal pew.

[3] A distinctive epithet of that branch of the Catholic Church which acknowledges the primacy of the Bishop of Rome and uses the Latin tongue in its rites.

[4] A figure by which an imaginary or absent person is represented as speaking or acting.

[5] In the 1569 Bible it is written thus: *The Book of the Preacher* xii. 4 and 5.    'When the milners [teeth] stand still because they be so few, and when the sight of the windows [eyes] shall wax dim.    When the doors [mouth] in the street shall shut, and when the voice [chawes] of the milner shall be laid down, when men shall rise up at the voice of the bird [cockcrow—because they cannot sleep] and when all the daughters [ears] of music shall be brought low.'    The words in brackets are from notes in the margin.

CHARACTER (*continued from p.* 482)

As she grew older Queen Elizabeth still retained that charm of manner which so struck every stranger coming into her presence for the first time.

'Her Majesty spoke most graciously to every one, even to those of the vulgar who fell upon their knees in homage,' states an eyewitness (1595).

Her godson, Harington, writing some time after her death, said: 'Her speech did win all affections, and her subjects did try to show all love to her commands. . . . When she smiled, it was a pure sunshine, that every one did chose to bask in; but anon came a storm from a sudden gathering of clouds, and the thunder fell, in wondrous manner, on all alike.'

Not until she had been Queen of England for at least twenty years did Elizabeth indulge in the great extravagance of finery with which her name is associated. The Queen firmly believed in the principle that it was necessary to be 'most Royally furnished both for her person and for her train, knowing right well that in pompous ceremonies a secret of government doth much consist, for that the people are naturally both taken and held with exterior shows.'

Her lavish taste for dress and her vanity did not pass uncriticized, for Sir John Harington tells us that 'one Sunday my Lord of London preached to the Queen's Majesty, and seemed to touch on the vanity of decking the body too finely—Her Majesty told the Ladies that if the Bishop held more discourse on such matters she would fit him for Heaven, but he should walk thither without a staff, and leave his mantle behind him; perchance the Bishop hath never sought Her Highnesse's wardrobe, or he would have chosen another text.'

Yet the same writer elsewhere declares that Elizabeth 'did love rich clothing, but often chid those that bought more finery than became their state.'

The ingratitude and fall of Essex in 1601 had a great effect upon Elizabeth and almost drove her to frenzy. Sir John Harington's letters give us instances of her temperamentality in old age. He writes: 'She is much disfavoured and unattired and these troubles waste her much. She disregardeth every costly cover that cometh to her table and taketh little but manchet[1] and succory pottage.[2] . . . She walks much in her privy chamber, and stamps much at ill news: and thrusts her rusty sword at times into the arras in great rage.' Again, 'The dangers are over and yet she keeps a sword by her table.' 'So disordered is all order, that Her Highness has worn but one change of raiment for many days, and swears much at those that cause her griefs in such wise.'

So late as 1602 Elizabeth would not admit to any sign of physical weakness; she suffered sorely from gout (only no one dared to call it gout), so that the coronation ring, which she had worn night and day since her accession, had to be filed off her finger.

---

[1] The best kind of white bread.      [2] Succory, a form of chicory.

ACCOMPLISHMENTS (*continued from p. 484*)

Elizabeth's health was never very robust, but during the latter part of her life she kept herself fit by taking bodily exercise, chiefly riding and dancing.

A visitor at Court during the Christmas festivities of 1589 wrote that it was the Queen's habit to dance six or seven galliards every morning. No small effort for a woman of fifty-six!

Even towards the end of her days she indulged in her favourite pastimes of music and dancing. De Maisse, Ambassador from France, writes in December 1597: 'I departed from her audience at night and she retired half dancing to her chamber, where is her spinet which she is content that every one should see.' '24th December. The same day I went to see the Queen and she sent me her coaches. I found her very well and kindly disposed. She was having the spinet played to her in her chamber, seeming

Fig. 699. Pentagonal Spinet, 1552

very attentive to it; and because I surprised her, or at least she feigned surprise, I apologized to her for diverting her from her pleasure. She told me that she loved music greatly and that she was having a pavane played. I answered that she was a very good judge, and had the reputation of being a mistress of the art. She told me that she had meddled with it divers times, and still took great pleasure in it.'

Again, on 31st December: 'She takes great pleasure in dancing and music. She told me that she entertained at least sixty musicians; in her youth she danced very well, and composed measures and music, and had played them herself and danced them. She takes such pleasure in it that when her Maids dance she follows the cadence with her head, hand, and foot. She rebukes them if they do not dance

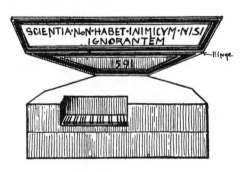

Fig. 700. Virginal, 1591

to her liking, and without doubt she is a mistress of the art, having learnt in the Italian manner to dance high. She told me that they called her "the Florentine."'

The minuet, 'menu pas,' and called by the Italians the 'passe-mezzo,' appears to have been known at the French Court. Brantôme describes seeing Elizabeth de Valois and Mary Stuart 'dance the Italian pazzemeno' in these words: 'Now advancing with grave port and majesty, doing their steps so gravely and so well; next gliding only; and anon making most fine and dainty and grave passages, that none, princes or others, could approach, nor ladies, because of the majesty that was not lacking.'

Fig. 699 is a pentagonal spinet or virginal dating 1552. The name 'virginal' was in earlier days restricted to the smaller forms of the instrument, pentagonal or rectangular: it was kept in an ornamental case, and taken out and laid on a table for use. A virginal in the Gruuthuse, Bruges, which measures sixty inches in length is shown in Fig. 700. It has a lid hinged in two places, on which is a Latin inscription and the date 1591. There are twenty-seven white and eighteen black notes.

The following excerpt throws an interesting light on the subject of orchestras at this time. At a masque given by the Earl of Hertford at Elvetham in 1591 'the Fairy Quene and her maides daunced about the garden singing a song of sixe parts, with musicke of an exquisite consort wherein was the lute, bandora,[1] base-violl, citterns,[2] treble violl, and flute.'

Fig. 701. Rebec    Fig. 702. Harp

On 28th April 1602, eleven months prior to her death, Queen Elizabeth opened a ball with the Duc de Nevers, dancing a galliard 'with a disposition admirable for her age,' says de Maisse. Two months later she kept the Scottish Ambassador waiting when he called to see her. He was led into a room adjoining her own, and seated where, by peering around a curtain carefully turned back for the purpose, he could see the Queen dancing to a lively tune from a small fiddle or rebec (Fig. 701). This was the last time she ever danced. A modern painting illustrates this incident.

Fig. 703. Trumpet

The Queen's skill in languages became more famous as time went on, and was a continual surprise, not only to the university professors, but to ambassadors of foreign powers whom she often addressed in their native tongues.

---

[1] *Bandora, bandurria,* a small kind of Spanish guitar of deeper pitch than the mandoline. *Mandora,* a lute with four strings.
[2] *Cittern,* a lute-shaped instrument, though with a flat back, having wire strings, usually four pairs.

De Maisse remarks that 'she spoke to me of the languages that she had learned, for she makes digressions very often, telling me that when she came to the Crown she knew six languages better than her own; and because I told her that it was great virtue in a princess, she said that it was no marvel to teach a woman to talk; it were far harder to teach her to hold her tongue.'

Although Elizabeth frequently drove in her coach, and she had many, she did not in her latter years give up riding on horseback, and was still very fond of hunting.   We hear that in her old age, and as late as August 1602, the 'Queen hunteth every second or third day, for the most part on horseback, and showeth little decay in ability.'   Not bad for an old woman of sixty-nine!

## Queen Elizabeth's Wardrobe, 1580–1603

This period opens with the end of one of Elizabeth's many political love affairs.   'Froggy [Elizabeth's pet name for the Duc d'Anjou] would a-wooing go' no longer—he died 10th June 1584, and his 'forlorn widow,' as the Queen called herself, wept for three weeks on end.   In six months Majesty completely recovered herself and we are assured that during the Christmastide festivities, 1584, when all her ladies- and gentlemen-in-waiting were very gorgeously apparelled, the Queen, as complimentary mourning for the Duc d'Anjou and the Prince of Orange, was dressed in black velvet sumptuously embroidered with silver and pearls.   From her headdress to the hem of her skirt fell an ample veil of diaphanous silver.   On either side of her crisp crimped hairdressing hung a great pearl about as large as a hazel-nut.

The 'Ermine' three-quarter-length portrait by Nicholas Hilliard, now at Hatfield (Plate XXXII D), is dated on the sword handle 1585, a fine example of the goldsmith's art.   The lines of the black velvet dress, pounced all over with cuttes and engraved gold buttons, headdress, and circular ruff, suggest that the style is of the same make as described under the 'Portland' portrait on p. 497.   The cutwork, of which the circular ruff and cuffs are composed, is a very beautiful specimen of the lace-makers' craft, and is reproduced in Fig. 693.   The jewels worn are diamonds, rubies, emeralds, and pearls. An ermine climbing up the Queen's left wrist and peering into her face has given the title to the painting.   As an emblem of chastity, the ermine was an especially appropriate compliment to the Virgin Queen.

'The Queen of England wears mourning for the Queen of Scotland' is stated in a letter bearing date, 'March 27 1587.'

The end of the year 1585 finally brought about friction between Spain and England: the breach widened—although both Philip and Elizabeth had an intense aversion to war.   Disquieting news of the Spanish Armada under the command of the Duke of Medina Sidonia, waiting at Lisbon, reached England in the spring of 1588, and on the 12th July 'the Kinge of Spaines Navy was Abroad,' sailing up the Channel in crescent form on the 19th. On the 29th the English fleet under Lord Howard of Effingham, supported by

Fig. 704.  Fig. 705.  Fig. 706.

TILBURY, 8TH AUGUST 1588. 'LORD BLESS YOU ALL.' 'MY LOVING PEOPLE'

Drake, Hawkyns, and Frobisher, inflicted a final blow on the 'Invincible' off Gravelines, after which the mighty Spanish galleons rounded the north of the British Isles, and so the remnants returned home.

The Earl of Leicester was in command of the land forces stationed at Tilbury to intercept the advance of the Spaniards if they landed, and to this army Elizabeth resolved to appeal.

On 8th and 9th August, 'she passed like some Amazonian Empress through all her army,' mounted on a richly caparisoned war-horse. For this occasion the astute Elizabeth adopted a semi-military outfit and Fig. 705 is a conjectural drawing, but made partly from contemporary descriptions. The dress is of cloth of gold, and the under-skirt of white stain embroidered with emblems, in which the rose and fleurs-de-lys are important features of the design. A cuirass of polished steel, damascened with gold and surmounted by a large circular ruff, the Crown poised upon an immaculately dressed auburn wig, a marshal's truncheon in her hand, and quantities of gems and jewels, are all calculated to increase Her Majesty's regal appearance and impress the loyal hearts of her devoted people. The military helmet, with crown and plumes of white ostrich feathers, is too cumbersome for the Queen to wear, so it is carried by a gentleman-in-waiting or a page (Fig. 706), who is dressed in sleeves, trunks, and hosen of green with a white jerkin—the Tudor livery colours. A similar costume is worn by the groom, who in Fig. 704 is leading the white charger which the Queen rode on this occasion. The horse is drawn from its portrait, painted in 1594, which now hangs on the staircase at Hatfield House. It should be noticed that the feet of the Queen rest upon a footboard, as was her usual custom when riding in full dress and on State occasions. A lady riding side-saddle with a pommel is seen in Fig. 714.

Another good illustration of this notable event is to be found in the mid-nineteenth-century picture by Sir John Gilbert, R.A., and made familiar in many history books.

By this time Elizabethan costume had reached the stage of elaborate development so familiar to every one. Queen Elizabeth in 1588 is shown in Plate XXXVIII. This is reproduced from the delightful brown ink and thin water-colour drawing by Isaac Oliver preserved in the Royal Library at Windsor Castle. The original measures twelve by eight inches, and was made in that year. The photograph is published by gracious permission of His Majesty the King. It is considered by authorities to be an excellent likeness of Queen Elizabeth, and is said to represent the dress in which she went in State to St. Paul's, to return thanks for the defeat of the Armada. It is the earliest portrait of the Queen showing her dressed in full band or ruff, long stomacher, veil, and wheel-farthingale. The farthingale in this picture shows the cart-wheel effect described on p. 618. The bodice, long hanging sleeves, and over-skirt are composed of white satin brocaded or embroidered with a gold scroll design. The full sleeves, stomacher, and under-skirt with cart-wheel arrangement on top are of cloth of gold, covered

PLATE XXXVIII. QUEEN ELIZABETH, 1588: Water-colour drawing by Isaac Oliver
Royal Library, Windsor. *By gracious permission of H.M. the King*

Th'admired Empresse through the worlde applauded
For supreme vertues numell Imitation
Whose Scepters rule fames lowde-voyc'd trumpet laudeth
Vnto the eares of euery forraigne Nation
Cannopey'd vnder powerfull Angells wynges
To her Immortall praise sweete Science singes.

Willm Rogers Sculp

PLATE XXXIX. QUEEN ELIZABETH, 1588: Engraving by William Rogers
British Museum. *By kind permission of the Governors*

with diagonal puffings of fine white silk: alternate intersections are decorated with groups of five pearls each, and rubies set in gold mounts, and a large pearl poses in the centre of each lozenge of the gold foundation.

Down the front of the stomacher and skirt, and round the hem, is a line of larger puffings, interspaced by larger jewelled ornaments of the same character, but including emeralds. Diamonds are liberally besprinkled over the whole costume. A gold band, set with groups of four pearls, interspaced alternately by rubies and emeralds, edges the stomacher, the over-skirt, and the long hanging sleeves.

Fig. 707. Burse

Other important items to be noticed are the much-becurled wig, ornamented with groups of pearls mounted on pins and with clusters of jewels; the festoon of pearls, finishing in a peardrop pearl on the forehead; the crown surmounting all; the girdle; the earrings, lace, ropes of pearls, sceptre, and orb. The ruff and veil are described on pp. 623, 626. Note the glimpse of a white satin petticote, the gold fringe of which just clears the ground.

The print shown in Plate XXXIX is a rare one, engraved by William Rogers. He took the details from Isaac Oliver's drawing (Plate XXXVIII).

Working some years after Oliver, Rogers has made the Queen look older, and many of the other details differ. The crown is much more open, and its design less reliable than that shown in Plate XXXVIII; the hair is differently adorned; the neck pendant is not the same; the rope of pearls, instead of being caught and festooned, hangs only from the shoulders to the point of the stomacher; jewels set in mounts are introduced on the ruff; no single pearls are placed between the puffings; a gold fringe edges the hem of the skirt; and the orb is jewelled. The details of the chair are interesting, and should be compared with those in Figs. 354 and 571, vol. ii, and with Fig. 215 in this volume.

The order in which the Court progressed and precedence prescribed is always interesting and often useful. The following composite description is based upon various accounts of eyewitnesses at Court. When the Queen processed in State or semi-State in the precincts of the palace or in public, the Lord Chamberlain walks first, being followed by all the nobility, ladies and gentlemen (the latter bare-headed), who are in the Court; and after them, near the Queen's person, walk the Knights of the Order of the Garter that are present, such as the Earl of Essex and the Admiral Lord Howard of Effingham (born 1536, Earl of Nottingham, 1596; died 1624). After come the six heralds who bear maces before the Queen. Immediately in front of Her Majesty comes the Lord Chancellor, bearing the seals in a red silk embroidered Burse or bag (Fig. 707), between two noblemen, one of whom carries the Royal Sceptre, the other the Sword of State, in a crimson velvet scabbard, studded with golden fleurs-de-lys, the point upward. Then comes the Queen's Majesty. She is guarded on each side by the Yeomen of the Guard, and the Maids of Honour follow, 'very handsome and well-shaped, and for the most part dressed in white.' After her march fifty Gentlemen Pensioners, also with halberts.

Plate XL is reproduced from a portrait said to be Queen Elizabeth, and dating some time between 1582 and 1589. It is one of a set of four portraits by the same artist, two of which are of Lady Southwell *née* the Lady Elizabeth Howard and the remaining one of Kate Carey, the celebrated Countess of Nottingham. Three of these portraits may have been painted at the time of the Lady Elizabeth's first marriage in 1582. In any case Plate XL shows the salient features of the height of fashion during the 1580's and onwards.

The entire dress is of white satin covered with embroidery in gold, silver, and coloured silks, obelisks forming an important item in the pattern on the skirt. It should be noticed that the embroidery on the bodice and sleeves is of a different design. The ruff, its surface powdered with jewelled brooches representing arrows, and the veil of gold and silver gauze, are described on pp. 626, 778. The headdress, which dominates the curled auburn wig, comprises seven upstanding points of flashing jewels finishing in pearls. These points are fixed to a band which fits round the head behind the front puff of the wig.

The three-quarter portrait at Woburn Abbey was painted in 1589–90 by Marcus Gheeraerts to commemorate the defeat of the Armada. A similar portrait in which the costume is the same but the background omitted is in the National Portrait Gallery, No. 541 (Plate XLI A). This latter shows the Queen in full dress such as she wore when giving audiences or on any other ceremonial occasion. The bodice with long sleeves hanging behind (*see* Plate XLII) and the skirt are of black velvet with borders of rows of pearls between narrow gold lines. These borders have, set at right angles to the borders, loops of silk in three shades each—pale yellow, rose, and grey, with rubies and emeralds in the centres. The sleeves and under-skirt are of white satin embroidered with red roses and pearl centres set in squares, and golden flowers of ten petals with ruby centres set in hexagons. A circular ruff of elaborate reticella, seven ropes of pearls and many other jewels, and a Royal crown set upon the usual auburn wig stuck with singularly large pearls complete the effect.

The 'Ditchley' full-length portrait, bequeathed by Viscount Dillon to the National Portrait Gallery, No. 2561, is dated 1592 and painted on canvas; it shows Queen Elizabeth at the age of fifty-nine (Plate XLI B). Her costume is not unlike that shown in Plate XXXVIII, of white satin diagonally cross-barred with white silk puffings, having roses superimposed with ornaments of goldsmith's work set at the intersections. These gold ornaments vary in design; some have groups of four pearls, others oval rubies, and others again rectangular sapphires. The long-pointed bodice and sleeves are decorated in the same manner, but the long-hanging sleeves have these ornaments set along the edges. The wired-out portions are the only parts of the veil visible. The headdress of crown-shape is a mass of rubies, pearls, and some spherical jewel of a brilliant red, with a pearl apex surmounting the whole structure. Other interesting details are the ropes of pearls hanging from the neck and the pearls on the wig, the pink rose set on the ruff, the decorated brown leather gloves in the left hand, and the Chinese fan, made to open and shut, attached by a coral-coloured riband to the waist girdle.

At Hardwick Hall is a full-length portrait of Queen Elizabeth, painted on canvas ninety by sixty-six inches, by the same artist (Plate XLI C). The Queen is shown wearing a dress of black velvet worked with gold and an under-skirt of white satin embroidered with many wonderful objects (*see* p. 585), the general style being similar to that just described.

On the 22nd September 1592 Queen Elizabeth paid her second visit to Oxford and, as on the first occasion, was housed at Christ Church. Long, tedious orations and elaborate productions of impossible plays were her chief entertainment. 'Hir Highnes departed from the University this day [28th September] about eleven of the clock in the forenoon, in hir open and princely carriadge.' Unfortunately no descriptions of the Queen's costumes, worn on her first or second visit to Oxford, are to be found in the documents relating to these events. From which it may be inferred that the Cambridge reporters of the day were more observant than their Oxford contemporaries.

To this same period may be assigned the portrait of Queen Elizabeth reproduced in Plate XLII and painted on canvas, seventy-six by forty-three inches, by Marcus Gheeraerts. It hangs in the drawing-room of the Master's Lodge at Trinity College, Cambridge, and represents the Queen at about sixty years of age.

Her costume is particularly interesting as it is exceptional in colouring. The bodice, long hanging sleeves, and back-skirt with train are all of a rich purple velvet. The long hanging sleeves and skirt have a border consisting of two lines of gold passamayne edged with pearls both planted upon the purple velvet. Between these lines are rubies in gold mounts set alternately with pink five-petalled roses in silk embroidery with seeded gold centres. The hanging sleeves are lined with white damask; the long pointed stomacher and the large leg-of-mutton sleeves are of white satin embroidered with a beautiful design in gold and pearls. The under-skirt mounted on the wheel farthingale is of apricot satin covered with a diaper design of conventional roses and flames. The roses, alternately rose colour and green, are worked in shaded silks outlined with gold and pearls, each having a large pearl centre. The flame ornaments are worked in gold and pearls, with ruby centres. The border at the bottom of the skirt is composed of two double rows of gold passamayne enclosing a design of connected squares and ovals carried out in gold lines, the centre of each feature being alternately rubies and emeralds surrounded by pearls. A beautiful pendent jewel (*see* Fig. 929) hung on a mauvish-pink riband is attached to the point of the stomacher, and caught up on the right side. (The 'Darnley' portrait in the National Portrait Gallery, London, shows the same detail).

The unseen headdress would be either a French hood, without tube, or a network caul enclosing the hair at the back, and to this is attached the upstanding jewel and feather. Pairs of pearls, mounted on pins, are stuck at intervals into the outside edge of the orange-golden wig. Seven ropes of pearls hang from the neck to the waist. A detail drawing of the lace which edges the band is given in Fig. 695. Other items of interest are the jewelled collar (Fig. 922), fan handle (see Fig. 937), and shoes (see Fig. 906), but no earrings are worn. A similar dress is worn by the Queen in a portrait at Jesus, and in yet another at Christ Church, Oxford.

The chair, upholstered in scarlet velvet, has elaborately carved arms, and is of French make. The design of the arm includes a figure whose headdress is in the style of those worn in the reign of Francis I. The cover of the table is green velvet edged with gold and fringe. Her Majesty stands upon a foot carpet of vermilion velvet fringed with gold.

A three-quarter portrait on canvas of Queen Elizabeth at the age of sixty-one, belonging to the Marquess of Salisbury and known as the 'Rainbow' portrait, was painted by Marcus Gheeraerts in 1594 (Plate XLI D). It is somewhat emblematic, which accounts for the rainbow—possibly referring to the prosperity which her skilful statecraft had brought about (suggested by Genesis viii. 22 and ix. 14, 15), though the words 'Non sine sole iris' (No rainbow without the sun) on the background may indicate the impersonation of the sun by the Queen. The serpent is symbolical of subtle wisdom ('wise as serpents'), and the eyes and ears on the orange drapery or lining of the fawn outer robe imply that Her Majesty saw and heard everything. The Crown mounted upon a turban-like headdress is suggestive of the heart-shaped headdress of the early fifteenth century; and the bodice of linen, embroidered with floral designs, is the first example of a vogue very popular during the following reign. Contrary to her usual custom, the Queen is wearing her hair in ringlets, perhaps to give the illusion of youth, while the chin ruff serves to mask her sinewy neck.

A description of the Queen, given by a German gentleman who had an interview with her in 1595, states that on this occasion she was seated upon a throne under a canopy of cloth of gold. Her dress was a silver robe, adorned with magnificent gems and jewels beyond compare, and on her head a Royal crown of pearls.

Later in the same year the aforesaid gentleman was present at Court during a meeting of the Knights of the Garter, awaiting an audience:

'Then Her Majesty stepped out of the Privy Chamber, arrayed in silver cloth. On her robe were embroidered two obelisks crossed, which in lieu of a button had at the top a beautiful oriental pearl. The robe was further adorned with rare costly gems and jewels. On her head she wore a very costly royal crown. Her Majesty was escorted on either side by Knights and

A

B

C

D

PLATE XLI. QUEEN ELIZABETH
A. *c.* 1589.   B. The 'Ditchley,' 1592: Portraits by unknown artists
National Portrait Gallery.   *By kind permission of the Directors*

C. The 'Hardwick,' 1592–4: Portrait by an unknown artist
Hardwick Hall.   *By kind permission of the Duke of Devonshire*

D. The 'Rainbow,' 1594: Portrait by Marcus Gheeraerts
Hatfield House.   *By kind permission of the Marquess of Salisbury*

PLATE XLII. QUEEN ELIZABETH, 1590: Portrait by Marcus Gheeraerts
Trinity College, Cambridge. *By kind permission of the Master and Fellows*

Earls.  Her train was borne by a Maid of Honour.  On stepping out of the chamber Her Majesty greeted all present.'

In the autumn of 1597, when receiving certain foreign officials, Queen Elizabeth wore a dress of red interwoven with threads of gold.  On her head was the usual crown of pearls, from which hung a long openwork veil; but what astonished one of the onlookers was a hideous large black spider which sat upon it and looked so natural and alive that many might have been deceived by it.  One is shown in Fig. 935.

The French Ambassador, De Maisse, who was much interested in Elizabeth's wondrous robes, tells us that on one occasion, in 1597, when he had an interview with the Queen in the privy chamber she was standing by the window.  'She looked better in health than before.  She was clad in a dress of black taffeta, bound with gold, and like a robe in the Italian fashion with open sleeves and lined with crimson taffeta.  She had a petticoat of white damask, girdled, and open in front, as was also her chemise, in such a manner that she often opened this dress and one could see all her belly, and even to her navel. . . . She had bracelets of pearl on her hands, six or seven rows of them.  On her head-tire she wore a coronet of pearls, of which five or six were marvellously fair.  When she raises her head she has a trick of putting both hands on her gown and opening it insomuch that all her belly can be seen.'

Evidently there was something wrong with De Maisse's powers of observation on this particular occasion or else he has a very coarse way of explaining some characteristic movements adopted by ladies at this time.  In Elizabeth's reign such indelicacies as those he describes could not possibly have been indulged in by any ladies of the Court, much less the Queen.  Obviously he was speaking metaphorically.  The two statements refer to the action of taking the sides of the open overdress and parting them with a graceful movement of the hands so as to display the underdress to full advantage.

A little later De Maisse tells us that 'she was strangely attired in a dress of silver cloth, white and crimson, or silver gauze as they call it.  This dress had slashed sleeves lined with red taffeta, and was girt about with other little sleeves that hung down to the ground, which she was for ever twisting and untwisting.  She kept the front of her dress open, and one could see the whole of her bosom, and passing low, and often she would open the front of this robe with her hands as if she was too hot.  The collar [ruff] of the robe was very high, and the lining of the inner part all adorned with little pendants of rubies and pearls, very many, but quite small.  She had also a chain of rubies and pearls about her neck.  On her head she wore a garland of the same material and beneath it a great reddish-coloured wig, with a great number of spangles of gold and silver, and hanging down over her forehead some pearls, but of no great worth.  On either side of her ears hung two great curls of hair, almost down to her shoulders, and within the collar of her robe, spangled as the top of her head.'

On 24th December 1597 when De Maisse surprised the Queen when playing the spinet, 'She was clad in a white robe of cloth of silver, cut very low and *her bosom uncovered*.   She had the same customary head attire, but diversified by several kinds of precious stones, yet not of any great value. She had a little gown [1] of cloth of silver of peach colour, covered and hidden, which was very fair.'

'Bosom uncovered' seems to have struck the gentleman as unusual.   All unmarried women had their bosoms, that is their throats and necks, exposed.   Some portraits of Elizabeth show this, especially those painted in later life, although there are some in which she is covered right up to the circular ruff.

On New Year's Eve of the same year, De Maisse informs us that 'this day she was habited, as is her custom, in silver tissue, or gauze as we call it in French; her robe was white and the over-vest of gold and silk of violet colour.   She wore innumerable jewels on her person, not only on her head, but also within her collar [ruff], about her arms and on her hands, with a great quantity of pearls round her neck and on her bracelets.   She had two bands, one on each arm, which were worth a great price.'

For the description of a costume worn by the Queen in 1598 see p. 597.

When giving an audience in 1599 Elizabeth was, we are told, 'most lavishly attired in a gown of pure white satin, gold-embroidered, with a whole bird of paradise for panache, set forward on her head studded with costly jewels, a string of huge round pearls about her neck, and elegant gloves over which were drawn costly rings.   In short she was most gorgeously apparelled, and although she was already seventy-four [she was only sixty-six], was very youthful still in appearance, seeming no more than twenty years of age.'

On the 16th June 1600, Queen Elizabeth honoured the Earl of Bedford with her presence at the wedding of his daughter, the Lady Anne Russell, with Lord Herbert, son of the Earl of Worcester (*see* Plate XLV).

The Queen is carried in a litter shoulder high by four gentlemen and is very gorgeously gowned all in white, the style and decoration being much the same as shown in Plate XXXVIII, and in the 'Ditchley' portrait.   The hairdressing is very lofty, much bejewelled, and surmounted by a Crown. An elaborate jewelled ornament is fixed high up on the left sleeve.

A portrait head of the Queen is in the Library of the Master's Lodge, St. John's College, Cambridge.   It appears to have been painted at this time as the hairdressing and ruff are almost the same as in Plate XLV, but the Crown is omitted, and she does not wear so many jewels.

Queen Elizabeth gave audience to the Persian Ambassador in February 1601.   It is recorded that 'the Queen, though very feeble and tottering on account of her illness, nevertheless appeared on this occasion adorned and bedecked with great pomp and right royally.'

The British Museum possesses an engraving of Queen Elizabeth opening her last Parliament on 27th October 1601.   Plate XLIII is a reproduction of it.   Her robes consist of a long pointed bodice and an all-round skirt of

---

[1] This is an erroneous translation from the French.   It refers to the under-skirt.

PLATE XLIII. QUEEN ELIZABETH IN PARLIAMENT,
1601: Engraving by an unknown artist. British Museum. *By kind permission of the Governors*

brocade open over an under-skirt of a different-patterned brocade and colour with the Spanish farthingale beneath. Over them is the parliamentary mantle of crimson velvet with a cape and lining of ermine fastened in front by long cords and tassels. A headdress,[1] like the French hood, but with a rolled front, and a circular ruff of moderate proportions, are worn, and the sceptre and orb carried. It is recorded that the weight of these Royal robes caused Her enfeebled Majesty to stagger on this occasion. The chair of State with crown fixed to it just above the Queen's head, dorsal, and cushions of brocade are other interesting features of the engraving.

So late as 6th February 1603, a little more than a month before her death, Elizabeth gave an audience to an envoy from Venice. In spite of her years, she still made a regal figure dressed in silver and white taffeta embroidered with gold: the Royal diadem surmounting hair 'of a light colour never made by nature,' and multitudes of pearls, rubies, diamonds, and other gems scintillating from all parts of her person.

Examination of the effigy of Queen Elizabeth, erected in Westminster Abbey by order of James I, will enlighten the student on some practical points of detail of the Queen's costume as worn by her during her last years.

The following is a list of garments taken from the Queen's wardrobe account dated 1600:

| | | | | | |
|---|---|---|---|---|---|
| Robes | 99 | Foreparts | 136 | Juppes | 43 |
| French gowns | 102 | Peticoats | 125 | Dublettes | 85 |
| Round gowns | 67 | Cloakes | 96 | Lappemantles | 18 |
| Loose gowns | 100 | Cloakes | 31 | Fannes | 27 |
| Kirtells | 126 | Saufegards | 13 | Pantobles | 9 |

Apparell, Jewelles, Kirtells, Coronation Robes, Mourning Robes, Parliament Robes, For Order of Garter. Sondrie P'cells.

The following descriptions of some of these garments are taken from the same wardrobe account:

'One Frenche gowne of russet stitched cloth, richlie florished with gold and silver, lyned with orange colour taphata, and hanginge sleeves, lyned with white taphata, embrodered with *antiques* of golde and silke of sonderie colours, called China-work.'[2]

'One rounde gowne of white cloth of silver, with workes of yellow silke, like flies, worms, and snailes.'

'One rounde gowne of Isabella colour[3] satten, cut in snippes and raised up, set with silver spangles.'

'One rounde gown of heare coloured raised *mosseworke* embroidered all over with leaves, pomegranets, and men.'

---

[1] The Cap of Maintenance was not generally worn after coronation.

[2] 'China work' refers to the pattern. China was a country vaguely known in the Middle Ages under the Tartar name of 'Cathay.' In the sixteenth century the Indian name of 'Chin' was latinized by the Spanish and Portuguese adventurers into 'China.'

[3] See List of Colours, p. 133.

'One loose gowne of Ladie-blushe satten, laide with bone-lace of Venice golde and silver, with spangles, with buttons downe before of the same lace.'

'One loose gowne of white tillyselge [tinsel] like grograine, bounde aboute with a small lace of golde, the hanging sleeves beinge cutt and bounde with the like lace and tufts of golde threede, and some golde spangles.'

Fig. 708. A Snoskyn

'Kirtells' refer to the under-skirt: 'foreparts' were equivalent to stomachers.

'One peticoate of white satten, embrodered all over with black flies, with a border of fountaines and trees, embrodered rounde aboute it, and waves of the sea.'

'One cloake of heare-colour raised mossworke, embrodered like stubbs of dead trees, set with fourteen buttons embrodered like butterflies, with fower pearls and one emerode in a pece, lyned with cloth of silver, prented.'

'One juppe and saufegarde of orenge-colour, or marigolde-colour vellat, cut and uncutt, the sleeves and downe before garnished with a lace of Venice silver, like essefirmes, and laide aboute with twoe plate laces of Venice silver.'

Safeguards were outward petticoats put on to protect an elaborate dress in bad weather. This name was also applied to the surcote since it had sleeves and made of rich material. The same may be said of loose gowns.

'One lappemantle of white plush, with a pane [a breadth] of redd swanes downe in the middest.'

'Lapmantle' was another name for apron.

Other items of dress which appear in different wardrobe accounts and inventories follow:

MUFF, *snoskyn* or *snuftkin*, an item of costume introduced towards the end of this reign. The shape of these muffs is obvious. Unfortunately,

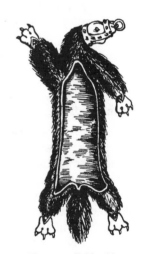

Fig. 709. Sable skin

representations of them in portraits of this period are scarce and the only example known to the author appears in a miniature of the 1590's in a private collection. It is of brown fur, rectangular in shape, and well padded, yet soft like a feather cushion as shown in Fig. 708.

'One snoskyn of crimson saten, laide upon with perfumed leather cut, embrothered with Venice gold, silver, and silk,' was a New Year's gift to the Queen in 1600.   At the same date a pair of snoskyns was given to Her Majesty—one for each hand.   They were 'of cloth of silver, embrothered all over with flowers and braunches of Venice, silver and silk of sondry colors.'

Sable skins were used by ladies to place around their shoulders for extra warmth.    When not required for this purpose they were carried in the hand (*see* Figs. 674 and 679).   Queen Elizabeth had one presented to her by the Earl of Leicester in 1584.   It is described as 'a sable skin, the head and four feet of gold fully garnished with diamonds and rubies of sundry sort.'   In Fig. 709 is shown a sable skin lined with silk and edged with a piping of the same.

*The Officers of the Household* of the Queens-Regnant, Mary and Elizabeth, were the same as in the households of kings, and with two exceptions they performed the same duties.

*Maids of Honour*, the daughters and granddaughters of the nobility, under the special supervision of the *Mother of the Maids*,[1] took the place of Gentlemen of the Privy Chamber.   They formed an aristocratic background for their Sovereign, and were also her personal companions.   While Gentlemen of the Privy Chamber were retained, but were exempt from any intimate duties, esquires of the body were replaced by *Ladies-in-waiting* and *Gentlewomen of the Bedchamber*.

Those who superintended the Queen's wardrobe were naturally ladies of influence and the highest importance, and correspondingly autocratic in their methods.

First and foremost comes Mary, whose father Sir John Shelton of Shelton, Norfolk, had been Controller of Elizabeth's household (1538); she was Maid of Honour about 1571, and married in 1576 James (later Sir James) Scudamore.   When the Queen heard of this she was furiously angry, but forgave and appointed Mary Scudamore a gentlewoman of the bedchamber.   After a time she held the important and difficult post of *Keeper of the Queen's Wardrobe*.

Rauff Hope was 'Yeoman of the Queen's Robes' in 1578.

---

[1] At a much later date the title 'Mistress of the Robes' was given to this official, who was usually a duchess.

Tailors and dressmakers of the Elizabethan era did not have an easy time, and the following quotation from Harrison gives some idea of the fussiness of their clients, gentlemen as well as ladies.

'How long time is asked in decking up' the body with much finery. 'How curious, how nice also, are a number of men and women, and how hardly can the tailor please them in making it fit for their bodies! How many times must it be sent back again to him that made it! What chafing, what fretting, what reproachful language, doth the poor workman bear away! And many times when he doth nothing to it at all, yet when it is brought home again it is very fit and handsome. Then must we put it on, then must the long seams of our hose be set by a plumb-line, then we puff, then we blow, and finally sweat till we drop, that our clothes may stand well upon us.'

It has been mentioned that Queen Elizabeth was enamoured of both French and Italian fashions, and it was not beneath her dignity to make surreptitious inquires about them for her own benefit. Thus at her instigation Lord Burleigh writes to Sir Henry Norris, then Her Majesty's representative in Paris, as follows: 'The Queen's Majesty would fain have a tailor that has skill to make her apparel both after the French and Italian manner, and she thinketh you might use some means to obtain such one as suiteth the Queen without mentioning any manner of request in the Queen's Majesty's name . . . as she does not want to be beholden to her.' The reference is, of course, to Catherine de' Medici, who would have been justifiably annoyed if she had known of such an attempt to entice away not only the creators of Court fashions but also the skilled dressmakers who carried out their designs.

A tire-woman (see Chapter II, p. 209) was the Tudor expression for a lady's maid, but the name was also applied to a dressmaker; likewise a tire-glass was a mirror, chiefly of polished metal as glass mirrors were very rare at this time and were of Italian, especially Venetian, manufacture. These glass mirrors were imported into England during this period and were very expensive. Both varieties, metal and glass, were set in frames of period design, which stood upon the tire-table; and a tire-room or tiring chamber was a dressing-room. A small mirror was sometimes attached to a lady's girdle, but more frequently was fixed into the centre of a feather fan. A small rectangular or circular mirror, with a frame and handle, was sometimes used.

Gentlemen carried very small looking-glasses, often worn in the hat as a brooch or ornament which could be detached when required.

Here are a few items from the Queen's privy purse expenses which may amuse those interested in dressmaking bills and sundry items, bearing in mind the value of money at this time, and the fact that Queen Elizabeth's household expenses were £55,000 per annum.

From 8th July 1566 until 23rd April 1567.

| | | | | | | |
|---|---|---|---|---|---|---|
| *To* David Smyth, embroderer | . | . | . | . | . £203 | 15 7 |
| William Middleton, embroderer | | . | . | . | . 25 | 11 11 |
| Robert Careles, pynner | . | . | . | . | . 127 | 8 9 |

*To* Raphell Hamonde, capper . . . . . £ 68 1 6

Thomas Ludwell, tailor, for apparell, and other necessaries for Robert Grene, the Quene's fool and Nicholas
Knyghte Smyth, his servant . . . . . III 13 9

Expenses and chardges of Robert Grene, the Queen's
fool, and to Nicholas Knyghte Smythe, his servant, for
wage and bordewage at sondry times. 1569 . . 17 0 0

[The last items show that the Queen supplied her Court jester with raiment
and also that he kept an attendant with a much more aristocratic name.]

Mrs. Mary Radclyffe, one of the maidens of honoure, for
her stipend of £40 per ann. for two years and a half,
ended at the Annunciation of Oure Lady, 1569. . 100 0 0

This lady was the daughter of a romantic marriage. Her father, Sir
Humphrey Radclyffe, a younger son of the first Earl of Sussex, fell in love
with Isabella, the beautiful daughter
of a rich London merchant named Edmund Harvey. Mary became a Maid
of Honour to the Queen about 1561,
and served her mistress 'honourably,
virtuously, and faithfully for forty
years.' Like the Queen, who was much
attached to her, she remained a spinster
all her life: the Queen's 'merry
guardian' the courtiers called her. At
the end of the reign Mary Radclyffe
held the responsible post of Keeper
of the Queen's Jewels.

Blanche Parry was another very close
attendant on the Queen. Born at New-
court Bacton, Herefordshire, in 1507,
she had known Elizabeth from the
cradle and served her mistress most
faithfully all her life, at first as Gentlewoman of the Privy Chamber, and
later as Keeper of the Queen's Jewels.
This lady died in 1589, and her effigy
in Bacton Church shows her kneeling
before the Queen. In it she is habited

Fig. 710. Blanche Parry, 1589

in a simple and comfortable costume, suitable for an old woman of eighty:
in black or some dark-coloured surcote with hanging sleeves, over an ordinary
gown (*see* Fig. 710). Some of Elizabeth's cast-off dresses became the per-
quisites of her gentlewomen-in-waiting, and the altar cloth presented by
Blanche Parry to Bacton Church, and still shown there, was, in all probability,
made up from one of them.

'For jewels of gold, stones, and pearles bought and provided for
Her Majestie within the time [10 months] of this accompte      £2,294 3 3½'

Seed pearls, which were very much used *en masse* for the decoration of
dresses, cost 1*d*. each.

'Silkes bought of sundry persons to the Queen's Majestie's use £101 14  2

'Gold lace bought by Walter Fisher, the Queen's Taylor, for Her
Majestie's use .    .    .    .    .    .    .    .    .    32 10

'Mrs. Taylor, the Queen's laundress, for her wages at £4 per ann. . . .
with £6 paid her for her livery gown £10.' 1568.   Fig. 719 shows a laundress,
and who knows but that she is the Queen's own?

'The Italian, Carlo Lanfranchi, a trader who was with the Prince of Parma
at Brussels a few days ago [about 1586], has requested His Highness's permission to purchase some silk wares and take them to the Court of the Queen
in England.   So this merchant has bought nearly 12,000 pounds Flemish
worth of all sorts of silk wares and started for England with them yesterday.'
Lanfranchi was a merchant resident at Antwerp; later with one Andrew de
Looe chief partner in a big Italian firm in London.


## 'NYGHT STUFFE'

### LADIES AND GENTLEMEN

What a wonderful vision young Gilbert Talbot must have beheld at eight
of the clock on the morning of 3rd May 1578—the Virgin Queen in her
nightdress!   He writes to his father:

'I happened to walke in the Tylte-yard, under the Gallery where her Ma^tie
useth to stande to see the ruñinge at tylte; where by chaunce she was, and
lokynge out of the wyndow, my eye was full towards her, and she shewed
to be greatly ashamed thereof, for that she was unreddy, and in her nyght
stuffe.'

Elizabeth was then in her forty-fifth year, an age when modesty grows upon
a woman; so naturally 'much ashamed thereof she was,' as she told her Lord
Chamberlain afterwards.   All Gilbert received was 'a great phyllyp on the
forehead.'   We wish he had remembered more, for then we should have had
first-hand particulars of these interesting garments.   Unfortunately they must
be more or less left to conjecture.   In shape, ladies' as well as gentlemen's
nightdresses or 'night-railes' were, without much doubt, similar to those worn
during the reign of Henry VIII (*see* Chapter II, p. 262), and decorated in various
ways.   A few paintings and some original nightdresses reputed to be of the
Elizabethan era show lace insertion, used in vertical, horizontal, and diagonal
lines in parts or over the whole garment.   A night-raile traditionally said to

have been worn at Rycote by Elizabeth, and once owned by the Earl of Abing-don (a substantial proof of its genuineness!), is now exhibited at the London Museum. Fig. 711 is a half-diagram made from it. It is of fine linen with embroidery, insertion, and lace all white.

Amongst items in the Queen's lists of New Year's gifts and wardrobe accounts are the following:

'A smock of cameryck wrought with tawny sylke and black, with ruffs and collar edged with bone lace of silver' (1577).

'A smock of fine Holland, and the bodies and sleeves wrought all over with black silk' (1588).

These garments may be equivalent to chemises, yet on the other hand would serve equally well as nightdresses.

'A nightraile of camberick wrought all over with black silk' (1588).

'A night gown [i.e. a dressing-gown] of tawny satten, allover embrodered, faced with satten heare collour, for the Queen from Sir Francis Walsingham' (1578).

The shape of night-caps, both for men and women, has altered little from time immemorial (*see* vol. ii, p. xi, and Chapter II, p. 262). One at least appears in the list of New Year's gifts to the Queen: 'By Mrs. Crokson a night coif of white Cipers florisshed ouer with silver' (1578).

All these night-garments were worn by fashionable women in imitation of the Queen, and even by men.

So elaborate did the embroidery on night-caps become, that gentlemen began to wear them in the day-time—

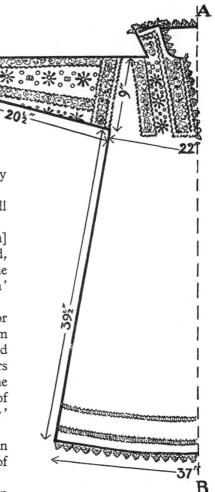

Fig. 711. A Night-raile

especially the elderly who needed protection for their bald pates. Several portraits show them wearing such caps with ordinary day dress, and some in official robes. The full-length painting of Charles, Baron Howard of Effingham (1536–1624), in the Royal Hospital, Greenwich, shows the Lord High Admiral of England (1585–1618) in the full robes

Fig. 712. Dr. Thomas Nevill

of the Order of the Garter and wearing one of these embroidered caps.

In shape they were like a bag round at the top, the end turning up to form a brim and the whole surface usually embroidered. Fig. 712 is drawn from a portrait of Dr. Thomas Nevill, Master of Trinity College, Cambridge, from 1593 to 1615. He built and paid for Nevill's Court.

This cap is made of linen, embroidered in black and white silk and silver gilt thread. Often the embroidery was in coloured silks, and frequently spangles were introduced.

Caps of this type may be seen in many museums and private collections.

## NOBILITY—WOMEN, 1580–1603

### THE FARTHINGALE (*continued from p. 504*)

The Spanish farthingale held its own during the remainder of the reign of Elizabeth, being a more conveniently proportioned garment than its close rival the wheel or drum farthingale. This was a development of the earlier Spanish farthingale, and came into use in England only about 1586–8 (Fig. 243). It was a petticoat of linen into which bands of steel or whalebone were inserted horizontally, and it resembled a drum in shape. It differed from the Spanish version in that the bands were all of the same circumference. Steel or cane spokes supported the top band to a waistbelt. This was not placed in the centre of the circle, but close to the frame; in fact, the frame rested on the stomach pushed out by tight lacing, the edges of the circumference bowing out over the hips and the widest part being in the centre of the back. Over this two or three voluminous petticoats were added before the underskirt was put on, followed by the overdress. The skirt of the overdress was drawn out at right angles to the body over the farthingale and then fell to the ankles showing the feet. In some portraits of great ladies of this period a circular top piece is seen on the farthingaled skirt, with box pleats radiating from the waist, resembling the spokes of a wheel; and for this reason it is referred to as the wheel farthingale. This is plainly shown in Fig. 725.

The wheel farthingale, however, had its merits. A dress displayed upon this structure showed the rich and costly material of which it was composed to greater advantage, consequently it became very popular at Court and for ceremonial and full dress.

It required no little skill to wear the cumbersome farthingale with grace and dignity; but use is second nature, and it was not a difficult matter for ladies of quality of the late Elizabethan era to manipulate these hoops with dexterity and effect. The art was born in them, for it must be realized that the farthingale had been worn by their mothers, grandmothers, and great-grandmothers for seventy years or more past.

The correct way to hold the arms when wearing a farthingale was to rest the wrists upon the edge, as shown in Fig. 725, one hand usually carrying a handkerchief, the other perhaps a fan. Two lines from a poem dated 1599 refer to this pose:

> Placing both hands upon her whalebone hips,
> Puffed out with a round circling farthingale.

Amongst the customs for which the wheel farthingale is responsible is that of sitting on piles of cushions on the floor.

The style and shape of chairs in use during the first eighty years of the sixteenth century can be seen from Fig. 215, were, one can understand, quite unsuited for sitting in comfort when the wearer was enveloped in the wheel farthingale. The arms and normal width of the seat were found inconvenient; consequently cushions, always a popular item of furnishing in medieval and Tudor times, were brought into much more general use. As the lady, decked out in all the paraphernalia Court and high society demanded, approached these piles of cushions, in order to avoid disarrangement of the skirt she turned and raised herself high on her toes, and then sank elegantly into their midst and sat upon a soft pedestal, so to speak, encircled by the voluminous skirt and farthingale.

Queen Elizabeth frequently seated herself on the floor on cushions, especially when carrying on a friendly discourse with a lady or gentleman. Taking this into account, it does not appear so incongruous that, during her last illness, this great Queen should prefer to remain upon her cushions instead of going to bed.

It was not until the end of the century that wide chairs, with or without arms, known as farthingale chairs, came into use.

In the Audience or Presence Chambers of the Royal palaces, and houses of the nobility, the number of stools was now greatly increased, amounting to anything from fifty to a hundred and fifty; and in some households cushions of velvet or embroidery were provided for a few of them, being tied by

Fig. 713. Hip Pad

cords and tassels to the legs. Thus, numbers of cushions, or 'quysshens,' are found in household inventories of the sixteenth century, elaborate descriptions being often given. Of oak, these *joint stools* of the mid-Elizabethan period remain with us to-day. Their name does *not* imply that they were used at table for carving; they were so called because made and finished by a joiner. These now took the place of cushions on the floor, and although harder to sit upon were not complained of by the much be-petticoted ladies. Nor was the discomfort of a hard wooden seat noticeable to the gentlemen,

Fig. 714. From an Engraving, 1603

in the days when bombast Venetian breeches were the mode. But in the 1590's fashion decreed a return to the round slops of earlier years *minus* the bombast, as is shown in Figs. 739 and 740. This loss of posterior padding was most likely responsible for more comfortable upholstered seats or 'buffet stools,' so called because they were stuffed with padding or 'buffet' of all kinds. The upholstering was of velvet, damask, brocade, or embroidery—

embroidery of similar design to that shown in Fig. 689. The same privileges connected with the use of stools in the Presence Chambers in the Royal palaces of France, described on p. 664, were adopted in England at this time.

Fig. 715. A Squeamish Townswoman

A faldstool was a similar stool of common make, used by ordinary people in England.

The French farthingale was introduced at the Court of Henry III as late as 1580. It consisted of a single padded hoop, and its modified version was a bolster-like pad (Fig. 713). It fastened round the waist sloping from the back to the point of the stomacher. This was set on top of some petticoats, one or two other petticoats being worn over the hoop or pad. This French type is seen worn by the lady (Fig. 755) in which the very full skirt of rich satin, cut on the circle and gathered into the waist, hangs in many graceful folds well on to the ground. A feature characteristic of the French type is that its widest part is level with the waist-line, the folds of the skirt slightly falling in towards the feet when supple fabrics, such as silk or satin, were used. But when the skirts were of stiff brocades, and some made stiffer by gold metal weaving, the folds took the reverse line and stood out at the hem, having almost the same effect as if the Spanish or wheel farthingale was worn. For example see Fig. 731.

It must have been quite impossible to sit a horse when wearing a Spanish or wheel farthingale, but sometimes the bolster was used.

The French or Italian lady (Fig. 714), taken from a contemporary engraving, is seated upon a special saddle with a very low cantle, and wears a bolster farthingale under the cart-wheel arrangement. Her full skirt drapes over her right leg, which is supported by a pommel, and over the horse's back in quite a pleasing manner. As was the discreet custom with ladies of quality when in public, she is masked, and carries a large feather fan, perhaps as an additional protection.

Fig. 715 is a reproduction of a contemporary engraving, and shows the farthingale as worn by middle-class women. The first impression is that faulty draughtsmanship is responsible for the bottom edge being too much curved and too short, thus showing a very decided and ungraceful ridge when the skirt was let down. Actually this bourgeois lady has hitched up her farthingale with both hands *under* the drapery of her skirt to avoid the canine scavengers; thereby revealing to us the lines of the canes or whale-bones which are very clearly defined.

### The Corset (*continued from p. 504*)

A change in the shape of the corset took place approximately at the time when the wheel farthingale was adopted, in order to accentuate the line of the farthingale.

The Queen was approaching her fiftieth year and her figure, always of slim proportions, became in middle life even more so. All fashionable women wished to emulate the Great Gloriana, consequently a long narrow tapering figure had to be acquired. The construction of steel corsets, without doubt, improved since their first introduction about the year of Elizabeth's birth; and this may account in some measure for the abnormal slenderness of late Elizabethan ladies as seen in their portraits. It is true that the artists who painted them may have exaggerated their narrowness of body, but on the other hand it is extraordinary what impossibilities women of all ages can achieve to be *à la mode*.

The Queen's narrow, flat-chested figure was well adapted to the new style of corset such as is shown in Fig. 716, a drawing made from an original. The front bands of steel extend downwards in a long tapering point as far as the pit of the stomach, and the sides converge as low down as the hip bone will permit. It is the line from this to the lowest point of the corset that deceives the eye and makes the figure look longer and the waist smaller than they really are.

There is no evidence that these corsets hooked, bolted, or padlocked; they were fastened by tight-lacing the back. As previously, the steel work was lined and covered with thin silk or other material, and often decorated with *flat* embroidery which could not add to the bulk. The lady (Fig. 243) is wearing a corset of this kind. The bodice of the dress was cut to fit the corset without a crease, and the front of it was generally covered by the stomacher, which took the lines of the constructional converging bands of steel.

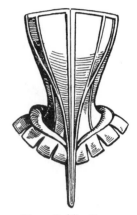

Fig. 716. The Corset

A less expensive contrivance was a broad slightly convex piece of wood which was used by the middle-class women to keep their busts flat, and make their figures straight and erect.

The following lines from *Pleasant Quippes for Upstart Gentlewomen*, by Stephen Gosson, 1596, describe the type of corset worn by both men and women of the middle classes:

> Those privie coats by art made strong,
> With bones, with paste, and such like ware,
> Whereby their backs and sides grow long.

### The Ruff or Band (*continued from p. 505*)

During the latter half of this reign the ruff assumed vast dimensions, its width varying from nine to fifteen inches from the neck on either side. When unset and drawn out to its full length the band was sometimes eight yards long. The Queen wore hers higher, wider, and stiffer than any one else in Europe, save the Queen of Navarre, Marguerite de Valois, who had a 'yellow throat,' and desired to conceal it with the addition of 'chin ruffs.' These consisted of one or more frills, themselves small circular ruffs worn close up under the jaw, which also helped to mask the line where the main ruff surrounded the back of the neck. These wonderful face frames of lawn were edged with exquisite lace, cutwork, and insertion. They were also decorated with embroidery, and sometimes in complete contrast were quite plain with the edges cut out in points like the head of a small spear.

In 1599 the Countess of Worcester presented the Queen with 'One ruffe

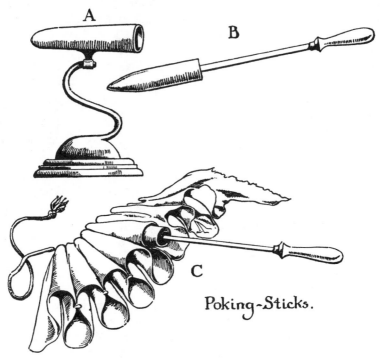

Poking-Sticks.

Fig. 717. Poking-sticks

of lawne cut-worke, set with 20 small knottes of gold like mullets [heraldic stars], gar' with small sparkes of rubyes and perle.'

Item 'a sute of ruffes of Lawne, wrought with Spanisshe worke.'

A poking-stick or setting-iron of this period is shown in Fig. 717 drawn from one found at Cowdray. The top of the iron or steel stand, shown at A, was heated in the fire. The stick B was thrust into it, and when sufficiently hot was then placed in that part of the band already damped with starch. This process was repeated all along the flutes of the band until it was complete and well stiffened. This process is seen at C.

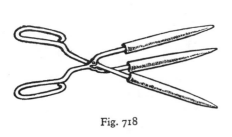

Fig. 718

Fig. 718 shows another kind of poking-stick or setting-tongs made on the principle of modern curling-tongs, except that two sticks were rigid and the third was worked on a pivot, so that three flutes could be goffered at one operation.

Fig. 719 shows a laundress in the act of goffering the set of a ruff. The 'band,' having been dipped in starch, is tied round the ruff-stand and the steel poking-stick is taken from its sheath in the charcoal brazier and thrust into the fold of linen with the aid of the fingers of the left hand. This action is repeated until the ruff is finished; then it is hung up to dry. A complete ruff with one edge attached to a piece of linen, which is fixed inside the collar of the dress, is seen hanging on a rod in the illustration. When the time came for the delivery of the band to its owner, it was placed in a circular box specially made for its reception and known as a 'band-box.' One is shown in the right-hand corner.

Fig. 719.
'There she sat with her poking-stick, stiffening a fall'

Bands and wristbands usually matched, and were made chiefly of lawn. In 1591 Queen Elizabeth paid £10 10s for 'three suits of good lawn cutwork ruffs edged with bone lace'—i.e. three ruffs and three pairs of cuffs.

Three ruffs, one on top of the other, were known as 'three-piled ruffs.'

That arch-craftsman in the art of grousing, Philip Stubbes, has much to say which is worth repeating with regard to the ruff:

'They have great and monsterous ruffs, made either of cambrick, holland, lawn, or else of some other of the finest cloth that can be got for money, whereof some be a quarter of a yard deep, yea, some more, very few less, so that they stand a full quarter of a yard and more from their necks, hanging over their shoulder points, instead of a veil. But . . . if the storms chance to hit upon the crafty bark of their brused ruffs, then they go flip flap in the wind, like rags flying abroad, and lye upon their shoulders like the dish-clouts of a slut. . . . They have them wrought all over with silk work, and peradventure laced with gold and silver, or other costly lace of no small price.'

Gentlemen 'have now newly [1595] found out a more monstrous kind of ruff, of twelve, yea, sixteen lengths apiece, set three or four times double, thence called three steps and a half to the gallows.'

Referring to the stiffening of the ruff he tells us they have 'a certain kind of liquid matter which they call starch, wherein the devil hath willed them to

wash and dive their ruffs well, which, when they be dry will then stand stiff and inflexible about their necks. And this starch they make of divers substances, sometimes of wheatflour, of bran, and other grains; sometimes of roots, and sometimes of other things, of all colours and hues, as white, red, blew, purple, and the like.' Ben Jonson mentions goose-green starch, but one does not find these coloured ruffs depicted in portraits.

Despite these stiffening methods it appears that the breezes still played havoc with the ruff.

Fig. 720. Supportasse

Stubbes describes 'a certain device made of wires, crested for the purpose, whipped over either with gold thread, silver or silk, and this be called a SUPPORTASSE or underprop. This is to be applied round about their necks under the ruff, upon the outside of the band, to bear up the whole frame and body of the

ruff from falling and hanging down.' Fig. 720 shows one of these supportasses made from a sixteenth-century Flemish engraving. Rebarto was another name for it.

Late in the period another kind of support was used with large circular ruffs. This contrivance originated possibly in Spain, and is seen in Fig. 886. It was a circular gold or silver wire frame fitting the neck, whence wires or spokes radiated to the circumference. To this was sewn a narrow fringe in gold, silver, or silk giving a very pleasing effect.

### THE VEIL (cont. from p. 505)

Now that fashionable costume had undergone various changes both in shape and

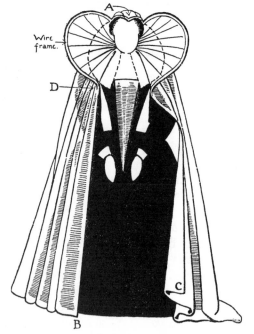

Fig. 721. The Wired-out Veil

decoration, elaborate yet grotesque, a new method of arranging the veil was devised. This was brought about chiefly by the increase in the width of the ruff. In shape this new veil was a large *square* of filmy transparent gauze or other material edged all round with cutwork, reticella, or gold or silver lace. Its arrangement, shown in diagram (Fig. 721) was as follows:

One corner, A, was attached to the headdress or coiffure; if to the latter, the corner was usually brought well on to the centre of the forehead. In the former case it was slightly gathered and fixed to the headdress, whatever shape it might be. It was again gathered or pleated into the nape of the neck, forming a cap over the back of the head. From the nape the edges of the veil were wired out in two large semicircles or three-quarter-circles on either side of the head behind the ruff, the wire being secured to the bodice just in front of the armpit at D. This arrangement kept the veil free from entanglement with the ruff, and did not impede the movement of the head. From the armpit and from over the shoulders two corners of the veil, B and C, fell to the feet. The remaining fourth corner trailed upon the ground behind: E, Fig. 722. The dotted line indicates the edge of the ruff worn *over* the front of the veil. The earliest example of the veil treated in this manner is seen in the 'Siena' portrait of Queen Elizabeth, 1578, and the more elaborate arrangement is shown in Plate XXXVIII and other illustrations in this section.

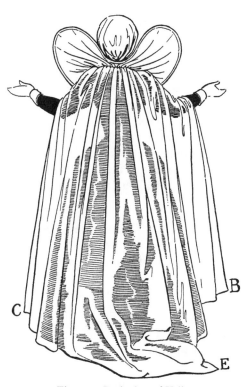

Fig. 722. Back view of Veil

In the National Portrait Gallery portrait, No. 2471 (Plate XXXII B), the gauze veil is decorated with bands of cutwork but not wired; as an alternative, a circular collar worn behind the ruff distends the veil beyond the shoulders.

### THE SLEEVES

To balance the width of the wheel farthingale and so enhance the effect of squareness, sleeves were large, of leg-of-mutton shape, and padded out at the shoulders.

In nearly every case there were long loose over-sleeves, cut as an oblong about twenty-five inches wide and forty inches long, though sometimes falling to the hem of the skirt, as seen in Plates XXXVIII, XLI B and C,

XLII, and Figs. 726 and 729. These over-sleeves were gathered or pleated into the armhole, starting from the shoulder and going round the back to the armpit.

## THE FAN (*continued from p. 507*)

The feather fan, as described in Section I, held its own in spite of the rivalry of a new type. It was greatly appreciated for its graceful line, and for the seductive flow of its plumes; besides, no one could possible deny its picturesque advantages. In France, the feather fan was pre-eminent, its use being stimulated by that leader of fashion, Marguerite de Valois, who had an extraordinary passion for magnificent fans. These cost a very great deal of money, which naturally aroused her husband's justifiable displeasure. Towards the end of the century the feather fan had become an almost indispensible item of the wardrobe of all ladies and gentlewomen, and even of the wives of the minor merchants. Some lines dated 1598 show for what other purposes the feather fan might be used:

> Were fannes and flappes of feathers fond
> To flit away the flisking flies . . .
> But seeing they are still in hand,
> In house, in field, in church, in street
> In summer, winter, water, land,
> In colde, in heate, in dry, in weet,
> I judge they are for wives such tooles
> As bables are in playes for fooles.

Some of these fans had very long handles and were found very useful as husband beaters.

A jewelled fan-handle is shown in Fig. 937.

## THE SEMICIRCULAR OR FOLDING FAN

It was during the late 1580's or early 1590's that a fan made to open and shut first appeared in England. Such fans were used much earlier in China, and the first European country to adopt them was Italy, where they were represented in paintings earlier in the sixteenth century. In France and Spain they came into vogue at much the same time as in England. One of the first English ladies to possess such a fan had her portrait painted displaying it very prominently: she was evidently very pleased with it, and with reason, since at this time such fans from far-off Cathay were very rare. Many of these fans of European make are seen in portraits of English ladies of the late years of the sixteenth century, but there are unfortunately none

shown fully open.  Fig. 723 is a larger-scale drawing
of the fan carried by the Countess of Nottingham
(*see* Fig. 728).  The 'guard' is wider than that of
a modern fan: it is black, inlaid with ivory, with
puff-balls of silk down the outside and along the
top.  Fig. 724 is a drawing from a portrait dated
1590, and is given because it is one of the earliest
examples of a fan painted half open.  It will be
seen that the same principle of carved sticks and a
decorated 'leaf' that we know to-day was adopted
by fan-makers [1] of the sixteenth century.  The sticks
are of carved ivory, the two guards tapering, but the
sticks are of uniform width and are fixed by stitches
of gold thread between the two layers of white gauze
which form the 'leaf': the guards are whipped across
with red silk.  The edges of the gauze are bound
together with fine stitches of gold and a row of small
gold knots.  The leaf is very finely embroidered in a
design of roses and pansies in their natural colourings.

Fig. 723.
Closed semicircular Fan

The pivot is kept in place with a gold filigree ornament set with a ruby.

Fig. 724. Fan, 1580

This fan has no ring to take
a riband, but many fans had
one as shown in some of the
drawings.

Mica or vellum was often
used for the leaf.

Whether it was a feather
fan on a rigid handle, or one
made to open or close, Brantôme does not say; but he
mentions that Marguerite,
Queen of Navarre, 'on one
occasion . . . gave Queen
Louise of France a fan made
of mother-of-pearl enriched
with precious stones and pearls
of price, so beautiful and rich
that it was called a masterpiece and valued at more
than fifteen thousand crowns.'
This fan certainly appears to
have been of the semi-
circular shape.

[1] The Fan-makers' Company was not incorporated until 1709.

It was customary for ladies, when out of doors, to have a page or servant to carry the fan.

Even men used fans; at least, Pierre de l'Étoile relates that Henry III fanned himself like a woman with a richly ornamented fan of this kind, which opened with a simple flick of the finger, and fell closed. Some of the courtiers also used fans, chiefly of taffeta decorated with gold and silk embroidery.

## STOCKINGS (*continued from p. 546*)

As late as 1595 stockings of worsted are mentioned as being worn by smart folk. Silk gradually superseded worsted for best wear, and so great a reputation did English silk stockings attain on the Continent, that Duke Frederick of Württemburg commissioned his secretary, Hans Jacob Breuning von Buchenbach, who was on a visit to this country in 1595, to replenish his stock. He writes to his master:

'The twelve pairs of stockings I have bought as cheap and as best I could. They are according to Your Grace's wish, in various colours, but no black or green. They are of excellent quality and picked from a large assortment. Twelve pair fine silk stockings, at 6 French crowns a pair.'

## THE STOCKING FRAME

In 1589 William Lee invented the stocking frame, a device which enabled stockings to be mechanically knitted. He was a clergyman, having matriculated at Christ's College, Cambridge, and was a B.A. of St. John's College. He resigned his living and devoted himself to the manufacture of stockings in worsted at Calverton, the scene of his ministerial labours. When he came to London his work was brought to the notice of the Queen by Lord Hunsdon, but this fastidious lady who had already worn hand-knitted silk stockings turned up her Royal nose with scorn at hosiery of such coarse make and refused to grant him a patent of monopoly. The inventor adapted his frame to the use of silk in 1598, but Elizabeth feared that the invention would prejudice the hand-knitters, and therefore discouraged the reverend gentleman. For the same reason, James I was not interested; but Henry IV invited Lee to settle in France. At the very moment when he was about to obtain the promised privileges, Henry IV was assassinated (1610), and Concini, the virtual Regent of France, was not willing to assist Lee in his enterprise. The disappointment so distressed the poor man that he gave way to despair, and died of privation and grief the same year. James Lee, his brother, returned to England with his craft and frames, and eventually obtained the patronage of James I; and with the assistance of a former apprentice of William's he became successful, and his trade increased rapidly. From this time knitted stockings in silk, worsted, and other materials became general throughout Europe.

The foregoing items of costume are seen illustrated in the portraits of the Queen already reproduced, as also in the drawings of Court and Noble ladies which follow. For example, the costume worn by the lady (Fig. 725), which was in vogue during the 1580's, shows large sleeves, long pointed stomacher,

Fig. 725. La Mode, 1580's

Fig. 726. The Lady Elizabeth Howard, 1582

skirt over the wheel farthingale with the cart-wheel effect on top and the huge ruff and high-dressed coiffure surmounted by a coronet like a stephane. The dress is without much decoration, and would be made of satin, silk, velvet or brocade, although the last does not appear to have been much favoured during this decade.

### The Lady Elizabeth Howard, 1580-90

The portrait of Lady Elizabeth Howard (Fig. 726) illustrates further the hanging sleeves, as well as a new method of draping the skirt over the wheel farthingale. She was daughter of the Earl and Countess of Nottingham, and is shown in one of the many dresses she wore as Maid of Honour to the Queen. It was Elizabeth's wish—nay, command—that all her ladies-in-waiting should dress in white and silver when in attendance, so as to form an ameliorative background for Her Majesty. Some of them strongly resented being mere backgrounds. Many made excellent marriages: the Lady Elizabeth wedded Sir Robert Southwell about 1582. Fig. 726 depicts an interesting costume of hers. The bodice and skirt are of plain white satin; the very large sleeves and stomacher of this material are decorated with oval ornaments of clusters of pearls. Behind these sleeves are pleated into the armholes at the back of one the *hanging sleeves*, a feature appearing here for the first time. These hang behind the skirt; the outer edge, and probably the inner also, is serrated and stiffened by flexible wire so as to carry projecting ornaments of pearls or tiny buttons in groups of three. The skirt cut all in one, a large circle, is pleated into a waistband and falls in folds over the wheel farthingale. No cart-wheel effect is here, but instead, the skirt is draped very skilfully at, and over, the edge. The Lady Southwell's headdress is composed of fern-like leaves in silver, pearls, and diamonds and worn over high hairdressing. There is no lace edging to the ruff: instead, it is cut out in points like *little spear-heads*, while the inner edge is masked where it rests on the neck by puffings of gauze.

### Catherine Carey

#### *Countess of Nottingham, died 1603*

The Lady Southwell's mother (Fig. 728) is 'Kate' Carey, eldest daughter of Henry, first Baron Hunsdon, and a granddaughter of Mary Boleyn, and so first cousin to Queen Elizabeth. She was one of the Queen's many Maids of Honour, and in 1563 married Charles, second Baron Howard of Effingham (1573), who was created Earl of Nottingham in 1596. The Countess's portrait is interesting because it shows distinctly the new arrangement of the veil. One corner is attached to the head in a series of pleats, the lace edging forming a coronet effect. The lines of the very transparent veil can be traced, first wired out behind the ruff, secondly fixing in front of the armpit, and thirdly descending to the ground behind the skirt. Her ladyship's dress is of black velvet, made on fashionable lines, the bodice and sleeves embroidered with silver of a different design from the skirt—a new feature. The skirt draped over the wheel farthingale is also embroidered in silver, and up the front is a puffing of gauze fixed with jewels. She is holding in her right hand a profusely decorated fan of the newest shape.    Below a dog-collar of jewels, and surrounding the throat, is placed a twist or ruche of gauze—a beneficent fashion for those who have scraggy necks—which also masks the edge of the elaborately worked ruff.    From beneath this, long ropes of pearls fall to the point of the stomacher.    These ropes of pearls and chains of jewels worn round the neck were now given the name of NECKLACES, carcanets being the former appellation for them.    Her hair—or is it a wig?—is closely curled, and adorned with numerous tiny horse-shoes of pearls.

Fig. 727. Noble Lady

*Reproduced by kind permission of Archibald G. B. Russell, Esq.*

The Countess is celebrated for having withheld the Earl of Essex's ring, confessing to the Queen on her death-bed in 1603 (*see* p. 780).

Quite a different style of dress is worn by the lady of quality (Fig. 727), which shows that the Spanish farthingale was still in favour.    The original drawing was made by Nicholas Hilliard in the 1580's.    The lady portrayed is in full dress wearing large sleeves, but not padded so stiffly as those worn for full State, as shown in some of the preceding and following illustrations. The stomacher is moderately long, but the Spanish farthingale is immoderately voluminous.    This figure is especially interesting as it reproduces all the important features seen in some of Queen Elizabeth's portraits, thereby allocating them within this decade. One of these portraits is shown in Plate XLI A. In Fig. 727 the bodice has tapering rolls converging from the shoulders to the point below the waist. They are studded part of the way with groups of gems, and on the shoulders with bows caught down with jewels. These bows are repeated down the front and hem of the skirt, and down the centre of the under-skirt. This garment displays rich embroidery between bands of gold set with rows of pearls. A circular ruff surrounds the head, and the headdress with attifet front closely resembles the French hood.

There is a portrait, in a private collection, of a young woman wearing a costume very much on the lines of the foregoing. Her dress is composed of green and gold brocade; the headdress is of the same shape as Fig. 727; and round her neck a heavy gold chain is wound four times, descending to the low point of the stomacher—and this portrait is dated 1597.

### MARY STUART, 1580–7 (continued from p. 517)

In 1580 Mary Queen of Scots was in captivity at Sheffield Castle, where she spent in all fourteen years until 1584. During the two following years the Queen was retained at four different places until the tragedy at Fotheringay, 1587.

After the death of Bothwell in 1576, Mary appears to have adopted plain black velvet for her gowns, as exemplified by the many well-known portraits of her. The full-length by P. Oudry at Hardwick Hall and the three-quarter, No. 429 in the National Portrait Gallery, which are practically identical, are pronounced the most authentic likenesses of the Queen at this time. A similar portrait, said to have been painted in 1578, originally belonged to the Earl of Darnley and is now in the Scottish National Portrait Gallery. The costume is exactly the same in all three portraits. The dress has a close-fitting bodice, rounded at the neck opening, over a partlet of goffered lawn surmounted by a moderate-sized ruff. The sleeves, fairly large at the shoulders and a little raised, taper towards the wrists. The waist-line is pointed and outlined by a small girdle of jet; from this hangs a Latin cross in gold from which is suspended a rosary of beads, some gold and others of dark metal enamelled with a design in red. From the headdress, reproduced in Fig. 876, hangs a fine white transparent veil edged with lace and wired out as described on p. 748.

Queen Mary's wardrobe was not well stocked, and her dresses were few. Queen Elizabeth took compassion on her 'dear sister,' and sent her as a gift some cast-off garments of her own which Mary haughtily declined.

On the first day of her trial in October 1586 at nine of the clock, Her Majesty of Scotland entered the Great Hall of Fotheringay escorted by a guard of Halberdiers and took her seat.[1]   She was dressed, we are told, in a gown with

---

[1] This fourteenth-century chair in carved oak used to stand by the altar in Fotheringay Church. It was brought into the Castle Hall especially for the Queen's use; and can now be seen in the church at Connington. Mary Queen of Scots at Madame Tussaud's is seated in a replica.

an over-robe like Fig. 602 of black velvet, and over her pointed coif a long gauze veil (*see* Fig. 875). Her train was borne by her Maid of Honour, Renée Beauregard.

On the fatal morning, 8th February 1587, the Queen of Scotland and Queen-Dowager of France robed herself in a skirt and bodice of black satin over an under-skirt of russet-brown velvet. Above these she wore a long-sleeved mantle (*see* Fig. 602) of black satin embroidered with gold and edged with sable.

From a contemporary manuscript other details are gathered, but they vary slightly from the foregoing. The original text is as follows:

'Her borrowed hair a BOURNE (*see* p. 515) having on her head a dressing of lawn edged with bone lace, a pomander chain, an Agnus Dei about her neck, a Crucifix in her hand, and a pair of Beads at her girdle with a golden Cross at the end of them, a veil of lawn fastened to her caul bowed out with wire and edged round about with bone lace, a gown of black satin printed [of formal cut] with a train, and long sleeves to the ground set with acorn buttons of jet garnished with pearl, and short sleeves of black satin cut [cutte] with ɔ pair of sleeves of purple velvet, whole under them a whole kyrtle of figured satin black, her petticote upper body's unlaced in the back of crimson satin, and her petticote skirts of crimson velvet, her shoes of Spanish leather with the rough side outward, a pair of green silk garters, her nether stocks of worsted coloured watchette, clocked with silver, and edged on the tops with silver, and next her legs a pair of Jersey[1] hose white.'

The purple sleeves mentioned above were 'false sleeves.'

One authority mentions that the Queen was 'putting on a paire of sleeves with her owne hands which they [the executioners] had pulled off.'

Another description of the Queen on the scaffold is afforded by the memorial portrait in Blairs College, Aberdeen, which was painted at a little later date under the supervision of Elizabeth Curle, for eight years a personal attendant of the Queen's, and who was, with Jane Kennedy, present at the execution. Her brother, Gilbert Curle, was the Queen's assistant secretary. The picture is an excellent authority for the dress and other details of this mournful event, and the portrait of the Queen, as she appeared at the end of her life, is pronounced an authentic likeness. In it she is robed in a black gown with close-fitting sleeves finishing in plain lawn cuffs; the over-robe, also black, has wider sleeves to the elbow cut up the front and edged with fur, and a stole-like effect of fur edges the fronts of the garment. A plain circular ruff and a black riband carrying a small crucifix surround the neck; and the usual coif (*see* Fig. 876), and wired-out veil are worn. In her right hand she holds an ebony cross with the Body of Our Lord in carved ivory, and in her left a vellum-bound book of prayers.

After the head had been severed from the body by three strokes of the axe, the executioner 'did lift up her head to the view of all the assembly, and bad God save the Queene. Then her dressing of lawne falling of from her head

---

[1] Jersey was the finest kind of wool, separated from the rest by combing.

it appeared as grey as one of threescore and tenn yeares old polled very shorte. . . . Then one of the executioners pulling of her garters espied her litle dogg which was crept under her clothes which could not be gotten forth but by force, yet afterward wold not departe from the dead corpes but came and lay betweene her head and her shoulders.'

Brantôme reports that the executioner 'uncoifed her in derision to show her hair, now white; which, however, she had never shrunk from showing, twisting and curling it as when her hair was beautiful, so fair and golden; for it was not age had changed it at thirty-five years old (being now but forty); it was the griefs, the woes, the sadness she had borne in her kingdom and in her prison.'

The charitable Brantôme is a little out with his calculations when he says the Queen died at the age of forty.   She was forty-five.

'IN MY END IS MY BEGINNING.'

Fig. 729 is a great lady of the English Court dressed to the full in the very latest vogue of the 1590's.   During this decade it was most modish to have the bodice and sleeves of a different material from the skirt.   In this dress they are of a metallic fabric—a sort of cloud design in gold or silver upon a ground of coloured silk or satin, perhaps shot with one or the other metal. The long hanging sleeves, instead of falling at the back of the skirt like those in Fig. 726, are draped over the top of the farthingale and fall half-way down the skirt.   The outer edges and the ends are decorated in the same fanciful manner as is affected by Lady Southwell.   The skirt of plain velvet or silk suggests the cart-wheel effect, but the spoke-like folds are not so regular; and an unusual note is the width of brocade let into the front, extending up to the point of the stomacher.   The wired-out ruff is of cutwork in a simple design, and edged with tiny white balls at the apexes of stiffened threads or covered wires, and puffings of lawn or gauze mask where the ruff meets the neck.

'MRS.' MARY FITTON, 1578 until 1603

A portrait of Mary Fitton or Phytton is reproduced in Plate XLIV by courtesy of the owner.   This lady was the younger daughter of Sir Edward Phytton of Gawsworth, Cheshire.   In her earliest portrait (1592) at Arbury,

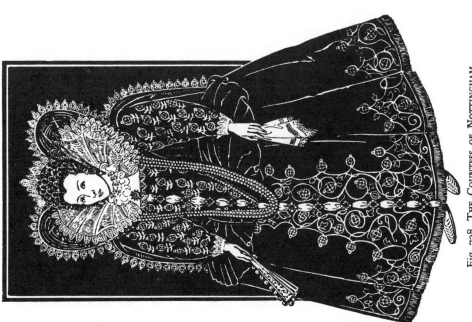

Fig. 729. ENGLISH COURT LADY

Fig. 728. THE COUNTESS OF NOTTINGHAM

wherein she is shown with her elder sister Anne, she wears a dress very like Fig. 732 except that the ruff is circular instead of fan-shaped, and that the leg-of-mutton sleeves resemble those of Plate XLIV.   In 1595 Mary became Maid of Honour to the Queen.   She was a clever vivacious girl, and her good looks, and especially her fair complexion, brown hair, and grey eyes, were much admired.   A beautiful dancer—she led a masque [1] in the character of 'Affection,' performed at Lady Anne Russell's wedding festivities in 1600 —she played havoc with many hearts; in fact, she was an arrant flirt, and about the same time carried on a serious intrigue with Lord Herbert (born 1580), 'a proper person, well set, and of graceful deportment.'   This young man succeeded to the Earldom of Pembroke in the following year, but no marriage took place—at least, not with Mistress Fitton!   This indiscretion caused her father to take her from Court, and Mary was packed off home to Gaws-worth forthwith.

The portrait (Plate XLIV) was, of course, painted before this disaster, and the costume exemplifies the climax of late-Elizabethan fashion and elabora-tion.   In style it resembles that shown in Fig. 729.   The stomacher and sleeves are of white satin, very elaborately embroidered with silver and cuttes. The decoration of the hanging sleeves is even more ornate than that worn by the lady before mentioned, for the points edge three sides of them.   The skirt of pale strawberry satin draped over the wheel farthingale is covered with embroidery of cross-bars of silver to suggest a basket, over which flowers and leaves are mingled with frogs, flies, beetles, butterflies, caterpillars, snails, and slugs, all in their natural colourings.   A charming accessory is a miniature (of whom?) in a black enamel case with a gold rim, and suspended at the neck by a fine black cord.   The ruff is fairly simple, but the head attire of silver wires, spangles, and pearls is indeed wonderful.   Sir Edward must have been a wealthy man to supply his daughter with a dress like this!

Fig. 730 is a drawing of the portrait of Anne Fitton's chief friend, Elizabeth, daughter of Edward Nevill, Lord Abergavenny, and wife of Sir John Grey, eldest son of Lord Grey of Groby; this dates about the same time as Plate XLIV; it shows another example of the fashionable mode of having the bodice and sleeves of a different material from the skirt.   In this illustration they are of white satin, worked in half-circles of silver from which hang tiny drop-pearls.   Notice the jewelled pendant hung from the left sleeve, and the gold and enamelled necklace (see also Fig. 912).   The usual long hanging sleeves are of black silk with escalloped edges; a jewelled ornament (see inset) is sewn on each.   These sleeves hang in the correct manner from the shoulders, back, and front, behind the skirt—the very latest mode—almost to the ground.

The skirt is pleated into the waist, puffed over the edge of the farthingale, and falls in heavy folds to the ankles.   The material is a rich white satin, or

---

[1] At the close of the masque 'Mrs Fitton went to the Queen, and wooed her to daunce. Her Majesty asked what she was?   "Affection," she said.   "Affection? Affection," said the Queen, "is false!"   Yet Her Majesty rose and daunced.'   The ingratitude of Essex was no doubt in her mind.

PLATE XLIV. MARY FITTON, AGED 17, 1596: Portrait by an unknown artist
Arbury Park. *By kind permission of Mrs FitzRoy Newdigate*

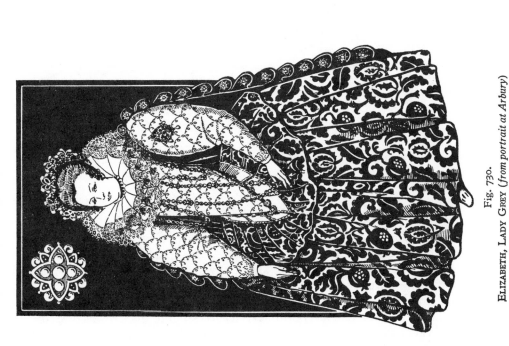

Fig. 731.
THE LADY ARABELLA STUART, 1603 (*after Marcus Gheeraerts*)

Fig. 730.
ELIZABETH, LADY GREY (*from portrait at Arbury*)

it could be a pale tone of (say) pink or blue, with a meandering pattern of pomegranates and leaves in two-pile black velvet woven on the satin foundation.

The large nebulée-set ruff edged with delicate lace; the hairdressing surmounted by a wreath of pearls and silver wire—a veritable billement—complete the *tout ensemble* of this fashionably dressed Court and Society lady of the 1590's.

Fig. 732. The Lady Anne Russell, 1600

### THE LADY ANNE RUSSELL

Lady Anne Russell (Fig. 732) was daughter of the Earl of Bedford and, like her sister Elizabeth, was Maid of Honour to the Queen. In 1600 she married Lord Herbert, and their wedding is the subject of the painting, Plate XLV. She is shown in bridal dress of white satin, the bodice and sleeves being embroidered with pearls, silver, and diamonds. Over the shoulders and covering the edges of the ruff are puffings of white and silver gauze, the triple ruff itself being plain and edged with tiny points. The skirt is without any decoration, and is puffed out over the wheel farthingale, hanging to the feet in radiating box-pleats—altogether a simple yet rich and effective costume for such an important occasion.

### THE LADY ARABELLA STUART, 1575 *until* 1603

The Lady Arabella, born 1575, was the daughter of Charles Stuart, Earl of Lennox (younger brother of Henry, Lord Darnley), and his wife Elizabeth, daughter of Sir William Cavendish and his wife Elizabeth, known as 'Bess of Hardwick' of architectural fame.

Lady Arabella was first cousin to James VI of Scotland, and therefore until 1594 (when Prince Henry was born) next in succession to the Crowns of Scotland and England. Owing to her exalted position she was the cause of much anxiety both to Elizabeth and to James, but the latter treated her with the consideration and affection due to a cousin.

There is a delightful full-length portrait of this lady at Woburn Abbey, painted by Marcus Gheeraerts, when she was about twelve years of age (1587). She wears a dress of what appears to be white brocade made in exactly the same way as that shown in Fig. 726. Her fair hair is flowing over her shoulders, and is surmounted by a wreath of silver and pearls. She evidently had a number of exotic pets, for she is painted with a parrot, a macaw, a monkey, a little dog, and two small parrots which nestle in her right hand. The Lady Arabella was somewhat odd; very vain, extravagant, fond of rich raiment, fantastic costumes (there is a portrait of her in one at Hampton Court), and particularly of jewellery.

Several portraits of this lady exist, and one owned by the Duke of Portland, painted in 1589, shows her wearing a plain white satin dress with long pointed stomacher over the bolster farthingale. Red and gold enamel ornaments decorate the front of the skirt, and smaller ones are set upon the full sleeves. No ruff is worn, which is unusual—she had eccentric tastes!

Fig. 731 is drawn from a very old photograph, dating about the 1880's, of the original by Marcus Gheeraerts in the possession of the Duke of Northumberland at Syon House.[1] It shows the most up-to-date style for February 1602–3, and the Lady Arabella's tall and stately figure carries it off to advantage. The bodice is close-fitting, but the straight lines terminate a little below the waist in striking contrast to the long point of the stomacher previously worn (see Fig. 732). The bodice finishes with tabs at the waist, and has pronounced shoulder pieces or wings and close-fitting sleeves. The skirt hangs in heavy folds over the bolster or wheel farthingale surmounted by the cart-wheel. The whole dress is made of a deep green and gold brocade. The collar of Italian needlepoint lace, 'punto in aria,' is backed by a second collar of starched white lawn; the wrist-cuffs match the two collars; the same lace edges the décolletage; from the right shoulder two strings of magnificent pearls are draped across the figure, and more pearls also encircle the waist. The hairdressing has not changed appreciably since Fig. 732, though an aigrette is fixed by jewels to the left side—the very latest vogue—already worn in Spain.

The artist's mannerism by which a cushion is placed over the arms of the farthingale chair, merely to support the right hand, is a feature of several of the portraits painted by Marcus Gheeraerts the Younger.

## MOURNING ROBES

At Sir Christopher Hatton's funeral, 1591, Lord Cobham was Chief Mourner (Fig. 733), whose train was held by a trainbearer. He wears a hood with liripipe of the old fashion, but tasselled; and the sleeves of his doole-robe, which

---

[1] No recent negative of this portrait exists, otherwise His Grace would have allowed the author to use a print from it. The portrait itself is inaccessible at the moment.

bulges over his slops underneath, are padded on the shoulders.    The ladies accompanying him are Countesses, whose only period details are the small ruffs and the curve of the veils over the foreheads.

For widows' weeds, see p. 715; and for the French style, pp. 752, 753.

Fig. 733. Doole-robes, 1591

## NOBILITY—MEN: 1580–1603

### PERSONAGES OF DISTINCTION ABOUT THE COURT

### William Cecil (*continued from p. 533*)

### *Lord Burleigh, 1580–98*

Lord Treasurer Burleigh during the remaining years of his life attained the highest honours of the State, including the Garter, but received no greater title than baron, which was intensely galling to him.

The National Portrait Gallery portrait, No. 2184, was painted in the early 1580's when he was about sixty.    In it he is wearing the same dress as in No. 604, but with the addition of the Collar of the Garter.    Another, No. 362, was painted later still when he was a white-haired old man.    He is fully dressed in the Robes of the Garter, still holding his rod of office.    The bulkiness of the crimson velvet surcote or robe around the hips is due to the padded slops worn underneath.

His death, which took place 15th August 1598, was greatly lamented by his Royal mistress, whom he had faithfully served for the greater part of his life without once thwarting her.

### Sir Christopher Hatton, 1580–91 (*continued from p. 535*)

Having incurred the Queen's displeasure over some money matters—he was some £56,000 in her debt—Sir Christopher Hatton withdrew from Court in 1584 and sulked at Holdenby. 'The Queen seldom gave boons, and never forgave due debts. She rigorously demanded the payment of some arrears which Sir Christopher did not hope to have remitted . . . failing herein in his expectations, it went to his heart.' However, Elizabeth desired his return and wrote him two letters to that effect. He obeyed, and was appointed a member of both Commissions which in 1586 tried the conspirators who favoured Mary Stuart. He was also on the Commission which tried this unfortunate Queen. In 1588 he was appointed Lord Chancellor and made a K.G. On Lord Leicester's death the same year he became Lord Chancellor of Oxford. There is a curious portrait of him (National Portrait Gallery, No. 1518), painted at this time, showing him in his robes and holding with great pride the Lesser George which hangs around his neck by a triple chain.

During his last illness the Queen was very attentive, 'bringing cordial broths unto him with her own hands, but all would not do.' He died at Ely, 20th November 1591.

### Robert Devereux

#### *Earl of Essex, 1566–1601*

Robert Devereux was the son of Walter, Earl of Essex and Eu, Viscount Hereford and Bourchier, and Baron Ferrers of Chartley, Bourchier, and Louvain; and was born 10th November 1566. He succeeded as second Earl of Essex at the age of twelve, and entered Trinity College, Cambridge, taking his M.A. degree in 1581. His first appearance at Court was made in 1584. 'There was in this young lord,' says Sir Robert Naunton, 'a kinde of urbanity or innate courtesy, which both won the Queene, and too much tooke up the people to gaze on the new adopted son of her favour.' For on the death of the Earl of Leicester he succeeded him in the Royal affections.

His complexion was pale with brown eyes and hair, his beard of a golden red, and his moustache lighter and more yellow.

'A body hath he made of iron,' 'of straight and goodly stature,' tall and strong; but he 'did bend a little in the neck, though rather forward than downwards, and he was so far from being a good dancer, that he was no graceful goer.' He is said to have 'exceeded in the incomparable fairness and fine shape of his hands, which . . . he took from his father.'

In 1590 the young earl secretly married Frances, daughter and heiress of Sir Francis Walsingham, and widow of Sir Philip Sidney; and in 1588, at the early age of twenty-two, he was created a Knight of the Garter.

Fig. 734. The Earl of Essex

There are many portraits of the second Earl of Essex, and the costumes he is wearing in nearly all of them are similar. Fig. 734 is adapted from these portraits. He wears a suit entirely of white silk decorated with lines of stitchery, the doublet with wide wings, close sleeves, and a basque which stands out at right angles at the waist. Attention is called to the stitchery round the armholes. The panes of the hip-pad are folded into a series of oblique tucks, but the decoration of this garment varies in the different portraits. The canions and netherstocks are of plain white silk, and the shoes are black. Both waistbelt and swordbelt are gold-embroidered and have a narrow edging of deep red: the sword is elaborate, and the usual dagger is stuck through at the back. The Lesser George is hung by the blue riband, and the Garter is worn. A special feature for notice is the turned-down collar, similar to those shown in Figs. 625 and 627, worn in conjunction with the ruff. In his right hand he holds a baton of command. In one portrait at least the costume is carried out in a pale dove-grey satin, woven with a small silk spot diapered all over its surface. This kind of material was very fashionable at this time.

Fig. 735

Fig. 735 is a detail of the braid with which a suit similar to that described above is decorated. It is from a three-quarter portrait dated 1599 in the Dining Hall, Trinity College, Cambridge, wherein Essex wears a suit of white silk banded with this braid in gold having small pearls set in the middle. A circular ruff of several layers and the Lesser George on a blue riband are worn.

In 1593, when only twenty-seven, Essex was admitted to the Council, and forsook 'all his former youthful tricks,' carrying himself with 'very honourable gravity.' Nevertheless, he became recklessly extravagant and improvident, so that even the most generous allowance that the Queen could afford to make him proved quite inadequate to meet the growing expenses of an elaborate household. The details of his toilet which follow illustrate that of a fashionable and influential courtier of the period. 'The Earl as he grew more and more attentive to business and matter, so less and less curious of clothing, insomuch as I do remember those about him had a conceit, that possibly sometime when he went up to the Queen, he might scant know what he had on: for this was his manner; his chamber being commonly stived with friends or suitors of one kind or other, when he gave his legs, arms, and breast to his ordinary servants to button and dress him with little heed, his head and face to his barber, his eyes to his letters, and ears to petitioners, and many times all at once; then the gentlemen of his robes throwing a cloak over his shoulders, he would make a step into his closet, and after a short prayer he was gone: only in his baths he was somewhat delicate.'

Essex had reached the pinnacle of popularity both with the Queen and her people when, in 1596, he was sent on the Cadiz expedition; and on his return the Queen, 'loving him for his beauty, gallantry, and devotion to her,' entrusted him with the still more difficult task of pacifying the Irish. 'The General of our Gracious Empress' completely mismanaged everything, and was recalled and confined in the Tower, but shortly afterwards released. He then sought to win back by force the favour which the Queen still withheld from him, and in 1601 madly put himself at the head of a revolt of the Londoners, hoping by their help to drive from power his enemy, Sir Robert Cecil, Keeper of the Privy Seal, and to recover his position. 'His misconduct in Ireland, and his project of displacing his enemies, would have been more easily pardoned by the Queen, than the vulgar and opprobrious words reported by Sir Walter Raleigh to have been spoken by him: "the late Earl says, he told Queen Elizabeth, that her conditions were as crooked as her carcase," but it cost him his head, which his insurrection had not cost him but for that speech.' He was in consequence sent back captive to the Tower, and after a trial condemned to death. His execution took place 25th February 1601, and his tragic fall only established Cecil the more firmly in the Queen's favour.

## Sir Francis Drake, 1540–95

Prominent amongst the 'Sea Lions' was young Francis Drake, who was born at Tavistock about 1540, and educated at the expense of his kinsman, Sir John Hawkyns. It was not until he was approaching forty that he leapt into fame on account of his voyage round the world. On his return from this voyage he finally moored his ship, *The Golden Hind*, at Deptford, and on 4th April 1581, 'the Queen made Drake a visit on board, and there, on the deck of the first English ship to have encompassed the Globe, did she Knight the first man of any nation who had commanded through such a voyage.' Knighthood was conferred upon him ostensibly in recognition of his fame as a naviga-

Fig. 736. Sir Francis Drake

tor, but no doubt also because of the rich spoils, estimated at £200,000, which he was able to lay at Elizabeth's feet.

In appearance Drake was 'of small size with a reddish beard, and is one of the greatest sailors that exist.'

Fig. 736 shows Sir Francis about this time. It is constructed from one or two portraits, all of which show a similar style of dress. His costume consists of a doublet with sleeves which button into loops up the front seam showing a sleeve of a different colour underneath, and venetians in a small patterned damask of some dark shade, the edges being braided or bound with silk or velvet. A goffered ruff with plain cuffs of lawn or linen, kersey netherstocks, and leather shoes, sometimes decorated with cuttes or sometimes plain, are worn. In later life he possessed a small medallion portrait of the Queen which he wore hung by a riband or a chain round his neck. Notice that he is raising his hat in the approved style.

Drake was Vice-Admiral under Lord Howard of Effingham, and assisted in repelling the Armada in 1588; in fact, men held him in such honour that none had the effrontery to sit in his presence, nor did they presume to keep on their hats without his permission.

The West Indian expedition of 1595 cost the lives of both Drake and Hawkyns. Admiral Sir John Hawkyns died at sea off Porto Rico, and 'as quiet as a sleeping child the sea-king died' off Porto Bello; but neither his own countrymen nor the Spaniards could believe it, and long expected his return.

### Sir Walter Raleigh, 1552–1603

A newcomer to Court, introduced by Lord Leicester in 1582, was Walter Raleigh, aged thirty.   This young man was born at Hayes, Budleigh, Devon, and entered Oriel College, Oxford, in 1566, where he remained three years but took no degree.   He then took rooms in the Temple, it being fashionable for a young man to take chambers there as a sort of finish to a gentleman's education, and to qualify him as a man of affairs.   In 1569 Raleigh was one of a hundred young gentlemen sent by the Queen to France to assist Marguerite de Valois, and there served with the Huguenot Army.   He was at sea during 1578, and in Ireland in 1580.   Returning to England as Captain Raleigh in 1581, he first came to the notice of Queen Elizabeth.   It is said that his cloak was primary instrumental in obtaining the Queen's favour.   So popular did he become at Court that even his strong west-country brogue was not only tolerated, but even adopted, by the smart set!   He obtained a patent for the settlement of 'Virginia'; and though he never visited it himself, it gave to England potatoes and tobacco.   He was

Fig. 737. Sir Walter Raleigh, 1588

knighted by the Queen in 1584, who commissioned him Captain of the Yeomen of the Guard, which post he held from 1587 until her death.   Fig. 737 shows Sir Walter at the age of thirty-six, and is taken from a portrait in the National Portrait Gallery, No. 7, dated 1588.   There is another in America, but full length, painted in the same year, in which he is wearing a slightly different doublet and slops, but the same cloak.

In Fig. 737 the white silk doublet is pinked in squares, but otherwise unornamented except for the large silver buttons.   The square collar has a second of cambric folded over it.   The silver embroidery on the black velvet waist and sword-belts is repeated on the black velvet panes of the slops. Over one shoulder is hung the cloak in the modish manner: it is of black velvet lined and turned back with sable, with sun-rays worked in seed pearls or silver and ending with three large pearls.

His attentions to Elizabeth Throckmorton, one of the Queen's Maids of Honour, checked his progress in the Royal favour.   Their marriage so enraged

Her Majesty that she sent them both to the Tower for two months.    Their son (Fig. 743) was born there.    With the idea of establishing colonies in the West he set out on voyages of discovery, and also made an expedition against the Spaniards at Cadiz (1596) and the Azores in 1597.

Duke Frederick I (succeeded 1593, died 1608) of Württemburg and Teck had, since 1592, conceived the idea that Queen Elizabeth would confer upon him the much coveted Order of the Garter.    It is not known if she actually made the promise, or, having made it, had any intention of fulfilling it; but the Duke in his impatience sent his envoy, Herr Johann Jacob Breuning von Buchenbach, to London to remind the Queen of her plighted word.    In spite of reams of correspondence, the Garter failed to materialize.    In slighting the Duke the Queen little realized that one of the descendants of this disillusioned potentate would one day occupy her throne.    He received better treatment, however, from James Stuart, who conferred it in 1603.

To further his master's suit, Herr Breuning equipped himself with a new Court dress, made by London tailors.    As will be seen from the following account, this cost him £14 4s. in English money, and all to no purpose!

### An Account for a Court Dress, 1595

|  | Gulden | Batzen |
|---|---|---|
| For velvet for breeches 6¾ yds., the yard at 3 crowns makes 20 crowns 3½s. | 32 | 6 |
| Four yards fustian or corduroy, 4s. | 1 | 1 |
| ½ ell double taffeta, 1 crown | 1 | 9 |
| Cloth for a cloak 3¼ yds., the yard 13s., that makes 42s. 3d. | 11 | 4 |
| 1 yard of lining, 2s. 9d. | | 11 |
| Gold braid for cloak 2¼ oz., gold lace for the dress, 1⅛ oz. at 10s. an ounce makes 33s. 9d. | 9 | |
| For silk 2½ | | 10 |
| Besides this for lining, 9s. 3d. | 2 | 7 |
| For a pair of silk hose, 6 crowns | 9 | 9 |
| Three dozen buttons for the doublet, 2 crowns | 3 | 3 |
| For making the cloak, 6s. | 1 | 9 |
| For making the doublet and breeches | 2 | 2 |
| | 75 | 11 |

Plate XLV is a reproduction of the painting by Marcus Gheeraerts of the wedding procession at Blackfriars (16th June 1600) of Lord Herbert, eldest son of the Earl of Worcester, and Lady Anne Russell, daughter of the Earl of Bedford.    There are two pictures of this subject, both by the same artist. The original from which Plate XLV is taken is owned by Colonel Wingfield-Digby, who has kindly given permission for its reproduction.

PLATE XLV. QUEEN ELIZABETH AT BLACKFRIARS, 1600: Painting by Marcus Gheeraerts
Sherborne Castle.  *By kind permission of Colonel Wingfield-Digby*

Fig. 738. KEY TO PLATE XLV

Fig. 738 is a key plan, giving the names of the principal persons and the predominating colourings of their clothes.

1. The Queen . . . White
2. Lord Howard de Walden . Rose colour, grey netherstocks
3. The Earl of Nottingham . White
4. The Earl of Cumberland . Pale scarlet
5. Lord Hunsdon . . . Grey
6. Lord Cobham, with sword . Deep peacock-blue
7. Sir Robert Cecil . . White, dove jerkin, pale green netherstocks
8. The Earl of Worcester . Pale pink
9. The Earl of Bedford . . Dark bottle-green, dove jerkin
10. Lord Herbert . . . White
11. Lady Anne Russell . . White

Fig. 739.          Fig. 740.
Noblemen, 1600

Most of the costumes are of silk or satin embroidered with gold and pearls, and all the cloaks are black velvet decorated with gold or silver. Nos. 2, 3, 4, 5, 6, and 8 wear the Collar of the Garter, and Nos. 2, 3, 6, and 8 have each a portrait miniature of the Queen suspended by a riband from his neck.

Yeomen of the Guard and Gentlemen Pensioners line the way.

The young bridegroom (born 1577), Fig. 740, is dressed (as all bridegrooms should be) entirely in white silk brocaded with a fine trellis pattern. The whole costume is extremely simple, yet thoroughly up to date and most elegant.

Fig. 739 is taken from the same painting and represents Henry Brooke, Lord Cobham, K.G., carrying the Sword of State. His suit, in deep peacock-blue satin with a tiny silk spot woven diaperwise in the material, is of the fashionable style as worn at the end of the century. The doublet is without the peascod paunch and has close rather rucked sleeves and a moderate basque. The buttons and waist- and sword-belts are of gold. The slops are quite plain, without any bombast or padding, being gathered or pleated round the waist and thighs. The canions or upperstocks are of the same material. Netherstocks and shoes are of white, the cloak is of black velvet braided with gold, and the Collar with Badge and the Garter are in evidence. Lord Cobham wears a triple ruff; and from a blue riband hanging round his neck is suspended a cameo portrait of the Queen in a jewelled frame with three peardrop pearls attached.

Fig. 741. A Nobleman's Son

The baby boy, Fig. 741, a nobleman's son, comes from a portrait painted about the 1590's. His white silk gown and hanging sleeves are banded with black velvet, and the full sleeves slashed with black. The black hat with a gold rim to the brim, worn over a white biggen, is decorated with a white feather and a rose of red ribbon. A pouch of black velvet and gold is attached to the waist-belt, and the silver and coral teether is slung on a red ribbon round the neck. Both are inset.

At the age of fifty (1602) Sir Walter Raleigh is seen in a portrait by Marcus Gheeraerts, in company with his son. Fig. 742 is made from this portrait. The doublet, slops, and canions are of white silk; oblique tucks edged with silver decorate the panes, and there is a line of silver down the seams of the somewhat rucked sleeves and down the front of the doublet, which is fastened by small silver buttons. Pearl and silver embroidery worked on very fine white cambric is laid on the brown velvet jerkin, and converges down the fronts and down and across the rather deep basques and round the pronounced wings. The waist, sword-belt, and hanger are of buff leather covered with silver embroidery. Pale buff netherstocks, tied with white silk garters having silver fringed ends, are worn with buff leather shoes. The black beaver hat of the newest shape, obviously having its origin in the same source as that worn by the Duke of Infantado (*see* Fig. 853), but slightly modified, has a jewelled feather and is tilted at an angle. Raleigh's pipes and pipe-case are in the Wallace Collection.

Figs. 742–3.
Sir Walter Raleigh and Son, 1602

A coming young man of the seventeenth century, Master Raleigh, unfortunately died in youth. In Fig. 743 he has a complete suit of dark blue silk braided with silver. The waist- and swordbelts and miniature sword are of silver.

'Sir' John Harington is introduced here with apologies. His only interest with regard to this book is that he gives us considerable information on numerous details which have been taken chiefly from his *Nugae Antiquae*. He was born in 1561, the son of Sir John Harington and Isabella Markham, a Maid of Honour to Elizabeth when Princess. 'Boy Jack' was a godson of the Queen—'my saucy godson,' she called him; and as he himself admits, he both loved and feared her greatly. He went to Ireland with the Earl of Essex, from whom he received a knighthood (1598) which was not altogether to the Queen's liking, as she had not conferred the honour herself. Sir John had the reputation at Court of being a wit of more than usual brilliancy.

One item of his wardrobe has become historical: 'The Queen loveth to see me in my last frize jerkin,' he writes, preening himself complacently, 'and faith its well enough cut. I will have another made liken to it.' He proceeds to put on record a most lady-like action of the Great Tudor Queen. 'I do remember,' he writes, 'she spit on Sir Mathew's fringed cloth, and said, "the fool's wit was gone to rags."' No wonder he took the precaution of ordering a second frieze jerkin: 'Heaven spare me from such jibing,' concludes Boy Jack.

He remained the Queen's affectionate if 'saucy godson' throughout her declining years, and helped to cheer her last days. In 1612 Sir John died, at the age of fifty-one.

His own mordant words, descriptive of the fashionable man of his time, may fittingly close this account of Sir John, who as a man of the world ought to know what he was talking about.

'We goe brave in apparell that wee may be taken for better men than wee bee; we use much bumbastings and quiltings to seem fitter formed, better shouldered, smaller waisted, fulled thyght than we are; wee barbe and shave often to seeme younger than wee are; we use perfumes both inward and outward to seem sweeter than we bee; we use courteous salutations to seem kinder than we be; and somtymes graver and Godly communications, to seem wyser than wee bee.'

In the sixteenth-century hall of Christ's Hospital, Abingdon, hangs the portrait, dated 1602, of a smart young man—William Bostock. Born in 1572 he was governor of the hospital from 1602 until 1624, when he was removed 'by reason he is departed the Towne.' He died some time before 1642. In Fig. 744 the fashionable doublet is of white cloth pinked, or cutte, the edges being overcast with black silk and outlined with six French knots. It has small overlaying picadils or tabs at the waist-line, and a dagger is stuck through the waist-belt on the right side. The collar of lawn is edged with beautiful

Fig. 744. William Bostock, Esq., 1602

lace and the cuffs match the collar. There is not sufficient indication in the painting to decide whether he is wearing slops or galligaskins; they are of black velvet, decorated with double rows of silver passamayne. The high-crowned white beaver hat, 'well brushed a mornings,' lying on the table has a rich silver hatband and a panache of *uncurled* ostrich feathers standing up high in the approved fashion. In the right hand he carries leather gloves banded with silver lace—altogether an excellent specimen of a well-dressed man of the first few years of the seventeenth century.

With the help of Jeffrey Chorlton and Sir Thomas Overbury, we may here picture an elegant coxcomb of the end of the reign. He has decked himself out in doublet, trunks, hosen, hat, and cloak, all in the height of fashion and of the latest cut. From one ear hangs a pearl, above the other is tucked a rose or other flower in the most fetching manner. In his hat, or mouth, he carries a pick-tooth; in his pouch a tobacco pipe.   He indulges mincingly in every eccentricity of mannerism: 'the brush upon the beard, the kiss of the hand, the stoop of the head, the lear of the eye.'

> 'Behold, a most accomplished Cavaleer,
> That the World's Ape of Fashion doth appear,
> Walking the streets, his humours to disclose
> In the French Doublet, and the German hose:
> The Muffes [1] Cloake, Spanish Hat, Toledo Blade,
> Italian ruff, a shoe right Flemish made.'

## FRENCH FASHIONS: 1580–1603

### HENRY III

*King of France, 1580–9*

(*continued from p. 560*)

The Duc d'Anjou, on ascending the throne of France in 1574 as Henry III, became so spoiled by his favourites that he lost the respect of every one.

Fig. 745. Henry III of France

Like his brother, Charles IX, he was indolent, and left the administration of the kingdom to his mother while he indulged in all kinds of frivolities and debauchery.   Very fond of dress, this 'King of fashion and pattern of the exquisite' invented 'novelties' in which he was assisted by his gentlemen friends.   These were designated 'Les Mignons,' and copied every detail and gesture of the King.   'Le Roi s'amuse,' we are told by the Duc de Sully, who writes: 'I found him in his closet, a sword by his side, a short cloak on his shoulders, little turban on his head, and about his neck was hung a basket, in which were two or three little dogs, no bigger than my fist.'   Teaching parrots to mimic and monkeys to perform tricks were other accomplishments of this puerile monarch, who also played at cup-and-ball,[2] an occupation which was copied not only by the courtiers, but also by the pages and lackeys who were perpetually engaged in it.

[1] A contemptuous term for a German or Swiss.

[2] The ball could also be caught on a peg; see Fig. 751, inset.

So vain had this last Valois become that he cosmeticized his face, stained his eyes, lips, and ears, and dyed his hair and beard. The result was premature baldness, necessitating the wearing of wigs and fantastic turbans, as seen in all his later portraits. Fig. 745 is a drawing from one of these. To keep his hands white and delicate he slept in perfumed and unctuous gloves.

Of the numerous portraits, the one in the Louvre, given in Fig. 746, is chosen as being the most eccentric costume. It is entirely in black—so becoming to a slim tall figure; the doublet of black satin is banded with velvet, but is without the peascod effect. It finishes at the low-cut waist-line, where there is a massive gold girdle with four pendent ornaments in goldsmith's work set with rubies. Similar ornaments are set up the front and on the cloak, and a large diamond in front of the turban. The moderately close sleeves are of plain black velvet, and the hosen extending from waist to toe, and the short cloak faced with sable, are of the same material. Wodges of silk, covered in priceless pearls, which look like corn-cobs, are fixed to the doublet in two places by jewelled ornaments, and extend from the right shoulder to the waist. The Badge of the St. Esprit or Holy Ghost is suspended by a blue riband round the neck, and the star is embroidered on the cloak as being the outer garment. The ruff is circular and small-pleated: a false hair front is tucked into the turban with a made-up white feather, and one peardrop pearl earring is worn. The

Fig. 746. Henry III, King of France, 1585

velvet-covered feet have scarlet heels attached to white kid heel pieces which fasten round the instep. A masculine touch is given by the sword hung high at the waist, and the indispensable laced cambric handkerchief is carried in the left hand, the right resting on the velvet-covered table.

In 1578 Henry III had instituted the Order of the Holy Ghost. The insignia consisted of a Collar of fleurs-de-lys of gold cantoned with flames of the same enamelled red, interspersed with three monograms of gold composed of the letters H, L, and HL, in white enamel.

The Badge (Fig. 747) is a gold cross of eight points enamelled with an edge of white, and gold fleurs-de-lys at each angle; upon a circular centre of green is a white dove, the wings, tail, and head extending downwards over part of the principal quarters of the cross.    The Badge hung from the collar or from a sky-blue riband—'the Cordon Bleu,' as the Order is sometimes designated.

A Star of silver, formed exactly like the Badge with the same details in the centre, was embroidered on the left side of the *outer garment* by all members of the Order.    The surcote was of white cloth of silver; and the mantle of black velvet, lined with orange taffeta and besprinkled with gold flames diaperwise, had a border of gold fleurs-de-lys and lacs d'amour—true lover's knots—of silver arranged alternately.    A short mantle of green cloth of silver was sometimes worn in place of the black velvet mantle; it was embroidered diaperwise with doves in silver, and lined with orange taffeta.

Fig. 747. Badge of Saint-Esprit

After the murder of the Duc de Guise, 1588, for which the King was rightly blamed, he became hateful to his subjects, and shortly after this event a Bull from Rome excommunicated the assassin.    The wrath of the Catholics forced the King to make a reconciliation with Henry, King of Navarre, and together the two monarchs marched on Paris; but the knife of the Dominican, Jacques Clément, ended his life—the last of the thirteen kings of the House of Valois—sovereigns who were for the most part brave, magnificent, and lovers of the fine arts.    With his dying breath Henry III recognized the right of Henry of Navarre to the French throne, and expired 2nd August 1589.

His younger brother, François, Duc d'Anjou, paid a second visit to England, an official one this time, in May 1581 to see the Queen.

During this time there was quite a lot of love-making going on between the mature spinster of forty-eight and her young man of twenty-seven—her 'Frog' or 'Froggy,' as she lovingly called him after her manner, just as she named his Ambassador 'the Monkey.'    This pleasant time induced the Duc d'Anjou to pay a third visit in October 1581, which lasted until February 1582: things seemed to be going most favourably, when fever carried off this unfortunate Prince in June 1584, before he could carry off his prize.

There are two paintings in the Louvre representing balls at the Court of Henry III.    One dated 1581—Ball No. I—was given in honour of the marriage of the Queen's sister, Marguerite of Lorraine, with the Duc de Joyeuse. The other—Ball No. II—is dated 1585, and shows some courtiers engaged in a round dance.    Both of these are valuable as authorities for the costumes of their respective dates.    The painting, Ball No. I, is attributed to François Clouet.    On the left is seen Henry III seated under a crimson velvet canopy; next him is his mother, and on her left his Queen, Louise of Lorraine.    The bride and bridegroom occupy the centre of the scene, advancing hand in hand;

the crowd of courtiers includes Henry, Duc de Guise, who stands on the King's right. On the opposite side is the consort. From this picture are taken Figs. 749, 754, and 748. In Ball No. II the King and Queen, as also the Queen-Mother, stand on the left. This picture has been used for Figs. 750, 755, and 756.

Anne, Duc de Joyeuse, was a great favourite with Henry III; they were very close friends, and Anne was a less covetous and self-seeking courtier

Fig. 748.                    Fig. 749.
Duc and Duchesse de Joyeuse, 1581

than the general run of such ambitious noblemen. Honours were heaped upon him. First, he was made a Peer of France, then a Duke, an Admiral, first Gentleman of the Bedchamber, and Governor of Normandy; and lastly became brother-in-law of Queen Louise. In fact, the King could deny him nothing, and could be led by Anne as easily as one of his own lap-dogs, whimpering when the Duke was absent: so that the people used to say that there were three Kings of France: Henry, the *nominal* king; Anne, the *King's* king; and Henry de Guise, the *people's* king. He is shown in Fig. 749 as he appears in the Ball picture No. I, wearing a suit—a doublet, venetians, and hip-roll in deep green satin. The short cloak is of reseda green velvet lined with rose satin, and turns back forming revers with a step-back collar. The hat is black, with a panache of white plumes. The stockings are rose and the shoes green.

The gentleman (Fig. 750) is one of those taking part in the dance, Ball No. II. Some may argue that he is wearing a masquer's costume, but in the same painting Henry III is represented wearing a dress almost identical, except that a short cloak and turban headdress are added.

In Fig. 750 the peascod doublet and hip-roll are of light-coloured silk, velvet, or cloth cutte in perpendicular slits. The bombast sleeves are very

Fig. 750. A French Courtier, 1585          Fig. 751. A Mignon

wide at the shoulders and taper to the wrists; and venetians, gradually decreasing in circumference from hip to knee, match in colour (as do the shoes and stockings), but are banded transversely with coloured braid or gold lace. A circular ruff and a black hat with an upstanding ostrich feather are worn.

The mignon in Fig. 751, or mignonette, dainty, sweet-smelling, and green(?), is playing with his 'bilboquet.' Here, again, the prevailing scheme of black and white is exemplified. The slight peascod doublet with bolonnoise or bouillon sleeves is of white satin, folded or cutte perpendicularly between transverse bands of black velvet. The panes of the hip-roll are of the same material and are edged with black silk braid and worn over white silk hosen and shoes. A black velvet turban with white feather surmounts his own dyed hair, brushed back and upward, and sprayed with violet-scented powder. In bed the made-up face is protected by a face mask, and the delicate white hands by gloves. His eyebrows, and (when old enough) his moustaches, were plucked so as to form thin lines.

Most of these mignons were expert swordsmen, and in later life became men of some worth. Chief among them were Bussy d'Amboise; Anne de Joyeuse (see Fig. 749) and his brother, Henri; François d'O, Seigneur d'O, de Maillebois, and de Fresne, Master of the Wardrobe, first Gentleman of the Chamber, Superintendent of Finances, Governor of Paris and the Isle of France; and Jean Louis Nogaret de la Valette (born 1554), also known as Caumont, later created Duc d'Épernon, Lord High Admiral, Colonel-General of the line, and Governor of half the provinces of the kingdom.

It is appropriate that Mr. Punch should make his début upon the stage of history in these days of folly. His name is said to have been crossed in its orthography with the Italian *Pulcinello*, a buffoon of Acerra, and *paunch*. The original puppet Pulcinello had a face like a Greek mask, and a nose like the beak of a bird. Punch's dress is of this period—a large ruff, peascod paunched doublet, and venetians. His cap and bauble are those which appertain to fools. During his travels over the Continent he acquired a humpback, and when he arrived in England he was thus deformed.

In a similar way, the conventional appearance of Mephistopheles illustrates the eccentric fashions prevailing at the French Court. In fact, he may even be a caricature of Henry III as suggested by Fig. 746.

## Henry IV

### King of France and Navarre, 1589 until 1603

Henry of Navarre was the first of the Royal House of Bourbon. Born in the Castle of Pau in 1553, he was the son of Antoine, Duc de Vendôme, and Jeanne d'Albret, Queen-Regnant of Navarre and Béarn. As a young man, Henry devoted little attention to dress. He is accused of rough manners, of 'Gascon inelegance,' and of a despicable disregard for clothes, at a Court of such an exquisite coxcomb as Henry III. His slovenly habits caused his mother much uneasiness of mind, although she did all she could to reform him. She procured first-class tailors and expert broderers to supervise his wardrobe, without much success.

A sketch portrait of Henry as a young man is given in Fig. 842.

In 1572 he married Marguerite de Valois, sister of Henry III; his wedded life was not too pleasant, and in consequence he solaced himself with many an intrigue with lovely ladies, chief among them being Gabrielle d'Estrées and Henriette d'Entragues.

In 1589 Henry of Navarre became King of France.

His claim to the French throne was not undisputed (he was eleventh in descent from St. Louis IX of France), largely because he had been brought up in the Protestant faith.   The Catholic nobles refused allegiance to him; and the intervening ten years were occupied in warfare against the League.   Most of his time was spent in camp and field, experiencing to the full their inevitable hardships, with a few brief intervals of relaxation.   These opportunities were seized by the King for flying visits to his lady friends.

We have it on authority that during this period his usual garb was of

Fig. 752. Henry IV, King of France, 1596

burgher-like drabness and modesty, and the shabbiness of his *grey* doublet was almost openly ridiculed by the nobles in attendance.   It appears that he nearly always wore this neutral hue. When he entered Paris, September 1594, he was dressed in a suit of grey velvet, laced with gold, and wore a grey hat and white plume. Even the horse he rode was mottled grey.   His reply to the deputation of clergy, who came to remonstrate against the edict upon the Parliament of Bordeaux (1599), has point: 'My predecessors,' he said, 'gave you words with a great deal of glittering parade.   I, in spite of my grey doublet, would give you deeds.   I am grey without, but inside all gold.'   Hardship and poverty caused him to complain to his friend and minister, the Marquis de Rosny, that 'my shirts are all torn, and I have no doublet which is not out at elbow, and not a suit of armour I can wear.'

Always of simple taste in dress, he endeavoured to encourage his courtiers to curb their lavishness in apparel; he even tried the Spanish method of issuing a pragmatic in 1594.   This prohibited the ornamentation of costume with gold and silver, but it proved quite ineffective.

An earlier effort met a similar fate.   For, according to de l'Étoile's journal, fifty young women of good  family had been imprisoned for 'contravening both in clothes and jewellery the edict of reform promulgated several months before.'   These failures did not deter Henry, for in 1601 and 1606 he issued two further ordinances, of which one forbade 'any of the inhabitants of the kingdom to wear either gold or silver on their clothes, except the *filles de joie* and pickpockets, in whom [the King said] we do not take sufficient interest to trouble ourselves about their conduct.'

On the other hand, when absolutely necessary, the King made a very good appearance and was quite in the vogue. For the ceremony of his Act of Abjuration, by which he renounced the Protestant for the Catholic faith, he appeared magnificently attired in *pure* white satin embroidered with gold, a black velvet cloak, and black hat and feather.

The well-known portrait by Pourbus (in the Louvre) of Henry IV, at the age of forty or forty-five, is reproduced in Fig. 752, as it gives the 'line' worn in Europe during the latter years of the sixteenth century. The suit is all black, having the doublet of velvet and the close sleeves and full breeches of black satin. There is nothing elegant about the cut of these garments; the waist is normal and rather short, with no suggestion of a peascod paunch; the gallyhosen or galligaskins —*Chausses larges à l'Antique* —do not enhance the figure

Fig. 753. Collar of Saint-Esprit

of a man, be he tall and slim or short and stout. The hat which lies upon the table is of black blocked felt, with high crown and wide brim, the hatband composed of twisted silk or cords with a rose of black silk on one side. Roses also decorate the shoes—a new mode. The Cordon Bleu suspends the Badge of the Holy Ghost. Henry IV made considerable changes in the Collar of the Order of the Holy Ghost. Only the fleurs-de-lys remained; and for the original monograms were substituted a trophy of arms, and the letter H, surmounted by the Royal Crown, with ducal coronets in gold on each side and cantoned with flames. These emblems were linked to the fleurs-de-lys by golden chains (Fig. 753).

There are portraits of Henry wearing the robes of this Order, and very dignified he looks in them, a great contrast to his earlier slovenly self.

A very beautiful equestrian painting of the King is at Chantilly, in which he wears a doublet with close sleeves, hosen and shoes of white satin with gold roses. The panes of his white slops are black and embroidered with gold in a design not unlike that shown in Fig. 625. The short cloak of black velvet is heavily embroidered in gold and lined with a rich white and gold brocade, with the Star of the Holy Ghost on the left side. The Badge is suspended by a sky-blue watered riband round his neck. His hat, shaped like the one shown in Fig. 752, is black with jewelled ornaments round the brim and short white ostrich feathers on either side; possibly there are two or three round the back as well.

Another portrait shows Henry wearing a suit shaped exactly like that in Fig. 752, but made of a brocade, the groundwork being in black silk with a trellis design in black velvet.

In 1599, Pope Clement VII granted Henry and Marguerite a divorce; and in December of the following year he married Marie de' Medici (born 1573), daughter of Francesco de' Medici, Grand Duke of Tuscany, and of the Archduchess Joanna of Austria.

The children of Henry IV and Marie were:

Louis, born 1601, who succeeded his father.
Elizabeth, born 1603, married Philip IV of Spain.   Died 1644.
Gaston Jean Baptiste, Duc d'Orléans, born 1608.
Christiana, married the Duke of Savoy.
Henrietta Maria, born 1610, married Charles I of England.

Not until Henry had forced his last enemy, the Duke of Savoy, into submission in 1601, was he firmly established on the throne of France.   He made an excellent King, and was most popular, ruling with admirable wisdom and patriotism, and earning for himself the title of 'le Grand.'   His subjects called him 'a father and friend.'   He was affable, indulgent, quick-witted, good-hearted, of a great courage, and skilled in reading the characters of those about him.

Maximilien de Béthune, Marquis de Rosny,[1] the great statesman, was born in 1560 of an impoverished Huguenot family.   At the age of twelve he entered the service of Henry of Navarre, and later did good administrative work for his master with untiring industry and perfect method.

François de Bassompierre was born in 1579 of a noble family in Alsace. After being educated in Germany and Italy, he arrived in Paris in 1598. He captivated the King, who at once took him into his service: in course of time he became Colonel-General of the Swiss, and Maréchal of France.   His *Memoirs* may be dull, but they contain some interesting passages.

## NOBLE LADIES: 1580–1603

### LOUISE

*Queen-Consort of Henry III, 1580 until 1603*

(continued from p. 564)

In the picture, Ball No. I, Queen Louise is seated, and Fig. 754 is a standing version showing the dress she wears.   It is in a deep shade of velvet, and the bodice has sleeves à la Bolonnoise slashed with white, and a long tapering stomacher.   The skirt is very full, being cut as a complete circle, with a short train, and worn over the bolster.   The circular ruff is open in front and surrounded with very fine lace standing out from the goffered edge.   This

---

[1] In 1606 he was created Duc de Sully.   His celebrated *Memoirs* were written in his later years.

portrait is of exceptional interest as it shows Queen Louise in a different style of dress from that of most of her portraits.

Louise of Lorraine was of a very religious turn of mind, spending most of her time in good works and prayer. After the King's death in 1589 'she did the same, employing her time in mourning and regretting him, and in praying to God for his soul; so that her widowed life was much the same as her married life.'

Queen Louise had a sister, Marguerite de Lorraine, who became the wife of Henry III's favourite, the Duc de Joyeuse. She is reproduced with her husband in Fig. 748, taken from Ball No. I, and is garbed as a bride should be in white satin. The bodice and skirt are made like those of the Queen (Fig. 754); but the sleeves are not so bolonnoise and are ornamented with horizontal bands of gold embroidery or lace between rows of pearls mounted on red velvet. Over these are worn long, hanging sleeves, but a new fashion note, originating in Spain, is struck here: the edges of these hanging sleeves are caught together by a rich jewel, showing the lining of white and gold-figured silk. The circular ruff and cuffs are edged with reticella. The head-dress is a cap of red velvet edged with gold, like the front of a French hood, having a jewelled ornament with three prongs of black enamel tipped with a pearl in front of a made-up white feather.

Fig. 754.
Louise de Vaudemont, Queen of France, 1581

The Duchesse de Joyeuse was left a widow; 'she was a good and virtuous princess, who deserves honour for the grief she gave to the ashes of her husband for some time, although she remarried in the end with M. de Luxembourg. Being a woman, why should she languish?' as Brantôme aptly asks.

In both the ball paintings the ladies wear costumes similar in most details, although there is a space of four years between the dates. Two of the ladies in Ball No. I are dressed in much the same style as those in Ball No. II, and the noble lady (Fig. 755) is a generalized version of the costumes of these ladies. The dress is entirely of white satin or of a delicate tone of colour, with attenuated stomacher, bolonnoise sleeves, and full circular skirt. The well-stuffed sleeves afforded a good excuse for all kinds of decoration: in this figure one or two rows of gold or silver cord or braids, caught at intervals

with jewels set in mounts, form oblique lines.    The same arrangement outlines the pointed stomacher.    The deep lawn collar is edged with lace, its
lower points descending well below the waist-line and revealing a plastron
front, over which the pearl and jewelled carcanet or collier falls.    A back
view of the hairdressing is seen in the following Fig. 756.

The seated lady (Fig. 756) is seen in the foreground to the left of the painting of Ball No. II.    The front of her dress is exactly the same as that in
Fig. 755, and is of satin in a pale shade.    The sleeves are embroidered with
a design arranged diaperwise over the whole surface.    Other small motifs or fancy ornaments were used to decorate such bolonnoise sleeves.    A modish note is the manner in which the collier or riband, or both, worn round the décolletage is fastened with an orna-ment or bow in the centre of the back.    Also the back of the coiffure should be noticed.

Fig. 755.
Lady of the Court of Henry III, 1581

At Penshurst Place is a French paint-ing of a ball scene said to represent Queen Elizabeth dancing with the Earl of Leicester at Kenilworth.    It must have been painted at the same time as the two ball pictures in the Louvre; the costumes, especially those of the ladies, are precisely similar, and a lady sitting on a stool in the left foreground is a duplicate of Fig. 756.    The figure said to be Leicester does not in the least resemble the Earl.    There must be some mistake in the title of this paint-ing, which is much more likely to be a representation of yet another ball at
the French Court; or possibly the artist, knowing that Queen Elizabeth had a
great passion for dancing, conceived the idea of painting her engaged in this
pastime with the two Louvre pictures in his mind.

The seat shown in Fig. 756 is of peculiar interest.    Such seats, or rather,
stools, superseded at the French Court the use of a cushion or piles of cushions
heaped upon the floor: the embroidered border of one such cushion is shown
inset.    Many of these stools or 'tabourets' stood along the walls of the
salons in the various Royal palaces and castles for the convenience of
the company.    In a short time a custom grew up whereby the wives of the
highest personages should have the privilege of occupying tabourets nearest
the Royal presence.    These were placed, or brought into the chamber by
lackeys for those entitled to sit upon them, including the wives of princes,

dukes, and some of the high Court dignitaries. The right to occupy a tabouret depended upon the rank of the husband, and was supposed to be relinquished at his death, unless great exertions and much influence were brought to bear to retain it. Late in the century this article of furniture was adopted in England for the same purpose, but the rule of precedence was not quite so rigidly enforced.

Fig. 756. Lady of the Court of Henry III, 1585

*A note on etiquette at the French Court:*

To receive a visitor of great distinction, the King or Queen, if amiably disposed, would advance from the Royal group 'to the middle of the room, not a step beyond, and rather nearer the door than farther from it.' A lady on such occasions would, on reaching the sovereign, make a very low curtsy.

### Marguerite de Valois

*Queen of France and Navarre, 1580–1615*

(continued from p. 566)

For three and a half years Queen Marguerite of Navarre spent her time in Gascony, probably but not necessarily with her husband. Their undomestic life was definitely unusual according to the sixteenth-century standard of morals: whether they lived together or with someone else, they remained on very friendly terms, and Henry would often appeal to his wife for sympathy and help on important affairs. In 1581 Marguerite took up her residence at the French Court. She was then a remarkably intelligent, good-natured, handsome woman of twenty-eight, and a resolute setter of fashion. As years rolled by, and as a means of holding on to her reputation as a high society beauty, she resorted to all kinds of washes and receipts for the preservation of her skin, so much so that by the time she reached forty-five she had completely ruined her complexion and was a victim to erysipelas and pimples.

By 1585 she had begun to quarrel openly with her husband, Henry of Navarre, and also with her brother Henry III, so that for the time being she was regarded as Queen by courtesy only, much to her annoyance. She therefore sought refuge in the impregnable fortress of Carlet in Auvergne, with her ladies-in-waiting, wardrobe, furniture, coaches, and horses; a lengthy business. By Henry III's orders she was removed to the Castle of Usson in 1587, where she was practically a prisoner in charge of the Marquis de Canillac. Her warder, however, proved too susceptible to the lady's charms,

LA REINE MARGOT.

Fig. 757

so that she gained entire control of the castle, where she remained until the troubles of the League were well over. It is said that 'many common frailties happened there, but less odious than are told by bitter and dishonourable chroniclers, the only authorities for the tales they put forth,' yet during this period she frequently corresponded amicably with her husband.

The King had meanwhile tentatively suggested a divorce: Marguerite was at first very unwilling, being suspicious that her husband, now King of France as well as Navarre, wished to marry Gabrielle d'Estrées. Only after the death of the latter, in 1599, did she consent, and in the same year the Pope granted the decree. If their marriage was commonplace their divorce at any rate was Royal: and before the end of the year the King had married Marie de' Medici.

Fig. 757 is from an engraving by Crispin van de Pass the Elder of 'La Reine Margot.' The portrait is dated 1598, and was therefore made while she was in retirement at Usson. It gives a good example of the large collar made of transparent lawn and edged with lace, insertion, and wire. The part which rested on the shoulders was also of wire, and from this framework uprights of wire supported the collar. A detail of the lace is given in Fig. 694.

Marguerite, still by courtesy Queen of France and Navarre, returned from Usson to Paris in 1605 where she held her Court at the Hôtel de Sens. After her long retirement she found herself on her re-entry into the fashionable world completely out of date, and no longer able to reign as the arbiter of fashion. Her attempt to do so met with much ridicule.

Queen Marguerite made a last magnificent appearance at the coronation of Marie de' Medici at Saint-Denis, 13th May 1610. This ceremony is commemorated by Peter Paul Rubens (1577–1640) in the painting in the Louvre. Marguerite is seen seated on the left, crowned and attired in Royal robes, and at fifty-seven the possessor of a very pronounced double chin. She died in Paris 27th March 1615, aged sixty-two; 'sole remains of the Race of Valois, who did no harm to any but herself,' says a contemporary writer.

## MARIE DE' MEDICI

### Queen-Consort of Henry IV, 1600 until 1603

Even before her marriage, Marie's interest in dress was well known to her future husband. She herself took pains to see that he was informed of her preferences in this important matter: 'Fontenac [the King's messenger] tells me,' Henry writes, 'that you desired to have some models of the fashion of dress in France. I am sending you some dressed dolls, and will send you with the Duc de Bellegarde [his proxy] a good tailor.'

In her widowhood, Marie still gave much attention to the subject of dress. When she returned from her exile in 1620, she occupied herself with the embellishment of her newly built Luxembourg palace, and commissioned Peter Paul Rubens to paint a series of twenty-one canvases illustrating her history. Rubens did not become famous until after 1603. These pictures were painted between 1621 and 1625 and are now in the Louvre. The allegories were entirely Rubens's own ideas, but the Queen-Mother supervised and directed him in all details concerning the historical matter; therefore, it is safe to rely on the earlier subjects of these pictures as correct representations of the personages, costume, and other details of the years 1600–3. All his preliminary designs and sketches were submitted to the Queen, and we are told that during the time that Rubens was thus occupied, she spent many hours with him in the gallery, eagerly watching the artist at work and delighting in his conversation.

In No. V of the series, 'Her Marriage by Proxy,' Marie de' Medici wears a costume of white and gold brocade made exactly like that shown in Fig. 774,

except that the neck of the bodice is cut low and the skirt is heavily braided with gold down the front and hem. Loops and aiglettes decorate the front. The dress the Queen wears in No. VI, 'Her landing at Marseilles,' is illustrated in Fig. 758. It is of plain substantial white satin, the bodice and sleeves being of the same pattern as shown in Fig. 774 and trimmed with gold and jewels. The skirt hangs in rich and heavy folds, most probably over the Spanish farthingale, and has a moderately long train. In both paintings the ruff is of large gofferings and surrounds the back of the neck leaving the throat bare. There is a string of pearls round the neck, and clusters of the same encircle the head behind the high hairdressing. The costume is, in fact, exceptional because of the small quantity of jewels displayed upon it. At the end of the century the costumes of the French Court ladies became not only very costly because of the rich materials

Fig. 758.
Marie de' Medici, Queen of France (*after Rubens*)

used, but also uncomfortably heavy by reason of the excessive quantities of gold and silver bullion and jewels which ornamented them. It is said that the wearers were often scarcely able to move, or even stand, in these gorgeous gowns.

### ITALIAN INFLUENCES, 1580–1603

A gentleman of Verona (Fig. 759) is taken from a plan of that city dated 1580. His suit is of the fashion shown in many of the preceding figures, both English and French. The hood of the cloak is of a large size. Hoods were fixed to the cloak, or they were separate garments. The one shown here is probably of a new fashion which later found its way into the wardrobes of western Europe from Italy.

Fig. 759. A Gentleman of Verona, 1580      Fig. 760

The hood shown in diagram (Fig. 760) is all in one with the cloak, cut as a segment of a circle about $3\frac{3}{4}$ yards long and about 30 inches at its widest. The points A and B on the straight edge, $\frac{7}{18}$ of its length from the ends, are caught together; and when the cloak is worn, this junction is placed in the centre of the back of the neck as seen at C. The loop forms a hood 'à la burnoise.'

In Fig. 759 the cloak has a double border of cuttes on the curved edge, and a simple band of gold braid on the straight. The part between A and B is set with a row of tiny silk tassels. The left side of the cloak is draped over the left arm, and the right side hangs from the shoulder. The hairdressing is curious, and the boots are of the fashion in England at the end of the fifteenth century.

Fig. 761.
A Gentleman of Florence, 1590

A representative costume of the next decade is given in Fig. 761, a young gentleman of Florence in the 1590's. His doublet, sleeves, and venetians are well padded, and are of cloth or silk decorated with black or coloured billets set at alternate angles on the doublet and venetians. The sleeves are treated in a slightly different arrangement. The band of embroidery up the seams of the venetians is common to all nationalities of breeches, but the pocket slit incorporated with it is a novelty, as is also the semi-circular decoration at the knee. A cloak with a collar attached to it, velvet hat, jewelled ornament hung by a riband, and sword complete the characteristic costume of an Italian noble.

The lady (Fig. 765) is taken from an engraving (1597) which shows her in the company of a Roman gentleman, shown back view. He wears a small ruff, doublet, trunks, and hosen in the French fashion. His hat has a high crown and a moderate-sized brim; the circular cloak of brocade has a plain velvet border and a hood of the same fastened up the fronts with laces and aiglettes.

## ITALIAN LADIES, 1580–1603

The same difficulty is encountered in Part II as with Part I; space allows of only a few drawings of Italian ladies being given, and it is difficult with so much material to find characteristic examples.

The materials used by Italian ladies were exquisite: they always had been, but in the sixteenth century, and especially in its second half, they excelled anything previously created. Italian silks and 'broccate' were of exceptionally fine workmanship and design, and were woven at Bologna, Florence, Genoa, Milan, Modena, and Venice. These factories supplied every country in Europe.

The lady of the 1580's, shown in Fig. 762, is a composite drawing embodying modes borrowed from Rome and Venice. The bodice, the close-fitting sleeves with (probable) puffs on the shoulders, and skirt are both Roman and Venetian, and were the models on which French fashions of the middle of the century were founded. The over-robe or surcote is Venetian, and claims kinship with the surcote of Spain, from which country the high collar is derived. The moderate circular ruff is international; the fan is one of the new models made to open and shut.

Fig. 763 shows a noble lady of Florence; the authority from which it is taken dates 1589. The main features to be noticed are the normal waist-line, the bodice open in a V at the throat and surrounded by a goffered ruff such as is seen in paintings of many Italian ladies, including the well-known portrait of Bianca Cappello by Bronzino. The armholes and waist are

Fig. 763. A Lady of Florence, 1589

Fig. 762 (*left*). An Italian Lady

decorated with a row of small tabs or ruchings, and the sleeves are much like the Spanish, but with under-sleeves of soft silk, lawn, or gauze. The skirt of rich brocade hangs stiffly without folds, and is *not* worn over a farthingale. It opens up the front, and fastens if desired by buttons and loops attached to tulip-like motifs. The neck-chain is of massive rectangular gold links, and the fan, of characteristic Italian design, is framed square and fixed to a long handle very like a flag.

The Grandes Dames of Venice were always very richly attired. The city produced magnificent brocades, lace, and jewellery, and the ladies took the opportunity of displaying these commodities on their persons. The matron of Venice (Fig. 764) wears a gown of simple though definitely Venetian style. Of some stiff brocade in gold and colour, the skirt is ample and forms heavy folds: it is quite plain, and gathered in to the sloping line of the waist.   The portly figure is accentuated by the point of the stomacher being padded, rather like the peascod paunches worn by men.   The sleeves are unattached at the shoulders, but tied to the bodice by laces and aiglettes, which also appear just above the wrists.   Escaping from the space between them is

Fig. 765. Roman Lady, 1597 (*after Boissard*)

Fig. 764 (*left*). A Noble Lady of Venice

a row of beautiful point de Venise lace, which also surrounds the stand-up collar or ruff.   This is all in one with the partlet and stomacher, and made of transparent silk-gauze, sometimes shot with gold or silver.   The fan when not in use hangs at the end of the chain girdle.

Italian ladies are accused of excessive painting, so that this lady of mature age has no doubt attempted to add to her charms by adopting this pernicious habit.

The ladies of Rome were simply, yet very beautifully, dressed, as is shown by Fig. 765.   This is a copy of an engraving by Jean Jacques Boissard, published in 1597, and therefore can well be taken as a fashion of the 1590's. The dress, with close-fitting and puffed sleeves, bodice cut low, and ample trained skirt gathered to the hip-line, is of rich silk or satin. The partlet is edged with a small frill, suggesting a miniature ruff, and the same frill is repeated at the wrists. Attached to the hair is a wide veil, soft and transparent; one corner is caught in the left hand together with the skirt. The corresponding corner is fixed to the ornament at the point of the bodice. This vogue was a very usual one with Roman ladies, and often both corners of the veil were fixed at the same point.

## SPANISH STYLES, 1580–1603

### PHILIP II, 1580–98

(continued from p. 576)

The eyes of all Europe, especially of Rome, were at this time turned towards one man—Philip of Spain, who was crowned King of Portugal at Lisbon in 1581, thus adding to his many titles —and cares.

As the hostility of Spain became more definite, culminating in the Invincible Armada, anything Spanish naturally fell into disfavour. Nevertheless we see the current influences of Spain influencing English costume via France.

From this time forward His Catholic Majesty is said to have dressed entirely in black. Plate XLVI shows him so garbed in a plain suit of dull black silk. His moderate-sized slops are the only part decorated with cuttes on the piped panes. Nether stocks are rolled up over the upper stocks, and the cloak and collar of black velvet are lined with a glossy black silk. The hat of blocked felt has a twisted silk band and a rose.

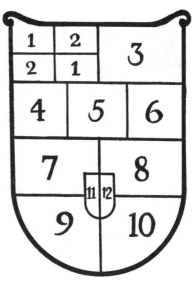

Fig. 766. Key to Armorials

Following his invariable custom he is wearing the Golden Fleece suspended by a small gold chain, well set off by its sombre background.

In striking contrast we see the brilliant tinctures of the Armorial Bearings of the States ruled by Philip before he became King of Portugal in 1581. Fig. 766 gives the names of these quarterings:

(1) Castile, (2) Leon, (3) Aragon, (4) Jerusalem, (5) Hungary (*unseen*), (6) Sicily, (7) Austria, (8) Modern Burgundy, (9) Ancient Burgundy, (10) Brabant, (11) Flanders (*unseen*), and (12) Tyrol (*unseen*). They are surmounted by the Spanish Royal Crown.

Although it is said that Philip usually dressed in unrelieved black, there are one or two portraits which show that the black suit was sometimes ornamented with a minimum amount of fine gold. He also wore a muceta of black silk or velvet, also relieved with gold, and sometimes lined with sable.

Fig. 767. Philip II of Spain, 1586

A head-and-shoulders drawing taken from a portrait of Philip II at the age of fifty-nine and dated 1586 is given in Fig. 767.

The King appears to have been too busy with affairs of State to trouble much about his subjects' apparel, for after 1564 no more pragmatics were issued for some time.

A description of the costume worn in the meantime by men (for women *see* p. 683) is given in the writings of Camillo Borghese, who came to Madrid in 1593 on a mission from Pope Clement VIII. The following is his account: 'The dress of this country is as follows. The men wear long breeches, with a surcote and hat or else a cloak and cap, as it would be a great breach of decorum with them to wear a hat and cloak together. This costume would certainly be very pretty if the breeches were not cut so long as to be disproportionate. Some men have taken to wearing hose in the Seville style, which they call galligaskins, and with these it is proper to wear a cloak and hat instead of a cap.'

Philip made a final attempt to check the extravagance of his subjects in the matter of dress; having found them, perhaps, reluctant to follow his own sombre example, he issued a last pragmatic in 1594:

'No man may wear either at his neck or wrists on any sort of ruff or frill, fixed or loose, any trimming, fringe, ravelling, or netting, starch, rice, gums, rods, wires, gold or silver threads, or any brass wiring or anything else to extend or support them, but only a plain holland or linen ruff with one or two little pleats, on pain of forfeiture of shirt and ruff and a fine of 50 ducats.'

These restrictions aroused so much indignation that the Council of State solemnly gave the subject its attention: and in the matter of ruffs a compromise was reached by which these adornments might be worn so long as they did not exceed three inches in width from band to hem, and were pure white. The penalties were enormous. Similar concessions were made regarding the materials of men's doublets, jerkins, and breeches, which might now be made of gold or fancy silk material (whose manufacture in Spain had of recent years much declined), as also of quilted silk, satin, or taffeta, while for the first time for many years stamped patterns might be used; trunk hose might be slashed and double-stitched at the edge of

Fig. 768. Don Enrique de Guzman, 1595

the slashings, and breeches stiffened by a single thickness of baize. Thus, luxury in dress was allowed to continue unchecked during the last years of the reign.

Philip II, who suffered from a lingering, loathsome disease, died in his palace-monastery on 13th September 1598, and is buried in the Escorial church. His reign marks the climax of Spanish power, and the commencement of its decline by secession of its New World possessions.

On the south side of the high altar is a monument to himself and his family. The effigies, five in number, are in gilt bronze, by Leoni. The King kneels in front at a prie-dieu and wears full armour under a State mantle with ermine cape quartering the armorial bearings of the Hapsburg inheritance. Grouped

Fig. 769. Don Luis de Velasco

around him are three of his wives—Marie of Portugal, Elizabeth of France, and Anne of Austria, and, behind, his son Don Carlos, all wearing armorial mantles in their proper tinctures.

As an example of the great simplicity of the costume worn by Spanish nobles of the highest degree in the 1580's and 1590's, the head-and-shoulders drawing (Fig. 768) of Don Enrique de Guzman, Conde de Olivares, Spanish Ambassador to the Holy See from 1584 onwards, is given. An unpretentious doublet of black silk, slashed on the breast over black and buttoned up the front, has a high collar, small ruff, and close-fitting sleeves with small shoulder rolls. This doublet must have had a narrow basque, although this is not shown. The rest of the dress consisted of equally plain nether garments—slops and hosen, and in addition an ample black cloth Spanish cloak and a high crowned almost brimless black felt hat.

Fig. 770.
Philip, Prince of the Asturias, 1596

Don Luis de Velasco, Viceroy of Mexico (Fig. 769), was a knight of the Order of St. James of the Sword in Spain. This Order was instituted in the twelfth century, but the Emperor Charles V made some additions and alterations. The badge (inset) was a red-enamelled cross of gold formed like a sword, the pommel like a heart reversed, and the guards terminating in fleurs-de-lys. Upon the centre was a white escallop shell. This badge was hung from a red riband round the neck, and on ceremonial occasions from a triple gold chain.

The robes of the Order consisted of a tunic of black silk or velvet, and the white mantle had a red cross embroidered on the left shoulder. A black velvet hat adorned with white ostrich feathers had a small red feather in the middle.

Don Luis is not wearing these full robes in his portrait (Fig. 769), but those worn for semi-State. The red badge on the black tunic is without the escallop shell, and is repeated on the shoulder of his *black* mantle. The hat he wears, with three rolls round the brim, is typically Spanish, and his gold-rimmed spectacles are attached to his ears by black leather straps.

Ladies were admitted to this Order; their robes were black, with the badge and cross.

The costume worn by a Spanish nobleman at the end of the century is illustrated in Fig. 770. It is taken from a portrait at Shottesbrooke Park, and is said to be of the Infante Philip, afterwards Philip III: if not, it represents some Spanish grandee. It was painted by Pantoja de la Cruz about 1596. The 'line' or cut of the doublet and trunks is different from that of the previous era, and shows the emergence of the form characteristic of the first part of the seventeenth century. The very angular effect of the trunks or slops should be noticed. The doublet and trunks are composed of vertical bands of dark green velvet embroidered in scarlet, white, and gold. The black velvet cloak is draped in the latest mode over the left upper arm; it is lined with white satin covered with lines of narrow gold cord set about one and a half inches apart and forming double loops. The sleeves are of the same embroidered white satin. A small plain circular ruff, black velvet belts, white silk hosen, and golden satin shoes with gold lace roses complete the attractions of this young Prince.

## PHILIP III

### *King of Spain, 1598 until 1603*

Philip, son of Philip II and Anne of Austria, was born in Madrid, 14th April 1578, and ascended the throne in 1598.

His long face with lack-lustre eyes, black hair, and heavy Hapsburg lip and jaw was anything but pleasing, as is evidenced by the crayon drawing by Daniel Dumoustier from which Fig. 771 is made.

Fig. 771.
Philip III of Spain

He was a sickly young man and subject to scrofula, with the mind of a silly pious child given over entirely to futile pleasures. The exact opposite of his father in everything except his beliefs, he squandered fabulous sums on Court festivals. He lacked his father's industry and intelligence, leaving the administration of the kingdom to Francisco de Sandoval y Rojas (born 1552), the chief minister, who was created Duke of Lerma in 1599. Later (1611) the Duke was superseded by his son, the Duke of Uceda. Philip married Margaret of Austria in the same year.

The sumptuary pragmatics had been ignored for many years, and extravagance in dress had reached such a pitch that it had become a national scandal. Hence in 1600 Philip issued a new pragmatic, quite different from previous ones, which formed the pattern of all similar enactments for the next hundred years. No one except the King and the Royal family might wear any sort of brocade or cloth of gold or silver, or silk in which these metals were woven, nor might ornamentation of any kind, or embroidery or pearls or jewels, be used on garments. Ruffs, however, could now be four and a half inches wide, as long as they had no lace edgings or ravellings and were pure white.

The following dress is alone prescribed: the cape or other over-garment may be of any sort of silk with stripes, on each edge of which may be an ornamental stitching. Surcotes and ropillas (a sort of half-tight over-jacket with double sleeves, the outer ones hanging loose from the shoulders) may be also of silk and trimmed in the same way, and, if desired, a piping of another sort of silk, but not the same, may be put between the stripes. The inside of the capes may have similar stripes of silk, satin, or taffeta, but not velvet. Shoulder-capes may be made of velvet, and the hoods of riding-cloaks or rain-capes may be lined with the same. Silk gimp and frogs may be sewn on to *duffel* cloaks, etc. The trunks may be worn of any kind of silk, and each slashing may be edged with a velvet or silk piping and an *eyelash* border. If the slashing is a wide one, this edging may be worn on both sides of it, but if otherwise only on one side. The slashings may be lined with taffeta. Silk gimp or braid of any sort may be worn on the trunks excepting *lutestrings* or crewels. Galligaskins may also be made of silk, but with no trimming but a row of gimp on each side and at the opening. Dressing-gowns for women and men may be of any material or fashion, so long as gold or silver is not used. Doublets, ropillas, or trunks made of satin may be ornamented by silk stitching of any colour, but on no account may the stuff be pinked, ravelled, or fringed.

The rules generally apply to women as well as men, but the former are allowed to wear *jackets* of light cloth of gold or silver, which may be trimmed with a braid of the same over the seams, and the whole jacket may be covered with 'whirligigs' or scrolls of gold or silver, so long as there is no working in the stuff itself. The frills and flounces of these garments may also be ornamented in the same fashion. Hats, belts, baldricks, etc., were all treated in the same way; gold or silver gimp, braid, and lace were allowed to be sewn on, but not embroidered or woven in, the texture.[1]

It should be explained that *eyelash* was a stitching very like what is known as 'blanket stitch.' Lutestring was a glossy silk cord or ribbon.

Philip's gloomy forebodings as to what would happen when the Crown should pass to his incompetent son were more than realized.


## NOBLE LADIES, 1580–1603

### THE GREAT INFANTA, 1566 *until* 1603

Isabella Clara Eugenia, eldest daughter of Philip II and Elizabeth or Isabel de Valois, was born at Balsain, near Segovia, in 1566. She was named after Queen Isabella the Catholic and her mother; Clara because she was born on that Saint's day, 1st August; and Eugenia out of gratitude to the efficacious body of St. Eugène which had restored her mother to health.

---

[1] The whole of this description is taken from Martin Hume's *The Year after the Armada*.

Fig. 772. THE INFANTA ISABELLA CLARA EUGENIA

Her father, who was devotedly fond of her, describing her on his death-bed as 'le miroir et la lumière de ses yeux,' endeavoured to bring about a marriage between her and Henry, Duc d'Anjou.   This project was extremely unpopular in France, especially with the Huguenots, and was the subject of much satire on account of her age and swarthy complexion.   The negotiations did not mature.   This middle-aged spinster—she was nearly thirty—was still left without a husband or a crown, despite the fact that was she the greatest catch of Europe 'ever since Elizabeth of England had definitely retired from the matrimonial market.'   However, as some compensation, her father bestowed upon her first the Netherlands (21st May 1598) and then her cousin the Cardinal Archduke, Albert of Austria, whom she married in 1599, the Pope releasing him from his religious vows.   As Governess of the Netherlands conjointly with her husband, the Archduchess persecuted her new subjects with zest, as was usual with some members of the Hapsburg family.   The famous siege of Ostend in 1601 was undertaken with this object.

The Great Infanta was frequently painted at different periods of her life by such artists as Pantoja de la Cruz, Coello, Liano, Pourbus the Younger, and—in late life—by Rubens: these portraits may be seen in the Prado, at Versailles, Munich, and Hampton Court.

Fig. 772 is founded on more than one of these portraits.   There are several apparently trifling details about the costume which repay study.   The characteristic surcote of Spain, mentioned as far back as 1550 (see Fig. 516), is still in vogue, and continued to be so well into the seventeenth century, but the shoulders and back are now cut to fit close as evidenced by the way the folds of the skirt part, gored behind at the waist, hang.   The slits on the breast remain; but turning the front back to waist-level instead of fastening it at the throat (see Fig. 592), and raising the hem in front, are new ideas. So also are the lace wrist-frills which form the transition from the turned-back cuffs of the sixteenth century to the flounces of lace worn during the whole of the seventeenth and eighteenth centuries.

The hanging sleeves, farthingale, hairdressing, and headdress are truly Spanish.   In Fig. 772 the whole dress is made of one of those magnificent brocades so much used at this time; it has a raised velvet pattern of more delicate design than hitherto, on a different coloured satin ground.   The surcote and underdress have a fancy gold lace set on all edges, and in some portraits there are two rows and even three placed close together.   In more than one painting the whole surface of the surcote and underdress is covered with bands of gold lace, about an inch in width, set close in horizontal, per-pendicular, and oblique lines.   The underdress is shaped like that shown in Fig. 774 and nearly always made of the same material as the surcote.

Portraits of the Archduchess's younger sister, the Infanta Catherine Michela, who was born in 1567, show her as a very good-looking girl with a round face, beautiful dark eyes and hair, and without any Hapsburg charac-teristics.   The one by Coello, in the Prado, is a specially good example. Fig. 773 is drawn from it.

Fig. 773. THE INFANTA CATHERINE MICHELA.  After Sanchez Coello

The Infanta married before her elder sister, her husband being Emmanuel I, Duke of Savoy; and their wedding festivities were so magnificent as to call from this very haughty young Princess the remark that such ostentatious display was unnecessary for a 'mere duchess.' However, she had nine children, and died at the age of thirty in 1597.

Although the art of weaving brocades, damasks, plain velvets, and silks had reached such a high standard in Spain during the fifteenth century, owing to the excellent craftsmanship of the Moorish weavers who were alone responsible for the textile manufacture (see vol. i, p. 218), a certain quantity of silken material was imported from Italy.

Fig. 774. Spanish Lady of the Court

Spanish woven fabrics had been entirely of Moorish design; but with the advent of the Renaissance, the pomegranate and the method of spacing out patterns in pointed ovals became incorporated with Morisco features. Towards the end of the sixteenth century the oval motif gave place to a lighter and more flexible ornament, such as are seen in the brocades worn by Spanish ladies of this time in their portraits. When the Moriscos were finally banished from Spain by Philip III in 1609, the country was deprived of the services of these expert silk weavers and designers. Henceforth Spain had to rely on Italy and France for the gorgeous stuffs wherewith to create magnificent clothes, upholder furniture, and decorate apartments.

The noble ladies of Spain who were in the entourage of the Great Infanta, and later the Archduchess, followed her example in their toilets and sumptuous apparel, and were entirely outside the pale of any pragmatics.

Fig. 774 is a representative costume carried out in a brocade of rich colouring, in which the most important motif is the tulip—a new flower lately introduced from Turkey. The bodice, cut high at the neck, and the farthingale, were regulated for the dress of Royal ladies, the Court, and the aristocracy. Usually the neck was high, having a stiff collar almost reaching the lobe of the ear. The circular ruff was attached to the top of this collar, as shown in Fig. 772; but there are a few instances in portraits of great ladies turning the edges and corners down, showing a little of the bare throat, the circular ruff being supported at the sides and back as seen in Fig. 774. In this, the bodice is cut to fit the corseted figure, descending in a point well below the waist; it has three lines, sometimes more, of gold set with jewels in gold mounts converging from shoulders to waist and point. Tabs surround the armholes and the sloping waist-line.

The hanging sleeves of deep-toned velvet are the most distinctive feature of this typical Spanish costume. Fig. 775 is a diagram of one. It is cut in two sections; AB is pleated or gathered into the armhole; from B to D it is seamed, leaving a reversed T opening at C; DE is the wrist; and from E it is seamed along the curved portion to A.

These sleeves were ornamented in many different ways, but usually with rows of gold braid, as seen in Figs. 774 and 775, showing a decidedly Moorish influence. Loops and aiglettes were often added, and as a matter of course the sleeve could be worn on the arm or hanging behind. The close undersleeves, of different but plain material, were almost covered with transverse braids, the joins and front and back seams being masked with a single row of braid. The skirt is without folds in front and at the sides, being cut on the circular plan; but sometimes a train was worn (see Fig. 772), when the skirt would become an oval. The seams are joined with care so as not to mutilate the pattern more than possible when

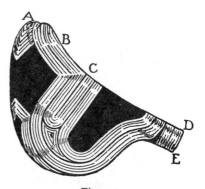

Fig. 775

using brocade or damask. If, of necessity, there must be a seam down the centre of the skirt, which was often left open, it was marked with braids. Velvet, satin, and silk were other materials much used for these costumes.

With regard to the costume of the Spanish ladies in general, we are told by Camillo Borghese in 1593 that it was usually of black relieved only by the large circular white ruff. Ruffs were not so frequently worn as voluminous black veils: 'They have a veil round their faces like nuns, their heads being enveloped by their MANTILLAS in such a way that their faces are hardly visible.' This is a very early reference to that very characteristic item of Spanish costume, as the mantilla of lace did not become important until much later. Velazquez's two portraits of a lady of middle class, one belonging to the Duke of Devonshire, the other, No. 88, in the Wallace Collection, are perhaps the earliest paintings which show the mantilla.

Straight-cut jackets with sleeves reaching to the elbow, or even sleeveless, were frequently worn over ordinary dress. These used to be very elaborately braided with gold or silver round the edges and over the seams, and were of Moorish origin; for this reason such decoration was no longer allowed by the pragmatic of 1594, but this restriction was not enforced by Philip III in 1600 (*see* p. 677).

Spanish ladies were notorious for painting their faces. Being dark-skinned they used many kinds of paint and cosmetics to make themselves appear fair, blonde complexions being greatly admired by all Spaniards. 'Though small of stature they wear pattens to make them look tall,' a method of increasing their height which had been in use from the early part of the century (*see* Fig. 248).

## MARGARET OF AUSTRIA

### *Queen-Consort of Philip III*

This Queen, the daughter of the Archduke Charles of Styria, led an uneventful life, and brought up her children to the best of her ability.

They were:

Fig. 776. Marguerite of Austria, Wife of Philip III, 1602

Anne, born 1602, married Louis XIII of France.

Philip, born 1605, succeeded as Philip IV, and married Mary, daughter of the Emperor Ferdinand III.

Mary married Ferdinand III.

Margaret realized from the outset that she was unequal to the task of supporting the important position thrust upon her, though bidden by her relentless parents to sacrifice everything to duty; tending the poor and sick in her native land, where she led an almost nun-like life, was much more suited to her temperament. However, she was much loved and venerated by her Spanish subjects.

The jacket mentioned on p. 678 was a garment often worn, but seldom seen in portraits or illustrations. Fortunately, in a full-length engraving by Crispin van de Pass the Elder, dated 1602, Margaret of Austria is wearing this interesting jacket. Fig. 776 is a drawing of it, in black or some dark-coloured velvet, the surface covered with a beautiful scroll design in gold and, possibly, some silver. The borders and shoulder pieces are edged with gold braid. It should be noticed that the funnel-shaped sleeves give the same effect as the fashionable sleeves worn by the lady (Fig. 774) but lack the lower part. This jacket is worn over a dress, of which the dark front of the bodice set with jewels is the only part visible; the close-fitting sleeves, finishing at the wrists with the new style of wrist-ruffs, are of light-coloured satin or silk. The skirt hanging in stiff folds over the Spanish farthingale is of white and gold

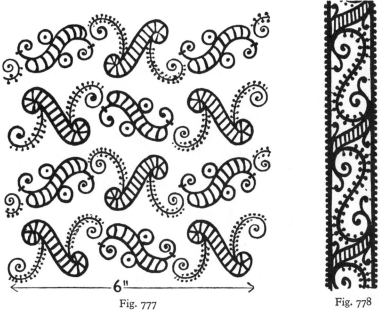

Fig. 777

Fig. 778

brocade, and opens over an embroidered underskirt. The fronts, like those of the jacket, are formally turned back to show the silk lining. A circular ruff edged with picadils, and a high jewelled coronet, are worn.

A three-quarter portrait by Gonzalez of Queen Margaret with her hand on the head of her dog 'Valliante,' in the Prado, shows her in a dress of white with a black pattern (Fig. 777) fashioned somewhat on the lines as that seen in Fig. 774, but heavily braided with black silk braid, a portion of which is given in Fig. 778. She wears a circular lace edged ruff and a coronet of up-standing pear-shaped pearls at the back of her head.

## TENYSE (*continued from p.* 196)

Tennis still remained a popular game, and in 1584 a Fellow of Oriel College, Oxford, wrote with reference to this enjoyable pastime, that it 'exercises all parts of the body alike and greatly delighteth the minde, making it lusty and cheerful, all which commodities may be found in none other kinde of exercise.' The racquet in use had not altered much, as may be seen in Fig. 490; the top is now rather more rounded.

According to Lupold von Wedel, who visited England in 1584, tennis balls were made of wood, though it was much more usual for them to be made of leather and stuffed with hair (*see* p. 196). Perhaps Herr von Wedel's observation was at fault.

It was not until 22nd September 1591 that tennis was first played upon a smooth lawn with marked-out courts. This was at Elvetham, the Earl of Hertford's seat: 'Ten of the Earle of Hertford's servants, all Somersetshire men, in a square green court, before Her Majesties window, did hang up lines, squaring out the forme of a tennis court, and making a cross line in the middle. In this square they (being stript out of their doublets) played, five to five with the handball, at bord and cord (as they tearme it), to so great liking of Her Highness, that she graciously deyned to beholde their pastime more than an hour and a half.'

As tennis began to be played more and more out of doors, shuttlecock became popular as an indoor winter game; and in 1602, we read that:

'24 Dec. 1602. The play of shuttlecock is become so much in request at Court that the making of shuttlecocks is almost grown a trade in London.'

## THE YEOMEN OF THE GUARD (*continued from p.* 424)

During the first years of Queen Elizabeth's reign the number of the 'Yeomen in Ordinary' was increased to two hundred, and that of the 'Yeomen Extraordinary' reduced to one hundred and seven. There were thirty 'Yeomen of the Crown' who were usually in attendance near the Queen's person, and four 'Yeomen Ushers,' a number subsequently increased to fifteen and ultimately reduced to eight.

The predominating colours of the State liveries of the Yeomen of the Guard during this reign are shown in contemporary illustrations as red, black, and yellow.

One of the corps in attendance at Queen Elizabeth's coronation is given in Fig. 779, reproduced from the pen-and-ink drawing referred to on p. 485. Comparison of A, Plate XXIII, with the rough drawing, will show that the only difference in their dress is the hat, which in Fig. 779 is a trifle larger. It is noticeable that in the original drawing the yeomen do not wear hats all of the same shape; there are three varieties, as shown inset. Some wear high-crowned hats, others a large bonet with a feather.

The captain of the Yeomen of the Guard, Sir William St. Loo (second husband of the Countess of Shrewsbury, 'Bess of Hardwick'), rides at the head of the corps on a finely caparisoned horse like Fig. 957, and wears rich clothes exactly as shown in Fig. 610, but with a high-crowned hat and feather.

Some time after the accession of Elizabeth the black gards shown on the sleeves and bases of the tunic in Plate XXIII A were edged with a narrow gold braid.

B in Plate XXIII illustrates the livery of the Yeomen of the Guard in use from about 1575 to 1595. The body part of the tunic is decorated in the same manner as the last example, the only differences being that some time before 1580 the black gards were edged with narrow gold and the Royal cipher was added, the letters 'E.R.' in gold being placed on either side of the rose. From this time onwards to the present day, the initials of the sovereign, together with the rose and crown, have been embroidered upon the breast of the State liveries. The gold-embroidered gards, which descend on each side of the tunic front, are repeated round the neck opening. The collar is attached to the doublet and supports the band.

The puffed sleeves finish with a gard of black velvet through which pass the close sleeves of the dark purple doublet. The basque seen in Plate XXIII A has been superseded by a reversion to the earlier bases—hence the opening up the front (seen in the basque) has disappeared

Fig. 779. 1559

—descending to the middle of the thigh and showing a small portion of the lower part of the dark purple slops. The legs are clothed in kersey hose, also of dark purple, and over them are drawn netherstocks of white kersey, tied with dark purple garters below the knee. Black shoes with black roses are worn.

From 1570 onwards Yeomen of the Guard wore a hat of black velvet, in place of the earlier bonet, as seen in the drawing (B Plate XXIII). Round the crown was folded a band of white silk or linen with a rose of the same on the left side, securing a bunch of white ostrich feathers.

A gilt halberd, together with a gilt-handled sword in a black scabbard slung from a black sword-carriage and belt, was carried.

The Yeomen of the Guard were present on all occasions of State and ceremony in numbers graduated according to the importance of the function. Thus Samuel Kiechel writing in 1586 says: 'Before the Queen marched her bodyguard. They are all tall, strong, picked men. There are said to be two hundred of them, but this day they were not all present. They bore gilt halberts and wore red coats trimmed with black velvet. On their coats in front and behind are the Queen's arms in beaten gilt silver.'

In the great Presence Chamber the Yeomen of the Guard, drawn up in lines in various positions, kept order. On occasions when a State banquet was given, or when the Queen dined in public,[1] one detachment was on guard as previously noted (p. 50), while the other served the different courses. The men of this latter detachment performed their duties bareheaded; and while serving, or when addressed by the Queen, they always knelt on one knee. These two customs, it should be remembered, were in use only during the reign of Elizabeth.

Since the Yeomen wore their hats at all other times when in attendance on the Sovereign, whether indoors or out, it is difficult to understand why they are shown in black *skull-caps* in the picture of Elizabeth at Blackfriars (Plate XLIII); or why the Gentlemen Pensioners in the same picture are bareheaded. Perhaps special consideration for the bald heads of these old men superseded a general order that no *hats* should be worn on this particular occasion.

Fig. 780

The French Ambassador, 1598, informs us that 'the Queen for her ordinary Guard has about one hundred and fifty Englishmen clad in red *velvet*, who live in the first chamber of her palace; and besides she has sixty Gentlemen that she calls her Pensioners, who are an ordinary part of her household, scions and gentlemen of good family.'

A slight change occurred in the tunic during the last ten years of Elizabeth's reign. The full puffed sleeves became shorter, little more than shoulder puffs; the horizontal gards disappeared from these reduced puffs, and were transferred to the elongated 'cuffs' on the upper arm. Sometimes one, sometimes two, gards are shown (*see* Fig. 780).

The Yeomen of the Guard numbered one hundred and fifty in the year 1601. Their active service equipment at this time is recorded as follows: 'The cuirass complete with breast and back pieces; taces, and tassets, and arm pieces; gorgets, morions (*see* Fig. 512), targets, muskets and musket rests, bandoliers for carrying ammunition, and long and short pikes.'

On the occasion of the funeral procession of Queen Elizabeth on 28th April 1603, the Yeomen of the Guard carried their halberds reversed and veiled in black.

[1] A custom very prevalent among Royalty.

## GENTLEMEN PENSIONERS

At the coronation of Queen Elizabeth the Gentlemen Pensioners wore rich suits of crimson damask and carried gilt battle-axes.

'This Princess in imitation of her father, Henry VIII, did admit none about her for Pensioners, Privy Chambermen, Squires of the Body, etc., but persons of station, strength, and birth.' Queen Elizabeth's pensioners and guard were 'always the tallest and goodliest gentlemen and Yeomen in the Kingdom,' though they were by this time evidently ceasing to be men of small fortunes: in fact, the wealth of the Corps must have been as noticeable as the high birth and physical prowess of its members. The Gentlemen Pensioners were held in very high esteem by Elizabeth, who treated them as personal friends and liked to have them in attendance near her on every possible occasion, and seldom, if ever, went on her progresses without a considerable number. When out in the darkness of the night they carried 'torch-staves' as well as their battle-axes.

It is stated that the Gentlemen Pensioners were at some time during this reign dressed all in black with black cloaks and golden chains about their necks; but this must have been when they were attending the Queen at some funeral ceremony. On the other hand, Elizabeth was fond of display and pageantry, and it is beyond all doubt that on other occasions these Gentlemen of Blood made a brave show in the Tudor colours of white and green, or crimson. In the picture of Elizabeth attending a wedding at Blackfriars, 1600, the Gentlemen Pensioners are seen, though not very distinctly; they all wear black cloaks with gold chains over their shoulders, but the other parts of their dress are of different colours, without uniformity.

At the Queen's funeral the corps were dressed entirely in black, if we may rely upon an Illum. MS. depicting this event. They were attired like ordinary gentlemen in doublets, slops, upper and netherstocks and shoes, ample cloaks, and high hats with round crowns and wide brims. They carried their halberds, of gilt garnished with crimson and gold like those in Plate XXIII B, point downwards, and covered with black.

# SECTION III: 1558-1603

## MIDDLE CLASSES—MEN

The social position of the *professional* classes was assured. Originally of the middle class, the learning of many gained them titles, sometimes, and so raised them to a higher sphere—the nobility. Harrison explains all this most aptly:

'The King doth dubbe knights, and createth the Barons and higher degrees,

Fig. 781. A Bishop

so gentlemen whose ancestors are not known to come in with William, Duke of Normandy (for of the Saxon races yet remaining we now make none account, much less of the British issue) do take their beginning in England, after this manner in our time. Whosoever studieth the laws of the realm, whoso abideth in the university, giving his mind to his book, or professeth Physick and the liberal sciences, or beside his service in the room of a captain in the wars or good council given at home, whereby his commonwealth is benefited, can live without manual labour and thereto is able and will bear the port [style of living], charge, and countenance of a gentleman, he shall for money have a coat of arms bestowed upon him by heralds, who in the charter of the same do of custom pretend antiquity and service, and many gay things, and thereunto, being made so good cheap, be called master.'

The Bishop of Lincoln (Fig. 781), although an ecclesiastic, appears in these pages from the funeral procession of Mary Queen of Scots, 29th July 1587, on account of his biretta, which is now in process of development into the square-shaped cap. It shows one of the earlier examples of the transition of the academic cap—a skull cap with a soft square top to it. After the Reformation 'a square cap without any stiffening which causes such corners to flap' took the place of the biretta amongst the Protestant clergy.

A square cap stiffened is seen in Fig. 854.

The scarlet robes of a judge are shown in Fig. 782, and consist of a long gown with sleeves turned back at the wrists with budge, a hood with deep cape edged with the same fur, a mantle lined with white and edged with budge, and a square black velvet or cloth cap, worn when not on the bench or tucked

into the black satin waist sash on State occasions. Underneath is the coif,
the 'principal and chief insignment of habit wherewith serjeants-at-law on
their creation are decked.' It should be noticed that the mantle is placed
*on top* of the cape, the hood being turned back over it. The mantle was worn
only at coronations, opening of Parliament, cathedral services, and on the
first day of term. A broad black silk scarf was sometimes hung round the
neck, stole fashion, when the mantle was dispensed with. These robes
remain in use up to the present day.[1]

Fig. 782. A Judge        Fig. 783. A Physician

In portraits of judges of the following centuries a 'modern' detail is always
in evidence, and that around the neck. In the Elizabethan and early Stuart
period it was the ruff; in the late Stuart the 'rabato'; in the Georgian, the
'cravat'; and in the nineteenth century the collar and tie.

Some judges were privileged to surround their shoulders with a collar consisting of a rose in the centre between two portcullises, SS, and cord knots,
like that worn by the Lord Mayor (Figs. 797 and 431).

The earlier austere monastic garb affected by the medical profession is now
out of date, and in Fig. 783 we see a physician of the Elizabethan era. His

[1] During the second half of the seventeenth century the periwig was worn over the coif which
was completely concealed by it; and in the reign of George II the white curled wig took the place
of the periwig, and this, with some modifications, became the judge's wig of the nineteenth and
twentieth centuries.

underdress is a suit of the period, and so is his flat black velvet cap.   The
wrap-over cloth gown of a dark colour or black, lined throughout or turned
back only with fur, has sleeves of the fashionable shape; and to the waist-belt
is attached a commodious pouch.   The professional coif of white linen, the
only symbol of his calling, is worn under the cap.   At the neck there is sure
to be a small ruff.   For a cap worn by an Italian doctor of medicine see Fig. 666.

A case of *cuir boulli* (Italian, of the sixteenth century, containing surgeons'
instruments) may be seen in the British Museum.

Fig. 784.        Fig. 785.
A Doctor and Student

Fig. 786.
A Schoolmaster

A don reprimanding an Oxford student (Figs. 784 and 785) clearly shows the
caps and gowns worn at the universities during the greater part of Queen
Elizabeth's reign.   These garments of black were, of course, worn over the
ordinary everyday dress of the period.   According to Anthony Wood 'the
Scholars are supposed in their dress to have imitated the Benedictine Monks,
who were the chief restorers of literature,' so that the gowns must have been
made of a soft woollen material.

Lord Burleigh's orders as Chancellor of the University of Cambridge
(1585) were as follows: 'They might walk in cloak and hat to and from the
fields.   Also within his College, Hall, Hostel, or Habitation it was lawful for
any student to wear a gown, or gaberdine of plain Turkey fashion with a
round falling cap without gard, welt, lace, cutte, or silk except one cutte in the

sleeves thereof to put out his arms only. . . . Also that every graduate wearing the above gown and gaberdine within the University or town out of his chamber or lodging do wear withal in the daytime a square cap and none other, no hat to be worn except for infirmities sake with a kerchief about his head, or in going to and from the fields, or in the street or open air when it shall happen to rain, hail, or snow; the hat which shall be worn to be black, and the band or lace of the hat to be of the same colour, plain, and not excessive in bigness, without feather brooch or such like uncomely for students.'

The gown of a schoolmaster is illustrated in Fig. 786, from the brass to the memory of Edward Harris, M.A., born 1534. He matriculated at Oxford 1564, and was appointed in 1570 first head master of Lord Williams's Grammar School, Thame. Master Harris was especially instrumental in founding the school, and was, in consequence, nominated for the period of his life, which ended in 1597. His hood, not worn in the brass, would have been of black cloth lined with white fur of superior quality. A bachelor's hood was similar, but lined with less expensive fur, which it retains to this day. Even undergraduates wore hoods at this period, longer in the point which hung behind (liripipe) and without any fur lining (see vol. ii, p. 213). Over his ordinary suit of cloth he wears his academic gown of black cloth slit up the sides and falling back down the open fronts. The conventional tubular sleeves are edged and frogged with black braid. His ruff is by no means smartly dressed.

Fig. 787.
A Gentleman, 1578

## GENTRY

The sixteenth-century opinion of what constituted a gentleman was very different from that held in the twelfth and following centuries (see vol. ii, p. 68).

According to William Harrison, any one who had the means to live comfortably without doing manual labour could be termed a gentleman. If he could afford to buy a coat of arms and register himself and his family at the College of Arms, he was, without doubt, a gentleman and an armiger, and would be addressed as 'esquire' or 'master.'

The gentleman dressed all in black (Fig. 787) is attending a society interment; nevertheless, his clothes are of the fashionable cut of the 1570's. His slightly padded doublet, with full sleeves and shoulder roll, has remarkably deep and full basques. His venetians are not stuffed, but form folds round the thigh, the lower part of the legs being clothed in netherstocks and ankle-boots.   The hat is of the Italian shape.

The two young gentlemen (Figs. 789 and 791) are escorting their lady friends to Bermondsey.   They come from the picture at Hatfield House painted by Joris Hoefwagel between 1582, when he came to London, and 1590.   Some authorities suggest that the painting dates 1570.   The ladies' costumes, if not the gentlemen's, have characteristics of that year.   The

Fig. 788.       Fig. 789.                    Fig. 790.            Fig. 791.
Ladies and Gentlemen at a Marriage Feast

clothes of the gentlemen are on the fashionable lines as worn by the nobility, and would be made of cloth.   The high-crowned hats, whether with wide or narrow brim, are much in vogue at this time.   Fig. 789 wears a buff doublet over dull pink trunks and hosen; his hat and cloak are black.   Fig. 791 is dressed entirely in black.

Two bright young people of the gentlefolk (Figs. 792 and 793) are performing a bow or 'reverence' prior to taking part in a dance.   They have gained their instruction in deportment from Thoinot Arbeau in his *Orchéso-graphie*, published at Langres in 1588.

'At the moment when the musicians begin to play make your reverence, holding the damsel by the hand.   To perform the reverence you will keep the left foot firmly on the ground and, bending the right knee, carry the point of the toe a little to the rear of the left foot, at the same time doffing your bonet or hat and saluting your damsel and the company as you see in this picture. When the reverence has been performed, straighten the body, and replace your bonet: then, advancing your right foot, bring and keep the two feet together. The reverence done, assume a goodly modest attitude.'

Fig. 792.        Fig. 793.
The Reverence of the 1580's

The pleasing young man (Fig. 793) is well dressed in a doublet of simple cut, having sleeves puffed on the shoulders; a fine lawn collar surrounds the high collar of his doublet. His slops are paned, and his hosen cross-gartered.

He is uncovered at the moment, and shows his hair dressed à la Don Juan.

Fig. 794 is a woodcut of Gabriel Harvey as caricatured by Thomas Nash in 1596. He is a fashionable young man, with his high-crowned hat and fierce moustaches, and is wearing rather antiquated paned slops, which is a vogue revived. The attitude of this young gentleman in getting out his purse to stand treat makes it obvious that *trouser pockets* were inserted in the amplifications of the slops. He is a good specimen of a gentleman of this decade.

The exploits of the sword-and-buckler man were somewhat handicapped by Proclamation. Two examples are given below:

'viij May 1562. Proclamation of the Acts of Array and great ruffs and great breeches, and that no man to have but a yard and half of kersey, that no sword be but a yard and a quarter in length of blade, and daggers but xij inches the blade and that bucklers shall not have long pikes, but of a fixed form.'

In 1580 another proclamation ordained further reduction in the length of

Fig. 794. Gabriel Harvey, 1596
*Have with you to Saffron Walden*

Fig. 795.
Young Gentleman, 1577

the sword blade to three feet. Pikes on bucklers were to be no more than two inches.

Fig. 795 shows a young gentleman of the 1570's and 1580's who is an expert in the art of sword-and-buckler play. He looks very smart in his doublet of cloth garded with black or dark velvet, but it is more in the fashion of the previous reign than of this. His hat with a high crown bulging at the top is more up to date, and his shoes are decorated with cuttes and loops. He is armed with a good long hefty sword and a *small* buckler known as a 'rondel,' 'rondelle à poing,' or 'boce.' This particular art of self-defence or aggression began to decline towards the end of the century owing to the increasing popularity of the rapier, which caused a certain amount of dissatisfaction.

One of the characters in *The Two Angry Women of Abingdon*, 1599, expresses public opinion in the following words:

'Sword and Buckler play begins to grow out of use . . . if it be once gone, this poking fight of rapier and dagger will come up: then a good *tall* Sword and Buckler Man will be spitted like a cat or rabbit.'

The word 'tall' was often used to mean courageous.

This country esquire (Fig. 796), Justice of the Peace and of the Quorum and Custos Rotulorum, 'who writes himself armigero [1] in any bill, warrant, quittance, or obligation,' is soberly and substantially clad in a gown with tubular sleeves of cloth decorated with bands of velvet. It is a comfortable garment worn over a suit of sombre hue, and girded with a leathern belt to which a pouch is attached. A set of small goffered cuffs and ruff, a hat perhaps of velvet, and a medallion or mounted jewel hung round the neck, add to the old gentleman's dignity.

Fig. 796. A Country Gentleman

## MERCHANTS AND BURGHERS

'Citizens and burgesses have next place to gentlemen, who be those that are free within the cities and are of some likely substance to bear office in the same. . . In this place also are our merchants to be installed as amongst the citizens, although they often change estate with gentlemen, as gentlemen do with them.'

English burghers and yeomen were all wealthy, and all, high and low, displayed great ostentation. Merchants still kept to the former gravity befitting burgesses, but their young wives were more frivolous than women of higher estate.

A Lord Mayor's show of the sixteenth century was very much as we see it on 9th November in our time. Several contemporary descriptions of it are extant, and mention that His Worship was accompanied by the sheriffs, aldermen, burghers, and craftsmen of the various city companies all mounted on goodly horses, and richly garbed with heavy gold chains about their necks. The Elizabethans loved pageants, and these played an important part in the procession; but a comic touch was given to the otherwise dignified proceedings by a row or two of servitors, who walked in front carrying squirts,

---

[1] One entitled to armorial bearings by birth, and very superior to those who have merely purchased them.

'such as are used for quenching a fire.    With these they squirted water at the crowd, for the street was full of people, so that they were forced to make way.'    An excellent idea for dispersing crowds.

The chief actor on the municipal stage was dressed, according to an eye-witness (1585), as shown in Fig. 797.    The robe or gown, worn over a very smart yet sober suit, was of scarlet velvet or cloth; some state that it was lined with ermine, others sable.    The cut of the gown is familiar, but from effigies of Lord Mayors and aldermen of this time one sees that the material is

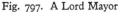

Fig. 797. A Lord Mayor                 Fig. 798. Lawrence Sheriff

gathered or pleated into a yoke at the back, and also that the tubular sleeve was intricately shaped at the back as shown in the drawing.    It is particularly mentioned that over the gown 'hung great golden chains, which before and behind reached to the girdles.'    A detail of the Lord Mayor's chain or collar is given in Fig. 431.    On the day of his election—28th October—both the retiring Lord Mayor and his successor wore gowns of pimpillo-brown cloth faced with ermine.    Over these they wore fig-brown hoods lined with squirrel. The hats on both occasions were of the usual Italian fashion in black velvet.

The mayors of Oxford, according to the brass to the memory of Randolph Flexney, who died in 1578, wore a gown shaped like the preceding but of red cloth; it appears to be quite plain, without any fur.    Round the neck is hung a black silk scarf or stole which reaches to the knees.

In Fig. 798 is seen a drawing of Lawrence Sheriff, a native of Rugby, who was apprenticed to a grocer in London and afterwards owned a first-class grocery establishment in Newgate Street.  He supplied the household of the Princess Elizabeth with groceries, and after she became Queen she made him an esquire and granted him a coat of arms.[1]  In 1561 he presented the Queen with a New Year's gift consisting of 'a sugar loaf; a box of ginger; a box of nutmegs, and a pound of cynomon,' and she returned the compliment by sending him 'oone guilt salt with a cover per oz. 7 oz.'  Sheriff was nominated

Fig. 799.
A Merchant of the 1570's

Fig. 800.
A Merchant of the 1590's

Vice-Warden of the Grocers' Company in 1566, and would have been Lord Mayor had he not died in 1567, leaving a wife, Elizabeth, but no children. He was the founder of Rugby School.

The gown in Fig. 798 is of the usual shape, which as a rule had long tubular sleeves with a slit at elbow level; but in this drawing, taken from a contemporary one, the top part forms a small shoulder cape with a long pendent end, somewhat similar to that shown in Fig. 797.  Livery gowns were at this time bereft of their gay colourings, being no longer made in the livery colours of the various companies, and as Stow relates (see p. 788) 'of the saddest.'

The best were of black silk, others of a kind of black material having the appearance of modern repp.  Lawrence Sheriff carries his chaperon (see

[1] Now the armorial bearings of Rugby School.

description under Fig. 623), parti-coloured crimson and violet, the livery colours of the Grocers' Company, by the tippet over his shoulder. The cap is of the fashion of Henry VIII's time in black velvet. For a description of the headgear of city aldermen refer to Stow on p. 788. Underneath the livery gown is worn the usual costume of the time; the sleeves on the forearm, the band or ruff, and the shoes only are visible.

This opulent burgher (Fig. 799), clutching his money bag, comes from a painting of Abingdon Bridge dated about 1590, and now in the hall at Christ's Hospital. It is supposed to represent Geoffrey Barbour, who took a leading part in the building of the bridge during the reign of Henry V. He is dressed, however, as a rich burgher of the sixteenth century, and affords another blatant example of the custom, arising from sheer ignorance, of painting people of past ages arrayed in costume of the artist's time. Barbour died in 1417; and the little that is seen of his dress, depicted in his brass in St. Helen's Church erected at this date, suggests it is exactly the same as shown in Fig. 582, vol. ii, except that he is wearing in addition a hood thrown back off his head. The costume in Fig. 799 is reminiscent of that worn during the reign of Henry VII: long under-robe with close-fitting sleeves, over-robe with tubular sleeves and lined with fur, and bonet. The only Elizabethan touches are the tiny ruff, and the slight raising of the sleeves on the shoulders.

Fig. 801. A Schoolboy

Fig. 800 shows the unpretentious dress of a well-to-do burgher of the 1580's and 1590's. His suit of cloth is of the ordinary cut, and with it he wears netherstocks over his upperstocks, and an ample cloak reaching down to his knees. This is a good example of the ordinary dress of the people in general.

As has been mentioned before, boys of all periods were dressed like their fathers. This may appear, to their modern counterpart, excessively uncomfortable as restricting their freedom of movement; but, because for many generations these garments had been customary, such complaints would not even occur to William Brome (Fig. 801). He is shown at the age of ten on his brass in Holton Church, Oxon, wearing a slightly padded doublet, full slops, upperstocks and netherstocks, and (for additional comfort or because he is in full dress) an ample cloak.

All readers of this book will agree that a tailor was a very important person despite the fact that Harrison classifies him with 'the last sort.' The Queen and both sexes of the nobility thought differently, and thoroughly appreciated his skill. Besides creating marvellous costumes, tailors manufactured 'pavilions for our Kings, robes of State for our nobles, and tents, etc., for our soldiers.' They also condescended to become 'makers of ordinary garments by stitching jerkins for our prentices, doublets for our shopmen, and trunk-hose for our cooks.' Linen armourers, makers of linen garments to wear under armour, were associated with the tailors.

A Spanish tailor is shown in Fig. 672, and an Italian tailor was honoured by having his portrait painted by Moroni. It can be seen in the National Gallery, London, No. 697.

## LONDON APPRENTICES

Here is an apprentice (Fig. 802) of the early years of Elizabeth's reign. Compared with Figs. 337 and 338 the dress has not altered much, the only difference being in the collar of the tunic, which is surmounted by a neatly goffered band.

Fig. 802.
Apprentice of the
1560's–70's

Luxury in clothing prevailed amongst the London apprentices as it did amongst people of all degrees. The merchants, naturally enough, disapproved of such ostentation on the part of their apprentices: and in consequence the Lord Mayor and Common Council enacted the following *Regulations recommended for the Apparel of London Apprentices* in 1582:

'That from thenceforth no Apprentice whatsoever should presume, (1) To wear any apparel but what he receives from his Master.

(2) 'To wear no hat within the City and Liberty thereof, nor anything instead thereof, but a woollen cap, without any silk in or about the same.

(3) 'To wear no ruffles, cuffs, loose collar, nor other thing than a ruff at the collar, and that only of a yard and a half long.

(4) 'To wear no doublets, but what were made of canvas, fustian, sackcloth, English leather, or woollen cloth, and without being enriched with any manner of gold, silver, or silk.

(5) 'To wear no other coloured cloth or kersey, in hose or stockings, than white, blue, or russet.

(6) 'To wear little breeches, of the same stuffs as the doublets, and without being stitched, laced, or bordered.

(7) 'To wear a plain upper coat of cloth or leather, without pinking, stitching, edging, or silk about it.

(8) 'To wear no other surcote than a cloth gown or cloak, lined or faced with cloth, cotton, or bays, with a fixed round collar, without stitching, garding, lace, or silk.

(9) 'To wear no pumps, slippers, nor shoes, but of English leather, without being pinked, edged, or stitched; nor girdles, nor garters, other than of crewel, woollen, thread, or leather, without being garnished.

(10) 'To wear no sword, dagger, or other weapon but a knife; nor a ring, jewel of gold, nor silver, nor silk in any part of his apparel.

'That no apprentice should frequent, or go to any dancing, fencing, or musical schools, nor keep any chest, press, or other place for the keeping of apparel or goods, but in his Master's house.'

Here are two of these jolly fellows (Figs. 803 and 804), apprentices of the 1580's and onwards. They filled the pit at the theatre, and indulged in all kinds of pranks and escapades, to say nothing of smashing windows and pates with their cudgels. They are dressed as regulations prescribed. The caps should be noticed: Fig. 803 has a knitted woollen cap, like that

Fig. 803.     Fig. 804.
Apprentices of the 1580's-90's

in Fig. 855, while his companion, wearing his winter 'surcote' or cloak, sports a wool cap of the only type which might bear slight ornamentation in needlework.

## YEOMEN

'Yeomen,' says Harrison, 'are those, which by our law (and lawyers) are called "Legales hommes," free men born English, and may dispend of their own free land in yearly revenue to the sum of 40s. sterling—or six pound as mony goeth in our times.'

'Yeoman—a settled or staid man—married and of some years, betaketh himself to stay in the place of his abode for the better maintenance of himself and his family.'

But the yeoman soon ceased to be a stay-at-home.

'This sort of people have a certain pre-eminence and more estimation than labourers, and (the common sort) of artificers, and these commonly live wealthily, keep good houses, and travel to get riches. They are also for the most part farmers to gentlemen, and with grazing, frequenting of markets, and keeping servants (not idle servants as the gentlemen doth, but such as get both their own and part of their masters' living) do come to great wealth, insomuch that many of them are able, and do buy the lands of unthrifty gentlemen, and often setting their sons to the schools, to the universities, and to the Inns of Court; or otherwise leaving them sufficient lands whereupon they may live without labour, do make them (their said sons) by those means to become gentlemen.'

Yeomen were not addressed 'Master,' but 'Goodman,' as 'Goodman Smith.' 'In matters of law these and the like are called thus Giles Jewd, yeoman, by which addition they are exempt from the vulger and common sorts.'

The wealth of English yeomen always attracted the envious attention of foreigners. 'Many a yeoman here keeps greater state and a more opulent table than the nobles in Germany. He must be an unskilled farmer who does not possess gilt silver salt-cellars, silver cups and spoons.'

Fig. 805. A Farmer

A yeoman in his best attire would pass for any well-to-do burgher, and his costume is exemplified in Fig. 800.

An opulent farmer living in the wilds of the country is seen in Fig. 805. His cote or coat is not unlike that worn by Fig. 610, except that it is made of cloth or linen.[1] It is worn over his shirt, to which the small ruff is attached, but he has a doublet at home. Trunk hose, hosen, long boots of soft leather, and a curiously shaped straw hat comprise his outfit when attending a market at the nearest town.

## LOWER CLASSES

A young man of the people (Fig. 806) is quite smartly dressed. Over his linen shirt with turned-down collar and cuffs, he might wear a doublet, but our friend here has a jerkin of soft leather with a turned-down collar,

---

[1] Ancestor of the smock worn by countrymen.

and fastened by pewter buttons. To this, sleeves of cloth are tied at the
shoulders by ribands, so that when the fancy takes him he can wear his jerkin
without sleeves, exposing those of his shirt which he could roll up at will.
His trunk-hose or slops, of moderate proportions, are of cloth braided and
stitched with a contrasting colour. The hosen are hand-knitted, or perhaps
they are the latest machine-made, and are tied with garters. A cloth cloak

Fig. 806.
A Dashing Young Fellow

Fig. 807. A Master Seaman
(late sixteenth century)

is slung from the back, and the hat of beaver or felt has pheasants' feathers
stuck through the band. Altogether a pleasing costume.

No history of costume of the Elizabethan era is complete without a description of the dress worn by seamen. It must be understood that at this time
there was no recognized uniform, but a serviceable outfit was provided for
men attached to the Navy.

Fig. 807 is taken from a woodcut on a work on *Navigation* by Mariner Mar-
tine Curtis, and shows a master seaman of the latter part of the sixteenth
century. The jacket, sometimes with sleeves, sometimes without, is cut to
fit the shoulders, and hangs in folds to just below the waist-line; this one has

close-fitting sleeves, and fastens with one button at the throat, and is not unlike that worn by Chaucer's shipman (Fig. 374, vol. ii). Under this was worn a shirt with small collar of white Hamborough linen or canvas. The galli-gaskins of coarse cloth, cut very wide and pleated into a waist-band buckled in front, taper down and fasten round the knee. These and the jacket were made of woollen cloth or rugge lined with canvas. His stockings are of thick knitted wool or kersey and his shoes of strong leather. The high crown cap of cloth lined with canvas turns up round the head to form a brim. A seaman always carried a dagger or knife slung to the waist-belt,

Fig. 808. An Admiral's Whistle

and some more important seamen had a whistle hung round the neck, a master mariner's being of silver and a high officer's of gold.

Fig. 808 shows a mariner's whistle and chain from the painted glass in Castle Hedingham Church. It was the badge, charged with a mullet, of the thirteenth Earl of Oxford as Lord High Admiral.

The power of the magnet was known as early as the twelfth century, and by the sixteenth century the mariner's compass became the germ of the new science of navigation, and was being used by all the seamen of Europe. The seaman (Fig. 807) holds one in his left hand, and in his right a 'cross-staff' or 'forestaff,' a contrivance for measuring the angles between the fixed stars or the sun and the sea horizon.

The seaman (Fig. 809) comes from an Illum. MS. and belongs to the 1590's. His doublet is just an ordinary one like those worn by people in general, but his leg-coverings called 'trousers' are a distinctive item of nautical dress. These were made of coarse white linen and frequently striped with colour: in the drawing a spiral band of two colours encircles the leg. Socks or stockings of any shade and black shoes were worn ordinarily, but on deck seamen

Fig. 809. A Seaman, 1580's–90's

often went bare-footed; and a full-fledged seafaring man was hardly ever without his tobacco and pipe. Fig. 810 shows a sixteenth-century clay pipe four and a half inches long from bowl to mouthpiece. According to a foreigner the art of smoking has changed very little since Elizabethan days; for he tells us that 'the English are constantly smoking tobacco and in this manner: they have pipes on purpose made of clay, into the farther end of which they put the herb, so dry that it may be rubbed into powder, and putting fire to it, they draw the smoak into their mouths, which they puff out again through their nostrils, like funnels, along with it plenty of phlegm and defluxion from the head.'

The flat cap worn by the seaman (Fig. 809) was of knitted wool, and known at this time as a 'Monmouth cap' (see p. 734). A 'thrum cap' was also worn by sailors (see inset) and this is described on p. 734.

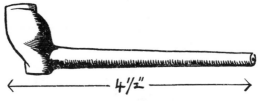

Fig. 810. A Clay Pipe

A person of no importance volunteered his services under Don Juan of Austria for the extermination of the Turks.    On the morning of the Battle of Lepanto, this soldier lay sick of the fever in the *Marquesa*, the flagship of Giovanni Andrea Doria,[1] but rose, sought, and obtained the command of twelve soldiers posted in a position of importance exposed to the hottest of the enemy's fire.    There he remained until the battle was over at four of the clock, receiving the only distinction ever conferred upon him—the loss of 'the movement of his left hand for the honour of the right.'    Don Juan, Doria, and Colonna, world-wide heroes of the sixteenth century, joined their ancestors and were forgotten, for who in the twentieth century has ever heard of them?    The warrior sleeps in the Convent of Trinitarian Nuns, Madrid; his work is known to all the world, for every one has read *Don Quixote*.

Fig. 811. Cervantes, 1571

Miguel de Cervantes was baptized at Alcalá de Henares, 9th October 1547, and studied at Salamanca and Madrid.    His early career was adventurous; some time after his Lepanto experiences he was captured by Algerian pirates (1575), and made galley-slave for five years until he was ransomed.    From 1582

[1] Nephew and heir of the great Andrea Doria (see p. 386).

he was writing copiously for the stage, so that it seems unlikely that he served at sea again. The immortal *Don Quixote* appeared in Madrid in 1605, and instantly attained such popularity that it was translated into almost every language.

Cervantes died in his house in the Calle de León, Madrid, 23rd April 1616. Fig. 811 is from a portrait pronounced by a great authority on the subject to be a good likeness, and shows the kind of hat sometimes worn by Spanish seamen (*see also* Figs. 342 and 343).

## PEASANTS AND THE POOR

'The Last sort of People of England are day labourers, poor husbandmen, and some retailers (which have no free land) copyholders, and all artificers,

Fig. 812. A Peasant or Farm Hand    Fig. 813. A Peasant

as tailors, shoemakers, carpenters, brickmakers, masons, etc. As for slaves and bondmen we have none'—which is not quite true about bondmen. 'Labourers have neither voice nor authority in the commonwealth, but are to be ruled, and not to rule others.' 'Husbandmen and artificers were never so excellent in their trades as at this present.'

Although we of to-day may think that the lower classes of the sixteenth century were downtrodden, they loved their Queen and were very grateful to her.   They were certainly happier during her reign than they had ever been before and long retained an affectionate regard for her memory.

In Fig. 812, a well-to-do farm hand in working kit wears a heuk of coarse linen over an ill-fitting doublet or shirt bound at the waist by a leather belt; his breeches are of cloth, his stockings of thick knitted wool, and his rather clumsy shoes of black leather.   Various hats were worn, but most of them had wide brims and were made of cloth, felt, or straw.   A leather wallet is slung over his shoulders, and he carries a shepherd's crook with shovel-like end.

As regards the real poor, their style of clothing was much the same as that of the early Tudor period, its chief characteristics being a long-sleeved tunic reaching to the knees, cloth hosen, and a felt or straw hat. They were usually content with the cast-off clothing of their betters.

Fig. 814.
Leper's Rattle

There is a trace of the medieval lingering in this (Fig. 813) costume of a peasant.   The tunic is loose, made of a coarse material fastened up the front by two straps and bound at the waist with a strap to which a pouch is attached.   Sometimes full slops are seen worn under the tunic; the legs are covered with ill-fitting hosen, often tied below the knee, and the feet thrust into cockers.   A hood sometimes took the place of a hat, but often both were worn, as of old.   If necessary a cloak would be thrown over the shoulders.

A poor man is described at this time as 'having an old ragged doublet, and a torn pair of breeches with his hose out at heels, and a pair of old broken slip shoon on his feete, a rope about his middle instead of a girdle, on his head an old greasie cap, which had so many holes in it that his haire started through it.'

The enclosures for sheep pasture had been going on since the beginning of the century and in consequence many peasants were deprived of their livelihood and turned adrift.   The dissolution of the monasteries (1536–9) greatly increased the number of beggars, outcasts, and vagabonds, many of whom had previously lived in the service of the monasteries, and now had to take to the roads and huddle on common or waste land.   These, the genuine paupers, known as the 'upright,' swelled the lawless throng considerably, joining dispossessed monks and 'rufflers'—men disbanded from the army, with their families.   'Counterfeit cranks' simulated all kinds of ailments and diseases, including leprosy if they cared to ostracize themselves from the public (though not from their fellows) by carrying a leper's rattle (Fig. 814). Of wood, the centre was rigid, the two flaps being attached to it by a piece of leather.

'Clapperdudgeons' ingeniously disfigured their persons with artificial sores and wounds, besides being ever ready with a dagger.   Most of them were addicted to strong liquors whenever they got a chance of purloining any; in fact, the word 'booze' first came into use among them.

Fig. 815 is a vagabond of the most dilapidated sort, whose threadbare and ragged garments beggar description. The hat (probably stolen) is the only respectable part of his attire: cloak, 'patched and unseemly' cote, hosen in process of separation into fashionable upper- and netherstocks, and single shoe, all combine to produce a picturesque ensemble. His wallet is interest-

Fig. 815. A Vagabond      Fig. 816. A Gaoler with Keys

ing because it shows the primitive method of rolling up his few belongings in a piece of material and tying it to a strap over the shoulder, as first mentioned under Fig. 91.

From such a plausible vagabond to a gaoler is but a step. One can hardly place a gaoler (Fig. 816) socially, but his position *after* a vagabond is suitable. His clothes are very ordinary: a leather tunic over the doublet as a safeguard against molesting, slops, hosen, and shoon. The block felt hat has a twisted hatband. A bunch of keys (*one inset*) is attached to his waistbelt by a chain, and he carries a rod. This drawing is made from an engraving of Alexander Andrew, the brutal gaoler of Newgate.

## MIDDLE-CLASS WOMEN

Foreign visitors were naturally interested in Englishwomen, and commented favourably upon their good looks and smart appearance; the amount of liberty they enjoyed caused no little surprise. Thus: 'The women are charming and by nature so mighty pretty. They do not falsify, paint, or bedaub themselves [?] as in Italy or other places; but they are somewhat awkward in their style of dress: they dress in splendid stuffs, and many a one wears three cloth gowns or petticotes, one over the other.' Again: 'The women are beautiful, fair, well-

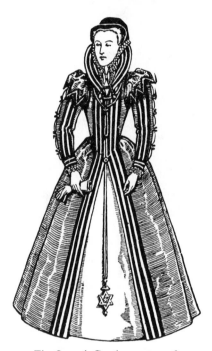

dressed, and modest—they go about the streets without any covering either of huke or mantle, hood, veil, or the like. Married women only wear a hat both in the street and in the house; those unmarried go without a hat. Ladies of distinction cover their faces with silken masks or vizards.'

'The women have much more liberty than perhaps in any other place; they also know well how to make use of it, for they go dressed out in exceedingly fine clothes, and give all their attention to their ruffs and stuffs. All English women are accustomed to wear hats and gowns cut after the old German fashion.'

In fact, 'the womenfolk in England wish to be in at everything.'

### GENTLEWOMEN

The disdainful lady (Fig. 817) steps from her portrait dating 1567. Her high collar and ruff have been alluded to under Fig. 607, but the shoulder pieces

Fig. 817. A Gentlewoman, 1567

are rather unusual. The dress is of black silk banded with black velvet, and is of the style worn by gentlewomen in both town and country during the first half of the reign, indoors as well as for walking. An Elizabethan lady when out walking had one man servitor before, and another behind.

The drawing (Fig. 818) is of Catherine, the second wife of Randolph Flexney, Mayor of Oxford, and is taken from the mural enamelled brass in St. Michael's Church. She died in 1567 and her husband in 1578, so the costume shown is that worn as a 'best gown' during the 60's and 70's. There is an old-fashioned touch about the black velvet partlet and the turned-back sleeves of the red cloth dress; as also about the false sleeves of cloth of gold

and the white waist scarf. The skirt with a short train edged with passamayne opens over a black velvet underskirt. The headdress is shown in

Fig. 818. Mistress Flexney, 1567

Fig. 819. fflorence Wyndham, 1572

more detail in Fig. 887. This costume was worn by the lady when she joined
her husband at municipal ceremonies.

This lady (Fig. 819) possesses the unusual name
of fflorence.[1] She is the wife of John Wyndham, Esq., of St. Decumin's, Watchet, who died
in 1572, to whose memory this dutiful spouse
erected the brass which includes herself, although
she did not pass out until twenty-four years
later. The style of dress is that worn during
the period 1565–75, and the material would be
cloth or perhaps velvet, braided with silk or gold.
The mahoitered sleeves are very up to date
with their slashings and braidings. Fig. 820
gives this sleeve on a larger scale. The cross-
barred braided sleeves on the forearms are in
the fashion of the moment. Fig. 949 is a rubbing
of the pattern on the under-skirt (not shown in
Fig. 819) which doubtless was a brocade. The

Fig. 820. Mahoitered Sleeve

[1] It has usually been understood that Florence Nightingale was the first to bear this name, having
been born at Florence in 1823.

reader should notice the French hood and the ornament at the end of the girdle. Her shoe is described under Fig. 902.

One of Mary Stuart's many faithful attendants is represented in Fig. 821, which is taken partly from a portrait and partly from a contemporary engraving, dating 1572, of Mary Ann Waltham, who was with the Scottish Queen during her imprisonment at Fotheringay Castle. Her dress is of black silk garded with black velvet. The bodice is cut low off the shoulders; the sleeves fit closely below the elbow, and are mahoitered above; surrounding the waist-line are small loops of the same materials. The chemisette is

Fig. 822. A Lady of 1571
(Crest of the Goldsmiths)

Fig. 821 (*left*). Mistress Waltham, 1572

embroidered with fine black silk over the folds of the white cambric round the throat, low-cut shoulders, and bust. There is a necklace of jet beads; and a girdle of black leather, decorated throughout with cut steel, holds the black velvet pouch with mirror. The headdress is given in Fig. 868.

The original grant of crest and supporters to the arms of the Goldsmiths' Company, dated 1571, shows the crest of a demi-lady rising from clouds above the crest-wreath. This was 'tricked' and tinctured at the time, and the lady is dressed in the fashion of that year. She is drawn to a larger scale in Fig. 822. The dress is violet velvet trimmed with gold passamayne, and notice should be taken of the lines on the bodice. Mahoitered sleeves are of velvet, with close ones of turquoise blue silk banded with gold, and white puffings; the under-skirt is of cloth of gold. A small ruff surrounds the face above a stand-up collar of black velvet, to which the white lawn partlet is attached; over this is placed a carcanet of jewels. The headdress of blue silk and gold has an attifet front which surrounds the puffed-out hair. Scales of the period are just like modern ones, only these have a loop with a tassel hanging from the top (*see also* p. 763).

The two ladies (Figs. 788 and 790), although visiting Bermondsey some time in the 1580's, are not so up to date in their costumes as the gentlemen accompanying them. The all-in-one garment worn by the lady (Fig. 790), of maize colour braided with black over an under-skirt of turquoise blue, is very similar to the over-robe shown in Fig. 607, but the fawn hat and feather,

| Fig. 823. Mistress Southcote, 1585 | Fig. 824. Mistress D'Arcy, 1593 |

as also the black hat worn by the other lady (Fig. 788), are definitely of a later period. The latter wears a fawn dress with a gold-coloured under-skirt. Each lady carries a small wrap draped over the right forearm, and both are obviously unmarried—their partlets being open at the throat.

Fig. 823 represents the dress with over-robe worn by many women of gentle birth and position during the latter part of the reign, and frequently met with in effigies and brasses. This is from the effigy of Elizabeth, wife of Sir John Southcote at Witham, who died in 1585. The plain underdress is of black silk, the front of the pointed bodice being buttoned up to the high collar supporting the small ruff. The overdress is of black velvet, with two rolled shoulder pieces and full sleeves. It is turned back with sable. The whole, which resembles that of Mary Stuart (Fig. 602), is of dignified richness and simplicity. It must be borne in mind that such ladies were shown wearing their best gowns, which often dated twenty years earlier.

The gentle damosel (Fig. 792) wears a simplified edition of fashionable attire of the 1580's, although the sleeves are not very up to date and at the neck is a wide frill instead of a goffered ruff. The hairdressing, of course, is quite stylish.

Margaret Syllyarde, the wife of Thomas D'Arcy of Tolleshunt D'Arcy (Fig. 824), well represents the costume of her class, and dates 1593. The dress is in the same style as Lady Southcote's underdress, but with the

Fig. 825. Dame Steward, 1596        Fig. 826. A Widow        Fig. 827

skirt open up the front. The full sleeves are decorated with embroidery after the French fashion.

There is quite a French flavour, too, about the dress worn by Dame Steward (Fig. 825) and yet it is not unlike Fig. 824. The only differences are that the former wears a larger ruff and the sleeves are spirally puffed or padded, a mode quite usual at this time. The French hairdressing is un-covered, whereas Mistress D'Arcy and Lady Southcote wear French hoods. The front of the bodice in both figures shows the same lines and absence of decoration; though Mistress D'Arcy's is formed of folds of silk, the other being of braids. The effigy of Dame Steward at Teversham, Cambs, dates 1596.

The kneeling figure (Fig. 826) of Dame Constantia, 'widdow' of Sir Thomas Lucy, Kt., of Charlecote, Warwickshire, who died in 1603, shows widow's garb at the end of the century. The plain black silk or cloth dress is of fashionable cut, worn over the wheel farthingale, and has a wide fold of the same material hanging from the shoulders down the back and well on to the ground. Over this is worn a hood lined with white, wired out to frame the face and ruff. A side view is given in Fig. 827.

'Mistress Minx, a *Merchant's* wife, that will eat no cherries forsooth, but when they are at twenty shillings a pound, that looks as simperingly as if she were besmeared, and jets it as gingerly as if she were dancing the canaries:

Fig. 828. A Merchant's Wife

Fig. 829.
Fig. 830.
Town Gossips

she is so finical in her speech, as though she spake nothing but what she had first sewed over before in her samplers, and the puling accent of her voice is like a feigned treble, or one's voice that interprets to the puppets. What should I tell how squeamish she is in her diet, what toil she puts her poor servants unto, to make her looking glasses in the pavement? How she will not go into the fields, to cower on the green grass, but she must have a coach for her convoy; and spends half a day in pranking herself if she be invited to any strange place?' The merchant's wife in Fig. 828 well illustrates Thomas Nash's description of 1592; she might be one of the Merry Wives of Windsor.

The details of the doublet are taken from the original in the London Museum, made of a dull red woollen stuff spotted with white. The black braidings down the front and forearms are frayed at the ends, and fixed down with a button in the centre. The welts, wings, and cuttes are edged with the same braid. A bolster sets her skirt well out at the back. 'The women also hath doublets and jerkins, as men hath here, buttoned up the breast, and made with wings, welts, and pinions on the shoulder points, as man's apparel is in all respects.'

'Good morrow, Mistress Gossip; how by my truly I am glad to see you in health.' No doubt the conversation soon turns to the subject of clothes,

Fig. 831. An Elizabethan Spinster

in which Fig. 830 would have a decided advantage by reason of her smarter costume—in fact, her companion seems to be meditating a reply *when* given the opportunity. Both are typical women of the bourgeois class. They step from an Illum. MS. dated about 1568. Fig. 829 is the simpler of the two, and in the original her dress is of grey woollen material with a collar and garding of black velvet. The under-sleeves are treated somewhat in the same manner as shown in Fig. 819, but appear to be tucked and banded with braid. The under-skirt is a dull pink, and she wears a posy on her bosom.

The other (Fig. 830) is in a rich brown garded with black velvet; her under-skirt is pink ornamented with appliqué work. A white sash is tied round the waist, and both carry gloves.

## LOWER CLASSES

The spinster (Fig. 831) of the latter part of the century, is a cheerful little person and sits all alone, so the contemporary saying 'Women's tongues are like lambs' tails which seldom stand still' cannot apply to her. She is using the old-fashioned wheel to wind bobbins, revolving the wheel with her left hand and with the other guiding the flax or wool from off the winder to the bobbin which is set in the spindle.

Spinning-wheels with a treadle attached were invented by a German in 1533, but they were not in general use in England until about this time.[1]

This woman (Fig. 831) is plainly dressed in a dark gown, with just a touch of smartness in the rolled shoulder pieces and well-fitting pointed bodice. The starched collar denotes that she belongs to the latter part of the century.

The dress of the laundress (Fig. 718) is homely, but a certain modishness is given to it by the turn-over collar, puffs on the shoulders, and smart little ruff. The sleeves which extend to the wrists are rolled up, as she is so much engaged with her goffering.

This sober matron (Fig. 832) going to market is not above doing a bit of charing now and again. 'Chare-women' were pretty general in the second

Fig. 832. A Market Woman

half of the century, and some of these ladies had a liking for the bottle. 'Brains waxt as mellow as a pippin at Michaelmas' was said of an old woman who drank too much. This good woman (Fig. 832) appears in her best gown of substantial woollen cloth, in dull greens, browns, or blues and banded with black velvet. Under the bodice and over the shift or chemisette was often worn a corset-like bodice, usually without sleeves, but occasionally with close-fitting ones. The apron is almost indispensable with this class of person, and so is the pouch. It must be a fine day for her marketing, otherwise she would have a cloak.

Fig. 833. A Farmer's Wife

The country woman (Fig. 833) is clothed in brown homespun, a white linen apron, ungathered and pinned round the waist like a towel, a folded kerchief round her shoulders, and a muffler over her mouth as a protection against cold.

[1] No spinning-wheel of the late sixteenth century seems to have survived in England.

It should be noticed that some of these women of middle and lower class are wearing goffered ruffs and turnover collars to their bodices, and carry gloves, thus adding greatly to their respectability.

A young country girl of the early and middle part of the reign is shown in Fig. 834. The plain stuff dress has a full skirt gathered to a bodice which is tied up the front with bows of riband: the full sleeves are also tied on in the same way, and could be dispensed with at will. This dress is lined with cotton, perhaps of ochre colour, which is seen on the turned-down collar and where the skirt is turned up to show a striped petticote. The stand-up ruff is attached to the chemisette, and the sleeves of the latter are rolled up because this young person is very business-like.

Fig. 834. A Country Girl

Another treatment of a bodice is shown in A. This would be worn over a similar chemisette, with a skirt of the same or of a different material. A third bodice is shown in B, which was attached to the skirt. It buttons up the front, and has a roll collar, loops on the shoulders, and sewn-on sleeves.

Since a wedding interests only the womenfolk the following description of

*A Tudor Country Wedding Procession*

is inserted in the section devoted to them, although it also includes the costume of the men. The details are taken from an account of an actual wedding at which it was hoped the Queen, who was staying in the neighbourhood, would be present. Those taking part were marshalled thus:

'First, all the lusty lads and bold bachelors of the parish, suitably every one with his blue buckram bridelace upon a branch of green broom (cos rosemary is skant there) tied on his left arm (for at that side lies the heart), and his alder pole for a spear in his right hand, in martial order ranged on afore, two and two in rank: some with a hat, some in a cap, some a cote, some a jerkin, some for lightness in his doublet and his hose, clean trussed with a point [of the doublet] afore: some boots and no spurs, he spurs and no boots, and he neither nother: one a saddle, another a pad or a pannell fastened with a cord, for girts [girths] were scarce; and these to the number of sixteen active riding men and well beseen: but the bridegroom formost, in his father's tawny worsted jacket (for his friends were fain that he should be a bridegroom before the Queen), a fair straw hat with a capital crown steeple-wise on his head: a pair of harvest gloves on his hands, as a sign of good husbandry: a pen and ink-horn at his back; for he would be known to be bookish: lame of a leg that in his youth was broken at football: well beloved yet of his mother that lent him a new muffler for a napkin that was tied to his girdle for loosing. After these horsemen, a lively Morris dance, according to the ancient manner, six dancers, Maid Marian, and the fool. Then, three pretty pusels, as bright as a breast of bacon, of a thirty year old apiece, that carried three special spice-cakes of a bushel of wheat (they had it by measure out of my Lord's bakehouse) before the Bride: coyly with set countenance, and lips as demurely simpering, as it had been a mare cropping of a thistle. After these a lonely lubber walked, freckle-faced, red-headed, clean trussed in his doublet and his hosen taken up now in deed by commission, for that he was so loth to come forward, for reverence belike of his new cut canvas doublet; and would by his good will have been but an onlooker, but found to be a meet actor for his office: that was to bear the bridecup, formed of a sweet sucket barrel, a fair turned foot set to it, all seemly be-silvered and parcel gilt, adorned with a beautiful branch of broom, gaily begilded for rosemary: from which, two broad bridelaces of red and yellow buckram begilded, and gallantly streaming by such wind as there was (for he carried it aloft). This gentle cupbearer, yet had his freckled physiognomy somewhat unhappily infested as he went, by the busy flies, that flocked about the bridecup for the sweetness of the sucket that it savoured on: but he like a tall fellow, withstood their malice stoutly (see what manhood may do) beat them away, killed them by scores, stood his charge and marched on in good order.

'Then followed the worshipful Bride, led (after the country manner) between two ancient parishioners, honest townsmen. God wot, and an ill-smelling was she; a thirty year old, of colour brown bay, not very beautiful indeed, but ugly, foul ill favoured; yet marvellous fain of the office, because she heard say she should dance before the Queen, in which feat she thought she would foot it as finely as the best. Well, after this bride came there by two and two, a dozen damsels for bridesmaids: that for favour, attire, for fashion and cleanliness; were as meet for such a bride as a wooden ladle for a porridge pot.'

A few notes are necessary to explain some of the details in the above.

The 'lusty lads' escorting the bridegroom would be wearing clothes of all styles, the genuine country louts in garments like Figs. 812 and 813. The more polished, if such there were, might appear garbed as Fig. 805, or even 806. Each lad carried an accessory to show that he was a good horseman, and also to suggest that he formed one of a mounted escort. The 'pannell' carried was a saddle, a treeless pad without cantle, such as was generally used when riding a donkey. The awkward 'lonely lubber,' like so many of his type, looked most unsuitably dressed in his smart new-cut doublet. Had he the good sense to appear in his everyday peasant togs, clean and tidy, he would have cut a much more presentable figure. 'Sucket' was a confection of fruits preserved in sugar, either candied or in syrup. The bridegroom himself would certainly endeavour to rig himself out smartly, either as shown in Fig. 806, or even 800. It is particularly stated that he wore a jacket or jerkin, which was probably at least twenty years old, having been worn by his father. The crown of his hat was high—quite in the fashion of the time. The costume worn by Fig. 806 would suit this young man admirably.

The three 'pretty pusels' or maidens of not too tender years would be in the style shown in Fig. 834, but, of course, with the skirt let down. The bridesmaids were clothed much the same, and probably had made themselves new dresses for the occasion.

For a description of the wedding dress of a Tudor bride of middle class, we use the *Delectable Historie of Ihon Winchcombe*, as this work was not published until 1596. The descriptions nevertheless apply to the costume of the reign of Henry VIII as well as to that of Elizabeth.

Winchecombe's first wife was a widow much older than himself, and possessed a considerable fortune. In fact, it was her money which financed the business of the wealthy clothier 'Jack of Newbury,' as he was familiarly known.

The second Mistress Winchecombe was a young woman, and we have a description of her as she appeared on her wedding day. She wore 'a gown of sheep's russet and a kyrtle of fine worsted: her head attired with a billiment of gold and her hair as yellow as gold hanging down behind her curiously combed and plaited after the manner of those days. Shee was led to Church between two sweete boyes, with Bridelaces and rosemary tied about their silken sleeves.'

Her head attire consisted of a network caul on either side of the head, but no veil is mentioned because such an accessory was not included in a Tudor bride's wedding dress. The special adornments of a bride of the sixteenth century were rosemary and bridelaces; little posies of the former were set in the headdress or worn on the left side of the bodice, and attached to these were long narrow streamers of silk in green and blue known as 'bridelaces.'

# SECTION IV: 1558–1603

## HAIRDRESSING—MEN

Men's hair during the reign of Elizabeth was generally short, and several variations were introduced from abroad during the period. There was the French mode, which was short and sometimes included a wisp of hair on the cheek; the Italian, short and curled with tongs; and the Spanish, short, but long at the ears. The English nobility and gentry as a rule preferred the French (*see* p. 725) and Spanish (*see* p. 726) styles to the Italian.

While the above national characteristics will be found to be generally correct the differences between them are actually small, so that a fashionable man of any country might adopt any style which pleased or suited him.

Perhaps the simplest and most convenient style is that shown in the drawing (Fig. 835) of Philip II about 1565. The hair is quite short and straight, and smartly brushed from the forehead and temples.

The style of hairdressing worn by fashionable men in the early years of the reign is seen in Figs. 609, 611, 618, and 619. The hair was brushed forward from the crown of the head, forming curves of hair on the forehead and temples; sometimes it was long at the ears and curled. This is the early Spanish mode, and a side view of it is seen in Fig. 537.

Fig. 835. Philip II of Spain, 1565

The portrait of Sir Philip Sidney, 1577, No. 2096 in the National Portrait Gallery, shows slightly wavy hair brushed up off the face—an intermediate stage between Figs. 835 and 843.

Soon after 1571 (Lepanto) a new Spanish mode, set by Don Juan of Austria and shown in Fig. 843, was adopted by self-respecting men of all ages. The hero's hair was naturally beautifully waved, worn fairly long all over the head, and moderately brushed back: his admirers, less blessed by nature, imitated this style artificially. It is worn by the courtier (Fig. 621); the gentleman (Fig. 630) has adopted this Spanish method of brushing his hair back, but the embryo lovelock is French.

Hair curled by nature or artifice in the Italian style was becoming more

721

favoured, and we see it in the portrait of Sir Henry Lee dated 1568, No. 2095 in the National Portrait Gallery. Fig. 836 is a drawing of it.

For a typical style of hairdressing for men of middle class during the greater part of the reign, the portrait of the tailor by Moroni, No. 697 in the National Gallery, is a good example.

Harrison writing about the middle of the reign, and commenting upon the variety of styles, 'will say nothing of our heads, which sometimes are polled, sometimes curled, or suffered to grow at length like women's locks, many times cut off, above or under the ears, round as by a wooden dish.'

The fashions in hairdressing for the period covered by Part II are well illustrated in the various drawings commencing with Fig. 734.

The young gentleman (Fig. 837) has his hair smartly brushed off the forehead and sides in the true Don Juan style, but he has included a wisp of hair

Fig. 836. Sir Henry Lee, 1568

Fig. 837. Aetat. xxiij

or lovelock in front of his ears. His moustaches are dressed with a sticky preparation and neatly twisted into small points; his beard of fluff is as much as he can grow at the early age of twenty-three.

Toward the end of the century it was the mode for gentlemen to 'cut their hair close on the middle of the head, letting it grow on either side. The noblemen (Figs. 739 and 740) wear their hair decidedly long over the ears, but it is anything but close cut on the middle of the head.

It was at this period that gentlemen with scanty locks, who yearned to be in the mode, had resource to 'perriwigges' (1595); Shakespeare refers to this when he describes one of the actors in *Hamlet* (Act III, Sc. ii) as a 'periwig-pated fellow,' a ruffian whose length of hair hung about the ears and 'curled like the two ends of an old cast periwig.'

Regarding these fashions we learn from Stubbes that the barbers 'have invented such strange fashions and monstrous manners of cuttings, trimmings, shavings, and washings, that you would wonder to see. They have one manner of cut called the French cut, another the Spanish cut; one the Dutch

cut, another the Italian; one the new cut, another the old; one of the bravado-
fashion, another of the mean fashion; one a gentleman's cut, another the
common cut; one cut of the court, another of the country, with infinite the
like varieties, which I overpass. They have also other kinds of cuts innumerable; and therefore when you come to be trimmed, they will ask you
whether you will be cut to look terrible to your
enemy, or amiable to your friend, grim and
stern in countenance, or pleasant and demure
(for they have divers kinds of cuts for all these
purposes, or else they lie).'

Beards and moustaches were very general
among men of all classes, and the fashions in
dressing the beard are too numerous to describe. Many kinds may be seen by referring
to the various drawings; Figs. 712, 851, and
854 give three varieties. Harrison writes:
'Neither will I meddle with our variety of
beards, of which some are shaven from the chin
like those of Turks, not a few cut short like
to the beard of Marquess Otto, some made
round like a rubbing-brush, others with a
*pique de vant* (O! fine fashion), or now and then

Fig. 838. The Pique de Vant

suffered to grow long, the barbers being grown to be so cunning in this behalf
as the tailors. And therefore if a man have a lean and straight face, a Marquess
Otto's cut will make it broad and large; if it be platter-like, a long, slender
beard will make it seem the narrower; if he be weasel-beaked, then much
hair left on the cheeks will make the owner
look big like a bowdled hen, and so grim as
a goose, if Cornelis of Chelmeresford [1] say
true: many old men do wear no beards at all.'
The dressing of the beard known as pique de
vant, (Fig. 838) is seen worn by Henry III of
France (Fig. 745), Henry of Navarre (Fig.
842), and Dr. Nevill (Fig. 712).

Besides these numerous styles and cuts of
beards there were the following: the swallow-
tail cut mentioned in 1596; this was also called
a fork-beard, and is seen in Fig. 839; it is
worn by Prince Philip (Fig. 670) and by the
gentlemen (Figs. 845 and 854). 'The broad

Fig. 839. The Swallow-tail

or cathedral beard, so called because bishops and grave men of the Church
anciently did wear such beards.'

---

[1] Nothing seems to be known of this worthy, but from the context he would seem to have been
the author of a book on hairdressing. How interesting such a book would be if only a copy could
be discovered.

'The British beard has long mochedoes [mustachios] on the higher lip, hanging down either side the chin, all the rest of the face being bare; the mouse-eaten beard is when the beard groweth scatteringly, here a tuft and there a tuft.' A 'bodkin beard' was pointed; a spade beard is shown in Fig. 840, and a 'great round beard like a glover's paring-knife' in Fig. 841. This tool, now obsolete, is shown inset. A Cain-coloured beard was small and yellowish red, so called because in old tapestries Cain (and Judas) were represented with such beards.

Fig. 840. The Spade

'Then when the barbers had wasted a lot of time and concluded all these feats . . . it is a world to consider, how their mustachios must be preserved and laid out, from one cheek to another, yea, almost from one ear to another, and turned up like two horns towards the forehead.'

The barber asks in 1591: 'Will you have . . . a pent-house on your upper lip [a straight tooth-brush moustache] or an ally on your chin? A low curl on your head like a Bull, or dangling locke like a spaniell? Your Mustachoes sharpe at the ends like shoemakers' aules, or hanging downe to your mouth like goates' flakes? Your love-lockes wreathed with a silken twist, or shaggie to fall on your shoulders?'

Small brushes, carried in the panes and cuttes of the slops, were made expressly for the use of the beard and moustache: these, together with ornamental beard combs and 'an instrument for dividing the hair'—a comb —known as a 'gallon,' were much used, even in public.

Although the Earl of Essex is shown in Fig. 734 as a comparatively young man, he wears a full beard. It should be borne in mind that during the Elizabethan period the beard was a very much coveted appendage, and all young men of fashion anxiously cultivated its growth. Remembering this, Rosalind's kind offer, made in the epilogue of *As You Like It*, has considerable point:

Fig. 841. The Round

'I would kiss as many of you as had beards that pleased me.'

This is particularly so if the part was played by a boy!

### FRENCH HAIRDRESSING

The French style of hairdressing during the middle of the sixteenth century was similar to that worn at the present time, the hair being cut short.

After 1571 the hair was allowed to grow a little longer, and was brushed off the forehead in the Spanish fashion. This is shown in Figs. 654 and 655; in the nobleman (Fig. 658) it is even more pronounced.

A 'lac d'amour,' nœud, or wisp of hair, known in England as a 'love-lock,' and worn on the cheeks in front of the ears, originated amongst the coxcombs of France, and was adopted by some gentlemen of England (*see* Fig. 630). The style adopted by young Henry of Navarre about 1580 (Fig. 842) is decidedly distinctive. His hair was naturally wavy and wiry, and stood up from the head, while that of his brother-in-law, the Duc d'Anjou (Fig. 656), fast falling off from too much application of dye, is probably a periwig. 'Per-ruque' was the French for a lock of hair, and the words 'peruke' and 'periwig' are derived from it. In his later portraits as King Henry III a peruke is obvious (*see* Figs. 745 and 746). He evidently retained a certain amount of hair on his forehead which enabled him to brush it up over the peruke, thus masking the hard line.

Fig. 842. Henry of Navarre

The youth (Fig. 751) has his hair rolled back to perfection, equal to any of the ladies. By the time Henry of Navarre came to the throne, his hair must have become more amenable, or the Royal barber, in his 'checkerd-apron,' must have been specially at work for the 'sitting' of this (Fig. 752) portrait. It is certainly not so wild, and more in the mode of the day.

The type of beard worn at the French Court during the reigns of Francis II and Charles IX is illustrated in Fig. 845. Later, under Henry III, they became very pointed—the pique de vant—with little if any hair growing on the sides of the face; and moustaches were narrow with the ends turned up and sometimes down (*see* Figs. 745, 746, and 749). In Henry IV's time moustaches became more normal.

### ITALIAN HAIRDRESSING

The styles of hairdressing worn by the Italian aristocracy are illustrated in Figs. 662 and 663. The young noble (Fig. 761) has adopted the earlier Spanish style, while the later Spanish mode is to be recognized in Fig. 664. Hair crimped with curling tongs was fairly general among Italians, but the coiffure worn by the gentleman in Fig. 759 suggests the East End of London in the twentieth century.

Beards dressed in the style most usual all over Europe are worn by the noble in Fig. 848 and by the doctor (Fig. 666) as well as in Fig. 759.

Only the length of hair over the ears distinguished the hairdressing characteristic of Spaniards from their contemporaries in other countries.    Most of the hair was cut close to the head like that worn by the upper classes in England and on the Continent.

Fig. 843 is made from the colossal statue of the Hero of Lepanto, 1571, Don Juan of Austria in full armour.    It was erected at Messina in 1572, and

is one of the masterpieces of Andrea Calamech.    It shows the method with which he dressed his golden hair—the envy of all the young bloods of Europe. Admiring him, most likely, more for this than for all his feats of military or naval glory, they made haste to cultivate the same style.    The hair is waved and left moderately long, and is brushed and combed up and back off the forehead and puffed slightly above the ears, the ends mingling in waves with the hair on the back of the head.    The more sober of the Spanish grandees displayed nothing out of the ordinary in their hairdressing; Fig. 768, typically Spanish of the earlier period, is an example.    The hair is allowed to grow rather long over the ears and to curl slightly at the ends.    That worn by the Spanish Infante (Fig. 770) has the ends rolled back over the ears.

Fig. 843.
Don Juan of Austria,
1571

With regard to beards, reference to Fig. 671, the usual style, and to Fig. 670, the forked or swallow-tail type, will show those generally worn during the period 1556 to 1580, when mustachios were quite normal.

During the latter part of the period—to 1603—those shown in Figs. 767 and 768 illustrate the style usually worn.    The beard and mustachios seen in Fig. 769, were not unusual and certainly have distinct character.    In Fig. 853 very little beard appears, and the ends of the mustachios turn up slightly.

## HEADGEAR, 1558–1603

In this section the division hitherto adopted, into two periods and separate countries, cannot be followed, as it is practically impossible to distinguish the various national styles.    During the first twelve years of Elizabeth's reign, the flat velvet cap, described in Chapter III, was the usual headgear of the nobility, gentry, and (in other materials) of the lower classes.

Afterwards, the crown of the cap became slightly fuller. Those shown in Figs. 653 and 611 are definitely of the flat or plate variety of older fashion, the former worn by a French, the latter by a Scottish, nobleman. The cap worn by the gentleman (Fig. 610) is in this later mode; and to prove how

Fig. 844. Charles IX, 1566         Fig. 845. Duc de Guise

universal the wearing of this type of headgear was at this period, Fig. 844 gives a French cap. It is from a portrait drawing of Charles IX made by Clouet in 1566; the same shaped cap is worn by this King in Fig. 650 (1569). In Fig. 845, a similar shaped cap, the decoration of portions of passamayne set at angles on the crown and brim, is shown; the braiding and aiglettes on the doublet of this French nobleman should be observed. Fig. 670 shows the same kind of cap worn by Philip II, and Fig. 666 by an Italian doctor.

## HATS

It was about 1570 that a new shaped hat, imported from Italy, came into general fashion among well-dressed men everywhere, and became a serious rival to the flat cap. For the first appearance in this book, refer to Figs. 662 and 663—two Italian gentlemen of the late 1560's and onwards. The crown of the hat is much fuller, and the material—velvet or silk—is lined with something moderately stiff, such as a coarse muslin or fine buckram, to give richness to the folds and to prevent them from flopping too much. The crown is pleated into the brim of moderate width in Fig. 662, with a hatband to conceal the join. Fig. 663 has the same kind of crown, but the brim is very narrow and almost covered by a rouleau of twisted velvet which forms the hatband.

Possibly the introduction of this new kind of hat from Italy into England was due to the young Earl of Oxford in 1573. It is seen in Fig. 846, a drawing from his portrait; and has a much more exaggerated crown of folded velvet, a narrow brim, and a band of two rouleaux fixed by pairs of gold buttons at intervals. The hat is most rakishly worn on one side, this being a feature of young coxcombs at this period. The dignified Knights of the Garter (Fig. 623) wear similar hats, but of much more reasonable proportions and poise.

Fig. 847—this is Mr. Edward Hoby (born 1560, knighted 1582, died 1617), a smart young gentleman in his eighteenth year, who as a nephew of Lord

Fig. 846.
The Earl of Oxford, 1573

Fig. 847.
Edward Hoby, Esq., 1577

Burleigh had the entry into High Society. His youth must be the excuse for his outrageous headgear. It is made on the same principle as that worn by Lord Oxford, but is tilted at a more moderate angle; it has some beautiful gold ornaments set round the hatband, and a straight plume of deep crimson. The two gold buttons and acorn placed towards the top strike one as odd; but such fancies often took modish men. The same eccentric arrangement of the crown is apparent in the hat worn by the Duc d'Anjou in 1573 (see Fig. 656); the hatband is of gold cords caught by jewels in gold settings.

Lord Burleigh (Fig. 624), Lord Leicester (Fig. 625), and Sir Christopher Hatton (Fig. 627), all wear this type of hat, but with moderate-sized crowns, much more like the original Italian hats, shown in Figs. 662 and 663.

An Italian hat of 1589, worn by an Italian nobleman, is shown in Fig. 848. Made of velvet, usually black, the crown is cut and pleated, as mentioned earlier, into a stiff and slightly rolled brim. The join between this and the crown is masked by a fold of silk or a band of velvet, a rose or bow being placed at the side. The appearance of the crown clearly indicates that it is mounted on a stiff lining or foundation. The skull-cap worn underneath probably suggested to the ladies of Europe the use of cauls beneath their chapeaux à l'Italienne. The patterned or embroidered material used for the doublet of this gentlemen (Fig. 848) should be noticed; it is of a bold and effective design in keeping with the Italian mode.

The hat worn by Philip III of Spain (Fig. 771) although of later date (1598) is of the same shape.

Hats with stiff or hard foundations appeared in fashionable England about 1575. An actual hat of this period is in the London Museum, and Fig. 849 is a drawing of it. The crown is hard and shaped like an inverted flower-pot, and covered with a small patterned black silk and velvet brocade. The brim

Fig. 848. The Italian Hat

is bound with a small fancy braid; and the hatband is of folded satin twisted

Fig. 849

round with a braid three-eighths of an inch wide, with loops of braid one-eighth wide forming bows along its length (*inset*). The dimensions of the hat are: brim of plain black velvet $1\frac{1}{2}$ inches wide and $30\frac{1}{2}$ in circumference; the crown is $5\frac{3}{4}$ inches high and 23 round the base. The hat worn by Sir Henry Unton, 1586 (born 1557, died 1596) (Fig. 850), is shaped very much like Fig. 849, except that the top of the crown is rounded. The black silk is moulded to the foundation by silk thread worked into a pattern. The hatband of twisted silk is very wide, and almost covers the moderately wide brim. The ornament at the side is of a new design in gold and black enamel, and from it spring the fronds of an ostrich feather and an aigrette.

Sir John Hawkyns (Fig. 851) wears a hat of similar fashion which has a brim very much curled up at the sides.   The stiff crown is covered with black velvet pleated down to the hatband, the latter being ornamented with pearl and diamond buttons.   The button with the silver pin stuck through it is, indeed, a pretty conceit.   This Italian hat, worn at a jauntish angle by the admiral, shows that this famous sea-dog did not disdain the latest fashion even at the age of fifty-eight.

In Spain this type of hat was the vogue, and it is seen in Fig. 767.

Fig. 850.
Sir Henry Unton, 1586

Fig. 851.
Sir John Hawkyns

Simultaneously with the hats last described was worn another of a slightly different kind (Fig. 852) from the original in the London Museum.   It is of soft light-biscuit-coloured leather, blocked stiff and decorated with cuttes and brown silk stitchery.   The lining is rose-coloured satin which is pulled through the cuttes.   Descending from the top of the crown across the brim are strips of leather with brown silk braid down the centres and brown silk stitches set diagonally (see at A): the hatband is trimmed in the same way. A button fixes the top.   The flat brim, which is of double thickness, has the under-part of brown leather, cutte as shown in the portion B.   The dimensions are: brim, $1\frac{1}{2}$ inches wide and 34 in circumference; crown, 8 inches high and $28\frac{1}{2}$ in circumference at base.   In the centre front is embroidered a coat of arms of seven gold fleurs-de-lys on a blue shield.   In the drawing, the centre back is shown where there is a holder of leather and brown braid fixed to take the quill of a feather. Most feathers were attached to the hat in this manner. Hats of soft or blocked felt having high crowns and small brims were worn in England and on the Continent from about 1570 onwards. Figs. 616 and 617 show two of this kind.

In France, headgear, as lately described, was popular at the Court of Henry III, although this monarch adopted the turban (Figs. 745 and 746) which was copied by a very select few (*see* Fig. 751).

The blocked felt worn by the courtier (Fig. 750) is high-crowned with parallel sides and a moderately wide flat brim, and is decorated in front with an upstanding plume. The Duc de Joyeuse (Fig. 749) wears a similar one, but with a narrower stand-up brim edged with gold and a panache of ostrich feathers in front. Henry IV has placed his hat on the table beside him (*see* Fig. 752). Its brim is rather wider than usual. In Spain these blocked black felt hats were very general; the crowns varied in height (*see* Plate XLVI

Fig. 852

and Fig. 769) and their brims were usually narrow, a Spanish characteristic (*see also* Fig. 767). Brims also went to the other extreme, and were very wide; but these were worn by the Spanish people of all classes as a protection from sun or rain, the name 'sombrero' being applied to them.

The life-size equestrian portrait by Rubens, painted in 1602, of the Duke of Infantado, chief of the family of Mendoza and first Grandee of Spain, furnishes us with a very smart and *becoming* hat at the beginning of the seventeenth century (Fig. 853). It is probably made of black felt, but its shape could also be carried out in black velvet, silk, or satin. Its wide brim is caught on one side to the fez-shaped crown by a large ornament of jewels, in which is set a brush of black feather-fronds.

This style of hat soon found its way into England, for we find Sir Walter Raleigh painted in the same year wearing one (*see* Fig. 742). It is true it is not so large as the Spanish original, and the brim is just caught by the pointed bejewelled feather with peardrop pearl.

The date of the appearance of this stylish hat in England may be earlier if the satirist, John Marston, in his lines of 1598 is referring to this style: 'His hat, himself, small crown and huge great brim, and all the band with feathers he doth fill, which is a sign of a fantastick still.'

It is interesting to reflect that this particular befeathered shaped hat became a very handsome piece of headgear in the seventeenth century.

However, hats with high crowns were in very general use at the end of the reign, as evidenced by many contemporary illustrations.

The 'copatain' hat, i.e. coppid-peaked, of high conical or sugar-loaf shape, is represented in several drawings (Figs. 789, 791, and 798). It was usually made of blocked felt with a brim of varying width.

Fig. 853. The Duke of Infantado

Two hats of curious shape are shown in Figs. 795 and 805. The former is of blocked felt; that of the farmer is in plaited straw: both have twisted hatbands, one of silk, the other of cloth with a cord round it.

A hard blocked hat of cloth with a twisted hatband is worn by the gaoler, Fig. 816. This type of headgear was in very general use during the latter part of the reign.

A soft felt hat of conical shape, such as was used in the fifteenth century, was still worn by the commonalty, a thong of leather or cloth being tied round it to make it fit the head. The shape of one is well seen in Fig. 806, where it is decorated by a band of colour and three pheasant's feathers, but the peasant (Fig. 813) has only a plain band of cloth or leather. (*Refer also to* Figs. 90 and 105.)

Stubbes, as usual, unburdens himself of many caustic gibes at the expense of the headgear worn by his better-dressed fellows:

'Sometimes they wear them sharp on the crowns, pearking up like a sphere, or shaft of a steeple, standing a quarter of a yard above the crown of their heads; some more, some less, as please the phantasies of their minds. Othersome be flat and broad on the crown, like the battlements of a house. An other sort have round crowns, sometimes with one kind of band, sometimes with an other; now black, now white, now russet, now red, now green, now yellow, now this, now that, never content with one colour or fashion two days to an end . . . their Hattes be made diverse also; for some are of silk, some of velvet, some of taffetie, some of sarcenet, some of wool: and which is more curious, some of a certain kind of fine hair. These they call Bever hattes of xx, xxx, or xl shillings price fetched from beyond the seas, from whence a great sort of other varieties do come. And so common a thing it is, that every servingman, countryman, and other, even all indifferently, do wear of these hattes. For he is of no account or estimation amongst men, if he have not a velvet or a taffatie hatte, and that must be pincked and cunningly carved of the best fashion; and good profitable hattes be they, for the longer you wear them the fewer holes they have. They have also taffeta hatts of all colours quilted, and imbroydered with gold, silver, and silks of sundry sorts, with monsters, antiques, beasts, foules, and all manner of pictures and images upon them, wonderful to behold. Besides this, of late there is a new fashion of wearing their hatts sprung up amongst them, which they father upon the Frenchman, namely to wear them without bands; but how unseemely (I will not say how assy) a fashion that is, let the wise judge. . . . An other sort (as phantastical as the rest) are content with no kind of hatt without a great bunch of feathers of diverse and sundry colours, peaking on top of their heads, not unlike (I dare not say) cockscombes.'

Unfortunately, few of these curiosities have been handed down to us in portraits.

## CAPS

A 'mortar-board' of the latter part of this reign is worn by Gabriel Goodman, Dean of Westminster 1561–1601, in his portrait bust in Ruthin Church, Fig. 854. The square top is thick, about an inch, and is attached to a cap pointed on the forehead and covering the back of the head to the level of the lobes of the ears. For the headgear of another Doctor of Divinity, see Fig. 781; of the Law, see Figs. 782, 783, and 666. Caps worn by members of the universities are shown in Figs. 784 and 785.

A cap, a development of the French bonet, is worn by the liveryman (Fig. 798), and hats modelled on the Italian fashion are seen in Figs. 797 and 796.

Knitted wool caps were much worn by apprentices and young men of the lower orders. School-boys were supposed to wear caps, and the Colloquies contain directions

Fig. 854. The Dean of Westminster

as to what was to be done with them: but boys went bareheaded when they could and despised the cap as effeminate.

The construction of these caps is explained under Fig. 377; and Fig. 855 shows an Elizabethan boy wearing one of these wool caps.

Another kind of wool cap, chiefly worn by apprentices, is seen in Fig. 804; this is flower-pot shape, and round it some kind girl friend (or his mother) has worked three rows of coloured wool.

Sailors also wore a knitted woollen cap, something like Fig. 855, but more

Fig. 855. Woollen Cap

of the nineteenth-century tam-o'-shanter shape. This kind was known as a 'Monmouth cap,' and is well shown in Fig. 809. During the first part of the sixteenth century the best were made at Monmouth. In 1590 the manufacture removed to Worcestershire, but the name of Monmouth caps[1] was still retained.

For extra warmth seamen often wore a cap that fitted tight, and could not be blown off. It was composed of coarse canvas shaped like a shallow flower-pot; the ends of the wool, cut off from woven lengths of cloth, were knotted through the canvas like wool mats to-day. Such caps, known as 'thrummed caps' (see inset, Fig. 809), had a shaggy appearance, and were dyed a brown or blue.

The master seaman (Fig. 807) wears a superior cap of cloth made like an elongated flower-pot and fairly stiff to stand up high: the base of it is turned up to form a brim and show the lining. The hat worn by the Spanish marine (Fig. 811) is exactly like the felt hat with a brim which one often sees to-day.

For the description of *night-caps* see p. 617.


### ETIQUETTE CONNECTED WITH HEADGEAR

Raising the hat was a fashion in vogue at the Court of Burgundy towards the end of the fifteenth century, and became universal on the Continent during the sixteenth century and in England during Elizabeth's reign (see Fig. 736). Towards the end of the century it became the general custom for gentlemen to remove their hats indoors, and in the presence of the Queen out of doors. Certain people had the privilege granted them by the sovereign to wear their hats in the Presence. This hereditary privilege was recognized in France from this time almost to the beginning of the nineteenth century. In the two celebrated paintings of a Court ball given at the Louvre in the 1580's, several of the gentlemen have their hats on, and, of course, the bridegroom (Fig. 749), who was a special friend of Henry III.

The custom of remaining uncovered in the presence of the Queen, which had grown up (perhaps more in compliment to her womanhood than to her

---

[1] Fluellen in *Henry V* says that Welshmen wore leeks in their Monmouth caps (Act IV, Sc. vii). It must be remembered that this play was first acted in 1599, and Monmouth caps were well established before this date. But in the days of Henry V they were unknown. Another snag!

sovereignty) during the early years of her reign (if not during Mary's) became firmly established before the end of the century. Thus: on one occasion in 1597 when the French Ambassador was summoned to an audience with the Queen, who was awaiting him in the Privy Chamber, De Maisse writes that he was led 'across a chamber of moderate size wherein were the Guards of the Queen and thence into the Presence Chamber, as they call it, in which all present, even though the Queen be absent, remain uncovered.' The same observer relates that when in the Queen's presence 'because I was uncovered, from time to time she signed to me with her hand to be covered, which I did. Soon after she caused a stool (*see* p. 619) to be brought, whereon I sat and began to talk to her.'

Visitors from abroad noticed that all the gentlemen in attendance on the Queen were bareheaded. 'Whoever speaks to her, it is kneeling; now and then she raises some with her hand.'

It was considered bad form to appear in a hat on public or ceremonial occasions without a cloak or gown over the doublet. The privilege of remaining covered, not only at Court, was fairly common during the sixteenth century in cases of *baldness, ringworm,* or *other scalp diseases.*

It may be surprising to learn that the male portion of the congregation kept their hats on in church, and more astonishing still that they were covered during the celebration of Mass.

## HAIRDRESSING—WOMEN: 1558–1603

At the commencement of the Elizabethan period the hair was dressed simply, as in the two previous reigns. The portrait of the Queen (Fig. 571) shows it so arranged, with the side hair brought slightly forward in a small puff. This method is also seen in Fig. 575. Fig. 540 exemplifies the usual style adopted by most ladies when wearing the French hood, as described in Chapter III.

A side view, showing the hair somewhat raised on the top of the head, is seen in Fig. 549. This also shows a small caul of gold network and pearls used to encase the hair at the back of the head. In several figures the caul may be seen worn in this manner. It was the usual way of decorating the knob of hair when the headdress worn exposed the back of the head (*see* Fig. 592).

During the period that the French hood was of narrower proportions (*see* Fig. 867), the hair was very little puffed, to make it conform with the line then in vogue.

For some years after Elizabeth had ascended the throne, hair of all natural colourings was the mode. As the popularity of the Queen increased, the ladies of the Court and aristocracy craved for hair of the same colour as the Queen's. This was easily achieved, of course, by the aid of dye, and before the end of the period covered by Part I every woman of fashion wore hair of auburn, gold, or bright yellow. These colours predominated during the remaining years of Elizabeth's reign, few ladies having the courage to differ from the rest.

The machinations of fashionable women are thus described by a contemporary:

'They are not simply content with their own hair but buy other hair, dyeing it of what colour they list themselves. And if there be any poor woman that hath fair hair these nice dames will not rest, till they have bought it.'

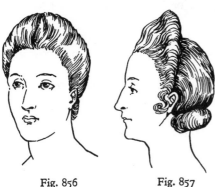

Fig. 856          Fig. 857

The fashion for using the crescent-shaped pads worn in France (*see* p. 738) was not popular amongst English ladies. Sometimes one sees in portraits the style described under Fig. 860, but in a much modified and less rigid form, which suggests that the hair was arranged without the use of pads.

To magnify their height, these winged and farthingaled Court ladies of the latter part of the reign built up their heads with quantities of curls and puffings mounted on false hair pads known as 'attires of false hair,' or—a simpler way of achieving the same ends—wore immense wigs called 'bourns.' At the opening of Part II the fashionable hairdressing is seen in Fig. 725, where the hair is drawn up high over pads placed on *top* of the head. A tiara (1555) is set above this.

The mysteries of the coiffeur's salon are thus revealed to us by a mere man, and he a Puritan: 'Then followeth the trimming and tricking of their heads in laying out their hair to the show, which of force must be curled, frisled, and crisped, laid out on *wreaths* and *borders* from one ear to an other. And least it should fall down, it is under-propped with forks, wires, and I can not tell what, rather like grim stern monsters, that chase Christian matrons.' 'Wreaths' and 'borders' here mean plaits or braids of hair encircling the head.

Lady Southwell (1582) (Fig. 726) has her hair dressed in the same manner as Fig. 725, and surmounted by a wreath of silver work and jewels (*see* p. 750).

The development of this high hairdressing can be traced through Figs. 728, 729, and Plate XLIV, all of which have accentuated the height by adding wreaths or garlands, cunningly and curiously wrought. The hairdressing of Fig. 732 is completed by a high jewelled ornament, almost like a crown, which gives increased height. Queen Elizabeth obviously much liked this style of hairdressing, it being easily adopted by means of built-up wigs. Many of the Queen's later portraits show her high 'hair frizzled, crimped and curled beyond the limits of nature. This added height was sometimes bought at the price of Royal dignity. 'Coming once to visit Lord Burleigh [1591], being sick of the gout at Burleigh House in the Strand, and being much heightened with her head attire (as the fashion then was), the Lord's servant who conducted her through the door said, "May your Highness be pleased to stoop," the Queen returned "For your Master's sake I will stoop, but not for the King of Spain's."'

At other times Elizabeth wore wigs of circular shape, not so lofty, and a mass of curls.

Ladies of the provincial aristocracy and gentle-folk in the early 1590's began to adopt the earlier French fashion of using crescent-shaped pads as a foundation for their hair. This style is frequently met with in the effigies of noble families to be found in country churches. It is seen in Figs. 856 and 857. In front the hair is taken up over one pad, moderately high in the middle and tapering down to the ears. The side view shows that the hair forms a decided ridge at the back. In front it is slightly puffed in the centre, and

Fig. 858. 1590's

the hair at the back is smoothly taken down into a small roll in the nape. Sometimes a row of small curls surrounds the forehead and temples as shown in Fig. 858, which shows the coiffure of a young girl. It is doubtful if a pad is used in this case; but the hair is pushed up high on top to give the same effect by the gold band set with jewels, whence the hair flows freely on to the shoulders.

The lady (Fig. 872) wears the same style of hair-dressing as shown in Figs. 856 and 857, but with a row of curls on the forehead like Fig. 858.

## FANCY HAIRDRESSING

The hairdressing worn by Venus, referred to under Plate XXVIII, is shown in Fig. 859. It is simple compared with that seen in Fig. 413, and much more attractive.

Fig. 859. 'Venus'

The very wavy golden hair, bespangled with gold, is parted in the centre and drawn upward and back from the temples: the ends are plaited, and entwined with a very narrow silver riband and a string of black pearls. The extremities of the plaits are formed into a loop or 8, and bound by one of the encircling plaits to the centre over the parting. At this point a red enamelled star, in a narrow gold setting, is fixed, and from it hangs a pendent sapphire.

Another example of fanciful French hairdressing combined with a head-dress is to be seen on the arm of the French chair in the portrait of Queen Elizabeth (Plate XLII).

### FRENCH HAIRDRESSING

By the time Charles IX ascended the throne in 1560 a new way of dressing the hair came into fashion.   Straight or waved hair was combed off the fore-head and temples over two pads shaped like crescents, called ARCELETS (Fig. 860), forming two bandeaux and producing the effect of a top-of-a-heart or Cupid's bow: the point where the ends of the two pads met coming in the centre of the forehead.   The remainder of the hair was dressed in a flat coil in the nape of the neck, or sometimes a little higher.   This arrange-ment of hair is much more pronounced and formal than that shown in Fig. 540, which is the earlier style both in France and England.   In some instances a little curl of hair is worn in front of the ears, and this may be seen in Fig. 882 and later in Fig. 757.   Queen Elizabeth of France is shown in several of her por-traits wearing her hair dressed in this manner, chiefly

Fig. 860. 'Arcelets'

with a headdress.   In Fig. 659 she wears a jewelled escoffion shaped like that of Mary Stuart (Fig. 599).

Queen Louise (Fig. 660) is coiffured in this type of hairdressing without any headdress or ornament.   Later, during the 1580's, this Queen of France is seen in Fig. 754 with an ornament of small black feathers, made up into a triangle with a few pearls.   This is fixed rather forward on the head just behind the arcelets.   The ladies of the Court of Henry III dressed their hair as shown in Fig. 755: the pads lost their crescent shape and became a single, semicircular pad, quite flat at the top, or a series of such pads one behind the other, framing the forehead.   A back view of the same style is given in Fig. 756, which shows that small plaits of hair, arranged horizontally, are attached to the head by bows or other ornaments.   Low in the nape of the neck the ends of hair were done into a coil.   An aigrette fixed with a jewel was often set at the side.

The coiffure of Marguerite, Queen of Navarre, and after 1589 Queen of France, is arrived at by the same methods, but (as can be seen in Fig. 757) it is much larger and altogether more massive.   It has a small, hardly notice-able puff in front, springing from a peak high up on the forehead, a new touch.   This hairdressing is framed at the back with pearls arranged in points.

Marguerite de Valois had very beautiful black lustrous hair, of which she was very proud; but as time went on much of its beauty and substance dis-appeared.   'She did not like the fashion in vogue much and seldom used it, but preferred perukes most daintily fashioned.' Towards the end of her life, when she returned from Usson to hold her Court in Paris, she became antiquated, with no black hair of her own to dress; but ever resourceful, she made great display of blonde perukes. For these she kept a brigade of golden-haired footmen, who were shorn of their locks from time to time to supply Her Majesty's wigmakers. Unconventional as ever 'she never hid behind a mask like other ladies of our Court, for nearly all the time she went uncovered,' it being the custom with most ladies in high circles to wear masks in public.

As would be expected, Marie de' Medici, on her arrival in France on 6th December 1600, was wearing her hair in the Italian mode—that of Rome, if we are to rely on Rubens's portrait (see Fig. 758).

Fig. 861.
Gabrielle d'Estrées, 1560

Fig. 861 is a portrait drawing of Gabrielle, daughter of Antoine d'Estrées, who was born in 1573. She was first seen by Henry IV when she was seventeen, and immediately made a lasting impression by reason of her beauty and grace. On the authority of two contemporaries, we know that she possessed 'a beautifully shaped head, covered with an abundance of fair hair; blue eyes of a peculiar brilliancy; a lily-white complexion, only faintly tinged with rose, . . . the nose well formed, the lively, humorous curves of the mouth set off with fine teeth.' The poet, Guillaume du Sable, praised 'her coral lips, her ivory teeth, and her lovely double chin.' The last, a blemish in these days; but so great was her charm that she was able to carry it off as an attraction.

Sainte-Beuve tells us: 'She was white-skinned and fair, with blonde hair of the finest gold heaped up in a mass on her head and crisping on the sides in little curls.' But La Belle Gabrielle sometimes removed her attractive 'little curls' as Fig. 861 proves. The simplicity of her coiffure is seen in this: she has brushed her hair off the forehead and temples in a perfectly natural manner, perhaps a little high, but that was to conform to the mode of the day. At the back, it is woven into a coil or knob, very like the Roman lady's (see Fig. 765).

To throw a flimsy veil over the intrigue, she was married to one Nicolas d'Amerval de Liancourt, a gentleman of fortune if not otherwise attractive. This was in accordance with the usual practice under such circumstances, the match being arranged by the King, or (as some say) by her father: but she lived at Court as a Princess of the Blood, though actually the King's mistress. Gabrielle was created in 1595 Marquise de Monceaux, and later, in 1597, Duchesse de Beaufort.

She was remarkable, not only for her beauty, but for her great luxury and extravagance, which shocked not only the populace but even the courtiers!

The schedule of toilet articles left by her and drawn up at her death mentions nineteen mantles of the utmost sumptuousness, cotillons (under-petticoats) of Turkish cloth of gold, robes of satin of the colour of *brown bread*, doublées (camisoles, chemises) of incarnadine taffeta, etc.

She also had the distinction of being painted, with her sister, by Frans Pourbus the Younger in her bath, attired in fashionable hairdressing and a pearl earring, with an obvious allusion to the birth of her son, César, created Duc de Vendôme, in 1594. Her second son, Alexandre de Bourbon, was born in 1598.

This celebrated courtesan, and all but Queen of Henry IV, died 'from eating a large citron' in 1599.

### ITALIAN HAIRDRESSING

The hairdressing of Italian ladies, like their headdresses, was very varied. Sometimes it was extremely simple, but more often very elaborate, not to say extraordinary.

The coiffure of Fig. 667 is simple, the line over the forehead being *the* mode for every self-respecting well-dressed woman of Europe. The hair is braided at the back, rolled round in the classic manner, and fixed with bows of riband.

The ladies of Rome dressed their hair somewhat on French lines, as shown in Fig. 762. The hair is slightly waved and taken up off the forehead, in this case over two pads, and is worn in conjunction with a black velvet cap fitting close at the back and having a deep rounded point on the forehead, as seen inset.

Sometimes one sees illustrations of Roman ladies at this time with their hair dressed close to the head in a series of very formal curls.

Later, in the 1590's, we find the front hair combed off the forehead over a small pad, and the back hair taken upwards to form with it a coil or knob on the angle of the cranium: this in Fig. 765 is partly hidden by the veil (*see also* Figs. 758 and 861). The effect is less rigid and much more natural than the original stiff and formal French style (*see* Fig. 860) and altogether more pleasing.

The Florentine lady (Fig. 763) wears an extraordinary coiffure. The hair is taken high up over a pad in front like Fig. 856, with the back hair dressed close to the head and ending in a twist, from which a long gauze veil floats. An ornament of pearls on wires is fixed to this twist, and a string of large pearls rests upon the rolled-up hair on the forehead and the puffs of hair at the sides.

The ladies of Venice dressed their hair in a most eccentric manner, with frisettes or curls, or both, mounted on wire frames or pads resembling horns. Fig. 764 is a typical example of the style: compared with some seen in illustrations this is quite inoffensive. The hair on the head itself is dressed in the ordinary manner, being smoothly brushed back and braided into a coil. In front, however, it is curiously wound round horns of material or wire, from which tiny curls escape: in the centre the hair is drawn back off the forehead. A wire support for the hair was called a PALISADO.

## SPANISH HAIRDRESSING

Judging by her portraits, Elizabeth de Valois continued to wear the French style of hairdressing after she became Queen-Consort of Spain, and most of the ladies of her Court followed her example. Many of these were French, who had accompanied her to the land of her adoption.

The hairdressing and headdress worn by the lady (Fig. 679) is definitely French, although her dress retains the Spanish characteristics. Similarly, Philip's fourth wife, although Austrian, adopted the French manner of dressing the hair with arcelets and over it the French escoffion, like Fig. 882.

During the first part of the period covered by Section II there was no Queen-Consort of Spain, and the first lady in the land was the Great Infanta. In Fig. 772 she has adopted the style popular in England and France, of dressing her hair high over one or more pads, with small curls on the forehead and temples. The same style is worn by the lady (Fig. 774), but she has arranged some additional curls in front of her ears.

At a little later period, the Infanta changed her style of hairdressing, and Fig. 886 shows her new ideas. The hair is brushed right off the forehead, and arranged in two reversed pronounced high-standing waves. At the sides, waves of hair lie close to the head: the remainder is made into a flat coil at the back.

The coiffure worn by the Infanta Catherine (Fig. 773) is composed of a mass of curls very like the wigs used by Elizabeth of England.

## HEADDRESSES: 1558–1603

### THE FRENCH HOOD

Without doubt the ladies of the aristocracy and upper classes emulated the young Queen by wearing the same kind of French hood as Her Majesty did. That worn by the Queen at the time of her accession is seen in Fig. 571. It is the same as that worn by Lady Jane Grey (Fig. 516) and described on p. 451, and, like it, is entirely without jewels or other ornamentation. On occasions when the Queen appeared in public, her French hood was more elaborate, having a *wide* coronet or PARURE of jewels like that shown in Fig. 575.

A later type of French hood worn during the 1560's is seen in Fig. 589: a three-quarter view of the same is given in Fig. 862, and a profile in Fig. 863. The front piece of black velvet followed the contour of the head and de-

Fig. 862. The French Hood　　　　　Fig. 863. The French Hood

scended well on to the ears.　It was shaped like a bow, lay flat on top of the head, curving outward at the sides, the angle level with the eyes, and then

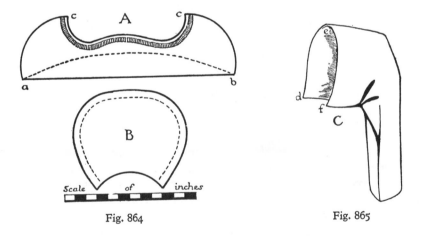

Fig. 864　　　　　　　　　　Fig. 865

descending in a graceful curve to the back of the neck, almost covering the ears.　This curve was achieved by the use of wire as described on p. 452. The front top edge was outlined, for a certain distance only, with gold cord or pearls. Behind this was generally a band of gold passamayne or gimp. Joined to the back was the 'coronet,' which, in this example, is headed by a row of ornamental and enamel beads, the parure. In front of it, and resting on the back portion of the headpiece, is a small, shaped band or slip of coloured or white silk tapering to ear level. Attached to the back of the upstanding 'coronet' was a rectangular piece of black velvet—the tube, so arranged as to form two or more pleats on each side of the back of the head, which fell down the back in definite folds. This was, of course, lined with silk.

Fig. 864 gives diagrams, A and B, of the main sections in the construction of the general type of French hood worn in Queen Mary's reign and in Queen Elizabeth's. It is exemplified in Figs. 862, 863, and 866. A shows the front portion which rests on the top of the head, the straight edge, a B, being fixed to the back, B, round the broken line. CC in the front piece A are the corners which come level with the eyes. A band of passamayne ornaments the front. The coloured silk slip covers the portion below the

Fig. 866

broken line. B is the back with the 'coronet'—often surmounted by a parure of jewels—shown between the solid and broken lines. C, Fig. 865, is the hood or tube, the front edge, D E F, being attached to the back of B at the broken line.

An important detail to be remembered is that the French hood was mostly made of black velvet, only *occasionally* was silk or even satin used and then always black.

Lady Denton (Fig. 595) wears a French hood of 1566. Fig. 866 shows the top of her head, as seen by looking at her recumbent effigy from behind. It shows all details which decorated the head portion, and the side pleats of the tube.

The Queen is shown wearing this latest type of French hood in Plate XXIX.

By the middle of the 1560's the French hood became narrower and higher, as shown in the drawing of Lady Walsingham (Fig. 867), the original being painted by Hans Eworth in 1572. This type was worn by all the fashionable ladies of the Court, as is seen by their portraits. The Countess of Sussex wears the narrow French hood in Fig. 607.

There is a very pleasing three-quarter-length portrait group dated 1568,

Fig. 867. Lady Walsingham, 1572

in which the noble father wears a jerkin like Fig. 492 and a hat like that worn by Fig. 505. Four small sons, all dressed alike, form a row in front of their parents; but the group is introduced here because of the ladies. The wife is very smart in her fashionable dress, with the latest narrow and high French

Fig. 868
Mistress Waltham, 1572

hood, and small ruff reaching half-way up the ears; but the gaunt grandmother, aged sixty-one, still adheres to the gable headdress which was all the rage in her youth.

The quaint headdress worn by Fig. 821 and shown in Fig. 868 is definitely a French hood, but the front is so shaped as almost to suggest the brim of a hat and in one piece with the curved sidepiece, the corner overlapping it. A gold ornamental band secures it to the head.

The French hood, as such, went out of fashion among the well-dressed aristocracy at the end of the 1580's, the finish of the period covered by Part I. Many knights' wives, gentlewomen, and old ladies, however, still wore it during the early years of the seventeenth century. Lady Southcote, 1585 (Fig. 823), wears a simple French hood entirely of folded velvet and without any ornament. Another gentlewoman of about the same date (Fig. 819) wears one with a slightly different arrangement and ornamented.

A.        B.

Fig. 869. Dame Clopton, 1596

A French hood of a late date is shown in Fig. 869, worn by Anne Clopton on her effigy in Trinity Church, Stratford-on-Avon. She died in 1596. In A, we see the hood side view, coming down in a point well on to the forehead, and curving behind the formal arrangement of hair over pads to a point on a level with the mouth. The ridge or 'coronet' is of goldsmith's work set with floral motifs.[1]   In B, one sees the hood from behind, showing clearly the three sections which form the headpiece.   From behind the ridge hangs the tube pleated into several folds.

Two elderly and unfashionable ladies of the aristocracy are shown in Figs. 870 and 871.   The former is Lady Williams from her alabaster effigy in Thame Church dated 1559.   The front portion of her headdress is reminiscent of the gable, but the back part is the French hood arranged in folds like that in Fig. 823.   The hair is entirely concealed by a lawn cap worn underneath and gathered into a very narrow band which encircles the head.

Fig. 870. Lady Williams, 1560

The other lady (Fig. 871) is Dame Agnes Sanders, from her painted effigy in Hatfield Church.   This is dated 1588, a period of twenty-nine years having elapsed since Fig. 870, yet the headdress is practically the same.   One sees grey hair slightly waved on the temples, with a small frill of the under-cap of

Fig. 871. Dame Agnes Sanders, 1588

Fig. 872. In Shadow

lawn showing over it, and above this is placed the French hood of black velvet.   A band of tubular and spherical beads was often attached round

[1] The shape of these motifs is very undefined in the effigy.

the slightly padded fold A, and hitherto referred to as the coronet. This lady's dress is all in black, and is modelled on the same lines as Lady Southcote's (Fig. 823).

From time to time to the end of her life, Queen Elizabeth continued to wear a type of French hood. In some cameo portraits (a drawing of one is seen in Fig. 698) one sees the front fitting close to the head, but without the flat tube. This is very like the escoffion of an earlier date (see Fig. 547). The Queen wore a French hood when opening Parliament in 1600 (see Plate XLIII).

Fig. 873. Queen Elizabeth, 1575

Other headdresses, of great variety, worn by the Queen at different periods, are described under the sections dealing with her wardrobe and portraits, Parts I and II.

When the French hood was worn with a ruff of increased circumference, it was found that the *fall* of the tube part was deprived of its perpendicular line. In some instances it was removed from the hood. On the other hand a custom arose of turning it up and arranging the tube attractively over the top of the hood, so that the end projected over the front and shaded the face as is shown in Fig. 872. It was then said to be *à l'ombre*.

It was the ambition of a woman of the people to don a French hood whenever an excuse occurred. 'Every merchant's wife and mean gentlewoman wore her French hood, and every cottager's daughter her taffeta hat.'

To make a perfect 'lady' a husband had only to supply his spouse with a French hood and a silken gown.

## HATS

The hats worn during the first part of Elizabeth's reign were of various shapes and sizes. The one referred to under Fig. 597 was that fashionable during the 1560's: one like it is worn by the Countess of Lennox (Fig. 596). These are of the flat variety, with narrow brims. Both are decorated in the same manner, with a row of pearls round the brim and three strands crossing each other over the crown; a tuft of ostrich tips is set at the side. Under the hat the hair is puffed out moderately at the sides of the head and over the ears (*see* Fig. 540), the knob at the back being encased in a network caul of gold or pearls, or both (*see* Fig. 549).

It is said that Mary Stuart wore a 'chapeau à l'Italienne'; without doubt this refers to that shown in Fig. 597. (*Refer also to* Italian headdresses, p. 753.)

The curious high-crowned hat worn by Queen Elizabeth, mentioned under Fig. 578, is one that is seldom met with worn by ladies. It is obviously borrowed from men's headgear, and has the same curled brim as that worn by Sir John Hawkyns (Fig. 851).

Fig. 873 shows the hat the Queen sometimes wore while hunting or riding. It is the same style as is described under Fig. 849. A row of pearls surrounds the bottom of the crown, and a panache of ostrich feathers is set at the back, the hat itself being tipped slightly forward over a network caul at the back.

Amongst other hats known to have belonged to Elizabeth in the 1590's were two sent as a present by Lady Russell, who herself dilates upon their beauty and expensiveness: 'Two hats with two jewels, though I say it, fine hats; the one of white beaver, the jewel of the one above a hundred pounds' price, besides the pendent pearl, which cost me the £30 more.' For their shape we may rely on Figs. 849 and 852.

Fig. 874. Bourgeois

A hat such as was worn by the wives of the middle classes and merchants is seen in Fig. 874. Of felt, it is ornamented with a feather fastened by a piece of jewellery to the hatband. Another such hat has been chosen by the good lady in Fig. 828. Hats of a little later date, perhaps more *outré*, are worn by the two gentlewomen (Figs. 788 and 790).

Towards the end of the reign hats of this shape and higher in the crown, covered with velvet or silk, were worn by the wives of London merchants.

### OTHER HEADDRESSES OF MARY STUART

Headdresses worn by the Scottish Queen already illustrated and described are: Fig. 548, 1559; Figs. 597 and 599, 1560; and Fig. 601, 1561. Another headdress worn by her in 1561 is shown in Fig. 602. A headdress, which was more or less her usual coiffure during the seven years she lived in Scotland,

Fig. 875. Mary Stuart, 1567

Fig. 876. Mary Stuart, 1578

is given in Fig. 875. Here again the cap is of white lawn, with an attifet front edged with lace, the motif of which is seen in the four corners of the drawing; it is covered at the back by a long hanging veil of the same material. In the later years of her life and imprisonment, she changed her style of headdress to that shown in Fig 876. This is founded on the various portraits of her, chief among them being that by P. Oudry in the National Portrait Gallery, London. The usual cap, not quite so bowed or pointed as before, is of white lawn, the front part slightly gathered into the wire frame and edged with narrow lace; the back part is plain. Over this, the veil, edged with the same lace, follows the curve of the head round to the ear, thence curving out and down to the armpit, the bulk of the veil falling in many folds over the trained skirt. This style of headdress was worn by the ill-fated Queen, with very slight variations, during the last tragic months of her life.

Figs. 597, 875, and 876 show, as do many of her portraits, the usual way the ruff or band is arranged at the throat, in the same manner as in Fig. 862.[1] In Fig. 876 one also sees the jet ornaments, or black pearls, Queen Mary wore round her neck at this time: they consist of two larger ornaments, and on either side the letter M.

[1] Special notice should be taken of the arrangement of the ruff, and reference should be made to Fig. 862 and the description on p. 504. Mary Stuart was in the habit of wearing her ruff with the collar turned down on the right-hand side. This has misled a nineteenth-century authority into thinking that the ruff on this side was of a different formation from that on the left! Evidently he did not know how the Elizabethan ruff was constructed.

### Cauls and Caps

It has been mentioned that cauls worn on the knob of hair at the back of the head were used in England. In 1583, Stubbes describes the escoffion (*see* p. 453) as 'made netwise, to the end, as I think, that the cloth of gold, cloth of silver, or else tinsel (for that is the worst) werewith their heads are covered and attired withal underneath their cauls may appear, and show itself in the bravest manner, so that a man that seeth them (their heads glitter and shine in such sort) would think them to have golden heads . . . and some wear lattice caps with three horns, three corners I should say, like the forked caps of Popish priests, with their perriwincles, chitterlings, and the like apish toys of infinite variety.'

Fig. 877. 1584

One seldom, if ever, meets these later monstrosities of head attire, 'these glittering caules of golden plate wherewith their heads were richly dect' in illustrations of English women. Stubbes, exaggerating his countrywomen's head attire for his own purposes, has unconsciously arrived at the Italian coiffures, as may be seen on reference to Figs. 763, 764, and 885.

A caul of quite a new shape is shown in Fig. 877, worn by a gentlewoman of the 1580's. The part which covers the head is bag-shape, secured to the head by three bands or one bound three times round. The front, edged with a

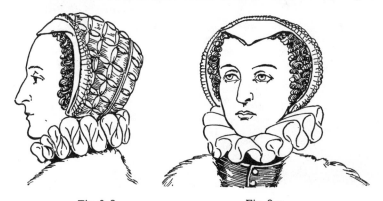

Fig. 878.  Fig. 879.
Anne Fiennes, Lady Dacre, 1594

fancy trimming, is bowed out by wire—the attifet—over the puffed hair at the sides, and this descends in a point on the forehead. A headdress of a similar type but definitely a cap, dated 1594, is shown in Figs. 878 and 879. It is made entirely of white lawn. The cap is a square trellis of puffings, with the horseshoe-shaped back joined to it with two rows of cording. On the front is a shaped piece of double lawn edged with a narrow pleated ruching, and being wired à l'attifet it bows out over the hair dressed in a mass of tiny curls. Underneath this cap is worn a kerchief folded cornerwise, the points coming well on to the forehead, and the sides curving out over the hair in front of the ruching.

Caps of this sort were much worn at the end of the century, and well into the seventeenth.

## HEAD ORNAMENTS, WREATHS, AND GARLANDS

The delightful fashion of wearing wreaths and garlands of wirework in gold or silver for the vain purpose of adding the desired cubit to the stature came in late in the 1580's. It is described by our friend Stubbes: 'Then, on

GLORIANA.

Fig. 880

the edges of their bolstred hair (for it standeth crested round about their frontiers, and hanging over their faces like pendices or veils with glass windows on every side) there is laid great wreaths of gold and silver, curiously wrought and cunningly applied to the temples of their heads.'

The first such wreath to be shown is in Fig. 726. This takes the form of fronds of fern and ospreys carried out in silver wire, and backed by a fan-shaped motif of the same mounted with diamonds and pearls. A rich jewel of rubies and diamonds in front sets off the whole headdress—a beautiful effect.

These head ornaments became more elaborate as time went on: an example may be seen in Fig. 729, obviously set in a comb inserted into the back of the hair or wig, and from it springs a spray of silver wires each carrying several hanging diamonds or bugles, giving the effect of lilies of the valley. The wreath which hangs on the hair in front is treated in the same manner.

The wonderful head attire worn by Mistress Mary Fitton in her portrait (Plate XLIV) is a very beautiful example of the mode of the 1590's. The foundation of this is of silver wire; and to its outside edge, as well as to the centre portion, are set sprays of silver wires on which are quantities of pearls interspersed with spangles and bugles. These would quiver and scintillate at the slightest movement of the head. Mounted on Mary's brown hair, dressed high, this would have a magnificent appearance, rather like a shimmering cluster of white and silver elderberries.

De Maisse was very much struck by the garland the Queen was wearing at an audience in 1597, though, unfortunately for our purpose, he omits to describe it. A portrait in St. James's Palace of Queen Elizabeth, shows her wearing a very lovely garland of the 1590's on top of her high hairdressing. It is reproduced in Fig. 880, and has a delicate framework of fine silver wire embodying scrolls, flowers, and leaves of silver gauze, beads, and diamonds, and further embellished with pearls set on upstanding wires forming a com- plementary design. Large peardrop pearls form a kind of fringe resting on the much-becurled wig. The whole structure tapers up very high in the centre, with wings descending the sides of the hair, the effect suggesting a Russian tiara but more delicate in design. Elizabeth was fully aware of the advantage gained by placing dazzling diamonds close to a face and neck much wrinkled and scraggy through advancing years.

## FRENCH HEADDRESSES

In the land of its birth the French hood, after reigning for many years, disappeared as a fashionable headdress by the time Henry III was on the throne.

A French example of it is shown in Fig. 881, which presents a French noble lady of the 1560's. It is worn over the hairdressing described under Fig. 860, and in consequence is placed rather far back on the head. Jewels in gold mounts alternating with double rows of four pearls form the parure, and also edge the front of the hood where it rests on a pleating of gold gauze. On the forehead is an ornament from which three peardrop pearls hang.

The escoffion was still fashionable in France, and in Fig. 599 we see it worn by Mary Stuart, drawn from a medal struck in 1560. The foundation is of silk or gold tissue cross-barred with gold: at the intersections pearls are set, and there are jewels in gold mounts (*see* inset) in the spaces.   A peardrop pearl is suspended from it and hangs well on to the forehead.

An escoffion worn by a French Noble lady is shown in Fig. 882.   It is composed of a dark-coloured silk covered by an intricate network of gold and pearls.   The edge fitting the head is of gold, set with jewels and shaped to

Fig. 881. French Lady in French Hood

Fig. 882. Catherine of Lorraine

come to a point in the centre of the head just behind the hair dressed as described under Fig. 860.   The escoffion disappeared as a headdress among fashionable women after 1560.   A smaller version of it remained in use to cover the knob of hair worn at the back of the head.


## WIDOW'S WEEDS

The Deuil Blanc, referred to on p. 514, and reproduced in Fig. 601, shows the characteristic weeds regulated by the Controller of French Court ceremonial for young widows.   To start with, the barbe, described under Fig. 191, vol. ii, and Fig. 149, vol. iii, is tied under the chin and over the head.   On the hair is placed a little coif of very fine lawn, a small portion only being visible on the forehead; and over it is the cap with the bowed attifet front.   Around the back of the cap is pinned the voluminous white lawn veil.

Widow's weeds, as worn by Catherine de' Medici, are referred to under Fig. 661 and Plate XXXV.   Fig. 883 shows another arrangement of the veil, and is taken from a portrait medallion of Catherine dating about 1574. This shows the arrangement clearly.   One corner of the black crêpe veil is pulled forward on to the forehead over the black cap with the attifet front, and tied with itself behind, the remainder falling to the ground. If, however, the edges were set out in curves on both sides of the head, the wire would be inserted at the line A. No barbe is worn. Catherine was apparently the first Royal widow to omit this, as henceforth it does not appear as an item of mourning amongst Royal and noble ladies. Possibly it was an Italian fashion introduced by this Queen of France.

The widow's weeds worn by Queen Elizabeth of Austria, are shown in

Fig. 883.
Catherine de' Medici

Fig. 884. Elizabeth of Austria,
Queen-Dowager of France

Fig. 884, taken from a portrait by François Quesnel dating shortly after 1574. A close-fitting black cap is first put on: then the black crêpe veil, wired into an attifet front, is placed over it. The wire at the sides continues below ear level, producing on a smaller scale the effect described under Fig. 721. This same type of widow's weeds was worn by Queen Jeanne of Navarre (see p. 453). For widow's weeds as worn in England at the end of the century, refer to Figs. 826 and 827.

### ITALIAN HEADDRESSES

The lady of Pisa (Fig. 669) wears a close-fitting coif composed of folds of soft material with semicircular ornaments of gold round the front. A series of loops gives a coronet effect at the back, from which falls a long gauze veil. No hair is visible.

The head-and-shoulders drawing of the Italian lady (Fig. 885) shows sufficient of her dress to give it a date—about 1550. She has mahoitered sleeves to her surcote, and the rest of the costume may be understood by referring to Fig. 521, remembering that Italy was in advance of England in fashions. The hat is of particular interest; it is typically Italian, and, together

Fig. 885. Bonet à l'Italienne

with the hats worn by Italian men, captivated fashionable women of England and France. It is of black velvet 'moulded on a porringer; a velvet dish—'tis a cockle, or a walnut shell.' Gold buttons set with jewels are placed round it, and on the right side an elaborate ornament of gold, jewels, and pearls stands erect. The hat is poised at an angle over a caul or escoffion, showing the hair through the network. Bunches of curls cluster in front of the ears.

### SPANISH HEADDRESSES

The same applies to headdresses as to hairdressing—Spanish ladies of *noble* rank wore much the same styles as English and French. In Figs. 676, 679, and 680, both Queens and the noble lady wear escoffions. The chapeau à l'Italienne is worn over a pearl and jewelled caul by Elizabeth de Valois in Fig. 674.

With the new style of hairdressing worn by the Great Infanta (Fig. 772), the headdress so popular in England was, curiously enough, adopted in Spain. Possibly the attention aroused in Spaniards to the nation of heretics may be the cause of this fantastic head decoration finding its way to Spain. In Fig. 772, the headdress takes the form of a coronet composed of pearls and jewels, and backed by a made-up plume of small feathers.

In Fig. 774 it has become

Fig. 886. The Great Infanta

more elaborate, and consists of a wire foundation of steeple shape, and in a scroll design, covered with pearls. An aigrette is fixed to the hair on the left side.

The head attire, shown in Fig. 886, is taken from a portrait of the Infanta Isabella by Pantoja de la Cruz. It is a wonderful erection of pearl scroll-work. From an ornamental holder on the left side of her hairdressing springs an aigrette.

The headdress worn by the Infanta Catherine (Fig. 773) is a Spanish version of the chapeau à l'Italienne, seen in Fig. 885. It is pill-box shape, covered with black velvet and encompassed by folds of the same set with oblique groups of three pearls and jewels in gold mounts. A short curled ostrich tip is fixed by a jewel on the upper side of the tilt. Whether a caul is worn or not it is impossible to see. The same style is seen in one or two other Spanish portraits.

## MIDDLE CLASSES

Besides those hats described on p. 747, there were other headdresses worn by the middle-class women and varying in shape.

Fig. 887 shows one of the blocked felt variety. It is in white, formed with

Fig. 887. Mistress Flexney, 1567

Fig. 888. Mistress Dorcas Martin, 1562

a point on the forehead and projecting at the sides; down the back hangs a flat tube. The townswoman (Fig. 830) wears a similar headdress.

Fig. 888 is a felt cap of another shape, or it could be made of cloth and seamed at the sides, worn over a plain linen under-cap.   It is taken from a portrait medallion of Dorcas, wife of Richard Martin, Queen Elizabeth's goldsmith.   He was Warden and later Master of the Mint, and Lord Mayor for part of the year 1588.

White linen caps worn by the lower orders and country people were very simple in construction.   The back part was horseshoe-shape, and to the curved edge was sewn plain or gathered a rectangular front piece (Fig. 889).   This

Fig. 889

Fig. 890

was always turned back off the face, as worn by the young girl (Fig. 834). Sometimes the front corners were rounded off.

Another kind of cap much worn is first seen in Fig. 352, and later in Figs. 718 and 831.   It has a shaped front piece like that of the French hood, but in linen; and most likely wired at the edge so as to lie close on the forehead, bow round over the hair at the sides, and come close to the cheek.   To this is gathered the bag-shaped back, as shown in Fig. 890.

These caps were always made of white or natural-tinted linen, and were worn indoors and out.   When it was required to be more dressy, a felt or straw hat was worn on top, as in Figs. 832 and 833.


## FOOTGEAR, 1558–1603

The Guild of Cordwainers was granted its third charter by Queen Elizabeth in 1562, which was followed by a grant of arms in 1579.   The armorial bearings (Fig. 891) are: azure, a chevron or between three goats' heads rased argent horned and bearded of the chevron.   Crest, a goats' head rased argent, the rasures (edges of the hair) gules, the horns wreathed or and azure, mantling gules lined or 'dobled' argent.

For some years after the accession of Queen Elizabeth, footgear was simple and more or less followed the shape of the foot.   The material used was chiefly leather: velvet, satin, silk, and cloth were employed by the shoemaker for special shoes.

Fig. 891. Arms of the Cordwainers

A man's shoe, such as was in general use, is shown in Fig. 893. This type was worn by all classes—by the nobility in the best Spanish leather. Most of the examples seen in portraits have no fastenings; they were close-fitting,

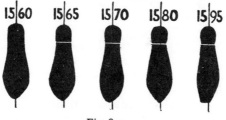

Fig. 892

but it was possible to pass the foot into the shoe with ease despite the rather high instep. Sometimes the shoe was open down the outer side (*see* dotted line at A) and laced; or a strap was cut in the vamp and fastened by a button. In Fig. 895 straps, fixed at the sides, tie in a bow on the instep. A buckle would serve the same purpose.

The soles of ordinary shoes were of uniform thickness, and as yet there were no heels. Shoes worn by the French nobility during the 1550's and 1560's were much decorated with cuttes, a fashion already noticed in Chapter III. Fig. 896 shows a shoe, dated 1561, and made of silk or satin; it has a row of loops over the instep, cuttes piped at the edges, and three ornamental buttons. Comparison with the earlier examples will show that these shoes do not differ

Fig. 893                Fig. 894.                Fig. 895
            Cordwainer's Knife

appreciably from them; in fact, this style remained in fashion during the greater part of the reign for dress purposes. As late as 1596 one meets it in a portrait of the Infante Philip at Vienna, painted by Pantoja de la Cruz.

Figs. 897 and 898 are drawn from shoes in the Archaeological Museum, Cambridge, which were found in Corpus Christi College. They are still in excellent condition. The soles are thin, and the shoes made of brown

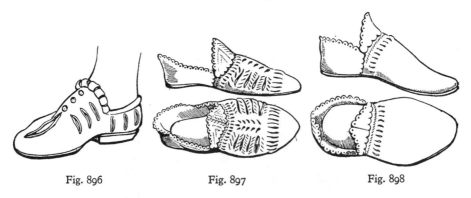

Fig. 896                Fig. 897                Fig. 898

leather, elaborately pinked, cutte and stitched. Their owner must have been a smartly dressed man. The method, known to the Greeks, of raising the foot at the back to give additional height, was not adopted in England until after the middle of the sixteenth century. As seen in Fig. 899, which is taken from an original, the sole of cork gradually increased in thickness from the toe to the heel. Another shoe, a lady's, with a corked sole is shown in Fig. 902.

Comment was, of course, made on this innovation. One such is quoted on p. 543, and we may be sure Stubbes would seize the opportunity of airing his disdainful, yet enlightening, remarks on footgear in general:

'They have corked shoes, pinsnets, and fine pantofles, which bear them up a finger or two from the ground: whereof some be of white leather, some of black, red, black velvet, white, red, green, raced, carved, cutte, and stitched

Fig. 899                              Fig. 900

all over with silk and laid on with gold, silver, and such like: yet not withstanding to what good uses serve these pantofles.'

Fig. 899 is of leather, decorated with cuttes on the toe joints, and with stitchery above them and on the heelpiece. Shoes were often 'stitched with silk, and embroidered with gold and silver all over the foot, with other gewgawes innumerable.' Heels to shoes began to make their appearance in France as early as the 1560's, for a low heel is seen in Fig. 896; this, however, is somewhat exceptional at this date.

In the portrait of Henry III of France, referred to under Fig. 740, there is

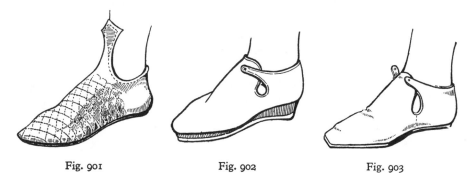

Fig. 901                    Fig. 902                    Fig. 903

shown a novel arrangement for attaching the heel (*see* Fig. 900). The sole is part of the black velvet hosen; the red heel is separate, attached to a heelpiece of white kid. No fastening appears, so the foot must have passed through the opening, which strikes one as not being very secure.

Fancy shoes were worn by courtiers during the latter part of the reign, and Fig. 901 shows one of a pair in white silk, satin, or leather, worn by Lord Leicester. An ornamental tongue stands up high over the instep, and the front part of the shoe is stitched with silver thread in a diamond pattern.

In the 1570's a new method of fastening the shoe came into vogue. The brass to the memory of Mistress Wyndham (*see* Fig. 819) furnishes us with an early example (Fig. 902). The side pieces are cut down rather low, the fronts curving up over the instep, and the backs curving forward to form a short strap with eyelet holes through which ribands were passed. These, being tied together in a bow, kept the top of the shoe secure round the ankle. Sir Walter Raleigh (Fig. 742) wears the same type of shoe at a later date and Fig. 903 is a detail drawing of it. This method in its primitive stage is seen in Fig. 630, but at that time shoemakers had not discovered the advantage of the larger open space at the sides which assisted the bend of the foot in a more comfortable manner. It should be noticed that the toe is cut rather square.

Fig. 904

'With two Provincial roses on my razed shoes.' This quotation from *Hamlet* (Act III, sc. ii) might perplex some, but the rose referred to was an ornament introduced to the shoe in the 1590's. 'Shoe roses' they were called, and were at first made up of loops of ribands resembling that flower. Henry IV is wearing them in his portrait (*see* Fig. 752). A little later they were made of gold or silver lace, as shown in the drawing (Fig. 770). In the following century these roses became the usual decoration for ladies' and gentlemen's smart footwear.

On the tennis court woollen slippers were worn lest ordinary shoes should distract the players by creaking.

The origin of the word 'pumps' is unknown, but it came into use in the middle of the century. They were shoes with thin soles and, later, low heels. As there were no fastenings, the foot was *slipped* into them (hence, also, the name slipper); they were used only indoors. Lackeys wore pumps because they were soft and quiet; and dating from the end of the century, the name 'pumps' was sometimes applied to a lackey.

The French 'pantoufle' means a slipper or mule. Fig. 904 shows one made of leather, having a row of cuttes, pinked at the edges, over the front, and a row of loops at the top of the instep. The heel rests on padded leather attached to the sole. The shape of the sole is given in Fig. 905 A. Pantoufles are worn by Sir Christopher Hatton (Fig. 627).

A　B

Fig. 905

One often finds these curiously shaped soles when examining the feet of ladies in their effigies recumbent upon altar tombs (Fig. 905 B).

Little of ladies' shoes can be seen when the skirts touch the ground: it may be assumed that their shoes resembled those of the men. In the 1580's and 1590's, when skirts became a little shorter, more of the shoes can be seen.

Two examples of shoes worn by ladies are given in Figs. 906 and 907, both dating about 1588–95. Those in Fig. 906 are taken from the portrait of Queen Elizabeth (Plate XLII), and are of white satin with numerous small cuttes. They are rather short from toe to heel, and broad across the toe joints, in contrast to Fig. 907, in which the shoes are tapering and flat. These

Fig. 906        Fig. 907

are of white satin, with the addition of three ornamental buttons, and the cuttes are differently arranged.

Long boots, generally worn for riding, but sometimes used for walking, were of the same shape as shown in Fig. 505. The French jack-boot (Fig. 559) is seldom met with in illustrations of English sixteenth-century gentlemen.

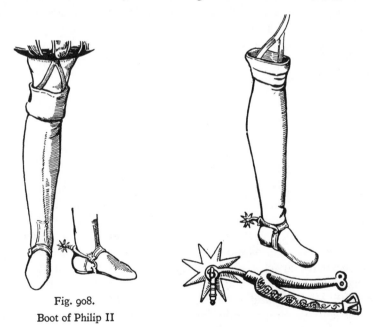

Fig. 908.<br>Boot of Philip II

Fig. 909. Boot and Spur

The long boot of soft fawn leather, and fitting the leg closely, shown in Fig. 908, is from a portrait of Philip II. The foot is sewn to the leg part underneath the spur strap, and also up the front in the form of a tongue, like that shown in Fig. 901. Above the knee the boot is turned down and up, and two straps sewn inside are attached to the waist-belt underneath the slops. The boot in Fig. 909 is similar, but more rounded in the toe, and without the stitching up the front of the ankle.  The top does not turn down, and two straps support the boot as described above.

'They have also boot hose—they be of the finest cloth that may be got, yea, fine enough to make any band, ruff or shirt needful to be worn: yet this is bad enough to wear next their gresie boots . . . they must be wrought all over, from the gartering place upward, with needlework, clogged with silk of all colours, with birds, fowls, beasts, and antiques purtrayed all over in comly sort, so that I have known the very needlework of some one pair of these boothose to stand, some in iiij pound, vi pound and some in x pound a piece. Besides this, they are made so wide to draw over all, and so long to reach up to the waist.'

Boot-hose, known as TRIQUEHOUSE, besides being a leg-bag to draw over the hose under a boot, was also a thick hose to wear instead of a boot.

Spurs worn for either riding or walking often had large loose rowels which caused a jingling sound.  Hence this excerpt: '. . . he walked the chamber with such a pestilent gingle'—an effect much sought after by cavaliers towards the end of the century.  At this time also a small metal ornament, called a 'jingle,' was hung to the axle of the rowel which made the same noise but more intensified.  The Elizabethan spur, set below Fig. 909, shows one of these jingles.  Another fancy was to have mottoes engraved upon the shanks.  In the sixteenth century Ripon was celebrated for the manufacture of the best English spurs, which were known as 'rippons.'


## JEWELLERY, 1558–1603

Though it hardly seems possible, the Court of Queen Elizabeth outshone that of her father in the lavish display of jewellery.  The craft of the goldsmith and jeweller underwent many improvements during Elizabeth's reign, owing to the greater influence of the Continent, and received much encouragement from the immense demands made by the nobility and upper classes for splendid and expensive articles of jewellery.  This applies also to the wealthy middle classes, who in this more prosperous era had more opportunities of bedecking themselves (and their wives) with goldsmith's work and jewels. Sumptuary laws, made specially for them, were (it seems) entirely ignored, as usual.

This prosperity, no doubt, prompted the Wardens of the Goldsmiths' Company to ask for an augmentation to their existing shield of arms (see p. 117), for in the Memorials of the company we find under date 14 Elizabeth— 1571—the following entry:

'Agreed that the Arms of the Company shall be renewed against the Mayor's feast—with helmet, crest and supporters.'  They are shown in Fig. 910.

The crest above mentioned is blazoned as a demi-lady rising from clouds above the crest wreath, holding in her dexter hand a pair of scales and in the sinister a touchstone. The dress is described under Fig. 822. The supporters are 'Two Unicorns or, armed, crined, and hoofed argent'; the motto: 'Justitia Virtutum Regina.'

The colours of the livery remained violet and scarlet, but these were confined to the hood, the gowns being of the lately introduced style—all of black and furred with foins. For an alderman in livery see Fig. 798.

Fig. 910. Arms of Goldsmiths' Company

English goldsmiths had serious rivals in Germany, where the craft had reached a very high standard and had acquired universal fame. Many German goldsmiths of an earlier generation had studied in Italy, and by this time they were outrivalling their masters by their delicacy of treatment and richness of invention. 'Never was the working of metals better understood, to bring out the highest brilliancy and mirror effects, to enliven plain flat surfaces with artistic engraving and, above all, how to combine the hard brilliance of precious stones with soft colours in enamels.'

Pure Classic lines gave way to a more mixed style in which strap and ribbon-work, architectural members, and the cartouche framing are prominent features.   The German craftsmen thus supplied a large proportion of the jewellery in use in Europe.

The reformed religion, which was occupying the minds of higher and lower classes, is responsible in a great measure for figures of saints and objects of religious significance going out of favour in the decoration of articles of jewellery.   They were not excluded altogether, but were replaced by mythological or allegorical figures and animals.   These were usually of white enamel with a mauvish hue, and modelled or raised in the round.   The design surrounding figures, especially for pendants and brooches, was of scroll and strap-work in enamels, and in the revived champlevé on gold.

Jewels of every sort were used, and diamonds became the most popular, since the method of cutting them was much improved, and the use of foil set underneath greatly enhanced their brilliance.

A great impetus to the popularity of rich jewellery was given by the capture of Spanish trading galleons by the Sea Dogs of the 1580's.

*The Handbook of Elizabethan Jewellery*, published by the London Museum, is particularly useful for the study of this extensive subject.

### CROWNS

The Crown Imperial worn by Queen Elizabeth is shown in Plate XXVII, and has the circlet set with rubies, sapphires, pearls, and diamonds.   There are eight crosses patées, from which rise four arches supporting a large cross. The orb, which makes its first appearance in this work in vol. i, Fig. 82, is of iron surrounded and arched with sapphires, rubies, and diamonds.   The reason for using iron is obscure: possibly to bring good fortune?

The Imperial Crown is shown also in Figs. 574, 575, and Plate XLIII.   It is probable that the crown shown in the coronation portrait, Plate XXVII, is the more authentic, as the artist no doubt painted it from the original. Fig. 575 is from a contemporary engraving.

The crown of France surmounts the drawing of Charles IX (Plate XXXVI); it will be noticed that the design has not altered since the time of Louis XII (Fig. 38).

Plate XLVI shows the Spanish Royal Crown, which consists of eight leaf-motifs rising from the circlet and supporting four arches.

The coronet of the Grand Dukes of Tuscany is seen in the drawing of Marie de' Medici (Fig. 758), surmounting the arms of the Medici family.

### COLLARS

The Collar of the Garter is seen in numerous portraits of the time, and the most satisfactory drawing of it in this book is that shown in Fig. 624. But there is always Fig. 339, vol. ii, for convenient reference.

It does not appear that Queen Elizabeth was painted wearing the Collar of the Garter, but she must, of course, have done so on certain occasions, particularly when attending a Chapter of the Order. Nor has the garter worn upon her arm ever been discovered in any painting. Unlike her sister Mary, Elizabeth had no kingly husband to take her place as Sovereign of the Order, and the drawing referred to on p. 495 is perhaps the only representation of her in the insignia and robes.

The following description of a George is found in an inventory of the Queen's jewels dated 1574:

'Item oone George, on horsebacke, the foreparte of the George of Diamoundes the maile of the Curettes and Renettes of the same silver haulfguilt, w$^t$ a sworde in his hand of golde, a Lozanged Diamonde like a shilde and a Dragone of gold, posz together iij oz iiij q$^a$rrt.'

The Lesser George, set in a jewelled frame and suspended on a black riband, is worn by Queen Elizabeth in her portrait (Plate XXXI C).

Below are the costs of some jewels of the insignia of the Order of the Garter:

A Garter of gold with diamonds and rubies, £48.

A George of diamonds, £60.

A wire chain to the same, £10 2s.

A Collar of gold, £210 5s.

Another George, £25.

And one must remember that these sums represent ten or twelve times as much to-day.

Elizabeth conferred the Order of the Garter upon the King of France, March 1586. 'The Garter is valued at fifty thousand crowns. In return the King is said to have prepared a magnificent coach with all fittings to still greater value for presentation to the Queen of England.'

### CHAINS

Chains worn by gentlemen during the Elizabethan era gradually lost their 'massy' proportions: their links were decidedly smaller, as for example, Fig. 621, and chiefly oval or round, but sometimes rectangular. In some portraits chains appear to be made of plaited gold wire, as are those described in vol. ii, under Figs. 503 and 513.

Not only were these chains worn once round the neck, but often two or three times, and they were frequently long enough to extend to waist level.

The French were more given to wearing chains than the English, and these were of more ornamental character, as already shown in the last chapter. The portrait, of which Fig. 650 is a drawing, shows a chain of gold beads of a more delicate nature; a cross of gold set with jewels is suspended from it.

That noble Frenchmen did wear the heavier gold chain to which a pendant is attached, is shown in Fig. 653; and a Spaniard wearing a longer one wound three times round the neck is seen in Fig. 671. Admiral Sir John Hawkyns (Fig. 851) has a very long chain of small links worn in like manner.

Attached to the neck-chain, or hung round the neck by a riband or chain, were *pick-tooths* and *ear-picks*, very generally used by both ladies and gentlemen and often richly gemmed and enamelled. These necessities were sometimes contained in an ornament in the shape of a whistle like Fig. 471. An excerpt from Queen Elizabeth's list of New Year gifts, 1576–7, gives an example of the decoration bestowed upon such articles.

'Item, a tothe and eare-picke of gold, being a dolphin enamuled with a perle pendaunte, 16 small rubyes being but sparcks, and 5 sparcks of dyamonds—geven by the Lady Cheake.'

Fig. 911.    Fig. 912.    Fig. 913.
Necklaces

## CARCANETS

The carcanet, which in the reign of Henry VIII was usually worn by gentlemen only, was now a very favoured decoration for the throat and shoulders of ladies also. The feminine carcanet was equally rich, and was composed of jewels in gold mounts and groups of pearls set between.

A very handsome carcanet is worn on the shoulders by the Countess of Sussex (Fig. 607); and Queen Elizabeth of Spain (Fig. 676) wears another close up round the throat.

See also the carcanets worn by Queen Elizabeth, p. 770.

## NECKLACES

In the 1580's the word 'necklace' came into general use with ladies in place of 'carcanet,' which gradually became obsolete. There was a great difference between the massive carcanet and the lighter necklace, the latter being a small linked chain in which ornaments and jewels were inserted. Figs. 911 and 912 are good examples.

The former, taken from a portrait dated 1589, has three differently shaped ornaments, in gold, black enamel, and pearls, strung together by three links.

Fig. 912 is a detail of the necklace worn by the lady in Fig. 730, and is also in gold, black enamel, and pearls. Fig. 913 shows a necklace taken from a portrait dated 1600; it is composed of three links, with ornaments in gold and two different coloured enamels with a pearl set in the centre of each. All these necklaces are very long, and are worn twice round the neck, extending to below the waist.

Ropes or strings of pearls were also referred to as necklaces. They were worn close up round the throat, and often consisted of two or three strands, sometimes with pearls in loops hung from the lower strand, as seen in Plate XLIV.

Many great ladies in full dress wore a number of long strands of pearls round the neck hanging well below the point of the stomacher; and it will be seen in some of the illustrations that these necklaces were sometimes knotted on the bosom. A graceful mode was to drape the necklace from the neck or shoulder and under one arm, as in Fig. 731.

## PENDANTS, JEWELS, MINIATURES

Pendants were most elaborate in design, quite different from the oval shapes in fashion previously. They were composed of all kinds of objects, from monkeys to ships in full sail, carried out in enamels and jewels, and hung from chains of jewels. Frequent subjects composing the designs were enamelled flowers, leaves, jewelled motifs perfect in themselves, and varied ornaments. Strap-work and scrolls also formed an important feature of the settings, especially of the frame.

Characteristics appear to be a cartouche-shaped frame with a comparatively unbroken outline, enriched with scroll ornament, and occasionally with human figures and grotesques, a slight use of open work, and the general employment of a central ornament.

Although of Spanish workmanship, Fig. 914 is a good specimen of the pendant with quaint animals introduced. A spotted dog in white enamel, and set with two diamonds, stands upon gold and enamel scrolls rising from a crescent of rubies. This is hung by two chains of gold and white enamel with four motifs set with rubies, from a red and gold ornament having an emerald in the centre. Five pearls form pendants. The total length is three inches.

A pendant worn by a gentlewoman, 1586, is given in Fig. 916. It measures two and a half inches without the three grey pearl pendants, and is cross-shaped, having an emerald in the centre surrounded by four rubies. The chain by which the ornament is hung is somewhat massive considering the small size of the pendant.

Fig. 918 is a pendant of rather unusual design in which enamel, rubies, sapphires, and pearls are arranged symmetrically. That shown in Fig. 915 is worn upon a lady's sleeve of 1590. The eagle of gold and enamel, bearing

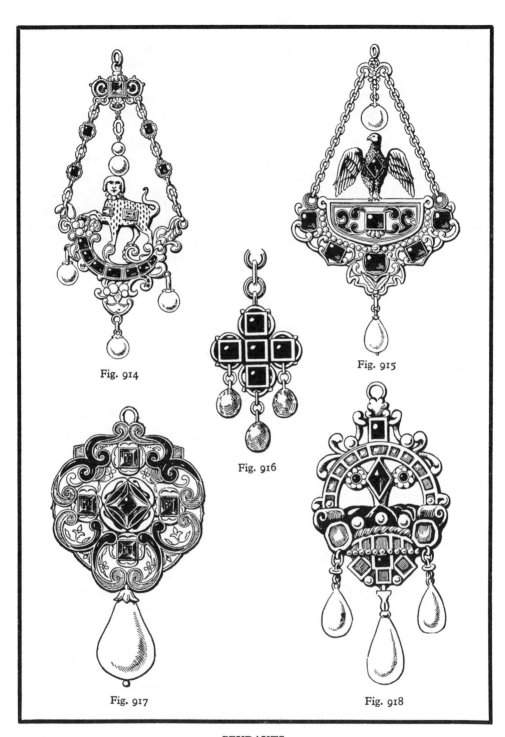

Fig. 914

Fig. 915

Fig. 916

Fig. 917

Fig. 918

PENDANTS

a lozenge-shaped ruby on its breast, stands upon a gold ornament decorated
with coloured enamels and a square emerald. Around the base are rubies,
emeralds, and small pearls set in gold
open-work scrolls with a pear pearl
suspended from it. The pendant is
hung by chains from a small ornament
with a pearl hanging in the centre.

A pendant of the usual shape is given
in Fig. 917, and is composed of two
coloured enamels, four small sapphires,
and a large one in the centre. The large
pear pearl is hung close up to the base,
which rather detracts from its beauty.

Fig. 919 is the celebrated Armada
jewel, produced after the defeat of
Philip II's fleet in 1588. Two and
three-quarter inches in length, it was
given by Queen Elizabeth to Sir
Thomas Heneage (died 1595), her Vice-
Chamberlain. On the front, which is
here reproduced, is a profile bust of
the Queen in gold upon an enamelled
ground of aventurine blue, inscribed

Fig. 919. The Armada Jewel

with the Royal title. On the reverse, and covered by a lid enamelled outside
with the Ark and inside with a Tudor rose, is a miniature of Elizabeth painted

Fig. 920.          Fig. 921.

Cameos

by Hilliard and dated 1580.
The jewel has a border in
blue, red, and white enamel
set with diamonds and rubies.
The original may now be seen
in the Victoria and Albert
Museum (M. 81–1935).

Cameos and intaglios be-
came very fashionable, especially towards the end of
Elizabeth's reign, partly owing
to the fact that the Queen was
very fond of such gems set in
jewelled frames. *Miniatures*
and cameos thus ornamented,
usually portraits of herself,
were presented by Her Majesty
as marks of esteem to such courtiers and other subjects as she favoured.
Several of the noblemen in Plate XLV wear these gifts at waist level, suspended on long ribands beneath the Collars of the Garter. Two examples

of portrait cameos are given in Figs. 920 and 921. The former is set in an elaborate frame of enamel and pearls, and the latter has a moulded gold frame with four square rubies 'garnished with their gold'—a period term for jewels in gold mounts.

Miniature cases, known at the time as 'picture boxes,' were among the most important of pendent jewels (*see* Plate XLIV). Such boxes were elaborately enamelled on the back and front, the latter being set with jewels as well.

Fig. E, Plate XVIII, shows the back of a miniature case, dated about 1580, three inches over all, enamelled with a lovely design of dolphins and arabesque scrolls in several colours on a black ground. The front is pierced in gold scroll work set with rubies and diamonds, through which the miniature portrait underneath can be seen. Such miniature cases were worn attached to the bodice, and often caught up round the neck by a cord as well (*see* Plate XLIV).

Many museums, notably the Victoria and Albert, possess original examples of Elizabethan pendants.

### Jewels of Queen Elizabeth

#### Carcanets and Pendants

We must here interrupt the description of jewellery in general to describe that worn by the Queen, as seen in her portraits.

Her great love of jewellery and the manner in which she loaded herself with jewels and pearls, already well known, is commented upon by the French Ambassador, de Maisse, in 1597:

'She wore innumerable jewels on her person, not only on her head, but also within her collar, about her arms, and on her hands, with a very great quantity of pearls, round her neck and in her bracelets. She had two bands, one on each arm, which were worth a great price.'

Attention is called to one of these bands in D, Plate XXXI.

The Queen was in the habit of frequently losing her jewels, as these were sewn on or even pinned to various parts of her dresses. Notices were issued to the effect that such and such a jewel was missing, and if found please return.

#### Carcanets

A very beautiful carcanet is worn over the ermine cape of the Queen's coronation robes in Plate XXVII. It is composed of table-cut rubies each set square and surrounded by six pearls, alternating with oval sapphires set in small diamonds; to each of these a pear pearl is attached. In the middle of the carcanet is a larger ruby set lozengewise and surrounded by six groups of diamonds; a pear-shaped pearl hangs from this. The carcanet encircling the throat is of the same design but on a smaller scale. The waist girdle is of the same jewels, but contains fewer pearls and no drop pearls.

In Fig. 575, the Spanish surcote being closed, the carcanet with pendant is worn over it. In Plate XXIX the carcanet with pendant of rubies and pearls is worn on the bodice and *under* the open Spanish surcote.

The carcanets seen in B, C, and D Plate XXXI, vary slightly in design, consisting of groups of pearls alternating with jewels set in gold mounts. They are worn close up round the throat.

The carcanet seen in D, Plate XXXI, has rubies in settings of enamel and gold alternating with groups of five pearls. The bracelets are bands, and match, being of the same jewels. To the carcanet is added a centre ornament of a large diamond or sapphire, and to this and to the rubies are attached peardrop pearls. An ornament in the form of a bracelet worn on the upper right arm is of rubies, sapphires, diamonds, and pearls. Quantities of pearls, sapphires, and diamonds are scattered with regularity over the whole dress and headdress.

In the Portland portrait, C, Plate XXXII, the jewellery worn by the Queen consists of a carcanet of jewels in gold mounts joined by groups of eight pearls, and from it hangs an oval pendant; another pendant of similar design with a pearl hanging therefrom is suspended by a riband from the girdle. This is quite a new fancy, and can be seen in the portraits A, Plate XXXI, C, Plate XLI, and Plate XLII. The jewels on the shoulder rolls, waist-girdle, and frogging down the front all match.

Fig. 922. Carcanet

Plate XXXVIII D, the Ermine portrait, shows one of the wider carcanets, and the arrangements of the eight pearls which come between the jewels is of quite a different design from any hitherto met with.

On close investigation it will be seen that the Queen in A, Plate XLI, is wearing the same carcanet as shown in Plate XLII. Fig. 922 gives a small part of it which is attached to the central jewel. This is a lozenge-shaped ornament in black enamel, framed in gold scroll work, and having a ruby set in the centre. The ornamental links, or rather hinges, connect oval rubies set in gold and black enamel mounts; and from each of these—and there must be at least a dozen to complete the carcanet—hangs a pear pearl on a gold chain. Three more pearls are suspended from the central ornament.

A few items referring to carcanets, and taken from various lists of New Year's gifts to Her Majesty, are set forth below:

'Item, one riche carkenet or collar of golde, having in it two emeraldes,

4 rubyes, and fully garnished with small rubyes and dyamondes.    Geven by the Erle of Lecetor [Leicester].

'A collar of golde contayning 13 peecies, wherein are 13 great emeraldes and 13 pieces of golde, with 13 troches [clusters] of perles, 5 perles in every troche, and in every peece 4 small rubyes, geven by therle Lecetor.'

'Item, a carkenet, upper and nether habilliment of christalles, and small pomaunders slightly garnished with golde.    Geven by the Countyes of Lyncolne.'

The 'upper' refers to a carcanet worn close round the throat, and the 'nether' to a larger one of the same design worn over the shoulders. 'Pomaunders' must mean that little filigree gold buttons or balls containing scents or disinfectants were used as additional ornaments to the carcanet.

## Pendants

The pendants worn by the Queen in her portraits are of varied design, yet some are very much alike.    For instance, that shown in Fig. 923, a detail drawing of the one worn by her in Plate XXIX, is very like the pendant worn on her left side in A, Plate XXXII; possibly it is the same.    The pendant in B, Plate XXXI, hung below a golden rose set with a ruby, is an eagle with widespread wings, trampling upon scorpions.

The pendant seen in D, Plate XXXI, appears to be a large square sapphire in a mount having scroll motifs on all sides, each set with a diamond; from this hangs a pelican in enamel perched on a rectangular ruby in a corresponding gold mount, and to this is attached a lace of pearls festooned round the bodice.

In the Siena portrait, A, Plate XXXII, Elizabeth has hung a beautiful pendant on the left side of her bodice.    It consists of an immense jewel in a gold setting, with two female figures supporting it; a round pearl is attached. The pendant shown in B, Plate XLI, is of square shape, with the frame of gold and red enamel.

Fig. 927 is a detail of the pendant worn in B, Plate XXXII.    It is an amber heart in a mount of black enamel and gold, surrounded by two rows of black enamel and headed by two rubies.    A third and smaller ruby holds the pendent pearl.

The Ermine portrait, D, Plate XXXII, at Hatfield, which the Marquess of Salisbury has kindly allowed to be reproduced together with the 'Rainbow' portrait, is particularly interesting.    Apart from the carcanet already referred to it has lately been discovered by the author that the Queen is wearing, suspended by a chain from this carcanet, the historic jewel known as the 'Three Brothers.'    Fig. 427, which is made from the Ermine portrait, is probably

Fig. 923

Fig. 924

Fig. 925

Fig. 926

Fig. 927

PENDANTS WORN BY QUEEN ELIZABETH

the earliest drawing of this unique jewel, which was then renowned throughout Christendom.[1]

The engraving by Rogers, Plate XXXIX, shows an ornate pendant reproduced in Fig. 924. The centre stone is a diamond set on foliated gold, flanked by oval rubies and surmounted by one of lozenge shape, all studded with pearls, with a pear pearl suspended at the base.

The pendant worn by the Queen in Plate XXXVII is reproduced in Fig. 926, and comprises three rubies, two rectangular and one round, in open scroll work with a little enamel introduced. A pendant of beautiful and simple design is seen in Fig. 925. A large square ruby is set in gold and framed with black enamel circles, whence two ruby drops and a pear pearl are hung.

Fig. 928.
The Three Brothers

In the portrait A, Plate XXXI, a very beautiful pendant of jewels, enamel, and two female figures is hung by a black riband from the Queen's waist-belt. This use of a pendant is also shown in Plate XLII where it is hung by a pink riband fastened with a bow to the point of her stomacher; a drawing is given in Fig. 929. A large oval ruby is framed in gold and a little black enamel, and surrounding this is scroll work in gold supporting six round pearls; a large pear pearl hangs from the centre.

As mentioned previously, pendants were sometimes fastened to the sleeve, as seen in Plate XLV, in which the Queen and the bride (*see also* Fig. 732)

[1] The remaining history of the celebrated jewel is as follows: In 1623 James I, in writing to his son Charles, about to journey into Spain to seek a wife, tells him he is sending for his 'Babies owin wearing . . . the Three Brothers that you know full well, but newlie sette, and the Mirroure of Frawnce, the fellowe of the Portugall Dyamont, quhiche I wolde wishe you to weare alone in your hatte with a little blakke feather.' 'Newly set' is misleading. In comparing the engraving (Fig. 928) taken from the work of Peter Lambeck, published in 1669, with the jewel shown in the Ermine portrait, it will be seen that not only have the jewels been reset, but apparently both rubies and diamonds have been recut and the pearls replaced by smaller ones—perhaps through loss or damage.

It is, on the whole, more probable that Hilliard, who was a careful artist and who had the original before him, is more correct than the Count's engraver.

The last record of the 'Three Brothers' is in 1625, when Charles, now King, sends the Duke of Buckingham and Lord Holland as Ambassadors Extraordinary to the States of the United Provinces. They are to take with them certain jewels, and among them 'A faire Flower of Goulde with three greate Ballasses in the middest, a great poynted Dyamond and three greate Pearles fixte with a fair Pearle Pendant, called the Brethren.'

These Lord Compton was commanded to deliver into the hands of Lord Conway, being at that time in Lord Compton's custody, to be pawned in Holland.

Henceforth all trace of this interesting jewel disappears.

A possible solution of the ultimate fate of this jewel is suggested. It would naturally have been pawned with one of the most important financiers or jewellers, in, say, Amsterdam, and retained by them for redemption. It may be that at some date, but not until the Civil War in England when English credit probably slumped, or after the death of Charles I when no hope remained of its ever being reclaimed, the 'Three Brothers' was dissected, and the diamond, rubies, and pearls sold separately.

Who knows whether Louis XIV, noted for his love of magnificence, or some other ostentatious monarch, did not acquire one, or some of them?

It would be an interesting mystery for someone with the necessary time, industry, and means to follow up.

are both wearing such a decoration. Another example is given in Fig. 730.

The following descriptions apply to other pendants belonging to the Queen:

'A juell of golde, being a catt, and myce playing with her.

'One green frog, the back of emeralds, smale and greate, and a pendaunte emeralde, and a smale chegne of gold to hang by.

'A juell of golde, being an anker.

'Two snakes wounde together.'

Some excerpts from lists of New Year's gifts which show the varied subjects introduced into pendants are given below:

'Item, a juell of golde, being a shippe, set with a table dyamonde of fyve sparcks of dyamondes, and a smale perle pendaunte. Geven by the Lorde Howarde.

'Item, one juell of golde, wherein is a pelly-cane garnished with small rubyes and dia-mondes, hanging by a small chegne, and one perle pendaunt. Geven by the Lady Mary Sidney. Geven by her Majestie to the young Countyes of Huntingdon.' 1572.

The above may refer to the pelican pen-dant worn by the Queen in the portrait, D, Plate XXXI.

'Item a Falcone or parret, the body christ-all, the hedd, tayle, leggs, and crest of golde;

Fig. 929. Pendant

fully garnished with sparcks of rubyes and emerauldes, hanging by a very short and small chegne of golde.' 1574.

'Item, a riche juell, being a clocke of golde, garnished with dyamondes, rubyes, emeraldes, and perles, with one very fayre rubye in the bottome, and a fayre emeralde pendante sett in golde, and two mene perles pendaunte, all 9 oz 3 ge. Geven by Mr. Hatton, Capitayne of the Garde.' 1575.

The following story illustrates the lengths to which Elizabeth would go to secure a coveted jewel—a greed which she shared with Catherine de' Medici. Soon after Portugal became a province of Spain under Philip II in 1581, the claimant to the throne, Dom Antonio, was driven out of the country and fled first to France and then to England. Arriving at the English Court penniless but with the bulk of the Portuguese crown jewels, Dom Antonio was made much of by Queen Elizabeth and Leicester, and treated with Royal honours solely on account of his great wealth in jewels. 'The greedy crew that sur-rounded the Queen soon scented plunder, and money for warlike preparations, the purchase of ships and the like [for the recovery of Dom Antonio's lost crown] was speedily forthcoming.' Elizabeth and Leicester managed to grab some of the best, advancing £5,000 for a magnificent diamond of the purest water, weighing eight carats and called 'The Portuguese.' After a good deal of haggling with merchants about loans, etc., the Queen annexed the diamond for £8,000 (it was valued at about £30,000) and in England it remained for forty-two years.[1] 'In dudgeon with the greedy English,' poor though he still had a considerable quantity of jewels left, Dom Antonio went back to France, only to be treated in like manner by that other coveter of rich jewels, Catherine de' Medici.

This finishes the list of a few of the Queen's jewels.

## HAT AND HEAD ORNAMENTS

There seems to be no rule as to the kind of jewellery worn by gentlemen in their headgear. Although there might be a particular vogue at a given time, men of fashion decorated their hats with whatever took their fancy at the moment.

The gold ornaments and the jewelled pin worn by Mr. Edward Hoby in 1577 (Fig. 847) are imitated by Sir John Hawkyns (Fig. 851). The decoration of young Oxford's hat, 1575 (Fig. 846), of fastening the hatband with jewelled buttons, is one that was frequently used on smart headgear for some time. Later we find Sir Henry Unton in 1586 (Fig. 850) wearing an elaborate jewel, such as at a later date (1602) is set upon a Spanish hat; and at a much later period

Fig. 930. Parure of French Hood

(beyond the limit of this volume) similar elaborate jewels in hats were very much in vogue.

The women copied the men, as with headgear, and their outdoor hats glistened with ornaments. The Spanish ladies of the aristocracy were profuse in the adornment of their hats, as seen in Fig. 674 (the Queen of Spain) and Fig. 773.

The band of jewels or parure which ornamented the arch of the French hood, referred to in this volume as a 'coronet,' varied very considerably, as will be seen by the many illustrations of French hoods. Fig. 930 shows part of a parure of unusual design in which jewels do not appear; instead, it is decorated with coloured enamels on a band of gold and set with large pearls. The portrait from which this drawing is taken dates about the 1570's.

Headdresses in the form of coronets or cauls, especially those worn by Queen Elizabeth, were masses of jewels; and the wreaths, or billiments as they were called (see especially Fig. 880), and tiaras such as were in fashion during the 1590's, are so elaborate as to be almost indescribable. Some illustrations are given in Figs. 729, 730, 732, 772, 774, and Plate XLIV.

---

[1] This diamond was ultimately given by Charles, Prince of Wales, to the Duke of Olivares in 1623.

Another head ornament much used during the second half of the reign was the bodkin. This was a kind of skewer, but for practical purposes it must have been shaped like a hairpin. At the top of this bodkin was usually set some jewel, often a diamond, or a round or pear pearl; sometimes a diamond suspended by pearls. A number of these ornaments were stuck over the whole coiffure. Queen Elizabeth was very fond of piercing her padded wigs with jewelled bodkins, as seen in her portraits, Plates XXXII A and XLI, A, C, and D, Plates XLII and XLV.

These ornaments might be termed buttons, as they could, without the pin, be used as such; and excerpts from an inventory of the Queen's are:

'Item, 3 dozen of buttones of golde, havinge 3 pearles and a sparcke of an emeralde or rubyes in every button.   3 ounces and a half.

'Item, 84 buttons of golde enamuled, and every of them sett with a small sparcke of emeralds, rubyes, and perles.   Geven by therle of Warwicke.

'Item, twoe bodkins of golde, thone a flye, thother a spyder, the spider's body being a perle and a sparke of a rubye, the fly garnished with sparks of dyamondes.   Geven by Sir Henry Lee, Master of the Armorye.'   1586–7.

'Item, a bodkinne of silver, with a little ostridg of gold, pendant, enamuled, and two waspes of golde lose enamuled.   Geven by Mr. Carmanden.

'Item, a bodkin of golde, with a pendant emrald with a smale perle therat. Geven by Mrs. Sakeford.'   1584–5.


## GIRDLES

The ornamentation of girdles with long ends reached its climax in the reigns of Henry VIII and Mary.   No new features are noticeable, and girdles worn were of the same styles as described in Chapters II and III.

By the 1580's the girdle with a long pendent end was definitely out of fashion.


## BRACELETS

Bracelets were not much used, as they could be worn only with sleeves of a certain kind; for instance, the one of embroidered linen shown in the portrait of Queen Elizabeth, Plate XXXI D.   Also bracelets were not consistent with the elaborate lace cuffs which were so general.   In some portraits one sees a single row of pearls between the edge of the cuff and wrist and falling well on to the hand (see Plate XXXII D, and Plate XLI D).

A wide band of jewels is worn round the upper arm by the Queen in D, Plate XXXI, and the Spanish Infanta (Fig. 772) also wears one in the same position.

That bracelets could be used as carcanets is verified by the following gift to the Queen:

'Item, a payre of braceletts, which may serve for a carkenett, fully gar-nished with ophales and rubyes very fayre, enamuleted with an ophall pendaunt. Geven by Mr. Hatton, Capitaine of the Garde.'

Fig. 931.
Cuff Ornament

Fig. 932.
Sleeve Ornament

A jewel fixed on to the lace cuff was quite usual, as shown in C, Plate XLI. This is given in larger scale in Fig. 931.

Fig. 932 shows another orna-ment which could be used for the same purpose, but this one is taken from a portrait of a lady dated 1599. In this she is wearing several of these ornaments sewn at the top of her full-puffed sleeves.

### EARRINGS

Earrings—when they were worn, which was not very often it appears—were, as a rule, circular or peardrop pearls. Other kinds were occasionally used, and Fig. 933 gives one of a pair worn by the Queen in D, Plate XLI; the main element in the design, thrice repeated, is a peardrop pearl and an almond-shaped ruby set in gold, both hanging from the same link.

Elizabeth preferred pearl earrings, and a peardrop hanging from a cluster of pearls is seen in Plate XL; in B, Plate XLI, the pear pearl is hung from an ornamental disc in gold and red enamel.

Mary Fitton, Plate XLIV, has chosen earrings each consisting of a hoop of pearls or diamonds, probably both, from which a peardrop pearl is suspended.

It has already been mentioned that gentlemen wore *one* earring, and that a pearl.

Fig. 933.
Earring

### RUFF ORNAMENTS

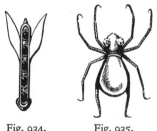

Fig. 934.       Fig. 935.
Ruff Ornaments

The use of jewelled ornaments pinned on to the ruff was a charming idea in vogue during the 1590's. These are particularly conspicu-ous in Plate XL, where they take the form of arrows in gold and red enamel set with rubies or diamonds, with the feathers in pearl (Fig. 934). It was noticed on one occasion that a large black spider was sitting on the ruff of Queen Elizabeth; this was a realistic piece of jewellery in jet with diamond eyes. Another spider is shown in Fig. 935, with the head and legs in gold and enamel, diamond or emerald eyes, and a pear-pearl body.

Some portraits of the Queen and noble ladies show a rose of the new variety fastened on the left side of the ruff, and there are several others where a rose or other flower is fixed to the bodice.

## AIGLETTES

Throughout the latter half of the sixteenth century the attractive decoration of aiglettes and loops plastered on sleeves and down the fronts of skirts was very much the mode. This fashion originated in Spain, where it was very generously used upon the elaborate dresses of the no-bility (*see* Figs. 674, 676, 680). These loops with ends are first seen worn by an English lady (Fig. 589), dating 1560, where the reason for their introduction is explained; but, as so often happens in the history of costume, utility soon gave way to decoration. Henceforth we find these aiglettes and loops much in evidence, but used only as ornaments mainly by ladies of the land of their origin, and of France, and in England from about 1600. Fig. 936 shows a pair of jewelled aiglettes of coloured enamel and gold, with spirals

Fig. 936.
A Pair of Aiglettes

Fig. 937.
Handle of Fan

of pearls. Each is attached to one end of a piece of silk or riband, which is knotted, forming an erect loop.

Fig. 937 is the jewelled handle of a feather fan carried by Queen Elizabeth in the portrait Plate XLII.

## FINGER RINGS

In the Bodleian is a book of original designs for finger rings by Pierre VVoerior of Lorraine, 1561; from this source Figs. 938, 939, and 940 have been reproduced.

Fig. 939 shows the side and end views of two of these rings. The ring (Fig. 938) with grotesque men's heads which terminate the shanks supporting the flange and bezel, is set with a pointed diamond. In Fig. 940 the shanks develop into rams' heads and forelegs, and are mounted by a circular watch. It is very ornate, and so minute that one wonders if it is practicable.

Another ring of the same kind, but dating the end of the century, is given in Fig. 941. Scrolls set with diamonds decorate the shanks, bezel, and lid, the latter covering a very small dial.  This ring is drawn from an actual example, which shows that a watch-ring such as is described above *could* be made.

Fig. 942 is a ring of romance — the Essex ring which the Countess of Nottingham failed to bring to Queen Elizabeth, with such fatal results.   The

Fig. 938.

Fig. 939.

Four Finger Rings, 1561

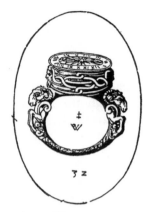

Fig. 940.

delicate shank, somewhat worn by age, supports a heavy flange engraved in lines with tiny globules surrounding the bezel.  This contains a cameo portrait of the Queen cut from a three-strata sardonyx.  A blue enamelled cinquefoil ornaments the top and base.  After the execution of the Earl of Essex, the ring was returned to his daughter, the Lady Frances Devereux, and thereafter it passed from mother to daughter for several generations.[1]

Fig. 941. Dial Ring

Fig. 942.
The Essex Ring

It was still not uncommon to wear a ring on the middle joint and one on the thumb as well as on the fingers.  Two rings worn on the right hand are shown attached for safety by a fine gold chain to the bracelet in the Arbury portrait of Katherine Nevill, wife of Francis Fitton, Esq., who was married in 1588.

It was stated recently that the wedding ring of Mary Stuart and Lord Darnley was a rather clumsy, rough one of tawny gold, bearing the initials M. H. entwined with true lovers' knots.  In her list of bequests (made in

---

[1] Later this ring came successively into the possession of six noble ladies, three peers, and four old bachelors, and was sold to Lord Michelham in 1910 for £3,412.   From him it was purchased in 1927 by an historical enthusiast, Mr. Ernest Makower, for £546 to present to Westminster Abbey, where it can now be seen upon the tomb of Queen Elizabeth.

1566) a wedding ring is mentioned of red and gold enamel set with a large diamond, and in her handwriting in the margin beside it are these words: 'Cest celui de quoy ie fus espousee. Au Roy qui la me donne.'

The English Envoy at Edinburgh, in his contemporary account of the Queen's marriage, writes: 'The words were spoken; the rings, which were three, the middle a rich diamond, were put upon her finger, they kneel together, and many prayers said over them.' The other two rings were plain guards.

## FRENCH JEWELLERY

The amount of jewellery produced in France during the reigns of Charles IX and Henry III was greater than at any previous period, and many French masters of the jeweller's art became famous. In design their work very closely resembled the Italian, being greatly influenced by the school of Cellini of the previous generation.

Some very delightful jewellery of about 1550–60 is to be seen in the portrait, French School, of the Duchesse d'Angoulême, No. 2617 in the National Gallery. She wears a pale mauve-grey dress; the carcanet, waist-girdle, bracelets, and the ornaments on her French hood all match. They are of gold with black enamel, and set with rubies and pearls.

A few of the presents, sent from the French Royal family to the Archduchess Elizabeth of Austria before her marriage to Charles IX in 1572, are quoted:

'List of the presents with which the Royal Princess of France has been honoured by His Majesty, his Lady Mother, and his brethren. The King of France caused to be given: To his Bride, the said Princess Elizabeth, the daughter of His Imperial Majesty: A necklace, that is valued in all at 50,000 scudi,[1] consisting of three diamonds in clusters, the least of which is valued at 10,000 scudi, four large rubies, sixteen large pearls, each one of which is valued at 100 scudi.

'A ring with a diamond hanging, set in four golden bands, so that it can be seen on all sides. It is valued at 12,000 scudi.

'To the Archduke Ferdinand: To lave the hands, a pitcher or can for water made of agate, set with pearls and a handle with an emerald to lift the lid thereof. . . .

'The Old Queen, Mother of the King of France, has presented: A chain' all of rubies, diamonds and emeralds from which is suspended a large diamond. At the top there is a large ruby, and thereunder hangs a large pearl like a pear. This all is valued at 20,000 scudi. . . .

'Besides these presents, four white harriers have been sent to Vienna as a gift to the Emperor. Each of these has a red velvet and gold collar. The value of all this is 500 scudi.'

Elizabeth of Austria possessed the largest oriental ruby in the world. It was the size of a hen's egg, and at her death became the property of her brother, the Emperor Rudolph II.

---

[1] An Italian coin worth about four shillings.

## JEWELS OF MARY STUART

Mary Stuart possessed many beautiful jewels of her own, chiefly of French workmanship. Amongst them were some remarkably fine pearls, including seven of exceptional size (*see* p. 277), the wedding gift of Catherine de' Medici. When Queen-Consort of France she had use of the French as well as the Scottish crown jewels in addition to her own, but the former she relinquished when she returned to Scotland in 1561.

In her will, drawn up in June 1566 by Mary Livingston, Keeper of Her Majesty's jewels, and Margaret Carwood, bedchamber woman in charge of the Queen's cabinet, Mary Stuart left certain jewels of her own to the Crown of Scotland in remembrance of herself and the Scottish alliance with the House of Lorraine. The items include seven jewels containing her largest diamonds for ornaments to the succeeding Queens-Consort of Scotland. To the Crown itself she devised a diamond cross, a chain enriched with rubies and diamonds, a carcanet of diamonds, rubies, and pearls, and the 'Great Harry.' This jewel contained a large diamond 'taillé à faces' set in gold, a cabochon ruby, and the cipher ℍ set in diamonds, hanging by a chain of gold 'with a ruby pendant thereat.' This was a gift to Queen Mary from her father-in-law, Henry II, whose cipher it bore.[1]

In 1570 the 'Great Harry' was bestowed by the Regent Moray upon his wife, and later much pressure was brought to bear upon the widowed Countess to give it up—apparently without success, as it was not until 1574 that she, now Countess of Argyll, was compelled by Parliament to restore it to James VI.

After 1567 Mary's own jewels and those of the Scottish Crown began an adventurous career. She left them behind, with most of her wardrobe, on her hurried escape from Edinburgh Castle in May 1567, some of them hidden, it is said, in a crevice in the castle rock. Others, chiefly those belonging to the Crown, including the Regalia, were discovered in the castle 'hidden in a wooden chest in a cave.' Her own personal jewels fared worse. At Carberry Hill (June 1567) Mary gave 20,000 crowns' worth (£6,000) to Bothwell, and these fell into the hands of the Confederate Lords, along with most of her belongings.

Shortly afterwards the Queen entrusted her own diamonds and pearls to the Earl of Moray, who was visiting her at Loch Leven. The trust was ill-kept; they passed, to the value of 20,000 or 30,000 crowns, into the hands of the Earl of Morton, and many of them were subsequently pawned or sold. Numbers of diamonds and pearls were pawned to many different persons, from whom the Regent Morton recovered them by powers granted by Parliament in 1574. Some came to London for sale, and among them were 'six cordons of large pearls, strung as paternosters; but there are five and twenty separate from the rest, much finer and larger than those which are strung; these are for the most part like black muscates'—the famous black

---

[1] In James I's reign the large diamond of the 'Great Harry' was incorporated in the more magnificent 'Mirror of Great Britain.'

pearls, the most magnificent in Europe. Many offers were made for them, but Queen Elizabeth, who had always kept a keen eye on her dear sister's jewels, bought the pearls [1] for 12,000 crowns, not a third of their value, in April 1568. This was done under the covetous eyes of Catherine de' Medici and, indeed, of most of Europe.

The little jewel casket, which afterwards became so celebrated, is described thrice—by the Regent Moray in 1568 as 'a silver box'; by the Privy Council in 1568 and 1571 as 'a silver box owergilt with gold'; and by Buchanan as 'a small gilt coffer not fully a foot long, being garnished in sundry places with the Roman letter F under a king's crown.'

Gabrielle d'Estrées was noted for the marvellous jewels she possessed, and at a Court function in 1594 her dress of black satin was so loaded with diamonds, rubies, emeralds, and pearls, that she was only able to stand for a few minutes at a time. By special permission this overweighted lady was allowed to sit in the Royal presence.

Another bejewelled lady, this time a Royal one, was Marie de' Medici, over whose gown were strewn 32,000 pearls and 3,000 diamonds. It was so heavy that she sat all through some State ceremony, but this was her privilege as Queen-Consort.

A beautiful Indian diamond of almond shape and faceted on both sides ultimately became one of the English Crown jewels, but not without a history of some interest.

Henry III's Ambassador at the Turkish Court was Nicolas Harlai, Seigneur de Sancy, who, while at Constantinople in 1570, bought this Indian diamond for a very large sum. On his return to France, Harlai sold it to the King, who prized it so much that he often wore it in front of his turban (see Figs. 745 and 746). At Henry's death in 1589 the diamond was returned to the Lord of Sancy, and henceforth this precious stone was named after him.

In order to raise money for the strengthening of his army, Henry IV borrowed the 'Sancy' from its owner, who had now become superintendent of the King's finances, and in course of time returned it. Later, when fulfilling his term of office as Henry's Ambassador to England, Harlai sold it to Queen Elizabeth.[2]

---

[1] The seven pearls, the gift of Catherine de' Medici, still form part of the crown jewels of Great Britain.

[2] After Queen Elizabeth's death this large diamond was taken, together with the diamond from the 'Great Harry,' to adorn a still more splendid jewel known as the 'Mirror of Great Britain,' and in an inventory dated 1605 it is described as follows:

'A greate and rich jewell of golde called the Myrror of Greate Brytayne conteyninge one verie fayre table dyamonde, one verie fayre table rubye, twoe other lardge dyamondes, cut lozengewyse, the one of them called the Stone of the letter H of Scotlande garnyshed with smalle dyamondes, two rounde perles, fixed, and one fayre dyamonde, cutt in fawcettis bought of Sauncey.'

So set, the Sancy remained among the British crown jewels until 1689, when it passed (detached) to the crown jewels of France, appearing again in an inventory of 1791. In the nineteenth century it came into the possession of the Princess Paula Demidoff, from whose family it was purchased in 1856 for the sum of £20,000 by the wealthy Parsee merchant, Sir Jamsetjee Jeejeebhoy. At his decease it returned to France and was shown at the Paris Exhibition of 1867, where it was priced at a million francs. Thence it passed to the Maharajah of Patiala, after whose death William Waldorf Astor purchased it as a wedding present to his daughter-in-law in 1906. This diamond is still in the possession of the Viscountess Astor.

The most confusing stories are told about famous jewels, but it is hoped that the accounts of those which have been given in this volume are reasonably correct.

## CLOCKS

Perpendicular standing clocks, anything from twelve to twenty-four or more inches in height, were very elaborate during the reign of Elizabeth, following the designs popularized by Holbein. A description of one is given on p. 501.

Another, mentioned in a list of jewels delivered into the custody of Mris Mary Radeclyffe, one of the gentlewomen of 'the Quenes Majesties privie chambre' by Mistress Blanche Parry, is described as follows:

'Item one clocke of golde curiouslye wrought with flowers and beastes with a Quene in the toppe on thone side, and on the other side a beare and a ragged staffe of sparkes of diamondes fullie furnished with diamondes and rubies of sundrye sortes and bignes one Emerode under it a faier table diamonde with a ragged staffe in the foyle thereof and a faier Rubie under it squared, and a pearle pendaunt on eyther side of the clocke.'

A clock in the form of a ship, dated 1580, can be examined in the Franks Room of the British Museum; and another, dated 1589, and resembling a three-storied tower, can also be seen there.

## WATCHES

In the second half of the century the clockmakers of southern Germany and France supplied an increasing demand for standing clocks, table clocks, and pectoral or pendent clocks—i.e. watches. By their ingenuity they were able to reduce the size of the works so as to take up as little space as possible, reducing the clock to a very small compass.

Watches were of different shapes, their dials being circular, square, octagonal, or oval; and in thickness flat, semi-spherical, pumpkin, or egg-shaped, the last being known as 'Nuremberg eggs.' 'Memento mori' watches were set in gold, silver, or ivory carved in the form of a skull, and were as much as three by two and a half inches; they were usually attached by a chain to the waist-girdle.

Circular watches were worn as pendants at the neck, on the hip, and at the waist or end of the girdle.

Mary Stuart possessed at least two octagonal watches or dials as they were often called. One of them, the work of D. du Chemin of Rouen, 1570, measures one and five-eighth inches in diameter, and has an engraved gold dial; the lid is of rock crystal set in a narrow gold frame. The other watch is almost identical in design, except that the dial is not engraved. Both these watches are similar to that shown in Fig. 945.

The Queen of Scots left to Darnley, by her will dated 1566: 'One watch garnished with ten diamonds, two rubies, and a cord of gold,' and 'one little dial curiously wrought and set with eight diamonds, two rubies, one pearl pendant, one little chain of gold to which is attached a pomander garnished with little turquoises and garnets.'

Fig. 943 is a German-made watch dating about 1560. Its case is flat, curiously shaped, and decorated with enamel. As a rule, German watches were circular boxes and struck the hours; they had the same appearance as a reliquary, being hung round the neck like a pendant. Augsburg was an important place for the manufacture of watches, and several of those now existing bear this name upon them. In 1558 it is stated that fashionable young men wore these circular watches suspended by a chain upon their breasts.

Fig. 943. German Watch, 1560

It is more than likely that the circular pendant worn by Queen Elizabeth on her right hip in the portrait (Plate XXXII C) is a jewelled watch. The Earl of Leicester presented her with a watch, sometimes called a dial or even clock, as a New Year's gift, 1578–9. It was 'a verey feyer juell of golde, being a clocke fully furnished with small diamonds pointed and a pendaunte of golde, diamonds, and rubies, very smale, and upon each side a lozenge diamond, and an apple of golde enamuled grene and russet.'

According to the design by VVoerior (Fig. 940) watches were sometimes set as finger rings, and perhaps the first wrist watch recorded in history was the Earl of Leicester's New Year's gift to Elizabeth, 1571–2. It is described as 'one armlet or shakell [shackle] of golde, all over fairely garnishedd with rubyes and dyamondes, having in the closing thereof a clocke, and in the fore parte of the same a fayre lozengie dyamonde without a foyle, hanging thereat a rounde juell fully garnished with dyamondes, and perle pendant; weying 11 oz. quᵃ dim. and farthing golde weight. In a case of purple vellate all over embranderid with Venice golde, and lyned with greene vellat.'

The portrait, dated 1586, of Joyce Frankland at Brasenose College, Oxford, shows the lady holding a circular watch in her hands (Fig. 944). She was the daughter of Robert Trappes, a goldsmith, and married first Henry Saxey and secondly William Frankland, both goldsmiths of London. It is said that she was the first citizeness to possess a gold watch. Being thrice associated with the goldsmith's craft, this is not surprising. Certainly the watch, which measures two and a half inches across, is an excellent specimen. The dial, A, of gold is plain with the exception of very delicate engraving in the centre. The hours are engraved, and round the edge is a cord moulding.

The lid, B, has an openwork design reproduced on a larger scale in E.    The back part, C, which shows in perspective in the original painting, has rectangular incisions forming a decorative border.    D is a section through the back.    To the watch is attached a black silk riband, and at the end is strung the golden key.

The pendant (Fig. 916) is worn by Mistress Frankland in this portrait.

Fig. 945 is a watch dating the 1590's, hexagonal and flat in shape, the dial

Fig. 944. Mistress Frankland's Watch, 1586                    Fig. 945

and sides being decorated with enamel.    The front and back are covered with rock crystal lids set in narrow moulded gold frames, and to it is attached a plaited gold chain bearing the key.

An instance of the diplomatic use of jewels—a very frequent occurrence —is cited below:

'Venice, 3 March 1600.

'We are advised from Constantinople that the Sultan has sent magnificent gifts of rubies, pearls, and diamonds to the Queen of England with a request that she should effect a peace between him and His Imperial Majesty.'

Should students of historical jewellery wish to pursue the subject more comprehensively, they will find H. Clifford Smith's book, *Jewellery*, 1908, most useful.

GUILDS AND TRADE (*continued from p. 464*)

In the early days of Elizabeth's reign, trade in the Mediterranean was made dangerous, even impossible, owing to the rise of the Turkish sea power dating about the middle of the century. Consequently, England was still dependent on the merchant galleys of Venice for her supplies of luxuries and gorgeous fabrics. In 1571 the Ottoman Empire received a tremendous blow at Lepanto, which completely crushed its naval ambitions. The first English representative was installed at Constantinople in 1578, and in 1580 the Charter of Liberties to English merchants, which opened trade relations with Turkey, was formally issued.

Russia had already, in 1553, made commercial overtures to the English nation, and again in 1582 a special envoy was sent by Ivan the Terrible to undertake matrimonial negotiations with one of Queen Elizabeth's relatives, but without success. A year later Sir Jerome Bowes was sent, as first Ambassador to Moscow, in order to obtain exemption from the duties on English exports to Russia.

Apparently Japan had trade relations with Spain in 1595, and China with England. The latter could not have been very extensive, for, according to a report dated 1599, 'a vessel richly laden with gold and silk is said to have reached England from China after a three years' voyage.'

Ever since it was established at the Styleyard, the Hanseatic League had enjoyed many and great privileges by special treaty; but owing to its arbitrary bearing, these were abolished by order of Queen Elizabeth in 1578. However, the merchants still remained at their headquarters, and continued to cling blindly to their old prerogatives; in consequence of which the exasperated Queen expelled them from London in 1598. A nasty blow was dealt them by Sir Francis Drake, who captured sixty-one of their ships. Piracy was a popular amusement carried on even against countries with which England was normally at peace; and the Queen herself thought no shame in protecting the pirates and in accepting a large share of the loot.

So remarkable was the development of the Merchant Adventurers in the Netherlands during this reign, that at the height of their prosperity they employed fifty thousand persons in Holland, and the annual value of the trade reached twelve million ducats. In 1578 the foreign headquarters were moved to Hamburg, whence the merchants were for a time expelled under pressure from the Hanseatic League, but after the Queen closed the Styleyard the Adventurers soon recovered their position in Hamburg, and there the Company continued to function until 1808.

In 1600 Queen Elizabeth granted a charter to the East India Company, whereupon the various Dutch societies trading in the Indies were consolidated in 1602 into the Dutch East India Company.

Alas! all the picturesqueness of the London Livery Companies disappeared with the Middle Ages, owing to the commercial instincts of Sir William Bayly, Draper, described on p. 367.

It is quite certain that the Queen did not approve of this change. She would have much preferred homage and ovations from a colourful crowd of City worthies rather than from a collection of black-robed Dominicans, as they might have appeared but for the coloured hoods they carried.

There is a note of regret in the following excerpt from Stow:

'But yet in London among the graver sort (I mean the Liveries of Companies) remaineth a memory of the hoods of old time worn by their predecessors: these hoods were worn, the roundlets [the roll part] upon their heads, the skirts [the shoulder part] to hang behind in their necks to keep them warm, the tippet [liripipe] to lie on their shoulder or to wind about their necks; these hoods were of old time made in colours according to their gowns, which were of two colours, as red and blue, or red and purple, murrey, or as it pleased their masters and wardens to appoint to the companies. But now of late time they have used their gowns to be all of one colour, and those of the saddest, but their hoods being made the one half of the same cloth their gowns be of, the other half remaineth red as of old time.'

For the dress of a member of one of the City Companies see Fig. 798 and the description given under it.

One of the most popular of the Livery Companies of London was 'the Fraternity of the Art and Mistery of the Haberdashers . . . indifferently called Hurrers and Milliners, the Latter from the Merchandizes they chiefly dealt in, which came from the City of Milan.' Their wares comprised all kinds of articles necessary for dress, adornment, and utility: such as aiglettes, buttons of silk, metal or bone, brooches and ouches, French and Spanish gloves, head ornaments of every kind, caps, hats, French hoods, cauls, escoffions, spurs, ink-horns and penners, earpicks and toothpicks, trinkets and gewgaws, needles and pins.

## WEAVING AND MATERIALS

During the course of the last two reigns there had been a repetition of many fraudulent practices in the making of cloth. Again in 1597 the same practices were denounced when 'flocks, sollace, flour, chalk, and other deceitful things' were mentioned as ingredients injurious to cloth, 'the use of which made them rewey, pursey, squally, cockling, light, and notably faulty . . . the same cloth having only for the most part an outward show, wanting that substance and strength which oftentimes it appears to have.' Fraudulent imitations of gold threads were made from copper-gilt wire, from gold leaf hammered upon vellum and afterwards cut into strips, and by covering fabrics with gold leaf.

The weaving industry received a tremendous impetus during this reign by the immigration of Flemings. Amongst them were a great number of weavers, dyers, and other skilled craftsmen, who fled to England to escape the persecutions of the Duke of Alba in 1568. A similar influx occurred in 1585, when the Duke of Parma captured Antwerp.

The prices of various materials will be found in Philip Henslowe's *Diary*.

## LIST OF MATERIALS

*Bays, bayze*, introduced into England in 1561 by the Walloons; so called from its colour, a reddish brown. In 1568 the Flemish refugees were granted permission to settle at Norwich, Colchester, Maidstone, Sandwich, and Southampton.

*Bewpers, beaupers*, some kind of cloth, but its character is unknown. Probably a light woollen stuff.

*Boulters, boulting cloth*, a thin woollen material of coarse mesh, like a sieve or bolter.

*Burra, borra*, diminutive *burrell*, a kind of stuffing or padding.

*Callimancoes*, material made of camel hair or wool in stripes, checks, patterns, or plain colours, and glazed in finishing.

*Cambric*. See *Lawn*.

*Carrells*, a material like bays and fustians, only mixed with silk, worsted, or linen yarn.

*Cobweb lawn*, an especially fine transparent linen, as the name implies.

*Crape, crêpe*, thin transparent cotton or silk material with a small crinkled surface, usually black, and used for mourning. Also in white, but smooth.

*Cyprus*, a very fine transparent curled linen. Both black and white were made, but the former was much more common. This was chiefly used for mourning. Originally introduced from Cyprus, hence its name.

*Damask*, first made in England by the Netherlands weavers, who sought refuge in this country in 1568 and again in 1585. Its price was from about nine to ten shillings per yard.

*Dornicks, dornock*, checked table linen.

*Estamel*, same as stammell.

*Harden*, a common linen made from the coarsest quality of hemp or flax, and sometimes even of tow.

*Galloon*, braid of gold, silver, or silk thread.

*Lawn*. Stow is not correct in stating that lawn and cambric 'began to be known,' and were first imported to England in 1562. Both materials had been known for more than a century (*see* vol. ii, p. 463).

*Luzarnes*, fur from the Russian lynx, the shade of which depends upon the climate, as described on p. 130.

*Mockadoes*, an imitation velvet; a fabric either of wool or silk on which a pattern was formed with loops, which being afterwards cut, in the same way that velvet was sheared, left the pattern in pile.

*Nettle cloth,* a material said to have been woven from the fibres of nettles.

*New draperies,* a term used to denote light woollen fabrics introduced into England from the Netherlands by Protestant refugees, hence a name given to any novelty in cloth weaving.

*Paillettes, pailles.*  See *Spangles.*

Fig. 946. Border, 1590

*Pampilion* also referred to a livery coat worn by servants, not necessarily furred.

*Passamayne,* gold or silver braid.  Also applied, after 1578, to coloured braids.

*Perpetuana,* a term used to denote substantial fabrics.  Also a strong *everlasting* glossy cloth, like parchment.

Fig. 947. Border, 1600

*Plush,* material made as shag having a long nap either in silk or of hair. Its use came in at the latter part of the sixteenth century.

*Sammeron,* a linen cloth 'between flaxen and hempen, finer than one and coarser than the other.'

*Satin* became so general and so inexpensive — about eight shillings, the

Fig. 948. Border, 1600

very best twelve shillings, per yard—that almost every one of any importance wore it.

*Say, saye, sayes.*  The craft of weaving this coarse woollen cloth was brought to England by some Flemings in 1567.  They settled at Braintree, Norwich, and Sudbury.

*Shag,* a rough hairy cloth woven with a single thread woof and a double warp; the one wool of two threads twisted, the other of goat or camel hair.

*Spangles, musers, pailles, paillettes.* Spangles were now much more scintillating. They were stamped in facets, and some were engraved.

*Stammell,* a coarse red cloth used by the commonalty as a substitute for the expensive scarlet cloth worn by the nobility. Estamel is another name for it.

*Swansdown,* the dressed down and skin of the swan fashionable for trimmings in the late sixteenth century. It was often dyed in colour.

*Taffeta,* a cheap substitute for the rich thin silk so popular amongst the nobility and upper classes, made in linen.

*Thrum,* the ends of the threads of the warp cut off from the extremities of the weaver's web.

*Tiffany,* a very transparent fine linen or gauze, sometimes classified under *Cobweb lawn.* Made in silk late in the sixteenth century as a silky transparent gauze.

*Velure,* a material something like velvet but made of cotton and sometimes wool.

*Velvet.* In the days of Queen Elizabeth velvet cost twenty shillings and thirty shillings per yard.

## PATTERNS

The patterns of materials used during the first half of Queen Elizabeth's reign were much the same as those used during the reign of Henry VIII.

During the late 1570's, when skirts became fuller and the surface was broken up into many folds, large patterns became distorted. The Italian designers and weavers realized this change, and were the first to adopt much smaller and more compact designs, chiefly floral and often of a diaper or semée nature. France produced brocades of similar design, which is accounted for by the fact that many Italian weavers had emigrated to that country and brought the newest ideas with them. The first appearance of this type of smaller pattern in this volume is to be seen in the Darnley portrait of the Queen, A, Plate XXXI: a semi-floral scroll design, in delicate curves and broken sprays of gold, is woven upon a white satin or silk foundation.

Later, in 1580, we find the Queen, Plate XXXII C, gowned in a very beautiful brocade in the very latest style; conventional flowers and leaves in colours alternate diaperwise with motifs in gold having a jewelled button sewn in the centre; the design is woven into the white satin ground.

A pleasing design is given in Fig. 949, taken from the brass of the lady (Fig. 819), and dated 1572, where the under-skirt is of a brocade of this pattern.

Fig. 950 is an Italian brocade showing one element of a floral design enclosed in ogival bands, which is repeated over the whole fabric. The

Fig. 949. English

Fig. 950. Italian

Fig. 951. Franco-Italian

Fig. 952. Italian

pomegranate is still prominent; and there are definite Japanese features introduced, e.g. the motifs on the ogival bands, which may have come direct from Japan or via China to Spain or Italy.

A very characteristic pattern of smaller and more compact design, used by the Italian and French weavers of the latter part of the sixteenth century, is shown in Fig. 951. The introduction of flowers and foliage springing from vases, coronets, and birds shows how very persistent these types of motifs were. The fabric would be woven in silk of two colours.

Fig. 953. Spanish

A good example of the single motif placed diaperwise or semée over the surface of a silken material of Italian weave is shown in Fig. 952. Each motif could be of the same design, but in this example two slightly different designs are employed, each occupying different rows—diaperwise, and two colours are used upon a light ground.

Fig. 953 is a motif, from four to six inches in width, showing Moorish influences. It is repeated diaperwise over the surface of the silken material. This brocade is of Spanish manufacture: it is taken from a portrait of the Great Infanta, and in this case the ground is cloth of gold with the central design woven in close globules of gold; the four scroll-motifs which enclose it are of silver.

A prevalent type of design used at the end of the century is illustrated in

Fig. 954. Spanish

Fig. 954, showing one lozenge-shaped floral motif. This might be woven in a coloured or black velvet upon a cloth of gold, silk, or satin ground.

The pattern (Fig. 955) is one section from a late sixteenth-century wall painting in which the squares set diaperwise contain a design suggestive of acanthus leaves and a vase with flowers; it is also a pattern that could be used for a material. In the original the ground is pale yellow and the pattern black.

The brocade worn by the Queen of Spain, referred to on p. 685, is of white satin with a pattern of the latest mode in black silk woven upon it. It is shown in Fig. 777, and consists of two motifs arranged diaperwise, one suggesting the letter N and the other a caterpillar.

A very serious rival to patterned fabrics and brocades at this time was embroidery: the former retired somewhat from the fashionable wardrobe for a time. All the same, patterned fabrics were worn, as is evidenced by the fashionable lady (Fig. 730) who wears quite a large pattern in velvet upon a satin ground.

Fig. 955. English

## LIST OF COLOURS

Ash-colour = grey: also *Cendré* (*see* vol. ii, p. 124)

*Beasar* = brownish like the bezoar-stone

*Bice* = a pale blue

*Blecche* = orange

*Carnaĉon* = carnation

*Claie-colour* = a deep cream

*Clodie-colour* = an off-white or light grey

*Dead Spaniard*: perhaps the colour of a corpse-like sallow complexion

*Devil in the Hedge*

*Dove* = a grey

*Drakes-colour*: possibly the flaming red of the Tudor 'dragon' or of the resin known as 'dragon's blood.'

*Fig-brown* = a brownish heliotrope

*Flax-seed-colour*. See *Isabella*

*Goose-turd-green* = a green darker and slightly more yellow than grass

*Gozelinge* = a pale yellowish-green

*Hearecolour* = brown, the colour of a hare

*Horsefleshe-colour* = a brown-pink

*Isabella-colour*. For the origin of this, *see* Chap. I, p. 133.

*Ladie Blushe* = pale pink or deep flesh colour

*Lion-tawny* = an ochre-orange colour

*Lust Gallant*

*Marigold* = an orange-yellow

*Peache* = yellow flushed with pink

*Pease-porridge-tawny* = a brownish-green

*Pimpillo* is a sixteenth-century name for a pin pillow. It is also applied to the prickly pear, from its appearance of a pin-cushion stuck full of pins.

A dye was prepared from the pulp of the prickly pear, of a colour between a raw umber, which is too red, and a raw sienna, which is too yellow

*Pincke* = pink

*Popingay-blue* = a blue-green

*Pounde-Gythrone*

*Virli* = a vivid green

*Watchet* = a light blue

The Dutch developed an extensive dyeing industry during the second half of the sixteenth century, and quantities of materials, chiefly cloth, were sent to Holland yearly to be dyed. According to Sir Walter Raleigh, as much as £400,000 per annum was spent out of England on this business.

The art of the dyer made much progress in France during the same period, and the following list gives the names of a few fancy French colours:

*Amarante* = amethyst-purple.

*Céladon* = sea-green.

*Nacarade* = pale orange-red.

*Zinzolin* = a red-violet.

*Astrée*. Astraea, the star-maiden, was a goddess who became the constellation Virgo, but what colour is intended, let another decide!

*Espagnol malade* = a variant of *Dead Spaniard*, above.

*Fleur mourante*
*Triste amie* } sad colour or neutral tint.

*Ventre de biche* = a reddish-white.

VEHICLES (*continued from p.* 466)

## THE LITTER

The litter continued to be a State vehicle, and according to custom Queen Elizabeth went to her coronation in an elaborately decorated horse-borne litter (Fig. 956), reproduced from the contemporary drawing in the College of Arms.

The body of the litter has ornate spiral ends, and the sides are decorated with lions' heads, scrolls, and a pelmet-like edging. The litter is borne by two richly caparisoned palfreys with nodding plumes on their heads, the first one led by Lord Giles Paulet and the second by Lord Ambrose Dudley. The Queen sits on a large chair, and over her a canopy of cloth of gold is carried by four noblemen. Her Majesty is preceded by an Earl carrying the Sword of State, and the Earl of Oxford as Lord Great Chamberlain of England. Behind the litter, Lord Robert Dudley leads the palfrey of honour (Fig. 957). On both sides walk 'Esquires and footmen near about Her Highnesses litter,' all dressed in crimson velvet; and outside them came 'The Gentlemen Pensioners on foot with polleaxes in their hands.' Both sets of gentlemen are garbed as shown in Figs. 609 and 610; the latter dressed in crimson damask and carrying gilded battleaxes. Altogether there were a thousand nobles and gentry, richly clad and mounted on gorgeously caparisoned horses. It is particularly stated that *all* were bareheaded.

An innovation in a French Royal litter, the use of *glass*, is described in the following:

Marguerite de Valois's journey to Flanders, in 1577, was undertaken ostensibly to partake of the waters of Spa, but in reality to gain partisans for her brother, the Duc d'Alençon, in his project of wresting the Low Countries from Spain.

'I went,' she says, in her *Memoirs*, 'in a litter with columns covered with rose-coloured Spanish velvet, embroidered in gold and shaded silks with a device; this litter was enclosed in glass, and each glass also bore a device, there being, whether on the velvet or on the glass, forty different devices about the Sun and its effects, with the words in Spanish and Italian.'

When Queen Elizabeth convened her fifth Parliament, 29th October 1586, she was not in the best of health. She therefore was conveyed 'in a semi-covered litter that looked like a half-canopied bed. The litter was entirely of wood upholdered all over with cloth of gold and silver. The cushions, too, on which the Queen reclined were of gold and silver material. . . . The litter was borne by two white steeds with yellow manes and tails; on the horses' heads and tails were plumes of yellow and white, their saddles and cloths being of gold material.'

Preceding the litter was 'a riderless horse, led by a Gentleman. The saddlecloth, the saddle, and the bridle were of pure cloth of gold, studded all

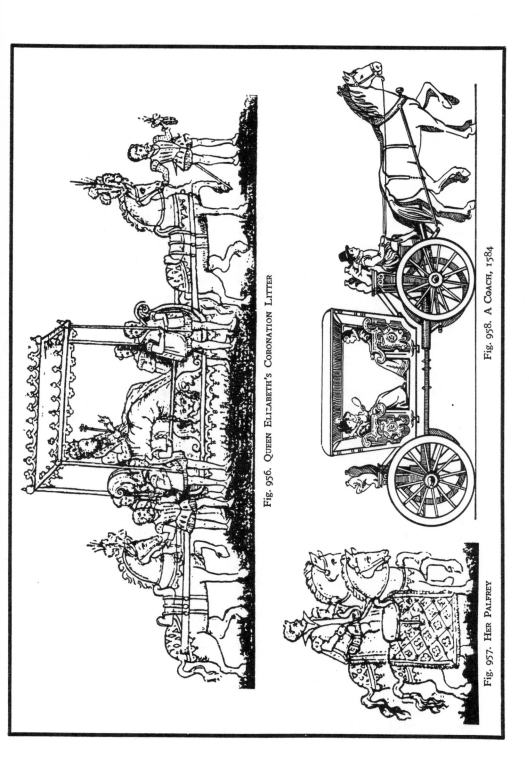

Fig. 956. Queen Elizabeth's Coronation Litter

Fig. 957. Her Palfrey

Fig. 958. A Coach, 1584

over with pearls.    The bridle was studded with precious stones and in front of the horse's head there hung a jewel with a beautiful large diamond and on either side near the horse's ears hung pearls of great size.'    'Behind the Queen was another led horse.    It had a red velvet saddle cloth garnished with gold borders and gold lace.'

A litter, carried on the shoulders of four gentlemen in 1600, is seen in Plate XLV.

### THE COACH

For some reason Queen Elizabeth discarded the coach made by Walter Rippon in 1556, so in 1560 she ordered another from Holland.    This was brought over by William Boonen, a Dutchman, who became the Royal coachman, which office he retained until the end of the century.

In 1564 Rippon built a 'hollow turning' coach for the Queen.    This term refers to the method adopted by Rippon, of scooping out the lower part of the front of the body to allow the wheels to turn on a greater circumference.

A coach was used for the first time for ceremonial when Queen Elizabeth opened her third Parliament in State, 2nd April 1571.

According to an inventory dated 1577, Archbishop Parker possessed two coaches.    One was 'covered with lether and furniture for two horses to the same'; the other was 'uncovered, with like furniture.'

We have no illustration of an English coach so early as this.    Two appear in Hofnagel's print dated 1582, but this is rather small.    However, at the Castle of Coburg is a coach used by Duke John Casimir, Elector of Saxony, in 1584, which appears to be in many respects of the same type as shown by Hofnagel.    Fig. 958 is a drawing based on the Elector's coach.    It should be observed that the body forms one piece with the roof, and that there is space enough for two people to sit side by side back and front.    Often two extra seats were added in the gangway, a box arrangement being built out at right angles to the sides.    On the axletrees, back and front, are set up high ornamental pedestals surmounted by the Elector's heraldic lions and made secure by iron braces; from the top of these pedestals leather straps suspend the body.    The wheels are less heavy, and the whole construction of this vehicle is more elegant, than hitherto.    Armorial bearings are blazoned on the side panels.    The coachman sits upon a stool placed on a board, with a foot-rest fixed to the front of the triangular under-frame (F in Fig. 480, and known as a 'futchel').    It should be noticed that this is a 'hollow turning' coach, the bottom front corner being *hollowed* out: this is repeated at the back to give uniformity to the design.    The two horses are fastened, first by a strap fixed to the shaft and strapped to the horse-collar, and secondly by traces attached to swingle-trees.

Mules were sometimes used, and in 1568 Sir Henry Norris was paid £210 'for provičon of cariadge moyles for her Highnes cariadge.'

It was about this time that coachbuilders on the Continent attempted an improvement on the leather strap suspension by introducing metal springs. Evidently springs of this kind were not in use in England at so early a date: otherwise Queen Elizabeth would not have made her confession (*see* p. 484) in 1568.

An early use of a coach with springs occurred in the marriage procession of the Archduke Ferdinand of Austria in 1582 when 'the betrothed Princess [of Mantua] appeared with her mother, and a stately retinue of ladies-in-waiting in elegant gilt litters, and *carriages on springs.*'

The decorations of Royal coaches were often very elaborate. The one belonging to Marguerite de Valois, discovered outside the lodging of Charles de Balzac d'Entragues by her suspicious brother, Henry III, was 'all gilded, and lined with yellow and silvered velvet.' 'I would wager she is there,' declared the King: but no evidence of any indiscretion was forthcoming, for examination showed that 'the birds have been there, but they have flown.'

In 1585 Queen Elizabeth owned at least three coaches and eighty-one horses. 'One of the coaches was so small that only two persons can sit in it; but it is so contrived that both the fore and hind wheels are attached far from the body of the coach. The second coach was of red leather and studded all over with gilt silver nails. On the third coach the wheels were placed under the axle in a way that I cannot describe. This coach had twelve wheels.' Another coach belonging to the Queen was of gold 'open all round, but having above it a canopy embroidered with gold and pearls. On the front and on the back of the coach were three plumes of various colours. The coach was drawn by four bays in Royal trappings. The coachman was clad in red velvet, and on his coat both before and behind was the Queen's coat of arms and a rose of chaste silver gilt.'

For her progress to St. Paul's to give thanks for the defeat of the Armada, Elizabeth rode in 'a chariette-throne made with four pillars behind to have a canopy, on the toppe whereof was made a crown imperiall, and two lower pillars before whereon stood a lyon and a dragon, supporters of the arms of England, drawne by two white horses . . . her footemen and pensioners about her.'

Whether the following stanza describes Elizabeth's coach accurately is doubtful. It was written by a poet who saw her on this memorable occasion.

> 'He happy was that could but see her coach,
> The sides whereof beset with emeralds
> And diamonds, with sparkling rubies red
> In checkerwise, by strange invention,
> With curious knots embroidered with gold.'

The use of coaches and carriages became more general among the nobility during the latter part of Elizabeth's reign. 'After a while, divers great ladies (with so great jealoussie of the Queen's displeasure) made them coaches, and rid in them up and down the country, to the great admiration of all the beholders.'   Towards the end of the century it was scornfully remarked that 'our wantons now in coaches dash.'

The celebrity of English-built coaches is shown by the following extracts. A German who came to England in 1595 on purpose to buy a coach, writes home and says that he had 'walked all over London, I did not overlook a single coachbuilder, and also saw a large number of coaches and carriages.' He eventually bought an English coach, with harness for the horses, for £34.

In 1599 'the presents sent by the Queen of England to the Sultan are said to be a very handsome timepiece and a coach with silver mountings.'   In September of the same year Elizabeth made Henry IV a present of 'a coach of great value and some fine horses.'

A mail-coach, 1592, is referred to on p. 563.

Towards the end of the sixteenth century long, immense-wheeled wagons —later known as 'stages'—for the conveyance of passengers and goods began to ply between the chief towns of England and on the Continent.

## THE CHAIR

In 1581 a seat enclosed in a box and carried on poles by two men made its first appearance in England.   Many years before, similar contrivances were used on the Continent to carry invalids.   The Emperor Charles V had one;

Fig. 959. An Italian Chair, 1590

and Henry VIII, when he became very gouty, was moved from room to room in such a seat or chair (see p. 257).   In the latter part of the century this chair became popular with the upper and middle classes.   It was found very convenient for getting about, especially along narrow streets, for visiting when 'dressed up,' and in inclement weather.

An Italian chair of the late sixteenth century is given in Fig. 959 from a contemporary engraving. The box is of wood covered with some kind of material inside and out, with waxed cloth between to make it waterproof; the window and door are at the side, and the roof is semicircular. Poles pass through the front and back of the box, and these are hung by straps over the left shoulders of the bearers.

The lady appears somewhat cramped but no doubt she is moderately comfortable.

## THE END

The following excerpts from contemporary writers give interesting details of the last days of the great Queen.

Sir Robert Carey, a relative of Elizabeth on her mother's side, writes in his *Narrative*: 'I found her in one of her withdrawing chambers, sitting low upon her cushions.' 'She took me by the hand and wrung it hard, and said: "No, Robin, I am not well," and then discoursed to me of her indisposition, and that her heart had been sad and heavy for ten or twelve days; and in her discourse she fetched not so few as forty or fifty great sighs. I was grieved at the first to see her in this plight; for in all my lifetime before I never knew her fetch a sigh, but when the Queen of Scottes was beheaded. Then, in 1587, upon my knowledge, she shedd many tears and sighs, manifesting her innocence that she never gave consent to the death of that Queen.'

'She remained upon her cushions four days and nights at least. All about her could not persuade her either to take any sustenance or to go to bed.'

Beaumont, the French Ambassador, relates that 'the Queen hastens to her end, and is given up by all her physicians. They have put her to bed, almost by force, after she had sat upon cushions for ten days.'

'The Queen kept her bed fifteen days,' reports her lady-in-waiting, Lady Southwell (Elizabeth Howard).

Archbishop Whitgift ministered to the dying Elizabeth at Richmond Palace. She died in her sleep, soon after he had left her, at 3 a.m. on 24th March 1603; and in sign that her soul had passed, Sir Robert Carey conveyed her sapphire ring to James VI of Scotland.

THE QUEEN IS DEAD—LONG LIVE THE KING.

Fig. 960.
Badge of James I

# GENERAL INDEX

*Note:* For names of Individuals and Places, see Index of Names, p. 819

# INDEX OF NAMES

This Index does not contain references to the Historical Data